Thomas M. Donnee
54 MULLEN HILL RD.
WATERFORD, CONN.

Encyclopedia of Pleasure Boating

Encyclopedia of Pleasure Boating

The Complete Illustrated Guide to Motorboating and Yachting

by

Arthur Liebers

New York: A. S. Barnes and Company, Inc.
London and Toronto: Thomas Yoseloff Ltd.

© 1961 by A. S. Barnes and Company, Inc.
Library of Congress Catalog Card Number: 61-13914
All Rights Reserved

A. S. Barnes and Company, Inc.
11 East 36th Street
New York 16, New York

Thomas Yoseloff Ltd.
123 New Bond Street
London W.1, England

Printed in the United States of America

CONTENTS

I	The Birth of the Boating Boom	9
II	Choosing the Outboard Motor	18
III	Selecting the Inboard Boat	23
IV	Guide to Outboard Cruising	27
V	Care of Boat, Motor and Equipment	50
VI	Maintenance for the Larger Pleasure Boat	57
VII	Small Boat Construction	73
VIII	Safe Small Boat Handling	89
IX	Boating Safety	102
X	Communication	111
XI	Anchoring and Mooring	120
XII	Aids to Navigation — Buoys and Other Aids	130
XIII	Cautions Concerning Aids to Navigation	140
XIV	Electronic Aids to Navigation	148
XV	Basic Small Boat Piloting	157
XVI	Fundamentals of Piloting	169
XVII	Weather Indications	180
XVIII	Rules of the Road	190
XIX	Marlinspike Seamanship: The Use of Rope Aboard Your Boat	195
XX	The Federal Boating Act of 1958	212
XXI	State Boating Laws	221
XXII	Refunds on Gasoline Taxes	249
XXIII	Yacht and Motorboat Insurance	254
XXIV	Something About Sailboats	264
XXV	The One-Design Sailboats	274
XXVI	Do It Yourself — Building from Kits or Plans	289
XXVII	Galley Cookery	306
XXVIII	Water Skiing and Water Skis	315
XXIX	Automobile-Marine Engine Conversion	321
XXX	Looking Ahead	330
XXXI	Federal Trade Commission and the Boating Industry	336
XXXII	A Boatmanship Quizzer — How Are Your Skipper Skills?	339
XXXIII	Free for the Boatman — Sources of Information	349
	Glossary of Nautical Terms	357
	Acknowledgments	365
	Appendix OBC Digest of State Boat Trailer Laws	366
	INDEX	375

Encyclopedia of Pleasure Boating

CHAPTER I

The Birth of the Boating Boom

The earliest available figures show that there were some 15,000 pleasure boats in use in the United States in 1904. Now, there are about 8,025,000 "recreational" boats in existence in United States waters, and an estimated 39,000,000 friends, relatives and neighbors join the boat owners in cruising and day-sailing.

Both the sailboat devotees and the inventive genius of men who discovered more efficient ways to propel people over

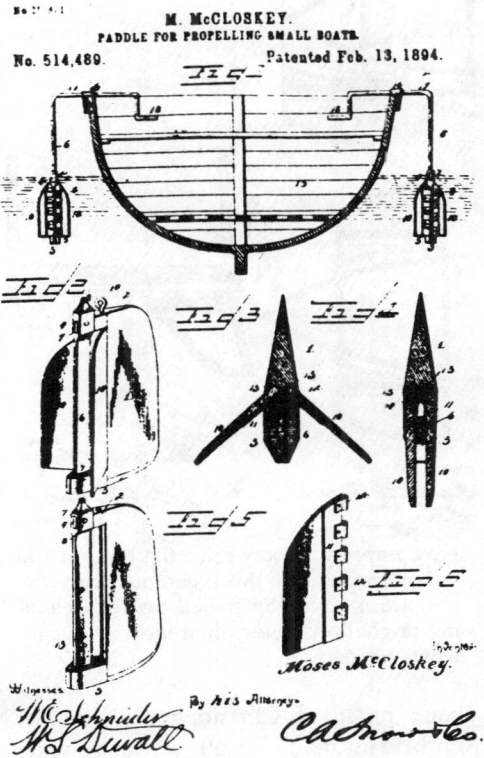

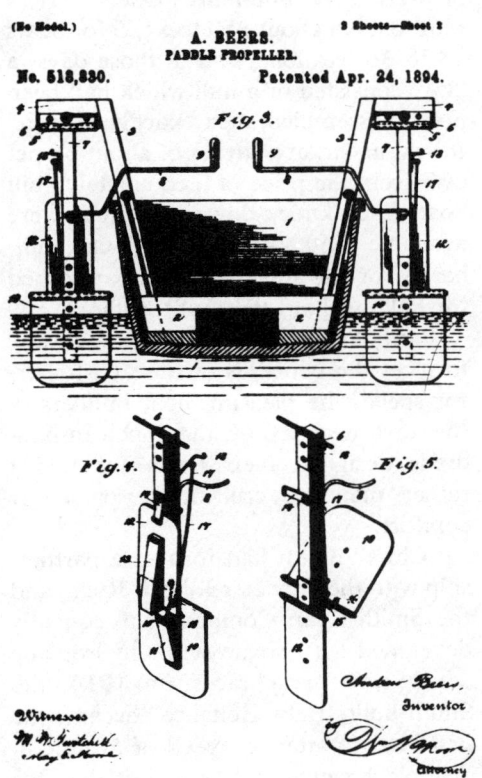

Mechanical devices to make the job of rowing easier were among the more frequently patented ideas. Above are sketches of two proposed solutions to the problem of getting a boat through the water.

the water made this tremendous boom possible. In the files of the patent office in Washington, the lists of patents in the field of boating make up one of the largest sections. Bringing pleasure boating to the general public had to await the development of an efficient marine gasoline-fueled engine. Steam launches were numerous at the turn of the century, but the boating laws of the early 1900's made it rather difficult to use them for personal pleasure cruising. These laws required that a steam vessel of any size must have a licensed steam engineer and a certified pilot aboard.

One of the pioneers in the pleasure boating field bore the somewhat pro-

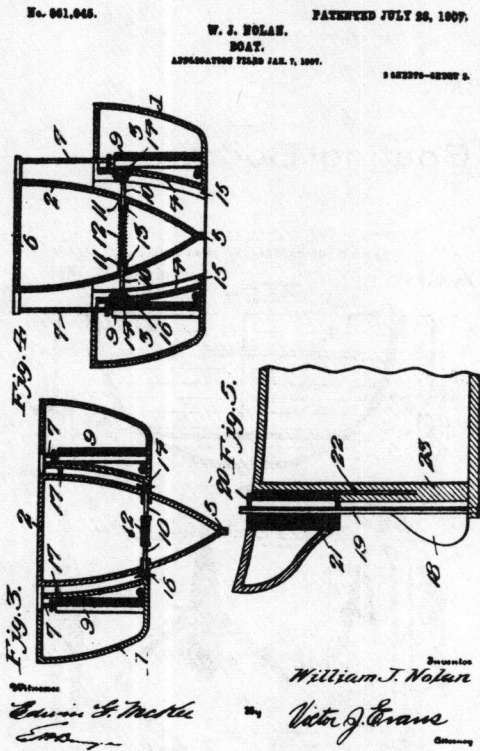

No compromise between a flat bottom and V-bottom here. In this ingenious craft, the V-bottom could be pulled up for beaching or shallow water, then let down again when needed.

phetic name of Christopher Columbus Smith. He made small wooden boats used by hunters in the marshes of the St. Clair River in Michigan. In 1894 he attached a small naphtha-gas engine to one of his boats—and the inboard pleasure boat industry was on the way. Two years later, he and his son tried using a newly developed gasoline engine, but with little success. It was not until an inventor named Charles Sintz showed up with a gadget called a carburetor that the marine engine became practical. Armed with this means of power, the "Chris-Craft Company" began building boats in earnest. By 1906, they were turning out a 26-foot boat that did 18 m.p.h.

Meanwhile, other boat manufacturers had entered the field. The first National Motor Boat Show was held in New York City in 1905, and manufacturers were already stressing boating as a family sport. In those early days a price of over $1,000 indicated a custom-built boat. For less than one hundred dollars it was possible to buy a 14-foot boat with a motor in the stern, cross seats forward and tiller steering, with storage room up front for camping equipment and the necessary tools for the motor. The hulls were of steel or wood and many were advertised as unsinkable.

The do-it-yourself enthusiasts were already at work in their carriage houses. A number of manufacturers were offering patterns and blueprints for their hulls. By 1909, it was possible to order a "knock-down" kit from among a choice of over fifty different models. Prices ranged from about $50 to $125 for boats 18 to 36 feet long, and in those days, a "kit" consisted of a hull which had been precut, assembled, then "knocked down" for shipment, at a saving of about 66 per cent from the price of a completely built boat. Even knock-down steel hulls were available with shaped sections numbered for assembly and holes punched for bolts to hold the hull together.

Partly to gain publicity for boating and to meet the demands of their customers for speed, the pleasure boat builders of the first decades of the nineteen-hundreds designed their boats for racing rather than for cruising or passenger comfort.

"Chris" Smith had formed a partnership with the financier John J. Ryan, and the Smith-Ryan Company subsequently developed a single-step hydroplane which won many races. In 1914, the Smith-built "Baby Reliance" became the first boat to attain a speed of 50 m.p.h. A typical racing hydroplane of the time was about 40 feet long, had more than one engine and aimed at a speed of 50 m.p.h. The craze for power and speed led to such oddities as a three-motor hydroplane with 750 horsepower, but because of design it was almost impossible to maneuver or turn her at high speeds. In 1916, "Miss Minneapolis" set a world speed record of 66.66 m.p.h. and a year later "Miss Detroit II," with a 350-horsepower engine, captured the Gold Cup at 67.72 m.p.h.

Chris-Craft and Gar Wood developed the first "Miss America" and in 1919 challenged the British for the Harmsworth International Trophy. This boat was a smooth-water hydroplane powered with two 125 horsepower aircraft engines and twin screws. On August 20, 1920, "Miss America" won the Harmsworth Trophy with a speed of 65 m.p.h., and captured the trophy again the next year. In 1932, the last of the "Miss Americas" flashed over a course on Lake St. Clair at 124.91 m.p.h., a record which stood unbroken for seven years.

Family Boats to the Fore

The trend away from the hydroplane design came around 1913. In that year the famed Hickman Sea-Sled made its appearance. This boat had a V-concave section in the forward half of its hull and only partially submerged propellers. Unlike the racing hydroplanes with their engines up forward, the Sea-Sled had its engine in the stern, allowing useable cockpit room. A 25 horsepower, 400-pound motor gave 26 m.p.h. to the 1,600 pound boat—considerably more efficient than the hydroplanes.

By 1920, exhibits at the Motor Boat Shows and in the salesrooms reflected a change in the public taste. Cruisers with family-living accommodations became the desired type of boat. Comfort, reliability, and more beam replaced the pre-

This mid-lake gathering shows the variety of boats and outboard power available these days. From the light, 98-lb. fishing skiff all the way around the clock to the family-sized cruiser, there's a boat and motor combination tailored for every need. *(Mercury Outboard Motors photo)*

mium formerly held by speed. This was still before the outboard boom, and the most popular boats were in the 35-foot-length range, selling from about $3,500 to $4,000.

One other group is believed to have had a considerable influence on "pleasure" boat development during the twenties. There were many boat purchasers with ready cash who were interested in buying medium-sized boats that could carry a small cargo of cases of whisky faster than a Coast Guard patrol craft could travel. The development of the speedy sea skiff is generally attributed to the impetus given the boating industry by these customers with a fervent desire to be able to serve their customers with beverages from the islands outside the prohibition zone.

By 1930, there were some 1,500,000 pleasure boats in operation and the boom was off to a good start.

SOME FIGURES ON PLEASURE BOATING

8,025,000 Pleasure Boats in Use in the United States.
Among these are:
550,000 motor boats (including all inboard boats, outboards over 16 feet and approximately 44,500 auxiliary-powered sailboats).
319,000 unnumbered inboard motor boats in use on waters not under Federal jurisdiction. Statistics on State-numbered boats not yet available.
4,000 larger inboard motor boats in use on waters not under Federal jurisdiction.
4,000,000 outboard boats in use (approx.) Thse are boats with transoms designed to accommodate outboard motors.
496,000 sailboats without inboard power on all waters.
2,500,000 rowboats, canoes, dinghies, prams and other miscellaneous craft in use. (A number of these are sometimes used with outboard motors.)
1,100 yacht clubs and boat clubs with waterfront stations in the U.S.
3,900 marinas and boat yards in the U.S.
7,000 launching sites for small craft in the U.S.
Also in use:
1,750,000 boat trailers, both home-made and factory-produced.

Meanwhile the Outboards

There are a group of conflicting claims as to the origin of the outboard motor. Some records profess to show that Gottlieb Daimler, one of the developers of the internal combustion engine, introduced the first outboard motor to the United States, which was shown at the Chicago World's Fair in 1893.

In 1902, a French inventor tried out an outboard motor on the Seine River. This was a single-cylinder engine which is referred to as the "Motogobile" and the "Motogodille" in different reports. Some sources attribute its failure to a balky engine which frightened off investors. It was a simple and fairly inexpensive device. The whole apparatus was self-contained and could be attached to the transom of a boat in a few minutes. The rig was almost seven feet long with the propeller extending over four feet from the stern. Speed was controlled by lowering and raising the propeller in and out of the water. Steering was accomplished by swinging the handle of the unit, which was available in two sizes.

The first commercially produced outboard motor and the first to use the name "outboard" was the Waterman Porto Motor, which was shown at the 1906 National Sportsmen's and Motor Boat Show. This was a two horsepower, single cylinder, water-cooled model, weighing about 40 pounds, that could drive an 18-foot rowboat about 7 m.p.h. and claimed to run about four hours on a gallon of gasoline. In the first year of production, about twenty-five Waterman outboards were made. The next year some six hundred were produced. This motor never caught on with the public, although the Waterman name was found in the field until the early 1920's.

The outboard motor industry is generally willing to accept Ole Evinrude as the "father" of the outboard motor. At the 1909 Boat Show, he presented a display of a single-cylinder, two-part, battery-ignition engine, developing one-half horsepower at about 1,000 rpm.

According to the story—which is given full credence by the Evinrude Motors Company—Evinrude, a girl named Bess, and several friends were picnicking on an island two miles from shore. Bess suddenly developed an urge for ice cream, and the gallant Evinrude immediately departed by row boat to get it. Rowing to shore was easy, but before he could travel the two miles against the wind on the return trip, the ice cream was in a liquid state.

It was hot, and as he pulled on the oars during the return trip, Ole thought, "Why not build a gasoline motor, hitch it to a propeller and stick it on the end of a row boat?"

After that weekend picnic, the Norwegian-born Evinrude returned to his pattern shop near the Kinnickinnic River in Wisconsin, and started working on the design for his "Evinrude Detachable Rowboat Motor." When he had a product finished and ready for a test run, he took two of Bess' brothers who worked with him down to the river for a trial run. The motor, hitched onto a rented boat, roared into life and pushed the boat along at about five miles an hour.

After the successful tryout Evinrude could hardly wait to get home to tell Bess the good news. Somewhere between the picnic and the building of the motor she had become Mrs. Evinrude. To her question, "Now that you have it, what will you do with it?" he had no ready answer, and her comment that it looked like a coffee grinder sent him back to the shop to make an improved model. Soon the second engine was completed.

It looked and performed better than the first model. One Sunday Evinrude loaned the new model to a friend for a spin on the river. When the friend returned on Monday he had in his hands orders for ten more, with cash payments in advance. Since the model weighed 62 pounds, Evinrude figured that a dollar a pound was a fair price and sold them for 62 dollars apiece. After the first twenty-five were sold, Evinrude inserted an advertisement in a Milwaukee paper and the outboard industry had started.

By 1911 the new firm was firmly established and working in new quarters. The outboard motor had lost its "coffee grinder" look and was on its way to being a national institution.

In 1914, the Evinrudes retired after selling their interest in the Evinrude Detachable Row Boat Motor Company to their partner of three years, C. J. Meyer, with a stipulation that Evinrude would not re-enter the outboard business for at least five years.

By 1921 Evinrude had perfected a new lightweight twin cylinder outboard motor which represented a definite advancement in the outboard field. Certain that the fisherman would be the best customer, Evinrude had incorporated new lightweight aluminum alloys and was able to produce a 47-pound unit which developed three horsepower. The Evinrudes established the Elto Outboard Motor Company, the name "Elto" being taken from the first letters of Evinrude Light Twin Outboard.

The new Elto firm flourished, but the old Evinrude Company which had changed hands several times began to lose ground. In 1928 it was sold to the Briggs-Stratton Corporation of Milwaukee—better known today for its powered lawn mowing equipment. The next year, the Outboard Motors Corporation was formed by a merger of the Elto Outboard Motor Company, the Evinrude Motor Company and the Lockwood Motor

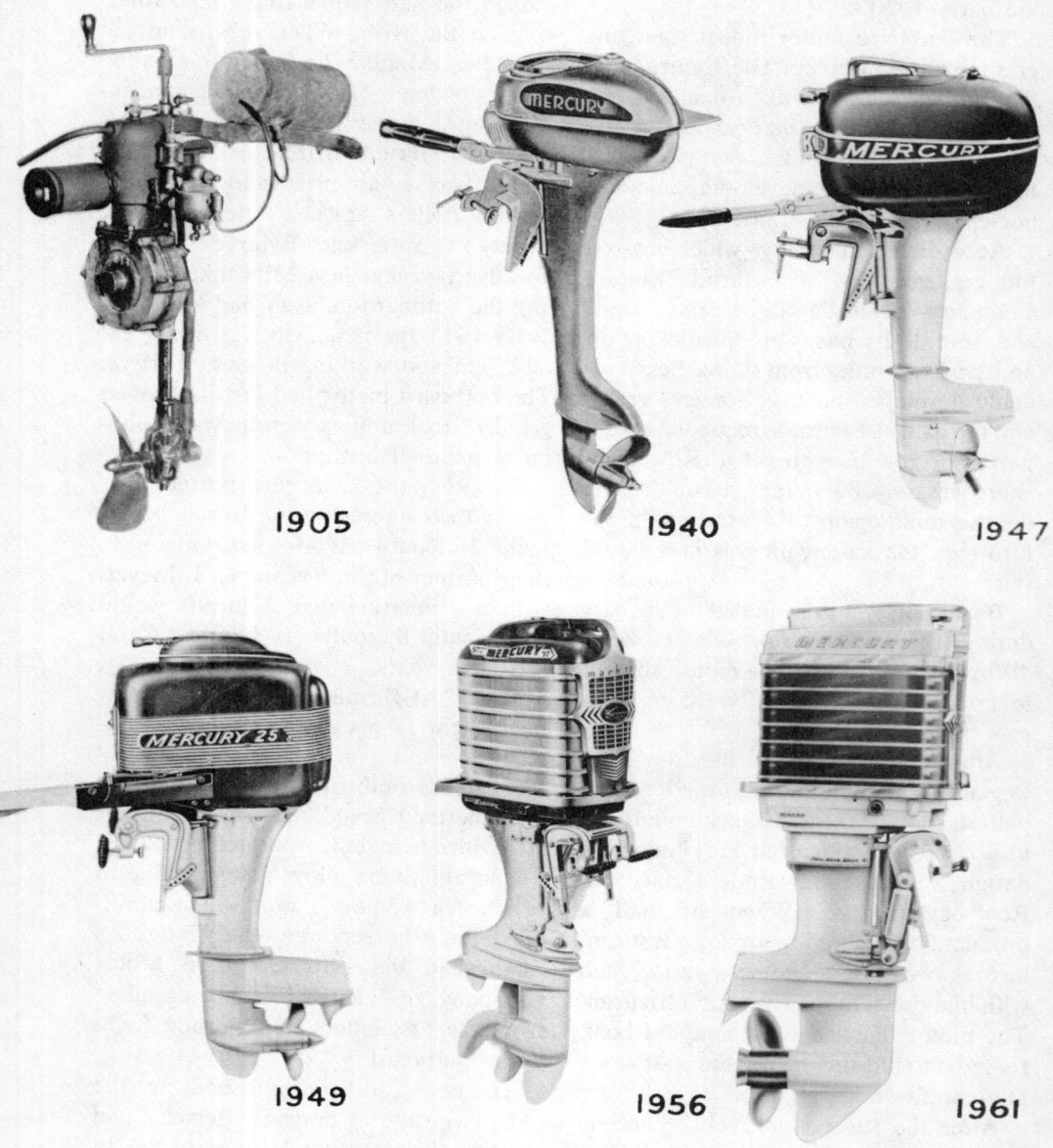

Fifty-six years of outboards: 1905, the first mass-production outboard, the single-cylinder Waterman Porto; 1940, a single; 1947, the Mercury Lightning, 10 horsepower; 1949, the Mercury 25, rated at 25 horsepower, the first four-cylinder-in-line outboard; 1956, rated at 60 horsepower, the first six-cylinder-in-line outboard; and 1961, the new Merc 800, rated at 80 horsepower.

Company. Ole Evinrude was president and chief stockholder, and Stephen F. Briggs was chairman of the board.

In 1929, the Elto Quad, the first four cylinder, two-cycle outboard motor to be built in the United States, appeared on the market. However, there were other competitors in the market during these years. Since 1922, Johnson had been in the market with a two horsepower Light Twin which weighed only 35 pounds, had an automobile-type carburetor, full pivot steering, and could be disassembled for packing in a carrying case. In the twenties outboards were produced by some thirty different companies, many of which failed after short business lives. Some of the larger outfits were Koban, Lockwood-Ash, Caille, Silverstreak, and Wisconsin. Many of these companies introduced refinements which are found in today's outboard motors.

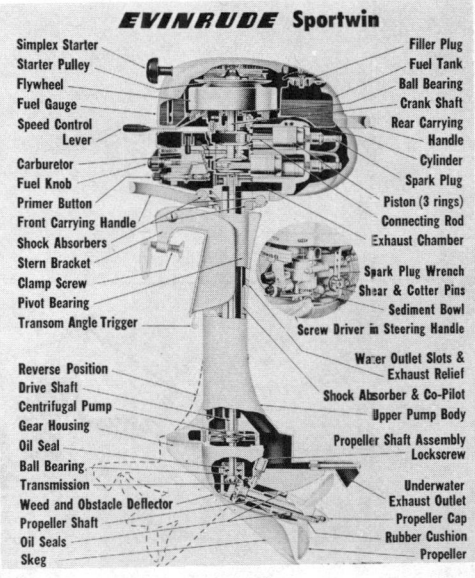

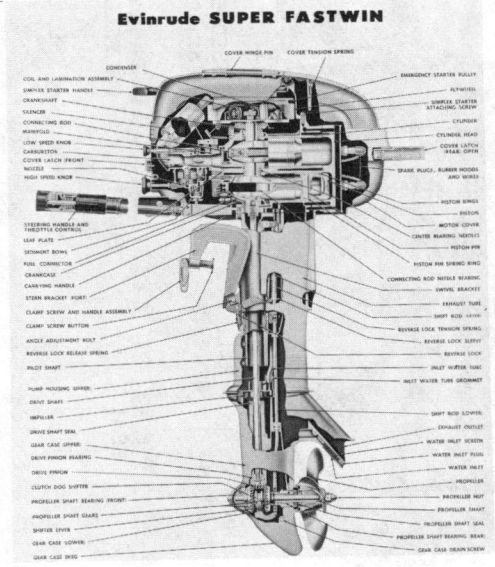

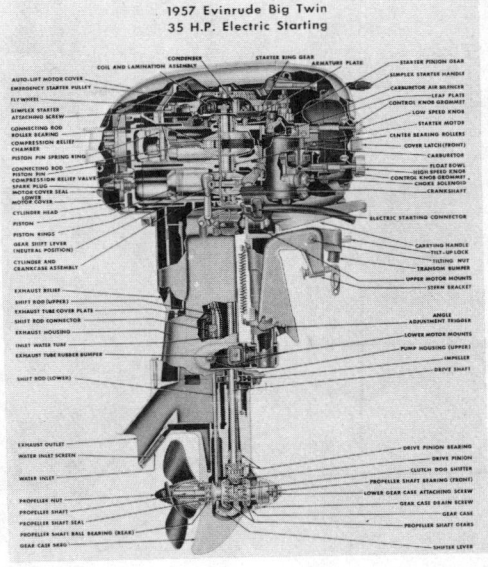

Basically, the outboard motor has changed little in recent years. Power has been increased, the electrical system has been improved, greater power has made manual starting difficult, and this has been overcome by electric starters; generators have been added to keep the batteries charged. Back in the middle fifties, a 15 horsepower outboard was considered a "large" engine. But essentially, today's 80 horsepower motors are very much like the 10 horsepower "Sportwin" which was introduced in the early fifties. *(Evinrude diagrams)*

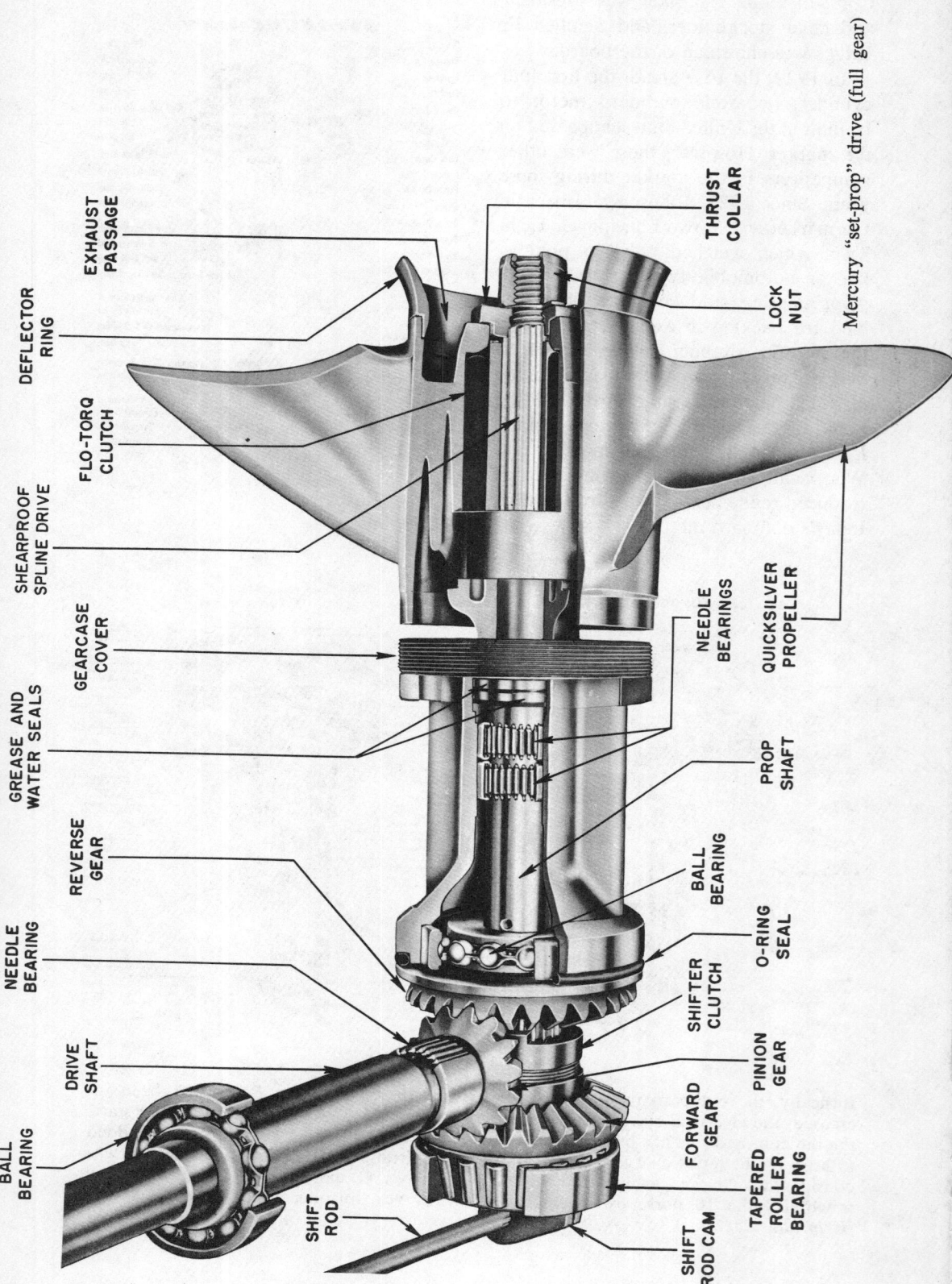

Mercury "set-prop" drive (full gear)

THE BIRTH OF THE BOATING BOOM

The outboard industry suffered two setbacks in the early 1930's. The first was the depression, which cut sales to a bare minimum. The second was the death of Ole Evinrude in 1934. More consolidations took place in the thirties. In 1936, the Outboard Marine and Manufacturing Company was formed by Outboard Motors Corporation which had taken control of the Johnson Motor Company. Now the "holding" company is known as Outboard Marine Corporation; and much of the promotional part of the outboard industry is handled by the independent Evinrude Foundation.

Major developments of the outboards shortly before World War II were the casting of parts to cut down production costs, the streamlining of motors, and the replacement of the opposed twin motor with the alternate firing motor. During the war the industry was engaged wholly in producing powerful outboards for military and naval use, but civilian production of outboards was resumed in 1946.

In the post war years, electric starting became popular. The gear shift was patented, and the separate fuel tank was introduced. Emphasis shifted from the production of light fisherman's models and high-powered racing motors to quiet, high-horsepower family outboards.

CHAPTER II

Choosing the Outboard Motor

The newest trend among manufacturers of outboard equipment is to offer a "package" including the hull, motor, and accessory equipment. The McCulloch Corporation, makers of the "Scott" line, has been the first to promote their "package" vigorously, but it is expected that the other outboard motor manufacturers will soon be following this pattern.

The majority of boat buyers still acquire their hulls and motors separately, however. The first consideration in matching the motor and hull is to follow the recommendation of the hull's maker as to the proper horsepower. The outboard hulls being offered by the larger companies carry a standard metal plate showing the approved horsepower according to the rating formula adopted by the Outboard Boating Club of America, a marine equivalent of the National Association of Manufacturers. The proper horsepower for an outboard hull is determined by multiplying the overall length in feet by the stern width in feet, and applying this figure to the "OBC Horsepower Curve" chart.

Horsepower Factors

Using a motor of lower horsepower will reduce the operating costs of the craft, but the performance will probably be sluggish, maneuvering will be uncertain, and the boat may lack sufficient power for safe use under adverse wind and sea conditions.

On the other hand, overpowering will generally not provide much additional speed since the speed is generally limited by the hull conformation. Attempting to add a few miles an hour to the top speed will impose a strain on the hull, probably cause severe vibration at high speeds, and create the additional hazards of capsizing or loss of control.

Shopping for the Outboard Motor

Selecting the outboard motor has become much like buying a new automobile. There are seven major manufacturers in the field and a number of independents. Prices are generally competitive. Until the past few years, the outboard makers have been in a "horsepower race" which brought the introduction of 80 horsepower motors into the market. Now, however, the emphasis in advertising and sales material has been away from sheer horsepower and more on design and mechanical refinements.

As in the automobile industry, the outboard motor field has become a place for mergers. While Evinrude and Johnson are competitors in the United States, they are both subsidiaries of the Outboard Marine Corporation and operate as one company for their foreign sales.

It is often possible to obtain an outboard motor at a considerable reduction from the list price. Many dealers have end-of-season sales; others offer substantial allowances for old trade-ins; and many of the discount stores carry a fairly complete line of outboard motors at substantial mark-downs from the list price. Also, in most waterfront areas, "asking around" will often locate a used outboard motor that is a good buy, and many motors are offered for sale in the "Boats" section of the local newspaper.

An Objective Report

The problem of selecting the "best buy" in the desired horsepower range is one that can become quite confusing. Usually, early each summer, "Consumer Reports" of Consumers Union of the U.S. Inc., Mount Vernon, N.Y., presents a report and ratings on the different current outboard motors. Each motor is tested to determine maximum speeds under light and heavy load conditions, cruising range per tank-full of gas, fuel economy, ability to keep running in rough water; also for the ease with which they can be handled, operated and maintained, and their noise and vibration levels.

The detailed reports also cover such features as starting, ease of spark plug replacement, safety features, etc. Color checks in the ratings indicate which motors, in the opinion of the experts, are judged superior in overall quality in their respective horsepower class and price range.

"Consumer Reports," is available on stands in the larger cities, and is on file in most public libraries.

The Outboard Motor Line-Up

Following are the specifications and details of the latest models of outboard motors:

Elgin: This is the line carried by Sears, Roebuck & Company. It offers eight different models, running from a 3.6 horsepower integral tank unit to a 170-pound, three cylinder Elgin 70 electric starting motor rated at 75.2 horsepower.

Available in 15 or 20-inch shafts, the top model develops its rated horsepower at 5,000 revolutions per minute. The unit has a remote fuel tank, full gearshift, a 12 amp. generator and reaches speeds up subscription, it is carried by many newsto 50 miles an hour.

Second in the line is the 40, available in both manual or electric starting models. The Elgin 25, rated at 27.7 horsepower, also comes with both manual and electric starting.

For the larger fishing boats, the Elgin 12 develops 14.1 horsepower. Also designed especially for fishing is the 7-1/2 horsepower. It weighs only 40 pounds, which the maker claims is 10 to 15 pounds lighter than competitive motors of this power.

Evinrude: Two models of 75 horsepower head the Evinrude line. Also available are two 40 horsepower models, and others at 18, 10, 5-1/2 and 3 horsepower. At the top of the list is the Starflite III Unicharger, a four cylinder, V-type engine that has fixed jet carburetion and a high output alternating current generator. In addition, the motor has been lined with a cellular sound-absorbing material to reduce noise. A companion model, slightly lower in cost, is the 75 horsepower Starflite III V-4.

The generator can be recharged while the motor is idling in neutral by use of a new transistorized voltage regulator. The Unicharger has automotive-type battery ignition. Improved fuel performance is claimed for the 40 and 75 horsepower models through the new carburetion system.

Full gearshift control for forward, reverse and neutral is included on all motors except the 3 horsepower.

Gale: Gale motors are available in eleven models in six horsepower ranges.

Leading the line is the V-Sovereign 60 horsepower, four cylinder motor with generator. Also in the 60-horsepower group is the V-Sovereign electric, and the V-Buccaneer with rope-starting.

In the 40-horsepower class are the Sovereign 40, two cylinder electric with generator; The Sovereign 40 electric, and the Buccaneer 40 rope-starter.

In the 25-horsepower group are two Buccaneer models, electric and rope-starting. The lower-powered Buccaneer models are the 15, 5 and 3 horsepower.

All motors in the line except the 3 horsepower operate on remote six-gallon fuel tanks. The single cylinder 3 has an integral half gallon tank. Except for the 60 horsepower models, all the others are two cylinder engines.

Johnson: With eight motors in six horsepower groups, Johnson is stressing greater mechanical efficiency and easier to handle controls. Recent developments are the introduction of an alternator generator and fixed jet carburetion.

Largest models offered are two 75 horsepower units, one with the alternator generator, the other without it. Other features emphasized by the company are: two-lever remote controls; reduction of engine noise; panel lights indicating engine overheating and ignition switch on; power cable permanently affixed in motor with the plug end enclosed in the junction box; and a safety interlock switch permitting starting at controlled speed in gear.

The Johnson line consists of the 75 horsepower V-75-A, a four cylinder vee-engine with an alternator generator; the V-75 without the generator; the twin cylinder Sea Horse 40 horsepower in electric and rope-starting models; the 18, 10, 5-1/2 and lightweight 3 horsepower Sea Horse twins.

The company claims that never before have boatmen been able to operate as many conveniences with their outboard motor as they can with the V-75-A. The alternating current generator is fully rectified to convert to direct current. A ship-to-shore telephone, depth finder, and refrigerator can all be used while the motor is idling with no strain on the battery.

Mercury: Mercury, the line of the Kiekhaefer Company, offers one of the two 80 horsepower motors on the market, heading the line of nine motors available.

The 80 horsepower Merc 800 and the 70 horsepower Merc 700 are both in-line six-cylinder engines. The 50 horsepower Merc 500 and the 40 horsepower Merc 350 are in-line fours. The 6 horsepower Merc 60 twin is a new fishing motor. All the Mercurys are offered with single-lever throttle and shift controls for remote operation. Mercury is the only company to adapt the simplified control system to its entire line. The models above were introduced in 1960.

Other models are the four-cylinder 45 horsepower Merc 400; the twin-cylinder 22 horsepower Merc 200; the 15 horsepower Merc 150, and the 9.8 horsepower Merc 100. The twins are described as being suitable for fishing boats and small runabouts while the fours and sixes are designed for water skiing, cruising, and off-shore fishing.

Automotive type fixed-jet carburetors, first used in 1958 by Mercury, are standard on every engine, and are said to eliminate the need for adjustable high-speed needle valves.

This company claims to offer the largest selection of options to motor buyers. Among these are a long shaft on six models, electric starting on the five most powerful models; counter rotating lower units on the six cylinder direct-reversing models; the single-lever controls for all motors and a choice of direct reversing or full gear with forward, reverse and running neutral on the 70 and 80 horsepower motors.

Scott: Ten motors in six power categories are offered by the McCulloch Corporation, maker of the Scott line. The most powerful model is rated at 75.2 horsepower and the company claims that this power has been raised from 60 horsepower with no increase in weight. Horsepower designations do not appear on the motor hoods to "emphasize intended use of the motor rather than sheer power."

Included in the line is the only three cylinder outboard on the American market, the Flying Scott and Flying Scott Custom, both electric starting and rated at 75.2 horsepower; the Royal Scott electric and manual and Royal Scott Custom, 43.7 horsepower; the Sport Scott, manual and electric, 27.7 horsepower; the Fleet

Scott, 14.1 horsepower; the lightweight Fishing Scott, 7.5 horsepower, and the 3.6 horsepower Scotty. All except the Flying Scott are twin-cylinder engines.

The electric-starting motors have an alternator generator with 12 ampere output, and are said to be 16 pounds lighter than conventional generators. The larger models have fixed-jet carburetion, which is claimed to give fuel savings of from 15 to 33 per cent over earlier models.

West Bend: The other 80 horsepower outboard motor is offered by this company which claims to present the broadest horsepower range of any manufacturer, with its smallest motor rated at 2 horsepower. In all, there are seven horsepower classifications.

The 80 horsepower Tiger Shark is a four cylinder engine including a 12 volt electrical plant which the maker says is the most advanced in any outboard. Between the 80 horsepower unit and the 2 horsepower Shrimp, which is air-cooled, are the Golden Shark 40 horsepower motors with electrical or manual starters; the Silver Shark at 25 horsepower with electric or manual starters, and 18, 12, and 7-1/2 horsepower motors.

One innovation recently adopted by West Bend is the practice of not providing a fuel tank with the motor, allowing the buyer, as the company says, "to choose any fuel tank he wishes." The Shrimp has a nylon propeller which is represented as not bending, cracking, chipping or breaking, and which will always maintain proper pitch.

The Golden Shark line's lower unit is claimed to be 24 per cent smaller in overall area and 16 per cent smaller in diameter than previous models, in order to increase boat speed by reducing underwater drag.

Motors in Disguise: The outboard motor buyer should be advised that several of the motors described above may appear under different names and with different types of covers among the chain stores and mail order houses which offer their own "brand" of motors. However, a comparison of the company-name brand with the descriptions above should enable an identification of the motor with its manufacturer. Then a comparison of the maker's catalog with the price being asked should be an aid to intelligent purchasing.

Independent Manufacturers and Imports

American Marc: This company offers a 9-1/2 horsepower *diesel* outboard. It is air-cooled with two opposed pistons in one cylinder.

Elk Marine of England: This company offers three light-weight, low-horsepower, air-cooled engines. Weight ranges from 21 to 40 pounds. In the line are: the Cub, 1-1/2 horsepower; Cadet, 3; and Captain, 4-1/2 horsepower.

Bundy: Introduced on the east coast in 1961, the Bundy is a new 30 horsepower motor developed by the Innocenti firm in Italy. The engine weighs 96 pounds, a fairly light weight for its power, and is built for 15-inch transoms although a five-inch extension kit is available. There is a choice of single or dual lever controls and a wide selection of propellers.

Marine Motors: A four-cycle, air-cooled 3 horsepower engine, weighing 35 pounds is made by this company.

Muncie Gear Works: Perhaps the "baby" of the outboard field is the Mighty Mite made by this company. Their 1.7 horsepower engine weighs 17 pounds.

Oliver Corporation: This company is a successor to Chris-Craft in the outboard field. Eight models are offered, all twin-cylinder engines ranging from 36 to 6 horsepower. The 35 horsepower B4 Bulldog is available in standard and long-shaft models, and in counter-rotating twin units. The K6, 16 horsepower model appears in manual and electric-starting units, with standard or long shafts. The J6, the 6 horsepower model, is also available with a choice of 15 or 20-inch transom shafts.

Seagull: This British import has been selected by a number of sailing classes as the preferred auxiliary propulsion unit. It is a single-cylinder engine, weighing about 28-1/2 pounds and is noted for low fuel consumption. Alternate shaft lengths for 16 or 22-inch transoms make it suitable for use on different types of sailing craft.

Outboard Motor Manufacturers

Elgin, Sears Roebuck & Co., 925 S. Homan Avenue, Chicago, Illinois.

Evinrude, 4143, North 27th Street, Milwaukee, Wisconsin

Gale, Gale Products, Galesburg, Illinois.

Johnson, Waukegan, Illinois.

Mercury, Kiekhaefer Company, Fond Du Lac, Wisconsin.

Scott, McCulloch Corporation, 2901 East Hennepin, Minneapolis, Minn.

West Bend, West Bend Aluminum Company, West Bend, Wisconsin.

American Marc, American Marc, Inc., 1601 West Florence Avenue, Inglewood, California

Elk Marine, c/o Robert Boomer Agency, 23016 Evalyn Ave., Torrance, Calif.

Bundy, 207 Sheffield St., Mountainside, New Jersey.

Marine Motors, 1001 Boyce Avenue, Towson 4, Maryland.

Muncie Gear Works, P.O. Box 1192, Muncie, Indiana.

Oliver Corporation, Outboard Motor Division, 135 Hamblin Avenue, Battle Creek, Michigan.

Seagull, Jake's Boat Yard, Kirby Lane, Rye, N. Y.

CHAPTER III

Selecting the Inboard Boat

Most of the inboard cruisers under 30 feet in length have their counterparts in outboard cruisers. However, there are certain inherent advantages in the inboard boat. The "selling" points of the outboards have been discussed in the section dealing with them. The engine used in most inboards is more efficient and quieter than a comparable outboard; its per-horsepower or gallon per hour consumption is usually lower, and it is lower in pound-of-weight per horsepower. Structurally, the inboard with its higher rear transom is a safer boat in any kind of rough water than an outboard. As to power, the practical maximum available today in outboards is a twin-sixty installation giving 120 horsepower. A number of 32 foot inboards offer engines of over 500 horsepower.

About Horsepower

The horsepower of the boat is one feature that calls for some caution on the part of a buyer. The race for horsepower in Detroit has been reflected on the waterways. Most marine engines are built on automotive blocks and the larger sized blocks used in automobiles mean larger and more powerful marine engines. In theory, the more powerful the engine, the greater the speed of the boat, although this is affected to some degree by the hull design. But buying unusable horsepower is a sheer waste of money. Before buying a boat it is suggested that it be tried out in the waters where it will be used. The novice boatman may find that the overpowered craft is too much for him to handle with any feeling of se-

Three popular types of inboards — the small utility-runabout; the family cruiser; and the sport fisherman.

curity, and that a boat with less power may be more suited to his needs. Also, the more horsepower the greater the fuel costs during a season. Many manufacturers offer hulls with options as to the type of power plant to be installed.

Some Hull Characteristics

Without being a naval architect, it is possible to tell something about how a boat will react in the water by examining it in its cradle on shore.

A barge, with its squarish, flat hull is the most stable type of boat, but it requires a great deal of power to move it through the water. Extending the length of a flat-bottom hull and giving it a prow will reduce the stability to some extent and it may roll a bit, but the flat-bottomed boat has these advantages: it has the greatest buoyancy and lift for its weight and will draw the least water. Boat builders have to effect a compromise.

Now, for a moment consider a perfectly rounded bottom. This is the most unstable type of boat, and generally a round-bottomed boat requires heavy ballast along the keel to keep it upright in the water. But the round-bottomed boat has the advantage that it sinks deeper into the water than a flatter boat and generally has an easier motion in the water. For the same weight, a round-bottomed boat will have a greater draft than a flat one.

The third possibility is a V-bottom boat. The V-bottom is a compromise between the flat and round-bottom types. It has less basic stability than the flat-bottomed boat, but is able to cut through the water with less slapping and pounding than a flatter-bottomed craft. The sharpness of the "V," what is termed the *deadrise*, largely determines the performance of the V-bottom hull.

As a rule, the broader the beam of a hull (its width), the greater its stability.

Consider the above factors when examining a boat with purchase in mind, keeping aware of the fact that all boats represent a comprise among the three types of hull characteristics. What is called a "round bottom boat" is usually about halfway between a round and flat hull. This kind of hull is rather sharply rounded at the chine (the longitudinal line along which the bottom and sides of the boat meet, in a flat or V-bottom boat. The perfectly round bottom would have no chine). Then the curve flattens out drastically across most of the midship part of the hull. Just as it is a compromise in design, it is a compromise in riding qualities, with water-borne characteristics being somewhere between those of the flat and round-bottomed boats.

Further compromises are possible by combining all three types of bottoms; part round, part flat, part V-bottom. The forward section may be V-shaped for maximum cutting power through the water, assuming a round shape and finally becoming flat towards the stern for greatest stability and lift. Also, there is the seasled type of flat bottom with an uprising prow.

Mention is often made of a "soft" or "hard" chine. The hard or sharp-cornered chine gives maximum static stability and buoyancy; the rounded or soft chine provides easier motion and greater ease in making turns.

Most of the larger inboard boats are of the "displacement" type. This means that they are designed to displace an amount of water equal to the weight of the boat and its load when moving through the water. For this purpose the boat should have somewhat rounded lines, tapering ends, and a narrow beam in relation to the length of the hull. Every displacement hull has what is known as "hull speed." This is the maximum speed to which it can be pushed despite the amount of power applied. Any additional power applied to propulsion will make the stern squat, the bow rise, and the wake become heavier.

Runabouts (both inboard and outboard) are what is known as the "planing" type. They are designed to climb on top of the water after hull speed is reached, and then plane or skim over the surface. Ideally, the inboard cruiser at top speed should operate in what is termed the "transition" zone, just a bit short of planing speed.

Also, keep in mind that a light boat will travel faster than a heavy one of the same shape and size, and that wind resistance is a factor to be considered. A boat with a high superstructure will be under "sail" influences from the wind which would not affect a similar boat with a more streamlined above-water construction. Still another point is the freeboard, or height of the boat above water. If the boat is low and is to be moored at a high dock it may be difficult for older persons to get in and out and to load and unload the boat.

The Sleeping Problem

The principle of *caveat emptor* applies to many of the boat advertisements which stress the number of persons that a boat will sleep. Generally a boat of at least 25 feet is required to sleep four persons in a reasonably civilized manner. In addition to the basic sleeping space, you must consider the need for room to hold clothing, food, water, fuel, cooking and sanitary facilities, and room to move about. The important feature of headroom must also be considered. There are few places more uncomfortable than a cramped galley or "head" in which there is no room to stand errect. The bunks should have sufficient height to sit up without banging against something, and there should be room for stand-up dressing and undressing near the bunks. Storage space is also important. There should be an adequate number of dry lockers and places to hang outer clothing.

While the bilge may look like a good storage area, in practice the only thing that should go down there is ballast. Another point is the interior lighting of the boat. There should be a way for a person to read in bed if he chooses to, and there should be no need to depend on a flashlight for getting around the boat after dark.

The "convertible" idea is one that has its drawbacks. Any boat that requires a complete rebuilding job from day to night use and vice versa will prove to be a serious problem. Makeshift bunks and sleeping arrangements that require shifting of partitions and furnishings may look satisfactory in the light of the showroom, but will prove a constant source of annoyance on the water.

Also, since many boats have fuel and water tanks that are inadequate for cruising, this point should be checked.

Check for Functional Layout

In some ways women have been the bane of the marine architects. In an effort to gain the approval of the distaff side of the buying team, they have created interior layouts as lavish as the powder room of a plush hotel, but some have overlooked the fact that a boat is a mechanism designed to carry people over the water, and that any mechanism can go wrong.

Make certain that you can reach any part of the boat. Plush upholstery and panelling will be of little help if there is a leak in some part of the boat that you can't get to, or if wiring and piping have become inaccessible because of some "pretty" feature of the boat. You should be able to reach any part of the operating machinery of the boat and have room to wield a tool there if necessary. You should be able to get down to the lowest point of the bilge and to reach any interior point in the craft. If not, look for another boat in which you can!

What Size Boat?

Here the important factors are what you can afford and the intended use of the boat. If you are new to the boating sport, your safest bet is to place yourself in the hands of a reputable boat broker or marine architect and follow his recommendations. River cruising obviously calls for a different type boat from those used in offshore sport fishing. If you are planning to stay within sheltered waterways, you do not need a boat that is built to take inlets and deep water.

For your first boat it is always safe to get a smaller boat than you think you want. Smaller boats of standard design are usually fairly easy to sell if you want to move up to a larger boat next year and not much should be lost on the trade-in. Also, a smaller boat is easier to handle, and with a smaller boat you are less likely to set out on a cruise that is beyond your boat-handling capabilities.

Another point is that the purchase of a boat is not the final investment. Operating and maintenance costs can only be learned from experience; there is little pleasure to be a boat owner and find that the monthly payments do not leave you with enough money to buy gasoline.

Here are some of the expenses that should be planned on in conjunction with boat owning:

1. *Insurance.*

2. *Maintenance.* This can be expensive if done professionally. If you plan to do it yourself, think in terms of the man-hours of labor and the energy you have, the volunteer help you can draft, and whether you have the know-how and strength to do this work.

3. *Mooring.* Unless you have a private dock or mooring place you will have to pay for a place to "park" your craft. Mooring fees are usually by the foot, and in many places there is keen competition for mooring places with the result that prices are going up each season.

4. *Winter storage.* This also includes charges for pulling up and setting your boat back in the water; usually figured by the foot. In addition many yards require that they be given the job of painting and hull repairs.

5. *Water transportation to boat.* Many moorings require the use of a dinghy to get to and from the mooring each time you use the boat. This may mean the purchase of a dinghy or an outboard for the trips back and forth.

6. *Yacht club fees.* Many find it no more costly to join a yacht club than to make deals for mooring, shipyard service, etc. Depending on the club there may be assessments, unexpected food and bar bills, etc.

7. *Incidentals.* There's an old saying, "it's going to cost more than you figured it was going to cost."

But, on the other hand, about eight million people can't be wrong, and they have boats!

CHAPTER IV

Guide to Outboard Cruising

A recent survey has found that boating rates third in preference among Americans' favorite recreations. Pleasure boating, largely due to the growth of the outboard, has crossed all class lines as a pleasant-weather sport. The bank president is likely to wave a friendly greeting to the waitress from the corner lunchroom as they pass in local waters.

No other sport has so much to offer

What could be more fun than a picnic? And getting to a place that is really different is easy by outboard. (*Johnson photo*)

A snow-covered mountain to look at, a quiet lake to fish in — and a good-looking boat and motor to enjoy both. *(Johnson photo)*

in terms of fun, leisure and a wealth of new experience. No other sport has so much to offer the family, for this is family fun and each member derives pleasure and satisfaction seldom found in other fields. No other sport is less demanding in the way of special skills, aptitudes, muscular coordination or strength. Its appeal is universal.

Thousands have discovered that an outboard-cruising family can find their winding way along the enchanting Oklawaha River in Florida, where the trees form arches overhead and are reflected in the glassy water. They can launch their boat from the hard, sloping beach on the shore of Coot Bay near the southern tip of Florida and from there explore the mysterious Everglades. They can follow the Gulf Coast Waterway between Venice and Clearwater along many shallow channels. They can explore the beautiful deep water river in New York which Henry Hudson first discovered 300 years ago and which now bears his name. From Hartford to its outlet on Long Island Sound, the Connecticut River vistas can be enjoyed. In the same years in which the Everglades are visited, it is possible to scoot around the Bras d'Or Lakes in Cape Breton, Nova Scotia, far beyond the northern tip of the United States. Many of the smaller outboard cruisers are as portable as a runabout.

Outboard cruising is one of the few forms of recreation which a family can enjoy together, especially if some thought and planning is given to the children's entertainment.

Most outboard cruisers run in length from 18 to 23 feet overall and have two regular bunks in the main cabin. The open cockpit space of the outboard usually provides enough room for at least

"Just cruising" is fun when you have a big, comfortable cabin cruiser with ample room for two couples. *(Johnson photo)*

two children (or grown-ups) to sleep on air mattresses or roll-up sleeping pads. And, with a hard or soft top over the cockpit and side curtains, a snug and roomy cabin is created.

It is far more difficult for a family to enjoy playing together on a golf course or tennis court than it is on an outboard cruiser where all can share, in accordance with their abilities, in the fun afloat and ashore. An outboard cruise helps to satisfy your instinct for exploration. With the aid of a boat trailer—or rental boats that are available in many areas—you can quickly reach distant waters and with the shallow draft of your boat you can reach waters inaccessible to other boats. In many places you can run the bow of your craft up against the bank for a stroll ashore or a picnic. Along waterways, rivers, canals, narrow lakes, and creeks, there are many interesting things to see: other boats and people, domestic and wild animals, birds of many varieties. And there are many beautiful scenes and colors to appeal to your aesthetic sense, whether the land is high or low.

Outboard cruising—no matter where you cruise—is the most practical type of cruising, especially for the family with children. The mobility of an outboard craft allows you to beach at will and to explore creeks and "gunkholes" not ordinarily accessible to larger craft. The constant change of scenery adds up to a change of pace. And the exploratory side-trips available with an outboard are a source of never-ending delight for youngsters.

Outboard cruising is relatively inexpensive. This writer doesn't know of any other type of cruising in a new boat in which you can get so much for relatively so little. With a trailer, you can usually store your boat in your own (or a friend's) back yard. If you need some work done which you don't want to undertake yourself, you can easily trail your craft to a boat yard.

It is fun to live in a movable home, to explore new waters and to revisit favorite haunts, to indulge in a healthy form of outdoor recreation which you can share with friends and children, to get off the crowded highways for a while, to enjoy weekends and vacations, to have family fun for moderate cost. The people you meet when you are cruising are almost

Whether at a well-equipped boat club, or on a gently sloping beach, launching the boat is always an exciting event, for it signals the beginning of carefree recreation, far from traffic jams and everyday problems. *(Kiekhaefer Corporation photo)*

Two increasingly common sights on the highways are the American compact car and the outboard boat and trailer. Together they can put hundreds of rivers and lakes within easy reach. *(Kiekhaefer Corporation photo)*

Cluster of Cruisers — The outboard cruiser continues to grow in popularity. Each of the models shown, complete with motor, sells for less then the average low-priced car. *(Kiekhaefer Corporation photo)*

invariably friendly and cooperative, and you will come back from your cruise with a higher opinion of human nature than you ever had before.

How to Plan Your Cruise

In planning an outboard cruise, it is well to take into account a number of things: your type of boat and water suitable for cruising in it; the location of your home port and the time which you have; frequency, convenience and accessibility of supply ports along the way (dockage, fuel, food, repairs, etc.) and the availability of secure anchorages or tie-ups. Possibilities for overnight accommodations or camp sites if you don't plan to live aboard should also be considered, as well as interests of your crew—such as in the scenery, points of historical interest along the way, or perhaps the location of friends and relatives. If you have the instincts of an explorer or like adventure and excitement, you may want to pick a different type of cruise than the one you would choose if rest and relaxation were your aims. Planning the summer cruise can well be the family activity for a winter week-end.

With a well-built seaworthy outboard cruiser, you don't need to be quite so careful in trying to avoid large lakes and open sounds when the weather is rough as you do in an open runabout with less freeway. But even with a runabout, if it is likely to be uncomfortably turbulent and wet on a stretch of wide water, you don't necessarily have to wait for the weather to change. If you are taking a really amphibious cruise, accompanied along the shore by your car and empty trailer, you can pick up the boat and circumnavigate the rough water by land, launching the boat again when conditions are favorable.

Weather conditions vary considerably in different parts of the country and it is important to know the waters in which you cruise. Once you get the feeling of being on water and learn the effects of tides and currents, you'll cruise with confidence.

Weather is most important. Changing winds, even the slightest breeze, exert their influence on the water. Always make it a point to check the water before going afloat. A call to the local Coast Guard station, airport, or weather bureau will fill you in with updated information on the weather.

Since the type of boat you have will determine to a considerable extent the waters you choose for your cruise, let's suppose that you do not already own a boat. What type should you buy for your outboard cruising—a runabout or a cruiser? As is the case with all boats, each has its advantages and disadvantages. No boat serves all purposes equally well.

A runabout costs considerably less in the first place, both for boat and equipment. It needs a smaller and less expensive trailer, and is easier to move from trailer to water and back. It costs far less for yearly maintenance, and half of a two-car garage makes an ideal winter storage place. If you decide to buy a runabout for cruising purposes, one of between 15 and 18 feet in length is ideal. But here a bit of advice could be injected. Don't be tempted into buying the lowest-priced boat you can find. Some runabouts may be all right for smooth waters and not too rugged use, but they may be poorly designed for rough waters or amphibious cruising. For instance, some runabouts tend to bury their bows in a choppy sea unless they are traveling fast enough to start planing. But in that case they will pound and throw out too much spray to be comfortable. For cruising, get a boat with enough fullness and flare in the bow to lift it out of the waves without requiring too much speed, while having enough beam and freeboard for reasonable stability and comfort.

Among the things to watch for in buying a boat are the following: (1) Is the

A 17-ft. runabout with a convertible top makes a comfortable and attractive family boat. Colorful stripes make the life jackets more appealing to the children. *(Kiekhaefer Corporation photo)*

Brisk cruising is a family recreation in this 20-foot overnighter. *(Kiekhaefer Corporation photo)*

FLOAT PLAN

of _____
(name of boat owner)

IF TROUBLE OCCURS while you're cruising on your boat, help will come faster if the Coast Guard or other rescue agencies know *where to look for you*. For your safety and your family's peace of mind complete this form—leave it with a responsible person whom you can depend upon to notify authorities if you're overdue.

IF OVERDUE, CONTACT _____
(name, phone number of nearest Coast Guard station or other rescue agency)

BOAT: Name of vessel_____ Length overall_____
Registry number_____ Color of hull_____
(white hull, blue top, etc.)
Power_____
(inboard, outboard, sail)
Radio aboard { (transmit frequency)_____
NUMBER OF PERSONS ABOARD_____ (receive frequency)_____

DEPARTURE FROM_____ DATE & TIME DEPART_____
DESTINATION_____ DATE & EST. TIME RETURN_____
ROUTE OR CRUISING PLANS_____

* * *

PREPARED IN THE INTEREST OF SAVING LIVES AND PROPERTY BY

MARINE OFFICE of AMERICA · 123 WILLIAM STREET, NEW YORK 38, N. Y.

LITHO IN U.S.A.   *Leading insurers of pleasure boats*   COPYRIGHT 1960

Just as a pilot benefits by filing a flight plan, you add a margin of safety to every cruise if you fill out a float plan and leave it with a responsible person ashore before you go. Then should something happen and you are overdue this person can notify the Coast Guard or local rescue agency of your destination and cruising plan so that help can reach you without delay. *(Plan courtesy Marine Office of America)*

outboard transom the right height? (15 inches is standard, though for bigger boats long-shafted motors and a 20-inch transom are desirable.) (2) Are the deck and cabin sides adequately supported with deck knees? (3) Are the frames sufficient in number and quality? (4) Are there enough strengthening reinforcements in the boat (knees, frames, clamps, etc.)? (5) Are the bow and stern corners adequately reinforced and braced? (See Chapter "Small Boat Construction")

These are just a few of the things to be aware of. But there are so many differences between a well built and a poorly built runabout that the safest plan is to have someone who "knows his stuff" advise you before you buy a runabout, new or old.

As to an outboard cruiser, it is important not only to bear in mind the points raised regarding a runabout, but also to consider what items of equipment are included in the price. For example, is there a "head" (toilet) with adequate headroom? Check also such items as a galley, sink, ice chest, water tank, mattresses, permanent or convertible top over the cockpit, anchor and anchor lines, fenders, and other items of equipment. The number and quality of such items is almost as important as the design and workmanship of your boat.

Where to?

In planning an outboard cruise, the next step after considering the type of boat you want and the kind of waters suitable for you is to pick the particular waters on which you would like to make your outboard cruise. If your time is limited, say to one week or two, you won't want to spend too much time on the road getting to or from your cruising area; possibly a day each way is all you will want to spend. Since this guide is written for people in all parts of the country, we can't recommend waters you should choose for your cruise. However, a few points to keep in mind are the following:

1. In figuring the mileage you expect to average per day, don't multiply the speed of the boat by the number of hours between breakfast and supper and expect to cover that mileage. You'll have more fun if you break your voyage several times during the day to allow for exploring and sightseeing. Also, if there are children aboard they need to work off steam. "Don't hurry too much" is the first prescription for a good time. The fun in cruising is going, not in getting to places.

2. If you are following a canal or narrow river, there are usually speed limits, especially on a canal. For example, on the New York Barge Canals (Erie, Champlain, etc.) there is a limit of 6 m.p.h. on the canal cuts and 10 m.p.h. on the rivers—statute miles per hour, not knots. And if you think you can get away with a greater speed than this, due to the absence of motor boat "cops" or radar, you may be fooling yourself. The lock tenders telephone your time of departure to the next lock and you may be held up at the lock for speeding.

3. It takes time to go through each lock, seldom less than 15 or 20 minutes per lock and often much more if commercial traffic is heavy. For unhurried, comfortable cruising, with several stops each day, we have found that from 60 to 80 miles a day is a good distance on which to figure—when there are no locks or speed limits.

4. Rough waters may limit your speed or make a fast passage too wet and uncomfortable for pleasure, and you may wish to wait in port for better weather. Also, in some parts of the country fog may hold you in for several days at a time. However, if you are on an amphibious cruise accompanied by a boat trailer, you can bypass the storm or fog by putting your boat on the trailer.

Supply Ports

You can learn a great deal about supply ports and tie-up or anchorage possibilities along your proposed cruising route by studying your charts. For instance, where the charts indicate a large community (by criss-crosses to show streets or black squares to show houses) you can be fairly sure of getting supplies and finding some sort of dock at which to tie up. Sometimes docks are shown on charts, although the type of dock is not shown. These charts will give you a good idea of how well protected a port is.

Overnight Sleeping Accommodations

It is generally possible to find accommodations in hotels, tourist houses, or motels in most moderate sized communities and often in or near smaller places, although it may take a considerable walk or taxi ride to reach these accommodations. In addition, the rapidly expanding number of marinas and "boatels" along the travelled waterways will make your search for a comfortable bed much easier.

Some runabouts can be rigged for sleeping—if you are young enough—by temporarily bridging the space between seats and putting up a top or tent of some kind over the cockpit. Sometimes along the route, public camp sites are to be found where you can pitch a tent and light fires. Camping out on someone's property along the way, without permission of the owner, may get you into trouble, though many people do this on the beaches and on out-of-the-way spots along deserted shores. In such cases, it is

Another Approach to Amphibious Cruising — A jeep provides the way to get there; a trailer for sleeping and a car-top boat complete the equipment. *(Johnson photo)*

Throughout the country, hotels and resorts are building attractive docking and dining areas for the growing numbers of outboard boaters. *(Kiekhaefer Corporation photo)*

very important not to light fires, especially when you are away from stony or sandy beaches.

Plan with a Purpose

Since having a good time is among the principal objectives of an outboard cruise, the wise skipper will take into account the kinds of things in which he and his crew are interested. Do they want to "get away from it all" or do they want to visit active yachting ports where a great deal is going on? Do they want to spend their nights in quiet, out-of-the-way creeks, rivers or coves, or in harbors where the lively tunes of a yacht club dance float—or perhaps bounce—through the evening air. Or do they want a movie or bowling alley for the evening's recreation? With a little advance planning, it is not difficult to arrange a little of both on many cruises.

Are they especially interested in scenery—spectacular or restful—or in exploring points of historical interest? Do they want to visit friends or relatives along the way? Are excitement and adventure a primary consideration, or is relaxation desired? Often you get some of both on a cruise, but a good plan can achieve a balance between excitement and relaxation.

These are a few of the many points to have in mind in planning a successful outboard cruise.

What You'll Need Aboard

Once you have selected your outboard boat, you will find there is no end to the amount of equipment you can put aboard. It is not too unusual to find a 21-foot cruiser equipped with a fathometer, direction finder, radio-telephone, a dashboard with a cigarette lighter, and a waffle iron in the galley.

This may be carrying things to the extreme, but with the generators found on the larger outboard motors and the new types of alternators, it's entirely possible to go afloat with almost as many appliances as you would find at home.

Let's be practical for a moment, and think in terms of outfitting the typical runabout. We'll assume she is a sturdy craft, with a walk-through forward cockpit and thwarts amidship or completely aft. There are several accessories which you will find extremely useful.

The first is a convertible top. There are a number of firms which turn out well designed convertible tops similar to those used on automobiles. Top and side curtains offer a good deal of protection for the helmsman, especially in foul weather or in rough seas when he might be ducking quite a bit of spray. The top and side curtains also make the going more comfortable during the late season when the temperature has dropped.

A cockpit cover is almost a "must." This, too, can be purchased as a stock item or can be easily tailored to the specifications of your boat by a competent sail or awning maker. A cockpit cover will protect interior paint and varnish when you are lying at mooring, and will make bailing easier after rainstorms. Make certain, however, that it is made of a material which "breathes", since condensation under the cover will cause many problems.

If you select a big, beamy, utility-type boat, you'll find that you have ample cockpit space. It's here that you can make good use of folding canvas chairs. Make certain the legs are tipped with rubber, for this will eliminate much of the scuffing of the cockpit floor boards. You might even wish to buy folding swivel chairs which attach to the thwarts.

Here's a rundown of additional equipment: one or two anchors (see the section on anchors, page 120), docking lines, and four fenders and a fender board which is useful if you lie alongside a seawall or dock, or if you lock through a canal in which there is considerable

Local landmarks take on a new aspect when viewed from the family outboard. The urge to explore, long an American trait, has been given a new means of satisfaction by the increase in boating facilities around the country. *(Kiekhaefer Corporation photo)*

turbulence. Make certain your craft has a combination lights or lights to meet the Coast Guard requirements. A flashlight is a handy item to keep aboard at all times. It should be checked frequently since dampness often affects flashlights. Binoculars, a liquid compass and a complete set of charts are other items in the "must" list.

Just a word about binoculars. If you are crossing a large lake or similar body of water, you'll find them extremely desirable to spot markers or buoys. But don't get a pair with too high power, for it is difficult to focus a high-powered pair of glasses on a distant object from a bouncing boat. For small-boat use, 7 x 50 power binoculars are recommended. The individual focusing type is advised as it is most resistant to dampness and fungus and has greater light-gathering power.

A tool kit, shear and cotter pins for the older model motors, and the owner's manual for your motor should always be within reach.

If you are fastidious about your boat, you'll probably want to stow a canvas bucket with a cellulose sponge, brush, cleaning powder and cloth. The urge to scrub the topsides is overwhelming for many skippers, so there's nothing like being prepared.

Your equipment should also include a horn, a paddle, and a lock and chain to fasten your motor to the boat. If you'll be doing a lot of trailering, you'll want a self-contained light to put on the transom of your boat while trailering at night and a red flag to fasten to the stern if you trail during the day. In all probability, you'll also want to take along several gasoline tanks, depending on the distance of the runs you make while cruising.

It goes almost without saying that most of the items recommended for a runabout also apply to the outboard cruiser—only more so. Naturally, the outboard cruiser is a larger craft, most of them running up to 21 or 23 feet in length. In itself, the increased size is a certain incentive for the cruiser-owner to invite guests to share his fun on the water. This munificence of spirit will undoubtedly increase operating costs. Even at that, the skipper-host should find himself spending no more money—and probably less—than if he entertained his friends at home for a weekend.

You can easily sleep two persons in the aft cockpit of most outboard cruisers as well as two in the cabin. It is here that sleeping bags or mattresses prove well worthwhile as additional equipment. They are relatively comfortable and they

Fast becoming the most important "First Step" for outboarders is the courtesy Coast Guard inspection. After such an inspection by experienced Coast Guard personnel, the owner can be sure that his craft is properly equipped for a safe boating season. (*Kiekhaefer Corporation photo*)

can be rolled up in the morning so that they stow in a minimum of space.

Towels, soap (including salt water soap), toilet paper, and extra deck cushions are all necessary additional equipment.

When it comes to equipment, remember one thing. The best friend to whom you can turn for advice is the local inspection officer of the Coast Guard Auxiliary. The Auxiliary is the civilian component of the U.S. Coast Guard, and the job it has done over the years is nothing short of admirable. If you are a complete newcomer to the field of boating, feel free to invite an Auxiliary member aboard. You'll find him kindly and sympathetic to your problems. His job is to make boating safer and it's a good bet that he will go out of his way to help you. The Coast Guard has the complete list of necessary safety items and will make recommendations of additional equipment C.G.A. considers necessary to make a boat more seaworthy.

OVERLAND CRUISING

There are various ways of conducting an amphibious cruise. The simplest is to use your car and trailer to bring your boat to the place at which you will start your cruise, put the boat in the water, leaving your car and trailer at that point, where you will pick them up again at the end of your cruise. Another very simple way if you don't want to retrace your steps is to arrange to have someone bring the car and trailer to the place at which you plan to end your cruise. You can do it yourself or get one of your crew to do it with the aid of a car, bus, or other means of transportation, or you can easily hire someone to do it, such as a garage or filling station man.

There is another form of amphibious cruising which requires a little planning, but which opens up intriguing possibilities for comfortable outboard cruising with runabouts not having sleeping accommodations. In this case, the car and empty trailer go along with the boat on roads which follow the waterways on which the boat is going. At various agreed upon points along the route the car with empty trailer meets the boat; sometimes several times during the day to exchange crews, sometimes at the end of the day's run. If your crew can drive a car it is easy to take turns at this kind of operation, with one or two of the crew in the car and the others in the boat. The ones on the mid-day car shift will have time to pick up a sandwich lunch for all, or find a good place for a shore meal at the noon rendezvous, when the entire crew can use the car while the boat is tied up. Those on the mid-afternoon car shift have the duty of finding quarters for the night near the place where the day's run is planned to end. If you have tents and want to camp out, perhaps the car crew can do some of the scouting while the boat crew watches for inviting possibilities along the way.

This kind of amphibious cruising is very flexible. If there are especially interesting places to visit along the way, perhaps a famous garden or a historic fort, the boat can be tied up at some convenient dock while the car does the transportation.

Speaking of such a cruise, Fessenden S. Blanchard, the noted boating writer, says: "This kind of amphibious voyage is not just an impractical theory as some of the old school might think. It is a very practical idea and mighty good fun as the writer, his wife and two friends found out in undertaking such a voyage from Troy, New York, along the Erie Canal to Oswego on Lake Ontario, then down the St. Lawrence River to Sorel, up the Richelieu to Lake Champlain, and down the Champlain Barge Canal and 'canalized' Hudson back to Troy again. We did this in two weeks with our 15-1/2 footer with a 30 h.p. Evinrude Lark, trailer and car. With the exception of two stretches, the

Trailering your boat gives you mobility to go boating in a variety of waters and provides convenient storage when you stay at home. Note tilting frame and dropping bolster on this trailer — two features that make launching and loading quick and easy. *(Lone Star Boats and Trailers)*

Meesdow made the entire trip successfully in the water. One of the two exceptions was by-passing Lakes Oneida and Ontario when the lakes were a mass of whitecaps from a 25 or 30 m.p.h. blow. We decided that a trip by car for this part of the journey would be less strenuous, although if we had been younger we might have felt differently.

"Launching Meesdow again at Thousand Islands Park, near where the St. Lawrence starts its flow eastward from Lake Ontario, we followed this river down to a short distance below Cornwall where we took the boat out again to avoid being delayed seriously in some crowded and out-of-repair locks. Again sliding Meesdow into the St. Lawrence just below Montreal, we continued for the rest of the voyage with our boat in the water though we had some rough going in a tide rip on the St. Lawrence and in a stiff blow on Lake Champlain.

"Thus we demonstrated to our own satisfaction the feasibility of this kind of amphibious cruising in a small runabout. And we found out how easy it was to skip a rough or unpleasant section, to dodge an area where several locks out of order would have seriously delayed our trip."

Amphibious cruising, for which outboard runabouts and cruisers are especially well suited, is still in its infancy and is due for tremendous development as more and more people take to boating and realize the possibilities which this kind of cruising opens up. Boat trailers are being improved yearly and the growth in their annual production has been phenomenal.

With home ports in back yards or garages, there is none of the concern a boat-owner feels over the fate of his boat when a storm strikes a crowded anchorage. With the boat near at hand, it is easy to work on it during spare hours. And with a boat trailer, you can turn seasonal cruising into a year-round affair. Winter outboard cruising in the southern states offers a wide variety of voyages.

Some skippers like to go it solo. Some find there's nothing they'd rather do than stow aboard wife, children and a week's supply of cold cuts; then take off for the most remote Shangri-la. This is an escape and it meets the need of many. On the other hand, there is the skipper who is naturally gregarious. He likes company and wouldn't dream of being on the water unless he made it a party. To him, there is only one kind of cruising—group cruising in the company of at least one more boat and perhaps with as many as ten or fifteen other craft.

Group cruising can be defined in two distinct categories. The first is the informal group cruise of four, five or ten boats. These outboard owners generally belong to the same boat club. If they are not club members, they keep their craft at the same anchorage. They simply get together and decide to make a group cruise, all of them running together to an agreed destination.

The second type group cruise is the mass cruise. These have proved extremely popular in Texas, Washington, Florida, Wisconsin, New York and other areas. Literally hundreds of families take part in Florida's annual Kissimmee River Cruise. These families trailer their boats to the Kissimmee River, then take off en masse, to enjoy a long weekend of barbecues, fish fries and square dances. They sleep aboard or pitch tents along the riverbank, frequently hauling their boats ashore for use as lean-to's.

When it comes to group cruising, there are many variations on the theme. There's a cruising club in Milwaukee whose members stage a *Smorg-Aboard*. The outboard owners shove off on a cruise and end up rafting their craft together for a big social gathering, at which they hop from boat to boat with each skipper playing host to his fellow club members. There is a group of outboard skippers on western Long Island Sound who get together informally and several times during the summer, cruise around Manhattan Island or head their craft northward on the Hudson River. The Connecticut Rivers, the TVA lakes, and many other areas are locales for informal cruises or annual get-togethers.

Once you get your boat, you will find you have no difficulty making friends on the water. And once you've made friends, you'll probably find yourself taking part in a mass cruise.

A skipper can shove off with his wife and children for a ten-day vacation and find at the end that they have spent considerably less money than they would have by vacationing at a resort or having toured extensively by auto. The informality of cruising immediately cuts the need for an extensive, and expensive, wardrobe. Meals cooked aboard, or at waterfront dining places are usually less expensive than those offered in resort-area hotels. Tipping is seldom encountered along the nation's waterways, where the boatman is accepted on the basis of friendship and not bankroll.

Houseboat Cruising

Houseboat cruising is still in its infancy and is due for a great increase in popularity as more people come to realize how well a houseboat driven by one or two outboard motors combines a maximum of room and comfort with sufficient mobility to move safely from place to place, even across rough water.

Although houseboats have not been promoted as strongly as other types of pleasure boats, there are almost thirty

The houseboat, once considered a waterborne shanty, has developed in the past few years into a glamorous recreational craft. Houseboats like this Holiday, have most of the comforts of home — and you don't have to cut the lawn. *(Kiekhaefer Corporation photo)*

Houseboating, the outboard way, may be a fairly slow way to travel but it is the most comfortable way without a doubt. Plenty of room to move around in — and bring all the friends you want. *(Johnson photo)*

companies in the business of making these floating "summer cottages." The great majority of houseboats are built for outboard power, although several types are available with inboard motors. Power and speed are minor factors since these boats aren't intended for much "going." A 40 horsepower outboard will push the average houseboat along at about 7 miles an hour in smooth water, and twin installations will provide slightly more speed and improved maneuverability.

While some of the houseboats are still made on the basic idea of a cottage on a barge, many of the newer models have V bows or sled-type hulls and a shallow enough draft to allow for easy beaching against any soft shore.

Prices range all the way from about $2,000 to $30,000 and up for the larger, plushier custom jobs. A fully-equipped houseboat offers all of the conveniences of a summer home and the advantages of a pleasure boat. They can be docked or anchored, and many have full house-size headroom and range from 8 to 12 feet in beam. One "savings" feature of the houseboat as compared to the summer cottage is that owners seldom pay property taxes.

A large number of houseboats are fitted with double wiring systems, one for battery use and the other for plugging into standard AC current when tied up at a pier. Such modern features as sliding doors and windows are used to save space and many are fitted with the decorative and useful jalousie windows. Other features found in many houseboats are: inside and outside steering for all-weather cruising; frames and awnings for sun decks; tile floors; canvas covered roofs; sun decks; formica counters in the galleys; folding tables and house-sized icebox. Walkways and decks may be rubberized as a safeguard against slipping. Cabins are insulated with rockwool. In short, the inherent features of a houseboat offer the maximum in usable and livable space afloat. In comfort and utility the houseboat is matched only by the largest yachts.

There is little doubt that outboard-powered houseboats are here to stay and will grow greatly in use. Many draw less than a foot and can tie up at almost any bank or dock in shallow water. If comfort rather than speed is your objective, if you want freedom of movement and love the water, look into the possibility of houseboating. Living on a boat instead of in a cottage is appealing to the increasing number of people who like to live in more than one place, suiting their movable home to the season or to their varied tastes and desires.

Keeping The Kids Happy

Stephen Leacock once told of a dashing cavalier who lightly vaulted into his saddle and rushed off madly in all directions. That isn't a bad description of the behavior of young children when they get off a boat after being confined to a small space for some time. So, as a parent, you have a real job on your hands to channel the activities of your kids along socially and nautically acceptable lines when traveling between ports of call. It takes imagination and leadership, especially with young boys.

To begin with, don't let the time between stops get too long. All day trips without stopping may be all right for a crew of adults, but not for children. A stop at a dock or anchorage for lunch is a good way of letting the children expend their extra energy. If the young fry are old enough to keep afloat, a stop for a swim off the swimming ladder would be a good idea. If no docks are handy, nudge up slowly to some steeply sloping bank and let the kids enjoy some needed exercise. You may find it best to make several landings a day for this purpose.

For shore and swimming, inflated rubber balls and perhaps a few tennis balls can add to the fun, and for nearby fields,

Two 15 horsepower outboards mounted on the stern brackets move the Large Pauline B along at a pleasant 8 miles an hour. *(Evinrude photo)*

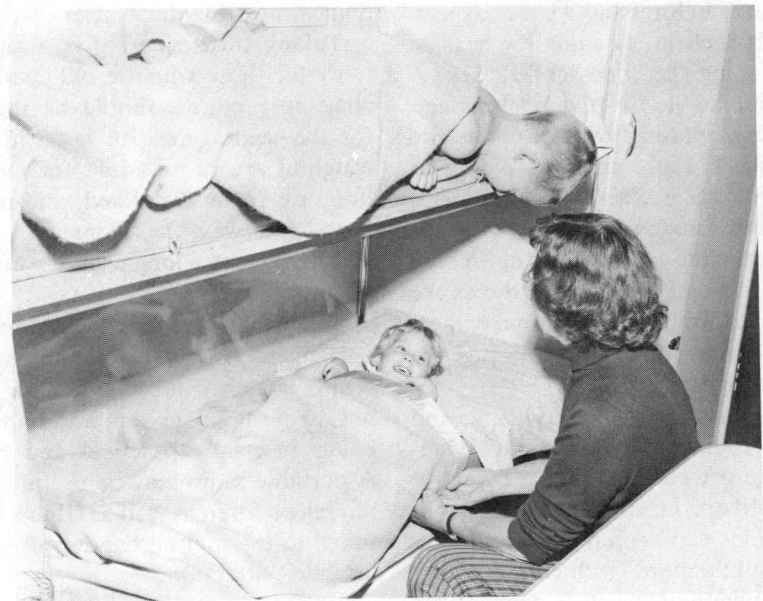

Sleeping accommodations on the houseboat can be as comfortable as those in the ranch house. *(Evinrude photo)*

if the kids are old enough, bring along a baseball and bat. For the water part of it, rubber or plastic rings or floats or some of the inflatable "animals" are a useful adjunct, with perhaps some fins or skin diving equipment for the older ones.

Knocking a tin can off a rock is a perennially favorite pastime that seems to give the competitive spirit a chance to express itself. Shell hunting on the beaches appeals to the more peaceful instincts. Bring along several small buckets for the shell hunters. For the very young, sandy beaches provide endless opportunities for castles with protecting dikes. The chief problem on these shore landings is to keep all of the kids within sight or sound, where you can find them when you are ready to start off again.

What to do with children on these shore or bathing stops is comparatively easy. But how to keep them happy in a small boat takes some foresight. For one thing, give each of them certain tasks and make it clear beforehand what is expected of each of them: cleaning the deck or floors, keeping the ropes coiled, sponging or pumping out the bilge if necessary, getting out or putting away cushions and if you have a cabin cruiser, folding or rolling up blankets and sleeping bags, wiping and stowing dishes, perhaps even doing some of the cooking. You'll probably think of many more duties for them to perform, but don't make them too onerous, or you may face a juvenile mutiny aboard ship.

Bring along some games and cards and plenty of reading and "looking at" material. Try to get material that is suited to the ages of your juvenile crew. Three- to five-year olds can keep happy for a long time filling in pictures with colored crayons or drawing things with a pencil. Older children may be interested in spotting birds along the waterways, and a good, illustrated bird guide and a pair of binoculars will keep them busy. This also applies to adult crew members who may

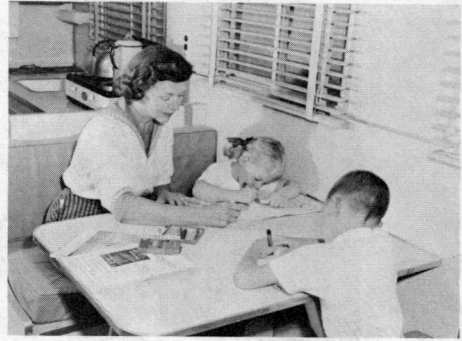

A pencil and crayon set provide the answer to "What to do?" especially on rainy days. *(Evinrude photo)*

become bored.

Fishing is an activity that doesn't depend too much on whether or not any are hauled aboard, so bring along a few hooks, lines, and artificial lures. And, if you want live bait, let your boys dig for clams or worms somewhere along the way. An unused shell bucket may be a good container . . . but keep in mind that fishing can do more to mess up a boat than almost anything else.

Taking turns steering is a useful activity for those who are old enough, and charting a course should be interesting for the teen-agers. But not without the watchful eye of an adult, for most children are easily distracted, and in a narrow waterway a moment's distraction may mean a long wait in a mudbank, if nothing worse.

Singing and musical instruments are a tremendously valuable adjunct to a cruise, whether for children or grown-ups, accordions, guitars and harmonicas being especially practical and popular. A portable radio may be useful in entertaining children as well as adults, and one tuned to the marine bands will keep the listeners' attention.

Unless you are one of those who flee to the waterways to avoid television, one of the new portable TV sets may prove helpful on rainy days when you're locked in a harbor and the children have tired of paint sets and building blocks.

Some Sources of Cruising Information

In open water, a young skipper takes his trick at the wheel. *(Evinrude photo)*

Upper deck of the houseboat makes an ideal sun deck — and a place for a family outdoor jam session. *(Evinrude photo)*

Being properly prepared for entertaining the little "darlings"—if you want that description to apply—may make a big difference in the success of any cruise which is accompanied by the patter of little feet and the joyful chatter of children.

There are numerous sources to which the outboard skipper can turn for information on where to cruise. With the sport growing so rapidly, it's almost impossible to keep completely up-to-date. However, through the expedient of a phone call or correspondence directed to the correct sources, the newcomer should have little difficulty in obtaining information on good cruising waters in almost any part of the country.

The first choice—a completely logical one—is to seek out friends of acquaintances who have done it before. If you are considering a cruise, start talking of the possibilities well ahead of time. Someone is certain to speak up and say something like this: "Oh, you ought to talk to Bill Smith—he and his wife made that trip a couple of years ago."

The boating magazines are an excellent source of information. There are about twenty national and regional boating publications, all of which devote considerable space to outboard cruising. If you happen to be a complete newcomer, stop by at your local newsstand and pick up several copies of boating magazines. Check your local library or boat club, for each will have back numbers on file, as will a "back number magazine" shop. It is here in the boating magazines that you will find colorful first person stories by boatmen who have actually experienced the type of venture you're planning. Cruising guides are another excellent source for basic information. Check your local bookstore for a publisher's list of titles. There are a number of such books written by F. S. Blanchard.

Many oil companies publish waterway guides for various parts of the country. These booklets may be obtained directly from each company or from their waterfront dealers. (See the section on "Free Materials" later in this book.)

State agencies often furnish useful information about waters within each state.

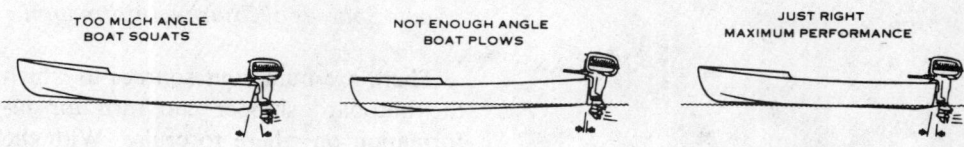

(Evinrude photo)

While the departments doing this vary in different states, usually a letter to the state publicity, public relations or recreation department will bring a reply steering you in the right direction. Frequently, local chambers of commerce will provide information on docking, marinas and waterfront facilities.

The larger newspapers are also a good source of information. Many now have a Boating Editor or a Boating Department that will be able to provide needed information or advise you how to obtain it.

If you are interested in cruising in your own area, you might check your local outboard dealer. Either he has cruised himself or he knows those among his customers who spend their leisure time cruising.

The Outboard Boating Club of America, 307 North Michigan Avenue, Chicago 1, Illinois, is a valuable source of information for anyone planning a cruise. The OBC's monthly publication "Outboard Boating" is one source for material about boating facilities throughout the country. In addition, the OBC maintains a file of boat clubs whose members are known to be active in the cruising field. The skipper who would like to know more about cruising in a specific locality might do well to write directly to the corresponding secretary of the club in whose area he wishes to cruise, or to the Evinrude Foundation, 4143 N. 27th Street, Milwaukee, Wisconsin, which also maintains a list of boating and cruising organizations.

Care and Feeding of the Outboard Motor

With proper care, the outboard motor should give you many years of sound performance.

To get the maximum performance from your motor, make certain you have it mounted correctly. The angle of the motor can make all the difference in the world when it comes to your boat's performance. The sketches above indicate how a boat will "squat," "plow" or "plane" depending on the angle of the propeller and the lower unit.

When you take your boat out, run the motor in all three positions. You'll feel the boat respond and know immediately how it best performs. To change the angle, just tilt the motor forward and take a look at the motor bracket which clamps to the transom. The motor bracket has a lever which slips easily into any one of three slots. By adjusting the lever, you adjust the tilt of the motor. Once you determine at which angle your motor best powers the boat, leave the motor set at that angle. The only time you might make a further adjustment is when you change the load. For instance, if you're headed for a long cruise and you have taken on additional weight in passengers or provisions, you may find your bow or stern "down in the water," depending on where the weight is placed. Naturally, this uneven distribution of the weight will affect the performance of your boat. However, this can be offset by redistributing the weight more evenly and by adjusting the tilt angle of the motor to compensate for off-balance, fore and aft.

A WORD ABOUT FUEL

You'll get the best performance from your motor if you use a good grade of regular gasoline. Correct lubrication of all working parts is extremely important. The lubrication of pistons, cylinder, crankshaft, and connecting rod bearings is supplied solely by oil which you mix with the gasoline.

SAE 30 outboard motor oil is your best bet as a lubricant. This is the outboard oil carried by most marine dealers, although a good grade of automobile motor oil may be used. Use a half-pint of oil for each gallon of gas, or one quart for the usual 6-gallon outboard tank. When the tank is being filled, pour gas into the tank, fill it only half way, then pour in the oil. Shake the tank or stir the mix thoroughly. The gas and oil must be thoroughly mixed to insure even distribution of the lubricant when the motor is running. The mixing of oil and gasoline is more important than the exact amount of oil.

While regular automobile gasoline is generally satisfactory for use in the older outboard motors, there is some controversy over the question of whether special oils and special fuels must be used in the newer, higher-powered outboard engines. Several manufacturers advise the use of white (marine) gasoline, as some types of engines may suffer damage from the effects of spark-plug fouling and pre-ignition from the use of regular gasoline and motor oil.

As a practical matter, it is difficult to obtain white gasoline in many areas, and several companies have discontinued the sale of white gasoline as they were unable to have sufficient turnover to maintain fresh supplies. But the engineers in the different companies generally agree that a cleaner running engine will result from the use of white gasoline. The use of leaded gasoline, particularly in the presence of phosphorus compounds, can cause accumulations in the engine and pre-ignition. This will normally evidence itself in a slowing down of the engine, which can be remedied by removing and replacing the fouled spark plug. However, in some types of engines this can cause serious damage. Also, some of the outboard oils can cause trouble.

It might be advisable for the purchaser of an outboard motor in the higher-power categories to check carefully whether the particular motor in which he is interested requires the use of white gasoline, and whether this fuel is available in the areas where he plans to use his boat.

When you buy your motor, you will receive an operating manual with it. Spend an evening with the manual. You will find it contains a wealth of easy-to-read information on the care and handling of a motor.

CHAPTER V

Care of Boat, Motor and Equipment

With the pleasure that comes with owning or operating a boat also comes the responsibility for keeping that boat, its power plant and equipment in first class condition. This can be part of the fun of boating, if it is tackled in the right spirit and done in the right way. Maintaining the appearance and efficiency of one's craft can be a source of great pride to the boat owner. Few compliments are more warming to the heart of the pleasure boatman than to hear his vessel described as "Shipshape and Bristol fashion."

The origin of that expression is somewhat obscure, but it is believed to have come from way back in the days of the sailing ships, when windjammers out of Bristol, England, had a lofty reputation for being scrubbed and polished and having their gear kept in the best possible shape.

An honestly made boat in which sound material and excellent workmanship have

Tinkering with the motor is part of pleasure boating — and important for full enjoyment of the sport.

been combined should last a lifetime with proper care along the way, but it can become a pitiful hulk in a few years if roughly used and neglected. There are fewer sadder waterfront sights than a once lovely boat blistering and rotting for want of attention, nor a happier one than a fine old-timer, shining and sound, reveling in her element like a two-year old.

There is nothing complicated or very hard about keeping a boat looking and acting like new. Timely and intelligent use of scraper, sandpaper, paint, varnish and scrubbing can do wonders along these lines. Naturally, the wooden hulls will require more care than the fiberglass. Most of the marine paint companies put out handbooks or pamphlets giving suggestions as to how to preserve the finish on your boat whether it be wood, canvas, plastic or metal. Get one of these books, follow its directions, and you will be surprised at how much paint and varnish will do for the appearance and life-span of your boat.

Normally boats are exposed to all sorts of weather—to sun and rain and hail and dampness—in addition to various marine growths. To combat these forces your boat must have the best possible protection. That comes from careful preparation of the surface to be treated and the use of quality paint and varnish. It is always best to make the small investment in the best quality marine products for use on your boat.

Here are a few tips on the care of wooden boats:

Do not leave bare wood exposed to the weather; get it painted at once. This is especially important in case of any exposed ends of plywood or other laminated woods.

If you keep your boat in salt water, use special anti-fouling paint for the bottom to discourage weeds and barnacles and to keep out the destructive teredo worm.

If you haul your boat up frequently on sandy, gravelly beaches, use either good marine bronze paint or a hard racing finish for the bottom.

If your boat has been out of water for a long period, it may leak when put overboard again. That means that the planking has dried out, thereby opening up the seams between the planks. If the drying out has not been too extensive, the swelling of the planking in the water may make the boat tight again. If not, then clean out the leaking seams and force into them a mixture of turpentine and marine glue. When the turpentine evaporates, the glue is left to seal the seams and it will give as the planks dry and swell. Prepared elastic seam compounds can be used if you prefer, and there are some new rubber compounds on the market for this purpose.

Bilges should be cleaned thoroughly of dirt and grease before painting. Also, remember that a good protective coating of paint makes wood less liable to absorb oil and grease.

Always paint from the top down and pick a dry day for your painting and varnishing jobs.

All boats should be kept clean inside and out and they should be kept dry. Boats get water aboard from rain, spray and wet bathing suits. It can be removed with a pump, bailing can or sponge, depending on the quantity. Several of the more recent outboards come equipped with electric bilge pumps.

A large chamois cloth is an excellent piece of shipboard equipment on the small boat. Use it to wipe moisture off the fire extinghisher, deck hardware and fittings. It is a good article to use, too, for wiping dew and water from seats, rails and varnished surfaces. If your cruising is on salt water, be sure to remove salt from varnished woodwork with fresh water. This little job will save you later from having to use varnish remover and sandpaper on dark, salt-pitted bright-work, and then building up new coats of varnish. It takes five of these coats to do the job well.

Dents, nicks and gouges in rails and topsides should be filled either with plastic wood or with the marine dough that is found in all marine supply houses; they should then be smoothed down, and then painted or varnished as required. Touch-up jobs like these keep your boat looking its best, and more important, prevent water and weather from getting at the wood.

Waterlines and topsides will, in certain waters, acquire soot and oil streaks. A scrubbing brush and a gentle abrasive cleaner will remove these disfiguring marks. If your boat is in water where marine growths attach themselves to bottom and waterline, get the boat up on a beach or float and give it a good scouring with a stiff brush. If it is merely slimy, rubbing it with canvas will do the trick. If, in the process of removing barnacles and other growth, you also remove so much paint that the wood or metal is exposed, then give her a coat of bottom paint before putting her overboard again.

Dock and anchor lines, life jackets, cushions, canvas-covered fenders, etc., are bound to get wet on boats, but that is no excuse for putting them away while they are soggy or damp, unless you want to encourage mildew and rot. Careless handling of these items of equipment means short life for them and expensive replacement. Dry your lines, cushions and such in the sun before stowing them away in a well-ventilated locker.

Motor Care for the Outboard

With a slight grain of salt, we can accept the claim of outboard motor manufacturers that anyone who can read and can tell the difference between a pair of pliers and a sparkplug can do an adequate job of keeping an outboard motor running. However, some of the current high-horsepower outboards are highly complicated mechanisms, whose treatment is best left to the trained mechanic. Most outboard manufacturers provide with each motor an owner's manual with detailed and diagrammed instructions on how to maintain, operate and repair the engine. The major oil companies also put out little handbooks containing similar information and the advice of proper lubricating and fueling procedures.

Normally, the outboard motor should give fairly free-from-trouble service once it has been broken in; although new motors—like automobile engines—may show up some "bugs" that call for adjustment, repair or even replacement of parts.

Basically, the operator should provide the proper mixture of oil and gasoline; keep the sparkplugs clean; keep the wiring in shape, and in general, look after his motor with common sense. One good suggestion is to look under the "Outboard Motors" heading in the yellow pages section of the telephone book and establish contact with a dealer-repairman for your brand of motor. The tool and spare parts kit that comes with your motor is important and should always be kept in the boat. Many outboarders have found that carrying an extra propeller, or "wheel" as it is known to the fraternity, is a wise precaution. Also, for the older models, generally '57 or earlier, extra shear pins, cotter pins, pliers and screwdriver are a "must," as these tiny pins, which are built to snap when the propeller strikes an obstruction can be replaced in a few minutes. Later models have special clutch construction which is intended to protect the propeller from impact damage.

Basically, there are three things that can put your motor out of commission: ignition, compression, lack of fuel.

Your engine manual will usually give you the whole story, but here are a few of the fundamentals. If the engine doesn't start — assuming the electric starter sounds healthy or the engine does not respond to a few healthy pulls on the cord, then:

CARE OF BOAT, MOTOR AND EQUIPMENT

1. Is the vent in the filler cap closed or clogged?
2. Is the shut-off valve open?
3. Is there gasoline in the tank?
4. Are there any obstructions in the fuel line or gas tank screen? Are there breaks or leaks in the gas lines?
5. Is the filter element on the engine clean? (This applies to motors with a separate gas tank.)
6. If your motor has a separate gas tank, check to see that the filler cap is tightly closed and sufficient pressure is pumped into the tank.

Next, have a look at the ignition:

1. Have the sparkplugs been fouled by surplus oil in the gas mixture?
2. Are the plugs corroded, cracked or chipped?
3. Do you have the correct gap between plug electrodes?
4. Are there any loose or broken wires?

Now for the fuel itself:

1. Are the gas and oil in proper proportion?
2. Is there water in the fuel? (It can get there by condensation if a partially full gas tank is left overnight with the vent open.)

If it is none of these things, then maybe the trouble is compression:

1. Cylinder head gasket blown out?
2. Piston rings clogged with carbon?
3. Pistons or cylinder walls worn?

If any of these, you have a job for the mechanic.

And, back to the older motors, if the motor is running, the prop not turning, and the boat not moving, it is likely that you have a broken shear pin, and the pin-replacement is fairly simple.

Perhaps the best insurance against trouble with an outboard motor is a careful check-up at the beginning of the boating season. If the boat has been stored with a dealer, chances are you can rely on his work. However, if you just pulled the motor off the boat and left it on a stand for some months, you had better give it a maintenance check before getting out on the water. The entire job is fairly simple, and should not take over an hour.

Start with the ignition systen. If you have many hours of running time on your spark plugs, the safest and simplest thing to do is to replace them. If you don't need new ones, clean carbon off the old ones and reset the gap. Check the spark plug connectors for corrosion, especially if you used your rig in salt water. Cracked or worn insulators should be replaced.

Next comes the fuel system. Remove the carburetor sediment bowl, which protects the carburetor from the gummy deposits present in fuel, and clean both filter and bowl with neutral spirits or thinner. Check fuel lines for cracks and leaks and replace the lines immediately if they show damage. This should include the fuel line to the portable tank.

As a word of caution, always be sure that your fuel tank lines are free of kinks and in such a position that other gear does not rest on them when you are operating. The best way to assure this is to coil the extra line around the top of the gasoline tank.

Another check point is the throttle linkage. All moving parts between the throttle, carburetor and magneto should be lubricated. Replace badly worn linkage. Fill grease fittings on the pivot shaft with grease and keep lubricated all year.

A thorough inspection of the lower unit is also recommended. Drain the fluid from the gear housing and refill with the proper lubricant. See that the drive pin on the propeller shaft is not worn and check the prop. If it looks nicked or bent, take it to your dealer and have it repitched.

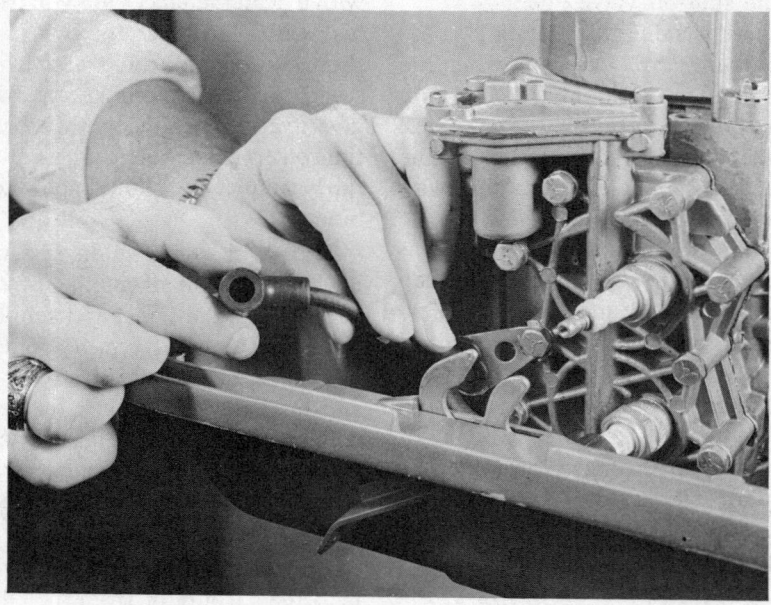

Check the ignition wires for wear and corrosion and pay particular attention to the spark-plug connectors. *(Evinrude photo)*

The carburetor sediment bowl should be removed and the bowl filter cleaned. *(Evinrude photo)*

CARE OF BOAT, MOTOR AND EQUIPMENT

If your prop looks like this, it should at least be repitched, and possibly replaced. *(Evinrude photo)*

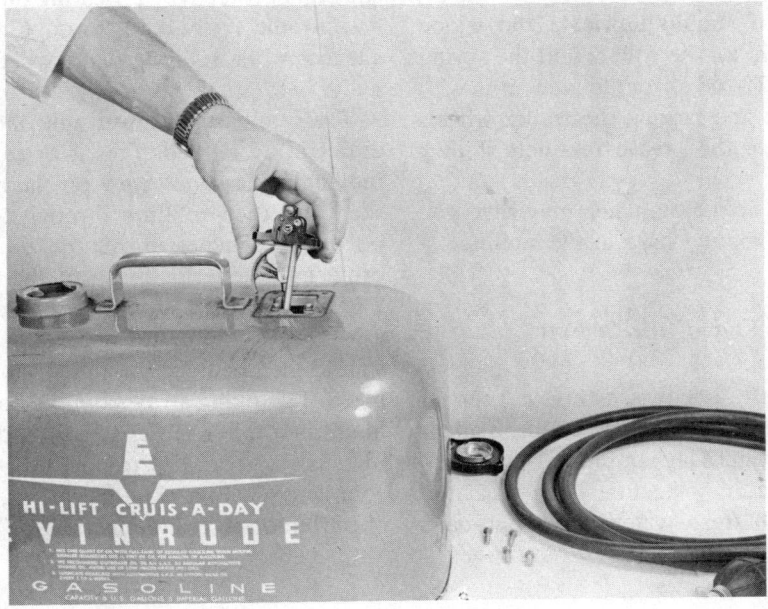

If gasoline was left over the winter in the fuel tank, remove the connector attachment, clean the tank thoroughly of any gum deposits and check the filter. Also check the fuel hose and connections for cracks. *(Evinrude photo)*

Also, if you happen to make a call on your dealer, you might have him check your motor's coil and condenser to see that they are operating properly.

If you left your portable tanks partially filled with gasoline last fall, there is a possibility gum deposits may have formed in the tanks. To be sure of getting these deposits out, remove the filler-cap casting and mechanism and scrub the gum loose with acetone or lacquer thinner. Then work this material through the fuel intake strainer to be sure it is not clogged. Again, a badly gummed tank can best be cleaned by your dealer.

On all electric start models, be sure your battery cables are in top shape. In addition, it is always best to start the year with a fully charged battery.

Remove the outer plate from your remote control box head and lubricate the entire head with a waterproof grease. Check to see that the steering cables are tight and in good condition, and also lubricate the steering pulleys.

While on the spring-cleaning program, you might also take care of your trailer. On it, you should lubricate the winch mechanism, all the rollers and the spring shackles. To save trouble later, it is wise to remove and repack the trailer wheels and replace the grease retainers if they show any wear.

This basic maintenance may save you possible difficulty later in the summer.

End of the Season

There are a few thoughts to keep in mind once you've enjoyed a season afloat and are about to lay your motor up for the winter months. The first is to flush the motor with fresh water. Most outboard motors built since 1952 are made to resist internal salt water corrosion and deposit. But if you want to do a thorough job, go ahead and flush by running the motor in fresh water. Salt deposits on the motor hood can be removed quickly with a cloth dampened in fresh water.

Water remaining in the cooling system should be forced out to avoid cracking cylinder walls or water jackets due to freezing. This is done by rotating the flywheel manually. Fuel should be drained from the carburetor to avoid collection of fuel gums and resins. This is accomplished by running the motor in a test tank until all fuel is exhausted. The carburetor sediment bowl should then be cleaned. The bowl can be removed for cleaning simply by easing the pressure on the screw type lock.

Spark plugs should be removed and several drops of lubricating oil should be squirted through the spark plug seats. The flywheel should then be rotated to distribute this oil evenly.

Internal parts can also be protected by squirting protective lubricating oil directly into the carburetor through the air silencer while rotating the flywheel manually.

The gear case, or lower unit, should be drained and refilled. This is done by removing a machine screw on the motor's skeg and then refilling through another port a few inches above the drain. To protect the exterior finish of the motor, a few drops of oil should be applied with a soft rag to the motor hood. The motor should then be hung on a rack, or a solid piece of planking away from the floor and in an area free from dirt, dust and moisture. It's a good idea to cover the motor completely with a piece of canvas, layers of burlap or an old blanket.

CHAPTER VI

Maintenance for the Larger Pleasure Boat

The following table of Maintenance Procedure can serve as a guide to the operator of a larger inboard pleasure boat in making his checkup at the beginning of the season and in going over his craft before setting out on a cruise of

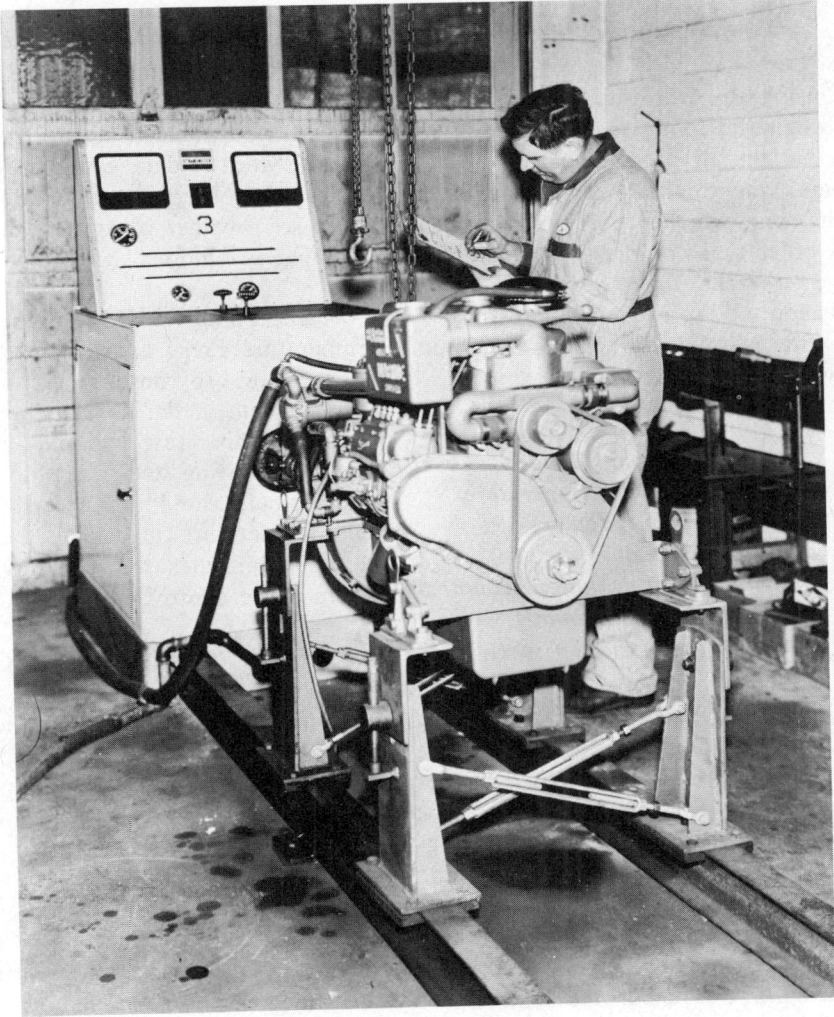

The marine motor is a carefully precisioned machine that gives best performance when kept in good running order. Here a marine diesel receives a factory check before installation. *(Barr Marine photo)*

any length. Even after a boat has been checked over by a mechanic and pronounced O.K., it might be worthwhile to utilize this chart to make certain that no important point has been overlooked. It may also be used as a review list to check the thoroughness of a seasonal overhaul.

Air Pressure
(Build Up) (Governor Cut-Off) (Low Pressure Indicator)

During the warm-up period operate the engine at idling speed, and observe whether the air pressure builds up at a normal rate to the specified maximum limits, and whether the governor then cuts off to stop compressing action. Observe whether the pressure indicator registers the approximate pressure as pressure is built up to the maximum limit.

Instruments and Gauges
(Oil Pressure, Oil Temperature and Hour Meter) (Ammeter and Voltmeter) (Tachometer and Revolution Counter) (Engine Temperature) (Fuel Oil Pressure) (Fuel)

Oil Pressure, Oil Temperature and Hour Meter. Observe the oil pressure and temperature to determine whether it is sufficient for safe operation of the engine, and whether the hour meter registers the accumulating engine running hours. Continue to observe the oil pressure and temperature to see that it is normal throughout the engine speed range. Also observe whether the hour meter continues to register at all times when the engine is running. *Caution:* If the oil pressure gauge indicates excessively low oil pressure, stop the engine immediately and investigate the cause.

Ammeter and Voltmeter. See that the ammeter and voltmeter are indicating normally. With the battery fully charged, charge should be indicated by ammeter for a short time after starting the engine (to restore the current used by the starter); the ammeter should return to slightly above zero, with all lights and electrical accessories switched off. When the battery is low, charge will be indicated for a longer period.

Tachometer and Revolution Counter. Observe the tachometer to see whether it operates normally without excessive fluctuation or unusual noises that might indicate worn or damaged gears or drive cables. Also observe the revolution counter to see whether it registers the accumulating revolutions.

Engine Temperature. Note the engine temperature gauge and exhaust temperature gauge (pyrometer) to see that they indicate in the normal range. The engine temperature should increase gradually during the warm-up period and normally should not exceed 180° F. The temperature at which the gauge hesitates indicates the opening of the thermostatic control.

Fuel Oil Pressure, Fuel. Observe whether the fuel gauges indicate the approximate amount of fuel in the tanks and determine whether the fuel pressure is sufficient for the proper operation of the engine.

Windshield, Windshield Wiper, Horn

See that the windshields are in good condition and secure, that the windshield glass is clean, that the wipers operate correctly through their full stroke without evidence of looseness in their motor mountings, and that the blades contact the glass properly. If the tactical situation permits, sound the horn to determine whether the signal is normal.

MAINTENANCE FOR THE LARGER PLEASURE BOAT

Clutch Drive
(Free Travel) (Linkage)

Observe whether the clutch lever has satisfactorily free travel (in accordance with the craft manual) before beginning to disengage or engage the clutch; see that it releases the clutch completely before the lever has completed its stroke and note whether there are any unusual noises in the clutch release mechanism that would indicate dry or defective release bearings, defective clutch plate or pilot bearings. When engaging the clutch and when the clutch is fully engaged, observe whether there is any indication of slipping and whether linkage is properly adjusted.

Gear Drive
(Lever Action) (Declutching)
(Vibration) (Noise)
(Control Synchronization)

With the craft in motion, operate levers of the driving units through all positions, noting whether the levers move easily and snap into each position. Observe whether there are any unusual vibrations that might indicate loose mountings, and whether the gears jump out of mesh. On multiple-engine-installations equipped with hydraulic or air controls, observe whether they appear to shift properly and whether the transmissions shift simultaneously. Continue these observations throughout the test.

Steering
(Gear)(Control) (Linkage)

Steering wheel should have minimum free play in accordance with craft manual. Rotate the steering wheel fully in both directions and note any indication of binding or bumpy feel. Examine the steering column and steering wheel to see that they are in good condition and secure. On booster control unit, observe the free play of the steering gear to see whether there is excessive lash in the steering mechanism, or any indication of binding. Notice whether the steering booster appears to operate properly to assist the steering mechanism, and notice any abnormal pull to one side.

Direct Drive Reverse Gear Mechanism

Operate the engine in both forward and reverse positions, observing whether fuel cut-off is automatic when stopping and reversing the engine. Observe the automatic braking of the engine, valve operation, interlocking reverse cycle sequence, pneumatic and manual speed regulation, and maneuvering controls for proper functioning.

Air Control
(Controlair) (Actuator)
(Pneudyne) (Valves)

Inspect these items for proper operation, and be sure that they are in good condition, correctly assembled, secure and adequately lubricated. Observe the action of:

Controlair, for proper control of maneuvering and speed regulation of the engine.

Actuator, for proper regulation of engine speed, as selected from the Controlair.

Pneudyne, for proper positioning of the engine camshaft and camshifting interlock and for shifting of engine clutch in accordance with the lever position of the Controlair.

Camshifting Interlock Valve, for the proper interlocking of pneumatic control equipment with the engine camshaft position.

Throttle Latch Pilot Valve, for the proper operation of fuel cutoff valve when changing engine direction.

Fuel Cutoff Valve, for the proper shut-off and control of fuel when engine is stopped, started or reversed.

Relay Air Valve, for the proper control of air as directed by the Controlair lever.

Reducing Valves, for the proper limiting of air pressure to Controlair and Pneudyne in accordance with craft manual.

Supercharger
(Operation) (Lube) (Vibration)

Observe operation of the supercharger, paying particular attention to vibration of rotors, indicating loose or worn parts or marred surfaces. Examine drive and coupling assembly for indications of excessive lash. Inspect unit for loose mounting, oil leaks, proper and adequate lubricant.

Engine
(Idle) (Acceleration)
(Power) (Noise) (Smoke)
(Governed Speed)

Idle. Observe whether the engine runs smoothly at idling speed and listen for knocks and rattles as the engine is accelerated and decelerated and while it is under light and heavy loads.

Acceleration, Power, and Noise. Observe whether the engine has normal acceleration, pulling power, and operating characteristics in each speed. Listen for other noises that might indicate damaged, excessively worn, inadequately lubricated engine parts or accessories, or loose drive belts.

Smoke. During operation of the engine test, look for any indication of excessive or unusual smoke from the exhaust.

Governed Speed. Slowly accelerate the engine and observe the tachometer reading. Notice that engine reaches but does not exceed the governed speed (rpm) specified on the caution plate or recommended by the craft manual. Do not accelerate engine beyond fast idle without load.

Safety Devices
(Overspeed Safety Trip)
(Low Oil Safety Shutdown)

Overspeed Safety Trip. With engine running, trip the overspeed safety trip to make sure that all parts are in working order. Reset trip lever. Examine linkage and controls for adequate lubrication.

Low Oil Safety Shutdown. Test cutout switch for low oil safety and excessive water temperature, to insure that all parts and units are in working order. Examine horn or howler if used in connection with switch. Any deficiencies in the operation of the safety devices must be corrected before engine is started again.

Leaks
(Fuel Oil) (Engine Oil)
(Water) (Air)

Check the engine compartment thoroughly, including the entire engine, for indications of oil, air, water, or fuel leaks and determine their source. This should be corrected.

Engine Stopped
Cylinder Head and Gaskets

Look for cracks or indications of oil, water, or compression leaks around studs, cap screws, and gasket. *Caution:* Cylinder heads should not ordinarily be tightened unless there is a definite indication of looseness or leaks. If tightening is necessary, use a torque-indicating wrench and tighten in the sequence and to the tension specified in the craft manual. When a new gasket is installed, tighten three times as follows: First, upon installation; second, after engine is warmed up, and third, after completing final test. On valve-in-head engines, adjust the tappet clearances to specifications after the final tightening of the head nuts.

Valve Mechanism
(Clearances) (Lubrication)
(Cover Gaskets)

On valve-in-head engines, examine valve tappet clearances while hot. Valve tappets, rocket arms, shafts, and springs should appear in good condition, correctly assembled, and secure. Oil should be delivered properly. Also make sure that the valve cover gaskets are in good condition. On L-Head engines perform the above service only as the need for such service is indicated by valve noises or engine performance. Remove valve mechanism covers, observe valve clearances and condition of valve mechanism.

Adjust the clearances to specifications, taking care that the lock nuts are secure when the clearances are last noted during the adjustment.

Diesel Fuel Nozzles and Lines

Observe whether these items are in good condition, secure, and do not leak.

Use fuel nozzle test stand, if available, taking every precaution to keep spray away from personnel. Observe whether there is any "after-dribble" from the spray nozzle. If the spray pattern is not normal or a dribble occurs, the nozzle should be replaced by a new or reconditioned and tested nozzle. Tighten all fuel nozzle mounting nuts, cap screws, and line connections securely.

Spark Plugs (Gaps) (Deposits)

Examine the installed spark plugs to see that their insulators are in good condition and clean, and that there is no leakage around the insulators or gaskets. When operating conditions require, the spark plugs may be removed for service.

Remove the spark plugs and examine for poor condition, paying particular attention to broken insulators, excessive carbon deposits, and electrodes which are burned thin. Replace unserviceable plugs. Report excessive deposits or damaged insulators. These conditions may indicate incorrect heat range. The porcelain insulators inside spark plugs of proper heat-range will be coffee-brown in color.

Clean deposits from the electrodes and insulators, and inspect again for cracks. If a plug cleaner is not available, install new or reconditioned plugs.

Adjust gaps to specifications. After completing this job, reinstall the plugs, using new gaskets and taking care not to overtighten them, as this may cause distortion and damage.

Compression Test

Gasoline. With all spark plugs out and engine warm, insert the compression gauge in a spark plug hole, and with the throttle wide open, revolve the engine at cranking speed until the maximum compression is indicated. Repeat this process for each cylinder. Refer to the craft manual for specified compression pressures and for variations due to condition and wear. If pressure in a cylinder is below normal, squirt sufficient engine oil on the piston head to temporarily prevent loss of compression, and recheck the compression of the cylinder. Low compression brought up to normal by oil sealing indicates piston, ring, or cylinder wear or damage. Low compression not brought up to normal by this method indicates compression leakage by valve or gasket.

Diesel. Attach pressure indicator to

cylinder, turn scale sleeve to bring red disk in register with letter "C" for compression readings. (Note: Set index sleeve to read about 50 to 100 pounds per square inch in excess of the expected maximum cylinder pressure.) Connect neon flasher to indicator valve and obtain reading of cylinder pressure. Repeat this process for each cylinder. Where the pressure indicator cylinder valve is not on the unit, use compression gauge and proceed as for gasoline engines.

Engine
(Mounting and Braces) (Ground Strap) (Side Pans)

See that engine is properly installed, taking care that all mountings and ground straps are securely tightened. Be sure engine side pans, if present, are in good condition, correctly assembled and do not leak.

Manifolds and Heat Control
(Intake) (Exhaust)

Note whether the manifolds and their gaskets are in good condition, correctly assembled, secure, and do not leak. Check for indication of leaks by looking for carbon streaks. Check exhaust temperature and temperature gauges. Equalize cylinder exhaust temperatures to the minimum appreciable variations. On a manually operated heat control determine if it is in good condition, secure, and set at the correct position. If the control is automatic, note whether the bimetal control spring is in good condition and securely connected to the heat-control valve shaft and mountings. See that the shaft operates freely and that the spring controls the shaft properly.

Tighten all manifold assembly, mounting, exhaust pipe, and carburetor connecting flange nuts evenly and securely.

Exhaust Pipes and Mufflers

Note whether they are in good condition, securely assembled, and mounted, and whether there are indications of exhaust leaks, usually indicated by carbon streaks. Be sure the drain holes in the mufflers are not clogged, so that all condensate may drain off.

Tighten all mounting bolts and connections securely.

Fuel (Tanks) (Vents) (Lines)

Inspect fuel tanks to see that they are in good condition and securely mounted. Examine caps for defective gaskets and note whether the vents are open and whether there are indications of fuel leaks from the tanks, lines or pumps. See that the filter necks are in good condition and the caps fit securely. Inspect fuel lines and fittings to see that they are in good condition, securely supported, and not leaking.

Remove the fuel tank drain plugs and drain off the accumulated water and sediment. Drain only until the fuel starts to run clean.

Fuel Filters and Screens

Note whether the fuel filters and cleaner bowls are in good condition, secure, and not leaking at gaskets or connections.

Clean. Remove fuel screens and cartridge-type elements, clean all screens thoroughly in dry-cleaning solvent, dry with compressed air, and reinstall. Observe whether the cartridge-type element is in satisfactory condition for further service. If so, clean and replace it, being sure that all element and cover gaskets are in good condition and in place. On disk-type filters, turn the handle one complete turn. Remove the plug, and drain the sediment bowl.

Serve and Clean. On a cartridge-type fuel filter, replace the cartridge, and clean all fuel screens. On a disk-type filter, remove the element from the cleaner bowl, and wash in dry-cleaning solvent until the disks are clean and free. Clean the bowl thoroughly, and reinstall the element, making sure all gaskets are in good condition and in place. Do not scrape or damage the disks.

Fuel Pump (Vacuum and Pressure)

See that the fuel pump lines are in good condition, secure, and not leaking. Attach the fuel test gauge properly and with the engine idling note whether the pump pressure is within specified limits, which are listed in the craft manual. Replace any pump that does not produce proper pressure, being sure to make a similar check of the new pump to see that it is satisfactory.

Fuel Injector Pump (Primer)

Note whether the pump (including any transfer pump) is in good condition, correctly assembled, securely mounted, and its connections do not leak. Determine the oil level in the pump with a dip stick. Add oil if needed.

Tighten all assembly and mounting bolts and cap screws.

Adjust the fuel injector pump timing according to the instructions and specifications in the craft manual. Note whether hand pump primer is in good condition and in operating order.

Drain the oil from the fuel injector pump and refill to correct level with specified engine oil.

*Throttle
(Linkage)
(Dual-Throttle Synchronization)*

See that the throttle and all of its connecting linkage are in good condition and securely connected. Also, on craft equipped with more than one engine, follow the instructions in the craft manual, and note whether the linkage is properly synchronized, so that the throttle valves open and close together. On those craft having automatic transmissions and transfer units, check according to instructions in the craft manual to see whether the throttle control linkage is properly synchronized with the controls of these units.

On craft equipped with automatic transmission and transfer units, follow the instructions in the craft manual, and adjust the relationship between controls of these units and the acceleration linkage so that they are properly synchronized.

Lubricate all linkage pins, fulcrums, joints and other connections requiring lubrication. Refer to craft manual and Lubrication Order.

*Engine Oil
(Tanks) (Coolers)
(Lines and Fittings) (Viscosity)*

Observe whether they are in good condition, correctly assembled, securely mounted, and whether there are indications of oil leaks. Measure the level of the oil in the supply tanks with the bayonet gauge. Inspect a sample of oil for grit, water or fuel dilution, and determine the viscosity with the use of "visgage."

Tighten all oil tank mountings and oil line support clips or brackets securely.

Drain all oil from the supply tanks, close the drain cocks, and fill tank approximately one-fourth full with light engine oil. Agitate with a clean stick or rod to loosen the sediment. Continuing to stir the oil, open the drain cock and drain the oil and sediment from the tanks. After flushing oil is thoroughly drained, close the drain cocks and fill the tanks to the proper level with specified engine oil.

Note: If crankcase oil change is due,

drain the crankcase and refill to the proper level with specified oil.

Engine Oil Filters (Reclaimers)

Inspect oil filters, coolers, and all external engine oil lines to see whether they are in good condition, secure and do not leak.

Clean. On disk type filters, turn the handle one complete turn, remove the drain plug, and drain off the contents.

Clean and Serve. When due or when oil filter cartridge condition indicates a filter cartridge change is necessary, remove the filter cartridge, clean the case with solvent and install a new filter cartridge of the correct type, installing new gaskets and tightening the cover securely. On disk type filters, remove the cover and element and without disassembling, clean them in dry-cleaning solvent. Blow dry with compressed air if available. If the element is serviceable, reinstall it; if not replace.

*Air Cleaners
(Carburetor) (Diesel)
(Air Compressor)*

Remove all carburetor, Diesel, or air-compressor air cleaner elements. See that all gaskets, seals, clamps, and any connecting hose or tubes are present and in good condition. Observe the condition of the cleaning elements, baffles and body. Note the oil in the reservoir of oil-bath cleaners, paying particular attention to the amount of dirt present in the oil. Also see that the oil level is satisfactory.

Clean and Serve. Wash cleaner element in dry-cleaning solvent, dry, apply engine oil to element, and drain excess oil. On oil-bath air cleaner, refill the reservoir to the correct level with clean engine oil. Reassemble, making certain all gaskets are in good condition and in place. Install air cleaner, being careful that it is pressed firmly into place and that the mounting is secure. If the air cleaner is equipped with an external air baffle, see that it is correctly alined with the air stream. Also note whether connecting hose is in good condition and properly clamped to the air cleaner and horn.

*Water Pumps
(Fresh Water) (Sea Water)*

Inspect pumps to see that they are in good condition and secure. See that the drive, belt, and chain are in good condition and properly adjusted and that the pulleys and sprockets are in good condition, secure, properly alined and not excessively worn. Examine shaft for end play and loose bearings. Note whether the valve control linkage is properly connected to the valves and operates them freely. Also see if the pump lines and strainers are in good condition, properly mounted, and secure. Particularly, see whether or not the strainers are clogged.

Adjust pump drive chain or belt according to instructions in craft manual.

Tighten all pump mounting and assembly bolts securely, and pump packing nuts cautiously. Over-tightening will score shafts and cause leaks.

*Accessory Drives
(Belt) (Pulley)
(Shafts and Couplings)*

See that these items are in good condition, correctly assembled, and secure. Pay particular attention to drive belts and pulleys, seeing that they are well alined and not excessively worn. Also note whether they are frayed, oil soaked, improperly adjusted, or bottoming in the drive pulleys. See that the universal joints of drive shafts are not excessively worn or loose.

Adjust all drive belts according to instructions and specifications in the craft manual, locking all adjustment devices securely.

Heat Exchanger
(Core) (Shutters) (Hose)
(Cap) (Zinc Plate) (Scale)

See that these items are in good condition, correctly assembled, securely mounted and do not leak. If air cooled, note whether the core air passages are obstructed with dirt or trash. Examine the shutter control linkage to see that it is in good condition, secure, and operates freely. Note whether the steam relief valve operates freely and is in correct position for the prevailing atmospheric temperature. Also examine coolant to see whether it is contaminated with rust, oil, or other foreign matter that would require the cooling system to be cleaned. Examine zinc electrodes for deterioration and replace if necessary.

If cleaning is necessary, clean the cooling system according to current directives, using only specified cleaner. Clean all dirt and trash from the exterior of the core.

Tighten all loose mountings, plates, and clamps.

Fresh Water Expansion Tank
(Antifreeze) (Cap) (Hose)

See that the items are in good condition, correctly assembled, securely mounted and do not leak. Also examine the coolant to see whether it is contaminated with rust or other foreign matter which would require the system to be cleaned.

If cleaning is necessary, drain, taking care to save drains to put back into radiator if ethylene glycol antifreeze is in use. Clean the cooling system according to current directives, using only specified cleaner. Flush cleaner from entire cooling system with clean water. Refill, adding specified inhibitor (if required) unless new antifreeze which contains inhibitor is used. If antifreeze is in use, determine its protective value. Clean all dirt and trash from the exterior of the core.

Tighten all loose mountings, plates, and clamps.

Generator
(Commutator) (Brushes) (Wiring)

Remove the brush head cover plate and check the commutator to see that it appears to be in good condition, clean, and not excessively worn. Observe whether the brushes are clean, free in their holder, properly spring loaded, and not excessively worn. Check giving connections for tightness and correct alignment of generator drive.

At each 200 hour service, clean the commutator by placing a strip of very fine sand paper (00 to 8/0) over a wood block of the correct size. With the engine running slowly, press the sand paper against the commutator until it is clean. Blow out with compressed air.

Tighten mounting bolt, and electrical connections securely.

Regulator Units
(Connections) (Voltage)
(Current) (Cut Out)

See that they are in good condition and all connections and mountings are secure.

Connect the low voltage circuit tester and observe whether the voltage regulator, current regulator, and cut-out, control the generator output properly. Follow the instructions in the craft manual or those which accompany the test instrument. Replace if test shows faulty operation. *Note:* This test should be made only after the regulator unit has reached normal operating temperature.

Carburetor
(Choke) (Throttle)
(Linkage) (Governor)

See that these items are in good condition, correctly assembled and securely installed; that the carburetor does not leak; that the control linkage, including the choke valve opens fully when the accelerating lever is fully depressed, and that the governor is secure and properly sealed. Drain the carburetor bowl and clean screen.

Coil and Wiring
(High and Low Voltage) (Supports)

Examine the coil to see that it is in good condition, clean, and securely mounted. All high voltage ignition wiring, including shielding or conduits, should be in good condition and securely fastened to all support mountings and terminals. See that all insulation and connections are clean. Inspect all low voltage wiring in the engine compartment in the same manner. On engines equipped with magnetos, examine the booster coils to see that they are in good condition, clean, and securely mounted.

Note: Do not tighten wiring connections unless actually loose, as overtightening of terminals will cause damage.

Clean all exposed ignition wiring with a dry cloth or compressed air.

Magnetos (Points)

Determine whether the magneto is in good condition and securely mounted. Note whether there is evidence of oil leaks at the mounting pad gaskets. Remove the breaker point inspection covers and check to see that the points are in good condition and clean; that the breaker points are well alined; that the mating surfaces engage squarely; and that point gaps are satisfactory (refer to craft manual). Replace unserviceable points.

Adjust the magneto breaker-point gaps according to instructions and specifications in the craft manual.

Distributor
(Cap) (Rotor) (Points)
(Shaft) (Advance Units)

See that the distributor body and external attachments are in good condition and secure. Inspect other parts of the distributor as follows:

Cap, Rotor, and Points. Blow or wipe the dirt or dust from the distributor cap. Remove the cap, and observe whether the cap, rotor arm, and the breaker-plate assembly parts are in good condition, correctly assembled, secure, and serviceably clean. Pay particular attention to cracks in the cap and rotor arm, to corrosion of terminals, and connections in these parts; also to burning off of the outer ends of the conductor strap of rotor arm. Also note whether the breaker points are in good condition and well alined, and that the gap is satisfactory. If the breaker-plate assembly is unserviceably dirty, remove the distributor, clean in dry-cleaning solvent, dry with compressed air, lubricate the parts as specified below, and reinstall the distributor in the correct position for timing. When cleaning the distributor, remove the wick and lubrication cup, clean and dry while removed, and reinstall them only after distributor assembly is cleaned and blown dry with compressed air. If the breaker points are pitted, burned, or worn to an unserviceable condition, install a new set. If the points are badly pitted, replace the condenser also, as it is probably the cause of the pitting. Install the new points so that they are well aligned and engage squarely. If the points are slightly pitted or burned, dress them with an American-Swiss No. 6 File (or equivalent) or No. 00 Sandpaper (do not use emery cloth), and blow off the filings with compressed air.

Shaft. Test by hand-feel for looseness, to determine whether the distributor camshaft is excessively worn in its bushings.

Centrifugal Advance. Install the rotor arm on the upper end of the distributor camshaft, and observe whether the camshaft can be rotated by finger force through the nominal range of movement which is permitted by the centrifugal advance mechanism, and whether it returns to its original position when the fingers are removed from the rotor arm. There should be no binding or hanging up in mechanism during these movements.

Special Lubrication. Lubricate the cam surfaces, the movable breaker-arm pin, the wick, and the camshaft according to the craft's Lubrication Order. Take care to keep lubricant off the distributor points, not to apply more lubricant than is specified, and to wipe the cam clean before lubricating its surface.

Adjust. Adjust the breaker-point gap to specifications. If suitable equipment is available, adjust dwell angle.

Battery
(Cables) (Hold-Downs)
(Gravity and Voltage)

Inspect the batteries externally to see that their cases, posts, and cell straps are in good condition and secure. Note whether the cases are leaking. Wipe dirt from and around the filler caps, remove, and see that the cap vents are open. Note the level of electrolyte in the cells. This level should be above the top of the plates, and may extend up to one inch above the plates. Before adding any water to the cells, test the specific gravity of each cell, with a battery hydrometer. As the samples of the electrolyte are in the hydrometer for the gravity test, observe whether the electrolyte is discolored to a reddish-brown color, which may indicate that the battery is being overcharged due to improper regulator action. Look for any gravity readings below 1.225 and variations of more than 0.025, and any reddish-brown discoloration of the electrolyte. Also take the voltage reading of each cell. Examine the battery cables, terminals, and terminal bolts to see whether they are in good condition, secure, and not corroded; if the battery hold-downs are securing the battery properly; and that the battery carrier is in good condition and secure. If the terminals are corroded, disconnect the cable terminals from the battery, clean, and lubricate the battery posts and terminals, and reinstall them securely.

Make a high-rate discharge test of the battery to see that the cells are in a satisfactory condition, taking care to make the test according to the instructions for a condition test which accompany the test instrument. A true test cannot be made if the gravity of the battery is below 1.225. If the difference in the readings obtained from the cells is more than 30 percent, replace the battery.

Clean. Clean top of battery with water of a soda wash, if available, and dry with a clean water or compressed air. Clean the battery carrier in the same way, and paint if corroded. Clean the battery cable terminals, terminal bolts and nuts and battery posts and grease them lightly.

Serve. Bring the electrolyte to the correct level with distilled water, if it is available, use any clean fresh water in preference to letting battery run dry. Inspect bolts for serviceability. Tighten terminals and hold-downs carefully to avoid damage to battery.

Air Compressor
(Unloader Valve) (Governor)
(Lines) (Tank)

Examine the air compressor to see that

it is in good condition, properly aligned with its drive pulleys, and secure. Observe the unloader valve for satisfactory valve clearance. See that the governor appears to be in good condition and secure; that all the compressor oil and air lines are in good condition and secure; and that the oil and air lines do not leak.

Clean. Clean the governor air strainer in dry-cleaning solvent; dry and reinstall. Drain water (condensation) from air-tank and lines.

Special Lubrication. Apply a few drops of engine oil on the unloader valve fulcrum pin.

Adjust. Adjust unloader valve clearances to specifications. (Refer to craft manual).

Gear Oil Levels

Inspect and check all gear cases to see that the lubricant is at the proper level, in good condition and not leaking.

Note: Sufficient time should be allowed so that the normal foaming may subside. If an oil change in these units is due, drain and refill with specified lubricant. (Refer to craft manual for lubrication requirements and levels).

Starting Motor
(Air) (Electric) (Controls)

Start the engine, observe whether the general action of the starter is satisfactory, particularly whether it engages or operates properly without excessive noise and has adequate cranking speed.

Note: As soon as the engine starts note whether oil pressure gauge and ammeter indications are satisfactory. See that the starter is in good condition and securely mounted; that all connections are tight.

Air. See that the starting air valve, check valves, lines, and controls are properly mounted, in good condition, and secure. Pay particular attention to air delivery pressure, to determine whether adequate cranking speed is developed; examine entire system for leaks, or sticking air valve stems.

Electric. Remove the commutator inspection block and inspect the commutator to see that it is in good condition and clean. See that the brushes are clean, free in the brush holders, and not excessively worn; that the brush connections are secure and wires neither broken nor chafed.

Handcrank Ratchet and Lever. Examine these items to see that they are in good condition and secure, and that the cranking box and ratchet operate satisfactorily to rotate the engine.

Clean. Clean the commutator end of the starter with very fine sandpaper or with compressed air.

Tighten. Tighten the starter mounting bolts securely.

Timing
(Diesel) (Gasoline)

With the engine running and the neon timing-light properly connected, determine the ignition timing of each engine according to instructions in the craft manual or current directives to see whether it is correct. Also observe whether the automatic controls advance the spark as the engine is accelerated gradually. When necessary, adjust the ignition timing to the specifications in the craft manual, taking care to see that the distributor is well secured when adjustment is completed. On engines equipped with magnetos, the timing is adjusted when the magnetos are installed.

Diesel: Bar engine over in direction of normal travel, the specified degrees (°) before top dead center for No. 1 cylinder. Check or adjust timing of fuel injection pump and nozzles according to instructions and specifications in craft manual.

may cause stuffing box to run hot, score the shaft, and cause leaks.

Bilge Pumps
(Drives) (Valves) (Control)
(Lines) Strainers)

Inspect the bilge pumps to see that they are in good condition and secure; see that the drive belt and chain are in good condition and properly adjusted; and that the pulleys and sprockets are in good condition, secure, properly aligned, and not excessively worn. Note whether the valve-control linkage is properly connected to the valves and operates them freely. Also see that the bilge pump lines and strainers are in good condition, properly connected, and secure. Pay particular attention to the strainers to see if they are clogged.

Tighten all pump mounting and assembly bolts securely, and pump-packing nuts cautiously. Over-tightening will score shafts and cause leaks.

Adjust pump-drive chain or belt according to instructions in the craft manual.

Propeller
(Seals) (Joints)
(Bearings) (Stuffing Box)

Observe whether they are in good condition, correctly assembled and secure. Pay particular attention to the alignment, the bearing mountings, stuffing box and propeller shaft tunnel bearings. See that the propeller drive control and coupling are in good condition, operate correctly and are not excessively worn. Note whether the thrust or forward bearings are excessively worn, and correctly lubricated.

Tighten the stuffing box packing flange cautiously. Do not overtighten since this

Rudder
(Shafts) (Arms) (Cable Sheaves)
(Rod) (Brackets) (Controls)

See that these items are in good condition, correctly assembled and securely mounted; that the control linkage and cable sheaves are adequately lubricated, and that the stuffing box does not leak. Look particularly for worn or broken cable strands. Turn the steering wheel to its maximum right and left positions; see that the rudder lever has about the same clearance in each position. If not, readjust the cables according to specifications. Check emergency steering devices.

Tighten all rudder and control assembly and mounting bolts securely. Tighten the rudder shaft stuffing box packing nut cautiously. Over-tightening may cause excessive binding and leaks.

Generator
(Commutator) (Brushes)
(Control Box) (Wiring)

Start the generator, observing whether it starts easily and runs at normal speed, and listen for any unusual noise that might indicate excessively worn, loose, or inadequately lubricated parts. Remove brush head cover plate and check the commutator to see that it appears in good condition, clean and not excessively worn. Check the generator output. Inspect the control box and buttons, ammeter and wiring to see that they are in good condition, correctly assembled and connected, and secure.

At each 200-hour service, clean the the commutator by placing a strip of very fine sandpaper (00 to 8/0) over a wood block of the correct size; with the motor running, press the sandpaper against the commutator until it is clean. Blow out the dust with compressed air.

Superstructure
(Doors) (Hardware) (Glass)
(Seats) (Safety Straps and Grab Rails)
(Stowage Compartments)
(Tarpaulins) (Ventilators)

Inspect these items to see that they are in good condition and secure; that the hardware and ventilators operate properly and are adequately lubricated; and that the doors engage their bumpers and strikers and latch properly in the closed position. Check safety straps and grab rails for correct mounting and secure them. Pay particular attention to tarpaulin condition and see that all fasteners, ropes, grommets and loops are present, in good condition and secure. See that stowage compartments, covers, and doors are property alined and hinges and latches adequately lubricated.

Hull
(Plugs) (Decks) (Ventilators)
(Plates) (Compartments)
(Bulkheads) (Frame)

Examine the hull to see that it is in good condition. Pay particular attention to the bulges that might cause leaks. See that hull sea cocks and plugs are in place and secure, and note their condition. Inspect the deck and hatch covers for good condition and see that they are properly aligned with their openings. Check deck ventilators to the engine compartment for good condition and proper operation; see whether the screens are clogged and whether the cover seals properly when closed. Examine hull compartments to see that the hull, frame, reinforcement plates, and bulkheads are in good condition and secure. Look for indications of water leaks between the bulkheads or in the hull, and see if the compartments and bilges are clean. All hulls should be hauled and the bottoms inspected and serviced in April and September. Wooden hulls operated in warm waters should be hauled for bottom scraping and painting in July and December, as well as in April and September. Wooden hulls operated in warm waters should be hauled for bottom service as soon as possible after any severe grounding or bottom scraping.

Wiring
(Junction and Terminal Blocks)
(Fuses and Spares)

Observe all exposed electrical wiring and conduits to see that they are in good condition, well supported, and whether or not the wiring is securely connected to its terminals. Also make sure that all junction and terminal blocks and boxes are in good condition and secure, and that all necessary fuses and spares are in place and in good condition.

Plumbing, Fixtures, Etc.

See that these items are in good condition, correctly assembled, and securely mounted; note whether there are any indications of fluid leaks in the control valves or fluid lines. Examine all control valves, gauges, and floats; inspect valves to determine whether they are operating freely, not clogged or corroded, and in serviceable condition.

Fire Extinguisher System
(Tanks) (Valves) (Lines and Nozzles)
(Mountings)

Inspect the tanks and valves feeding the fire extinguisher system to determine whether they are in good condition and securely mounted and whether the tanks are fully charged. The charge may be determined on gas type extinguishers by weighing with a scale; on a liquid type, by shaking. Examine the control cables and handles to see that they are in good condition and free to operate at a moment's notice. Note whether all the lines and nozzles are in good condition and securely mounted and connected and whether the nozzles are clean and properly aimed at the points most likely to catch fire. If there is any indication that the nozzles are clogged by dirt or corrosion, disconnect the main feed line between the tank control valve and the nozzles, and apply compressed air cautiously. *Caution:* If the fire extinguisher tanks are not full, they should be reported for recharge or exchanged for fully charged tanks immediately. Any cylinder containing gas under high pressure should never be dropped, struck, handled roughly, or exposed to unnecessary heat.

Special Lubrication. Apply a few drops of engine oil to all of the pulleys and guides through which the control cables operate.

Tighten. Tighten all assembly and mounting bolts and screws.

Paint and Markings

Examine the paint and markings on the entire craft; see that they are in good condition, paying particular attention to bright paint spots in the finish that might cause glare or reflection. Inspect craft markings and identification for legibility. Include identification plates, signs and their mountings, if furnished.

Compass
(Fluid) (Lamp)

Inspect the compass to see if it is in good condition and secure; look for low level or indications of bubbles in the fluid bowl. Fill the fluid bowl with ethyl alcohol if needed. Operate the compass lamp and switch to see that it operates properly.

Tow
(Chain) (Cable) (Rope) (Block)

Inspect provided towing lines and devices to see that they are in good condition, clean, and properly stowed. Tow chains, lines, and cables must be properly protected against rust when not in use. If snatch blocks are furnished, check to see that they are in good condition, properly lubricated and operate freely.

Anchor, Hand Bilge Pump, and Boat Hook

See that these are present, in good condition, securely mounted, or properly stowed. Operate the hand bilge pump in water to see that it functions properly.

Tools and Equipment

Check against craft stowage list to see if all items are present, in serviceable condition and properly stowed or mounted. Pay particular attention to see that all tool-mounting brackets and straps are in good condition and secure; also, that tools with cutting edges are sharp. Sharpen if necessary. In nautical operations, any tools or equipment that are mounted on the outside of the craft and have bright or polished surfaces should be painted or otherwise treated to prevent glare or reflection.

Note: Tools and equipment not in use should be treated with a rust preventive compound to prevent rust and to maintain tools in a serviceable condition.

First Aid Kit and Life Preservers

See that the items in the first-aid kit are present, in good condition, and properly packed. Inspect safety devices, such as life preservers, collapsible rafts and boats to see that they are in serviceable condition and complete with accessories.

CHAPTER VII

Small Boat Construction

As in any other sport, a knowledge of the proper terminology sets the "expert" apart from the novice. In boating, knowledge of construction of a boat and the use of correct terms is vital to the execution of commands and instructions and is an important safety factor under many different conditions.

Whether the small boat is constructed of wood, metal, or fiberglass, the basic structural features are alike.

The *keel* is the backbone of the boat. It is a longitudinal member extending along the center of the bottom of the boat—sometimes it projects below the bottom. The frames or ribs, stern, and sternpost rise from the keel. Often an extra piece is fastened to the bottom of the main keel to protect it; this is called the *shoe*. Ordinarily, a timber or stringer bolted inside as a reinforcing member to the keel is called a *keelson*.

A *stem*, common to all boats with the conventional type of prow, is a vertical member set up on the forward end of the keel. In wooden boats, it is usually of white oak, and may be either straight or curved. It is *plumb* if set up perpendicular to the waterline; but it is often *raked* at an angle to reduce water friction and improve appearance. Small boats are often equipped with ringbolts fitted through the stem and stern for hoisting or handling. An *apron*, also called *stemson*, is an inner stem fitted behind the stem to reinforce it. *Stem bands* of metal are usually fitted on the forward edge of the stem for protection. *Breast hooks* are reinforcing knees set horizontally behind the stem.

When the stern is shaped like the bow, drawing to point as in a canoe, or broad as in a ferryboat, the boat is a *double-ender*. Planking across the stern of the boat that forms a flat vertical bulkhead (as in most outboards) is called a *transom*. The transom stern is the most common. Various kinds of *knees* are used throughout the hull structure to connect members joined at an angle to each other. At the stern, the principal vertical member is called a *sternpost*. It is set up on the after end of the keel or on the shaft log; it is attached by the stern knee. *Deadwood* is solid timber placed on the keel at the stern to connect the end timbers. *Shaft logs* are timbers between keel and deadwood through which the propeller shaft passes. *Horn timbers* are used to fasten the shaft log to the *transom knee*. The *propeller post* stands vertically behind the deadwood and is attached to it and the keel. A *stern hook* in a double-ended boat is that reinforcing member which corresponds to breast hook at the bow. Breast hooks at the stern are also called *crutches*. When a boat has a transom stern, it has *quarter knees* at each side of the transom instead of one stern hook.

Frames are vertical members set up on the keel to form the skeleton over which the planking is laid. The frames may be curved as in a round-bottomed boat or straight as in certain types of V-bottomed boats. Some are sawed to shape, others are steambent. The stem is one of the main frame members at the bow. *Floors* in marine construction are transverse frame members which tie the lower ends of frames together at the keel. *Limber holes* are cut in the lower edge of frames to allow bilge water to flow into the deepest part of the hull. The

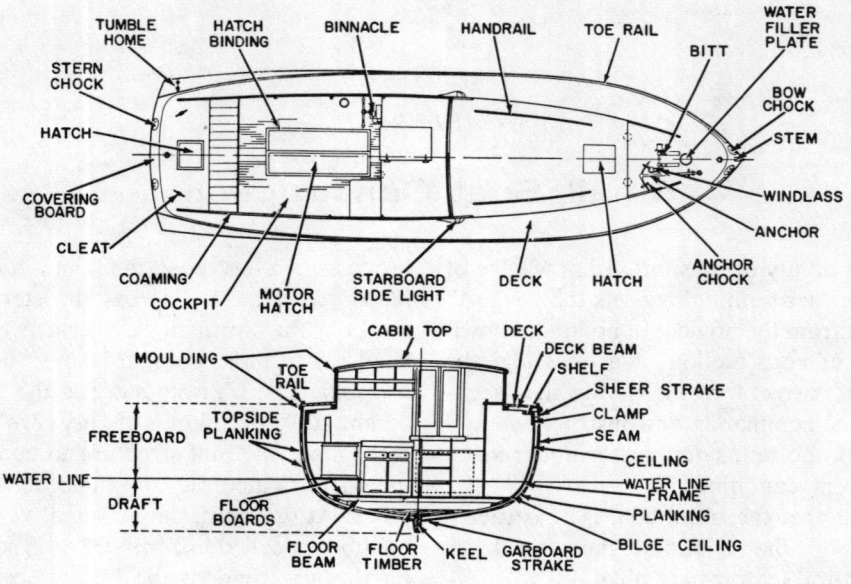

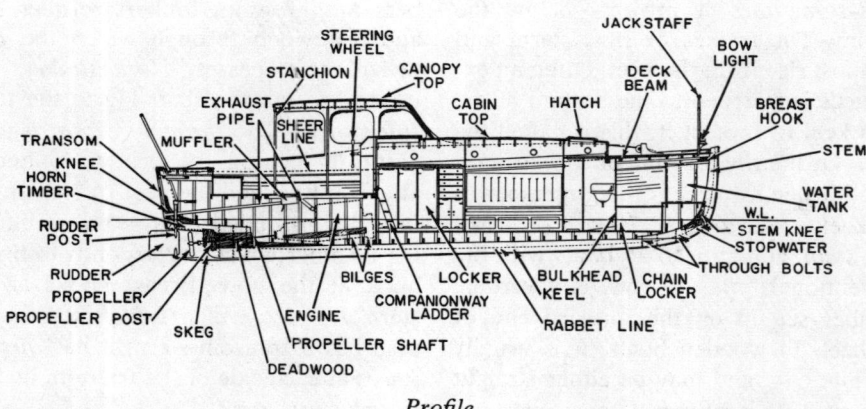

Profile

Typical small-boat construction

ceiling is inner planking applied to the inside of frames for strength and interior finish.

Planks are applied to the outside of the frames in constructing the hull. Each continuous line of planks from bow to stern is called a *strake*. When short planks are used in one strake, the ends are butted and jointed on *butt blocks*. The lowest strake, next to the keel, is called the *garboard*. The upper edge of the *sheer strake*, or top plank, of the *topsides*, is called the *gunwale* (always pronounced "gun'l"). The *taffrail* is the rail at the stern, farthest aft. Spaces between planks are called *seams*. They are calked to make them watertight by rolling or driving cotton into them. Then the seams are *paved* (filled) with white lead or seam composition. Frame members such as the keel and stem are *rabbeted* to receive the edges and ends of the planks.

The plank fits into the *rabbet*, which is a longitudinal recess, or cut, of the proper size in the wood. Plank ends at the stem and stern are called *hood ends*. *Deck beams* are the athwartship members that support the decks. *Carlines,* or stiffeners, are fore and aft timbers placed under a deck to reinforce it and to tie in the transverse and longitudinal framing.

Types of Wooden Boat Construction

Four general types of wooden-boat construction are commonly used by boat builders in the United States:

1. *Carvel.* In carvel construction, the planks which cover the sides of the vessel lie alongside one another without overlapping and the seams are calked. Where the construction is too light to permit calking, a narrow batten or riband is run along the seams inside. The calking in this case is limited to the garboard seams and hood ends of the planks. When heavy boats are built in this manner, a second layer of planking is sometimes used. The two layers are separated by canvas or compound. The seams of the inner planking are staggered from those of the outer planking.

2. *Clinker.* In clinker construction, the planks overlap at their edges as the clapboards on a house, and are fastened to one another as well as to the frames. Clinker construction has greater strength than carvel construction because the planks support each other. The added strength allows the frames to be placed farther apart. The seams are not calked as the swelling of the planks causes them to bind tightly one upon another. To keep the seams tight, the boat should be put in the water or hosed down frequently.

Strip planking construction. *(Owens photo)*

Ribbon carvel on batten seam construction. *(Owens photo)*

This cruiser is double-planked from keel to sheer. *(Owens photo)*

The Lapstrake "job" is readily recognized by the "clapboard" look. *(Owens photo)*

This "Express Cruiser" has an all-plywood Hull. *(Owens photo)*

3. *Diagonal.* In diagonal construction, the planks run diagonally, at about a 45° angle, from the keel to the gunwales; two thicknesses of planking are used at right angles to each other. This very strong construction is used chiefly for large boats carrying heavy weights. The diagonal and carvel methods are often combined by using two layers of planking, one carvel-laid and the other diagonally laid.

4. *Plywood.* In plywood construction, thin strips of plywood, impregnated with waterproof glue, are diagonally bent over a mandrel or mold to the desired shape. The skin is built up of several layers (laminations). The mold is then placed in a superheated steam-pressure room where the wood is curved to form a one-piece hull.

Metal Boats

The plating of metal boats is galvanized sheet steel or aluminum. The gunwales are sometimes of wood, but more often they are steel or aluminum angle bars. The keel, stem and sternpost are usually made of steel.

Many wood and metal boats are fitted with air tanks for reserve buoyancy. These tanks are made of copper or galvanized sheet steel. The position of the tanks is an important consideration because it affects a boat's center of gravity. Carrying the tanks low keeps the center of gravity low and helps to prevent capsizing. As a make-shift buoyancy "tank" some operators of smaller boats place inflated automobile tubes under the covered deck area of their vessels.

Decks. Decks usually have fore and aft curvature called *sheer,* and athwartship curvature called *camber.* Sheer, manifested in a higher deck line forward —and sometimes aft—provides reserve buoyancy for improved riding qualities, and normally results in a drier and safer vessel. A boat's deck is cambered (designed with a slightly convex surface) to drain water over the sides of the craft.

Hatches. Hatches are deck openings through which material or persons move vertically. They should be provided with hatch covers and battens or other means of making them watertight. Hatches exposed to the weather have *coamings,* the raised framework around the hatch to prevent water from getting below.

Masts. A mast is a straight piece of timber or a hollow cylinder of metal set vertically on the centerline of the vessel supporting yards, booms, or gaffs. It may be one piece or several pieces banded together to form a continuous pole. Masts are used principally as support for rigging, signal halyards, radio antennas, lights and such equipment as radar apparatus. In the event of engine breakdown, any sizeable mast can be used to rig sails for some control of the boat and to keep headway.

The mast situated farthest forward is called the *foremast.* On a two-masted vessel, the after mast is called the *mainmast.* On a three-masted vessel, the masts (in order from forward) are the foremast, the mainmast, and the *mizzenmast.* A mast rests in a foundation in the hull called a *step;* when the mast is upright, it is said to be *stepped.* The top of a mast is called the *truck* and the lower portion, the *heel.*

Due to their height and the weight they support, masts need *rigging* to keep them erect. A mast is supported by *standing rigging* or *wire-rope stays* running fore and aft and by *shrouds* that support the mast from the side. Stays on a boat include the *forestay,* running fore and aft from the bow to the fore truck; the *spring stay,* running from the foremast to the mainmast; and the *back stay* running from the mainmast aft to the stern.

Small vertical spars at the bow and stern are called *jackstaff* (forward) and *flagstaff* (aft). On some boats, a small spar called the *gaff* extending abaft the

SMALL BOAT CONSTRUCTION

mainmast, a short distance below the truck, is used to fly the national ensign when under way.

Boat Measurements

Measurements of pleasure boats in advertising material and builders' descriptions do not always conform to actual sizes. Some boat builders, for example, state their crafts' length as measured along the gunwale rather than straight fore and aft; others use different means of "expanding" the size of their merchandise. According to maritime practice, the following are the accepted methods of ship measurement:

Length: The *length overall* (LOA) of a vessel is the total length from the foremost to the aftermost points of a vessel's hull. The important *length between perpendiculars* (LBP) is the distance between the *forward* and *after perpendiculars*. The forward perpendicular is a vertical line drawn at the point where the forward side of the stem intersects the load waterline. The after perpendicular is a vertical line drawn where the after side of the sternpost intersects the load waterline.

Breadth: Extreme breadth is the greatest breadth between the outside surfaces of the planking or shell plating. *Molded breadth* is the greatest breadth between the outside edges of the frames.

Weight: The weight of a pleasure boat may be important as it will affect trailer-portability and this is generally included in the boat's specifications in pounds. For winter storage, etc., prices are generally figured by the boat yards on the basis of length-feet of the boat. As a matter of interest, however, the method of measuring the weight of a vessel is:

Gross Tons: The entire cubic capacity of the vessel expressed in tons of 100 cubic feet each, excluding the space occupied by the peak and other tanks for water ballast, open forecastle, bridge, poop, access and hatchways, certain light and air spaces, domes, skylights, etc.

Net Tons: The carrying capacity of a vessel expressed in net tons (100 cubic feet) is arrived at by measuring the cubic content of the cargo and passenger space.

Deadweight Tons: The carrying capacity of a vessel is expressed in tons of 2,240 pounds (long tons), and is the difference between light displacement and loaded displacement. Light displacement of the vessel is its weight excluding fuel, water, stores, dunnage and other items that are necessary on a voyage. This also excludes cargo and passengers. Loaded displacement is the weight of the vessel including fuel, water, stores, crew, dunnage, other items necessary on a voyage, and/or cargo and passengers.

Freeboard: Freeboard is the distance in feet and inches from the waterline of the vessel to the top of the main deck. It refers to the entire above-water portion of a vessel's hull. Technically, freeboard is the distance measured vertically at the side of a vessel amidships from the upper edge of the deck line to the water surface. On outboards, the important freeboard is that of the transom to which the outboard is attached. This has been standardized at 15 inches by the boating industry.

Draft: The draft is the vertical disance from the waterline to the lowest point of a boat's bottom. The draft may also be defined as the least depth of water in which a vessel will float. Naturally, the waterline, freeboard and draft vary with the weight of the load carried by the boat, and the greatest danger in overloading a small boat with passengers is that this reduces the freeboard and increases the danger of swamping the craft.

In the 1961 Motorboat Show in New York City, more than 50 percent of the boats on display were made of fiberglass.

Until very recently, this had been strictly an outboard and small motor or sailboat building material. However, in 1961, several of the fiberglass hulls were in the 30 to 40-foot range, and even larger fiberglass boats were in the planning stage. Manufacturers also announced that the plastic hull materials now being used were fire-retarding in addition to their other advantages.

Fiberglass Boats

Fiberglass is a glass, drawn or spun into fibrous yarn, in combination with a suitable plastic. Some manufacturers prefer to call their product "reinforced plastic" which is the same material.

The advent of reinforced plastics into the boat-building industry has raised a number of problems despite the fact that the material seems eminently suitable for the cheap and rapid production of certain types of hulls.

One of the greatest problems for the fiberglass manufacturers is the fact that design data for hull structures in wood, steel and aluminum are scarce. Indeed, the technical area of stress considerations has been seriously deficient in the conventional boat-building materials, with the prime criteria in construction volunteered by the old line builders being, "We built it that size and shape before and we have found it to be about right." Therefore the builders of plastic craft are faced not only with the problems of building, but also of determining the strengths of the hull structures they are replacing. Failure to do this by many fiberglass builders has resulted in a rash of poorly constructed boats which have proven unseaworthy, often at the expense of human life. Hence, the acceptance of reinforced plastic boats by builders and by the general public has been somewhat retarded. Possibly an even more difficult task facing the plastic boat builder is that of persuading the naval architect to design the hulls so that full advantages of the material can be gained.

Why Fiberglass?

One of the greatest advantages of fiberglass is the aesthetic. The molded forms can be used to create curving lines and even "fins" on the taildeck. Since many boats are purchased today by former landlubbers with little appreciation of the nautical aspects of a boat, a new set of values has become applied in the boating trade. In earlier boats, the emphasis was on seaworthiness and a Spartan purity of line. Today, probably inspired by the automobile designers, there is an attempt to sell boats by elaborate flowing lines and gaudy colors, and an obvious attempt in the fittings and decorations to appeal to the female taste.

The Maintenance Advantage

One of the practical advantages of the plastic boat is that of maintenance cost or effort. While the "old timer" seemed to enjoy the long hours of work in refinishing his boat each year before putting it in the water, the modern boat-buyer seems to want a craft that will skim around the water on weekends in the summer and that can be forgotten during the winter. Fiberglass boats offer about the minimum in required maintenance since they do not require to be caulked, scraped, sanded, refurbished or painted.

However, there have been greatly exaggerated claims regarding the maintenance of fiberglass boats. Although much advertising has stressed that there is no maintenance necessary, it is a fact that *fiberglass boats are not maintenance free*. They require a certain amount of yearly attention to keep them in prime operating condition. Many of the resins tend to absorb and retain stains present in some waters. The pigments used in many boats' gel coats are attacked by the ultraviolet rays of the sun and are prone to fade out after a few years. In essence, although fiberglass boats are reasonably free from maintenance, they lack the permanence of finish and color that the advertisers claim for them. (See section on "Federal Trade Commission and the Boating Industry.")

Fiberglass Hull-Making

Making the fiberglass hull involves molding a reinforced plastic by combining glass fibers with a polyester, or thermosetting resin. Reinforcement of plastic has been practiced for many years by utilizing such materials as chopped rags, asbestos fibers, cellulose fibers, and many others. In the last fifteen years, however, glass fibers have been widely used, and have become an important factor in the pleasure boat field within the last ten years. Glass fibers are especially suitable for hull reinforcement since they offer low moisture absorption and high resistance to chemicals and weathering; they also resist fungus attack and the glass itself is completely fireproof.

Fiberglass hull makers use a boro-silicate type of glass which is melted into a viscous liquid which is then stretched into fibers. This is done mechanically or by "attenuation" in fast-moving gas streams. The fibers produced in the gas streams are limited in length, but the mechanically-drawn fibers can be of any length. The fibers are then used much as any other fiber to produce a "cloth." The strands are twisted into yarns and the the yarns are woven into rather thin fabric. These thin cloths are then used as laminates to reinforce the plastic in a sandwich type of construction. However, not all builders use the cloth-laminate method of hull formation. Since the cloth is more expensive than chopped mats, some builders use only the chopped mats for reinforcement. In better quality plastic boats a sandwich type of construction is used which consists of a layer of woven cloth sandwiched between two layers of chopped strand mats. As is implied in the name, chopped strand mats consist of chopped strands bonded together in a random manner. The binder used is normally a resinous material.

On an equal weight basis, tests have shown that glass reinforced laminates can equal or exceed metals in certain mechanical strength qualities. However, the fabrication of the hull presents problems requiring careful temperature and humidity control during the "curing" of the polyester resins. An extremely rapid increase in temperature in a mass of resin during its transformation from a soft gel to a solid can set up internal strains leading to cracking. Under some conditions, bubbling within the mass can create voids in the cured resin, leaving spaces within the hull structure.

How the Hulls Are Made

Core Construction: Some of the companies making larger boats which must withstand rough water have incorporated cores of balsa wood or foamed plastic into the hull. These lightweight coring materials are used to build up very thick hull sections at a saving to the builder, since the materials are less expensive than the resin and glass matting. Thus, the overall cost of the boat may be reduced.

However, this construction has virtues other than cost-saving. It offers many structural advantages by allowing a better distribution of weight for more stability. Also, these light-weight substances provide flotation properties which make the boat virtually unsinkable. What is considered in boating circles even more important is the increase in rigidity in the basic hull structure. The cores increase the compressive or impact loads the hull will withstand since the core material itself will absorb and distribute loads. Coring materials of necessity must be resilient and tough, with high compressive strength. Of the materials available, balsa wood has the highest strength to weight ratio, but it is not used as widely as the chemically foamed plastics. These offer the advantages of lower price, easier molding to the compound curvature which is a feature of the plastic hulls, and chemical inertness to most elements.

Open Mold Fabrication

The open mold method of fiberglass hull-making was the first and is still the most commonly used method. One advantage is that it permits many complex shapes to be built into the finished design. However, one feature of this method is that only one surface can be smooth and accurate in contour—the surface which is in contact with the mold. In this type of construction, the ratio of glass to resin is high so that the finished hulls may be thicker and heavier than pressure-molded hulls of comparable strength.

A pattern or plug for initial mold casting is built up from wood to the desired hull design. This pattern must be made with extreme care and must be sanded, polished and waxed before it can be used for mold production. When this pattern has been completed, it is temporarily used as a male mold on which the female mold can be laminated. Chopped glass mats are generally used as reinforcements for the female mold, as these mats lend themselves to the concave curvature of the hull where woven mats might bridge the concavities. Once made, these "plugs" will last indefinitely and on each an infinite number of hulls may be made.

The shrinkage which occurs as "polymerization" causes the resin to settle down into the laminate, leaving the texture of the glass fiber raised on the surface of the molding. This effect can be quite pronounced and detract from the finished hull appearance. By coating the mold with a thin, even coat of thickened resin and allowing it to set before proceeding with the laminate, the desired smooth surface can be obtained. This *gel* coat is the only surface that will be visible and so only this surface is pigmented with the colors desired for the hull.

Problems arise at this stage of construction. The difference in the amount of shrinkage that takes place between the gel and the laminate may lead to warping or internal stresses which can affect the hull strength. If the gel coat is unevenly applied, the thicker areas may be brittle due to the absence of reinforcing fibers, which may cause premature cracking or flaking.

The fact that the external surface of the gel looks about the same in a poorly constructed boat as in one that is well constructed has misled many boat buyers and is a serious problem in appraising the worth of a fiberglass boat in the showroom.

After the application and drying of the gel coat, the reinforcing material mat is laid in place. Paint brushes or rollers are used to apply the resin and to remove entrapped air. Some manufacturers apply the resin with a spray gun, but the air must still be removed manually. The main task of the workman at this stage is to work out as much of the entrapped air as possible.

The process of laying up the reinforcing material and impregnating with resin is repeated until the desired thickness has been reached. Normally, two or three layers of matting are used. As mentioned before, some quality builders use a slightly more expensive sandwich construction which uses a layer of woven roving between two chopped strand mats.

As the resin cures, it passes first to the fragile gel state. Then, depending on exact process used, the hull may be removed in from two to twelve hours. In addition, some builders allow their boats to "mature" at room temperatures for periods up to four weeks.

Matched Metal Die Molding: Although this process will produce a hull of higher strength than the hand layup methods, it is in limited use because of the high investment necessary to build the huge presses required, and the fact that any change in the design would require a large capital outlay.

The construction technique is simple. Matched metal dies, constructed of flame-hardened steel, telescope within each other to place the resin under pressure in the same way that fluid is compressed by the piston in a hydraulic cylinder.

The method is basically similar to that used in automobile body manufacture.

Vacuum Bag Molding: This method is a compromise between the open mold method and the expensive matched metal die molding method. More uniform thickness throughout the hull can be obtained, although this is not always desirable, and a lighter-weight hull can be made since the ratio of resin to reinforcement can be lowered.

In this process, a flexible film or bag is used to apply pressure against a layup as it cures. In the vacuum bag process, atmospheric pressure is brought to bear against the assembly by applying a vacuum to the side of the bag adjacent to the mold.

The same type of molds are used as in the open mold method, except that a flange is provided for the evacuation apparatus. The catalyzed resin is sprayed and the need for rolling or brushing is eliminated. Generally mats that have been pre-moistened with resin are used.

Vacuum is applied until the entrapped air and excess resin have been removed. Heat is then applied and the hull is cured in the mold.

Sprayup Process: This is a newly developed method which is expected to grow in importance since it eliminates much of the hand labor required in the impregnation of the glass mats in the other processes.

The world's largest matched metal die, exerting 700 tons of pressure under a constant temperature of 240°F. guarantees a uniform molding of the fiberglass into the hull. This method makes the hull stronger than steel of the same weight and thickness. *(MFG Boat Co. photo)*

The first step in this process is the application to the mold of a pigmented gel coat of resin. A ply of glass reinforcement, carefully cut to fit, is then positioned within the gel and sprayed with resin by means of a hand gun. The process is then continued until the desired ply has been reached. These "guns" spray up to 35 pounds per minute a blend of promoted and catalyzed resins. It is claimed that this process results in a 10 percent weight (resin) reduction.

SOMETHING ABOUT PROPELLERS

There are few products in such common use as marine propellers and yet often so little understood. However, the operation of a propeller has been the subject of much study by marine engineers and can be explained in fairly nontechnical language.

The power developed by any marine

The installation of aluminum floor braces give stability to the floor plus added strength to the hull. *(MFG Boat Co. photo)*

The process of adhering the boat to the deck — rather than the deck to the boat — is done in this manner. When the "Gunk" is applied, the weight of the hull against the deck insures a completely air-tight waterproof seam when the "Gunk" has hardened. *(MFG Boat Co. photo)*

engine is available at the propeller shaft in the form of torque, or "twisting effort." Something is needed to convert this twisting effort into a thrusting effort, which can be used to drive the boat. The propeller does this job.

At this point, it will be helpful to become familiar with propeller geometry and dimensions. Propeller diameter is the diameter of a circle circumscribing the tips of the propeller blades. See *Fig. 1*. It is equal to twice the distance from the shaft centerline to the tip of one blade.

Propeller pitch is a linear dimension usually expressed in inches or feet and is equal to the advance of the propeller in one revolution at zero slip. *Fig. 2*. It is exactly the same thing as the pitch of a marine screw if one imagines the propeller to replace the screw and the water to replace the nut into which the screw is threaded.

Propellers commonly have three blades, but may be built with two, four, five or more blades for special purposes.

Propellers are either right hand or left hand turning, depending on the direction of rotation of the engine. Direction of rotation has no effect on performance as far as speed or engine load are concerned; it may, however, affect the "backing" of a single screw boat. (See Section on "Small Boat Handling")

A section through a normal propeller blade is of a shape called "ogival." See *Fig. 3*. The flat side of the ogival section faces aft and is called the "pitch" surface. It is the side on which all pitch measurements must be made.

Theory of Propeller Action

The function of the propeller is to convert torque to thrust. Thrust is another name for force, and a basic axiom of mechanics tells us that Force (thrust) is equal to Mass times Acceleration. In other words, if we impart an acceleration to a mass of water, we will generate a

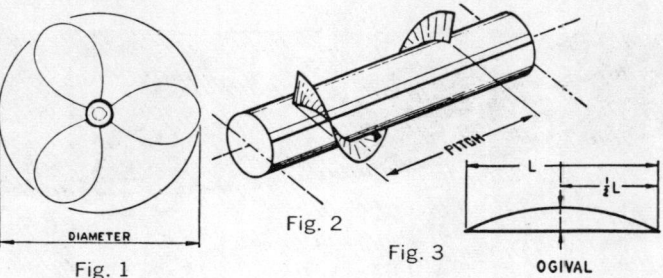

Fig. 1 — DIAMETER
Fig. 2
Fig. 3 — OGIVAL

thrust or push which will accelerate the boat forward while the mass of water is moved in the opposite direction.

The propeller blade is given a shape such that when rotated in water, it acts liked a pump and pushes a mass of water astern. Actually, it sucks water from ahead, gives it an acceleration as it passes through the propeller disc and discharges it astern. It is, in other words, a pump without a casing, operating submerged in the fluid it is pumping.

A propeller and an oar blade do the same job—both impart an acceleration to a mass of water, except that the oar blade does so intermittently whereas the propeller, because it is submerged and is a rotating device, does so continuously.

Propeller Slip

We have seen that the propeller, in order to generate thrust, must accelerate or move a mass of water astern. But the propeller, being shaped like a screw, might conceivably, as it rotates, slide through the water as machine screw would into a nut, without displacing any water aft. If this happened the propeller (and the boat) would, in one revolution of the shaft, advance a distance equal to the propeller pitch. This would be called *zero slip*. But in order to produce a thrust, we must accelerate or move some water aft, and therefore, it is apparent that the propeller will not advance the full amount of its pitch in each revolution, but will advance some lesser amount, depending on upon how much water it ac-

celerates astern in the process of producing enough thrust to offset the resistance of the boat to being driven ahead. If the boat were tied to a dock, the propeller would not advance at all, but would generate maximum thrust because full power would go into accelerating water astern. This would be called operation at 100 per cent slip. The term "apparent slip" is used to indicate the difference between the theoretical speed which the boat would obtain on the propeller pitch and the rpm of the propeller shaft, and the actual speed of the boat.

Fig. 4 illustrates the relation of slip to boat and propeller speed. The following formula may be used to determine the slip at which a given boat is operating:

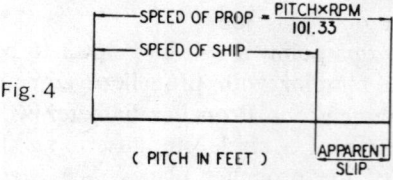

Fig. 4

Slip must not be confused with efficiency which is a measure of the percentage of engine power converted to thrust by the propeller. We have seen that we must have slip in order to generate thrust and the amount of slip will be proportional to the amount of thrust required by the boat. High speed runabouts, fast cruisers, and most pleasure boats require relatively low thrust and therefore operate at low slip, whereas tugs and other heavy vessels require high thrust and therefore operate most efficiently at high slip.

Selection of Efficient Shaft Speed

Since force (thrust) is equal to mass times acceleration, it would seem that we might get the same force whether we apply large acceleration to a small mass of water (small propeller turning fast), or a small acceleration to a large mass of water (large propeller turning slowly). In practice, however, there are other factors such as the relation of the propeller pitch to its diameter and energy losses due to friction between the accelerated water and the surrounding water that makes a proper relation between boat speed and propeller shaft speed essential to an efficient installation.

In general, horsepower available and shaft speed determine the propeller diameter (this may also be limited by the clearance available because of the construction of the boat), while shaft speed and boat speed determine propeller pitch. The pitch of a propeller divided by its diameter is called "pitch ratio." For example a propeller of 20" diameter and 20" pitch has a pitch ratio of 1.0; a diameter of 20" and a pitch of 15" a pitch ratio of .75, etc. For best efficiency, the pitch ratio of boat propellers should be in the range of .65 to 1.0 for heavy and average cruisers; .80 to 1.2 for medium and fast cruisers; and .90 to 1.5 for exceptionally fast cruisers and runabouts. Pitch ratios outside these ranges will generally indicate an unsuitable shaft speed.

Galvanic Corrosion

When dissimilar metals are in contact with one another in salt water, one of them suffers excessive corrosion. This is called galvanic corrosion. It follows that marine propellers, rudders, shafts, fastenings and other underwater fittings may be subject to galvanic corrosion.

In recognizing galvanic corrosion as distinguished from the ordinary corrosion of metals in salt water, it is important to remember two requisite conditions for corrosion due to galvanic action: There must be dissimilar metals located near to each other, and there must be an electrical (metallic) connection between them.

The following table of galvanic series may be used to select metals which are apt to be good neighbors underwater. Metals near the top of the list will be corroded rapidly if installed near metals having a lower position on the list.

Galvanic Series

Corroded End — Less Noble
Magnesium
Zinc
Aluminum
Cadmium
Steel
Cast Iron
Stainless (active)
Lead
Tin
Nickel
Brasses
Copper
Bronze
Monel
Stainless (passive)
Silver
Gold
Protected End — More Noble

Both theory and practice have shown that the group of bronze, copper and Monel may safely be used together in salt water.

Good Practice

1. Select metals listed as closely as possible to each other in the galvanic series.

2. Insulate between dissimilar metals.

3. Locate dissimilar metals as far apart as possible.

4. Never use fasteners of less noble material than the metal parts they are used to secure. For example, while bronze bolts might be used to secure an iron skeg, steel bolts would corrode rapidly if used to secure a bronze skeg.

The "Multi-Pitch" propeller allows the outboarder to manually select seven different pitches, on the water, to cope with his changing requirements for power, speed and gas economy. *(Lesnor-Maehr Marine Co. photo)*

Metallurgy

Propellers are generally available in several types of bronze, stainless steel, and aluminum, which is generally preferred for outboard motors because of its lighter weight. Also, a new appearance in the field is a propeller made of nylon which is claimed to "bounce" off obstructions it may strike and then resume its original shape.

As a rule, many of the dealers offer a choice of propellers for small boats depending on the use of the vessel. Different types would be recommended for the fisherman mainly interested in trolling at low speeds, the speedster, and the waterskier who needs more pulling power. It is generally safe to rely on the charts provided by the propeller manufacturers which describe the different types of propellers and their recommended uses.

CHAPTER VIII

Safe Small Boat Handling

Safe boat handling requires an understanding of the many varied and complex problems of seamanship. Too many persons enter the boating world with the feeling that "if you can drive a car, you can handle a boat." However, there are far more differences between driving and boat handling than there are similarities. As noted elsewhere in this book, your local Coast Guard Auxiliary and U.S. Power Squadrons offer many courses in boat safety and handling. These courses are free and open to all. Marine equipment manufacturers have available pamphlets and boating films that are loaned to interested groups. The National Safe Boating Association (611 East Marceau Street, St. Louis 11, Mo.) has a Speakers Bureau which can furnish your club or organization with a speaker on boating safety.

The following chapter will attempt to cover the basic principles involved in handling small boats, both inboard and outboard. Basically, an outboard craft is handled in the same manner as any other boat of the same size and power.

Vessel Characteristics

The "characteristics" of a boat that affect its control are its design, power, propeller action, and rudder action.

The "design" of a boat includes the size and shape of the hull, draft, trim, weight and amount of superstructure. Boats with shallow draft, low superstructure, and slim design normally handle more easily than those with high superstructure, deep draft, and wide beam because they are less affected by wind and current and respond more rapidly to the rudder. Deep draft vessels are normally more affected by currents; large superstructures impose a "sail" effect when maneuvering or when under way.

The "power" of the boat is a highly variable factor. Each phase of motive force has its own peculiarities as it reacts on the boat and no set of rules can be devised to cover all types. Every boat has its own power characteristics which the operator can only learn through experience in order to determine their effect on the handling of a particular boat.

The "propeller action" is generally not understood. A propeller draws its supply of water from every direction around the blades, forcing it in a powerful stream toward the stern. This moving current which provides the power for propulsion is called *screw current*. The water flowing into the propeller is called *suction screw current;* that being ejected is called *discharge current*. Basically explained, the suction current vaporizes off the tips of the blades and spirals back in a helical (bedspring) pattern.

There are three factors that affect propeller action:

1. Pitch. The pitch of a propeller (see illustration) is the distance the propeller would advance in one complete revolution if the water were a solid medium.

2. Slip. The differences between the speed of the boat and the speed of the propeller is known as the slip. Slip is caused by the yield of the water against the propeller thrust. In other words, it is the percentage of distance lost because water is a yielding substance.

3. Cavitation. When the blade-tip speed is excessive for the size and shape

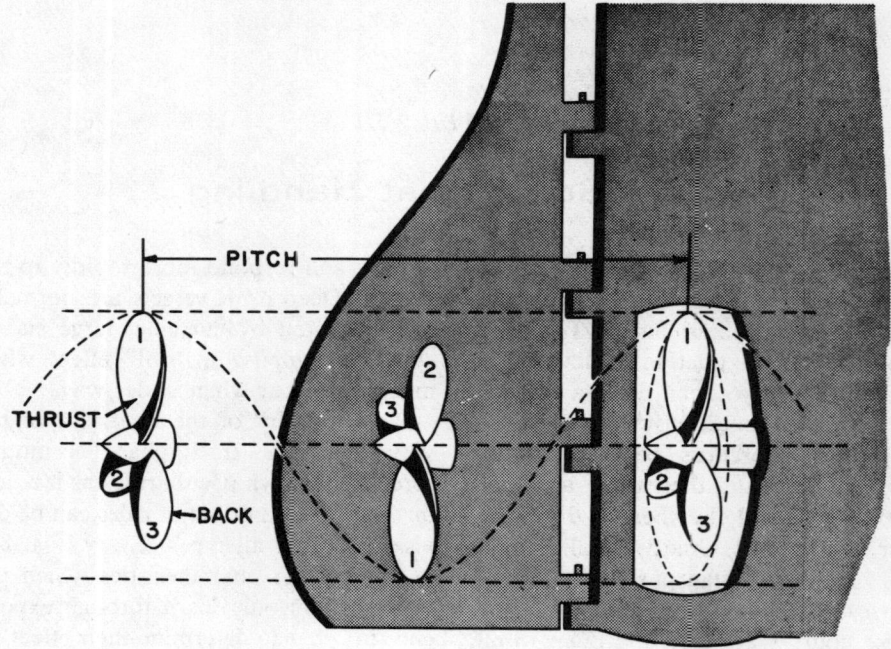

Propeller pitch

of the propeller, the boat will ride high in the water, and there will be unequal pressure on the lower and upper blade surfaces, producing cavities or bubbles around the propeller. This condition is known as cavitation. The result is an increase in revolutions per minute without an equivalent increase of thrust; thus, there is a loss of efficiency. When cavitation is fully developed, it limits a boat's speed regardless of the available engine power or the hull design.

The "rudder action" is the same on a large boat as on a small one. The rudder is normally placed directly behind the propeller to use the powerful discharge action to turn the boat. Moving the rudder to the right deflects the discharge current to the right, thus forcing the stern to the left. This action is reversed when left rudder is applied. At a very slow propeller speed and with very little headway there may not be sufficient control over a boat to maneuver it, especially if other forces (wind, water current, etc.) are acting upon it at the same time. When this condition prevails, the propeller may be speeded up enough to give it a more powerful thrust against the rudder. Using sudden thrusts of power to "kick" (move) the stern in this manner is one of the fundamental principles of boat handling. A vessel can often be turned in twice its length by kicking the stern.

Natural Factors Also Influence Control

Wind, tidal and ocean currents, waves or sea, and depth of water must be considered when handling a boat. Shallow water particularly affects deeper draft boats because of the cushion affect similar to that encountered when navigating in narrow channels. This will be taken up a few pages later.

Steering Orders

There are always times when a friend or relative will take the helm of the boat. This can be a serious strain on marital or social relationships when there is a lack of complete understanding between the person at the tiller or wheel and the one shouting commands. The novice at the "handle" of an outboard with no steering wheel will almost invariably push the handle to the right when told to "turn right," with a resultant left swing of the boat, or vice versa.

To avoid discord and possible accident, it might be well to insist that anyone who takes the helm be made to study the following ten steering orders—and orders should be given accordingly.

"Right rudder" and "Left rudder," are orders for the wheel to be turned to the right or left or the outboard motor to be swung in that direction. If your steering setup is a do-it-yourself installation, when the wheel is turned to the right, the rudder should turn to the same side. The wheel and rudder should not be rigged in reverse.

Commands

When a command is given to the helmsman, the first part of the order indicates the direction (right or left), allowing the helmsman to start direction of the wheel before the second part of the command which states the amount of angle. Steering commands commonly used are:

1. "Right (or left) full rudder." Full rudder designates a 30° rudder. When the rudder is turned past 30° (usually designated "hard right or left"), care must be taken to avoid jamming it against the stops.

2. "Right (or left) 5°, 10°, 15°, etc." This is used to indicate the angle in degrees that the rudder is to be offset.

3. "Give her more rudder." To increase the rudder angle already on when it is desired to turn the boat more rapidly in the direction in which she is already turning.

4. "Ease the rudder." To decrease the rudder angle. The order may also be: "Ease to (state number) degrees."

5. "Rudder amidships." To place the rudder on the centerline.

6. "Meet her." To check, but not stop, the swing by putting the rudder in the opposite position. Usually this order is used when it is desired to keep the boat from swinging past her new course.

7. "Steady" or "Steady as you go." To steer the present course while the ship is swinging. The course should be noted at the time the order is given and the ship steadied on that course.

8. "Shift the rudder." To change from right to left (or left to right) rudder, usually given when the boat loses her headway and commences to gather sternway and it is desired to keep her turning in the same direction.

9. "Mind your rudder." To steer more carefully or stand by for an order.

10. "Keep her so." To steer the course just reported, following a request for that course.

As most operators of pleasure boats are considered "Captain Blighs" by their passengers, you might point out that on merchant and naval craft the helmsman, to assure that orders have been correctly received, must always repeat, word for word, any command received. In addition, as soon as the command has been executed, the helmsman reports it to the ship's officer. The officer confirms the fact that the situation is understood by replying, "Very Well." Perhaps your "crew" will be different from most and follow that procedure.

Handling Characteristics of Single-and-Twin-Screw Boats

Handling Single-Screw Vessels

Characteristics such as the power, propeller, rudder and design of a boat affect handling in various ways. For the purpose of illustrating the effect of these factors, we may assume that the sea is calm, that there is neither wind nor current, and that the boat has a right-handed propeller as almost all single-screw pleasure boats do.

1. *Vessel and propeller going forward.* With the vessel and propeller going forward and the rudder amidships, the boat tends to move on a straight course. The sidewise pressure of the propeller is offset by the canting of the engine and shaft. When the rudder is put over, either to the right or the left, the water through which the boat is moving strikes the rudder face, forcing the stern in the opposite direction. At the same time, discharge current strikes the rudder face and pushes the stern over farther. As a result of these forces, the bow moves in the direction in which the rudder has been thrown.

2. *Vessel with sternway, propeller backing.* When backing, the sidewise pressure is opposite to that exerted when a vessel is moving forward. The discharge current from the propeller reacts against the hull. Since this current is rotary, it strikes the hull high on the starboard side and low on the port side when the propeller is backing. This current exerts a greater force on the starboard side and tends to throw the stern of the vessel to port *(1, Fig. 1)*. With rudder amidships, the vessel will back to port from the force of the sidewise pressure and the discharge current. When the rudder is put over to starboard, the action of the suction current against the face of the rudder will tend to throw the stern to starboard *(2, Fig. 1)*. Unless the vessel is making sternway, this force will not be strong enough to overcome

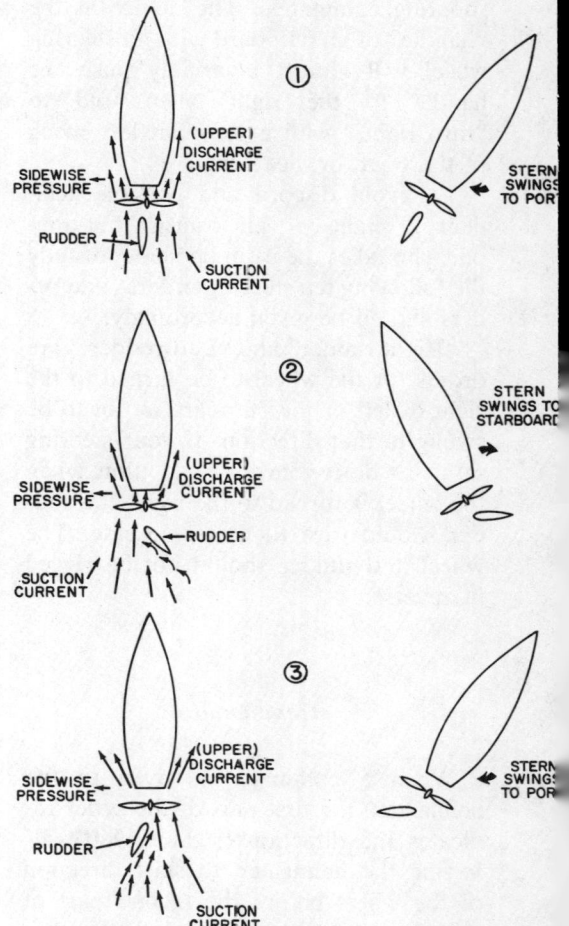

Vessel with sternway, propeller backing

the effect of the sidewise pressure and the discharge current — the stern will back to port. When the rudder is put over to port, the force of the suction current on the face of the rudder accentuates the effect of the sidewise pressure of the propeller and the discharge current and will force the stern rapidly to port. *(3, Fig. 1)*.

Because of these forces, *all right-handed single-screw boats tend to back to port.*

3. *Vessel with headway, propeller backing.* With the rudder amidships, (1, Fig. 2), the stern will go out to port

because the only active forces are the sidewise pressure of the propeller and the discharge current. With the rudder to starboard (2, Fig. 2), the stern rapidly goes to port, but as headway is lost and the vessel begins to go astern, the effect of the suction current on the face of the rudder slows the swing. However, since a single-screw boat tends to back to port when moving astern, the stern will tend to port unless the boat gathers considerable speed astern. With the rudder left, the normal steering tendency of the rudder will throw the stern to starboard. This starboard motion will occur when the vessel has considerable headway, but as headway is lost, the effect of the sidewise pressure of the propeller and the discharge current, in conjunction with increasing forces of the suction current against the face of the rudder, swings the stern rapidly to port (3, Fig. 2).

going ahead. In this situation, the sidewise pressure of the propeller and the discharge current are persistent factors and may offset each other. Therefore, if the rudder is amidships with no forces acting against it, the vessel will tend to follow a straight course (1, Fig. 3). With the rudder to the right, the action of the water on the back face of the rudder as it moves astern will tend to throw the stern to the starboard, whereas the action of the discharge current against the forward face of the rudder tends to throw the stern to port. Direction is determined by the stronger force. As the boat loses sternway, however, the direct steering action of the rudder takes over and the stern swings to port (2, Fig. 3). With the rudder left, the action is the same as with the rudder right; in either case, the rudder action is determined by the strength of the forces, and as the vessel loses sternway, the direct steering action of the rudder takes over and the stern swings rapidly to starboard. (3, Fig. 3).

The Outboard Propulsion Unit

The handling of the outboard motorboat is different from that of the conventional single-screw boat because in the outboard the propeller itself is turned to provide the turning force. The outboard motor is more maneuverable than the inboard since it can turn a craft in its own length.

Some of the older and a few of the smaller current models do not have a reverse, but the entire motor can be swept around 180° for reverse power. When the direction of the units is reversed, it is better to idle the engine while the propeller rotates to its new position.

Handling Twin-Screw Vessels

The twin-screw boat has two propellers—one on each side of the centerline.

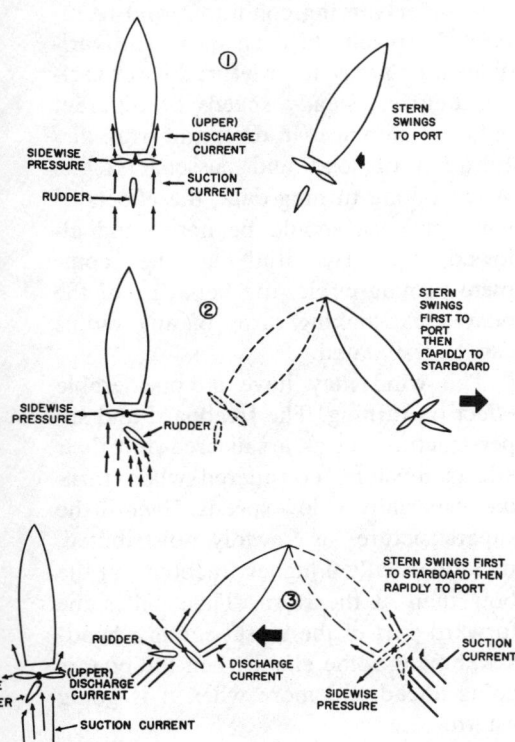

Vessel with headway, propeller backing

4. *Vessel with sternway, propeller*

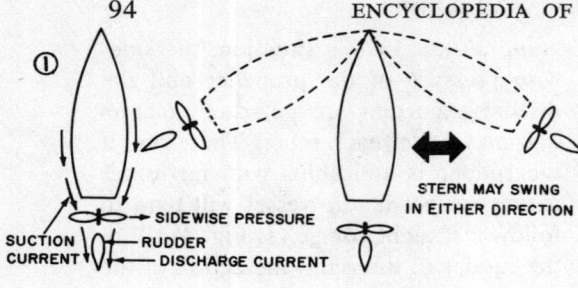

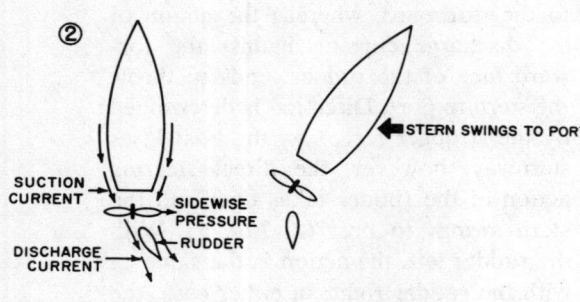

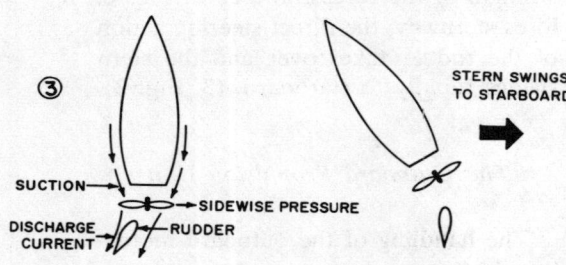

Vessel with sternway, propeller going ahead

They are maneuvered by separate throttle controls. Generally the propellers are outturning; that is, the starboard propeller is right-handed and the port left-handed. This balances the sidewise pressure of the propellers and makes it possible to keep the ship on a straight course with no rudder. Discounting outside influences, the twin-screw boat backs with equal facility to port or starboard.

The various forces affecting the action of a single-screw boat are still present, but normally a twin-screw vessel is not affected by these forces as much as a single-screw boat. This is because the forces from one screw balance the forces from the other screw.

One powerful force is the momentum of the boat, ahead or astern, acting through the center of gravity. Where a twin-screw boat is going ahead and one screw is backed, two opposing forces are set in motion; namely, the force of the backing screw acting in one direction and the weight of the ship acting in the other direction. This is in addition to the force of the rudder if it is put over. Other than this force and the turning action accomplished by one engine ahead and the other astern, the handling characteristics of a twin-screw boat are similar to those just explained for the single-screw craft.

Effect of Natural Factors on Turning

The standard method of finding the turning characteristics of any boat is to turn her in a number of complete circles under varying conditions and to record the results of each turn. The variables used are right or left rudder of various degrees, steady speeds of different values, differences in draft and trim, distribution of load and passengers, etc. When taking turning data, the effects of wind and sea should be noted and allowed for. By studying the complete turning circle, the behavior of the boat while making turns of any radius can be estimated.

The wind may have a considerable effect on turning. The freeboard and superstructure act as a sail area and their effects must be considered when turning, especially at low speeds. Even if the superstructure is evenly distributed, there is usually a higher freeboard at the bow than at the stern. This makes the forward part of the vessel act as a headsail, having some effect when the boat is going ahead and more when it is going astern.

A boat will usually back into the wind because the propeller acts as a pivot and the pressure of the wind in the bow and superstructure swings the craft around stern to. The stronger the wind, the stronger the tendency to back into the wind. The tendency can be used to facilitate a turn whenever maneuvering in narrow turning areas.

The condition and relative direction of the sea affect both the progress and steering of the ship through their effect on the underwater body. Any sea forward of the beam will retard the speed of the ship, whereas any sea abaft (behind) the beam will accelerate it. The general effect of the sea on steering is to cause the boat to seek the trough of the waves. When the sea is on the bow or quarter, it may be necessary to carry a definite amount of either right or left rudder to maintain the course. This will result in the loss of speed because of rudder resistance. When bucking a heavy sea in a high wind, it is usually necessary to slow down. The slow engine speed opposed to the force of the waves results in less steering control. Under these conditions, the tendency of the ship to *fall off* into the trough is more pronounced. With a following sea, a vessel wallows (yaws) excessively and tends to go off course; this requires the use of more rudder to keep her steady. This extreme rudder will slow the vessel and partially offset the advantage of a following sea. A ship with no deadwood aft (see sketch of ship profile), yaws more than one whose underwater body is continuous to the rudder. All of the effects of the sea described above are more noticeable at low speeds than at high speeds and may vary if the wind and sea come from different directions.

In their Boat-Owners Manual, the Chris-Craft Corporation advises: "When driving the boat in a heavy seaway, avoid allowing the boat to get parallel to the waves. An angle something less than 90° is the best way to cut waves. Under circumstances like these it is also important to watch the distribution of your load. Do not allow everybody to sit up front when you are in a particularly heavy seaway as this has a tendency to raise the propeller and rudder and when going over a wave you may lose traction and steerage-way. When driving in a following sea, always keep the boat going a little faster than the sea is moving. The natural tendency if the sea is heavy, is to slow down to avoid giving your passengers too rough a ride; but if you move slower than the waves move you will drench all the passengers. Remember this rule only applies when the waves are going in the same direction as the boat. If you are going against the direction of the waves, you can select any speed you choose.

"If it is necessary to turn around in a heavy sea, there will naturally be one instant when the boat will be parallel to the waves. Make this instant as short as possible. In other words, turn sharply, and quickly at the time you are passing through the parallel position.

"Do not let these directions frighten you as they are only important in very heavy weather and probably you will avoid being out in such weather anyway, but it is well to know these things in case of emergency."

A Note for the Outboarder

Because of the low transom freeboard on many outboards (15 inches is the standard height of transom above water), they are especially vulnerable to water pouring in over the transom from following seas. This may cause the motor to "die" or bring in enough water to affect the trim of the boat. A self-bailing well aft or a watertight bulkhead in front of the motor are wise for any outboards that may be out in rough water.

Effects of Current

Current affects the underwater body of the boat. It is especially important because its existence may not always be realized. Known ocean currents may be shifted, accelerated, diminished or even reversed by winds blowing steadily in one direction over a long period of time. Currents in harbors, straits, and bays are caused by the action of the tides. The currents at the entrances to certain harbors are strong at times and may run at an angle to the entrance course. The current may be reduced or reversed by the tide. The direction and probable force of currents in ports and along the coasts may be determined approximately by studying the tide tables and current charts. However, every effort should be made to verify the data found in these publications as wind and weather may make them inaccurate. Observation of the shape of the shoreline and the direction in which buoys and other anchored navigational aides are leaning will give a good check on the force and direction of the current running at any time.

The general effect of a current on the underwater body of a boat is to move it bodily in the same direction as the current is running. When turning in a current, the completion of the turn may find the boat well down in the direction of the current as contrasted to her position when the turn was started. When held at any point, as by an anchor, the ship usually assumes the position that gives the current least resistance. For this reason, an anchored ship heads into the current unless the wind or sea is strong enough to overcome it. Likewise, a ship at anchor will swing with the change of the tidal current. Current is often used to an advantage when docking or undocking a ship. Steering is always easier when heading into a current than when going with it. In relation to this, it might be noted that U.S. lightships are always moored with one bow anchor so that their direction of swing serves as an additional guide to mariners.

Turning in a Limited Space

A twin-screw boat with a single rudder can be turned by going ahead on one engine and astern on the other, using the rudder only when headway or sternway has been gained. When the boat is fitted with twin rudders that are directly behind the propellers, the rudder is placed over hard in the direction of the turn before the maneuver is begun and one engine is backed at the speed necessary to prevent headway.

Single-screw boats can be turned easily in tight quarters. To start the swing, the engine speed is set at full ahead and the rudder is put hard right; then the engine is reversed to full astern until way is lost. When way is lost, the rudder is again shifted and the engine put full ahead. This procedure is repeated until the boat is on the desired heading. This maneuver makes use of the tendency of the righthanded propellers to back to port. In strong winds, it is advisable to turn in such a way that the tendency to back into the wind can be used to increase the turn.

Using an Anchor as a Turning Aid

An anchor can be used to facilitate and expedite a turn in a restricted space. Before using the anchor, the local chart should be studied to make sure that there are no submarine cables in the immediate area. The anchor is dropped at short scope. Even when low engine speed is used, the anchor will drag a little. The engine can be operated ahead and astern as described above, but only slow speeds should be used and little steerageway gained. The turn should be made to starboard by pivoting on the anchor when going ahead and by exploiting the tendency of the stern to swing to port when backing.

Navigating in Narrow Channels

A boat will be set off the nearer bank when proceeding along a straight, narrow channel, especially if the draft of the boat approaches the depth of the water. This effect is called *bank cushion*. It is particularly noticeable in narrow channels that shelve rapidly. As the ship moves ahead, the wedge of water between the bow and the nearer bank builds up higher than that on the other side, and the bow is forced out sharply. The suction of the screw, especially with a twin-screw boat, and the unbalanced pressure of water on the quarter tend to lower the water level between the quarter and the near bank forcing the stern toward the bank. This is called *bank suction*. The combined effect of bank cushion and bank suction may cause the boat to take a sudden and decided sheer toward the opposite bank. When a single-screw vessel traveling at very low speed with her starboard side near the right bank takes such a sheer, she may be brought under control by backing full with left full rudder. A twin-screw boat under similar conditions has a chance to recover from such a sheer by going full ahead on the port engine, stopping or backing the starboard screw and putting the rudder full right. If the sheer should carry the boat across midchannel, an anchor should be dropped and snubbed if necessary. All engines should be reversed as the anchor is dropped.

In extremely narrow channels where bank cushion and bank suction may be expected, it is best to proceed at very low speed, to keep near the middle of the channel, to keep an anchor (or anchors) ready for immediate use, and to meet and pass other boats much closer than is usual. When approaching to pass another boat in a narrow channel, headway should be greatly reduced but not enough to lose steering control. As the boats come nearly abeam, each should give sufficient right rudder to head slightly toward its right bank. Shortly afterwards the boats should reverse their rudders to straighten up. Little right rudder will be required when the bows are abreast because the height of the water between them will counteract the bank cushion. As the bows come abeam of the quarters, the suction of the propellers tend to pull the bows to port, tending to swing to midchannel. This swing should be checked with right rudder. Next the sterns will be affected by the suction and will tend to straighten the boats up. The boats may then go ahead full to increase steerage way. Under some conditions in very narrow channels, it may be necessary for each vessel to drop an anchor at short scope and to pass very slowly.

Turning in a Bend

Bank suction, bank cushion, and currents are factors which affect a boat trying to turn in a sharp bend in a narrow channel. Bank suction and bank cushion are strongest when the bank of the channel is steep. They are weakest when the edge of the channel shoals gradually and extends into a large shallow area. The tendency of the vessel to continue along her original course when the rudder is put over is strongest when the banks of the channel are steep and the boat is deeply laden. Bank suction increases with the boat's speed. River and canal currents are usually strongest in the bend. There may also be eddies or countercurrents on the lee side of the point. In a long canal or channel, tidal changes may change the direction of the currents.

With a head current, the best position from which to start a turn is the middle of the channel. The eddy under the point and the increased current in the bend are both avoided. The boat should proceed at a very low speed so that it can be stopped quickly by the engines and the current or with the help of an anchor.

When making a sharp bend with the current, it is possible to make any one of the following maneuvers:
1. Hug the point.
2. Stay in the bend.
3. Proceed slightly on the bend side of the middle of the channel.

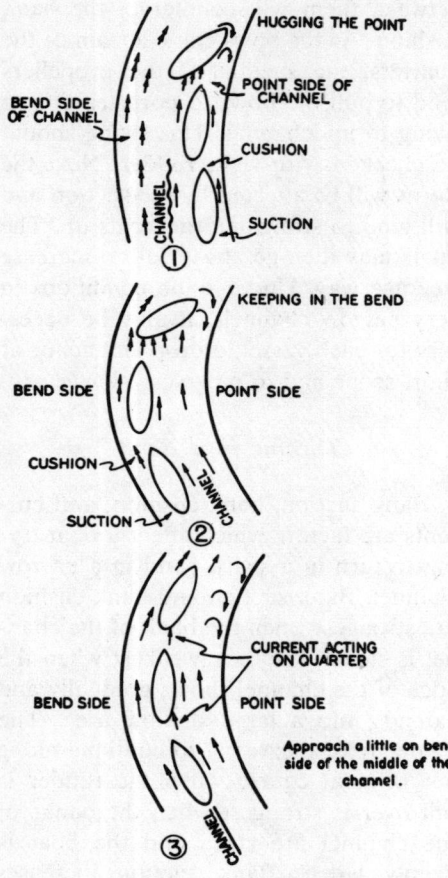

Turning in a bend

started too soon, the bank suction on one quarter added to the force of the current on the other may give the vessel a strong and sudden sheer. The bank cushion under the bow will increase the sheer. If the bow should enter the eddies under the point, the boat may pivot and run aground.

The safest way to turn when the current is from astern is to approach the turn on a course a little to the bend inside of the middle of the channel (*3*). By doing this, the eddies under the point and the increased current in the bend can be used to assist the turn. A current from astern tends to force a boat toward the bend side; consequently the turn should be started early in the bend. Conversely, a strong head current tends to force the ship toward the point side; therefore the turn should be started later. Generally, turns should be made at a very slow speed.

When the boat hugs the point (*1*), it requires but a small amount of rudder toward the bank to steer a straight course. Less rudder will be necessary as the channel begins to bend and the ship moves from the bank; this condition may be used as a sign that it is time to begin the turn. Slack water or eddies may be encountered around the turn and may make it very difficult to prevent a sheer toward the near bank, particularly in shallow water when laden. The current under the quarter may affect the stern, resulting in an increase in the sheer.

If the operator decides to make a turn in the bend, that is, away from the point (*2*), the problem is the timing of the turn. If started too late, the craft may ground on the bank in the bend; if

The Sea Anchor

The sea anchor, or drogue, is another safety device that should be carried aboard the boat that may possible encounter rough waters or have to run through dangerous inlets. Basically, the sea anchor is a canvas bag which is dropped over the stern or bow to hold the boat by creating a drag. Some sea anchors have a trip line connected to the tip of the anchor which can be pulled

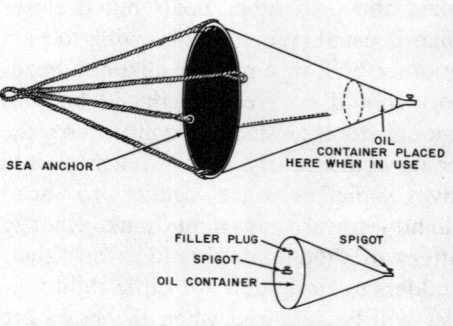

A sea anchor for a small boat

SAFE SMALL BOAT HANDLING

Stay clear of moored barges. River currents moving under the rake of a moored barge are dangerous, and can readily pull a pleasure boat under the barge. Arrows denote the direction of the stream's flow.

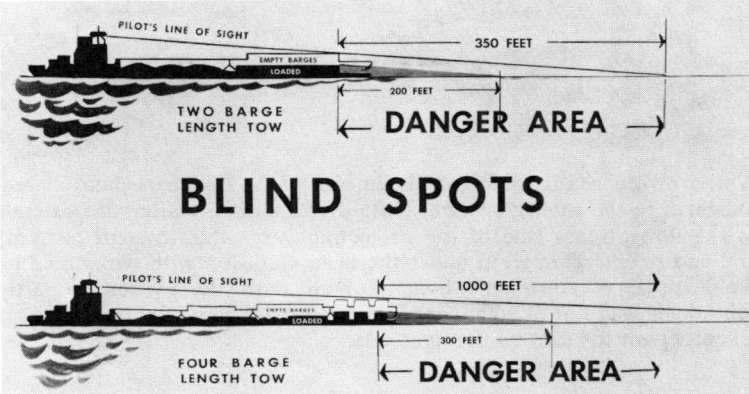

This diagram shows the danger area in front of river tows. The distances are based on the height of the average pilothouse. Do not water ski or cruise in front of tows. A water skier who falls in front of a tow will not be within the visual range of the pilot. It takes up to half a mile for a river tow to stop.

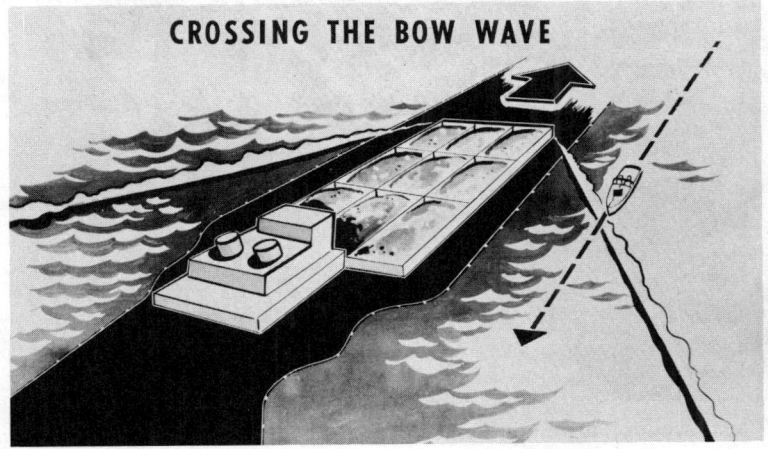

Use extreme caution when crossing bow waves. Proceed slowly and cross waves at about a 90 degree angle. Maintain as much distance between your craft and the tow as is possible. Note shaded danger areas.

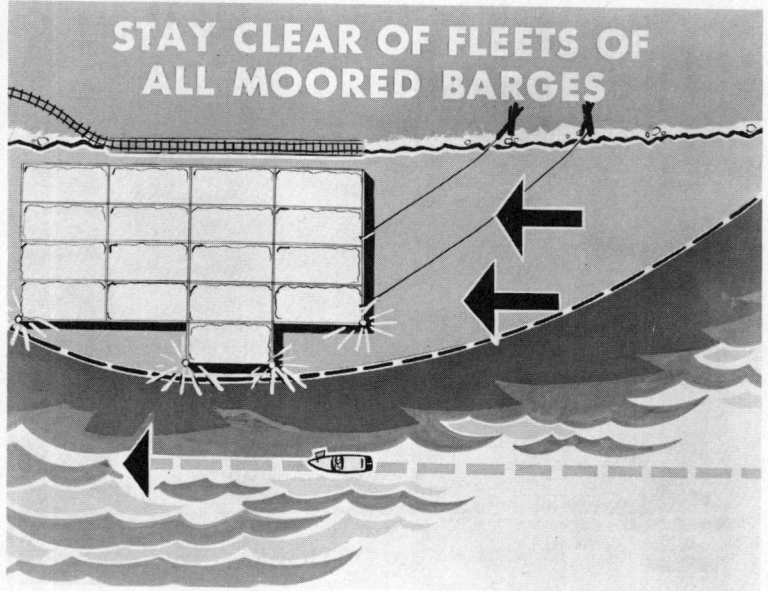

A fleet of moored barges expands the size of the upstream danger area, indicated in the shaded section. Note that the danger area also extends to the downstream side of the projecting barge due to swift currents and eddies emerging from under the fleet. Collision with wires holding the fleet may overturn small boats; in many cases these wires are partly submerged and out of sight. At night, watch for white lights located on all corners of the fleet on the river side.

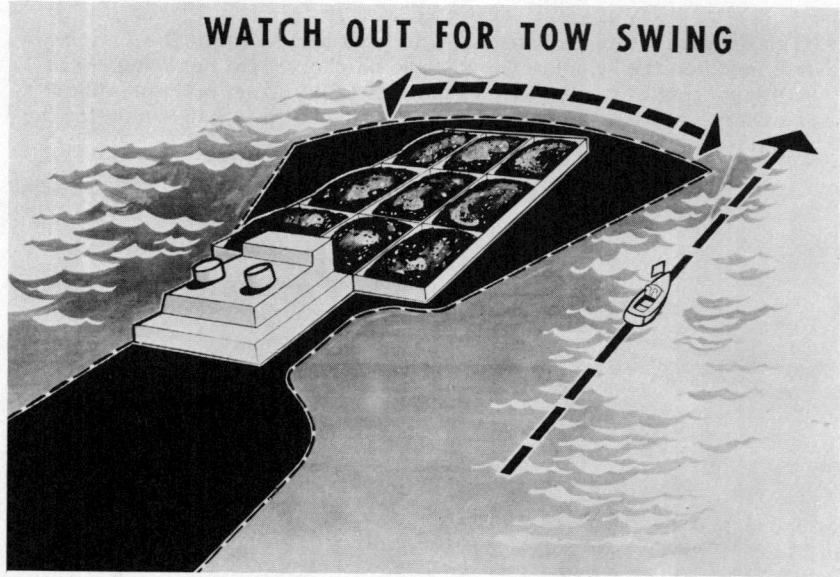

When meeting a tow in the bend of a river or when the towboat is maneuvering barges near shore, stay clear! The entire tow may be swinging either right or left as indicated in the shaded area. *(Photos of barges courtesy National Safe Boating Association)*

when it is desired to eliminate the dragging effect and pull the device aboard.

When the small boat is swept ahead by the seas, a sea anchor over the stern will enable the operator to have the control afforded by his engine for steering and headway while limiting the forward speed of the boat.

In a case where the boat is making no headway, either with or against the seas, the boat must be "hove to," that is headed so she will take the seas most comfortably. It must be remembered that different boats will heave to in a manner dependent on their design and trim; some will lay their quarters into the wind and others their bows. The sea anchor should be cast off to keep the boat from being flung about at the mercy of the sea.

Oil (to calm the seas) may be used in conjunction with the anchor. Technically, the use of oil is based on the fact that the adherence of water to air affords strong winds the opportunity of building up one large wave at the expense of others. These waves are dangerous to boats because of their size and speed, and the amount of water they can deposit on deck. This liaison between water and air can be reduced by spreading oil over a large area of water to decrease the formation of giant waves and deaden the cresting motion of all waves. Preferably, an animal or vegetable oil should be spread to the windward of the vessel at the rate of approximately 2 gallons an hour. The sea anchor fitted with an oil container will do this. However, too much reliance must not be laid on oil despite the old saying about oil and "troubled waters." In cold weather the oil may spread slowly and under some sea conditions it may be whipped away with relatively little effect.

Another way to spread oil is to hang over the side a canvas bag stuffed with oakum cotton or waste which has been soaked with oil.

CHAPTER IX

Boating Safety

Boating is essentially one of the safest of sports, but when accidents do happen, they are almost always traceable to human causes—ignorance, carelessness or some ingenious combination of both.

This is especially conspicuously true of fire (including explosion, which is fire in a hurry), which a casual reading of the newspapers will reveal as one of the most common type of serious boating accident. Even that well-publicized high explosive, gasoline, is harmless until somebody gets it in the wrong place at the wrong time and provides the means of setting it off.

Most boat fires and explosions happen to two kinds of boatmen—the ignorant, who don't know any better, and the careless, whose familiarity with potential causes of fires has bred not contempt for them, but a subconscious "it-won't-happen-to-me" psychosis. Many experienced boat owners in the latter category become ex-boat owners in a sudden and often spectacular manner.

This chapter will point out some of the more common causes of fires and explosions aboard boats and some of the ways to avoid them, but a reasonable amount of common sense and caution is the best way to keep your boat from catching fire.

Engine Fuel Fires

Engine fuel fires are probably the most common kind and also the kind most likely to begin with a loud explosion and get out of control before anything can be done—even if the operator of the boat is still around after the explosion.

Most boat engines run on gasoline, and everyone who can read should know by now that a half-cupful of raw gasoline spilled on the bilge can generate enough explosive vapor to blow a 50-foot cruiser to pieces.

When your automobile gas tank runs over from careless filling or its gas line or carburetor develops a leak, little harm is done since the gasoline usually drips onto the ground, evaporates and soon mixes with enough air to be non-explosive. But in a boat the liquid gasoline or the heavier-than-air vapor from a partly empty fuel tank may trickle down into the bilge or the corner of some compartment and lie there for hours or even days until a backfire, a spark from electrical equipment, or a carelessly dropped live ash from a cigarette sets it off.

The dangers of gasoline aboard ship are well known, and the safeguards against those dangers are observed by most competent yacht designers and builders. But even the employment of a recognized boat-builder or the purchase of one of the popular stock cruisers or runabouts is no guarantee that all these safeguards are included in the boat. Human nature being what it is, there may be sloppy workmanship or short cuts hidden away somewhere. Furthermore, there are a lot of back-yard built boats and patchwork engine and tank installations around, so every boatowner should check to make sure his craft complies with the standards. These are fully set forth in a 48-page manual, "Fire Protection Standards in Motor Craft," put out by the National Fire Protection Association, 60 Batterymarch Street, Boston, Massachu-

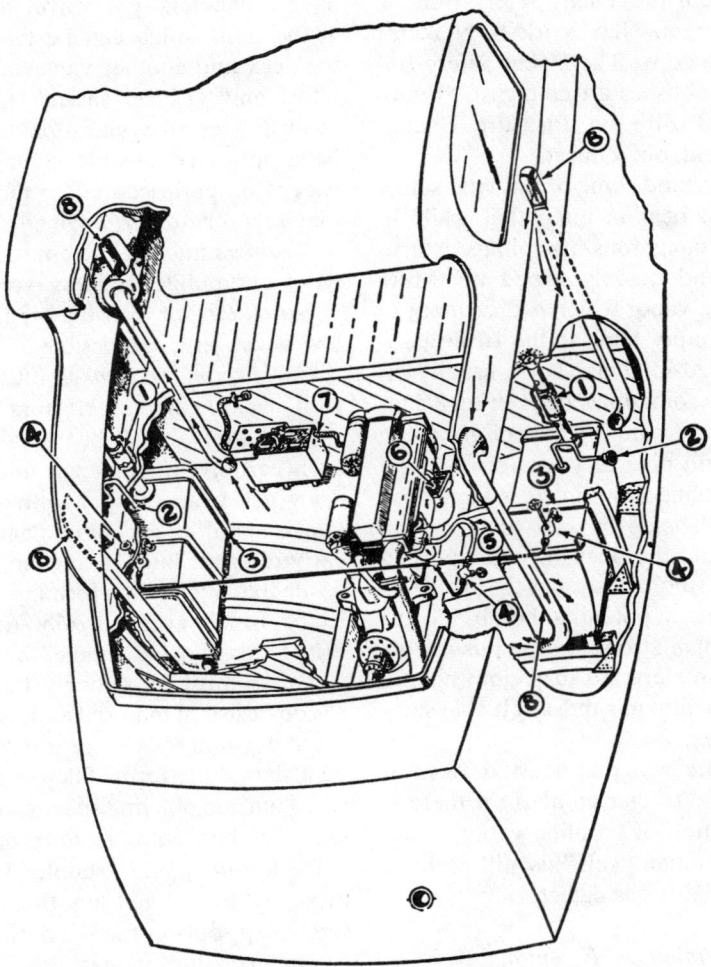

Several important fire prevention safeguards, detailed in NFPA No. 302, are illustrated in this diagram. The fuel pipe (1) should be of ample size, should run directly from deck plate to tank, and should be arranged to prevent overflow of fuel or vapors inside the hull. (Par. 323). The fuel tank vent pipe (2) should lead from top of tank and should have flame arresters to protect against flash-backs (Par. 323). The fuel tank (3) should be rigidly secured with holding straps insulated from the tank surface (Pars. 311-314.) Fuel cut-offs (4) are required at both tanks and engine (Par. 324.) Flexible tubing (5) should separate the fuel lines to the hull from those secured to the engine (Par. 324.) The carburetor (6) should have a drip collector and back-fire flame arrester (Par. 212.) Battery (7) should be securely installed and equipped with a protective shield (Par. 523.) Ventilation (8) requirements include two intake and two exhaust ducts of equal and large diameter terminating in large cowls or equivalent fittings, with exhaust blower installed as high above bilge as possible (Sec. 13). Paragraph references are to Marine Bulletin 302 of the National Fire Prevention Association. *(Yacht Safety Bureau)*

setts. The manual can be obtained from them or from the Yacht Safety Bureau, 21 West Street, New York 6, N.Y. for fifty cents a copy. The Yacht Safety Bureau also publishes a free digest, "Fundamentals of Fire on Pleasure Boats," which is sent on request.

To understand some of the vital safety precautions, bear in mind that while liquid gas is dangerous, its spillage is usually seen and quickly wiped up. More deadly is the vapor which is driven out of your part-empty tank as the fresh gasoline is poured in. This vapor, usually invisible, may sometimes be seen on a sunny day as a shimmering flow of gas rising out of the fill pipe of your auto or boat tank as gasoline flows in. It is highly explosive, and being heavier than air can flow back into the boat through an open hatch or porthole and turn the inside of the hull into a potential bomb. Fortunately, it has a strong and unmistakable smell, and an alert and suspicious nose is one of the boatman's most valuable safety appliances.

While there are a number of devices on the market to trigger an alarm if there is a concentration of gasoline vapor in the bilges, the human "sniff" is still perhaps the most reliable gas detector.

Installation Essentials

Fill Pipes for gasoline tanks must be at least 1-1/2" in diameter, tightly connected to outside decks outboard of cockpits and coamings, and as far as possible from hull openings such as ventilators. The pipe should run straight into the tank with no bends.

Tank vent lines of not less than 5/8" copper tubing must lead to the outside of the hull and must be open at all times. They should be equipped with flame arrestors and should be arranged so that water cannot run back through them into the tank. This is generally done by bending a high "gooseneck" up under the deck.

Each *fuel line* from tank to engine must have a packless-type valve (not a cock) at the tank which can be reached from the deck and another valve at the carburetor end. Lines should be secured against excessive vibration and should have approved flexible connections between the part secured to the boat and that secured to the engine.

Strainers must be the approved marine type; automobile strainers won't do.

No *outlets* for drawing off gasoline below decks are permissible.

Carburetor air intakes must be fitted with backfire flame arrestors.

Drip pans must be installed under each carburetor, screened and piped to draw gas from the pan into the engine intake manifold except on engines whose carburetor air intakes turn up at about a 45-degree angle, thus forming a drip collector which automatically returns any drip to the engine intake.

Tanks must be strongly built of corrosion-resistant material and securely fastened down in chocks, or if flat-bottomed on a slatted platform. They should be located outside of living spaces, and if practical, bulkheaded off from them.

Deck *fill plates* should be clearly marked "Fuel," not on the removable screw cap, but on the fixed plate. Water is embarrassing in gasoline tanks and vice versa.

Fire prevention authorities frown on openings for feed lines or other purposes anywhere except in the top of a gasoline tank. They also take a dim view of handhole-size clean-out plates even in the top of the tank.

Filling Precautions

Carelessness in filling tanks causes many fires—and common sense and caution will prevent them. The period of danger is during and *after* fueling your boat.

Before taking on fuel, all lights and

fires must be out, all electrical equipment switched off and smoking prohibited. All hatches, ports and doors should be closed —remember the vapor that will pour out of the tank. A fire extinguisher—filled and recently tested—should be ready at hand.

When fueling, keep the hose nozzle in metal-to-metal contact with fill pipe to avoid static sparks. Don't let the gas come through the hose fast enough to cause blow-backs from the tank. Take all precautions to keep gasoline from spilling into the boat. Don't fill the tank quite to the top — leave a little air space for possible expansion of the gasoline. Determine the quantity of fuel to be taken on board and advise station attendant. Do not attempt to overload tanks. Allow for at least 2 per cent expansion of the cubic air space under normal conditions and up to 6 per cent where gasoline in storage is below freezing.

When fueling is completed, screw down the caps, wipe up any spillage from the deck, open all ports, hatches, and doors and ventilate for *at least* five minutes, running the exhaust blower if one is fitted. Then take a good sniff in all compartments for gasoline fumes before starting the engine or stove.

If you are at a pier near another boat that is taking on gasoline, especially if she is to windward of you, it is a good precaution to close your ports and hatches and have no open flame or sparks on your own boat.

Diesel Fuel

Diesel fuel with its high flash point is far less dangerous than gasoline, but it is still a flammable liquid. Installations of tanks and the piping and handling of diesel fuel are subject to many of the same precautions as for gasoline. Once ignited, diesel oil, or wood that has ever been soaked with it, will make a hot, stubborn fire.

Galleys are For Cooking Food . . . Not Boats or People

A wide variety of galley stoves are in use on pleasure boats, most of them operating on various solid, liquid or gas fuels. Electric stoves are found on only a few large boats with high output electric power supplies.

Solid Fuels

The safest stoves and cabin heaters are those burning solid fuels—wood, coal and charcoal. Such a stove and its smoke pipe must be carefully installed with ample air spaces all around it and with sheet metal and asbestos insulation between it and any nearby woodwork or other inflammable material. The smoke pipe must pass through a properly designed deck iron. Care must be used in removing and disposing of hot ashes. These stoves may be a bit slower to start cooking than other types and they may make the cabin hot on a mid-August day, but they can be a comfort in cold or damp weather. You can almost always find driftwood alongshore to stoke them with.

A different type of solid fuel is solidified alcohol or "canned heat," which is burned in specially-designed stoves. This fuel rates well up in the safety scale. However, it is rather expensive for longtime use and may be hard to find in some areas.

Liquid Fuels

Gasoline as a cooking or heating fuel is extremely dangerous and must never be used in a boat.

Kerosene, which is cheap and readily obtainable, has a relatively high flash point and is a reasonably safe fuel. However, it must be burned under pressure, and the stove, pressure pump, tank piping, and burners must be maintained in good condition. They must be kept clean and free from leaks. The wick-type kerosene stoves are *not* approved for boat use.

Alcohol, in its normal liquid form, is one of the most popular galley fuels. While its flash point is lower than that of kerosene, it has the great advantage that an alcohol fire can be extinguished with water. Throwing water on a kerosene or gasoline fire only spreads the blaze over a wider area since the blazing liquid floats on top of the water. Alcohol requires some pressure, either from a pump tank or from a gravity tank located higher than the stove, and all joints must be kept tight. It burns clean and hot, but costs more than kerosene and may not be available in out-of-the-way harbors.

Both kerosene and alcohol stoves must be *primed* by pre-heating the burners. This is usually done by burning liquid alcohol in the priming can under each burner. A safer method is to burn one of the commercially available small, solid "heat pills" which can be placed in the priming pan and lit with a match.

Gas stoves, using liquified petroleum fuel in tanks under high pressure, are increasingly popular afloat, being more like what the lady of the ship is accustomed to at home. But the lady must be made to realize that gas stoves in boats are far more dangerous than the one in a kitchen and require careful handling. Most of these "bottled" gases are heavier than air and are odorless. If they get loose they may collect in the bilge or other unventilated corners, ready to explode with terrific force if a spark or flame reaches them.

Supply tanks of gas stoves must be installed above decks and must have shut-offs in the supply line above deck as well as within reach of the cook, between deck and stove. These valves must always be closed, as must those on the stove itself whenever the stove is turned off, and may be opened again only when the cook is ready to immediately light the stove. All piping, especially inside the cabin, must be frequently inspected for leaks. Test the joints with soapsuds—not with matches. On the cost basis, gas is relatively expensive and can usually be replenished only around major yachting centers.

All stoves must be securely fastened down and should have rails around the top for securing pots and pans over the flame in rough weather.

There are many varieties of "camp" stoves on the market that are sheer murder aboard a boat. Whatever type of stove you select, fuel-wise, buy nothing but a marine stove that has the approval of the marine insurance underwriters.

Grease can blaze up in the skillet aboard a boat as easily as anywhere else, so don't hang dish towels, clothing or other flammable objects in a position where a roll of the boat might drop them on the stove top.

Watch Your Electricity!

Faulty wiring, overloaded circuits, broken insulation and short circuits from various causes can start many boat fires. Fires are especially prevalent in boats where the electrical system has "just sort of growed" with piecemeal additions of appliances, wiring, and odds and ends of equipment. In these days when electricity is used for so many purposes even aboard small cruising boats, the electrical system should be designed and installed as a whole by experts in accordance with accepted standards.

These standards, as applied to the relatively low voltages used aboard most pleasure craft, are outlined in the two booklets, mentioned earlier. For voltages above 32, the authority is "Recommended Practices for Electrical Installations on Shipboard," put out by the American Institute of Electrical Engineers, 33 West 39th Street, New York, N.Y. Unless the boat owner is fully qualified to carry out these recommendations himself, he should have all electrical work done by a professional experienced in marine — not house or auto — electrical work.

Generally speaking, wiring, switchboards and electrical equipment should be kept as high in the boat as practicable, not only because it is drier there, but also because any possible sparks or hot wires must be kept out of the low places where combustible gasses may be trapped. For the same reason electrical units like generators, starters, etc. should be installed as high as possible on the main engines. Separate generating plants are best located on deck or, if in a large engineroom, well above the floor level.

Every electric circuit must be protected with a fuse or circuit breaker. If a fuse blows out, don't just screw in a bigger one. Find out what caused it to blow and have it fixed. That's what fuses are for.

Batteries, especially when being charged, give off combustible gases, so they should be located in well-ventilated compartments.

Keep the Air Moving

Ventilation is important to eliminate fire risks aboard a boat. Not merely ventilation of the living space, which you will want for your own comfort, but ventilation of the bilge, engine and tank spaces. Ducts of ample cross-section to carry a good flow of air should lead down into the very bottom of the bilge, especially in engine and tank spaces. Each should be topped by a cowl ventilator head and arranged to work in pairs, one turned forward so as to lead the air in while the other, turned aft, sucks air out. Four ducts are recommended for engine spaces. Natural circulation is more effective in boats at moorings or anchors, which usually lie head to wind, than in boats moored in slips or piers, which should have the cowls turned so as to be effective in prevailing winds.

An electric blower in at least one exhaust duct is desirable and should be of a design in which the electric motor is located outside the duct so that sparking cannot ignite gas being sucked out of the bilge. Cautious skippers turn these blowers on for at least five minutes and then try to detect the odor of gas in the engine compartment before starting the engines. This should be done especially after fueling or when the boat has been closed up and unused for some days.

Ventilation of lockers, drawers, and other small spaces is also important, especially in places containing such things as oilskin clothing, cleaning rags, paints, etc., which are possible sources of spontaneous combustion.

And while this has nothing to do with fire, good ventilation of a boat is the Number One enemy of mildew and dry rot — problems that shortens the lives of so many wooden boats.

About Fire Extinguishers

A minimum of fire extinguishing equipment for boats of different sizes is required by Coast Guard regulations and can profitably be supplemented by additional equipment.

Boat fires are of three types: Class A fires in wood, fabrics, papers, rubbish, etc.; Class B in flammable liquids, grease, etc.; Class C in electrical equipment, where the extinguishing agent must be a nonconductor of electricity.

The best antidote for Class A fires is usually found around boats—plenty of water. Of the various chemical extinguishers, the three that are most effective against both Class B and C fires are the vaporizing liquid types, using carbon tetrachloride or some similar liquid, or the carbon dioxide gas type and the dry chemical type using sodium bicarbonate. All three are non-freezing.

At least two hand-operated extinguishers, quart-size or larger, of one of these types must be aboard even a small boat, while four is the minimum, for a 50-footer. They should be strategically located, handy to likely starting points such as galley and engineroom, but should not be placed where a fire in one of those places might make it impossible to reach them. At least one should be on deck near the helmsman and one in any compartment below where a person might be cut off from escape by a sudden engineroom or galley fire.

Extinguishers should be checked at least once a year, the liquid type by discharging a few strokes and refilling—the others by checking their present weight as shown on an attached tag and refilling if they are lighter than the tag specifies.

In addition to the required hand extinguishers, permanently installed extinguishing systems are often piped to the likely starting points for fires, especially the engineroom. These may be manually discharged and they may also be equipped with automatic discharge devices which will take over if, for instance, things get too hot in the engineroom while you are ashore.

Coast Guard Safety Inspection

A service that is available in most boating localities and is well worth taking advantage of is the courtesy inspection given by the U.S. Coast Guard Auxiliary, a volunteer organization of boatmen who aid the Coast Guard in its duties. Your local auxiliary unit will make a date with you and inspect your boat thoroughly for compliance with all the official safety and other equipment requirements. They will also give some recommendations which go further than the actual law with regard to fire as well as other risks.

If your craft passes muster, they will give you a sticker to prove it, which will usually save you an official visit from the Coast Guard later on. If she is deficient

FOR SAFETY AFLOAT: The inspection of the Coast Guard Auxiliary covers everything from required life vests or pillows on an outboard to flame arrester on an inboard craft. (*Coast Guard photo*)

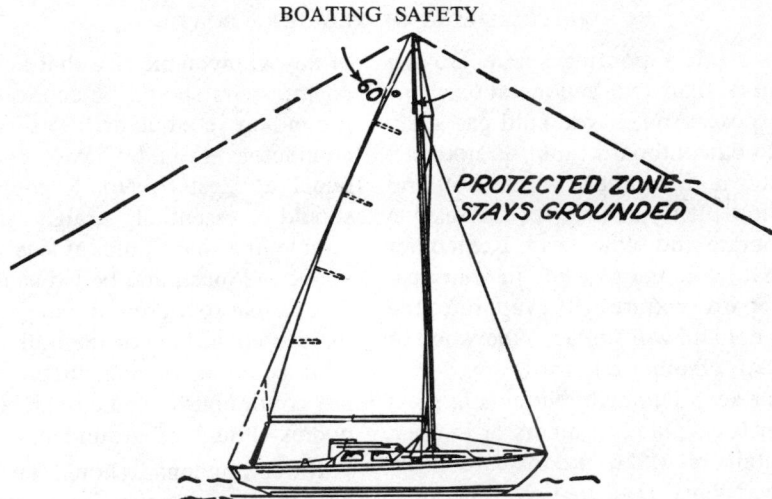

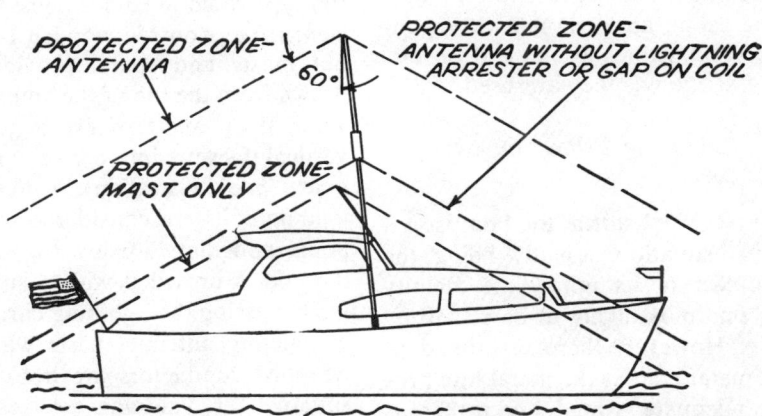

Diagrams above illustrate the "cone of protection" provided by a grounded mast or antenna. This protective zone is largely immune to direct strokes of lightning. No part of the vessel to be protected should extend outside the cone of protection. Thus in the cabin cruiser illustrated, adequate lightning protection is afforded only by the grounded antenna equipped with a lightning arrester or gap on the coil.

in any respect, they will list the things you should do to bring her up to standard, so that your boat will pass an official Coast Guard inspection. There is no charge, and no fine or report to the Coast Guard if they find anything wrong.

A Few Odds and Ends

A clean boat is likely to be a safe one. Be especially careful to keep the bilges free from grease and oil by an annual scraping and scrubbing and by putting one of the chemical detergent preparations which dissolve grease and oil into your bilge-water at least twice a month. The grease and oil can then be pumped out with the bilge water. If you are one of those lucky people with a tight boat with no bilge-water, toss in a few bucketsful of detergent and then pump it out again.

If you carry extra gas for an outboard motor, keep it above decks or in the cockpit in an approved, vapor-tight container with a safety pouring spout. Do not keep more than two gallons aboard for this purpose. And, if you spill gas when you fill your outboard tank, do not start the motor until you have wiped it off and then allow plenty of time for the residue to evaporate and blow away. Remember also, that while the gasoline in your gas-oil outboard mixture will evaporate, the oil will not and will sink into the wood of your boat, creating a hazard.

Never keep flammable liquids in glass or other breakable containers or in open top containers. Make sure the caps of the containers you do use are tight. The same goes for the reserve supply of matches.

Paint rags, oily waste, and used polishing cloths, however decorative they may be in the cabin, are a short cut to spontaneous combustion and should be disposed of as soon as they are used.

Lightning Protection

In an electrical storm, the boat is in a hazardous situation, usually being the tallest object in its immediate vicinity and the one most likely to be struck by lightning. However, there is little danger in a metal boat as the metal hull provides an adequate ground, and if there is good metal to metal contact between hull and metal masts, no further protection from lightning is necessary.

However, on non-metallic boats, especially those with masts, metallic fittings at extremities of wooden masts and yards should be effectively grounded and all metallic structural parts or accessories of any appreciable size that are installed on the spars should be connected to the grounding conductor. The grounding conductor should have conductivity equal at least to No. 8 copper cable, should be essentially straight, should terminate in a sharp point at least six inches above the mast, and be led as directly as practicable to a ground plate attached to the wetted surface of the hull. Also, metallic standing rigging, metal masts and any continuous metallic track on masts or booms should be grounded.

Radio antennas should be equipped with transmitting type lightning arresters or with some means of grounding during electrical storms. The grounding of metal rod type radio antennas constitutes sufficient protection for wooden boats without masts and spars, provided a line drawn from the top of the antenna downward at an angle of 60 degrees to the vertical does not intercept any part of the boat. (See illustration). Antennas with loading coils are considered to end at a point immediately below the coil, unless the coil is provided with a suitable gap for bypassing the lightning current. Non-conducting antenna masts with spirally wrapped conductors are not considered suitable for lightning protection purposes.

The boat owner should consider that lightning protection provisions are quite likely to receive scant attention, so he should be sure that their composition and assembly are strong and that the materials used are highly resistant to corrosion.

CHAPTER X

Communication

Distress Signals

Few situations in life are more fraught with loneliness than that of being on a boat that is having difficulties. A dead motor or a leak in the hull even a few hundred yards from shore can present a serious problem. Generally, the logical solution is to summon aid, which is usually close at hand. Others are always eager to help if you can inform them of your need.

Searching for a vessel in distress can be a difficult and lengthy procedure when incorrect or insufficient information is given. To increase your chances of rescue, know the distress signals and have the proper equipment on board. This signalling gear is not among the minimum legal requirements for a pleasure boat. Your needs of this type must be based upon the area in which your boat is operated and the size of your boat.

The radiotelephone is now a compact piece of equipment and a most valuable aid, and is seen in more and more outboard as well as inboard cruisers. Merchant craft, pleasure boats, Coast Guard ships listen constantly on 2182 kilocycles—the distress channel. This is a calling and distress frequency. A boat calling "Mayday," the code word for needing emergency assistance, stands an excellent opportunity of being heard in most areas. In some cases 2638 or 2738 frequencies may not be busy and may bring assistance sooner, but in an emergency you may use any available frequency to indicate your need for help. The Coast Guard has printed a 4 x 5 cardboard placard called "Distress Information Sheet" for posting near your radio (see below). It is a handy reference for the information desired by rescuers and will enhance the possibility of speedy rescue. These placards are available through the Coast Guard Auxiliary and at most Coast Guard units.

Many searching craft today are equipped with radar. This device enables searches to continue after dark and under conditions of poor visibility. However, boats made of wood and plastic do not make good radar targets. The placing of a radar reflector such as the small collapsible type high on the disabled boat will increase the chance of radar detection and rescue. Any signal that will attract attention and bring help is a satisfactory distress signal. However, if your signal is a known or recognized distress signal, your chances of obtaining assistance are improved.

The "Wave" for Help

The latest recognized distress signal for small boats on waters of the United States is that of slowly and repeatedly *Raising and Lowering Arms Outstretched to Each Side*. This is a distinctive signal that is not likely to be mistaken for a friendly greeting. To be as effective as possible, this signal should be given from the highest vantage point on the boat with consideration given to color contrasts.

A note should be added that while the flare gun is a highly effective night signalling device, in some areas these are legally considered as "concealed" weapons, and it might be well to check with a local police department for a ruling as to your right to obtain one.

DISTRESS INFORMATION SHEET

WHEN REQUESTING ASSISTANCE FROM THE COAST GUARD, FURNISH THE FOLLOWING INFORMATION AFTER ESTABLISHING COMMUNICATIONS. SPEAK SLOWLY AND CLEARLY.

(Coast Guard Station being called.) THIS IS *(your boat's name and radio call sign).* I AM *(nature of distress—disabled, sinking, grounded, etc.),* IN POSITION *(latitude and longitude or bearing (true or magnetic) and distance from a prominent point of land).* I HAVE *(number)* PERSONS ABOARD. I AM IN *(no immediate or immediate danger).* MY BOAT IS *(length and type, type of rig, color of hull, and color of topside).* I REQUEST *(source of assistance: Coast Guard or Commercial)* ASSISTANCE. I WILL STAND BY *(radio frequency).* OVER.

POST THIS CARD NEAR YOUR RADIO
TREASURY DEPARTMENT, U.S. COAST GUARD, CG-3892 (2-59)

✱ U.S. GOVERNMENT PRINTING OFFICE : 1959 O—502260

Ship Radiotelephone

There are two types of radiotelephone service available for pleasure boats, the "Maritime Service" and the "Citizen's Band Radio Service." The Maritime Service consists of special operating frequencies set aside for boat use while the Citizens Service may be utilized by any adult U.S. citizen for any lawful purpose and is a shorter range setup of the "walkie-talkie" type, requiring the establishment of separate transmitting and receiver stations. The Maritime Service gives a transmitting range from about twenty miles upwards, depending on the power of the set and atmospheric conditions, antenna height and other limiting factors. It gives ship-to-ship, ship-to-shore communications and it makes possible the reaching of shore telephones, Coast Guard Stations, etc.

Regulations on Boat Radiotelephones

The operation of marine radiotelephones is under the control of the Federal Communications Commission. The official rules are contained in the publication known as "Part 8" of the Commission's regulations. The first step towards obtaining or operating a boat's radiotelephone is to secure a copy of that regulation, "Stations on Shipboard in the Maritime Services." It sets forth in detail the requirements applicable to ship radio stations and must be kept available in every ship station. "Part 8" is located in Volume IV of the Commission's Rules which may be obtained for $2.50 from the Superintendent of Documents, Government Printing Office, Washington, 25, D. C.

The Radio Technical Commission for Marine Service publishes a pamphlet entitled "Marine Radio Telephony" which includes a summary of regulations governing voluntarily installed ship radiotelephone stations. This pamphlet may be of use as a source of additional information, but the F.C.C. advises that it is not an official publication of the Commission and contains some information not current. "Marine Radio Telephony"

Signal	Inland rules	Great Lakes rules	Western rivers	International rules*
A gun or other explosive fired at intervals of about a minute.	Yes (day and night)	Yes (day and night)	Yes (day and night)	Yes
A continuous sounding with any fog-signal apparatus.	Yes (day and night)	Yes (day and night)	Yes (day and night)	Yes
Rockets or shells, throwing red stars fired one at a time at short intervals.				Yes
Signal made by radiotelegraphy or by any other signaling methods consisting of the group ...━━━... (SOS) in Morse Code.				Yes
A signal sent by radiotelephony consisting of the spoken word "Mayday."				Yes
The International Code signal of distress indicated by N.C.			Yes (day)	Yes
A signal consisting of a square flag having above or below it a ball or anything resembling a ball.		Yes (day)	Yes (day)	Yes
Flames on the vessel (as from a burning tar barrel, oil barrel, etc.)	Yes (night)	Yes (night)	Yes (night)	Yes
A rocket parachute flare showing a red light.				Yes
Rockets or shells, bursting in the air with a loud report and throwing stars of any color or description, fired one at a time at short intervals.			Yes (day and night)	
A continuous sounding with steam whistle.			Yes (day and night)	
Rockets or shells, throwing stars of any color or description fired one at a time at short intervals.		Yes (day and night)		

*International rules do not distinguish between day and night use of signals.

Recognized distress signals *(From U.S.C.G. "Recreational Boating Guide")*

may be obtained for fifty cents from the Radio Technical Commission for Marine Service, c/o Federal Communications Commission, Washington 25, D. C.

Station and Operator Licensing

All radio stations and most operators aboard ship must be licensed by the Federal Communications Commission. The holder of the license is responsible at all times for the lawful and proper operation of his station. Licenses are granted only to United States citizens. Ship stations are licensed primarily for safety of life and property; therefore distress and safety communications must have absolute priority. Secondarily, however, certain frequencies which are not reserved for calling, distress, or other safety purposes may be used for radio-telephone calls to coast stations or between ships. The local telephone company or radiotelephone coast station can furnish information as to frequencies and charges for radiotelephone service.

Application for a regular-term (usually four years) ship radiotelephone station license is usually made on F.C.C. Form 501-A. All station license applications must be accurate and complete, must be signed before a notary public, and must be sent to the Secretary, Federal Communications Commission, Washington 25, D.C. Ship station licenses are not transferable. If you have purchased a vessel equipped with a licensed radio station, the previous licensee is required to return the old license to the Commission with a request for cancellation. In order to minimize the delay in issuance of a new license, you may enclose the old license and the previous licensee's request for its cancellation with your station license application. There is no charge for either the station or the operator's license.

When need arises for use of a ship radiotelephone station before a regular-term license can be issued by the Commission at Washington, D.C., an interim ship station license may be applied for at the nearest Commission field engineering office. It usually requires thirty to sixty days for the issuance of a regular-term license, and the interim permit is issued for three months.

Operator License

The transmitter aboard ship may only be operated by a licensed radio operator. The license usually held aboard pleasure boats is the Restricted Radiotelephone Operator Permit which may be obtained without charge or examination at any F.C.C. office by proper completion of Form 753.

You cannot make transmitter adjustments with such Permit. A first or second class operator license is required for adjustments which might affect the proper operation of the station. If the Restricted Radiotelephone Operator Permit was issued on or after November 15, 1948 and has not been suspended, it is good for life. Permits issued before that date have expired and should be replaced.

The licensed operator makes contact. Other persons may then talk over the set, but the operator must remain there and supervise the transmissions. He must also make the sign off announcement and the log entries. It is not necessary to post the Restricted Radiotelephone Operator Permit if it is kept on the operator's person. However, higher grade operator licenses must, in general, be conspicuously posted with the station license.

Some Regulations

Following is a summary of some of the more important regulations affecting ship radiotelephones:

2182 KC—This is the calling and distress frequency. Ship radiotelephones in the 1600–3500 kc band must maintain an efficient listening watch on 2182 kc while the station is open and not transmitting on other frequencies. All newly licensed and replacement shipboard transmitters in this band must be capable of transmitting on 2182 kc and at least one other frequency.

Intership Frequencies—There are four intership frequencies provided in the 1600-3500 kc band: 2003—Great Lakes area; 2638—all areas; 2738—all areas except Great Lakes area and Gulf of Mexico; 2830 kc — Gulf of Mexico. Use of these intership frequencies is limited to safety and operational communications, except that commercial transport vessels may also use them for business communications.

Intership Communication — The Commission's rules require that ship stations, before communicating on the intership radio channels, first establish contact by initially calling and answering on 2182 kc, unless another clearly understood operating procedure has actually been established in advance between the ship stations concerned. The operating procedures established in advance must encompass calls which are scheduled to be placed and received at definite times. There must be a mutually established specific time for the call, a time known by both vessels before the transmission or reception of the call. A general "understanding" that calls will always be on a certain intership working frequency does not comply with the rule requiring calling and answering on 2182 kc.

Certification—2738 and 2830 kc— No ship station licensee may operate a non-accepted type transmitter on 2738 or 2830 kc until he has certified that the transmitter will not cause interference to other stations on the second harmonic of 5476 or 5660 kc respectively. This is necessary because the second harmonics of such stations may disrupt aviation safety communications. Unless your transmitter has been type accepted, certification is necessary if you wish to use either of these frequencies.

Certification is made by a radio operator, technician or serviceman having an appropriate license or permit. Many manufacturers are now furnishing certifications to owners of their equipment to be completed and forwarded to the Commission. If these are not available for your transmitter, the local marine radio service company or the nearest F.C.C. office can supply further information about methods of measurement, filtering where necessary, and certification.

If you receive a violation notice for emission of a "harmonic," you will need the help of a competent radio service man. Harmonics are a fault of the transmitter. They are unwanted signals sent out on two, three, four or more times the licensed frequency to which the transmitter is adjusted. This wasted power interferes with other stations. You may need improvements to your ground system, repairs, adjustments, or an additional filter for the transmitter; or you may even need a better-designed transmitter.

Prevention of Interference—Always listen on the radio channel to be used before transmitting so that you will not interfere with others already using the channel—remember radiotelephone is a "party wire" situation.

Operating Procedures—You must give your call sign whenever you call another boat or coast station and when you finish the conversation. If the transmission lasts longer than fifteen minutes, you must break and announce your call sign. Make your calls short (not more than 30 seconds) and do not call that station again for one minute.

Radio Conversations are Private— If you hear a radio conversation not intended for you, you cannot lawfully use the information in any way.

Frequency Measurement—The licenseholder is made responsible for measurement of each frequency on which the transmitter will work (1) when it is first operated, (2) any time it is moved, and (3) any time any work is done on it that might affect the frequency. The frequency measurements must be recorded in the official records of the station. The measured frequency of each channel must be within the frequency tolerance limits set by the F.C.C. This tolerance is 0.02 per cent in the 1600–3500 kc band. This means, for example, that if you are operating on 2182 kc and a Commission monitoring station finds that your frequency is one-half of one kilocycle (more than 436.4 cycles to be exact) off to either side of 2182 kc, you will receive a violation notice. You must then have the transmitter adjusted, the frequency measured, and a full explanation on its way back to the Commission within ten days.

Modulation—F.C.C. rules require adjustment of the peak percentage of modulation of all transmitters for normal speech to 75 and 100 percent when they are installed, moved, or have any work modulation.

Ground—Effective radio grounds are required. For metallic hulled vessels a clean direct ground connection to the hull is required. For wooden or plastic boats, the most effective ground practicable is to be installed, preferably a bareplate or strips of corrosion-resistant metal of at least 12 square feet in area attached to the hull below the water line.

Logs—A radio log is required. Each page must be numbered, have the name of the vessel, call sign, and be signed by the operator. The licensed operator must enter a summary of communications exchanged between the ship radio station and other radio stations (except public coast stations in the United States). Such summary should include the name or call sign of the station worked and the time the station was worked. Entries must be made showing the beginning and end of each watch on 2182 kc. Distress, urgency, and safety communications made or intercepted should be put down in the log as completely as possible. A record of all installations, service, or maintenance work which may affect the proper operation of the station must also be entered by the licensed person doing the work, including his signature, address and the class, serial number and expiration date of his license.

The 24 hour system is used in a radio log. That is, 8:45 A.M. is written as 0845 and 1 P.M. becomes 1300. Local time is usually used, but Eastern Standard Time (EST) must be used throughout the Great Lakes. On international voyages vessels use Greenwich Mean Time exclusively. Whichever time is used, the appropriate abbreviation must be entered at the head of the time column.

Radio logs must be retained for at least a year; for three years if they contain entries concerning distress or disaster; and longer periods if they concern communications being investigated by the F.C.C., or against which claims or complaints have been filed.

Inspection and Monitoring—Ship radio stations (radio telephones) are inspected from time to time by F.C.C. engineers. In addition, transmissions on all ship channels are frequently monitored at the F.C.C. monitoring stations. Notices are issued for all violations observed by the F.C.C.

Violation Notices—If you receive an "Official Notice of Violation" from the F.C.C. you must reply to it within ten days after receiving it. If you cannot give a full answer that soon, you should acknowledge it and say you will make a full answer as soon as possible. If you are away from your permanent address, it is suggested that you make arrangements to have mail from the F.C.C. opened, acknowledged and forwarded.

An acceptable answer tells three things: (1) a full explanation of the incident involved, (2) the name and license number of the operator responsible, (3) what you have done to see that the violation is not repeated.

Citizens' Band Radio Service

Basically a form of walkie-talkie, the Citizens' Band Radio Service requires the installation of one unit aboard the boat and another ashore or on another boat to provide two-way communication. Under ideal conditions, this system gives a maximum range of about twenty miles over water. The installations generally cost in the neighborhood of two hundred dollars.

These sets operate on the 27 megacycle frequency band set aside by the Federal Communications system for a variety of personal, business and recreational uses. Twenty-three channels were provided on a "party-line" basis, with licensing requirements held to a minimum. A number of the twenty-three channels in any area may be shared by yachtsmen, farm-

> **FCC RULES REMINDERS**
> 1. Keep Part 8 of the Rules handy.
> 2. Post your station license prominently at the principal operating location.
> 3. Do not turn transmitter on without an operator license or permit.
> 4. Licenses cannot be transferred.
> 5. Keep your receiver tuned to 2182 kc.
> 6. Keep a log.
> 7. Give call sign clearly at the beginning and upon completion of each communication with any other station.
> 8. Stop conversation with another ship after five minutes. Do not contact the same ship again in less than five minutes.
> 9. Say only what is necessary, and sign off. Others are waiting.
> 10. Use of indecent language or profanity on the air is a criminal offense.

ers, and other radio set operators. Operation of a Citizens' Band set requires a license from the F.C.C., but about the only requirement is United States citizenship and some reasonable need for the license. In the last few years, more than 100,000 such licenses have been issued, not, of course, all to boatmen.

The "Long Island System"

One of the potential uses of this system is indicated by the manner in which it has been set up on Western Long Island Sound, New York. Six yacht clubs and a marina serving some 1,500 small boats are linked in the setup. The plan provides a flexible means of communication between small boat operators and their home bases, other yachtsmen, and shore stations operating on the Citizens' Band. Shortly after installation of the system, a dozen small sailing craft capsized during a race when northerly squalls moved into the race area without previous warning. The young skippers, trained to remain with their disabled boats, were picked up unharmed in a matter of minutes, thanks to the radio hookup which directed radio-equipped patrol boats in carrying out the rescue operation.

This system, worked out with the co-operation of Radio Corporation of America, works as follows: units have been installed near the dockmaster's station at each of the seven shore points. Other sets have been placed aboard launches at the marina and six yacht clubs. In addition, the racing committee yacht has been similarly equipped. More than 1,500 individual boat owners operating out of the marina and the six yacht clubs may be tied in by the simple installation of sets on their boats.

The western end of Long Island Sound was divided under the plan into channel zones, with only one participating marina or yacht club in any given zone.

The first of the four positions on the set's channel selector knob will tune in a system-wide "calling channel"— to be monitored by all craft when not engaged in other traffic, and to be used by boats attempting to make initial contact with onshore points or other skippers. Citizens' Band Channel No. 2 is being used for this purpose.

The second position (Citizens' Band Channel No. 4) is designated for communications between boats and shore points other than their own, as well as between the various clubs and marinas, again after initial contact on the calling channel.

A third position (Channel No. 7) will permit craft from different yacht clubs or marinas to talk directly with one another, after initial contact on the calling channel.

The fourth position will be for the primary use of specific yacht clubs and marinas and their members. Adjacent clubs

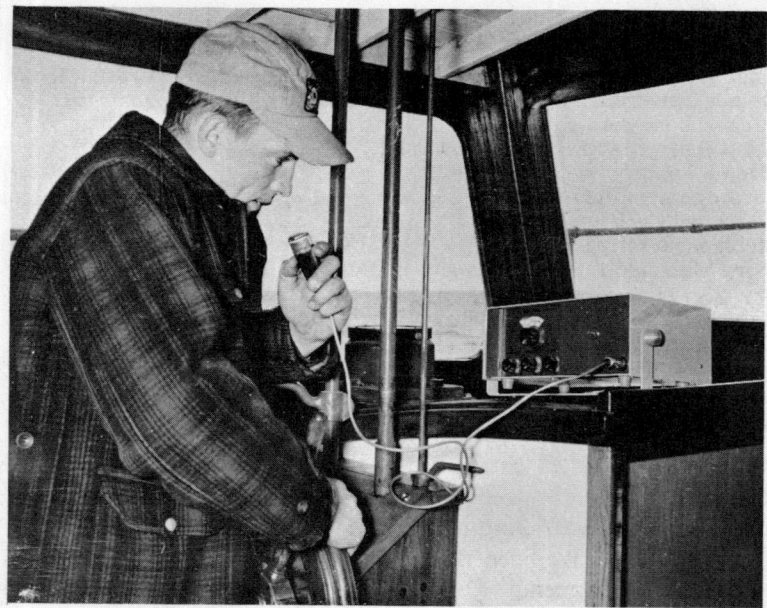

Compact, two-way radio, shown in use aboard a cabin cruiser, was designed by the Radio Corporation of American as a flexible, low-cost communications device both ashore and afloat. The Radio-Phone operates on the Citizens' Band of frequencies and is used in an ingenious communications system in Western Long Island Sound. The system links six yacht clubs and a marina, as well as small craft equipped with the shoe-box-size radio units. *(Radio Corporation of America photo)*

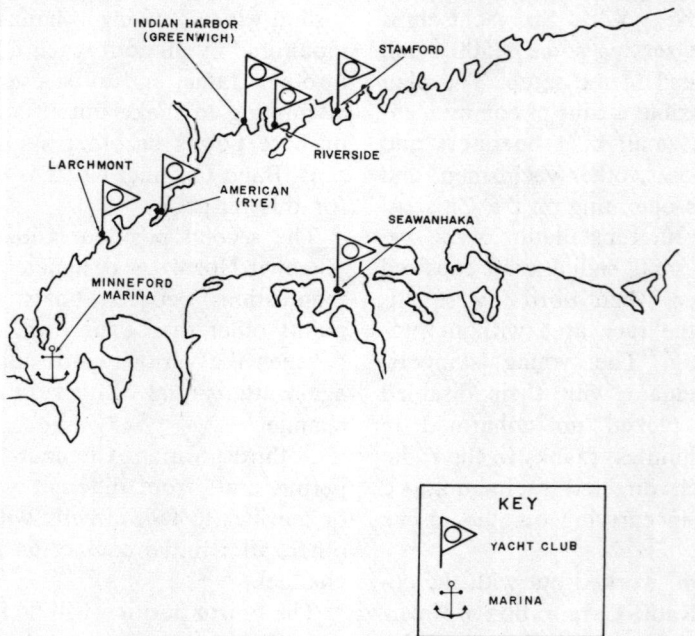

Western Long Island Sound Communications System

will utilize difference channels sufficiently separated in the 27 megacycle Citizens' Band to minimize overlapping on the airways.

Boat owners can obtain further benefits from the two-way system by having Citizens' Band equipment installed in their automobiles or homes within the sending-receiving area. For instance, a club member will be able to radio his dockmaster that he's on the way and ask that the boat be fueled prior to his arrival, or a skipper can inform his wife at home that he is ten minutes from docking and would she please meet him.

Flag Talk

Despite the electronic means of communication, the old nautical means of communication by signal flags and pennants is still widely used in the international language of the sea. In pleasure boating, the flags are most often seen when larger yachts dress up in their colors and use these flags for a decoration. However, they are still often used by merchant ships and Navy vessels. The boatmen who would like to know what these flags mean can get the whole story of flag talk in a government publication. "International Code of Signals," a publication of the Hydrographic Office of the Navy, H.O. No. 87 (Vol. I, Visual and Sound), will provide interesting hours of reading.

The chart of International Flags and Pennants gives the basic flag-meanings and the one-flag signals. In H.O. 87 are listed many two-flag signals and other keys to translate the whipping flags and pennants into ship-to-ship communication.

CHAPTER XI

Anchoring and Mooring

To the "salt," the term "ground tackle" is applied to all the equipment used in anchoring a boat, including the lines, connecting devices, anchors, and on larger boats, the windlass. Generally, a Manila line is preferred for the anchor "cable" for boats under 60 feet in length. Larger boats require a line that is too heavy to handle and for them an anchor chain is used.

By definition, an anchor is a heavy forging or casting that has a shank with a large shackle or ring at one end and two arms with palms at the other. It is shaped to grip the sea bottom and to hold a vessel by a cable or rope in a required position regardless of wind or weather.

For the smallest boats, a cement block will serve as an anchor under most conditions, with the line being tied through the openings in the block. However, modern anchors combine good holding power with relatively light weight. Anchors have different names according to type and use. The Danforth anchor is generally used on small and medium-sized boats. Cast in various weights, it fits the requirements of most pleasure boats and may be used for kedging. *Kedging* is using an anchor to move or turn a vessel. As a safety measure, many pleasure boats carry more than one anchor: one light for fishing or relaxation mooring, one heavy for emergency use. In nautical terminology, these are known as:

1. *Bower Anchor:* Carried in the bow, it is used for general anchoring; it can be further identified as a port or starboard anchor.

2. *Stream Anchor*. This is a medium weight anchor carried at the stern of the boat and used to prevent swinging.

3. *Stern Anchor*. Any anchor carried at the stern of a vessel is so named.

4. *Kedge Anchor*. The name is derived from its use in moving a ship by carrying the anchor out in a smaller boat, dropping it and then hauling the boat to it. This is usually a light anchor.

Depending on weather and bottom conditions, the *scope* or length of anchor line that will be let out should be between three and ten times the depth of the water in which the boat is anchored. In planning the scope allow for the fall and rise of the tide. As an aid in figuring the scope, the anchor line should be marked at intervals. Some prefer painted rings on the line, others whip rings of twine around the line. One simple method of marking for a small boat might be one ring at first fathom (6 feet), two rings at the second fathom and so on, or rings of different colors.

Anchoring Technique

In pleasure boating it is seldom possible to choose the depth of water or the type of bottom. However, reference to the chart of the anchorage area will indicate the bottom type and give you an idea of the possible hold of your ground tackle.

Generally speaking, the holding characteristics of bottoms are:

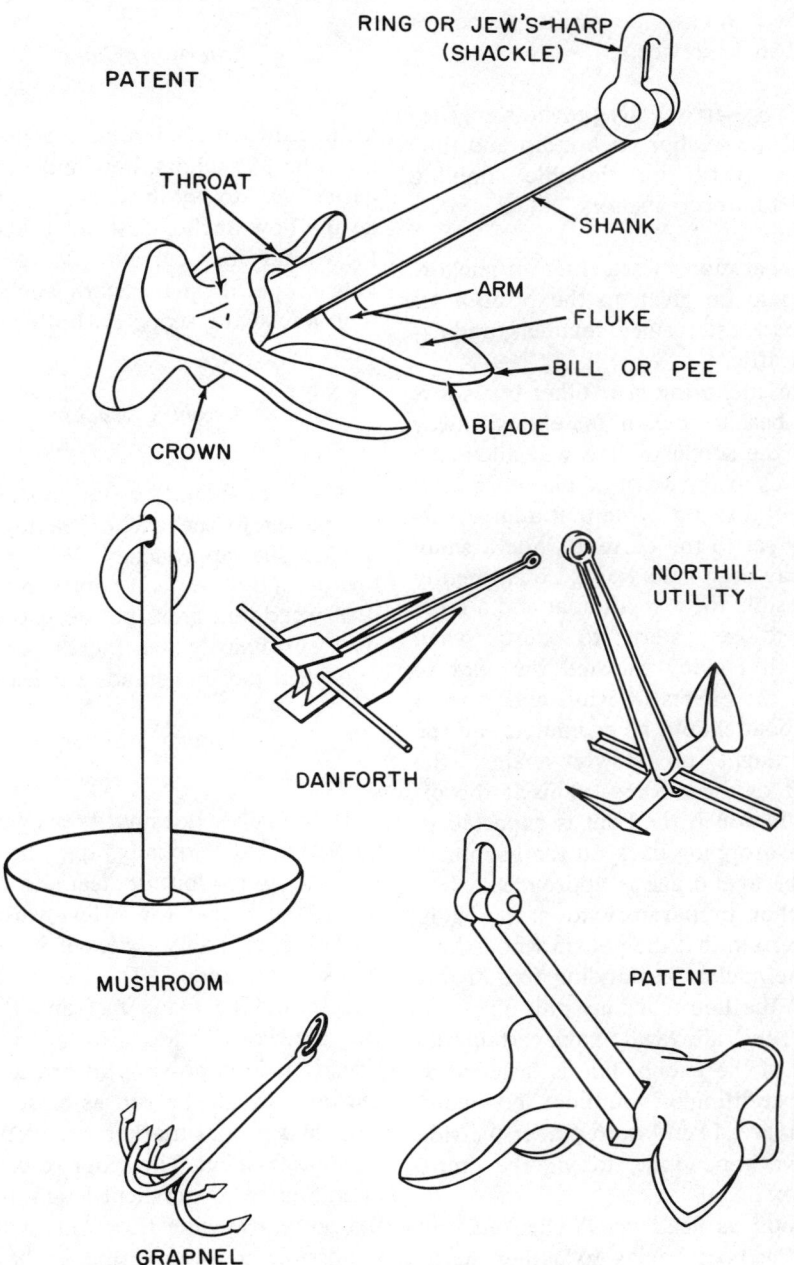

Types of anchors.

1. Firm sand—excellent and consistent.

2. Clay—excellent if quite dense but sufficiently plastic to permit good anchor engagement.

3. Mud—varies widely with sticky mud being fairly good and soft mud or silt quite questionable.

4. Loose sand—fair provided anchors engage deeply.

5. Rock—contributes nothing to holding power unless the anchor becomes hooked in a crevice.

6. Grass—frequently prevents engagement of the anchor on bottom and thus provides very questionable holding ground for most anchors.

Consideration in selecting an anchorage should be given to the position of other craft, established channels, and existing traffic.

When anchoring near other boats it is always best to anchor far enough away so that the scope of line will allow the boat to clear the stern of the other craft in case of a swing. Note that a large vessel may set to the current while a small craft may set to the wind, consequently it is possible for a small boat and a large vessel to set stern to stern when anchored. Having selected the spot to anchor, the effects of wind and current on the boat should be estimated and the ship brought up slowly against the stronger of these forces. This is the direction in which the boat is expected to lie after dropping back on the anchor.

As the anchorage is approached, free the anchor preparatory to dropping it. Make certain that the person who is lowering the anchor is standing free of any loops in the line that may pull him over the side; and, above all, make certain that the end of the anchor line is fastened to the proper fitting on your boat. Too many anchors have been lowered over the side and have gone down taking the entire line with them!

As soon as headway is checked, but before the boat begins to gather sternway, the anchor is dropped. With the anchor on the bottom and the boat backing slowly, the line is played out. When the line has been played out, it is snubbed to allow the anchor to get a good hold on the bottom.

With the boat brought up and the proper scope played out, the line can then be secured and the engine stopped.

Stern Anchors

In crowded anchorages, boats sometimes lie to anchors, bow and stern. The easiest way to lay these anchors is to let go the bow anchor first, drop back with the wind or current on an extra long scope, drop the stern anchor, and then adjust the scope on both as necessary.

Weighing Anchor

The boat should be run up slowly under power to the anchor, taking in the line as she approaches. Whipping the line up and down as it comes in will free it of weed and grass before it comes on deck. Ordinarily the anchor will break out when the line stands vertically.

Fouled Anchor

If an anchor does not break out when being hauled vertically, the line should be fastened to a bitt or cleat and the boat should go ahead for a few yards. The anchor is probably fouled if it does not break out then. To clear it, the line should be made fast and the boat run slowly in wide circles on a taut line. If it is impossible to break it free, the boat should be run as close as possible and a float marker attached to the line and then cut. The scope of the marker should be of sufficient length to reach the bottom at high tide. This will make it possible to retrieve the anchor later.

Several types of anchors with automatic release devices are now available. The Danforth Shearpin is one which is released by snapping a shear pin with a vertical pull. However, the utility of this type is limited as the anchor may become useless with changing wind or current. They are generally made only in the 4

ANCHORING AND MOORING

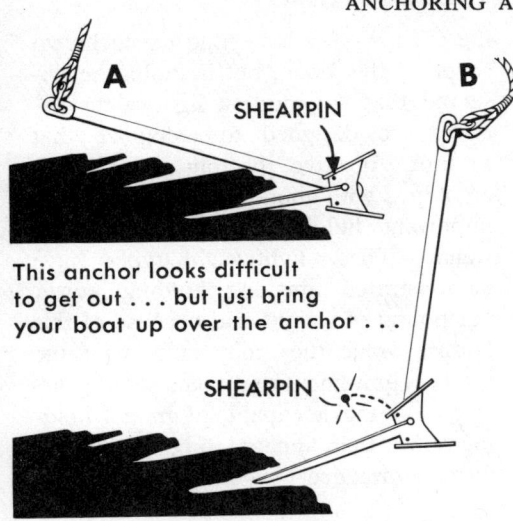

This anchor looks difficult to get out . . . but just bring your boat up over the anchor . . .

pull vertically . . . the shearpin breaks, the shank swings back, and out it comes, backward!

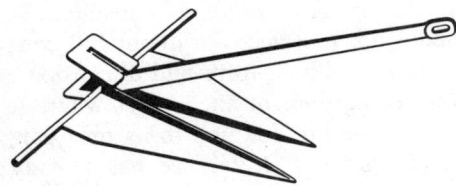

How the shearpin anchor works.

and 8-pound sizes for smallest boats, and the maker advises against leaving the boat unattended with this type of anchor.

Anchoring Precautions

Special precautions may avoid, the possibility of fouling on a rocky bottom. One trick is to attach a buoyed line to the crown of the anchor before letting it go. Then if the anchor fouls, the trip line can be hauled to bring the anchor up crown first.

It is difficult to tell from observation whether an anchored boat is drifting. However, one accepted practice is to take bearings on two identified objects on shore. If the bearings change, the boat is probably dragging anchor. Usually a check is made about fifteen minutes after setting the anchor and periodically thereafter, especially after each swing. One frequent cause of drifting at anchor is that a turn of the line or chain catches a fluke of the anchor and breaks it out.

More About Ground Tackle

In the opinion of safety experts, every small pleasure boat should carry at least two anchors—one being for service under ordinary conditions, the other a storm anchor for emergencies. When cruising away from home waters, a heavy third anchor should be carried as a safety spare.

A good way to estimate the desirable weight of service anchor is to consider the holding power requirements of the average cruiser as equal to approximately six percent of her displacement (weight) and to relate that to the generally accepted holding capacity of the yachtsman's stocked anchor which for this purpose and on bottoms likely to be encountered, is about seven pounds of holding power per pound of weight, although that ratio may vary widely under different conditions.

Thus, a 27-30-foot cruiser weighing 6,000 pounds would need 360 pounds of holding power, which would be provided by a stock type anchor of about 50 pounds as the service anchor.

The storm anchor should be from one and one-half to two times the weight of the service one.

The anchor weights and holding requirements suggested here are appreciably heavier than those usually suggested (even heavier than the suggestions of the anchor manufacturers who charge more for heavier anchors), but the Yacht Safety Bureau is interested in convincing boat owners to beef up the holding power capacity carried by the average pleasure boat.

After considering all the factors, if a boat owner decides to obtain anchors of one or more of the lightweight designs, it is suggested that the actual weights of the anchors be reduced conservatively so that full advantage of even more greatly increased holding power is taken.

A boat owner may well desire to carry a smaller anchor for various temporary anchorings in good weather, such as for swimming, fishing or even for lying-to overnight when staying aboard. If so, such an anchor can be considerably lighter, but in no sense should it take place of either the service or the storm anchor.

The load on ground tackle has three principal components. One results from wind action on all parts of the boat above water. Another component results from the effect of current, which is equivalent to the force required to propel the boat through still water at the speed of the current. The third load component results from swing and surge action of the boat. Of the three, that due to wind is probably most important. That due to current is of comparatively little importance unless hull resistance is unusual or current speed is relatively high. The swing and surge component is developed when the boat is set in motion by changes in wind and current, or by wave or wake action. It is difficult to assess but it can be very appreciable. This third component is the key one to consider in determining adequate cable lengths.

A reasonable idea of the magnitude of wind loads can be gained from the fact that under storm conditions with wind gusts of 60 to 120 knots, the average 35-foot cruiser can develop wind loads of from 800 to 3,000 pounds.

The Importance of Holding Power

Many designs of anchors are available for boat use. The principal types have been illustrated and all have features in their favor, but it should be emphasized that no anchor is so effective that it can be lowered away and forgotten.

The analysis of the various qualities of the anchor types is beyond the technical scope of this book, but it should be observed that the modern lightweight anchors are designed to recognize that prompt, positive bottom penetration combined with good fluke area are more important holding factors than sheer weight. These lightweight types have demonstrated amazing holding power per pound of weight and because of this feature alone they may help meet the safety requirement that boats should carry ground tackle capable of greater holding power than appears to be the current average practice.

Select the Right Anchor

The anchor itself is the primary factor in determining holding capacity. It should not be selected without full consideration of boat form and dimensions, types of bottoms at anchorages where it will be used, in addition to its own particular qualities. Reference has already been made to the three principal components of load on an anchor, namely windage, current drag, and surge. Of these, windage and surge are the ones needing consideration.

Since windage is the result of wind action on all parts of a boat above water, obviously a light, wide beam, shallow draft power cruiser with a high freeboard and an average superstructure can develop a considerable load on ground tackle, while a narrower, deep draft sailing craft of the same length would develop a somewhat lighter windage load. A similar generality prevails relative to surge loads during heavy weather that frequently cause anchors to drag or break out.

Unless these loads can be substantially reduced before their actual application to an anchor, it is practically certain that either the anchor will drag or break-out, or that some part of the ground tackle will give way. The length and make-up of anchor cables require careful planning to bring the impact from surge loads within range of accommodation.

The first condition to appreciate is that an anchor has maximum holding power when its cable pulls horizontally, or very nearly horizontally, along its shank. This means that the anchor cable must be long enough to give its catenary (curve) a zero or very small angle with the bottom at the anchor shackle. This is accomplished by using adequate scope—which is also defined as the length of cable under water to the depth of water. Under normal conditions a scope of 7 or 8 to 1 is adequate, but for heavy weather a scope of 10 or 12 to 1 may be required. It is to be emphasized that any lessening of scope means a great reduction in the anchor's holding power—hence this is another reason for being sure that the holding power potential of anchors is well on the safe side, for in many anchorages the swinging room available just does not permit use of adequate scope.

What Kind of Cable to Use

The type of cable used also has considerable effect on surge loads. Chain, because of its weight, absorbs much of the surge and thus reduces the impact at the anchor. Further, chain tends to assure the desirable low angle pull at the anchor, making a somewhat shorter scope permissible. However, handling requirements practically eliminate its use for most small pleasure boats; moreover, absorption of some of the surge load can be accomplished by use of a separate weight on a separate inhaul line rigged to travel along the anchor rode.

Wire cable, bronze or stainless, is sometimes used because of its strength and relative lightness, but for reasonable ease of handling special equipment is needed to reel it correctly. However, it is subject to kinking and, owing to its lightness, does not contribute to impact reduction. Also, many stainless cables have been known to corrode. Consequently, wire cable is not suggested for the average cruiser.

Manila rope is favored by many boat owners. It is easy to handle, light in weight, relatively cheap, and can absorb some of the effects of surge because of its fair elasticity. On the other hand, Manila requires care to prevent bacterial attack and unnecessary mechanical chafing.

Nylon rope is becoming increasingly popular although its cost is about two and one-half times that of Manila. Compared to Manila, it has about twice the strength, three times the elasticity, and is impervious to rot, mildew and deterioration by borer action. Thus, its greater cost is compensated for by longer useful life, provided it is not subjected to severe mechanical chafing.

Where anchor rope passes through chocks, a wrapping of heavy canvas is recommended to protect it from chafing.

A suggested anchor rode would be made of a short length of galvanized chain, perhaps from 10 to 20 feet, between the anchor and the Manila or nylon rope. This length of chain is highly desirable to prevent chafing of rope fibres on rock bottom.

The length of anchor rode required can be estimated by the relation between the depth of water at anchorages to be used and adequate scope. The sizes of chain and rope should be determined by a consideration of the maximum holding power required. Hence the chain should not be less than 5/16" for the service anchor, perhaps not less than 3/8" for the storm anchor and graded upward for the heavier anchors. The same principle applies to the ropes. If nylon is used the service rode should be 9/16" diameter and the storm rode of 3/4". For Manila, the sizes would be 3/4" and 1" diameter respectively. These sizes are suggestions for the average 30-foot cruiser carrying the suggested anchors. It would accomplish little to equip an anchor or probable inadequate holding capacity with a rode capable of handling a much greater load.

Tackle Inspection

In connection with ground tackle, it would be well to check on the reliability of chocks, cleats and bitts. These items must be rugged, smooth to prevent undue mechanical wear on lines, and they must be large enough to permit fastening by bolts (not screws) of good tensile strength. Decks in way of these fittings should be reinforced to spread the stress, and the securing bolts should extend through the reinforcing members.

As a vital part of spring check-up, inspect all ground tackle items thoroughly. The condition of anchors can be determined at a glance, but shackles should be checked for excessive rust and worn threads; chain for link wear and rust. All rope should be examined for cuts, dry rot, or mildew. The surface appearance of rope may be deceptive. Open up the lays and if the fibres are brittle, broken or colorless, get a new line.

Permanent Moorings

Much of the reasoning reviewed above applies to anchors used as permanent moorings, and it is certainly worth repeating that many boats dragged or broke free from inadequate moorings during East Coast storms in recent years.

The practical problem posed by the condition of crowding at many anchorages tends to the use of very inadequate scope. This can only partially and perhaps not even appreciably be bettered by increasing the weight of permanent anchors. Scope of 4 to 1, 3 to 1 and even less has been used. It is not sufficient under heavy weather conditions. Scope of at least 6 to 1 with an anchor of good holding power is required for reasonable security. This is especially important for modern cruisers which surge strongly during storms, causing heavy strain on mooring gear.

All manner of things are in use as anchors for permanent moorings — old flywheels, old engines, odds and ends of junk bound together in cement, old oil drums filled with cement, to mention just a few. All of these have limited holding power beyond their weight, and even this is compromised for the more bulky types because of the buoyant effect of the displaced water. Furthermore, when such anchors are once set they are never lifted, and this absence of a check on the condition of the mooring chain and its attachment at the anchor is a prime cause of failure.

The mushroom type of anchor is the popularly accepted permanent mooring. In design, it is ideal for 360 degree swing, being free of projections which might foul the chain, and it has good holding qualities. Weights of mushroom anchor recommended for power cruisers have approximately 10 pounds of weight for each foot of over-all boat length. This weight can be varied either way, within reason, on the basis of favorable or unfavorable bottom holding characteristics. At least 5/8" chain should be used.

In the light of storm and hurricane experience, one very important precaution should be taken each year. If permanent moorings are not lifted at lay-up time, which is preferred practice, they should be lifted and searchingly checked pior to August each season. Since it is surprising how quickly chain links and shackles can be weakened by wear and corrosion, boat owners should insist that this be done for moorings they rent and might be curious about the make-up of such moorings.

Boat owners should check mooring pendants periodically during the season and do so particularly prior to August 1

— the start of the storm season. Being subject to intermittent but practically continuous "wetting and drying" they are likely to deteriorate rapidly. Pendants are also subject to much chafing and any detection of cut or frayed fibres should be enough evidence to warrant a new replacement.

Those boat owners who tie to a dock or berth in a slip, instead of lying to a mooring, should also look to their lines. Neither docks nor berths are places where questionable mooring lines can be used.

Mooring the Boat

The lines used to secure the boat to a wharf or other boat are called mooring lines. They must be as light as possible for easy handling and at the same time be strong enough to take considerable strain when coming alongside or when holding a ship in place. (For details on types of lines see the section on "Marlinspike Seamanship.") Most boatmen use Manila line for mooring purposes. As a safety measure, make it a practice to keep the lines neatly coiled or

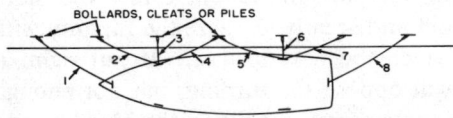

(1) BOW LINE, (2) FORWARD BOW SPRING, (3) FORWARD (BOW) BREAST, (4) AFTER BOW SPRING (5) FORWARD QUARTER SPRING, (6) AFTER (QUARTER) BREAST, (7) AFTER QUARTER SPRING, (8) STERN LINE.

Names and locations of mooring lines.

arranged to prevent fouling, eliminate hazards, and to keep the working area clear.

The illustration gives the names and locations of the mooring lines that would be used on a fairly large pleasure boat. A smaller boat may be secured with merely a bow and stern line.

In a proper mooring setup, the bow line and the stern line lead well up the wharf to reduce the fore and aft motion of the craft. Breast lines are run at right angles to the keel to prevent the boat from moving away from the wharf. Spring lines leading forward or aft prevent the boat from moving aft or forward respectively. Two spring lines placed close together and leading in opposite directions act as a breast line from wharf to boat.

Using the Lines

Lines assist in coming alongside or clearing a wharf. Before the boat comes alongside, the mooring lines should be readied, with eye splices or bowlines in the ends. Heaving lines (light lines with weighted ends) are used on larger vessels to carry heavier lines to the wharf. With small boats there is rarely any need to use a heaving line. Generally, someone can step ashore with the mooring line or throw it the short distance required.

One trick of seamanship is this: If two bights or eye splices are to be placed over the same bollard, the second one must be led up through the eye of the first and then placed over the bollard. This makes it possible for either line to be cast off independently of the other, and is called *dipping the eye*.

Effective use of mooring lines calls for some knowledge of the dynamics of the boat in water. The boat 1, in the illustration (p. 128) is lying off a wharf with a bow breast line secured to a bollard. When strain is put on this line the bow will swing toward the wharf while the stern moves out. It should be noted, however, that the stern does not go out as much as the bow comes in. Because the vessel is not held rigidly at the pivoting point, it will respond to the force acting at the bow with resultant motion like that in Figure 1.

When the boat is secured as described above, and the stern is held by a line to the wharf, as shown in Figure 2, the stern remains approximately the same distance from the wharf and the whole boat tends to move slightly forward as

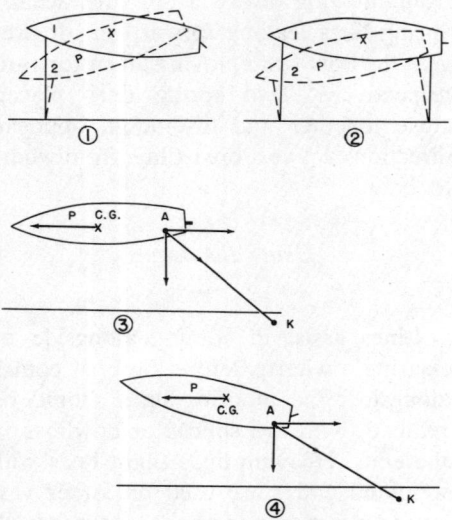

Handling a vessel around a wharf.

the bow swings toward the wharf. This requires much greater effort than turning the boat near her natural pivoting point as in Figure 1.

When the bow lines and quarter breast lines are hove in at the same time, the boat will be breasted in bodily but at greater expenditure of effort than in the preceding cases.

When the boat has way on, either ahead or astern, her momentum enters into the problem of her behavior. In Figure 3, the boat is moving forward parallel to the face of the wharf with engines stopped and rudder amidships. The afterquarter spring AK is taut. The motion of the boat results from her momentum along the original course and the tension along AK. One retards the boat along the line of her original course, directly opposing the momentum while the other moves her toward the wharf. The stern will swing in and the bow out. The momentum which is concentrated at the center of gravity forward of the pivot A opposes the turning and tends to keep the boat parallel. Thus the boat does not turn much but comes in nearly parallel to the wharf as shown in Figure 4.

If the boat in Figure 3 is moving ahead with an after spring from the bow instead of from the quarter, the forces are similar to those in Figure 2. But there is an important difference: the momentum increases the turning effect of the spring instead of opposing it. A comparison of Figures 1 and 4 will show the difference. Consequently, the bow of a boat moving ahead on an after bow spring turns sharply in towards the wharf and the stern swings out. When the ship is moving astern instead of ahead, the conditions are reversed. A forward quarter spring will turn the stern sharply, whereas a forward bow spring does little turning because its point of application is near the boat's pivotal point, P.

The boats in 3 and 4 could go ahead on their engines and apply left rudder to approach the wharf. As the steering effect of the rudder is a result of the action of the discharge current against the rudder and as the stern cannot move to starboard because it is held by the spring, the left rudder is capable of comparatively little turning. The right rudder, on the other hand, will help materially to throw the stern in. If, as in 2, the rudder is put left, it will throw the stern out and greatly increase the rapidity with which the bow turns in. If put right, it will oppose the turning, but not enough to overcome it. Since the rudder and screw aid in controlling the stern, the bow is normally worked into the wharf first.

In clearing a wharf, the same principles apply, but the procedure is reversed.

Consider the Tides

In securing alongside a wharf, especial attention must be paid to the tide. When securing at high water, enough slack must be left in the lines to insure that at low tide they will not part, carry away bollards, or in extreme cases, list the ship to a dangerous degree or even capsize a small vessel. Usually the water

ANCHORING AND MOORING

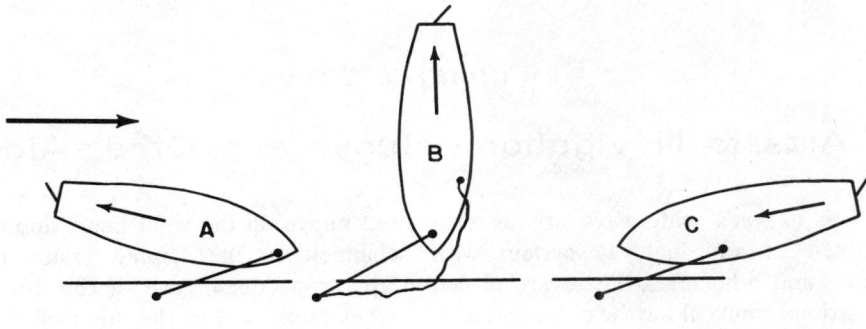

Winding ship.

marks on pilings will give you an idea of the tide situation at the time of mooring.

Making Landings

Wharves and piers may be built on piles which allow a fairly free flow of water under them and in the slips between them. Their underwater construction may be solid in which case there will be no current inside the slips, but eddies may whirl around them. Warehouses or other houses may be near the slips, varying the effect of the wind on the upper part of the boat when making a landing.

Making a landing is more hazardous when the wind and current are at right angles to the wharf than when blowing or running along its face. In coming alongside, as in all ship handling, the wind and current should be observed and used to advantage if possible.

Winding Ship or Warping

When it is necessary to turn a boat end-for-end at a wharf (wind it), the easiest way is to hail some friendly passing boat, throw it a line, and ask for a "lift." Failing that, it is safer both for inboards and outboards to pivot the boat on the bow to avoid the possibility of damaging the rudder or screws (or the hanging outboard motor) against the wharf. An after bow spring should always be held when the stern lines are slacked or let go. With a current from astern, the stern will usually start out by itself. Backing a single-screw boat down slowly, starboard side to, will usually start the stern out. If port side to, going ahead dead slow on the after bow spring will have the same effect. With a twin-screw craft, backing the inboard screw, or going ahead on the outboard, or doing both should start the stern out. The swing is made on the after bow spring line, but a forward bow spring line on the other side of the bow should be led from well aft to assist in controlling the swing and to take the strain after the swing is past 90 degrees as shown in the sketch. The bow is kept clear of the wharf by backing a little as needed. Should a strong current be running, a long after breast line could be used to slow down the first part of the swing. During the latter part of the swing the engines may be used to slow the spring and to prevent the boat from striking the wharf—and fenders should be hung to absorb the jolt. After the winding is completed, the boat can be spotted in position by using the engines or by hauling her ahead.

CHAPTER XII

Aids to Navigation—Buoys and Other Aids

The nation's waterways are as well marked as any highway system with buoys and other aids. These are placed at various points along the coast and navigable waterways as markers and guides to enable mariners to determine their position in relation to land and to hidden dangers. These aids to navigation mark isolated dangers, make it possible for vessels to follow natural and improved channels, and provide a continuous chain of charted marks for coastal or river piloting.

Probably most vital to the pleasure boatman—at least in his first hours on the water — are the buoys which mark the channels. One "easy" guide to the novice boatman is given in the Chris-Craft operator's manual:

"The system of placing the red and black buoys is described in the 'Pilot Rules,' but this may be somewhat confusing to the novice and the best thing to do in every case is to spot both a red and a black buoy and pass between them. This will give your cue so that for the rest of the trip you will know which side each color should be on. At night it is sometimes hard to see two buoys in which case steer first for the nearest buoy you see. Sometimes before you actually get to it you will see a buoy of the opposite color. This will let you know which side of the first buoy to pass. After you have passed this first one, steer for the second one and repeat the procedure. In watching for buoys, bear in mind that some channel buoys are sometimes right on shore. This means of course, there is deep water right up to the shore."

The principle in marking channels is that they run in from seaward, with the red buoys on the right hand side of the channel. In the United States Power Squadron course, one of the first messages implanted in the mind of the student regarding channel buoys is "Red to right returning," as a key to following a marked channel.

Now, to some more technical information on the aids to navigation.

Lighthouses

Lighthouses are found upon all coasts of the United States, along the Great Lakes, and along some of the interior waterways of the country. They are placed where they will be of most use, on prominent headlands, at entrances, on isolated dangers, or at other points where it is necessary that mariners be warned or guided. Their principal purpose is to support a light at a considerable height above the water. The same structure may also house a fog signal and radiobeacon equipment, and also contain quarters for the keepers. However, the fog signal and radiobeacon, and the operating personnel are usually housed in separate buildings grouped around the tower. Such a group of buildings constitutes a light station.

The location of a lighthouse, whether in the water or on shore, the importance of the light, the kind of soil upon which it is to be built, and the prevalence of violent storms have a direct bearing on the type of structure erected and the materials of which it is built. From the boatman's point of view, the materials used and the type of construction aid in daytime identification of the different lighthouses within his cruising area.

Lighthouses vary markedly in their outward appearance because of the points mentioned and because of the great difference in the distances to which their lights should be seen (these facts about the lighthouse appear on the chart). Where the need for a powerful light is great, and the importance and intensity of traffic warrants, a tall tower with a light of high candlepower is erected. Conversely, at points intermediate to the major lights, where the traffic is light, and where long range is not so necessary, a structure of more modest dimensions suffices.

The terms secondary lights, minor lights, and automatic lights indicate in a general way a wide variety of lights, each class shading imperceptibly into the next. These lights may be displayed from towers resembling the important seacoast lighthouses, or may be shown from almost any type of simple structure. The essentials of a light structure are: the best possible location dependent on physical conditions of the site; sufficient height for the location, a rugged support for the lantern, and a housing for the tanks of compressed gas or electric batteries from which the light is operated. Meeting these essentials are many types of structures — small tank houses surmounted by a short skeleton tower, a cluster of piles supporting a battery box and the lens, and countless other forms.

At present, many of the lighthouses which were originally cared for by resident keepers are now operated automatically by electricity. There are also a great many automatic lights on smaller structures, cared for through periodic visits of Coast Guard cutters or of attendants placed in charge of a group of such aids.

The recent introduction of much new automatic apparatus means that the relative importance of lights can no longer be judged on the basis of whether or not they have resident keepers, for a number of powerful lights in towers of great height are now operated without continuous attention.

Color is applied in varying patterns to lighthouses and automatic light structures for the purpose of making them readily distinguishable from the background against which they are seen and to distinguish one structure from another. The nighttime means of distinguishing lighthouses is by the cyclic flashings of their lights and their height above water, both of which are indicated on the chart.

How Flashes are Produced

The flashing lights of lighthouses and minor lights are produced in several ways. In some of the larger lights the flashes result from the rotation of the lenses in which various flash panels are incorporated. The use of electricity as the illuminant has made it possible to produce flashes by means of timing devices which interrupt the flow of current or conceal the light source at definite intervals.

In those minor lights where acetylene gas is used, the flashes are produced by interrupting the flow of gas by means of a bellows-like device, each small charge of gas being ignited at the burner by a constantly burning nonluminous pilot flame.

Electricity is the illuminant now used in all of the larger lighthouses. Electric incandescent lamps placed inside the larger sizes of lenses or reflectors produce beams of as much as 14,000,000 candlepower when such intensity is required. Lenses, which are aggregates of highly polished glass prisms, are assembled in a variety of types to produce the characteristics desired.

Visibility of Lights

The theoretical visibility of a light as shown on the chart depends on two factors, the height of the light above water and its intensity. The height controls what is known as the geographic range, while the intensity controls what is known as the luminous range.

As a rule, for principal lights, the luminous range is greater than the geographic, and the distance that such lights are visible is limited only by the earth's curvature. Under some atmospheric conditions the glare or loom of these lights, and occasionally the light itself, may be visible far beyond the computed geographic range. But unfortunately, it more frequently occurs that these distances may be lessened by fog, rain, snow, haze or smoke.

Lights on inland waters, where their radius of usefulness is not great, are frequently of insufficient intensity to reach the full limit of their geographic range.

Sectors

Sectors—whose arc of visibility is marked on the chart—are changes in the color of a light, but not in its characteristics, when viewed from certain directions. Sectors of colored glass are placed in the lanterns of certain lighthouses to mark shoals or warn mariners of the nearby land. Lights so equipped show one color from most directions and a different color or colors over definite arcs of the horizon. Note that the characteristic does not change, and a flashing white light having a red sector, when viewed from within the sector, will appear flashing red.

Sectors may be but a few degrees in width, marking an isolated rock or shoal, or of such width as to extend from the direction of the deep water toward shore. Bearings referring to sectors are expressed in degrees as observed from a vessel toward the light.

In most cases, water areas covered by red sectors should be avoided, the exact extent of the danger being determined from an examination of the charts. In some cases a narrow sector may mark the best water across a shoal. A narrow sector may also mark a turning point in a canal.

Fog Signals

Fog signals form an important part of the equipment of many lighthouses situated in sections of the country where fog or low visibility is prevalent. Identification is made in the same manner as with lights. Each fog signal station is assigned a signal consisting of a definite number of blasts recurring at stated intervals. The sound or tone of the signal, varying with the type of mechanism employed, also assists in the identification.

Any sound-producing instrument operated in time of fog from a definite point shown on the charts, such as a lighthouse, lightship, or buoy, serves as a useful fog signal. To be effective as an aid to navigation, a mariner must be able to identify it and to know from what point it is sounded. The simpler fog signals are bells and whistles on buoys. As such signals on buoys which are operated by the action of the sea do not produce sounds on a regular time schedule, positive identification is not always possible. However, pleasure boat operators should make a point of becoming familiar with those buoys which they may encounter on their home cruising grounds.

Fog signals at all lighthouses and lightships so equipped are operated by mechanical means and are sounded on definite time schedules during periods of low visibility, providing the desirable feature of positive identification.

The various types of apparatus employed for sounding fog signals are of interest to the boatman principally because each type produces distinctive sounds, familiarity with which assists in identification.

Fog Signal Characteristics

Fog signals are composed of blasts and silent periods. A definite time is required for each signal to perform a complete cycle of changes. This time, stated in the "Light Lists" is one of the means of identification. Where the number of blasts and the total time for a signal to complete a cycle is not sufficient for positive identification, reference may be made to the details in the light lists regarding the exact length of each blast and silent interval. The various types of fog signals differ in tone, and this facilitates the recognition of the respective stations. The type of fog signal apparatus for each station is stated in the light lists.

Diaphones produce sound by means of a slotted reciprocating piston actuated by compressed air. Blasts may consist of two tones of different pitch, in which case the first part of the blast is high and the last of low pitch. These alternate-pitch signals are called "two-tone."

Diaphragm horns produce sound by means of a disc diaphragm vibrated by compressed air or electricity. Duplex or triplex horn units of differing pitch produce a chime signal.

Reed horns produce sound by means of either a disc or a cup-shaped rotor actuated by compressed air, steam, or electricity.

Whistles produce sound by compressed air emitted through a circumferential slot into a cylindrical bell chamber.

Bells are sounded by means of a hammer actuated by a descending weight, compressed gas, or electricity.

Maritime Radiobeacons

An increasing number of pleasure boats are being equipped with radio receivers that utilize the maritime radiobeacon system. These are within the price range of good portable radio receivers—which is basically what they are.

The maritime radiobeacon system, effective for distances up to 200 miles and more, is an electronic system by means of which a navigator can determine position or lines of position quickly in practically any kind of weather. It makes use of radio transmitting stations (radiobeacons) and specially designed radio receivers equipped with a rotating coil antenna (radio direction finders).

Maritime radiobeacons, installed at lighthouses, on lightships, and at other charted locations, operate separately or as part of a group of two or three radiobeacons. Any one or all of a group of radiobeacons can be used by the navigator in determining position or lines of position.

These radiobeacons transmit radio signals on preselected frequencies from 285 to 325 kilocycles which radiate in all directions. The signals are emitted as groups of dots and dashes or a series of short dashes. The arrangement of the groups of dots and dashes is selected to permit identification of individual radiobeacons transmitting signals on the same radio frequency.

The majority of Coast Guard radiobeacons transmit signals for one or two ten-minute periods out of every hour in clear weather and for one minute every three minutes during periods of fog or low visibility. Other Coast Guard radiobeacons transmit signals continuously. Consult the light list for specific information.

In the radiobeacon system, a navigator uses the radio direction finder to determine the bearing or direction of the signal transmitted from a radiobeacon. The general problems and practices of navigation when using radiobeacon bearings are the same as when using bearings on lighthouses or other charted objects. While both radiobeacon and visual bearings are available in clear weather, the former have the added important advantage of being available at greater distances and under all conditions of visibility.

The signal emitted by a radiobeacon follows a great circle course. When the distance to the radiobeacon is short, the bearing is plotted in the same manner as a bearing on a visually-charted object. When the distance is greater than 50 miles, a correction must usually be applied to the radiobeacon bearing before plotting on a Mercator chart. These corrections are found in Radio Bearing Conversion tables published in United States Navy Hydrographic Office publication H.O. 205, titled "Radio Navigational Aids."

While maritime radiobeacons are specifically provided for the purpose of navigation, it should be noted that radio bearings can be obtained from any radio station which transmits identifying radio signals within the frequency range of the direction finder, and whose charted location is known or can be plotted. Caution should be exercised when using such stations for navigation purposes due to refraction and calibration problems.

Distance Finding in the Fog

Many Coast Guard radiobeacons are synchronized with the sound fog signals at the station for distance finding. During fog, a group of two radio dashes, one second and from three to five seconds in length, are transmitted every three minutes coincident with sound signal blasts of corresponding length. When within audible range of the sound signal, distance from the station can be determined with any radio receiver capable of receiving radiobeacons (even without the revolving antenna) by observing the time elapsed between hearing the radiobeacon and corresponding synchronized sound signal.

The elapsed time in seconds divided by 5 for statute miles and 5.5 for nautical miles will give the distance from the station. The error of such observations should not exceed ten percent.

The Coast Guard maintains and operates all marine radiobeacon stations along the coast of the United States and its territories and possessions. Complete information regarding these radiobeacons is available in the Coast Guard List of Lights and Other Marine Aids, and United States Navy Hydrographic Office publication H.O. 205, "Radio Navigational Aids."

Radiobeacon system charts showing general locations and operating characteristics of Coast Guard radiobeacons, suitable for ready reference by posting near radio-direction finders, are available in the various Light Lists: the Atlantic, the Pacific, and the Great Lakes. A detailed treatise on the radiobeacon system is contained in a separate Coast Guard publication, "Electronic Aids to Navigation," CG-157-1.

The Buoyage System

The primary function of buoys is to warn the mariner of some danger, some obstruction, or change in the contours of the sea bottom, and to delineate the channels leading to various points, so so that he may avoid the dangers and continue his course safely. The utmost advantage is obtained from buoys when they are considered as marking definitely identified spots (and for this, the charts should be used in conjunction with any buoyage system being followed). For if a mariner knows his precise location at the moment, and is equipped with charts, he can plot a safe course on which to proceed. Such features as size, shape, color, numbering, and signalling equipment of buoys are but a means to the end of warning, guiding, and orienting the navigator.

The Lateral System

The waters of the United States are marked for safe navigation by the lateral system of buoyage. This system employs a simple arrangement of colors, shapes, numbers and light characterics to show the side on which a buoy should be passed when proceeding in a given direction. The characteristics are determined by the position of the buoy with respect to the navigable channels as the channels are entered from seaward toward the head of navigation. As all channels do not lead from seaward, arbitrary assumptions must at times be made in order that the system may be applied consistently. The characteristics of buoys are based on the assumption that proceeding in a southerly direction along the Atlantic coast, in a northerly and westerly direction along the Gulf coast, in a northerly direction on the Pacific coast, and in a westerly and northerly direction on the Great Lakes (except Lake Michigan) and in a southerly direction on Lake Michigan is proceeding *from* seaward. On the Intracoastal Waterway proceeding in a general southerly direction along the Atlantic coast, and in a generally westerly direction along the Gulf coast is considered as proceeding from seaward. On the Mississippi and Ohio rivers and their tributaries the aids to navigation characteristics are determined as proceeding from sea towards the head of navigation, although local terminology describes "left bank" and "right bank" as proceeding with the flow of the river.

Special Purpose Buoys

In addition to the lateral system of buoyage, several special purpose buoyage characteristics, which have no lateral significance, are utilized to mark dredging areas, quarantine areas, fish net areas, anchorages, race courses, experiments or tests, etc.

Types of Buoys

The pleasure boatman can expect to encounter eight different types of buoys marking the waterways on which he cruises. Each kind is designed to serve under definite conditions. Generally speaking, all buoys serve as daymarks. Those having lights are also available for navigation at night, and those having sound signals are also more readily located in fog as well as in darkness. The following are the principal general types:

Spar Buoys: Large logs, trimmed, shaped and appropriately painted. Buoys of the same spar shape are also constructed of steel plates.

Can and Nun Buoys: Buoys built up of steel plates having the distinctive shapes designated by these names.

Bell Buoys: Steel floats surmounted by short skeleton towers in which the bells are fixed. Most bell buoys are sounded by the motion of the sea. In a few buoys, the bells are struck by compressed gas or electrically-operated hammers.

Gong Buoys: Similar in construction to bell buoys, but sounding a distinctive note because of the use of sets of gongs each gong of which has a different tone.

Whistle Buoys: These provide a sound signal which is useful at night and during fog or low visibility. As the whistle mechanism is operated by the motion of the buoy in the sea, these are buoys used principally in exposed locations. A type of sound buoy is also used in which a horn is sounded at regular intervals by mechanical means.

Lighted Buoys: These consist usually of a metal float on which is mounted a short skeleton tower at the top of which the lantern is placed. Tanks of compressed acetylene gas, or electric batteries, on which the light is operated, are placed in the body of the buoy, below the water level.

Combination Buoys: These are buoys

in which a light and a sound signal are combined, such as a lighted bell buoy, lighted gong buoy, lighted whistle buoy, or lighted horn buoy. Most modern buoys have corner radar reflectors designed into the superstructure to improve radar response. This also makes them a bit easier to locate with a searchlight.

Coloring of Buoys

All buoys are painted distinctive colors to indicate their purpose or, in the lateral system, the side on which they should be passed. The meaning of lateral system buoys (channel markers) when proceeding *from* seaward is indicated by their colors as follows:

Black Buoys mark the port (left) sides of channels, or the locations of wrecks or obstacles which must be passed by keeping the buoy on the port (left) hand.

Red Buoys mark the starboard (right) sides of channels or the locations of wrecks which must be passed by keeping the buoy on the starboard (right) hand.

Red and Black Horizontally Banded Buoys mark junctions in the channels, or wrecks or obstacles which may be passed on either side. If the topmost band is *black,* the preferred channel will be found by keeping the buoy on the port hand side. If the topmost band is *red,* the preferred channel will be found by keeping the buoy on the starboard hand.

(Note that when proceeding *toward* seaward, it may not be possible to pass on either side of these buoys, and the chart should always be consulted.)

Black and White Vertically Striped Buoys mark the fairway or midchannel and should be passed close to, on either side.

The meaning of special-purpose buoys is indicated by their colors as follows:

White Buoys mark anchorage areas.

Yellow Buoys mark quarantine areas.

White Buoys with Green Tops are used in connection with dredging and survey operations.

White and Black Alternate Horizontally Banded Buoys mark fish net areas.

White and International Orange Buoys Alternately Banded, either horizontally or vertically, are for special purposes to which neither the lateral-system colors nor the other special purpose colors apply.

Yellow and Black Vertically Striped Buoys are used for seadrome markings and have no marine significance.

Numbering of Buoys

Most buoys are given numbers, letters or combinations of numbers and letters which are painted conspicuously upon them. These markings facilitate identification and location of the buoys on the charts. Also, they serve as handy guide posts for pleasure boatmen. You will often hear a shout from one boat to another—or a radiotelephone message—such as: "They're biting today about one hundred and fifty yards east of buoy 32."

All solid-colored red or black buoys, except those in the Mississippi River system, are given numbers or combinations of numbers and letters. Other colored buoys may be given letters. Numbers increase from seaward and are kept in approximate sequence on both sides of a channel by omitting numbers where required. Odd numbers are used only on solid-black buoys. Even numbers are used only on solid-red buoys.

Numbers followed by letters are used on solid-colored red or black buoys when a letter is required so as not to disturb the sequence of numbering, or on important buoys, particularly those marking isolated off-shore dangers. An example of the latter would be a buoy marked "1DR." Here the number has the usual meaning as the first in a series of buoys, while the letters "DR" indicate the place as Duxbury Reef. Letters without numbers are sometimes applied to black and white vertically-striped buoys, red and black horizontally banded buoys, solid-yellow buoys, and other buoys not solid colored red or black.

In the Mississippi River system, unlighted buoys are not numbered, while the numbers on lighted buoys have no lateral significance, but indicate the mileage from a designated point.

Shapes of Buoys

For the purpose of ready identification, certain of the unlighted buoys are differentiated by their shapes.

Most important to the pleasure boatmen are these facts about unlighted buoys: The nun buoy is always found on the starboard side of the channel, entering, is always red, or red and black banded, with the red on top. The can buoy is always found on the port side, entering, is always black, or red and black banded with the black band on top. The shape has no special significance in the case of spar, lighted, bell, whistle, or similar buoys, and when those are sighted it is the color alone that indicates the side on which to pass, the number, sound, or light characteristics indicating the purpose of the buoy.

Color of Lights on Buoys

The lights on buoys are either red, green or white. Red lights serve to identify "red" buoys and are found only on red buoys or banded buoys with a topmost band of red.

Green lights mark only "black" buoys or those banded buoys with the topmost band of black. In other words, entering a channel, red lights mark the starboard buoys; green lights the port buoys. However, care should be observed before accepting a red or green light as marking a buoy. Such lights could be ship's running lights, or other lights.

As to a white light on a buoy, it has no special color significance, the purpose of the buoy being indicated by its color, and number or light phase characteristics.

Optical Reflectors

Many unlighted buoys are fitted with optical reflectors which greatly facilitate the locating of the buoys at night by means of a searchlight. Optical reflectors may be white, red, or green and have the same significance as the lights of these colors. And, as mentioned earlier, the corner radar reflectors will also show up in the beams of a searchlight.

Light Phase Characteristics

For nighttime navigation in marked waters, it is essential to know the characteristics of the four different light phases which are used on buoys.

Flashing Lights (flashing at regular intervals and at the rate of not more than 30 flashes per minute) are placed only on black buoys, red buoys or special purpose buoys.

Quick Flashing Lights (not less than 60 flashes per minute) are placed only on black buoys and on red buoys at points where it is desired to show that *special caution* is required, as at sharp turns or sudden constrictions, or where there are wrecks or dangerous obstructions which must be passed only on one side.

Interrupted Quick Flashing Lights (the groups consisting of a series of quick flashes, with dark intervals of about 4 seconds) are placed only on buoys painted with red and black horizontal bands, at points where it is desired to indicate junctions in channels, or wrecks or obstructions which may be passed on either side.

Short-Long Flashing Lights (groups consisting of a short flash and a long flash, the flashes recurring at the rate of about eight per minute) are placed only on buoys painted in black and white vertical stripes, at points where it is desired to indicate fairways or midchannel and should be passed close to, on either side. The lights are always white.

Daybeacons

There are many aids to navigation which are not lighted. Structures of this type, not buoys, are called daybeacons. Although a movement is underway to standardize them, they vary greatly in design and construction, depending on their location and the distance to which they must be seen. A daybeacon may consist of a single pile with a day mark at the top, a spar with a cask at the top, a slatted tower, or a structure of masonry. Daybeacons are colored, as are lighthouses, to distinguish them from their surroundings and to provide a means of identification. Daybeacons marking the sides of channels are colored and numbered in the same manner as buoys and minor light structures; red indicating the right side entering; black the left side entering. Many daybeacons are also fitted with optical reflectors to facilitate locating them at night by means of a searchlight.

THE INTRACOASTAL WATERWAY

The Intracoastal Waterway is a comparatively shallow channel lying parallel to and extending along the Atlantic and Gulf coasts from New Jersey to the Mexican Border. It is the "commuter" route of the pleasure boats which move south in the fall of the year to havens in Florida and other warm waters from the northeastern states. The special marking described here is applied to the so-called "inside route" proper and to those portions of all connecting waterways which must be crossed or followed in order to make a continuous passage. Although it is an "inside" route, it does include some portions of fairly rough water and while it has been covered by outboards, it should not normally be followed by a boat which is not designed for fairly heavy waters. A set of charts is a must for long trek and a complete set for the Atlantic coast portions runs somewhat over fifty dollars in cost.

Distinctive Markings

All buoys, daybeacons, and light structures marking the Intracoastal Waterway have some portion of them painted yellow, the distinctive coloring adopted for the Waterway. Buoys have a band of yellow at the top, daybeacons have a band or border of yellow, and light structures are similarly painted.

The coloring and numbering of buoys and daybeacons, and the color of the lights on buoys and light structures is on the same lateral system as that prevailing in other waterways. The basic rule is that *red* buoys and daybeacons are on the *right hand* side of the channel when proceeding from New Jersey toward Mexico, and *black* buoys and daybeacons are on the *left hand* side of the channel when proceeding in the same direction. This rule is applied in a uniform manner the entire length of the waterway, regardless of the widely differing compass headings of many sections, and the fact that rivers and other waterways marked on the seacoast system are sometimes followed.

Numbering of Intracoastal Waterway aids follows the basic rule, numbers increasing from New Jersey toward Mexico. Aids are numbered in groups, usually not exceeding 200; numbering begins again at "1" at certain natural dividing points.

Lights on buoys follow the standard system of red or white lights on red buoys, and green or white lights on black buoys. The color of the lights on fixed structures also follows this general rule. Range lights, not being lateral markers may be any of the three standard colors.

Dual Marking

Special markings are employed in order that boats may readily follow the Intracoastal Waterway route where it coincides with another waterway such as an important river marked on the seacoast system. These special markings are applied to the buoys or other aids which mark the river or waterway for other traffic. The special marks consist of a yellow square and a yellow triangle, painted on a conspicuous part of the dual purpose aid. The yellow square, in outline similar to a can buoy, indicates that the aid on which it is placed should be kept on the left hand side when following the Intracoastal Waterway from New jersey toward Mexico. The yellow triangle, in outline similar to a nun buoy, indicates that the aid on which it is placed should be kept on the right hand when proceeding south. By this marking, a boatman, when approaching a body of water such as the Savannah River, and knowing that he must follow it for some way before again entering a dredged cut of the Intracoastal Waterway, knows that his course lies along such buoys or other aids as are specially marked in yellow. He determines the side of his boat on which these aids should be passed by the shape of the yellow marks, always bearing in mind the basic direction of his travel.

Where coincidental marking is employed, the boatman following the Intracoastal Waterway disregards the color and shape of the aid on which the mark is placed, being guided solely by the shape of the yellow mark. Can buoys of the seacoast system may have painted on them yellow triangles or yellow squares, depending on whether the waterway which they mark is followed in the direction of the sea or in the direction of its headwaters, as the Intracoastal Waterway is followed in the direction of Mexico. Those not traversing the Intracoastal Waterway entirely can disregard the special yellow markings.

CHAPTER XIII

Cautions Concerning Aids to Navigation

The preceding section of this book may have given the impression that anyone with normal intelligence and a boat can set out and follow the aids to navigation to his destination. However, seamanship is not acquired in a few easy hours of reading, or even by taking a ten or twelve-week session in small boat handling. The other side of the coin is described now. Some of the deficiencies, derangements and unusual phenomena that occasionally occur and which are potential sources of danger, and conditions which require caution on the part of the boatman, are discussed in the following pages.

Lights and Fog Signals

The condition of the atmosphere has a considerable effect upon the distance at which lights can be seen. Sometimes lights are obscured by fog, haze, dust, smoke or precipitation which may be present at the light, or between it and the observer. These conditions need not be at the location of the observer, and possibly may be unknown to him. On the other hand, refraction may often cause a light to seem farther away than under ordinary circumstances. A light of low intensity will be easily obscured by unfavorable conditions of the atmosphere and little dependence can be placed on its being seen. For this reason, the intensity of a light should always be considered when expecting to sight it in thick weather. Haze and distance may reduce the apparent duration of the flash of a flashing light. In some conditions of atmosphere white lights may have a reddish hue. Colored lights are more quickly lost to sight under weather conditions which tend to reduce visibility than are white lights.

Brilliant Shore Lights

The increasing use of brilliant shore lights for advertising, illuminating bridges and other purposes, may cause marine navigational lights, particularly those in densely inhabited areas, to be outshone and difficult to distinguish from the background lighting. The Coast Guard would appreciate reports of such cases so that steps may be taken to improve the conditions.

The "loom" of a powerful light is often seen beyond the limit of visibility of the actual rays of the light. The loom may sometimes appear sufficiently sharp to obtain a bearing.

At short distances, flashing lights may show a faint continuous light between flashes.

The distance of an observer from a light cannot be estimated by its apparent intensity. Always check the characteristics of lights in order that powerful lights visible in the distance should not be mistaken for nearby lights showing similar characteristics at low intensity (such as those on light buoys).

If lights are not sighted within a reasonable time after prediction, a dangerous situation may exist requiring prompt resolution or action to insure the safety of the vessel.

Characteristics

The apparent characteristics of a complex light may change with the distance of the observer. For example, a light which actually displays a characteristic of fixed white varied by flashes of alternating white and red (the phases having a decreasing range of visibility in this order: flashing white, flashing red, fixed white) may, when first sighted in clear weather, show a simple flashing white light. As the boat draws nearer, the red flash will become visible and the characteristic will apparently be alternating flashing white and red. Later, the fixed white light will be seen between the flashes and the true characteristic of the light finally recognized—fixed white, alternating flashing white and red (or, as the abbreviations appear on the chart, F.W. alt. Fl. W. and R.).

There is always the possibility of a light being extinguished. In the case of unattended lights, this condition might not be immediately detected and corrected.

Also, if a boat has considerable vertical motion due to pitching in a heavy sea, a light sighted on the horizon may alternately appear and disappear. This may lead the unwary to assign a false characteristic and hence err in its identification. The true characteristic will be evident after the distance has sufficiently decreased, or it may be determined by increasing the height of the eye of the observer.

Problems with "Sectors"

Sectors of colored glass are placed in the lanterns of some lights to produce a system of light sectors of different colors. In general, red sectors, as we have noted, are used to mark shoals or to warn the mariner of nearby land or other obstructions to navigation. Such lights provide approximate bearing information since an observer may note the change of color as he crosses the boundary between sectors. These boundaries are indicated in the Light Lists and by broken lines on the charts. These bearings, like all bearings referring to lights, are given as true in degrees from 000° to 359° as observed from a vessel towards the light.

Altering courses on the changing sectors of a light or using the boundaries between light sectors to determine the bearing for any purpose is not recommended. Be guided instead by the correct compass bearing of the light and do not rely on being able to accurately observe the point at which the color changes. This is often difficult to decide because the edge of a colored sector cannot be cut off sharply. On either side of the line of demarcation between white and red sectors, and also between white and green, there is always a small arc of uncertain color. Moreover, when haze or smoke are present in the intervening atmosphere, a white sector might have a reddish hue.

The area in which a light can be observed is normally a small circle with the light as center and the range of visibility as the radius. On some bearings, however, the range may be reduced by obstructions. Also keep in mind that the visibility is predicated on a height of 15 feet above the water for eye level, which is far above the height of most pleasure boat skippers. In such cases the obstructed arc might differ with height of eye and distance. When a light is cut off by adjoining land, the arc of visibility is given, but the bearing on which the light disappears may vary with the distance of the vessel from which observed and with the height of eye. When the light is cut off by a sloping hill or point of land, the light may be seen over a wider arc by a boat far off than by one close to.

Circles drawn on charts around a light are not intended to give information as to the distance at which it can be seen, but solely to indicate, in the case of lights which do not show equally in all directions, the bearings between which the variation of visibility or obscuration of the light occur. Lights of equal candle-power, but of different colors, may be seen at different distances. This fact should be considered, not only in predicting the distance at which a light can be seen, but also in identifying it.

Hazard in Rip-Rap

At many lights rip-rap mounds are maintained to protect the structures against ice damage and scouring action. There have been collisions with the uncharted, submerged portions of such rip-rap by vessels attempting to pass the lights extremely close.

Fog Signals

Fog signals depend on the transmission of sound through the air. As aids to navigation, they have certain inherent defects that should be considered. Sound travels through the air in a variable and frequently unpredictable manner.

It has been clearly established that:

1. Fog signals are heard at greatly varying distances and that the distance at which a fog signal can be heard may vary with the bearing of the signal and may be different on different occasions.

2. In a fog signal having a combination of low and high tones, it is not unusual under certain atmospheric conditions for one of the tones to be inaudible.

3. There are occasionally areas close to the signal in which it is wholly inaudible. This is particularly true when the fog signal is screened by intervening land or other obstruction or a high cliff.

4. A fog may exist a short distance from a station and not be observable from it, so that the signal may not be in operation.

5. Some fog signals cannot be started at a moment's notice.

6. Even though a fog signal may not be heard when the engine is in motion, it may be heard when the boat is stopped, or from a quiet position.

7. The intensity of the sound emitted by a fog signal may be greater at a distance than in the immediate vicinity.

All these considerations point to the necessity for the utmost caution when navigating near land in a fog. The fog signals can never be implicitly relied upon, and the practice of sounding the depth of water and making comparisons with the chart should never be neglected. If possible, lookouts should be placed in positions where the noises in the boat are least likely to interfere with hearing a fog signal. Fog signals are valuable as warnings, but the operator should not place complete reliance on them in navigating his vessel. They should be considered solely as *warning* devices.

Regarding fog signals, you should never assume:

1. That you are out of ordinary hearing distance because you fail to hear the fog signal.

2. That because you hear a fog signal faintly, you are at a great distance from it.

3. That you are near to it because you hear the sound plainly.

4. That the distance from, and the intensity of the sound on any one occasion is a guide to you for any future occasion.

5. That the fog signal is not sounding because you do not hear it, even when in close proximity.

Lightships, Buoys and Radiobeacons

Courses should invariably be set to pass lightships with sufficient clearance to avoid the possibility of collision from any cause—although there is strong temptation to try to pass close enough to exchange friendly waves with the crew members.

Errors of observation, current and wind effects, other vessels in the vicinity, and defects in steering gear have been the causes of actual collisions and many "close shaves."

Experience shows that lightships cannot be safely used as leading marks to be passed close aboard, but should always be left broad off the course. When approaching a lightship or a station on a submarine site on radio bearings, the risk of collision will be avoided by insuring that the radio bearing does not remain constant.

It should be borne in mind that most lightships are anchored to a very long scope of chain and, as a result, the radius of their swinging circle is considerable. Furthermore, under certain conditions of wind and current, they are subject to sudden and unexpected sheers which are certain to hazard a boat attempting to pass close aboard.

The charted position of a lightship is the location of the anchor, but during extremely heavy weather and due to their exposed locations, lightships may be carried off station without the knowledge and despite the best efforts of their crews. Therefore you cannot rely on a lightship maintaining its precisely charted position immediately following severe storms. A lightship known to be off station will secure her light, fog signal and radiobeacon, and fly the International Code signal "PC" signifying "Lightship not at anchor on her station."

Watch buoys are sometimes moored near lightships to mark the approximate station should the lightship be carried away or temporarily removed and to give crews an indication of dragging. Since these buoys are always unlighted and, in some cases, moored as much as a mile from the lightship, the danger of a closely passing vessel colliding with them is always present, especially at night or in periods of reduced visibility.

Buoys

It is imprudent for a navigator to rely on floating aids to navigation to always maintain their charted position and to constantly and unerringly display their listed characteristics. The obstacles to perfect performance are of such magnitude that complete reliability is manifestly impossible to achieve. Buoys are likely to be carried away, shifted, capsized or sunk as the result of storms, ice conditions, collisions or other accidents. Lighted buoys may become extinguished or their lighting apparatus broken or deranged, causing them to show improper light colors or light phase characteristics. Practically all audible signals on buoys are operated by the action of the sea and may consequently be silent during periods of calm weather. They may fail to sound, regardless of wave activity, due to mechanical defects or damage to their sound-producing devices. Even if functioning properly, a sound buoy may not be heard at relatively close range due to the vagaries of sound in atmosphere as explained under "Fog Signals." Buoys that have been placed to mark shifting shoals may not always be properly located in relation to the obstructions they are meant to mark. This is particularly true after heavy storms when the shoals are liable to shift their positions away from the buoys.

Buoys are moored to scopes of chain of various lengths, in some cases, several times the depth of the water in which they are located. Like the lightship, the radius of swing should be taken into account. The position of a buoy, as shown on the chart, actually represents the location of its sinker to which the mooring chain is shackled. The buoy, however, does not maintain position directly over its sinker. Being moored as they are, buoys have a tendency to yaw about under the influence of the wind and current. The action is most unpredictable, and a boat attempting to pass very close aboard always risks collision with a yawing buoy.

Wreck Buoys

The idea seems to have developed among the uninitiated that a wreck buoy always occupies a position directly over the wreck it is intended to mark. This idea is entirely erroneous. Buoys must be placed in position by a vessel. It is usually physically impossible for these vessels to maneuver directly over a wreck to place the sinker without incurring serious underwater damage to themselves. For this reason, a wreck buoy is usually placed to the seaward or channelward side of a wreck, the proximity to the wreck being governed by existing conditions. If necessary to avoid the possibility of confusion, more than one buoy is used per wreck, in which case both may not be located on the seaward or channelward side of the wreck, but the wreck will lie between them. Obviously no attempt should be made to pass between buoys so placed.

Sunken wrecks are not always static. They are sometimes moved away from their buoys by severe sea conditions or other causes. The previously mentioned precaution regarding shoals shifting away from their buoys also applies to sunken wrecks and wreck buoys.

All buoys should therefore be regarded as warnings or guides, not as infallible navigation marks; especially those located in exposed positions. Whenever possible, navigate by bearings or angles on fixed objects on shore and by soundings rather than by reliance on buoys.

Radiobeacons

Exact rules cannot be given as to the accuracy to be expected in radio bearings. The accuracy depends to a large extent on the skill of the operator, the condition and type of equipment, and the accuracy of the boat's direction-finder calibration curve. Skill in the operation of a manual radio direction finder can be obtained only by practice and by following the operating instructions provided with the equipment. As the operator obtains bearings by manually revolving the direction finder loop or goniometer until the signal disappears or becomes a minimum, he can estimate by the magnitude of the arc of silence (null) or minimum strength the approximate accuracy of the bearing. Operator error is in addition to those due to other causes.

An automatic direction finder does not afford the operator an opportunity to judge the accuracy of the bearing. Automatic direction finders are also subject to additional errors because of the designed receiver bandwidth usually used. The wider bandwidth allows more spurious signals, from both interference and other signals, to enter the receiver. Since the automatic direction finder reacts to a composite of all signals, received, errors can result.

To be able to operate a radio direction finder accurately, the user should be aware of certain disturbing effects that can introduce an error into the observed reading. These can be:

Skywave Signals—Reliable radio direction finding is not possible if the groundwave does not exist, as the skywave is very unstable, i.e., its angle of earth contact (skip distance) varies in accordance with ionospheric conditions. Generally, radiobeacon signals transmitted in the 285 to 325 kc./s. and on 500 kc./s. bands have strong groundwave fields, and under normal conditions little or no disturbing skywave energy exists except at considerable distances from the radiobeacon station or ship.

Local Disturbing Effects—Erroneous radio direction finder bearings may result due to the following:

1. Distortion of wave front due to physical dimensions and contour of the vessel's hull.
2. Currents may be induced in the direction finder by structural features of the boat's superstructure, masts, stays, ladders, life lines, railings and any metallic objects forming closed loops which have a natural frequency greater than the frequency to which the direction finder is adjusted. These currents are generally in phase opposition to the currents, and bearings may be affected if corrective measures are not employed.
3. Currents may be induced in the direction finder by masts, grounded stays, or any metallic object or objects which can act as vertical antenna having a natural frequency greater than the radio direction finder frequency being used. Objects resonating at a harmonic frequency of the radio direction finder frequency may to a lesser degree affect the quality of the bearing. Such objects will cause the bearing null to be broad and obscured. Generally, these objects will not produce spurious currents of sufficient magnitude which will affect the apparent bearing of the obscured radio direction finder signal.

Since the conditions listed above are local in nature, they must be corrected or compensated for locally. Frequent checks of radio direction finder installations should be made to determine whether corrections or compensations remain the same by checking calibrations of the radio direction finder installation. The usual method of calibration is to obtain a series of simultaneous radio and visual bearings on a transmitter. This may be done while a boat swings at anchor, or more quickly by sailing in a circle within sight of a transmitter. It is essential that the radio direction finder be accurately calibrated in order that bearings may be corrected for quadrantal error. It should be recalibrated after any changes have been made to the set or its surroundings, whenever there is reason to believe that the previous calibration has become inaccurate, and also at periodic intervals. The calibration must be made on approximately the same frequencies as will be used to take bearings, because the deviation for several frequencies is not likely to be the same. Many radio direction finders are compensated and no calibration chart or curve is used. Compensation is just as vulnerable as calibration data to changes made in the set or its surroundings.

Night Effect—All radio direction finders are subject to night effect. This effect is apparent to the observer in one or more of the following:
1. Complete disappearance of all minima or directional characteristics.
2. Multiple minima.
3. Crisp, but displaced minima.
4. Minima normally placed but obscure.
5. Swinging minima.

Night effects should be expected during the periods of sunrise and sunset. Such bearings should be treated or accepted with doubt to their accuracy.

Land Effect — A radiowave crossing a coastline at an oblique angle undergoes a change of direction due to the difference in conducting and reflecting properties of land and water. It is avoided by not using, or regarding as of doubtful accuracy, bearings of waves which cross a shoreline at an oblique angle. If the transmitter is near the coast, negligible error is introduced because of the short distance the waves travel before undergoing refraction.

Moreover, many observations seem to indicate that such errors are negligible when the observing vessel is well off from the shore (scant comfort to the average pleasure boatman). Bearings secured entirely over water areas are to be preferred since any question of so-called land effect in producing error is thus eliminated.

Before taking bearings on a commercial station which broadcasts entertainment programs, the mariner should consider that the frequency may differ widely from the frequency to which his direction finder is calibrated. This also applies to aeronautical beacons. The published location of the station may be that of its studio and not of its transmitting antenna and, if the station is synchronized with other stations, it may be impossible to tell on which station the bearing is taken. As a majority of the standard broadcast stations are inland, their use is not recommended due to possible coastal refraction as explained above.

Due to the many factors which enter into the transmission and reception of radio signals, an observer cannot with any degree of accuracy estimate the distance from a radiobeacon by the strength of the signals received.

When steering a course for a radiobeacon, the same precautions should be observed as when steering for a light or any other mark. If the radiobeacon is aboard a lightship or on a submarine site, particular care should be taken to avoid the possibility of collision. Sole reliance should never be placed on sighting the lightship or light station, or hearing the fog signal in time to avoid collision.

The 180° Error Problem

Unless a radio direction finder has a

Harbor of Refuge Light Station.

Execution Rocks Light Station.

Ambrose Lightship.

Three "aids to navigation." Harbor of Refuge and Excution Rocks lighthouses are familiar sights to east coast pleasure boatmen. Note the extensive rip-rap at the base of Excution Rock station which cautions giving it a wide berth. The Ambrose Lightship is one of the old-timers in the Coast Guard navigation service. *(U.S. Coast Guard photos.)*

vertical sensing antenna, there is a possible 180° error in the reading. If such an error is discovered, one should take the reciprocal of the uncorrected reading, and apply the correction for the new direction. If there is a doubt as to which of two possible directions is correct, one should wait long enough for the bearing to change appreciably and take another reading. For a vessel on a steady course forward the true (re: relative) bearing: on a fixed transmitter should move aft (unless homing head-on or dead astern departure). If the bearing moves forward, it must be a reverse or reciprocal bearing and should be treated accordingly.

A course should be selected, whenever searoom permits, that will insure passing at a distance rather than close aboard, and repeated bearings of the radiobeacon should show an increasing change in the same direction.

During periods of radio propagation disturbance, observations may be unreliable. When using the radio direction finder the boatman should understand the limitations of the apparatus and the possible vagaries of the radiobeacon transmissions due to causes outside the control of the transmitting stations.

CHAPTER XIV

Electronic Aids to Navigation

The Radio Direction Finder

In earlier times the mariner could only navigate by visual means by making use of known coastlines, the sun, the moon, stars or other vessels. If the weather became foggy or overcast, navigation became extremely hazardous or impossible except by intuition.

The development of the magnetic compass during the twelfth century gave the mariner a fixed point (North) for navigation which was not obscured by overcast or foggy weather. This was a great improvement, but he was still compelled to make use of the sun and stars for cross-checks on his course of travel because of windage and drift.

During the twentieth century a new navigational tool, the radio direction finder, was made available for coastal cross-checks on magnetic compass courses. The radio direction finder operates independently of winds, tides and drift currents, and operates independently of visible "fixes." An increasing number of pleasure boats have been equipped with these devices which are now available in the "$150-and-under" price range, and even in the form of kits which the do-it-yourselfer may assemble at considerable savings.

Landbased and Mobile Finders

Early radio direction finders were landbased. The vessel desiring a position "fix" provided the radio signal by "wireless." The landbased stations communicated with the vessel and gave the vessel its position in relation to the station. Usually two or three landbased direction finders were used to determine and check the vessel's position.

More recently, mobile radio direction finders have been developed which use the same principle as the landbased radio direction finders, but in reverse. That is, landbased "wireless" stations provide the radio signal for one radio direction finder location aboard the boat. "Fixes" can thus be taken without the need of communicating with the shore.

Necessary Equipment

An accurate job of navigation can be accomplished with minimum effort with a radio direction finder aboard to augment the pelorus and magnetic compass. A list of landbased radio transmitting stations—and transmitting lightships—up to date charts showing the location of the transmitters, and parallels or protractor are needed to complete the navigational "kit."

The "RDF"

The radio direction finder is essentially an electronic extension of the pelorus, the standard equipment of mariners for taking bearings on visible fixed landmarks. In daytime, clear-weather operation with an easy, unrestricted view of the shoreline, the pelorus and the radio direction finder have about equal utility. The pelorus depends on the eye and fixed visible landmarks, whereas the radio direction finder replaces the visible landmarks with radio stations of known location, which are not necessarily visi-

The portable radio direction finder is found on an increasing number of smaller pleasure boats. *(Courtesy Bendix Corp.)*

ble, and converts the radio signals into audible or visible indications on the finder.

RDF Construction

Generally speaking, the radio direction finder consists of a directional antenna (usually a loop), a non-directional antenna, a radio receiver with aural and/or visual signal strength indicator, and an azimuth (compass card). The directional antenna locates the line of "sight" to the radio station with respect to the ship's heading or magnetic compass bearing. The non-directional antenna locates the line of "sight" to the radio station with respect to the ship's heading or magnetic compass bearing. The non-directional antenna called a *sense* antenna is used in conjunction with the directional antenna to determine the general direction of the incoming radio signal. The sense antenna is necessary because the usual loop provides two bearing indications 180° apart on any radio signal. The sense antenna determines which of the two bearing indications is correct. The radio receiver performs its usual function of converting the incoming radio signal into an indication sensed by the boat operator, such as sound, meter variation, or light. The azimuth dial converts the directional antenna position into directional bearings such as 0°, 125°, 330°, etc. with respect to the ship's heading or relative to magnetic compass points.

Types of Radio Direction Finders

All radio direction finders for use on the low and medium radio frequencies, 150 kc. to 4,000 kc., employing loop antennas will fall into one of the following categories:
1. Manually rotated loop, RDF
2. Automatically rotated loop, ADF
3. Manually operated fixed loop, RDF

4. Automatically operated fixed loop, ADF

Manually Rotated Loops

Two types of equipment fall into category one, (A) direction finders having rotatable loops *without* provision for *sense,* and (B) radio direction finders and adjustments for *sense*. Those without *sense* provisions are primarily used for "homing" on a radio station when the general direction of the incoming signal is known. It is possible to determine the direction of the incoming signal with a homing type direction finder by means of a bow and beam or beam and stern maneuver (described elsewhere in this book in the chapter on piloting). This maneuver is not necessary for radio direction finders having *sense* provisions. In each case the loop antenna is rotated by hand to secure a null and bearing.

Automatically Rotated Loops

The equipment in this category is the same as the manually rotated loop types except that the loop is rotated by an automatic drive mechanism which is controlled by the receiver null output. The loop and automatic drive mechanism automatically rotate the loop to the direction of the incoming radio signal when a station is tuned in. *Sense* is also automatically applied to eliminate bearing ambiguity. These types are usually equipped with a remote bearing indicator.

Manually Operated Fixed Loop

This equipment employs two fixed position non-rotatable loops which are mounted at right angles to one another. The output of the two fixed loops are usually fed into a device called a "Goniometer" which combines the loop outputs and reads the vector sum depending upon the position of the goniometer. Changing the position of the goniometer electrically rotates the loop output, thereby allowing bearings to be taken just as if a single loop were physically rotated. The goniometer is manually operated and is connected to the loops by means of electrical wiring only, and it is usually remotely located from the antenna at the receiver installation.

Automatically Operated Fixed Loop

These are the same as the previously described type, except that the goniometer is continuously rotated by a motor, thus continually scanning all directions for incoming signals like a radar. The motor rotation is synchronized with a circular sweep in an oscilloscope. When a signal is tuned in, the oscilloscope pattern shows a figure eight (propeller-shaped pattern) whose orientation depends upon the direction of the incoming signal. The orientation of the propeller pattern is measured with respect to a compass rose for relative and/or magnetic bearing reading. *Sense* is applied to eliminate bearing ambiguity.

Types 1 and 3 are the least expensive, but consume time to operate manually and bearing accuracy is largely dependent upon operator skill. Types 2 and 4 being automatic in operation are the least complicated to operate, but the most expensive to buy. Bearing accuracy is not dependent upon operator skill for types 2 and 4.

How It Works

The basic principle of operation of a radio direction finder is "triangulation" which is also the basic principle of operation of the pelorus. However, when a radio direction finder is used, the lights or landmarks are replaced by radio transmitting stations such as broadcasts or radio beacons which transmit in all directions simultaneously. Since the eye or ear cannot see or hear a radio signal, a radio receiver is used to convert the incoming radio signal to an audible or visual indication. A radio direction finder provides both—audible indication from the speaker and visual indication from a null meter or picture tube. A loop antenna provides the means of determining direction, and when rotated will provide *two* locations 180° apart where the received signal peaks (is loudest); and *two* where the received signal nulls (is of least volume). To determine which of the two is the correct direction a *sense* non directional antenna is required which, when properly mixed with the loop antenna signals will allow one to determine the correct peak indication and also to pick out the proper null.

The radio receiver, loop, *sense* antenna, and azimuth indicator comprise the complete system for converting a radio signal to an audible or visual indication and determining the direction of the signal transmitted from the ship.

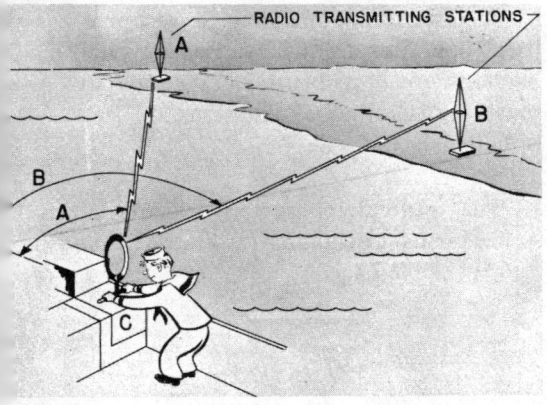

The figure illustrates the principle. Radio transmitting stations are located at points A and B. The radio direction finder is at point C aboard your boat. The radio transmitting stations radiate energy in all directions like a beacon light. The loop antenna in the direction finder only "sees" the radiated energy from Station A at angle A with respect to the boat's heading and Station B at angle B with respect to the boat's heading, providing the "sense" adjustment is employed properly. Here as in the case of a pelorus "fix," if angles A and B are laid out on a chart together with the geographical location of the two stations, an accurate determination of the boat's position can be obtained.

Using Radio Stations

Any radio station can be used for radio direction finding provided the signal it produces meets certain minimum requirements. Most radio direction finders are capable of tuning the Beacon Band 150 to 400 kc.; Broadcast Band 550 to 1600 kc., and Marine Band 1.6 to 5.0 mc.

Each of the different types of radio stations commonly used for radio direction finding is listed and identified by a special marker on the newer navigational charts. They are: marine radio-beacons on mainlands, islands or breakwaters; marine radiobeacons on lightships; marker radiobeacons on breakwater entrances or jetties; aeronautical range stations on mainlands and islands and standard broadcast stations.

As with other navigational aids, the "Light Lists" and the local charts will provide you with location and characteristics of nearby transmitters. At the present time, only the most recent editions of the Marine Charts are complete with respect to the locations of airways radio beacons and radio stations. Therefore it is necessary to employ aeronautical charts as well as marine charts to obtain maximum utility from a direction finder, and you can mark the locations of these "guides" on your marine charts.

In addition to the marine and aeronautical charts, the following publications will prove helpful:

H.O. Pub. No. 205, U.S. Hydrographic

Office, Washington, D. C. (Worldwide list of radiobeacons with call signs, frequencies and locations); *Flight Information Manual,* Office of Information of CAA, available from Coast and Geodetic Survey Offices. (List of aeronautical range stations with call letters, frequency, locations, etc.)

Note that all aeronautical and range and marine radio beacons are identified by call letters transmitted in International Morse Code. Familiarity with the code is helpful for the rapid identification of a station. This code with the latest approved phonetic alphabet is shown below.

Alfa	A	• —
Bravo	B	— • • •
Charlie	C	— • — •
Delta	D	— • •
Echo	E	•
Foxtrot	F	• • — •
Golf	G	— — •
Hotel	H	• • • •
India	I	• •
Juliett	J	• — — —
Kilo	K	— • —
Lima	L	• — • •
Mike	M	— —
November	N	— •
Oscar	O	— — —
Papa	P	• — — •
Quebec	Q	— — • —
Romeo	R	• — •
Sierra	S	• • •
Tango	T	—
Uniform	U	• • —
Victor	V	• • • —
Whiskey	W	• — —
X-ray	X	— • • —
Yankee	Y	— • — —
Zulu	Z	— — • •

International Morse Code.

Rules for Choice of Station

If the following rules are observed, greatest accuracy, satisfaction, and reliability may be obtained from a direction finder:

1. Choose the strongest stations available but never stations closer than one mile from your boat unless they are low power harbor beacons or other ships' transmitters.

2. Choose stations having a clear non-interference channel. Whistles, static or crosstalk on the station will cause bearing errors and sometimes produce additional null directions.

3. The station should not be further than 50 to 75 miles away. At greater distances wave bending and reflections will cause bearing errors and/or constantly changing bearings.

4. Choose stations having a clear, unobstructed transmitting path between your boat and the station. Stations located on islands and coastal points provide best results. Avoid stations which are inland or behind mountain ranges.

5. Choose stations on the lowest practical operating frequency. Beacon band stations are best, broadcast stations are next, and marine band stations are least reliable.

The general characteristics of the three bands are summarized in the table on the next page.

The Depth Sounder

The Depth Sounder is the electronic successor to the old lead line. It gives a continuous picture of the changing contour of the bottom. In addition to indicating depth, it shows whether the bottom is hard or soft, the depth of mud on a soft bottom, and whether a hard bottom is smooth, sand or rocky. As a navi-

	Daytime	Sunset	Night	Sunrise	Sky Wave Effect
Beacon Band	50-75 mi.	50-75 mi.	50-75 mi.	50-75 mi.	Bearing jitter during sunrise and sunset hours.
Broadcast Band	50-75 mi.	10-20 mi.	20-30 mi.	10-20 mi.	Large bearing errors on stations more than 10-20 mi. distant during sunrise, sunset and night hours.
Marine Band	50-75 mi.	0	5-10 mi.	0	Fading of stations during sunset, sunrise and night hours produce large bearing errors. Distant stations are heard loudly but are subject to large bearing errors.

Reliable Bearing Distance.

gational aid, in conjunction with a chart and other aids to navigation, it simplifies the task of locating your boat's position.

For the fisherman, this piece of equipment enables him to locate fishing grounds, wrecks and schools of fish, and can actually detect large individual fish such as tuna.

How it Works

A depth sounder takes advantage of the fact that water is a good conductor of sound. It works by shooting a beam of sound through the water to the bottom; an echo bounces back off the bottom and returns to the depth sounder which measures the time it takes for the beam to hit bottom and bounce back. The time the sound beam takes to make this trip is converted to read in feet or fathoms—the depth measurement. In addition, the depth sounder will indicate the depth of anything in the water which reflects the sound beam.

The depth sounder has three essential parts: the transmitter, transducer and receiver. The transmitter generates pulses of electrical energy. These pulses are converted into sound by the transducer, which is usually mounted on the outside of the vessel in direct contact with the water. The transducer also receives the echo and relays it to the receiver. In the receiver, the length of time of the sounding is translated to a depth measurement. Depending on the type of depth sounder used, the depth is read either by means of a flashing red light or a stylus mark on a sheet of depth sounder paper.

All depth sounders use essentially the same method of transmitting and receiving the sound beam. They vary according to their application in shoal, moderately deep or deep water, the frequency of the sound (from 40,000 to 200,000 cycles), the number of sound pulses per minute, size, weight, power consumption and type of transducer. The choice depends on the needs of the buyer—and the state of his purse. Prices range from slightly over $100 to well over $1000 for commercial models.

The major difference among depth sounders is the manner of presentaton of depth. Two general types of presentation are available—indicator and recorder.

Indicator depth sounders report depth by means of a red light flashing through a transparent scale calibrated in feet or fathoms. The red light is a tiny neon tube carried on the end of an arm rotating at constant speed. This arm assembly is so adjusted that a sound impulse is generated every time the arm passes zero. At zero, the sound impulse is sent through the water and also lights the neon tube. When an echo returns, it again lights up the tube at the depth reading. Since the tube rotates clock-wise, the left hand edge of the flash should be read for accurate depth.

With this type of unit, depths can be read quickly and accurately, but the scale must be observed constantly and a record of readings noted if a profile of the bottom is desired. Indicator models usually cost less than recorder types.

Recorder models actually trace the contour of the bottom on graph paper. A stylus passes over the paper at constant velocity and keys the sound impulses. As it passes the zero mark on the paper, it makes a mark and starts the sound beam on its way. When the echo energizes the stylus, it makes anther mark on the scaled paper which shows the depth. Some recorders offer two ranges or "phases"—shoal and deep. When the deep phase is used, the zero signal is not recorded.

The principal advantage of the recorder depth sounder is that it makes a continuous and permanent record of the soundings. It also shows the characteristics of the bottom and indicates the time of a run between given points on the bottom.

Using the Depth Sounder for Navigation

In a later chapter we will discuss the lead line. While it is a venerable means of depth sounding, it has obvious disadvantages and is somewhat inconvenient. Also soundings must be taken at fairly close intervals to be meaningful.

The depth sounder eliminates the labor of taking soundings and takes as many as hundreds in a minute, making it possible to have a continuous bottom profile while the boat is proceeding at normal speed.

In thick weather, when running close to land, or in the vicinity of rocks and shoals, soundings should be taken continuously and a check made of the characteristics of the bottom. To obtain information which can be used in getting a "fix," take several depth readings to develop a "chain of soundings," as would have been done with a lead line. Plot the soundings on a piece of tracing paper on a line representing the course of your boat, using time and distance intervals that are consistent with the chart being used and your speed. Then move the paper around on your estimated position until the soundings match or nearly match those on the chart. This should indicate your position quite accurately. Study your chart for the location of bottom irregularities on your course. Watch for them on your depth sounder.

Exact agreement with the soundings of the chart is rarely found since much depends on the date of the survey and thoroughness with which the survey was made. Allowance must also be made for the state of the tide and effects of wind on the tide level. Also, be sure to allow for the depth of the transducer below the waterline and make sure your depth sounder and chart readings agree as to the scale—feet or fathoms.

When you take a chain of soundings, try also to get a visual bearing on some fixed object, or a radio direction finder bearing to further check your position. If all factors are taken into consideration, excellent results are possible and piloting with a depth sounder can add the professional touch to your seamanship.

Interpreting Bottom Conditions

The basic factor in interpreting bottom condtions is that a hard bottom will reflect an echo more strongly than a soft one. When you want to read bottom echoes only, set the gain control at the minimum position that will give a good, consistent signal.

To understand how various types of bottoms affect echoes, consider the sound beam as a conical beam of light. If the bottom were perfectly hard and flat, there would be one bright, sharp echo.

ELECTRONIC AIDS TO NAVIGATION

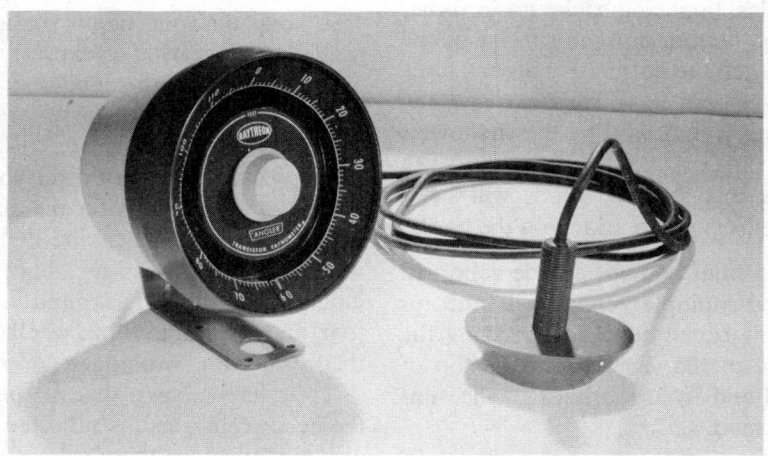

The Portable "Fathometer" has its own battteries inside the indicator unit at left. The transistorized "Angler" is six inches in diameter and five inches deep. Transducer, right, can be mounted permanently through the bottom of the boat or hung over the side for temporary use. *(Courtesy Raytheon Co.)*

The Portable "Angler" Fathometer depth sounder emits ultrasonic signals to indicate depth of water, tell type of bottom, and signal when boat passes over a school of fish. Powered by its own self-contained mercury battery or a boat's 12 volt DC system the depth sounder probes from 2 to 120 feet. *(Courtesy Raytheon Co.)*

Since this is seldom the case, the echoes from a hard bottom are reflected at various angles, bouncing back and forth between the bottom and the surface of the water. When the bottom is rocky, a large number of echoes will appear and the true depth is indicated by the shallowest reading. In the recording type depth sounders this shallow depth will be a clear, well-defined marking on the paper.

Over a mud bottom, a wide echo will show and multiple echoes will not appear. This broad echo is caused by the reflection of the signal from the top of the mud and from the hard surface under the mud.

Another indication of bottom conditions is the relative setting of the gain control needed in order to obtain echoes at various depths. The strongest echoes are obtained from a point where air and water meet. Echoes from other materials in diminishing order of strength are: rock, sand, metal, wood, mud, fish, plankton.

Multiple echoes are those received after the first echo and are caused by reflections back and forth between the bottom and the surface. These echoes show up as multiples of the true depth and they may be eliminated by reducing the gain control.

"Strays" are intermediate flashes of an indicator and random dark marks on a recorder. They may be caused by screws of a passing vessel, fish, faulty electrical equipment of your boat, your own shaft and stern bearing, or a rough or loose fairing which causes turbulence across the face of the transducer.

Finding Fish

In order to recognize a fish when you "see" one on your depth sounder, you need an idea of what to expect; also how to adjust your depth sounder so you will see it.

At their best, echoes from fish are relatively weak. Whether or not you obtain echoes at all depends on the size of an individual fish, the size and density of a school, where the fish or school is in relation to the sound beam and to the bottom, and most important, whether or not the fish has an air bladder.

Tests have shown that 40 percent of the echo from a fish is reflected from its air bladder. Since these echoes are quite weak in any case, it is necessary to run your boat at low speed and with the gain control of the depth sounder turned high in order to "see" any fish.

On indicator depth sounders, echoes from fish show as intermittent flashes between the zero and bottom echoes. These signals do not interfere with the bottom reading. With a recorder depth sounder, when the gain control is advanced to look for fish, you will notice that the paper darkens or smears. This is normal and fish will show up as very dark spots or clouds between the bottom and the surface.

"Fathometer"

The term "fathometer" is often used to describe the depth sounder, or depth finder as some manufacturers call it, but the "Fathometer" name is actually the exclusive trademark of the Raytheon Manufacturing Company and identifies their depth sounders.

CHAPTER XV

Basic Small Boat Piloting

Charts

Charts are the most basic of all piloting equipment used in coastal waters. They are issued by the Coast and Geodetic Survey of the Department of Commerce, the Hydrographic Office of the Navy Department, and the Corps of Engineers of the Department of the Army. The Corps of Engineers issues charts that show the Great Lakes and inland waterways; they also depict adjacent areas, the buoy systems (coastal and inland waterway), depth of water, lighted aids to navigation, manmade objects, danger areas, obstructions, and other features significant in safe piloting.

The frame of reference for all chart construction is the system of parallels of latitude and meridians of longitude. All portions of the chart are referenced in terms of latitude or longitude. A topographic survey determines the characteristics of the land and its adjacent water areas. A hydrographic survey determines the characteristics of the sea floor. The depths of the bottom are determined by taking many soundings of the area charted. The soundings are placed on the chart in correct relation to other objects. On a finished chart, areas in which the depth of water is up to 30 feet are usually shown tinted; areas where the depth is greater than 30 feet are usually shown untinted.

Figure 1 shows a portion of a Coast and Geodetic Survey chart. The scale is 1 to 400,000 (polyconic projection). The black dots on the chart indicate lights, the diamond shapes indicate buoys. True directions are given in degrees.

Types of Charts

Three methods of projection are used in the making of charts: Mercator, polyconic, and gnomonic. There are several other types of projections, but these are the methods used in marine navigation.

Mercator Chart: The Mercator chart (*1, Fig. 2*) is used most often. The chart is constructed by laying out the surface of the earth as represented by points a, b, c, and d when projected on the Mercator chart. The advantage of this chart is that a vessel's course can be represented on it as a straight line.

Polyconic Chart: The polyconic chart (*2, Fig. 2*) is laid out as a series of different cones, one for each unit of longitude. Distortion is less in this type of projection than the others. A vessel's course appears as a curved line on a polyconic map.

Gnomonic Chart: The Gnomonic projection (*3, Fig. 2*) is the one used principally for finding the course and distance by great circle sailing. The projection is drawn as though the earth's surface were seen by an observer from the center of the earth and projected on a plane tangent to the surface. As the plane of every great circle passes through the earth's center, the course line will appear as a straight line. The meridians converge toward the poles and the parallels crown toward the equator. The distortion for meridians increases toward the outer edges of the chart and decreases for the parallels toward the equator.

Each chart will show which method of projection was used in its production.

158 ENCYCLOPEDIA OF PLEASURE BOATING

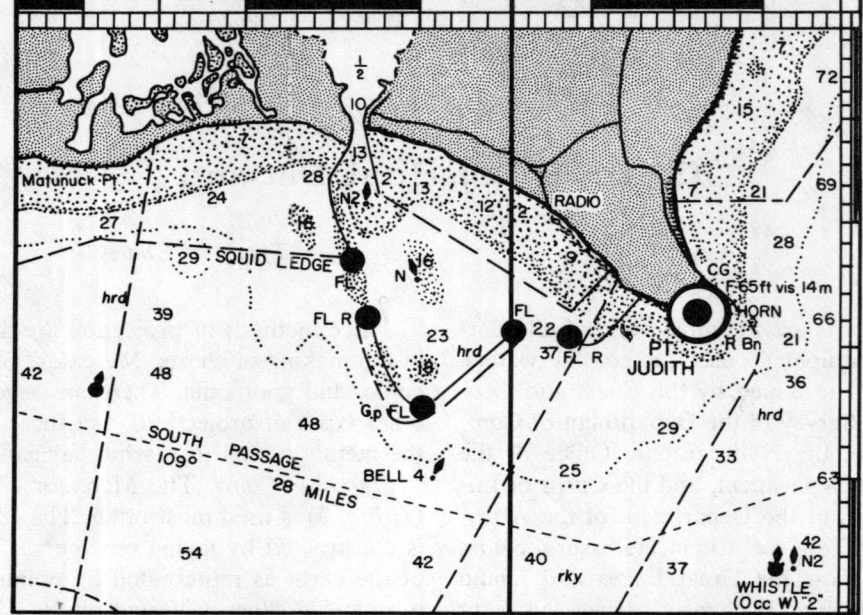

Fig. 1. A Section of a Coast and Geodetic Survey Chart.

Fig. 2. Mercator, Polyconic, and Gnomonic Projection.

Scales Used

Scales may be in inch, foot, yard, or mile units so long as the ratio is maintained. It is the responsibility of the user to verify the unit of scale used on the chart. Most sailing charts are plotted on a scale smaller than 1 to 1,200,000.

General charts of the coast are projected on a scale of 1 to 400,000 or 1 to 200,000, and are intended for coastwise navigation.

Coastal charts are usually drawn on a scale of 1 to 80,000; this large scale makes it easier to plot courses through channels when entering large bays and harbors.

Harbor charts are plotted on a large scale and are intended to meet the needs of local navigation.

The New Small Boat Charts

One of the problems of navigating a small boat is the size of the standard charts which are made for the wheelhouse of large ships. However, the U.S. Coast and Geodetic Survey has begun preparing a series of compact, folding type charts, about the size of the familiar automobile trip-ticks, just for the convenience of the small boatman. In addition to the information found on a regular chart, these charts will also contain such information as distances, magnetic courses, storm signals, Weather Bureau broadcast schedules, tide and current information, calls for local radiotelephone stations, and available boating facilities.

This type of chart is known as the Small Boat Chart. At the time of writing, two of these are available, No. 101 covering the Potomac River, and No. 140 covering the Miami, Florida boating area. One covering the Long Island, New York, area is being worked on.

Measuring Distance on the Chart

When the scale of miles is not given on the chart (and remember that they use the nautical, not the common statute mile), distance can be measured by using dividers on the latitude scales on the east and west edges of the chart. In Figure 1, the longitude scale is along the top of the illustration (the north) and the latitude scale is along the right (east) side of the chart. For instance, if the distance between Point Judith and the whistle buoy (lower right) is required, it can be obtained by:

1. Setting the points of a pair of dividers on Point Judith and the whistle buoy.
2. Transferring the dividers to the latitude scale and reading the distance in minutes and tenths. In this case, the distance would be approximately 1.1 minutes or 1.1 nautical miles. When the distance to be measured is greater than the span of the dividers, the dividers can be set at a minute or number of minutes of latitude from the scale, then *stepped off* (walked along) a line drawn between the points to be measured. The last span, if not equal to that set on the dividers, must be measured separately by bringing the points of the divider to the remaining distance and then measuring that along the line being measured. (The longitude scale is never used for measuring distance.)

Notes and Dates on Charts

The user of a chart must take care that the chart is of recent issue and contains up-to-date corrections. An outdated chart can be worse than no chart at all, as aids to navigation change; new obstructions appear; channels may shift; and a hundred things may happen to create a danger where an old chart shows clear sailing ahead.

The notes on the chart should be read attentively because they may contain important information that cannot be presented graphically. The units in which soundings are expressed vary on charts, so note carefully what unit is used on any particular chart.

Charts have *three* dates which must be understood by persons using them. These are, the month and year of the:

1. Edition—printed on the latest charts below the border in a central position.
2. Latest correction to the chart plates —printed in the lower left side, below the border.
3. Issue—stamped below the border and just to the left of the subtitle.

Charts show all essential corrections concerning lights, beacons, buoys and dangers which have been received to the date of issue. The latest correction date is printed in the lower left corner of the chart. Corrections occurring after the date issue are published in the *Notice to Mariners* (more about that later) and must be entered by hand on the chart.

Planes of Reference

The water-depth soundings plotted on charts actually express the height of water above the bottom at the position marked for a certain water level known as the *datum plane*. The datum is generally an average of low water level. The effect of this reduction of soundings to such a level is to indicate minimum depths during most periods; this provides the mariner with a margin of safety. However, the water can be lower than the indicated depth under some conditions.

The plane of reference for soundings on Hydrographic Office charts made from United States Government surveys and on Coast and Geodetic Survey charts of the Atlantic Coast of the United States is the mean of low water. On the Pacific Coast of the United States as far north as the Strait of Juan de Fuca, it is the mean of the lower low waters. From Puget Sound to Alaska, the Coast and Geodetic Survey charts show the *harmonic,* or Indian tide, plane which is roughly that of the lowest low waters observed.

In Lake Survey charts, the plane of reference is the mean elevation of the lake above mean tide of New York.

In using the chart for navigation, whenever soundings are used as a basis for determining positon, the datum plane and tide conditions must be considered.

Chart Symbols and Abbreviations

The nautical chart can convey much information to the user if he will familiarize himself with the symbols and abbreviations used on them, and study the information on the reverse of most charts. The illustration shows the symbols and abbreviations used on all charts made by the Coast and Geodetic Survey and the Hydrographic Office. Study of these will enable the amateur navigator to understand the meaning of these symbols and abbreviations.

The following facts pertaining to heights, depths and visibility of lights must be kept in mind when examining data on a nautical chart:

1. Soundings may be expressed in either feet or fathoms. The navigator must know which unit of measurement was used to record the data on the chart.
2. Heights of land or other conspicuous objects are found below the title and are given in feet above mean high water (unless otherwise noted on the chart).
3. Elevations of rocks, lighthouses, contours, and hills are also given in feet above mean high water.
4. Elevations of mountan peaks, if underlined, refer to heights in feet above mean sea level.
5. The coastline as charted represents the line of mean high water.
6. Visibility of lights is given in nautical miles and is computed on the assumption that the observer's eye is *15* feet above water level. (Note: This 15-foot level creates a bit of a problem for pleasure boatmen. In an outboard the operator's eye is only a few feet above water level; very few pleasure boats bring the boat's pilot to that height. In addition, many aids to navigation are set with this same assumption and the man in a low boat must proceed by dead reckoning from one buoy to another which would be visible from a higher deck.)
7. Dredged channels, with the depth, month and year of latest examination, are shown by limiting dash lines.

Temporary Changes

Caution must be observed with respect to temporary changes which affect lights, buoys and daybeacons. When an aid to navigation has been destroyed or removed, but is to be re-established (although temporarily replaced

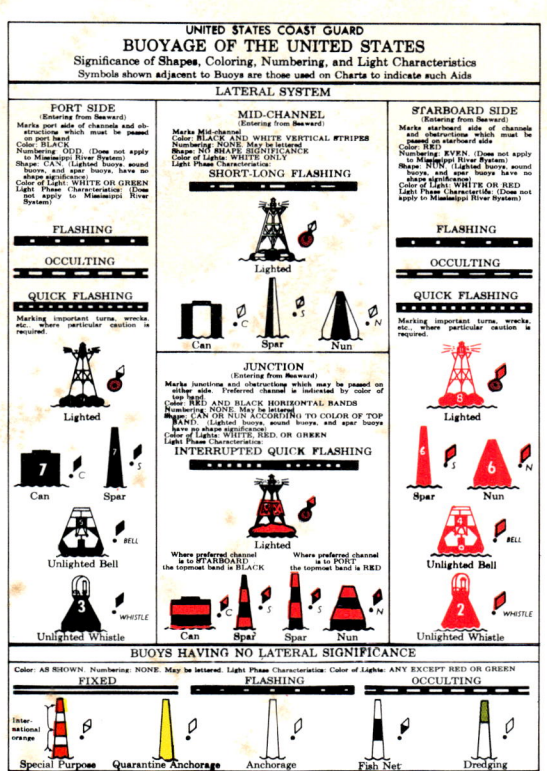

Buoyage system of the United States.

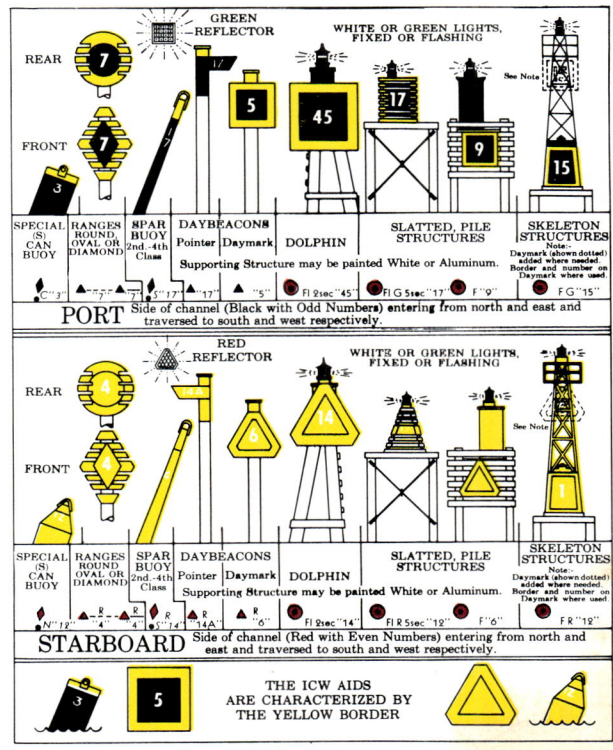

Types of aids to navigation Intracoastal Waterway.

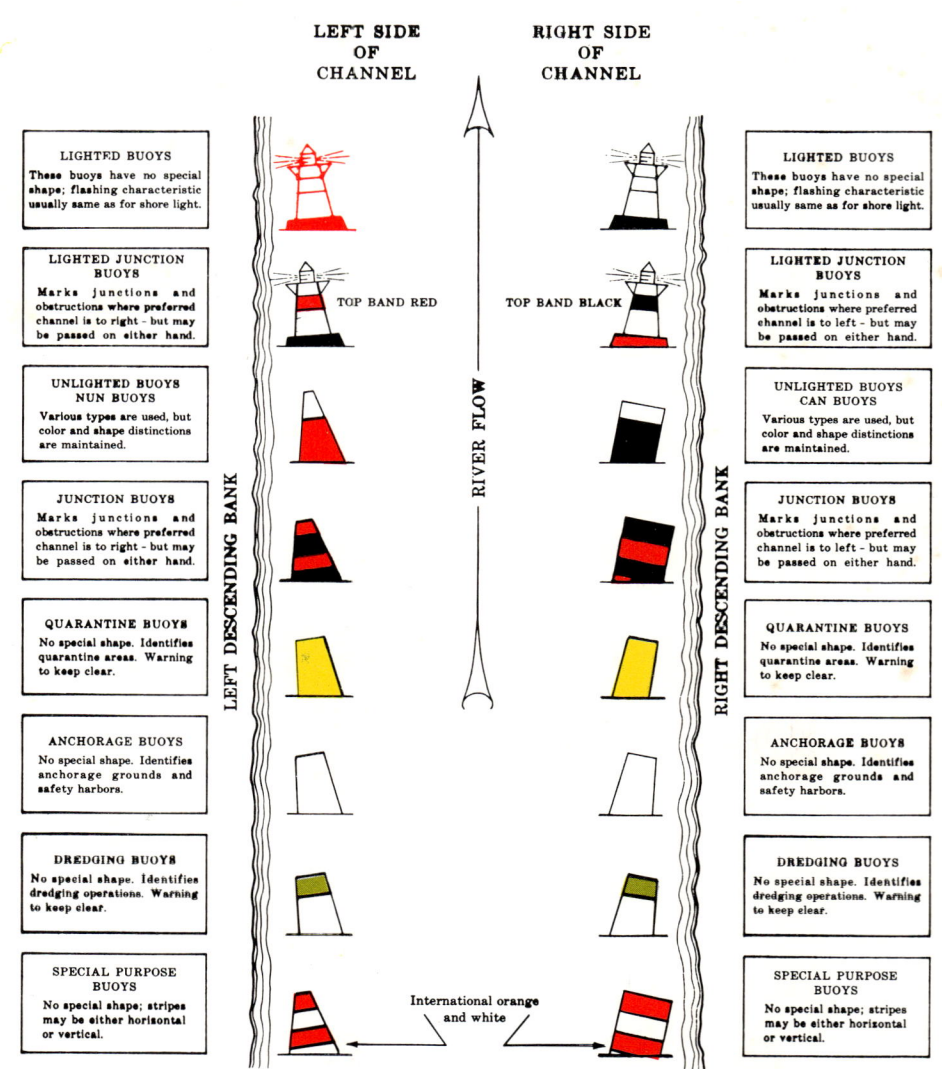

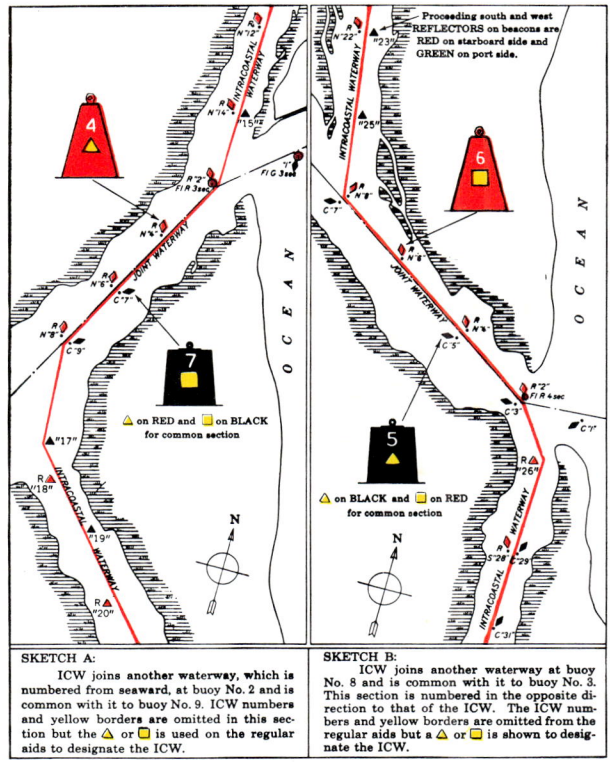

Illustrating the system of dual purpose marking where the ICW and other waterways coincide.

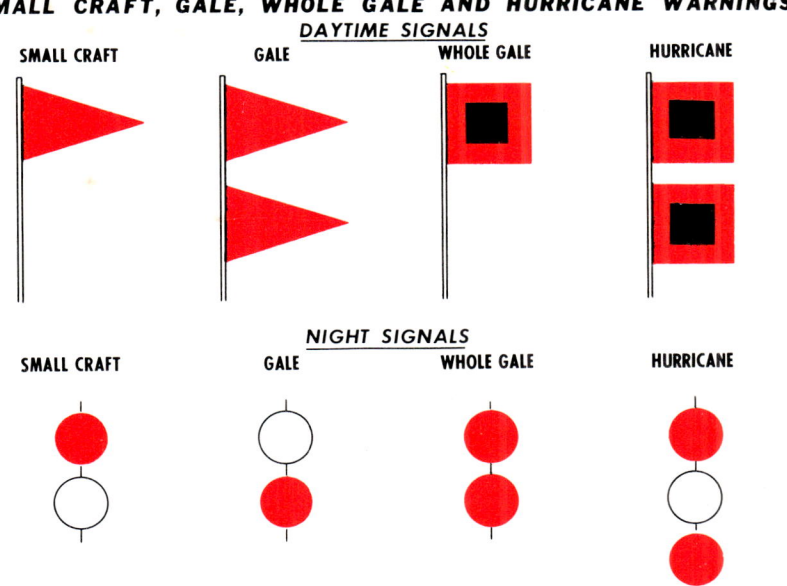

Storm warning signals.

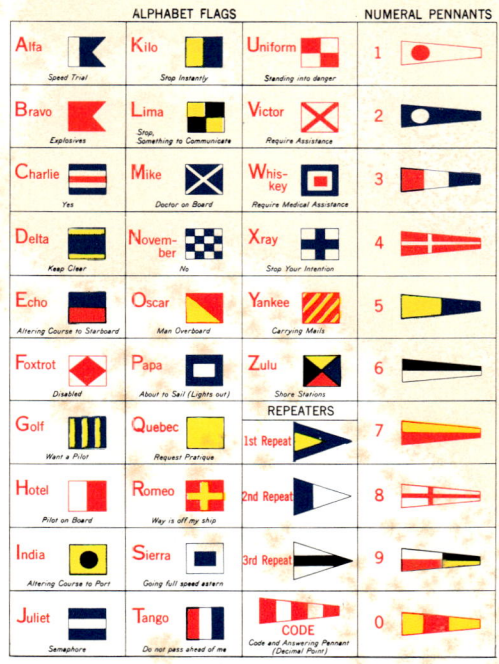

(U.S. Navy Hydrographic Office)
International flags and pennants.

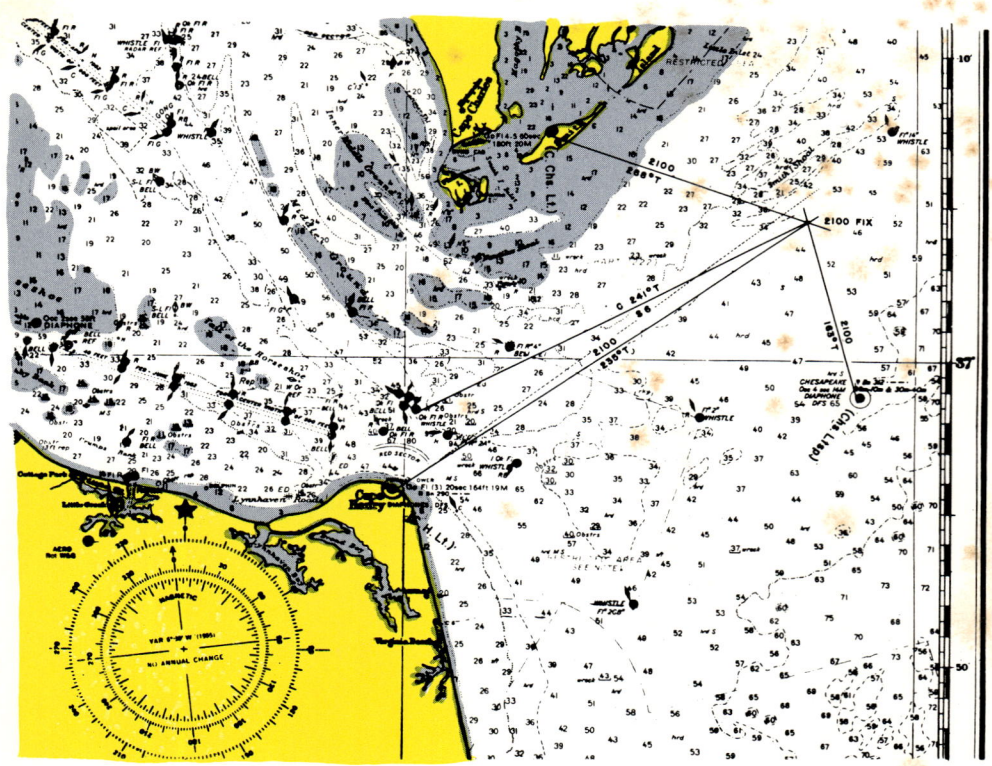

Section of a chart (Chesapeake Bay, southern part).

Group A of the new classification shows features of the coastline; B, abbreviations of coast features; C, the land; D, control points; E, abbreviations for units; and F, adjectives.

Symbols relating to harbors are included in Group G, those showing various characteristics of topography in Group H. At the right, in Group I, are given the symbols and abbreviations used in designating buildings on a chart. Charts are tinted tan, blue and green to aid in differentiating certain features. See key to colors at the right.

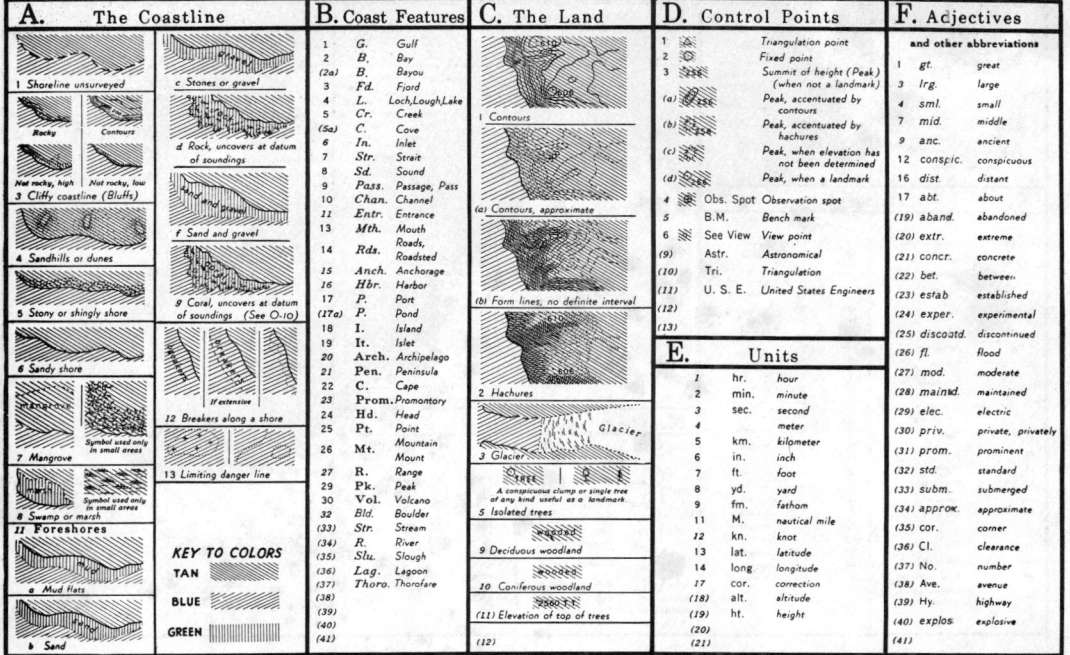

Chart symbols and abbreviations.

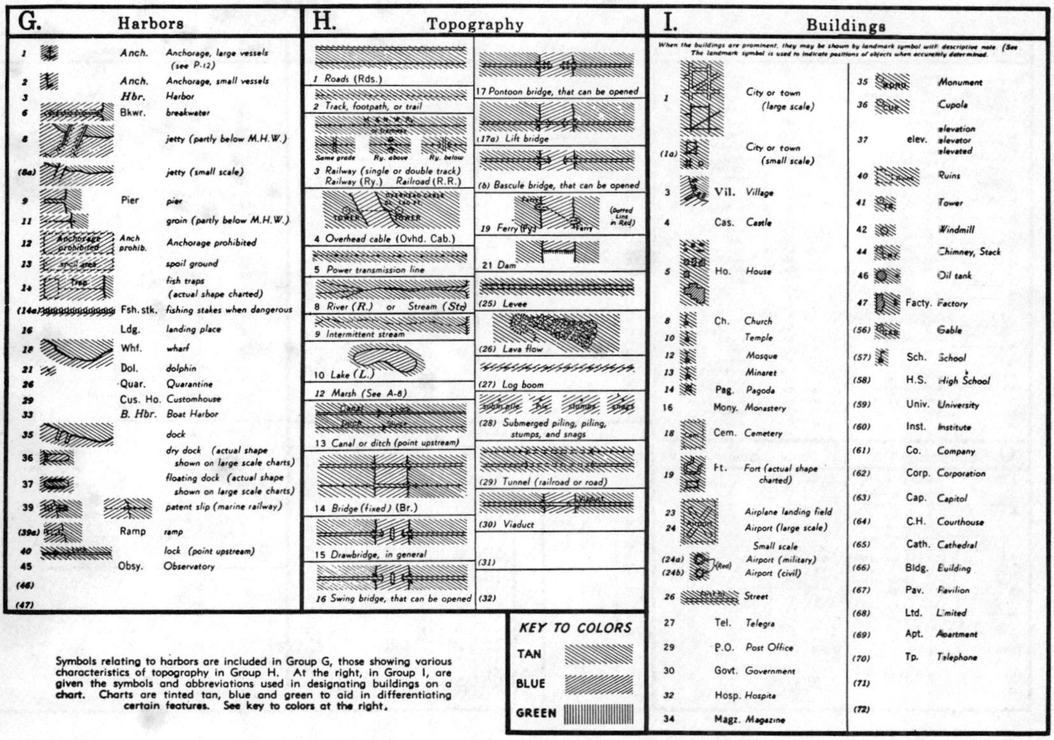

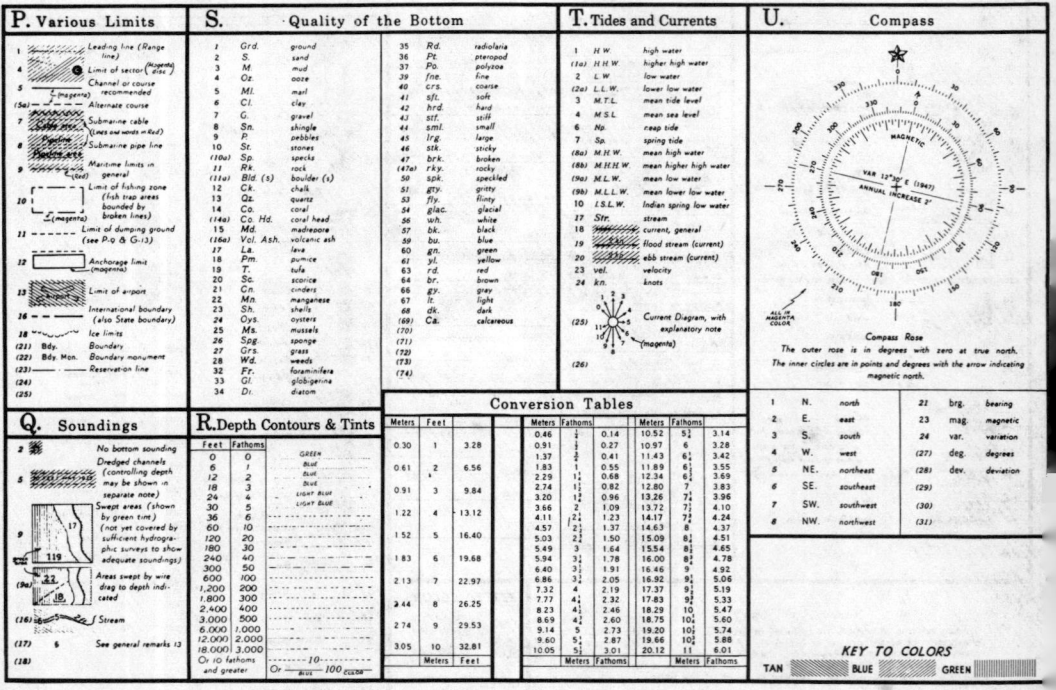

by an aid with a different characteristic), its status is indicated in red by the following abbreviations.
1. D—Destroyed, to be re-established.
2. TRB—Temporarily replaced by a red buoy.
3. TBB—Temporarily replaced by a black buoy.
4. TFB—Temporarily replaced by a fixed white-lighted buoy.
5. TFRB—Temporarily replaced by a fixed red-lighted buoy.
6. T FL B—Temporarily replaced by a flashing white-lighted buoy.
7. T FL RB—Temporarily replaced by a flashing red-lighted buoy.
8. T FL GB—Temporarily replaced by a flashing green-lighted buoy.

Government Nautical Publications

Because of the physical limitations on the amount of information that can be presented in chart form—and the many things which must be considered in piloting even a small boat—a number of government publications are necessary to supplement the chart; some of these should always be on hand during actual navigation on a long trip or in unfamiliar waters. The publications most frequently used will be discussed here.

Tide Tables

Tide Tables are publications of the Coast and Geodetic Survey that give the predicted times and heights of high and lower water for each day of the year at a number of reference points known as reference stations. Additional data for intermediate stations are tabulated in the section entitled "Tidal Differences and Constants." This data is of obvious interest to fishermen, and is carried by many local newspapers on their sports pages in addition to often being reported on local radio stations with the news and weather.

Current Tables

Current Tables, also published by the Coast and Geodetic Survey, give time of maximum flood, maximum ebb, and slack water. The velocity or strength of the current is given in nautical miles per hour (knots). The tables are published in three volumes—*Atlantic Coast, North America; Pacific Coast, North America;* and *Philippine Islands.*

Tidal Current Charts and Diagrams

Tidal Current Charts and Diagrams issued by the Coast and Geodetic Survey are available for eight important bodies of water: New York Harbor, Boston Harbor, San Francisco Bay, Long Island Sound, Narragansett Bay to Nantucket Sound, Delaware Bay and River, and Puget Sound. These charts provide valuable information which mean the difference between carrying the strength of the current throughout the entire passage or bucking an unfavorable flow for long periods. All current diagrams are included in the current tables except the one for Chesapeake Bay which is drawn on a large scale and issued as a separate publication.

You can find additional information on the use of tidal and current tables in Hydrographic Office Publication No. 9 (H.O. No. 9).

Notice to Mariners

Notice to Mariners is the free weekly publication of the Hydrographic Office by which charts and the other government publications may be kept up to date. Part I covers the Western Hemisphere; part II covers the Eastern Hemisphere. In addition—and these will be more useful to the pleasure boatman—local notices are issued by Coast Guard Commanders for their respective districts.

Coast Pilots

Published in ten volumes by the Coast and Geodetic Survey, these guides contain detailed and complete sailing directions between ports in the United States waters, including recommended courses and exact distances. They describe channels, giving their controlling depths and list all known dangers and obstructions in the channels and navigable areas.

Light Lists

Light Lists covering the lights and aids to navigation of the United States are published in six volumes by the Treasury Department, United States Coast Guard (CG 158). This contains the *North Atlantic List; South Atlantic List; Pacific List; Great Lakes List; Intracoastal List;* and *Mississippi River List.* These lists describe the lighthouses, lightships, radio beacons, and buoys maintained by the Coast Guard in all navigable waters of the United States. The information includes the official name of the aid, the characteristics of its light, sound, and radio signals, structural appearance, position and dimensions for taking angles. The Hydrographic Office publishes *Light Lists* also for foreign waters.

Pilot Rules

Pilot Rules, published by the U. S. Coast Guard, regulate navigation upon certain inland waters of the United States. These rules govern the display of lights, fog, passing and day signals, and speed.

Special Publications

The Hydrograhic Office also publishes the following special data for the pilot: *Sailing Directions; Hydrographic Bulletin; Daily Memorandum; Pilot Charts; Radio Navigational Aids (H.O. No. 205),* and *Radio Weather Aids (H.O. No. 206).*

PILOTING INSTRUMENTS

There are many different kinds of piloting instruments used to determine the position of a boat—which is the essence of piloting. Instruments in general use in pleasure boating will be briefly discussed here. More detailed information can be found in texts on navigation, or can be acquired through the advanced courses in piloting offered free of charge to pleasure boatmen (and women) by the United States Power Squadrons.

The Magnetic Compass

The magnetic compass is a magnet (actually, more often a number of long, thin magnets) suspended in a manner which allows absolute freedom of movement in a horizontal plane. The magnet aligns itself with the earth's magnetic field and thus points to the magnetic north and magnetic south. Every marine compass has a *lubber's line* marked on its case or mounting. This is a fixed reference line set on, or placed parallel to, the centerline of the boat and which indicates the heading of the ship with reference to the floating compass card.

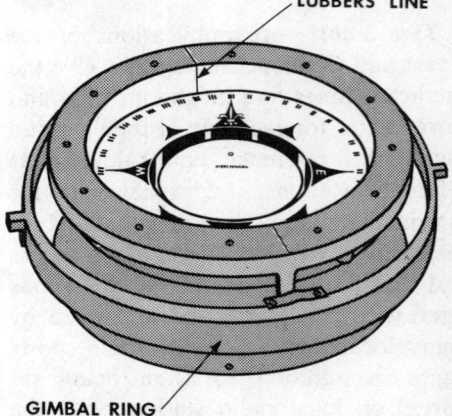

The magnetic compass.

The compass card is marked by degrees in a 360 circle with north as 000. Some compass cards are also marked with the cardinal and intercardinal points such as: *N, NE, S, SE, W, SW* and so forth. However, the numerical degree system is more adaptable to use in performing the necessary computations.

The magnetic compass is subject to two influences or errors which prevent it from pointing to the geographic North Pole and which must be considered when navigating.

One of these errors called *variation* is primarily caused by the earth's magnetic poles not being located in the same positions as the geographic poles, and their habit of shifting around over the years. The *compass rose* on the chart shows the amount of variation for points on the particular chart, and thus the correction that must be made to translate a compass reading to a "true" magnetic reading. The compass rose also shows the annual change in variation that must be figured for accurate piloting by compass.

The housing of the magnetic compass, called a *binnacle*, is made of nonmagnetic material, usually wood or brass. It contains features for compass correction, and, in the larger compasses, for illumination. However, attempting to correct a compass is not a job for the amateur, but for the trained adjuster. The best advice is never to meddle with the adjustment screws of the compass.

The correction devices may be used by the adjuster to compensate for the second type of magnetic error, called *deviation*. This is the error caused by the magnetic influences in the metal of the ship itself, its fittings, electrical system, the metallic mass of its motor, etc. Unlike variation, which is constant in any one locations and time, the deviation error changes with every different heading, or direction of the ship, and is seldom the same for any two headings. Even if the compass has been corrected, or a deviation table (a later topic) is drawn

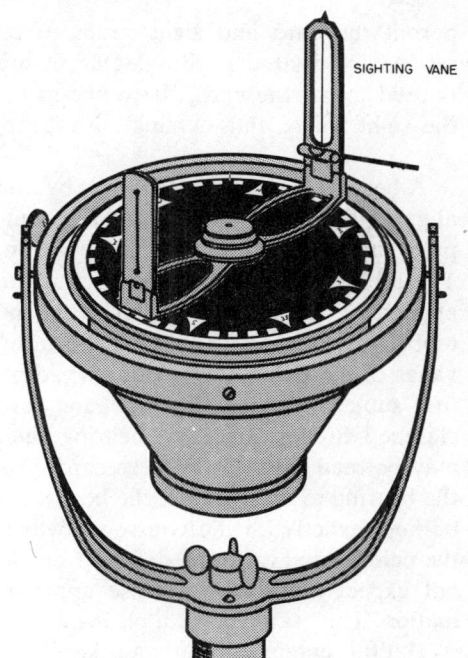

One type of Pelorus.

up, care should be exercised to keep "attractive" influences away from the compass. A portable radio; any piece of metallic equipment; even a heavy pocket knife in the belt or pocket of a person near the compass can cause a change in the deviation error of the compass.

The Pelorus

The Pelorus is a dummy compass fitted with sight vanes for taking bearings. It is generally made of brass and is wholly non-magnetic. The pelorus is suspended in gimbals and in the larger boats is mounted on a stand, although the hand-held type is generally used by pleasure boatmen. To keep it in a horizontal position, a weight is usually attached to the underside of the instrument. The dial, or card, has a compass rose painted or engraved upon it and is divided into 360°. The card and sight vanes revolve independently of each other upon a pivot. Two clamps, one above the other on the top of the pivot, permit the card and sight vanes to be set in any desired position. One clamp is used to set the card, the other to set the sight vanes, thus "fixing", any bearing.

A bearing is taken on an object by first aligning the pelorus card with the compass card and clamping it in position. The lubber's line of the pelorus must be aligned with the boat's keel—with the lubber line of the compass. The sighting vanes of the pelorus are then aligned on the subject of the bearing and are clamped in position. The bearing then may be read from the pelorus card. For the bearing to be accurate, the boat must be kept exactly on the course on which the pelorus dial is clamped. However, do not expect more than a close approximation. The "skipper" of a pleasure boat is skillful enough if he can keep his course within a few points, since current, wind and seas make it more difficult to hold course. If someone else is aboard, have them call out when the boat is closely on course, and take the bearing at that moment.

Keep in mind that the pelorus bearing is a compass bearing and must be corrected in the same manner as a compass reading (more of that very soon). The pelorus is also used to obtain relative bearings. In obtaining a bearing of this kind, the pelorus is clamped in position with 000 on the lubber's line. After the lubber's line is aligned with the boat's keel, a bearing can be taken, the sighting vanes clamped in position, and the bearing read. This bearing is relative to the boat's heading at the time the bearing was taken and must be added to the boat's heading to obtain the compass bearing of the subject.

The Hand Lead Line and Depth Finder

The echo-sounding device (sonic depth finder) is similar to radar except that sound waves are used instead of radio waves. The sonic depth finder is used to determine the depth of water under the keel of the boat. It uses the principle that sound travels in sea water at an average speed of 4,800 feet or 800 fathoms per second. Therefore, an elapsed time of one second between transmission of the sound and reception of the echo would indicate a depth of 400 fathoms. Indicators may not only indicate depth visually, but may also make a permanent record of depths by moving a stylus on a special type of paper. The depth-record can be matched with the chart's indication of water depths as another important aid to fixing the boat's location on the water.

The hand lead line is more likely to meet the needs of the average pleasure boat operator as a device for determining the depth of water. It consists of a suitable marked line and a shaped lead weight. The weight of the lead and length of the line will, of course, vary with the size of the vessel. Generally, a 25-fathom line with a 5 to 14-pound weight is sufficient for harbor and coastal use.

Marking the Line

It is possible to mark off distance on the line with tags to show the different depths, but the true nautical method of marking the line is as follows:

Fathoms	Mark
2	2 strips of leather
3	3 strips of leather
5	White rag
7	Red rag
10	Leather strip with hole
13	3 strips of leather
15	White rag
17	Red rag
20	Cord with 2 knots
25	Cord with 1 knot

Using the Line

The bottom of the lead is hollowed

out to allow it to be *armed*. *Arming the lead* consists of packing grease or tallow into this hollow. When the lead strikes the bottom, it picks up particles which may be compared with data on the chart showing the nature of the bottom. An excellent check of the boat's position is often obtained in this manner.

In taking a sounding, the lead is cast well forward so that it will strike the bottom directly below the leadsman as the boat moves slowly through the water. The soundings are reported by the leadsman by calling the fathom points that are marked on the line as *marks* and the fathom points between as *deeps*. Depths between marks are estimated. The voice of the leadsman calling out his soundings is one of the romanticized features of American river life, and the great writer who used the pseudonym of Mark Twain might as well have called himself "Two-Fathom-Sam."

The following are examples of typical reports and corresponding depths:

Report	Depth (in fathoms)
By the mark five	5
And a quarter five	5 1/4
And a half five	5 1/2

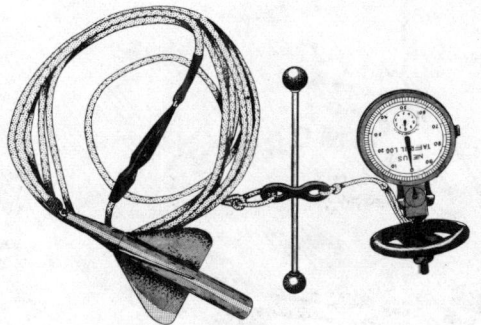

A Taffrail Log.

A quarter less six	5 3/4
By the deep six	6
And a quarter six	6 1/4
And a half six	6 1/2
A quarter less seven	6 3/4
By the mark seven	7

The Taffrail Log

The taffrail log is a device for measuring the distance run through the water. It consists of a rotator with spiral blades, a braided line for towing the rotator, and a mechanical device that registers the revolutions of the rotator and shows, on a dial, the distance run. To prevent erroneous readings, care should

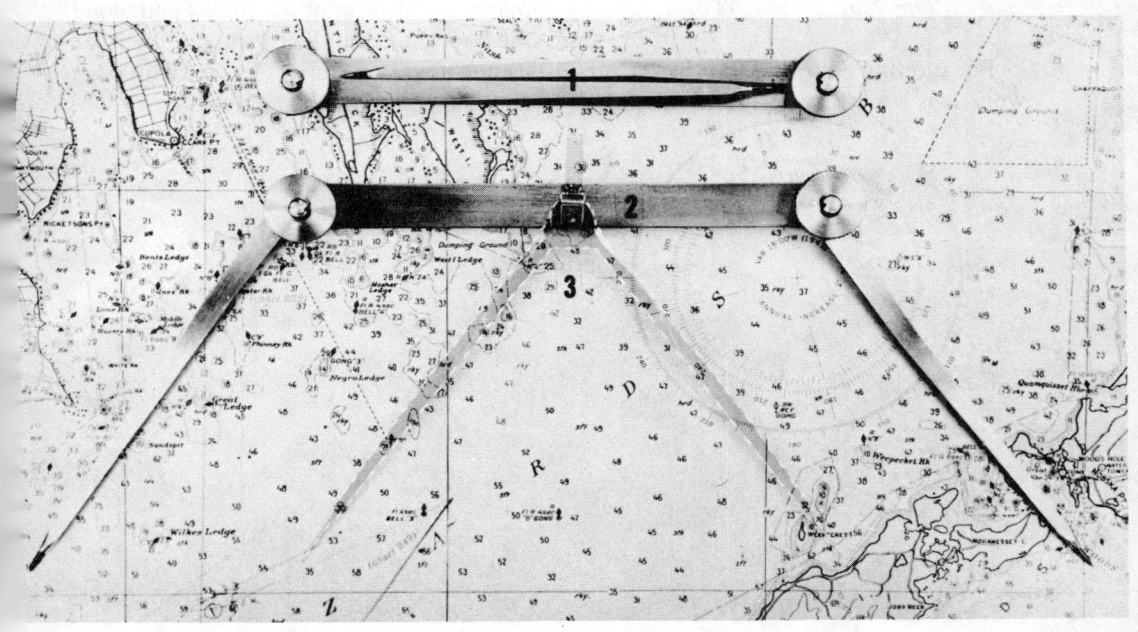

Dividers.

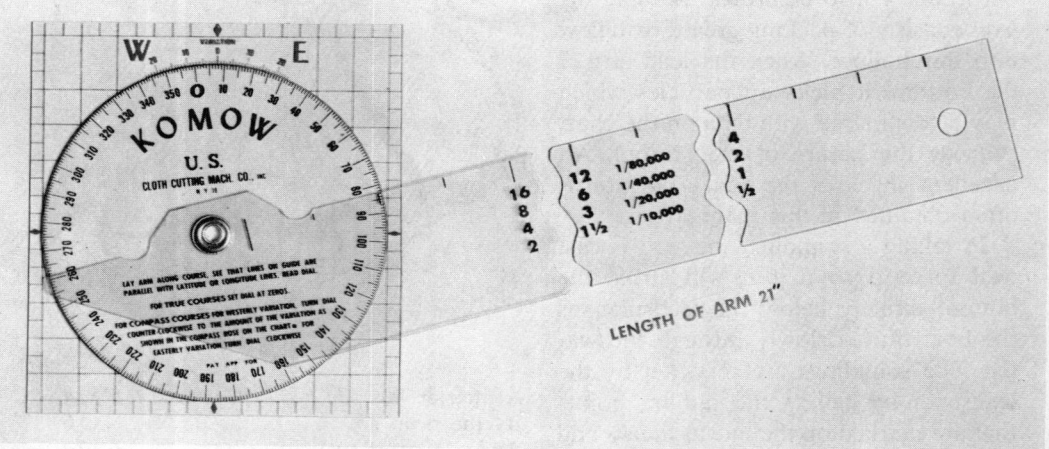

A course protractor.

be taken to insure that blades are not bent or fouled with seaweed. Dependent on the speed of the boat, the rotator should be approximately 70 to 100 percent of the vessel's length when trailed. The rotator is towed astern. Spinning as it is drawn through the water, it rotates the line and records revolutions on the counter in nautical miles. To secure it after use, the line should be streamed out from the counter end and coiled down, beginning with the rotator end.

The Navigator's "Tools"

For plotting courses and other "chart" work it is necessary to use dividers, and a course protractor or a parallel rule. The dividers are used for measuring distance on the chart. The course protractor consists of a clear plastic disc, marked in compass points and degrees, and a movable plastic arm pivoted at the center of the disc. It is used in transferring the line of bearing, or course drawn on the chart, to the compass rose on the chart to determine the bearing or course direction. The parallel rule (two straightedges joined by short, pivoted arms) accomplishes the same thing in a different manner. One arm of the rule is laid along the course line on the chart, and the ruler is moved in successive steps until an edge cuts the center of the compass rose.

CHAPTER XVI

Fundamentals of Piloting

Piloting is defined as the art of conducting a vessel in channels, harbors, and along coasts by determining the position of the vessel by the aid of terrestrial objects and by soundings — with reference to the appropriate chart. While much of the pleasure boatman's cruising may be safely managed by use of a chart and the visual aids to navigation, there is considerable satisfaction in being able to do a professional job of piloting in strange waters. In many pleasure boating areas the changing depth of waters and the dangers to navigation require constant watch and frequent changes in course for safe cruising.

Piloting is a complicated matter, requiring considerable experience and judgment.

Using the Compass

The basic tool of the pilot is the mariner's compass, and piloting would be much easier if the needle of the compass could be made to point to true north. The gyrocompass, which does indicate the true north, is far too cumbersome and expensive for the pleasure boat. Therefore, the amateur pilot must perform some fairly involved "figgering" to translate the direction in which his compass needle points to true north on the chart he is using.

The first error in the compass reading is caused by the fact that the magnetic compass points to what is termed "magnetic north." The angle of difference between magnetic north and true north is called *variation* and is usually expressed in degrees and minutes of arc. This variation, and the annual changes in variation, are indicated in the magnetic rose on the chart. Variation changes and is normally not constant for any given location. Therefore, all compass readings must be corrected for variation unless the boat happens to be in a rare area of "no variation" where the magnetic north and true north happen to be in the same line from the boat's position.

Variation, when present, is either easterly or westerly, depending on the location of the compass on the earth. If the magnetic pole is to the west of geographic north at the location, variation is west; if the magnetic pole lies to the east at the location, variation is east. For example, the variation at Fort Eustis, Virginia, is 6° westerly. This means that the compass needle while pointing to the magnetic north is actually pointing 6° west of true north, or 354°. If a ship were steering a course of 369° by the magnetic compass (no deviation considered), the true course would be 6° less than 360° or 354° — a considerable difference over any long run.

Note these two principles:

1. *When variation is west, the amount of variation should be subtracted from the magnetic course to find the true course.*

2. *When variation is east, the amount should be added to the magnetic course to find the true course.*

Deviation

In addition to variation, there is a second error in the magnetic compass which must be considered. This error is called *deviation*. This error is caused by magnetic influences of the ship itself: metal in the hull; particularly the magnetic "pull" of the engines or the outboard motor; magnetic influences set up by the wiring in the boat, etc. Deviation is not a fixed figure, it usually changes when the ship changes course.

An experienced adjuster can adjust a compass to correct for deviation and usually charges in the neighborhood of $50.00 for this service. However, any subsequent changes in the boat may induce new deviations, such as the installation of new equipment, electrical changes, etc. Most pleasure boatmen find it more feasible to prepare, or have prepared a "deviation card" or Napier diagram, which shows the deviation on different ship's headings and allows for correction by computation. (Incidentally, the United States Power Squadron's courses devote several sessions to this subject.)

Variation and deviation are usually handled together, their sum comprising the *compass error*. This error when corrected and correctly applied to the compass course in accordance with the directional symbol of E (east) or W (west) gives the true course. The mariner's rule is "east you add; west you subtract when correcting." This is the method used to convert a compass course to a true course. The reverse procedure is used to convert a true course to a compass course.

A Summary. A vessel's course, therefore, may be named in any one of three ways:

1. *True course:* True course is the angle between the boat's heading and true north.

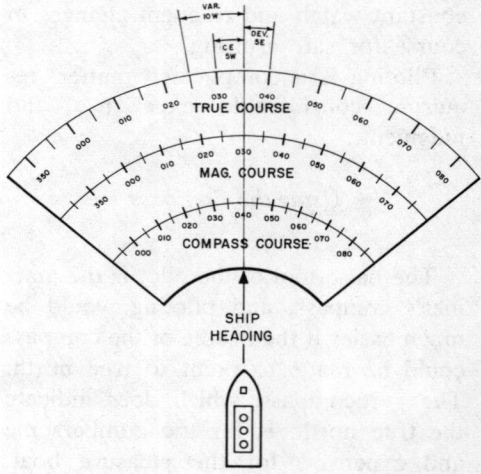

True, magnetic, and compass courses.

2. *Magnetic course:* Magnetic course is the angle between the boat's heading and magnetic north.

3. *Compass course:* Compass course is the angle between compass north and the boat's heading. Compass course represents the course that is actually read on the compass. The indications of this compass are termed *per standard compass,* usually abbreviated to *p.s.c.*

DEVIATION CARD

Ship's Name: FS-212
Date: July 15, 1955
Compass: Steering

Compass Course	Deviation	Compass Course	Deviation
0°	½°W	180°	1°W
15°		195°	
30°		210°	
45°	0	225°	1°W
60°		240°	
75°		255°	
90°	½°W	270°	½°W
105°		285°	
120°		300°	
135°	2°W	315°	1½°W
150°		330°	
165°		345°	

Lat. 37°N
Long. 74°W
W/O J. Smith, Adjuster

Typical compass-deviation card.

FUNDAMENTALS OF PILOTING

The Napier Diagram

To find a magnetic course from a compass course, or a compass course from a magnetic course, a simple Napier diagram may be plotted. To plot it, all that is required is knowledge of basic arithmetic and ability to read bearings from a compass and pelorus. However, it requires two persons working together, and the one at the helm should have enough experience to be able to keep the boat on a determined course, and preferably on smooth water.

Making a Deviation Table

The navigator of a boat, equipped with compass properly set on the boat so that the lubber's line is parallel with the keel, and a pelorus, selects a fixed object on shore and takes bearings on it in the following manner:

1. Instructs the helmsman to steer north by the compass.
2. Sets the pelorus with 000° on the lubber's line and clamps it there.
3. Swings the vanes of the pelorus around until he sights an object at least six miles away — a tower for example. When the helmsman informs him he is right on course, he reads the bearing — for example 068°. He then enters the bearing on a deviation computation table (See illustration).
4. Orders the helmsman to steer 015° by the compass.
5. Sets the pelorus with 015° on the lubber's line and clamps it there. Swings the vanes of the pelorus again until he sights the tower, and when informed by the helmsman that the vessel is on course, reads the bearing — for example, 060° — and enters this in the table.
6. This process is repeated for all headings 15° apart until the navigator has filled in the values in columns 1 and 2 of the table.
7. If the magnetic bearing of the tower is not known from the chart, the values of column 2 are then averaged (in this case 085°) to find the magnetic bearing of the tower.
8. The magnetic bearing of the tower is entered in column 3 of the table to make the arithmetic easier.
9. The difference between columns 2 and 3 for each heading gives the deviation to be entered in column 4.

Plotting a Deviation Curve on a Napier Diagram

The central line of the Napier diagram represents the outer rim of the compass card; the degrees from 000° to 360° are indicated by dots with each 5° interval being marked numerically. Deviations east or west are plotted along the inclined lines which are spaced at 15° intervals. If a deviation corresponds to a magnetic heading, it is set off parallel to the solid inclined lines labeled "mag-

(1) Ship's heading (p. s. c.)	(2) Bearing of tower (p. s. c.)	(3) Magnetic bearing of tower	(4) Deviation
°	°	°	°
000	068	085	17 E
015	060	085	25 E
030	055	085	30 E
045	055	085	30 E
060	060	085	25 E
075	068	085	17 E
090	078	085	7 E
105	089	085	4 W
120	097	085	12 W
135	102	085	17 W
150	104	085	19 W
165	103	085	18 W
180	098	085	13 W
195	094	085	9 W
210	090	085	5 W
225	089	085	4 W
240	090	085	5 W
255	093	085	8 W
270	096	085	11 W
285	098	085	13 W
300	097	085	12 W
315	094	085	9 W
330	087	085	2 W
345	078	085	7 E
	24)2043		
	085		

netic." If the deviation refers to a compass heading it is set off parallel to the dotted inclined lines labeled "compass." The two systems of inclined lines and the vertical line make a series of equilateral triangles. Therefore, deviations may be measured along the inclined lines as well as along the vertical line.

The deviation values in column 4 of the table are now easily placed on a printed form of the Napier diagram (available at any marine supply house) by:

1. Plotting the first easterly compass deviation in column 4 (17°E) along the dotted line (compass) which intersects the central line at 0° north, counting 17 dots from the central line and making a suitable reference mark.

2. Repeating this for the next easterly deviation (25°E) and marking it along the dotted line intersecting 15° on the central line.

3. Continuing this procedure for every deviation value for every heading recorded in column 1 of the table. In marking the deviations, care should be taken to note east or west deviation.

4. Drawing a smooth curve through the completed points on the diagram to represent the deviation.

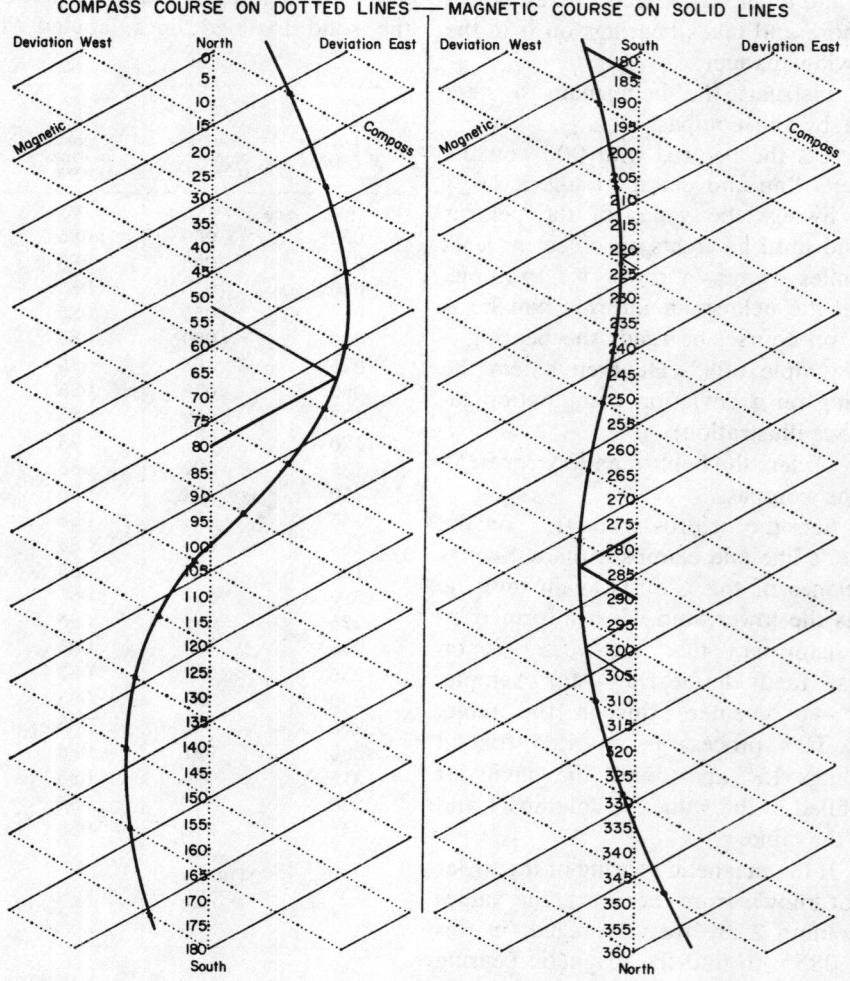

Napier diagram.

On most small boats, it is sufficient to record deviation from the Napier diagram every 45°. This deviation table should be posted near the compass for ready reference. It is important that this deviation card be dated and that deviations should be checked periodically, especially when the boat has been subjected to any disturbing forces such as engine or equipment changes. In a small boat, even the stowage of supplies or the bringing aboard of a portable radio can affect the deviation of the compass, and anything of a magnetic nature should be kept well away from the compass.

Labeling a Chart

In order that the information plotted on a chart may be of value to the navigator, a system of marking or labeling is required. The illustration (color section) showing part of Chesapeake Bay indicates the proper way to label a chart. All lines of position (bearings) and courses should be true (referring to directions). The alternate and intermingling use of magnetic bearings and true bearings can only result in errors. Lines of position and course should be drawn distinctly. Care should be taken not to draw heavy lines on the chart which may damage the chart or mislead the navigator when the chart is used again. Course lines should be labeled C (course) followed by the true course in three figures. On the lower side of the line, under the course label, S (speed) and numerals indicating the speed in knots should be written.

Over lines of position (bearing lines) the time of observation should be written in four figures; the three figures denoting the true bearing should be written beneath the time figure. The label now contains both a time notation and an abbreviation for the type of point identified. In the illustration these are the Cape Charles Light (C. Chs. Lt.); the Chesapeake Lightship (Chs. Ltsp.) and the Cape Henry Light (C.H. Lt.). Identification points are normally written to one side of the points they identify and at an angle to the course line or lines of position on which they lie.

The Cross Bearing

The chart illustration also shows how to make a "fix" using a cross bearing. The cross bearing is the most widely used method of obtaining a "fix." It affords a high degree of accuracy, especially when three bearings can be used for lines of position. The most accurate fixes are those obtained from lines of position that are at a 60° to 90° angle from each other and are made from established navigational marks. It is well to remember that whenever possible the navigational mark should be a landmark or a fixed light. Buoys may shift positions and are relatively hard to locate and identify from small vessels. It is most important to be sure that the mark being used for a bearing has been properly identified.

Obtaining a Fix From Two Visible Objects

For the purpose of explaining how a fix is obtained, assume that your are navigating a vessel approaching the Chesapeake Bay entrance. The last fix was obtained when the boat passed the Cape Charles lighted whistle buoy 14. The buoy was identified by referring to volume III of the *Local List of Lights and Other Marine Aids* which gave the latitude and longitude of the buoy and the characteristics of its light as FL. W. 6^s (2^{s}f) (Flashing-white, dark 4 seconds, duration of flash 2 seconds). At 2100, deciding to obtain a fix you adjust the compass card of the pelorus to correspond to the boat's compass and take a bearing on Cape Charles Light. You write this bearing down and immediately swing the sight vanes around and take a bearing on the Chesapeake Lightship, also writing it down.

Then you convert both bearings (compass) to true. The bearing taken on Cape Charles Light read "306°" and using the Napier diagram (assuming that the one a few pages back is the one for this boat), you convert that compass course to magnetic (294.30). Then noting in the center of the compass rose on the chart that the variation for this locality is 6°30′ W, you subtract this figure from magnetic, arriving at true (or 288°). Next, you place the edge of the parallel rulers through the exact center of the compass rose, and on 288° on the outer rose. Then, by alternately moving each ruler, you bring this bearing up on the chart until the edge of the ruler rests on the black center dot of Cape Charles Light. A line of position is then drawn on the chart as shown in the illustration. The same procedure is followed for the bearing taken on Chesapeake Lightship. The two intersecting lines of position make the "fix" as shown. Knowing your boat's exact position, you are now able to plot a course on the chart to pick up the whistle buoy at the channel entrance.

Obtaining a Fix From One Visible Object

In navigation, it is not always possible to see more than one established navigational mark at a time. Therefore, some means must be found for obtaining an accurate fix from one visible object. Several methods available to the navigator for accomplishing this are discussed in the following paragraphs. Fundamentally, these methods consist of using one bearing and a distance measurement. For example, if the first bearing taken in the previous example (288°) were used and if the distance from the light could be determined, a fix could be obtained by using only one line of position. Among the various available means of estimating distances — some of which are not readily available to the small boatman — are radar, loran, sextant angle of structures of known heights, range finders, and synchronized sounds, such as the diaphones of lightships and lighthouses. However, estimates of distance are never accurate and such fixes are always doubtful.

The Bow-and-Beam Method

The bow-and-beam method is used to determine position by taking a bearing and computing the distance over the ground which the boat has made. Currents and other factors must be considered when estimating distances run. The bow-and-beam method is shown in the illustration. The bearings used in this method of obtaining a fix are *relative bearings*. The term means that the bearing is in relation to the center line or keel of the boat. The bow of the vessel, therefore, is considered as being 000° and the stern as being 180°. Two relative bearings are used in this method, 45° and 90°. It makes no difference whether

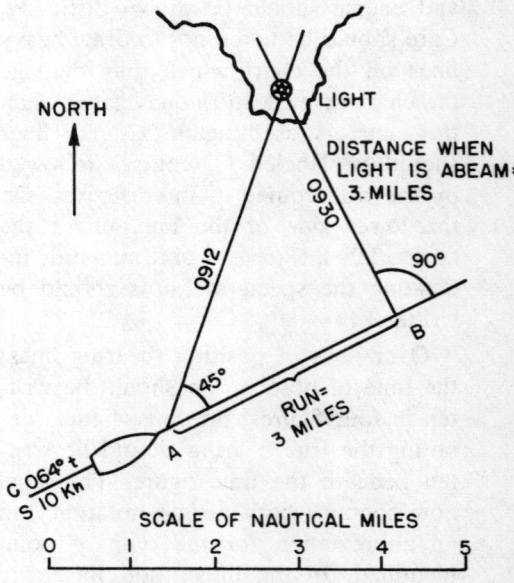

these bearings are taken to the left or right of the bow. The boat in the illustration has noted the exact time the light bore 45° to port. The time is again noted when the light bears exactly abeam, or 90° as at B. The run between points A and B is estimated from taffrail log revolutions during this time, or by other means available to the navigator. This estimated distance run is equal to the distance the boat is off the light when it reaches point B. This holds true only if the boat maintains the same course throughout the run.

A fix can be plotted on the chart from this method by noting that the boat's heading during the run was 090°. The line of position then, from B to the light must be 064° less 090°. In this case, 090° cannot be subtracted from 064°, therefore add 360° to 064° and then subtract, giving a *true* bearing from the boat to the light of 334° true. This line of position is drawn on the chart, then, with a pair of dividers, the distance run along this line is measured from the light to the ship, thus giving the desired fix.

The Seven-Tenths Rule

The seven-tenths rule makes use of two angles, 22-1/2° and 45°. Here, the time is noted when the navigational mark bears 22-1/2° off the bow. The time is again noted when the mark bears 45° off the bow. Again, the distance off is equal to the run between bearings. If the vessel maintains course until the mark is directly abeam, the distance off it will be seven-tenths the distance run between the first and second bearings.

The seven-tenths rule and the bow-and-beam bearings are two of the most valuable methods of determining position that are available to the navigator in coastwise navigation. For small boats not equipped with a pelorus, satisfactory results can be obtained if the 22-1/2°, 45°, and 90° points are marked in some manner, both port and starboard. Precisely placed thumb tacks in the railing can be used. It is not absolutely necessary to plot the estimated positions.

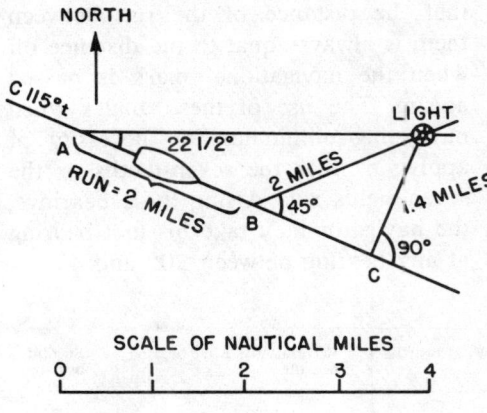

Doubling the Angle on the Bow

Study of the two preceding methods will reveal the simple mathematical principle involved. In each one, the angle on the bow of the second bearing was twice that of the first angle. This principle can be used by the navigator at any convenient time regardless of the angle of the first bearing. For example, a bearing is taken of a mark that bears 34° off the bow and the time is noted. Doubling the mark equals 68°; therefore the time is noted again when the mark bears 68° —vessel course and speed being unchanged. The distance run is equal to the distance off the mark at the time of the second bearing.

The Seven-Eighths Rule

This rule can be applied when the navigator has missed the 22-1/2° bearing necessary when using the seven-tenths rule. Just substitute 30° for the first bearing, 60° for the second bearing, and use seven-eighths of the distance run as the distance off the mark when it passes abeam.

Special Bearings

The bearings in the following table have such a relationship to each other that the distance of the run between them is always equal to the distance off when the navigational mark is passed abeam. The use of these angles when navigating eliminates the necessity of applying either the seven-tenths or the seven-eights rule. Using these bearings, the navigator may take his first bearing at any bearing between 20° and 45°.

First bearing	Second bearing	First bearing	Second bearing
°	°	°	°
20	30	33	61½
21	32	34	64½
22	34	35	67
23	37	36	69½
24	39	36½	71
25	41	37	72
26	43½	38	74
26½	45	39	77
27	46	40	79
28	48½	41	81
29	51	42	83½
30	53½	43	86
31	56	44	88
32	59	45	90

Special bearings.

Ranges and Their Uses

Range lights have been mentioned in the section on Aids to Navigation. When two beacons (or any two objects) appear to be in line as seen from the boat, that is, when one object is directly behind the other, the vessel is located somewhere on the straight line through these objects. Such a line is called a range and is the same as a line of position. Frequently two objects are placed so as to form a range that will mark the center of a channel. The boat is then steered so as to keep the markers in line. Ranges have been established for specific navigational purposes along the coast and within harbors and along the Intracoastal Waterway.

A typical range is shown in the illustration. When using such a range, the helmsman has only to keep the range closed to stay on course. Should the boat stray off course the range would begin to open; it could be closed by altering the boat's course. To be valuable in piloting, ranges need not be established navigational marks; they may be natural ranges, such as a church steeple and a water tower; a yacht club flagpole and a spire; a tree stump and a fence post, or two hills or mountains. In fact, many harbor boatmen have their own ranges that enable them to navigate prearranged courses without recourse to conventional navigational aids.

Piloting in Fog

The average pleasure boatman has no business being out in fog. Fog presents the pilot with his most difficult task by depriving him of visibility. Every aspect of navigation so far discussed requires

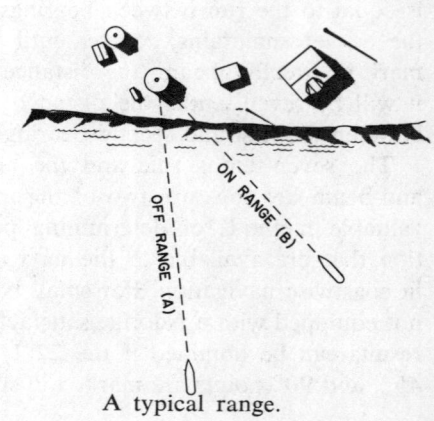

A typical range.

visibility. However, there is the ever-present possibility of being caught in the fog, and advance preparations can be made. Fog can be anticipated in several ways. Weather reports received by radio and visual indications are among them. Before fog closes in, the boatman should make every effort to get an accurate "fix" by any of the methods available to him. The appropriate chart, light list or coast pilot must be carefully checked for the location and characteristics of all buoys and lights within the area, with careful attention to those aids specifically useful in fog, such as sound signals, radio-beacons, bell and whistle buoys. The whistle should be blown in accordance with the covering rules of the road. (See that section in this book.)

For safety, it is most important that the speed of the boat be reduced in accordance with both the International and Inland Rules. *The speed of a vessel should be reduced to a speed that will make it possible to stop it in half the distance of visibility.* Running lights should be turned on, and, if others are aboard, lookouts should be stationed at the bow and stern. Special attention should be paid to watching the compass to insure staying on course.

The navigator must plot a course on the chart that will enable him to arrive at a recognized buoy equipped with a sound device. To do this, it may be necessary to sacrifice the time gained by a more direct course, but it will increase the chances of reaching the destination. With the course plotted, and the estimated time of arrival at the navigational mark figured, the boat can proceed until 1 minute of the time remains before the mark should be sighted. Then the engines should be slowed until the navigational signal (bell or whistle) is located. If not heard, the boat can proceed on course for 1 additional minute, at which time the same procedure should be followed. If the bell or whistle is then heard, the boat should proceed close enough to the buoy to identify it positively. After identification, the course for the next leg is followed with the same precautions. In such dead-reckoning navigation, the effect of current on the vessel track over the ground plays an important part. At such times current tables provide valuable information to the navigator. The tilt of the buoy is an aid in determining current set and drift.

Sounding the Way

Under other conditions, or when the navigator has "lost" his aids to navigation in a fog, a line of soundings may be the only way left to determine the boat's location, if the approximate location is known and a chart is available.

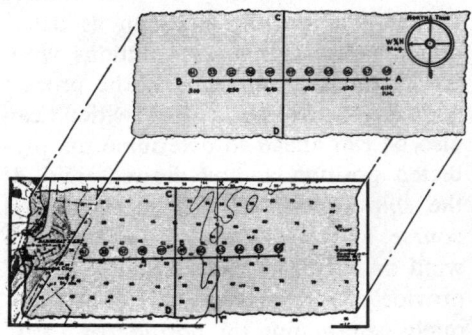

A line of soundings.

A series of soundings is taken at regular intervals throughout a portion of a run while the vessel maintains a steady course. These soundings are plotted on a piece of transparent paper and course line passing through them is labeled. The paper is then moved about on the chart until the sounded depths agree with the charted depths and the courseline is properly oriented.

In the foregoing paragraphs, the electronic aids to navigation, such as radar, radio direction finders and depth sounders have been purposely omitted from discussion. Although these instruments are invaluable when properly calibrated and handled, complete reliance on them could be disastrous — note the "Cautions Concerning Aids to Navigation" — and mechanical failure is possible. The boat operator who sets out beyond the confines of his home waters must know the fundamentals of piloting as practiced without the benefit of electronic navigational aids.

And, of course, there is still another way of handling a fog situation. Drop anchor, display the proper lights, use the fog signals and wait it out.

Dead Reckoning

Dead reckoning is the process of determining a ship's position by applying to the last well-determined position (fix or running fix) the run that has since been made, using only the true courses steered and the distance run as determined by log or engine revolutions, without considering current. By the process of dead reckoning, the position can also be run ahead to determine the predicted position at any desired time. If the ship kept exactly to the predicted course and speed and there were no wind or current, dead reckoning would provide at all times a method of accurately determining the position of a vessel.

Since this is rarely the situation, a dead-reckoning position must be considered as only an approximation of the true position. This does not mean that dead reckoning is unimportant or may be neglected. On the contrary, it is highly important to know the approximate position, for this is a great aid in determining when to make turns, predicting the time of sighting lights and other aids to navigation, identifying landmarks, and evaluating information or the absence of expected information.

To provide the necessary data for dead reckoning, the navigator must keep a navigation logbook in which he records the time and all other data pertaining to changes in course and speed, time of getting under way and anchoring and all other data. Before charts became reliable, dead reckoning was done entirely by computation. In modern practice nearly all navigators do their dead reckoning graphically upon the chart of the locality in which they are cruising, or upon *plotting sheets* published by the Hydrographic office.

Plotting Sheets are blank charts ruled for latitude and longitude in accordance with the Mercator projection and imprinted with one or more true compass roses. The use of plotting sheets has many advantages over computation; for example, there is less chance of making arithmetical errors and the navigator is able to see his work and the position of the ship with reference to dangers to navigation and to landmarks.

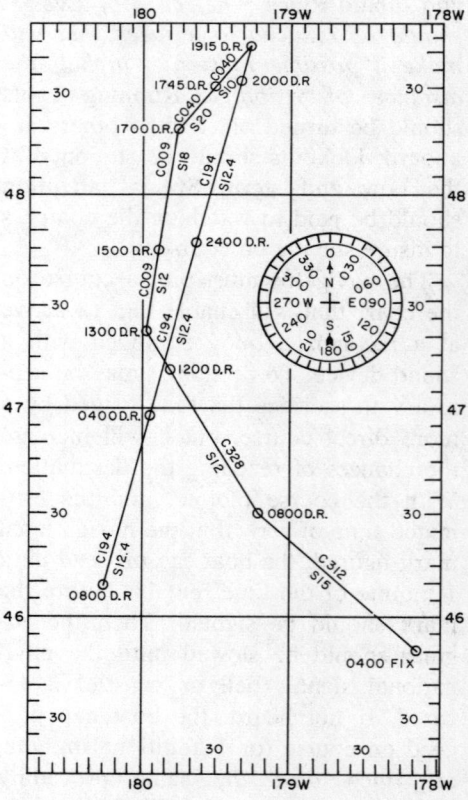

Dead reckoning plotted on a plotting sheet.

The Course Line is the direction prescribed for the boat's movement, or the direction in which it moves from one place to another. The prescribed direction can be represented on a Mercator chart by drawing a straight line (the course line will form an angle with the meridians equal to the true course).

In laying out the course line, it is customary to start from the boat's last known or well-determined position. The course line represents the path the boat would follow (or would have followed) if there were no wind or current, and it could be steered exactly at every instant. Obviously this is rarely, if ever, the case.

Along this course line, the navigator may plot dead reckoning (DR) positions for any given time by measuring off the distance he traveled (or should have traveled) through the water since the time of the "fix."

Distance may be determined by the taffrail log, but it is more usual to determine it by engine speed. A curve of engine revolutions per minute (rpm) against boat speed in knots is determined by a series of trial runs over a measured mile. From this chart, or curve, a table showing rpm's and corresponding speed can be made up. *The speed in knots multiplied by any time interval (hours or fractions thereof) equals distance traveled through the water in the interval.*

An Example. The problem presented below, and solved in the illustration (p. 178), illustrates a dead-reckoning plot.

1. Problem: The 0400 fix of a boat is lat. 45°50′N, long. 178°09′W. The boat is on course 312° true, speed 15 knots. At the hours indicated below, the following speed and course changes take place:

Time (in hours)	True course (in degrees)	Speed (in knots)
0800	328	12
1300	009	12
1500	009	18
1700	040	20
1745	040	10
1915	194	12.4

2. Requirement: To plot the DR track from 0400 the first day until 0800 the next morning.

3. Solution: At 0800 on the following morning, the boat arrives at rendezvous in lat. 46° 10′ N, long. 179° 46′ E. The solution is apparent from an examination and review of the illustration.

The Track Line

It might be well to note at this point that the course line when laid out from a fix, is really the *locus* of successive DR positions. It is a line generated by the constantly moving DR positions and is more properly called the *DR track line*. The DR track line is laid out from a known or well-determined position and continues as a graphic history of courses steered and engine speeds (calibrated in knots) until such time as another fix is obtained. Winds, currents, slight steering errors, and other factors, usually in unknown or variable quantities, combine to set the vessel to the right or left of its intended path, and to retard or aid the boat's progress along the track. It is therefore desirable to frequently fix the boat's position and replot the DR tracks from the new fixes. It is good practice to plot the DR position frequently; for instance, every hour in open waters and more often in restricted waters.

CHAPTER XVII

Weather Indications

Every boating area has its "old salts" who can look up into the skies, spit into the wind, and come up with a weather prediction as accurate as that of the official forecasters. Generally, this is due to an unconscious knowledge of the weather phenomena which the boatman can acquire from what the old seafarer would term "book-learnin'."

The three main factors which contribute to any type of weather are moisture (rain, snow, sleet), wind and temperature. Varying combinations of these factors produce fog, tornadoes, snowstorms, thunderstorms and cyclonic storms such as tropical cyclones, hurricanes, typhoons and other weather conditions. The terms for the various types of storms arise from the source of the storm or its location.

About the Weather Bureau

The United States Department of Commerce operates the Weather Bureau. It provides forecasts and general weather information to anyone desiring it. Most of these data are issued in the form of weather maps; one of the most widely used is the "Daily Surface Weather Map." Boatmen operating in harbors or inland waters can use these maps to advantage in preparing local forecasts.

The storm warnings issued by the Weather Bureau are conveyed to vessels during the day by flags and during the night by lights. These signals are shown at Coast Guard installations, and by many yacht clubs, marinas and other waterfront establishments. The "storm signals" are as follows:

1. *Small Craft Warning:* One red pennant displayed by day and a red light over a white light at night to indicate that winds up to 38 miles an hour (33 knots) and/or sea conditions dangerous to small craft operations are forecast for the area.

2. *Gale Warning:* Two red pennants displayed by day and a white light above a red light at night to indicate that winds ranging from 39 to 54 miles an hour (34 to 48 knots) are forecast for area.

3. *Whole Gale Warning:* A single square red flag with a black center displayed during daytime and two red lights at night to indicate that winds ranging from 55 to 73 miles an hour (48 to 63 knots) are forecast for the area.

3. *Hurricane Warning:* Two square red flags with black centers displayed by day and a white light between two red lights at night to indicate that winds 74 miles an hour (64 knots) and over are forecast for the area. (See color section, Illustration F.)

Weather Instruments

Various kinds of instruments are used for gathering the data necessary to forecast weather.

Although a great many barometers are hung in homes and yacht clubs as decorations, their utility in weather forecasting is too often neglected. The barometer is used to measure the atmospheric pressure. Atmospheric pressure at sea level is approximately 14.7 pounds per square inch; this mean height is expressed as a barometric reading of 29.53 inches of mercury. Variations of the atmospheric pressure serve

WEATHER INDICATIONS

to indicate changes in weather.

In the typical aneroid barometer the scale is calibrated from 25 to 31 inches, inclusive. These figures represent inches of mercury which are the standard means of expressing atmospheric pressure. The black pointer indicates the pressure at any given instant. It is actuated by a shaft-and-linkage arrangement from a metal bellows which expands and contracts as the pressure varies. The other indicator is a reference pointer which can be turned by hand to any position on the dial by moving a knurled knob at the center of the dial face. The reference pointer is used to indicate the pressure at the last reading of the barometer. Although the reading must be recorded, use of the barometer allows a quick visual determination of pressure changes between periodic readings.

A typical aneroid barometer.

Use of the Barometer

A record of barometric readings made at regular intervals will indicate the pressure being exerted on the earth's surface at the instant of observation. If several readings have been logged, as in the following table, they will serve as valuable weather guides.

Time	Pressure (in inches)	Changes (in inches)
0700	30.02	
0800	30.00	−0.02
0900	29.97	−0.03
1000	29.93	−0.04
1100	29.88	−0.05
1200	29.82	−0.06

Barometric pressure falling at an increasing rate denotes foul weather. A fall of 0.02 inches an hour is a low rate of fall and not particularly disturbing, while a fall of 0.05 inches per hour is a high rate and normally indicates stormy weather.

Note that there is a normal daily change in atmospheric pressure. It is usually at its maximum at 1000 and 2200 each day, and at its minimum about 0400 and 1600. The variation between minimum and maximum may be as much as 0.05 inch during the 6-hour intervals (about an 0.01 change per hour). If at 1200 the wind is backing east to north and the barometer is continuing to fall at a rapid rate, a severe northeast gale with heavy rain is on its way. On the other hand, given the same barometric reading of 29.82, with the barometer rising rapidly and the wind going to the west, clearing and cooler weather can be expected.

General Rules for Using the Barometer

Here are a few general rules that will help when using the barometer:

1. Foul weather is usually forecast by a *falling* barometer with winds from the east quadrants. Fair and clearing weather is usually forecast by winds shifting to west quadrants with a *rising* barometer.

2. When the wind sets in from points between south and southeast and the barometer *falls steadily,* a storm is approaching from the west or northwest.

Wind direction	Barometer reduced to sea level	Character of weather
SW to NW	30.10 to 30.20 and steady.	Fair with slight temperature changes for 1 or 2 days.
SW to NW	30.10 to 30.20 and rising rapidly.	Fair followed within 2 days by rain.
SW to NW	30.20 and above and stationary.	Continued fair with no decided temperature change.
SW to NW	30.20 and above and falling slowly.	Slowly rising temperature and fair for 2 days.
S to SE	30.10 to 30.20 and falling slowly.	Rain within 24 hours.
S to SE	30.10 to 30.20 and falling rapidly.	Wind increasing in force, rain within 12 to 24 hours.
SE to NE	30.10 to 30.20 and falling slowly.	Rain in 12 to 18 hours.
SE to NE	30.10 to 30.20 and falling rapidly.	Increasing wind and rain within 12 hours.
E to NE	30.10 and above and falling slowly.	In summer with light winds, rain may not fall for several days. In winter, rain in 24 hours.
E to NE	30.10 and above and falling rapidly.	In summer, rain probably in 12 hours. In winter, rain or snow, with increasing winds will often set in when the barometer begins to fall and the wind sets in from the NE.
SE to NE	30.00 or below and falling slowly.	Rain will continue 1 to 2 days.
SE to NE	30.00 or below and falling rapidly.	Rain with high wind, followed within 36 hours by clearing and in winter colder temperatures.
S to SW	30.00 or below and rising slowly.	Clearing within a few hours and fair for several days.
S to E	29.80 or below and falling rapidly.	Severe storm imminent, following within 24 hours by clearing and in winter colder temperatures.
E to N	29.80 or below and falling rapidly.	Severe NE gale and heavy rain; in winter heavy snow followed by a cold wave.
Going to W	29.80 or below and rising rapidly.	Clearing and colder.

Barometer weather table.

The center of the storm will pass near or north of the observer within 12 to 24 hours and the wind will shift to the northwest by way of south and southwest.

3. When the wind sets in from points between east and northeast and the barometer *falls steadily*, a storm is approaching from the south or southwest. The storm center will pass near or to the south of the observer within 12 to 24 hours and the wind will shift to northwest by way of north.

4. The rapidity of the storm's approach and its intensity will be indicated by the rate and amount of fall of the barometer. The above table provides a ready means of forecasting weather from wind-barometer data.

Hygrometer and Anemometer

Two other instruments used in weather forecasting are the hygrometer and the anemometer. A hygrometer consists of two thermometers mounted vertically in a ventilated case or box. One thermometer, known as the *dry bulb,* has a mercury bulb exposed directly to the air. The other thermometer, known as the *wet bulb,* has a bulb covered with muslin. In use, the muslin is kept soaked in water, stretched tightly around the bulb and kept moist by a wick immersed in a small cistern or cup filled with water. The muslin is kept thoroughly moist, but not dripping, at all times.

The dry-bulb thermometer records the temperature of the free air. The wet-bulb thermometer, exactly like the dry-bulb one except for the moistening materials, records what is known as the temperature of evaporation, which is always less than the temperature of the free air. The difference of the temperatures shown by the dry-bulb and the wet-bulb indicates how near the air is to state of saturation — the humidity. The

Beaufort No.	Knots	Descriptive terms	Sea criterion 1939 (provisional)	Approximate equivalent sea disturbance scale in open sea		
				Code fig.	Description	Mean height of waves in feet
0	Less than 1	Calm	Sea like a mirror	0	Calm (glassy)	
1	1–3	Light air	Ripples with the appearance of scales formed but without foam crests.	1	Calm (rippled)	½
2	4–6	Light breeze	Small wavelets, still short but more pronounced; crests have a glassy appearance and do not break.	1		1
3	7–10	Gentle breeze	Large wavelets; crests begin to break; foam of glassy appearance; perhaps scattered whitecaps.	2	Smooth (wavelets)	2½
4	11–15	Moderate breeze	Small waves, becoming longer; fairly frequent whitecaps.	3	Slight	5
5	16–20	Fresh breeze	Moderate waves, taking a more pronounced long form; many whitecaps are formed; chance of some spray.	4	Moderate	9
6	21–26	Strong breeze	Large waves begin to form; the white foam crests are more extensive everywhere; probably some spray.	5	Rough	14
7	27–33	Moderate gale	Sea heaps up and white foam from breaking waves begins to be blown in streaks along the direction of the wind; spray can be seen.	6	Very rough	19
8	35–40	Fresh gale	Moderately high waves of greater length; edges of crests break into spray; foam is blown in well-marked streaks along the direction of the wind.	7	High	25
9	41–47	Strong gale	High waves; dense streaks of foam along the direction of the wind; sea begins to roll; spray may affect visibility.	7		31
10	48–55	Whole gale	Very high waves with long overhanging crests; the resulting foam in great patches is blown in dense white streaks along the direction of the wind; on the whole, the surface of the sea takes a white appearance; the rolling of the sea becomes heavy and shocklike; visibility is affected.	8	Very high	37
11	56–65	Storm	Exceptionally high waves; small- and medium-sized ships might be lost to view for a long time behind the waves; the sea is completely covered with long, white patches of foam lying along the direction of the wind; the edges of the wave crests are blown in froth; visibility affected.	9	Phenomenal	45 or more
12	Above 65	Hurricane	The air is filled with foam and spray; sea completely white with driving spray; visibility very seriously affected.	9		

To record in knots the velocity of hurricanes exceeding force 12, the new scale is used: 13, 72–80 knots; 14, 81–89 knots; 15, 90–99 knots; 16, 100–109 knots; 17, 110–118 knots.

Beaufort wind scale.

relative humidity is found by reference to standard tables from the true and wet-bulb temperatures. Generally, the humidity over the ocean's surface is about 90 percent.

The *dewpoint* is the temperature at which moisture suspended in the atmosphere will begin to form dew. The *dewpoint spread* is the number of degrees between the actual temperature and the dewpoint. This, too, is determined by reference to standard tables.

The anemometer is an instrument for measuring wind velocity and, in most cases, wind direction. When this instrument is mounted aboard the boat, readings under way indicate apparent wind speed and direction; they should be corrected for vessel speed and direction to obtain a *true* wind reading. When measuring velocity and direction of wind, the high degree of accuracy usually essential in bearings is not required. It is sufficient if the velocity is estimated within one *Beaufort* number, and direction within 5°. The Beaufort numbers, obtained from a standard table, are used to indicate wind velocities for marine purposes.

Basic Elements of Weather

Uneven heating of the earth's surface causes differences in atmospheric pressure. This in turn causes wind. As the air is warmed it expands and becomes less dense; when it cools it contracts and becomes denser. This results in higher atmospheric pressure (higher barometric readings). Equatorial regions of the earth receive considerably more heat than the polar areas. This excess of heat at the equator is the basis of a definite world wind pattern, which affects the prevailing wind situation of any local area.

The prevailing winds of the regions of the world are:

1. *Doldrums* — The low-pressure belt extending around the earth in the vicinity of the geographical equator is known as the doldrums. It shifts slightly north or south with the seasons and is characterized by light winds, cloudiness, afternoon thunderstorms and showers, and a depressing humidity.

2. *Trade winds* — The relatively permanent winds on each side of the equatorial doldrums that blow from northeast in the northern hemisphere and southeast in the southern hemisphere are known as the trade winds.

3. *Horse latitudes* — These are zones of higher atmospheric pressure on the poleward side of each trade wind where calms and variable winds prevail. The conditions are unlike those in the doldrums in that the air is fresh and clear, and calms are not of long duration.

4. *Prevailing westerlies* — The prevailing westerly winds (winds blowing from the west) are those on the poleward sides of the horse latitudes.

5. *Polar fronts* — In the northern hemispheres, the air masses of the converging polar northeasterlies do not mingle readily with the southwesterlies of the temperate zone where they meet. Instead, the cold mass underruns the warm air from the south. The surface between these two air masses is known as the polar front. (Action similar to this occurs in the southern hemisphere.) The average position of this irregular front is 60° north latitude. It is important to realize that the polar front shifts. For example, in the northern hemisphere it may extend as far south as Florida and farther north than the 60th parallel.

Land and Sea Breezes

Land and sea breezes are caused by the alternating heating and cooling of coastal land and sea areas. The land, particularly in summer, is warmer than the sea by day and cooler than the sea

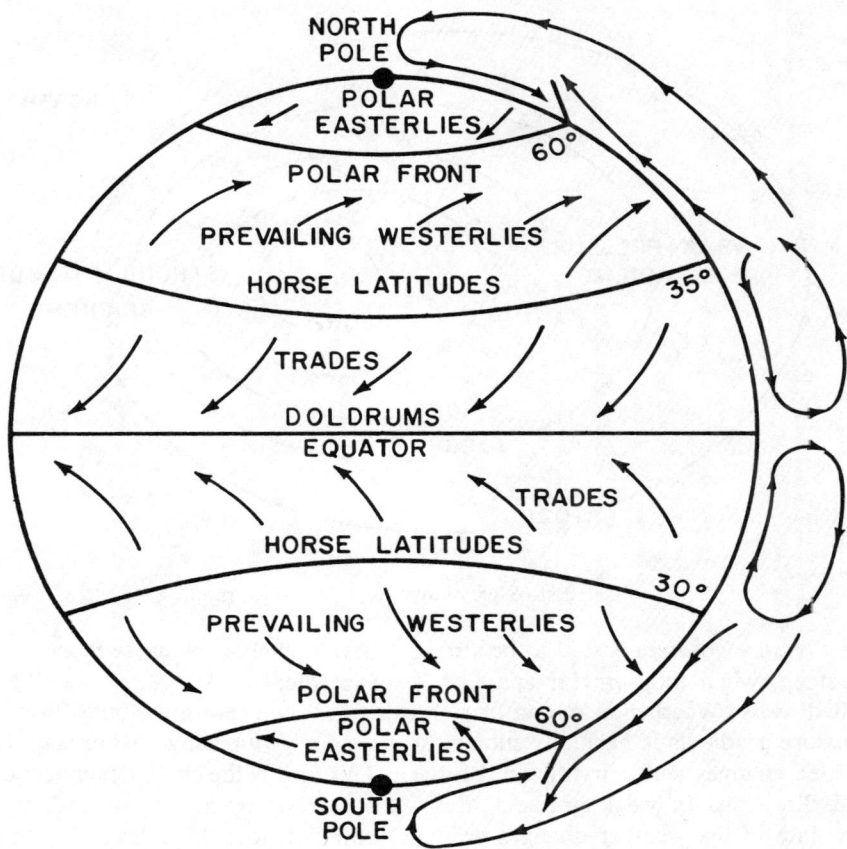

The general pattern of world winds.

by night. There is, therefore, a variation in atmospheric pressure over the adjoining land and sea areas. This causes a system of littoral breezes which blow landward during the daytime and seaward during the night. These land and sea breezes usually penetrate to a distance of about 30 miles on and off shore, and extend to a height of a few hundred feet.

The sea breeze begins in the morning hours, from 0900 to 1100, as the land warms. In the late afternoon it dies away. In the evening the land breeze springs up and blows gently out to sea until morning. In the tropics this process is repeated day after day with great regularity. In higher latitudes the land and sea breezes are often altered by winds of cyclonic origin. In many harbor areas or at the mouths of large river systems, the summer afternoon or evening breezes give rise to sudden squalls.

Pressure Gradient — A Key To Understanding Weather Maps

Lines drawn through points on the earth having the same atmospheric pressure are known as *isobars*. These lines of equal pressure enclose areas of either high or low pressure. A *pressure gradient* is the space found between isobars. It indicates an increase or decrease in atmospheric pressure per unit distance between isobars.

In the illustration, the isobars are spaced more closely in the eastern portion of the high-pressure area than in the western section. When isobars are close,

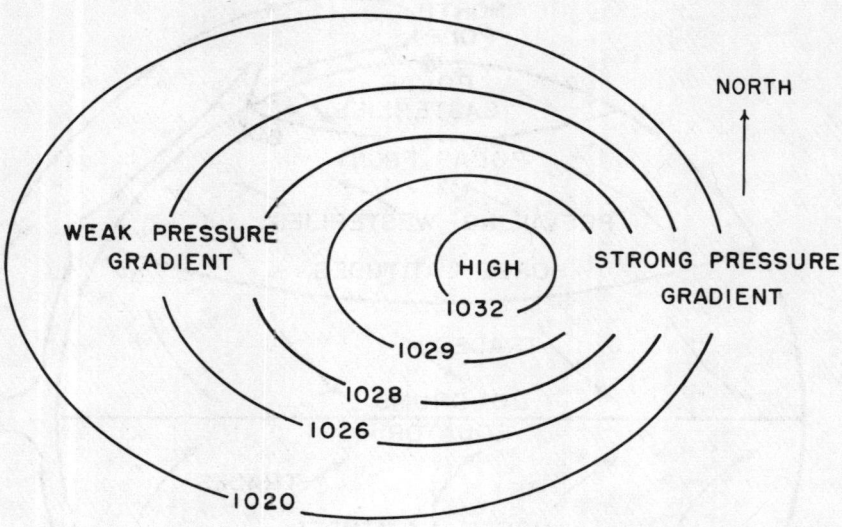

Pressure gradients on a weather map.

the *pressure gradient* is said to be strong or steep; when they are far apart, it is called *weak*. Weather in strong or steep pressure gradients is normally subject to sudden changes with varying wind force and direction. In weak gradient areas, the state of the weather changes gradually and predictably.

Wind Velocity and Direction

The velocity of the wind is determined by the pressure gradient. Strong gradients cause strong winds, whereas weak gradients result in gentle winds. When the pressure is about the same over a large area, the wind is light. Wind direction depends chiefly on the pressure gradient and the rotation of the earth. Wind direction is named by the direction *from* which it blows.

Clouds as Weather Indicators

The type, amount, and height of clouds have a direct bearing on weather. The cloud types in themselves are not of great significance, but their changes and developments (cloud sequence) are. For example:

1. When *cumulus* clouds form early on a summer morning, the air is quite moist. This means the clouds may become more numerous by afternoon and, if so, will build up to a high level, making afternoon thunderstorms likely. If the cumulus clouds do not appear until late morning, fair weather should continue throughout the day provided the air is stable. Unstable air will allow the clouds to build up to great height — thunderstorms are then likely.

2. *Cirrus* clouds mean little unless they increase in number and are followed by cirrostratus clouds. The latter may be rapidly followed by *altostratus* and then *nimbostratus* clouds — this indicates rain and stormy conditions in general.

3. When clouds are replaced by thicker, lower clouds, stormy weather follows. Because weather in the middle latitudes moves from west to east, the first signs of storm clouds are usually seen in the west. Similarly, blue patches in the western sky usually indicate a breakup of stormy conditions.

WEATHER INDICATIONS

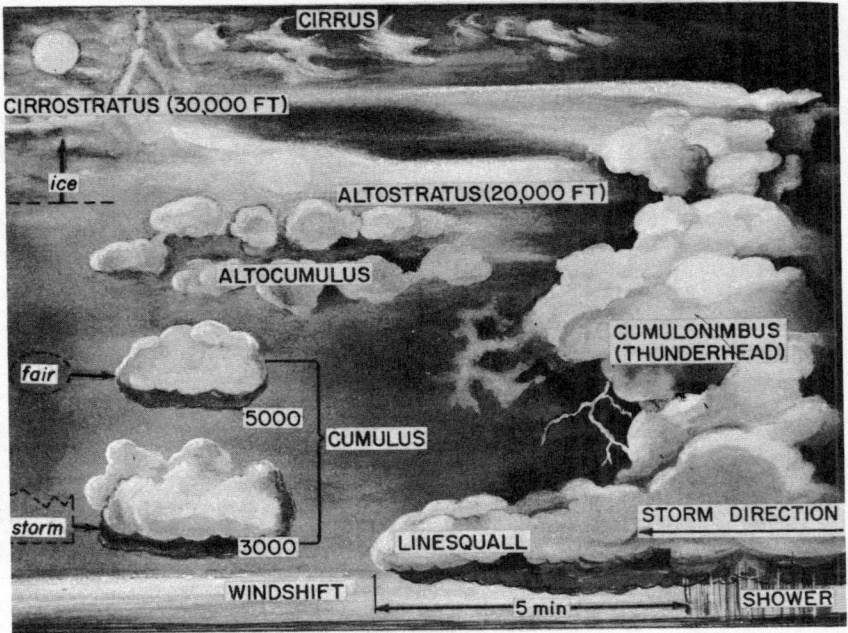

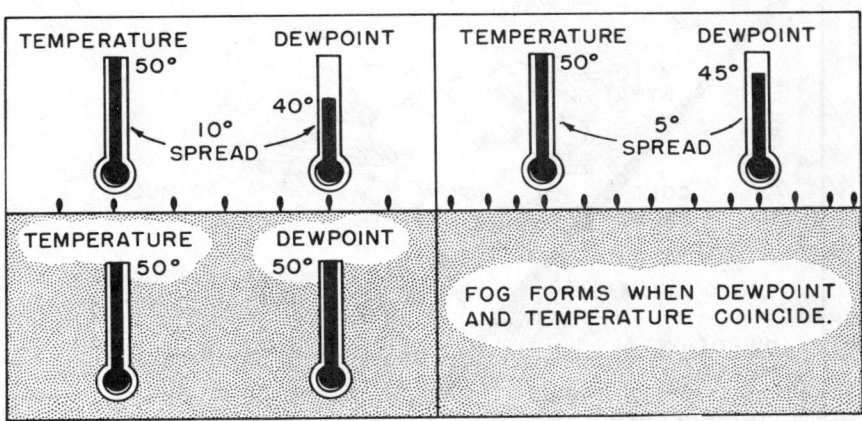

The formation of fog.

Fog

Foggy conditions are possibly the most hazardous for the pleasure boatman, and an early prediction that fog may occur may aid in avoiding a dangerous situation. Basically, fog results from cooling of the air that remains at the earth's surface. Cooling air and the resultant fog may come about in a number of ways:

1. Warm air flowing over a cold surface. Fog may form, day or night, when warm, moist air flows over water or land surfaces which are cooler than the air.

2. Radiation fog. Radiation fog is a night phenomenon. During the day the earth's surface receives and radiates warmth. At night, the incoming heat ceases, but the radiation continues and the earth's surface gets cooler. Although the lowest temperature is reached just before sunrise, fog sometimes forms soon

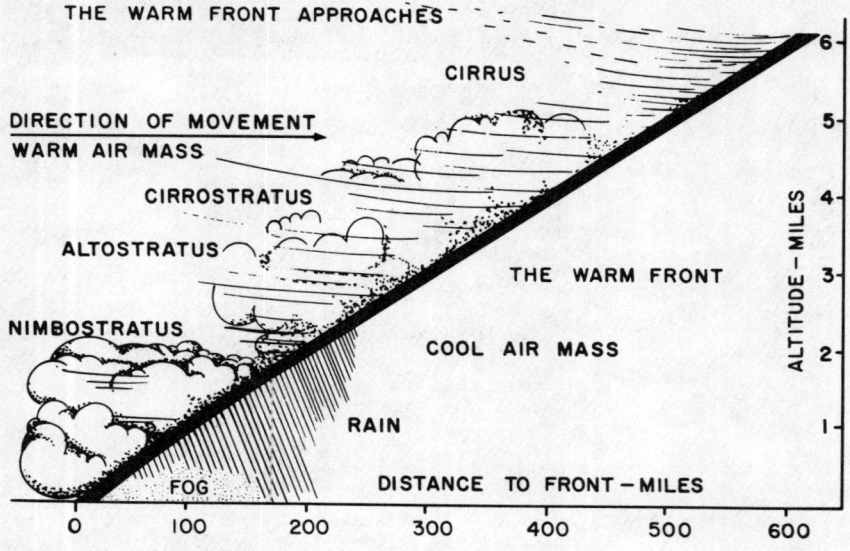

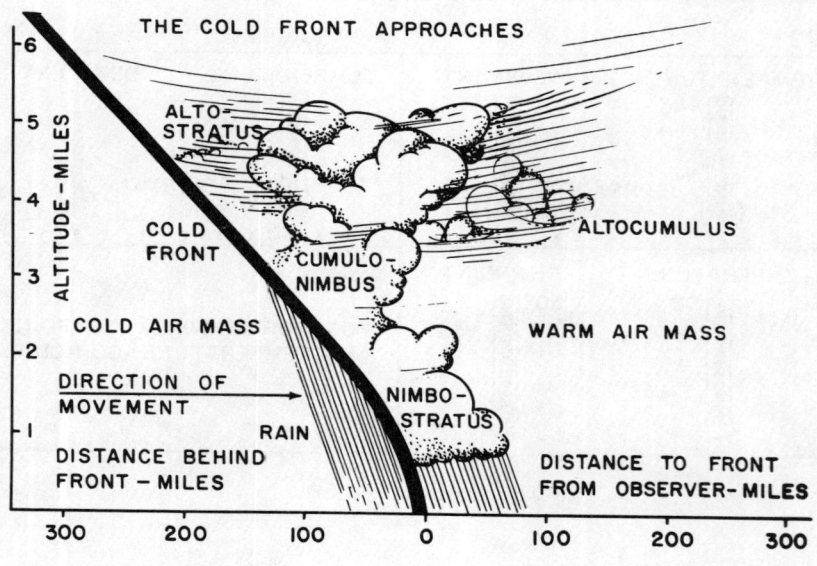

Characteristics of warm and cold fronts.

after sunset. Radiation fog is much more common over land than over water. It usually burns off within an hour or so after sunrise. If mixed with smoke, it will form a heavy, dark and greasy *smog* that will not quickly burn off.

3. Air moving from low to higher latitude. Warm, moist air moving from a low to a higher latitude may cool to such an extent that fog will form over large areas. This type is much more common over sea than land.

Forecasting Fog

Fog is likely to form as the spread between air temperature and dewpoint decreases. As the temperature approaches the dewpoint, fog is likely. Thus, watching the relationship between temperature and relative humidity can sometime give an indication of imminent fog.

Fronts

A *front* is the surface between warm and cold air masses. Adjacent masses with different temperatures and degrees of humidity tend to mix readily. Because the cold masses are heavy and the warm masses light, the warmer of the two converging currents tends to overrun the colder.

In general, there are three types of fronts — cold, warm and *occluded*. An occluded front is a mingling of the first two fronts. All occluded fronts should be watched closely because it is along these fronts that most adverse weather conditions occur. When a boat passes through a front, a noticeable change in the weather may be observed. This is especially true if passing through a cold front, because a cold front is sometimes accompanied by a sudden shift in the wind and a hard squall from a westerly quarter. Fronts are clearly marked on all weather charts by type. Their direction and proximity can be checked through daily weather forecasts.

Storms

Storms are caused by the coming together of air currents of differing temperatures, moisture content, speed and direction. In tropical hurricanes and extra-tropical cyclones, the air is forced to turn in the direction opposite its usual flow. Tropical hurricanes are whirlpools of wind and rain which rise over the ocean; storms that form outside the tropics are termed extratropical and are marked by discontinuities of cold and warm fronts. A cyclone is horizontal vortex in the troposphere; it rotates counterclockwise in the northern hemisphere and clockwise in the southern hemisphere. Tropical cyclones are known by various names — hurricanes if occurring in the western Pacific, willy-willies if near northwestern Australia, and cyclones if originating in the Indian Ocean. Only storms with a velocity of 64 knots (74 miles) or higher are classified as hurricanes; storms with winds of less violence are called tropical disturbances.

CHAPTER XVIII

Rules of the Road

The Rules of the Road are the traffic laws of the waterways, and they apply to every type of vessel. As with automobile traffic regulations, they were instituted to lessen the chances of marine collisions. Everyone operating a boat should understand the purposes of the rules and the strict necessity for observing them. All lights, sounds and signals on the water have a meaning under the rules and must be observed in day, and especially, in night cruising.

The basic rule of safety for boats is practically the same as that for automobiles — safety first, keep to the right, and proceed cautiously when in doubt.

The Rules of the Road govern *all* seagoing traffic from a rowboat to the largest liner. These rules apply to sailing vessels and to aircraft while operating on the water. There are certain provisions that apply only to sailing vessels and to power-driven vessels; for example the rules require that power-driven vessels when meeting or crossing keep out of the way of sailing vessels because sailing vessels cannot maneuver easily. However, nothing in the rules exempts sailing vessels from adhering to applicable rules of the road.

"Rules" Publications

The only official source of information on rules of the road is contained in the three pamphlets issued by the Coast Guard.
1. The basic booklet that will furnish the information most valuable to the majority of pleasure boat operators is "Rules of the Road, International-Inland," CG-169. The other two "rules" booklets are:
2. "Rules of the Road, Great Lakes," CG-172.
3. "Rules of the Road, Western Rivers," CG-184.

These may be obtained upon request from Coast Guard Marine inspection offices in the major ports, of the Commandant (CHS), United States Coast Guard Headquarters, Washington 25, D.C.

There are some differences between the Inland Rules, which generally cover the waters in which pleasure boats travel, and the "International" rules which govern marine traffic on the high seas. On the "Lights Required" chart in another chapter you will notice that there are some differences in the requirements for running lights, and there is also some difference in the sound signals.

However, in the following pages, we will concern ourselves with the "Inland" rules.

General Provisions

The rules of the road apply to all vessels which are under way. A vessel is under way, according to maritime practice, whenever she is not at anchor, made fast to the shore, or aground.

As to the risk of collision, the rules state that "risk of collison can, when circumstances permit, be ascertained by carefully watching the compass bearing of an approaching vessel. If the bearing does not appreciably change, such risk should be deemed to exist."

The rules of the road contain provisions to reduce the risk of collision, providing the boat operators are familiar with the rules and adhere to them. Even an unskilled boat operator should realize that a whistle signal from another boat at close quarters is not just a friendly greeting, but has a definite meaning.

Sound (Whistle) Signals — Inland Rules

A short blast of the whistle means a blast of about one second's duration.

A prolonged blast of the whistle means a blast of from four to six seconds duration.

One short blast of the whistle signifies intention to direct course to own starboard, except when two boats are approaching each other at right angles or obliquely, when it signifies intention of vessel which is to starboard of other to hold course and speed.

Two short blasts of the whistle signify intention to direct course to own port.

Three short blasts of whistle mean "My engines are going at full speed astern."

Four or more short, rapid blasts means the danger signal. This indicates that the responding boat does not understand the intentions of the other boat.

Cross signals are forbidden. Boats are forbidden to use what has become technically known among pilots as "cross signals," that is, answering one whistle with two, or answering two whistles with one. The signal given by the first vessel must be respected, or the danger signal given.

Boats passing each other: (The following provision is of course written with larger vessels in mind and should be applied with a modicum of common sense by the operators of small boats. For example, the "half mile" provision would hardly apply to two 14-foot outboards passing each other.) The signal for passing, by blowing the whistle, shall be given and answered by pilots, not only when meeting "head and head," or nearly so, but at all times when vessels are in sight of each other, when passing or meeting at a distance within half a mile of each other, and whether passing to the starboard or port.

The whistle signals are never used except when vessels are in sight of each other, and the course and position of each can be determined in the daytime by a sight of the vessel itself, or by night by seeing its signal lights. In fog, mist, falling snow, or heavy rainstorms, when vessels cannot see each other, fog signals only must be given.

The Five "Situations"

Boats approaching each other head and head, end on — When boats are approaching each other head and head, that is, end on, or nearly so, it is the duty of each to pass on the port side of the other. Either boat shall give, as a signal of her intention, one short and distinct blast of her whistle, which the other boat shall answer promptly by a similar blast of her whistle, and thereupon, such boats shall pass on the port side of each other. But, if the courses of such boats are so far on the starboard of each other as not to be considered as meeting head and head, either boat shall immediately give two short and distinct blasts of her whistle, which the other boat shall answer promptly by two similar blasts of her whistle and they shall pass on the starboard side of each other.

This applies only to cases where vessels are meeting end on or nearly so, in such a manner as to involve risk of collision. In other words, to cases in which, by day, each vessel sees the masts of the other in a line or nearly in line with her own, and by night to cases in which each vessel is in such a position as to see both the side lights (red and green) of the other.

It does not apply to cases in which a vessel sees another ahead crossing her own course, or by night to cases where

FIRST SITUATION

Here the two colored lights visible to each will indicate their direct approach "head and head" toward each other. In this situation it is a standing rule that both shall direct their courses to starboard and pass on the port side of each other, each having previously given one blast of the whistle.

SECOND SITUATION

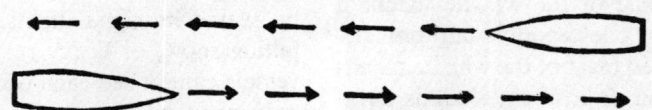

In this situation the red light only will be visible to each, the screens preventing the green lights from being seen. Both vessels are evidently passing to port of each other, which is rulable in this situation, each pilot having previously signified his intention by one blast of the whistle.

THIRD SITUATION

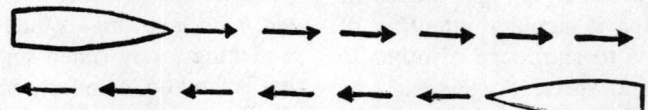

In this situation the green light only will be visible to each, the screens preventing the red light from being seen. They are therefore passing to starboard of each other, which is rulable in this situation, each pilot having previously signified his intention by two blasts of the whistle.

FOURTH SITUATION

In this situation one steam vessel is overtaking another steam vessel from some point within the angle of two points abaft the beam of the overtaken steam vessel. The overtaking steam vessel may pass on the starboard or port side of the steam vessel ahead after the necessary signals for passing have been given with assent of the overtaken steam vessel.

FIFTH SITUATION

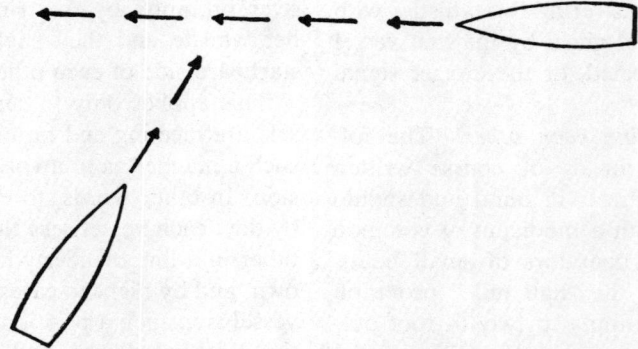

In this situation two steam vessels are approaching each other at right angles or obliquely in such manner as to involve risk of collision, other than where one steam vessel is overtaking another. The steam vessel which has the other on her own port side shall hold course and speed, and the other shall keep clear by crossing astern of the steam vessel that is holding course and speed, or, if necessary to do so, shall slacken her speed, stop, or reverse.

(From CG-169, "Rules of the Road")

the red light of one vessel is opposed to the red light of the other, or where the green light of one vessel is opposed to the green light of the other, or where a red light without a green light is seen, or a green light without a red light is seen, or where both red and green lights are seen anywhere but ahead.

Boats nearing bend or curve in channel; moving from docks — Whenever a powered boat is nearing a short bend or curve in the channel, where, from the height of bank or other cause, a vessel approaching from the opposite direction cannot be seen for a distance of half a mile, such vessel must, when she arrives within half a mile of such curve or bend, give a signal by one long blast of the whistle, which signal must be answered by any approaching vessel that may be within hearing. Should such a signal be answered by a vessel on the farther side of the bend, then the usual signals for meeting and passing should be given; but, if the first alarm signal is not answered, the first boat is to consider the channel clear and govern herself accordingly.

When boats are moved from a dock or berth, and other boats are liable to pass from any direction, they must give the same signal as in the case of boats meeting at a bend; but immediately after clearing the berths so as to be fully in sight, they are governed by the steering and sailing rules.

Boats running in same direction; overtaking vessel — When boats are running in the same direction, and the one which is astern wants to pass on the right or starboard side of the vessel ahead, she should give one short blast of the whistle to signify that desire, and the vessel ahead answers with one blast, she may direct her course to starboard; or, if she wants to pass on the left or the port side of the vessel ahead, she gives two short blasts, and if the vessel ahead answers with two short blasts, she may proceed, passing to port.

However, if the vessel ahead does not think it safe for the one astern to pass at that point, she must immediately signify that by giving at least four short, rapid blasts of the whistle. The overtaking boat should not attempt to pass until she has given a passing signal which is satisfactorily answered by the boat ahead.

Every boat coming up with another vessel from any direction more than two points abaft her beam (that is, in such a position that she cannot see either of the side lights of the vessel she is overtaking) is considered an overtaking vessel and is bound by this rule; in case of doubt, the burden is upon the overtaking vessel which must keep out of the way of the one ahead.

Boats approaching each other at right angles or obliquely — When two power boats are approaching each other at right angles or obliquely so as to involve risk of collision, other than in an overtaking situation, the boat which has the other on her port side shall hold her course and speed; the vessel which has the other on her own starboard side shall keep out of the way of the other by directing her own course to starboard so as to cross the stern of the other vessel, or, if necessary to do so, slacken her speed, or stop or reverse. (Note: As a general rule, if the operator of the boat can see the other boat's green light, he is the privileged boat with right of way; if he sees the red light of the other boat, he is the burdened vessel and must give way.)

If, from any cause, the conditions covered by this situation are such as to prevent immediate compliance with each other's signals, the misunderstanding or objection shall be at once made apparent by blowing the danger signal and both boats shall be stopped and backed if necessary, until signals for passing with safety are made and understood.

(International and Inland Rules)

When two sailing vessels are approaching one another so as to involve risk of collision, one of them shall keep out of the way of the other as follows, namely:

(a) A vessel which is running free shall keep out of the way of a vessel which is close hauled.

(b) A vessel which is close hauled on the port tack shall keep out of the way of a vessel which is close hauled on the starboard tack.

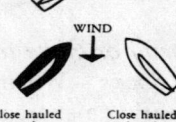

(c) When both are running free, with the wind on different sides, the vessel which has the wind on the port side shall keep out of the way of the other.

(d) When both are running free, with the wind on the same side, the vessel which is to the windward shall keep out of the way of the vessel which is to the leeward.

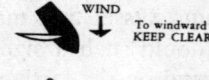

(e) A vessel which has the wind aft shall keep out of the way of the other vessel.

In the five situations for sailing vessels, the vessel required to *keep clear* is the burdened vessel; and the other vessel is required to hold course and speed—the privileged vessel.

Rules for sailing vessels. *(From CG.-340, "Recreational Boating Guide")*

Fog Signals

In fog, mist, falling snow, or heavy rainstorms, whether by day or night, signals shall be given as follows:

A vessel under way, except when towing other vessels or being towed, shall sound at intervals of not more than 1 minute, on the whistle or siren, three blasts in succession, namely, one prolonged blast followed by two short blasts, and no other.

A vessel when at anchor shall, at intervals of not more than 1 minute, ring the bell rapidly for about five seconds.

CHAPTER XIX

Marlinspike Seamanship: The Use of Rope Aboard Your Boat

In nautical language, marlinspike seamanship is the general term for the handling, knotting, splicing, seizing, rigging and care for the ropes used aboard the boat or in connection with ground tackle, mooring, etc. The knowledge and practical application of marlinspike seamanship is one of the basic skills that the pleasure boatman should acquire. Before he purchases his first yachting cap, he should be able to tie the basic knots—even in the dark—and be able to care for his lines.

Hints for Care of Lines

Care of ropes is a basic safety requirement. Many boat owners try to get "just another season" out of rope that obviously need replacement. They even take chances on the most important rope of all—the mooring line. But that's living and learning the hard way. Boats break away and drift out to sea. Good moorings are lost—chain, anchor and all! On the other hand, the price of a good, new rope, in the proper size is a small investment for the peace of mind you get in return. And it's the cheapest boat insurance in the world!

The first thing seasoned skippers do every year, before their boats hit the skids, is to make sure all their lines are strong and safe. What's more, they do this periodically during the entire sailing season, making replacements where necessary.

It's good practice to examine the entire length of all lines aboard the boat periodically and carefully. Look for cuts, dry rot or mildew. Don't be casual about the inspection of rope. Since the surface appearance of used rope is sometimes deceptive, you'd better twist it open and look between the strands. If you notice a musty odor or if the inner fibers seem colorless or broken, heave it overboard and replace it.

Rope deteriorates for several reasons: *mechanical action,* such as surface wear or internal friction between fibers; *biological action,* such as rotting by bacteria and mold, or boring by ship worms.

Running rigging can be run ragged if you are not careful. This is due to mechanical *action.* For running rigging really works its passage. It's in practically constant motion—running through chocks or around cleats or being hauled up or down. That is one reason why many yachtsmen prefer a stronger more durable rope for their rigging than ordinary Manila.

Reversing lines occasionally to keep the wear distributed is a good idea. Also, remember that the majority of ropes swell when wet, so blocks should have sheave-holes large enough to handle the added difference in diameter. This applies to fair-leaders of all kinds. Then, too, there is always a certain amount of friction present when rope is working over a sheave. And eventually, this friction breaks up the rope fibers.

Deck cleats, whether of metal or wood, should always have smooth surfaces. For hawse-pipes or any other metal fittings which hold rope, composition metal is preferable to iron. And your mooring line should be further protected by canvas or burlap wrapping—or even a length of rubber hose, where it contacts the chocks—to keep mechanical action at a minimum.

Keep your ropes clean and free from sand, mud, etc. Wash them in clear water. Otherwise, grit will work into the lines and act as a harmful grinding agent.

So-called "dry rot," which is due to the action of fungi, generally occurs when wet rope is stored in a poorly ventilated locker or otherwise not given a chance to dry out properly. Anchor lines and other ropes which are saturated with water should be spread out on deck to dry thoroughly. Your second choice is to coil wet rope loosely where fresh air circulates freely.

Common commercial acids are particularly injurious to rope fiber, and the same is true of uric acid or bilge water that contains traces of it. If drying must be long delayed, a rot resistant line, such as nylon or treated manila should be used.

Biological action such as rotting of fiber or infestation with borers can happen almost anywhere when untreated rope is used constantly under marine conditions, but the action is more severe in tropical waters. Untreated manila rope is hazardous when used as a mooring line.

Working conditions and other things being equal, ropes in the smaller sizes need replacing more frequently. For *all* the yarns in rope up to about 3/4" diameter are subject to surface wear. In larger rope, which contains center yarns, the inner fibers are protected from surface abrasion—which increases their life and the limit of safety of the rope before replacement becomes necessary.

About Rope

The word "rope" is generally applied to all sizes and types of rope, either fiber or wire. In military and naval practice, the sizes of wire and fiber rope are designated by *diameter* in inches; in commercial use, the size of fiber rope is designated by *circumference* in inches.

Cordage, in marine usage, is a collective term that includes all cord, twine, line, rope and string made from twisted synthetic or vegetable fibers. Cord, string, and twine are loosely used to indicate small line. Small cordage is known on shipboard as *small stuff*. It is designated either by the number of threads that it contains, such as 12-thread or 15-thread, or by its use, such as "ratline stuff," "seizing stuff," or "marline."

Generally the term "fiber rope" refers to heavy lines having three or more strands. As a rule in marine usage all fiber cordage larger than 1-1/2 inch in circumference or more than 21 threads is called fiber rope. Fiber rope larger than 5 inches in circumference is called hawser.

How Rope is Made

Ropemaking is essentially a series of twisting operations. A fiber rope consists of three elements: fibers, yarns and strands. Fiber rope is formed by three twisting operations. The procedure described below is standard and is known as *right-laid* or *plain-laid* rope (see illustration).

The steps are as follows:

1. The fiber is twisted from left to right to spin the yarn.
2. The yarn is twisted from right to left to form the strands.
3. The strands are then twisted from left to right *to lay* (or form) the rope.
4. To make left-laid rope, the twisting procedure is reversed.

Types of Fiber Rope

The three principal types of fiber rope are *hawser, shroud* and *cable-laid*. Each type of fiber rope is designated by the combination of strands that make up the rope. Hawser-laid rope consists of three strands laid up to the right. Shroud-laid rope consists of four strands laid up right-handed around a center strand or

MARLINSPIKE SEAMANSHIP — USE OF ROPE ABOARD YOUR BOAT

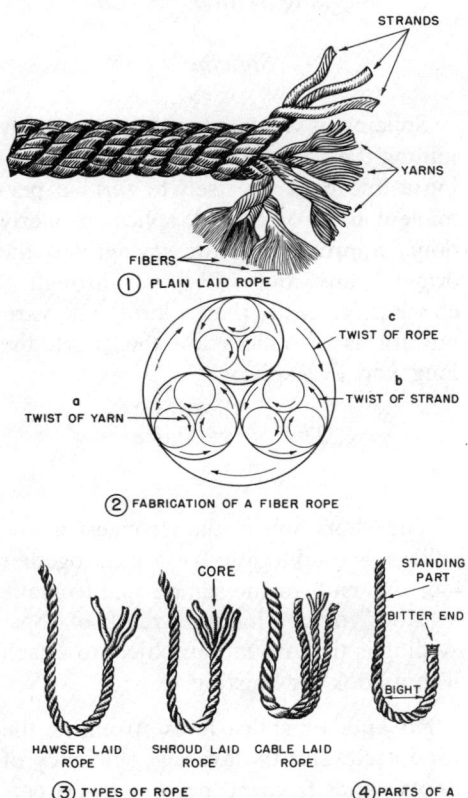

Parts and types of fiber rope; parts of a line.

core. Cable-laid consists of three right-hand, hawser-laid ropes laid up together in a left-hand direction.

Rope Fibers

Fiber rope is so named because it is made from natural or synthetic fibers, including Manila, sisal, hemp, jute, cotton, flax, nylon, dacron, polyethylene and polypropylene. In many instances varying percentages of natural fibers are combined to fabricate certain grades of ropes.

Manila rope should be used where strength, ease of handling and safety are important, such as mooring lines, towing lines, etc.

Sisal rope is lighter than Manila rope, but is only approximately 80 percent as strong. It has a coarse testure and stands sea exposure well. It is generally used as a substitute for Manila for towing and mooring purposes.

Hemp rope is usually used aboard ship as small stuff; it is generally tarred to keep it from deteriorating. Tarred hemp rope is known as marline, and is used principally for seizing, lashing, or other light work.

Cotton and flax rope have a limited use aboard a boat. Cotton line is sometimes used for a lead line on the taffrail log, and for lead and heaving lines. Flax (linen) is often used for signal halyards or for other light lines. Cotton and flax lines are usually braided instead of laid to give added strength to their relatively short fibers.

Nylon rope possesses high tensile strength, great elasticity and extremely high resistance to deterioration, as do the other synthetic fibers.

Dacron is often used for sheets and halyards. Its stretch and working elasticity are much less than nylon and only slightly greater than Manila. Size for size, dacron lines are 15 percent heavier than Manila.

Polyethylene rope is not affected in strength by wet condition. Its working elasticity is slightly greater than Manila; has been found superior to Manila in abrasion resistance and flexing properties especially under wet conditions. Its low elasticity recommends it for "tight" mooring or docking use.

Polypropylene lines have good wet strength, and manufacturer's tests have shown that their wet strength is actually 5 percent greater than dry strength. They are less slippery to handle than polyethylene, and under light load are slightly more elastic than Manila.

Some Hints on Selecting Rope

It is quite important to keep in mind the different characteristics of ropes when determining the proper type for specific use aboard your boat. When considering lines for marine use, one of the most important rope characteristics is stretch. Some ropes, like nylon, have high stretch. Others, like Manila, have low stretch. Dacron is intermediate between Manila and nylon, though closer to Manila. In some uses, high stretch is an advantage; for others, a disadvantage.

Nylon rope elongates elastically when loaded, but not like a rubber band. It recovers its original length after loading, but the time depends on the conditions under which it relaxes.

In end uses such as anchor lines and mooring lines, where the loading is usually repeated over short intervals with incomplete relaxation between loadings, nylon rope is superior because of its much higher working elasticity and, therefore, better shock absorption quality. A nylon mooring line and anchor line afford greater safety than Manila for a given scope. It also permits the use of less scope in crowded yacht basins with no sacrifice of safety.

Nylon rope, because of its high elasticity, is not recommended for main and jib halyard on racing yachts. Here the high "come and go" of nylon results in undesirable changes in set of the sail under changeable sailing conditions.

While the working elasticity of dacron rope is somewhat higher than that of Manila or linen, it is below that of nylon. Dacron rope has been found to perform satisfactorily as running rigging in extended use.

Working With Fiber Line

Splicing

Splicing is a method of permanently joining the ends of two lines or of bending a line back on itself to form a permanent loop or eye. A splice, properly done, approximates the strength of the original line and will pass through a chock more easily than a knot. The various forms of splices are the short, the long and eye splices.

The Short Splice

The Short Splice, the strongest of the splices, is used to join two ropes together —or two ends of the same rope, to make a "sling" or continuous wreath of rope. A sling is tied around an object to attach it to a hook for hoisting.

No knot or splice is as strong as the rope itself. But the average efficiency of knots varies from 50 percent to 60 percent of the rope itself—where a well-made splice will have 85 percent to 95 percent of the rope's strength. Splices are always to be preferred, therefore, when the load is heavy.

The Short Splice, though the strongest of the splices, can not be used on rope which is to run through a correctly sized pulley.

How to Make a Short Splice

1. Lash rope about twelve diameters from each end (A). Unlay the strands up to the lashings. Whip strands to prevent untwisting and put together as in diagram above, alternating the strands from each end. Pull up taut.

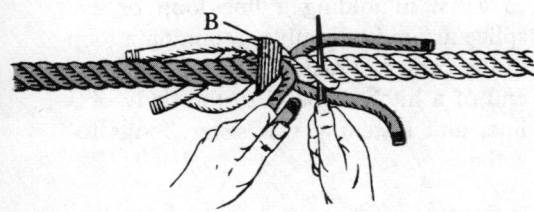

2. Now tie down all the strands temporarily (B). Take off the lashing from one side of the rope and raise one strand on this side, using a fid. Take the middle strand of the opposite side. Tuck it over one strand and under the raised strand. Pull it up taut. Every time you tuck a strand, let out a little of the turn. And be sure to keep some tension on the raised strand under which you are tucking. This prevents strand kinking.

3. Tuck against the twist or "lay" of the rope. What happens is that the tuck goes over one strand, under the second, and out between the second and third.

4. Roll the rope toward you. Pick up the second strand. Repeat the same operation. Then do it again with the third strand. You have now made one full tuck.

To taper this splice, first make one tuck just like the first one. Then make the third tuck the same way, but first cut off 1/3 of the yarns from the strands. For the fourth tuck, cut off 1/2 the remaining yarn.

For the untapered short splice, you do not cut the strands. You just make three more tucks, exactly like the first one.

5. Take both lashings (which were applied in No. 1 and No. 2) off the other side of the rope. Repeat above operations.

6. To finish, cut off ends of strands, leaving about one or two inches protruding.

To Splice Nylon Rope — The above procedure applies to splicing of nylon and other synthetic ropes except that one additional full tuck should be used.

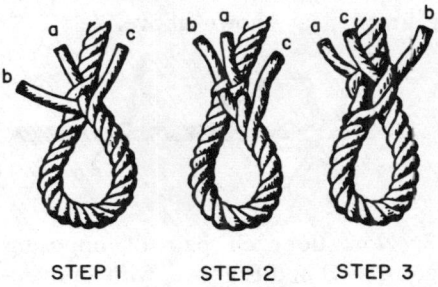

STEP 1   STEP 2   STEP 3

The Eye Splice

An eye splice is made in the same way as a short splice, except that the line is first brought back upon itself enough to give the desired size of the eye, and the strands tucked into the body of the line as shown in the illustration. For additional strength a thimble may be fitted and the eye and tucks seized.

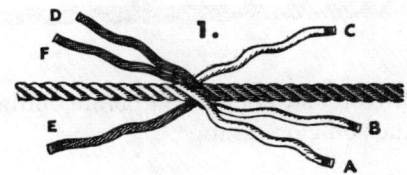

The Long Splice

The Long Splice is slightly weaker than a Short Splice, but allows the rope to run through a pulley without obstruction and lessens wear and chafing of the rope fibers at the point of splicing. A Long Splice should be made only with two ropes of the same size.

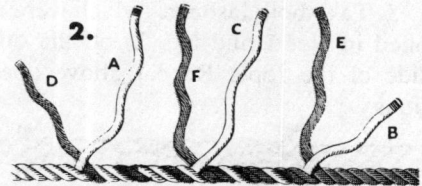

1. Unlay the end of each rope about 15 turns and place the ropes together, alternating the strands from each end, as shown above.

2. Start with any opposite pair, unlay one strand and replace it with strand from the other part. Repeat operation with another pair of strands in the opposite direction as shown above.

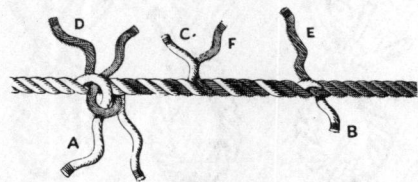

3. Now tie each pair of opposing strands, as B and E above, with an overhand knot, tuck each strand twice (see Figure 4), as in the Short Splice, and then twice more as for the Tapered Splice. Or, halve each strand (see A and D), and tie with an overhand knot before tucking. By this latter method a smaller splice results — but at a considerable sacrifice of strength.

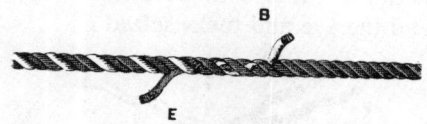

4. Roll and pound well before cutting strands off close to rope.

Seizing

Seizing is the lashing of two parts of line by continuous turns of small stuff. The seizing is then secured by a clove or other type of hitch. When two crossing parts of line are bound, the seizing is called a *throat seizing*. Seizings are used to assist in holding a line loop or eye splice around a thimble, retaining a loop in the center of a line, holding the short end of a hitch or bend to the body of a line, and fastening two sister hooks together.

Worming, Parceling and Serving

Line that is intended for exposure to weather over long periods or for exceptionally hard wear is protected by worming, parceling and serving. For generations, apprentice seamen have learned the sequence and procedure by memorizing this: "worm and parcel with the lay; turn and serve the other way."

Worming consist of following the lay of the line between strands with tarred small stuff. This prevents moisture from penetrating to the interior of the line and at the same time fills out the round of line, giving a smooth surface for the parceling and serving.

Parceling consists of wrapping the line spirally with long, narrow strips of canvas, following the lay of the line. Each turn of the parceling overlaps the preceding turn as shown in the illustration.

Serving consists of wrapping small stuff snugly over the parceling, each turn bring hove as taut as possible so that the whole forms a stiff protective cover for the line. A serving mallet is used for passing the turns and heaving them taut.

Knots, Bends and Hitches

The skill with which he handles his lines is one of the chief marks of the experienced boatman, and everyone who gets out of the landlubber class should be able to employ any of the knots, bends, and hitches described on the following pages. Almost as important as

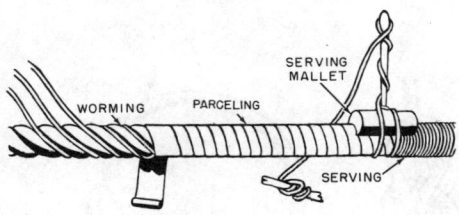

Worming, parceling, and serving.

knowing marlinspike seamanship is the ability to call the different kinds of knots by their proper nautical names. It is customary to speak of the different parts of the line as follows: the *bitter end* is the very end of the rope; the *bight* is a loop formed by turning the rope back on itself; the *standing part* is the long, unused portion of the rope. (Refer to the illustration.)

Knots in a Single Line

These knots are used to fasten a line upon itself or around another object:

(1) Overhand Knot. This simple knot is formed by passing the end of a rope over the standing part and through the bight.

(2) Bowline. One of the most common and useful knots, the bowline forms an eye which may be of any length and cannot slip. It is used for lowering men over the side and for rescue work; for forming eyes in mooring lines and for a great variety of similar purposes. A bowline is made by forming a bight in the line with the end part on top; bringing the end part up through the bight; then passing it under the standing part above the bight, and back through the bight.

(3) The Running Bowline. This is made by tying the regular bowline around a loop of its own standing part. This makes an excellent slip, commonly used to retrieve spars, rigging, etc. And, with lighter rope or twine, it makes a good knot for tightening at the beginning of tying a package.

(4 & 5) Bowline on a Bight. Here is a useful knot to know when you want to attach tackle to, say, the middle of a line when both ends of it are made fast. To tie: Grasp the rope where you want the new knot. Shape it into a loop in one hand and strike this against the two lines leading to the loop, held in the other hand. Then complete the first bight used in tying a regular bowline. Now, open the loop after it has passed through the bight and bring the whole knot through it. Pull the loop tight over the standing part.

(6) Cat's Paw. A convenient, secure, double loop is formed by twisting two bights of a rope and passing the hook of a tackle through them.

(7) Sheepshank. The bight of the rope is laid in three parts, and each part half hitched around the bight of the other two parts. This knot is used to shorten a rope and will hold under tension.

(8) Figure of Eight. This knot resembles the figure eight and is used to prevent the end of the rope from unreeving when rove through blocks. The end of the rope is passed around the bight, over its own part and through the loop. Basically, it is a "saltier" version of the overhand knot.

(9 & 10) The Blackwall Hitch. A hitch, either single or double, around the back of a hook, with the bitter end on one side of the hook and the standing part on top of the other side of the hook is called a Blackwall Hitch.

*Knots Used for Bending
Two Lines Together*

The following knots are used to fasten one rope to another or to some other object:

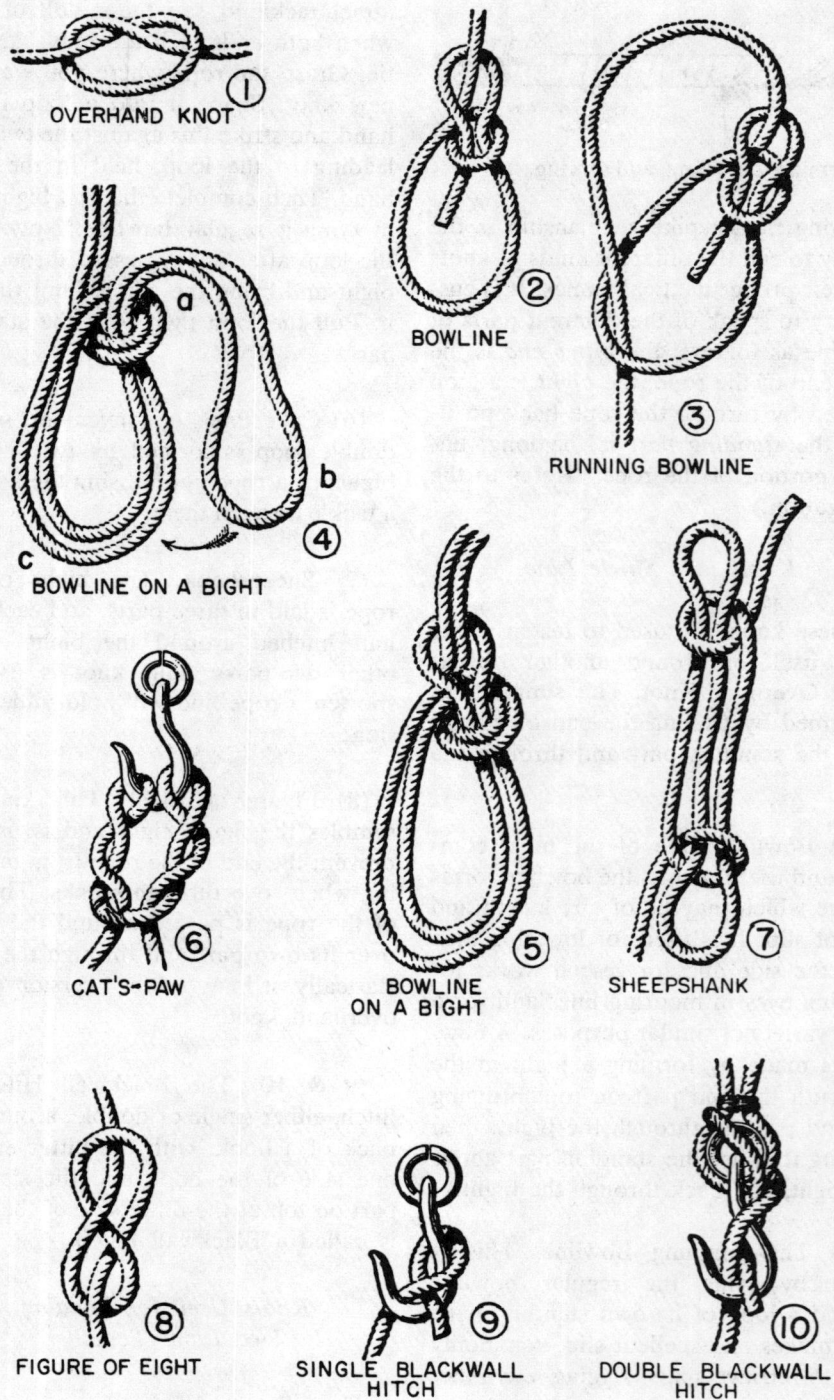

Making knots in a single line.

(1) The Square or Reef Knot. This is simply the old reliable package knot for parcels and bundles. Aboard boat, you will find it useful for reefing or furling sails or similar purposes. Don't use it for tying two ropes together though, since it unties too easily when either free end is jerked. To tie: Pass the left end *over* and *under* the right end. Curve what is now the left end towards the right. Cross what is now the right end *over* and *under* the left. Draw up tight. Take warning that you do not end up with the Granny Knot (2) which won't hold at all. Note that the Granny has one end over, one end under on both loops.

(3) Sheet or Becket Bend, Single. This is probably the best knot to join two ropes. It is made by forming a bight in one of the ropes, bringing up the other rope end through the bight, twisting it over and under the bight, and then bringing it under itself.

(4) Sheet Bend, Double. Here, the end of the bending line is passed twice around the standing line and through its own part, giving added security.

(5 & 6) Single Carrick Bend. This knot is made by first crossing the end of one rope and then passing the end of the other down through the bight, under the standing part, over the end and down through the bight again. The ends are seized in their own parts. This is good bend for tying two heavy ropes.

(7, 8 & 9) The Double Carrick Bend. This bend, with both ends coming out on different sides, is more secure than the single carrick. The ends are seized to their own parts.

(10) Two Bowlines. This is a safe, slipproof and convenient way of bending two ropes together, but the result is somewhat bulky if the lines are to be veered out through a chock.

(11) Reeving Line Bend. This knot is made by taking a half hitch with each end around the other rope and seizing the ends. This method connects two ropes in such a way that they reeve through an opening with as little resistance as possible.

Knots Used in Securing a Line to a Ring or Spar

These knots, shown in the illustration, are generally called "hitches" from their purpose of securing or hitching to an object.

(1) Studding Sail Tack Bend. This is a useful hitch for a variety of purposes. It is especially suggested where there is a danger of the line coming adrift as a result of flapping.

(2) Studding Sail Halyard Bend. This bend is formed by taking a round turn, with the end coming around the standing part, under both turns and tucked over and under the turns. The greater the pull on the halyards, the more tightly the parts of the bend are jammed against the spar.

(3) Fisherman's Bend. This is formed by passing the end twice around the ring and under the turns, and seizing the end back. This bend is used for securing a rope to a buoy or a hawser, to the ring or jew's harp of an anchor.

(4) Timber Hitch. Useful when towing spars, or similar objects, this hitch is formed by passing the end around the spar and its own standing part; then passing several turns around its own part.

(5) Timber Hitch and Half Hitch. In this knot, the half hitch is taken first and the timber hitch formed afterward with the end.

(6) Rolling Hitch. The end is passed

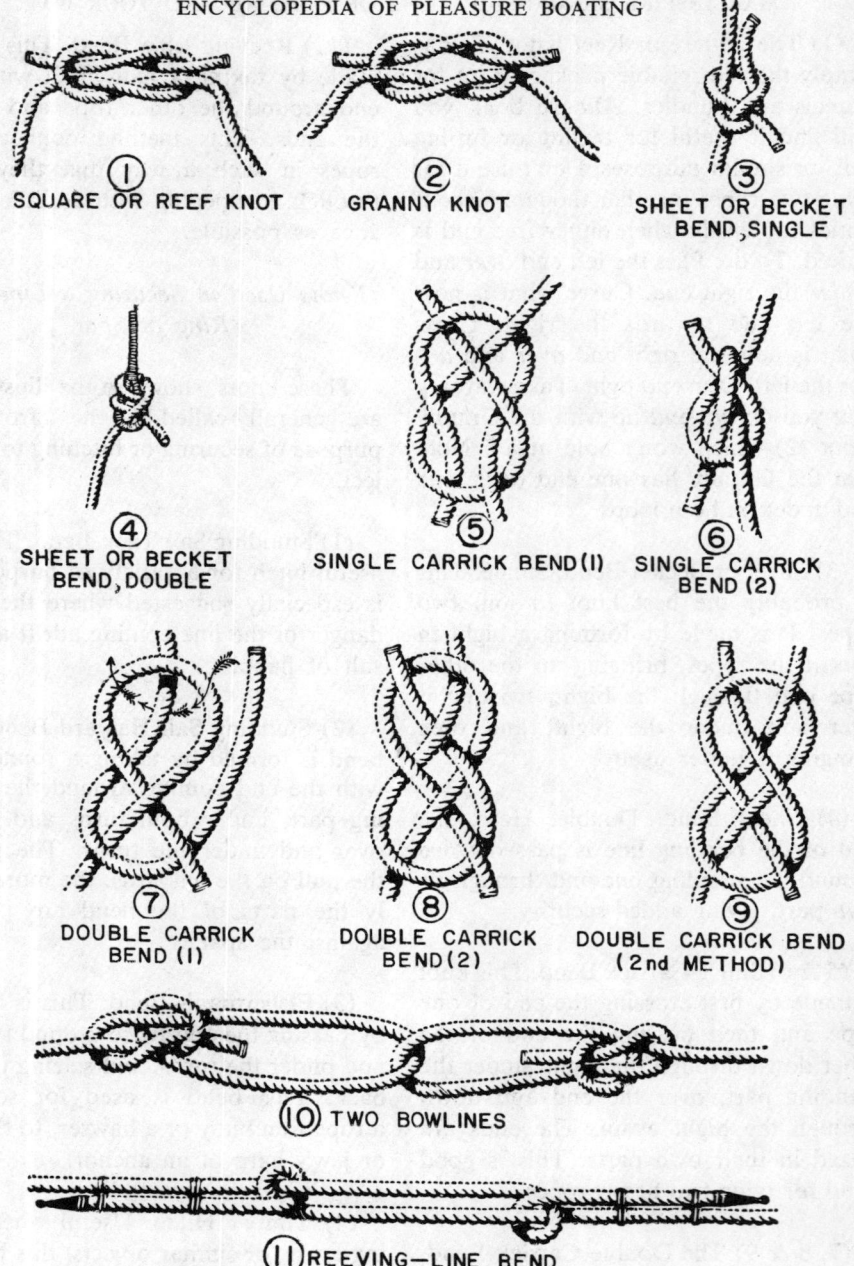

Knots for bending two lines together.

around the spar or rope—crossing the standing part on the top side each time; then the end is hitched around the spar or rope of the opposite side of the two turns. The rolling hitch is very useful when a rope is bent to a spar or to the standing part (not the end) of another or to a chain.

(7) Round Turn and Two Half Hitches. This is formed by encircling a bollard, spar, or other rope twice; passing the running end over and under the standing end and through the space between the bollard and crossover. Repeat crossover with running end and pass

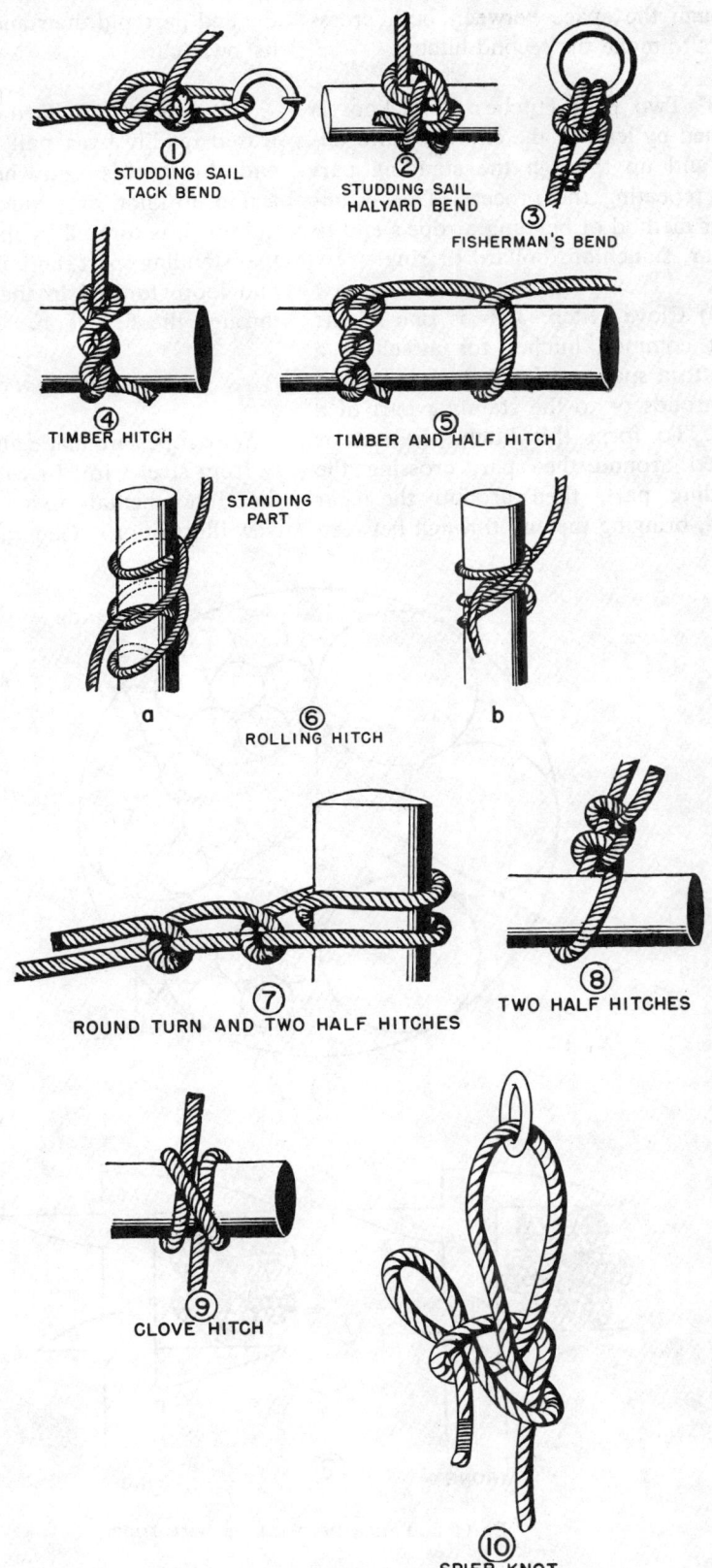

through the space between both crossovers to make the second hitch.

(8) Two Half Hitches. This knot is formed by leading the end over and under and up through the standing part and repeating the process. This is another method of bending a rope's end to a spar, stanchion, bollard or ring.

(9) Clove Hitch. This is one of the most common hitches for attaching a rope to a spar and for fastening ratlines to shrouds or to the standing part of a rope. To form this hitch, the end is passed around the spar, crossing the standing part, then around the spar again, bringing the end through between the end part and the standing part under its own part.

(10) Spier Knot. Tied quickly and released readily by a pull on the running end, this knot is used when a fixed loop, a nonslip knot, or a quick release is required. It is formed by making a loop in the standing part and drawing a second loop, formed in the working part, through the first loop.

Wire Rope

Wire ropes are made almost exclusively from steel wire. In wire ropemaking, the fundamental unit is the strand (see illustration). Generally, the strand

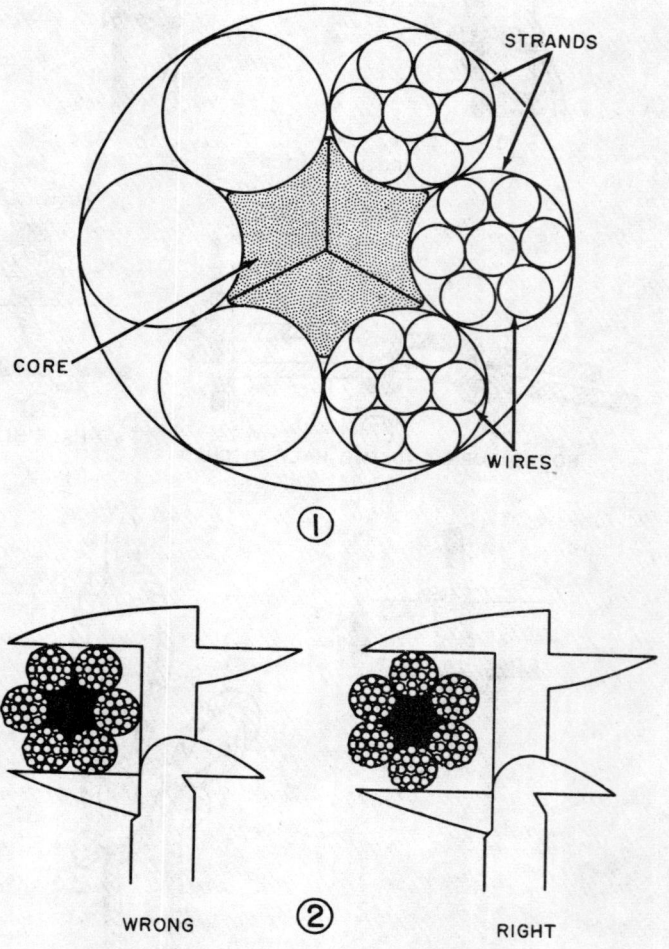

Parts and measurement of wire rope.

is made by spirally winding 6 wires around a center wire or core, then, depending on the required strength and flexibility, adding successive layers of 12 and 18 wires each.

Standard wire rope is formed of 6 strands and a fiber core. The use of a fiber core for the center of the rope gives the rope more flexibility and elasticity which reduces the effect of sudden stress. Wire rope may be made from various kinds of metal and may be galvanized or uncoated. Galvanized wire rope is used as standing rigging and where it will not be subjected to excessive wear; uncoated wire is used for running rigging.

The size of wire rope is designated by its diameter in inches. The right and wrong ways to measure the diameter of wire rope are shown in the illustration above. To measure the rope correctly, place it in a micrometer so that the outermost points of the strands will be touching the jaws of the micrometer. Because of friction and tension, the diameter of a used wire rope will be 1/8 to 1/64 of an inch less than a new one of the original size. Wire rope is also designated by the number of strands per rope and the number of wires per strand.

Care of Wire Rope

Wire rope needs better care than fiber rope and far better care then it generally receives. It is particularly important to avoid kinking wire rope as a single kink in the finest wire will ruin it. When not in use, wire rope should be kept on a reel or drum.

Wire rope needs occasional treatment with linseed oil or other preservative. When the rope is not to be used for some time, it should be coated with a heavy petroleum lubricating oil to which graphite has been added. When wire ropes have been subject to wetting by salt water they should be washed down with fresh water and oiled. It is important to remember that whatever kind of lubricant is used, it must be thin enough to penetrate through the wires to the core of the rope and thick enough to adhere to the wire for a reasonable length of time.

There is one hazard in the use of wire rope. A broken wire can inflict a serious cut, occurring most often on the hands or arms. Wear should be watched carefully and wire rope should be discarded when the outside wires are worn down to half their original diameter or when it is apparent that the rope has been severely damaged by kinking or excessive strain.

When cutting wire rope, a whipping of soft iron wire should be made on each side of the point where the cut is to be made to prevent the rope from unlaying. If wire is not readily available, fairly heavy seizing stuff may be used — the turns being passed very tautly.

Working Wire Rope

Working with wire rope differs from working with Manila in that special tools and equipment are required. The tools used in working with wire rope including a *rigging screw* are shown in the illustration. An ordinary vise may be used in place of a rigging screw, but it is less efficient.

Three types of splices are worked in wire rope — long, short, and eye splices. The first two are used to join pieces of wire rope; the third is used to form loops in the end of a rope or around a thimble. Long and short splices are rarely used by boatmen as all runners, stays, pendants, etc., are made up in the proper length for use. For this reason, only instructions for making the Liverpool eye splice (spiral splice) are shown here.

1. Make a stout seizing at least a foot from the working end of the rope. This distance depends on the size of the rope. To determine the required length from the end of the rope to the seizing, take

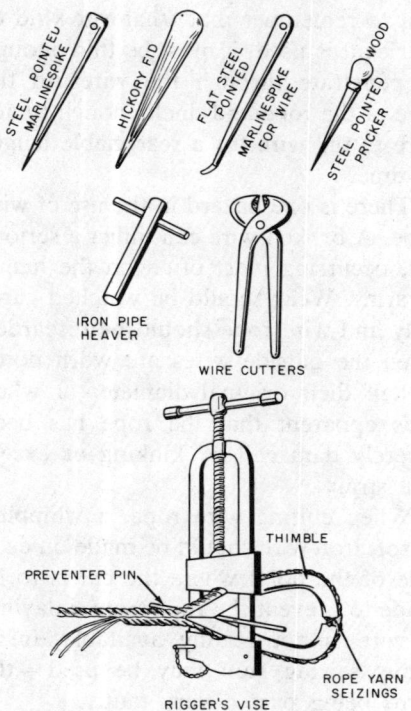

Tools for working with wire rope.

the diameter of the rope, assume it to be feet (not inches) and multiply it by three. For example, the distance required for a 1/2 inch rope would be 1-1/2 feet. Whip the ends of each strand, unlay, and cut out the core of the rope.

2. Bend the wire to form an eye of desired size, place it in the rigging screw and seize it in place. Stretch the wire taut with a selvage strap and a handbilly. Using the heaver, take enough turn out of the rope to permit easy entrance of the marlinspike.

3. Open the standing part through the center with a marlinspike, entering through strands E and D, keeping the core to the right (1). Roll the marlinspike back between the strands, keeping the point of the marlinspike in a convenient position to insert strand 1. The number of turns the marlinspike is rolled back depends on the size and composition of the rope. Large and/or stiff wire requires a longer roll to avoid kinks. As the marlinspike is rolled back, bring strand 1 around the standing part, following the point of the marlinspike. Then insert strand 1 through strands A and B and out through strands E and D and under the marlinspike. Roll the marlinspike back around the loop, forcing the first strand into a locked position at the base of the splice. Then withdraw the marlinspike.

4. Insert the marlinspike between strands E and F, and tuck in strand 2 as

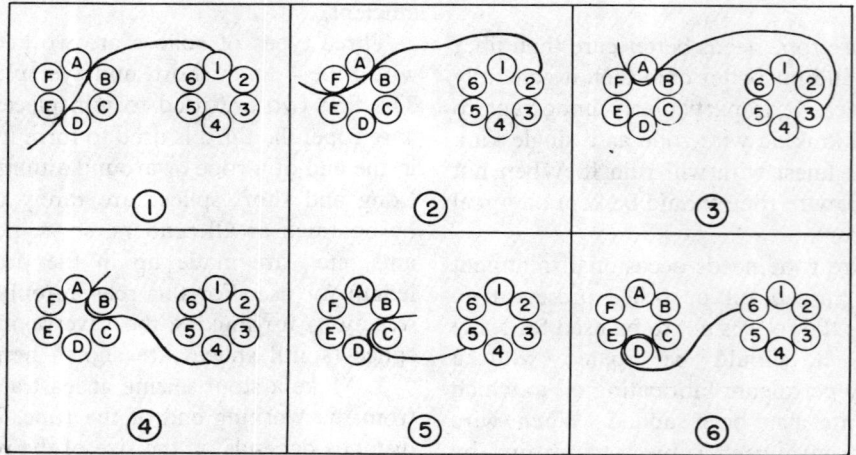

Steps in making the Liverpool splice.

THIMBLE EYE, SPLICED AND SERVED

THIMBLE EYE WITH ROPE CLIPS

OPEN END SOCKET   CLOSED END SOCKET

SHACKLE   HOOK AND THIMBLE

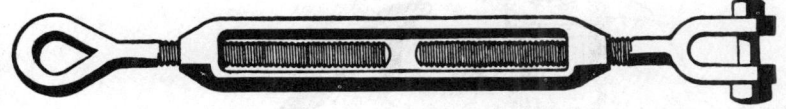

TURNBUCKLE

JOINING THE ENDS OF ROPE

Fittings used with wire rope.

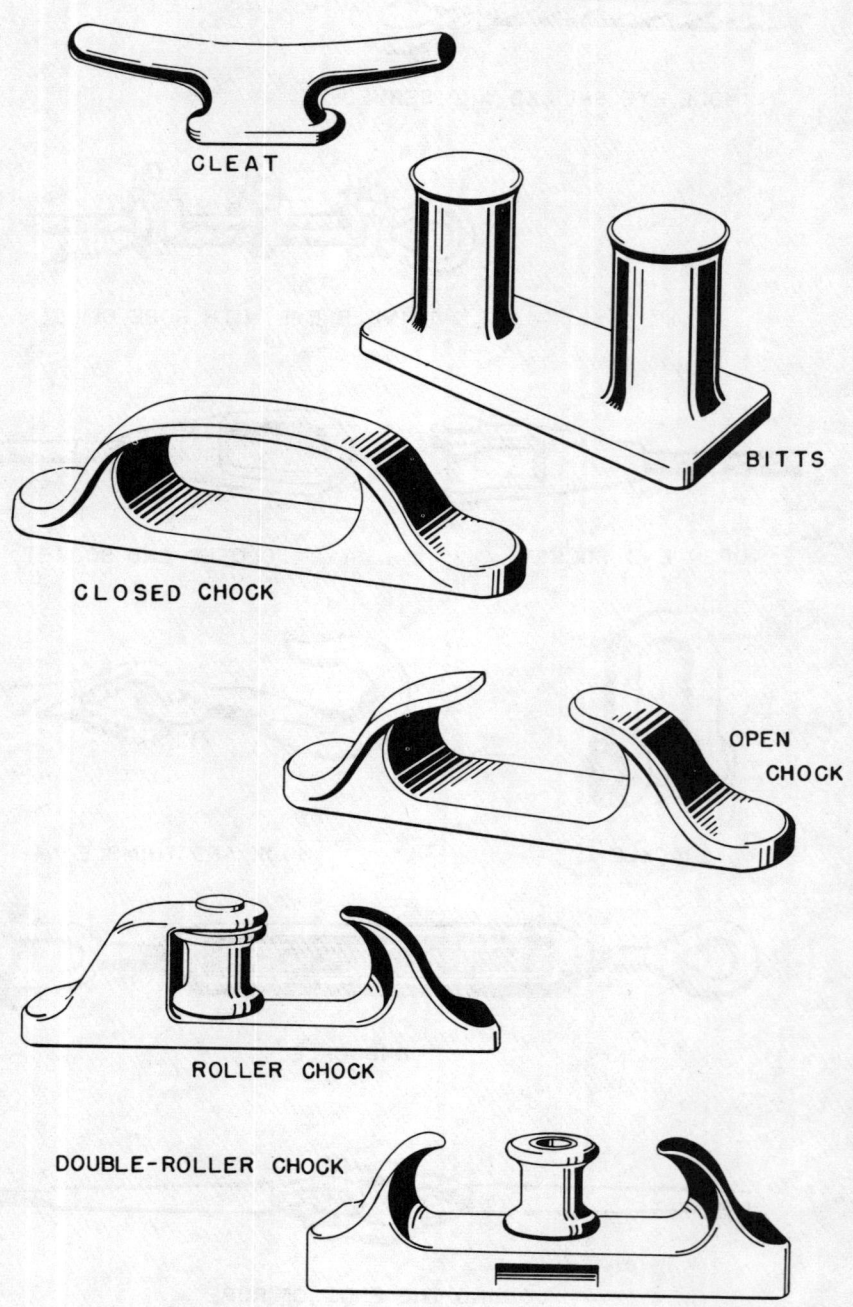

Deck fittings.

shown in (2) in the sketch below. In each step, follow the same procedure of rolling the marlinspike and locking the strands as described above.

5. Care must be taken to correctly identify strands C and D for inserting strands 5 and 6, because strands C and D often become buried near the center of the splice and it may be difficult to determine which is strand C and which is strand D.

6. After inserting strand 6, roll the marlinspike back one complete turn and make the second tuck with strand 6. Then follow through with two more tucks to complete the strand.

7. To complete the splice, tuck each of the other 5 strands 3 times, following the procedure described above. Then remove the wire from the vise, pound it into shape and cut off the ends of the tucking strands close to the splice.

Fittings for Wire Rope

Because of its nature, ends of wire rope cannot be tied together. Most of the fittings used with wire rope are designed to provide an eye in the end of the rope. This affords a convenient means of connecting two ropes or otherwise securing a rope. The illustration shows a number of these appliances and their uses.

U-bolt clamps can be applied in a few minutes, while a wire rope splice means several hours of steady work. Note that the *U* of the clamp is always applied to the bitter end of the rope. Generally, at least four clamps should be used for a safe fastening. A more attractive and permanent eye is provided by the use of the *socket,* which makes the rope easier to handle as the nuts of the clamps can catch a hand and inflict a nasty wound. The two types of socket are the open and the closed.

CHAPTER XX

The Federal Boating Act of 1958

This new law made no change in the requirements respecting lifesaving equipment, fire extinguishers, lights, or other equipment, nor did it extend the water areas over which the Coast Guard has jurisdiction. Numbers and certificates of number issued under this act are for vessel identification only and do not authorize engaging in trade.

Numbering

On April 1, 1960, the Coast Guard began assigning new identification numbers to all undocumented vessels operating on the navigable waters of the United States, which, regardless of length, are propelled in whole or in part by machinery of more than 10 horsepower unless the state in which the vessel is principally used has assumed the numbering. The states may assume this function at any time by enacting a suitable law and the approval of its numbering system by the Secretary of the Treasury.

All numbering must conform to an overall numbering system. In this new uniform system the first part of each number is an abbreviation of the state of principal use as indicated in the application. If principally used on the high seas, the vessel will be numbered according to the state in which it is usually docked, moored, housed or garaged.

An undocumented vessel principally used in a state which has assumed numbering will not be numbered by the Coast Guard.

Unpowered vessels and those of less than 10 horsepower will be numbered on request. (Note: This is suggested as an aid in boat identification.) A number of states require that all powered boats be numbered without regard to the horsepower.

Vessels of more than 10 horsepower which have not previously been numbered will, pending receipt of a permanent certificate, be furnished a temporary certificate which must be carried on board whenever the vessel is in use. Documentary proof of title and ownership is not required by the Coast Guard with the application for number.

A numbering fee may be charged by the state. Estimated Coast Guard fees are: original numbering — $5; renewal of number — $3; re-issue of lost or destroyed certificate of number — $1. A number issued by the Coast Guard will be valid for three years from the date of the owner's next birthday after the certificate is issued. Each renewal will be for three years. In line with this, a certificate issued by a state may not be valid for more than three years.

Certificates are of pocket size, of water-resistant material, and must be on board whenever the vessel is in use.

A change of address must be reported within 15 days, and when a vessel is lost, destroyed, abandoned, or transferred to another person, the certificate must be surrendered within 15 days. If the certificate has been destroyed, notice to that effect must be given to the numbering authority. (Note: It is advisable to remove the numbers from any boat which is sold prior to making delivery to the new owner. Also, allowing the new owner to operate the boat, even for a limited time, with the former owner's certificate is illegal and subjects the seller to responsibility for any liabilities incurred as a result of accident, etc.)

A change of motor is not required to be reported.

If the state of principal use is changed, the owner must make application for a number for the new state and surrender the old certificate within 90 days. A certificate may be canceled and the number voided prior to expiration for a false or fraudulent certification in the application.

Application for renewal of a Coast Guard-issued number may be made within 90 days before expiration. If not renewed, a number is automatically invalid on the expiration date shown on the certificate. Applications for renewal received after the expiration will be treated as original and involve the higher fee. The same number may be re-issued if the renewal application is filed within one year after expiration.

On sale or transfer, where the vessel continues in use in the same state, the old number will be issued to the new owner. (Note: This practice is not followed in a number of the states.)

The number awarded to the boat (and no other) must be painted on, or attached to each side of the bow (each side of the forward half of the vessel). They must be so positioned as to be clearly legible. The numbers must be in block character, at least three inches high, of a color which will contrast with the background, and must be maintained so as to be clearly visible and legible.

Numbers awarded to boat dealers or manufacturers may be printed upon or attached to a removable sign temporarily but firmly mounted upon the boat being demonstrated or tested.

Each state must for a period of 90 days recognize the validity of a number issued to the vessel by another state or by the Coast Guard.

Boating Accidents

The operator of any boat involved in an accident is required by law to stop, render assistance, and offer identification.

A written report must be filed within 48 hours if the accident caused death. If it injured any person so as to incapacitate for more than 72 hours, or if the accident resulted in physical damage to property in excess of $100, the report must be filed in 5 days.

Boating accident report forms (CG-3865) are obtainable at any Coast Guard office or unit. They must be submitted by the operator to the nearest Coast Guard Officer in Charge, Marine Inspection, unless the operator is required to file an accident report with a state having an approved numbering system. These accident reports furnish information for use in accident prevention. Information from individual reports will not be publicly disclosed.

Law Enforcement

Coast Guard boarding vessels may be identified by the Coast Guard ensign. Their personnel will be in uniform. A vessel underway, upon being hailed by a Coast Guard vessel or patrolboat, is required to stop immediately and lay to, or maneuver in such a way as to permit the boarding party to come aboard. Failure to stop to permit boarding may subject the operator or owner to a penalty of $100. A civil penalty (fine) may be imposed by the Coast Guard for reckless or negligent operation, for failure to obey the rules of the road, or for failure to comply with regulations (on equipment, etc.).

Both under the 1940 law and the 1958 revision, there is a provision for a fine of up to $2,000 and imprisonment of not more than one year for the criminal offense of reckless or negligent operation of a vessel which endangers the life, limb or property of any person.

Documentation and "Yachts"

"Documents" are ship's papers issued by the Bureau of Customs according to the trade in which the vessel is engaged, and may be a "Register," an "Enrollment and License," or a "License." As most motorboats were not eligible for documentation but their number was steadily increasing on the waters of the United States, some means of identification became necessary. In 1918, the first numbering act was passed which required that every undocumented vessel owned in the United States, using Federal waters, and propelled in whole or part by machinery must display on each bow an identifying number which is "awarded" upon application, and required, with certain exceptions, that this Certificate of Award of Number be kept on board when the vessel is in use. This act did not apply either to boats not over 16 feet in length temporarily equipped with detachable motors, or to public vessels.

Under the Navigation Laws, administered by the Bureau of Customs, a vessel of five tons or over owned by a citizen of the United States and used exclusively for pleasure may be documented as a yacht.

The principal privileges are:

1. Authority to fly the yacht ensign.

2. Provision for recording and retaining copies of mortgages, bills of sale, and other instruments of title in the offices of collectors of custom. Mortgages which are so recorded may, upon compliance with the applicable requirements, become preferred mortgages, giving additional security to the mortgagee.

In addition, with the states taking over the numbering of boats, many owners of larger pleasure craft prefer the Federal documentation. Another advantage is that crew members of a yacht are eligible for medical service at public health service hospitals and clinics.

Also, for the boats which are large enough to consider cruises outside United States waters, the yacht documentation which is open only to United States citizen-owners is more readily accepted at foreign ports of entry than pleasure boat registration which may be held by non-citizens.

Owners who enroll and license, or license vessels as yachts must effect renewals annually. Requests for documentation should be made through the custom-house at or nearest the port where the owner resides. The Coast Guard will not issue a number to a vessel documented as a yacht.

EQUIPMENT REQUIRED
Outboard Motorboats

Outboards must meet the same requirements as to safety equipment that apply to other boats of identical length, with the exception of the requirements for ventilation and carburetor flame arrestor. Outboard motorboats less than 26 feet in length, of open construction, not carrying passengers for hire, are not required to carry fire extinguishers. Note that for the application of regulations as to equipment, pleasure boats are divided into four classes.

Motorboats of Class "A" — Less than 16 Feet in Length

Light: See "Lights Required" chart.

Lifesaving Devices: One Coast-Guard approved life preserver, buoyant vest, ring buoy or buoyant cushion in good and serviceable condition for each person on board.

Fire Extinguishers: See table, p. 218

Ventilation: Two or more ventilators with cowls or equivalent capable of removing gases from the bilges in the engine and fuel tank compartments on boats constructed or decked over after April 25, 1940, using gasoline or fuel of a flashpoint less than 110°. (Note that diesel fuel has a considerably higher flash point than 110°). Motorboats so constructed as to have the greater portion of the bilges under the engine and fuel tanks open and exposed to the natural atmosphere at all times are not required to be fitted with such ventilators.

Flame Arrestor: Carburetors on all engines on motorboats, other than outboard motors, must be fitted with an approved device for arresting backfire. Installations made before November 19, 1952, need not meet the detailed requirements of the specifications and may be continued in use so long as they are in good condition.

Motorboats of Class "1" — 16 Feet to Less than 26 Feet in Length

The same equipment as required by a Class "A" motorboat is required on this class boat. The only addition is a hand, mouth or power-operated whistle or horn capable of producing a blast of at least 2 seconds duration and audible for a distance of at least one-half mile.

Motorboats of Class "2" — 26 to less than 40 Feet in Length

Lights: See "Lights required."

Lifesaving Devices: Same as for Class "A" boats.

Bell: One which, when struck, produces a clear, bell-like tone of full round characteristics.

Horn or Whistle: One hand or power-operated whistle or horn capable of producing a blast of at least 2 seconds duration audible for a distance of 1 mile.

Fire Extinguisher: See table.

Ventilation: Same as for Class "A" motorboat.

Motorboats of Class "3" — 40 Feet to not more than 65 Feet in Length

Lights: See "Lights required."

Lifesaving Devices: One Coast Guard-approved life preserver, or ring buoy for each person on board (buoyant cushions or buoyant vests will not meet the requirements on this class boat).

Bell: Same as for Class "2" motorboat.

Horn or Whistle: Must be power-operated, capable of producing a blast of at least 2 seconds duration and audible for a distance of at least 1 mile.

Fire Extinguisher: See table, p. 218.

Ventilation: Same as for Class "A" motorboat.

Flame Arrestor: Same as for Class "A" motorboat.

Note: Signalling Equipment

The Rules of the Road place upon the owners and operators of motorboats responsibility for giving and answering passing signals on whistle, fog, horn or bell as prescribed, although the law does not specifically require such signalling equipment aboard certain classes of motorboats. In cases of accident or casualty, the courts would undoubtedly give great consideration to any lack of such equipment in fixing responsibility.

In addition to the above legally prescribed equipment, the Coast Guard Auxiliary suggests the following:

At least one hand portable fire extinguisher for all outboard boats.

Class "A" boats should be equipped with at least one paddle or oar; distress flare; adequate pump or bailer; and anchor and line suitable to the locality.

Coast Guard Approved Equipment

"Coast Guard Approved Equipment" is equipment which has been approved by the Commandant of the Coast Guard after it has been determined to be in compliance with the various Coast Guard specifications and regulations relating to the construction and performance of such equipment. Names of manufacturers of approved equipment and approval numbers assigned to them for various types of equipment are contained in the Coast Guard Booklet *CG-190, "Equipment Lists,"* which is published approximately once each year. This publication may be obtained upon application to any Coast Guard District Office or any Officer in Charge, Marine Inspection.

Lifesaving Devices

Life Preservers: Construction: Approved life preservers are of jacket design, constructed with pads of kapok, fibrous glass, cork, or balsa wood in a cloth covering which is fitted with the necessary straps and ties. Adult and child sizes are available and are so marked. Since 1949, all approved life preservers have been required to be Indian Orange in color.

Markings: Approved life preservers must bear two markings, the manufacturer's stamp indicating the approval number, and the inspector's stamp indicating that the preserver has been inspected and passed. Current stamps follow:

Adult (or Child)
Model No. ....
Manufacturer's Name and Address
U.S.C.G. Approval No. ......
INSPECTED AND PASSED
Date
Place
U.S.C.G. Inspector's Initials

Buoyant Cushions: Construction: Currently approved buoyant cushions may have as buoyant material, kapok, fibrous glass, or plastic foam covered with various fabric or plastic covering materials and fitted with grab straps. They come in a variety of sizes and may be of any color.

Markings: Approved buoyant cushions currently being manufacturered are all marked with a cloth tag attached to the boxing or border of the cushion on which is printed the following information:

BUOYANT CUSHION
Size (width, length, thickness)
Contains .... ozs. (kapok or fibrous glass) or .... Cu. In. Foam
Approved for use on motorboats of Class A, 1, or 2 not carrying passengers for hire
U.S. Coast Guard Approval No. ....
Lot No. ....
Instructions for Care of Cushion ....
....
Name and Address of Manufacturer

Ring Buoys: Construction: Approved ring buoys are available in 30", 24", and 20" sizes and may be constructed of cork or balsa wood, with a canvas cover, or plastic foam with special surface. All buoys are fitted with a grab line and they may be either white or orange in color.

Markings: Cork and balsa wood ring buoys must bear two markings, the manufacturer's stamp and the inspector's stamp, which are similar to those described above for life preservers. Plastic foam ring buoys bear only one marking, a metal nameplate attached to the buoy on which appears the following:

Name and Address of Manufacturer
Size of Buoy (30", 24", or 20")
U.S.C.G. Approval No. ......
Date ....
U.S.C.G. Inspector's Initials

Buoyant Vests: Construction: Approved buoyant vests are of vest design, constructed of pads of either kapok or fibrous glass, with a cloth covering, and straps and ties attached. They are made in three sizes, two child sizes and one adult size, and may be of any color.

Markings: Approved buoyant vests are all marked with a cloth tag attached to the cover on which is printed the following information:

BUOYANT VEST
Model ....
Adult (or Child)
Approved for use on motorboats of Class A, 1 or 2, not carrying passengers for hire
U.S.C.G. Approval No. ......
Lot No. ....
Instructions for Care of Vest ......
....
Name and Address of Manufacturer
Weight Ranges for Child Sizes

Unapproved Equipment

There is much boat safety equipment on the market which does not bear the Coast Guard stamp of approval. This does not mean that these other devices are unsafe. Many are designed for special purposes — such as for racing — and some are more comfortable to wear than the approved types. Still others, such as the inflatable types, are in categories which the Coast Guard does not approve. These "unapproved" types of lifesaving equipment may be carried aboard the boat, but they must be in addition to the required approved equipment for the different classes.

Fire Extinguishers and Flame Arrestors

Approved types of fire extinguishers are identified by make and model number. The markings on the extinguisher's nameplate can be checked against the model number listed under the company's name in the Equipment Lists booklet, CG-190. Similarly, the marking on flame arrestors can be checked in the booklet.

With few exceptions any equipment which has ever been approved by the Coast Guard or the former Bureau of Marine Inspection and Navigation will be accepted as legal equipment so long as it remains in good and serviceable condition. When no longer serviceable, or when the required approval stamps are no longer legible and the equipment cannot otherwise be identified as being approved, such equipment must be replaced with currently approved equipment. Any questions regarding the status of approval of any item of equipment should be directed to a Coast Guard district Office of an Office in Charge. Marine Inspection, together with a complete description of the device and its markings.

When purchasing approved equipment insist on a sales slip describing the article as Coast Guard approved.

Approved Fire Extinguishers

Each fire extinguisher is classified, by letter and number, according to the type of fire it may be expected to extinguish, and the size of the extinguisher. The letter indicates the type of fire ("A" for fires in ordinary combustible materials; "B" for gasoline, oil, and grease fires; "C" for fires in electrical equipment). Extinguishers approved for motorboats are hand-portable, of either B-I or B-II classification.

The number of approved extinguishers

FIRE EXTINGUISHERS REQUIRED

Class of motorboat	Without fixed system in machinery space	With fixed system in machinery space
A (less than 16 ft.)	1 B–I	None.
1 (16 ft. to under 26 ft.)	1 B–I	None.
2 (26 ft. to under 40 ft.)	2 B–I or 1 B–II	1 B–I.
3 (40 ft. to 65 ft.)	3 B–I or 1 B–II and 1 B–I	2 B–I or 1 B–II.

Classification (type-size)	Foam (minimum gallons)	Carbon Dioxide (minimum pounds)	Dry Chemical (minimum pounds)	Carbon Tetrachloride (See note)
B–I	1¼	4	2	Approval discontinued.
B–II	2½	15	10	

NOTE. *Effective 6 December 1958 all approvals were withdrawn of carbon tetrachloride extinguishers and others of the toxic vaporizing-liquid type such as chlorobromethane. However, such of these extinguishers as were in service on that date may be continued in service as approved equipment until 1 January 1962 provided they are in good and serviceable condition.*

required depends upon the class (or length) of the motorboat. One B-II extinguisher may be substituted for two B-I extinguishers. When the engine compartment of the motorboat is equipped with a fixed (built-in) extinguishing system of an approved type, one less B-I extinguisher is required.

Numbering Your Boat

Under the Federal Boating Act of 1958, motorboats of more than 10 horsepower which are operated on the navigable waters of the United States must be numbered in the state of principal use.

The Coast Guard is continuing to number motorboats in the following states: Alaska, Connecticut, District of Columbia, Hawaii, Idaho, Iowa, Maine, New Hampshire, New Jersey, Pennsylvania, Tennessee, Washington and Wyoming. In these states, apply for the Coast Guard card application for number at any post office and purchase the Federal Boating Stamp at that time. The postmarked stub will serve as your temporary proof of numbering until the certificate is received from the Coast Guard.

In Other States

Motorboats principally used in the following states are numbered by those states. Applications should be filed with the state or local agency indicated:

ALABAMA: All undocumented motorboats, all sailboats and all boats for hire. Department of Conservation, Montgomery 4.

ARIZONA: Every watercraft. Motor Vehicle Division, Boat Number Section, 1739 W. Jackson Street, Phoenix.

ARKANSAS: All undocumented motorboats of more than 10 horsepower. County Clerk.

CALIFORNIA: All mechanically propelled undocumented boats (except those having electric motors of 10 horsepower or less) and all sailboats of more than 8 feet in length. Department of Motor Vehicles, 2570 24th Street, Sacramento 18.

COLORADO: Every motorboat of more than 10 horsepower. State Park and Recreation Board, 221 State Services Building, Denver 3.

DELAWARE: Every motorboat. Small Boat Safety Division, Delaware Commission of Shell Fisheries, Dover.

THE FEDERAL BOATING ACT OF 1958

LIGHTS REQUIRED ON BOATS UNDERWAY BETWEEN SUNSET AND SUNRISE

ANCHOR LIGHTS. Vessels at anchor must display anchor lights except those of not more than 65 feet in length in a "special anchorage area."

Manually propelled vessels shall have ready at hand a lantern showing a white light which shall be temporarily exhibited in sufficient time to prevent collision

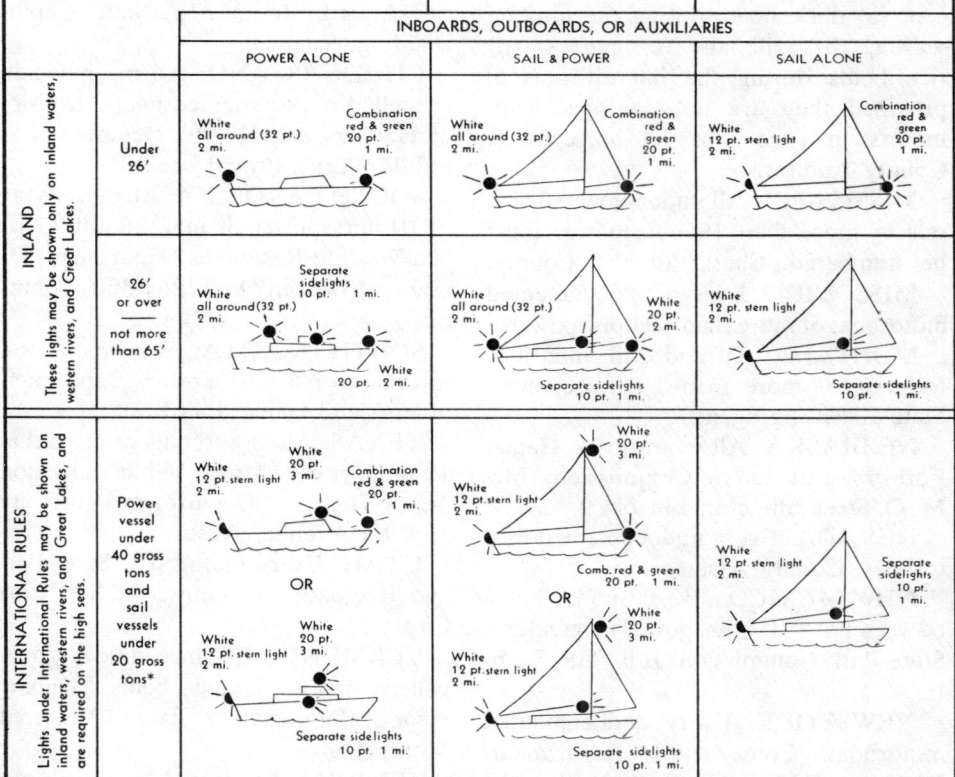

* Under International Rules powerboats of 40 gross tons or over must carry separate sidelights, visible 2 miles, and a 20-point white light visible 5 miles. Sailing vessels of 20 gross tons or over must carry separate side lights, visible 2 miles. Under sail, only boats of less than 20 tons may use a combination lantern. (Note: A vessel under sail alone on the Great Lakes is not required to display a stern light.)

FLORIDA: All motorboats of more than 10 horsepower. County Tax Collector.

GEORGIA: Every undocumented motorboat of more than 10 horsepower. State Game and Fish Commission, Motorboat Registration Unit, 401 State Capitol, Atlanta 3.

ILLINOIS: Every undocumented motorboat. Department of Conservation, 400 South Spring Street, Springfield.

INDIANA: Every motorboat of more than 6 horsepower. Department of Conservation, 311 West Washington Street, Indianapolis 9.

KANSAS: All motorboats of more than 10 horsepower. Kansas Forestry, Fish and Game Commission, Pratt.

KENTUCKY: Every undocumented motorboat. Circuit Court Clerk.

LOUISIANA: Every undocumented motorboat of more than 10 horsepower. Wild Life and Fisheries Commission, 400 Royal Street, New Orleans.

MARYLAND: All undocumented vessels of over 7-1/2 horsepower, and all sailboats over 35 feet in length. Department of Tidewater Fisheries, State Office Building, Annapolis.

MASSACHUSETTS: Every undocumented motorboat of more than 10 horsepower. Apply to Registry of Motor Vehicles (numerous branch offices).

MICHIGAN: Every motorboat. Sheriff's department in every County.

MINNESOTA: All undocumented watercraft are required to be numbered except (a) duck boats during the hunting season, (b) sailboats, (c) canoes, (d) rice boats during the harvest season, provided they are not equipped with motors in excess of 10 horsepower. County Auditor.

MISSISSIPPI: All undocumented vessels of more than 10 horsepower must be numbered. Sheriff of the County.

MISSOURI: Every undocumented motorboat of more than 10 horsepower.

MONTANA: All undocumented motorboats of more than 10 horsepower. State Licensing agents.

NEBRASKA: All motorboats. Game, Forestry and Parks Commission, Mr. M. O. Steen, director, Lincoln 9.

NEVADA: Every undocumented motorboat. County Assessor.

NEW MEXICO: Every undocumented vessel of "10 horsepower or greater." State Park Commission, Box 958, Santa Fe.

NEW YORK: Every undocumented motorboat. Conservation Department, Division of Motorboats, State Campus Site, Albany.

NORTH CAROLINA: All motorboats of more than 10 horsepower. Motorboats Registration and Licensing Section, N.C. Wildlife Resources Commission, P.O. Box 2919, Raleigh.

NORTH DAKOTA: Every motorboat having 10 horsepower or more. North Dakota Game and Fish Department, Bismarck.

OHIO: Every watercraft. Administrator, Division of Watercraft, Department of Natural Resources, 1106 Ohio Department Building, Columbus 15.

OKLAHOMA: All undocumented motorboats. Properly licensed boat dealer.

OREGON: All motorboats of 10 horsepower or more. Oregon State Marine Board, Room 311, State Capitol Building, Salem.

RHODE ISLAND: All mechanically propelled undocumented boats. Division of Harbors and Rivers, Department of Public Works, Providence 3.

SOUTH CAROLINA: All motorboats of 10 horsepower or more. South Carolina Wildlife Resources Department, Division of Boating, P.O. Box 360, Columbia.

SOUTH DAKOTA: Every motorboat in excess of 6 horsepower. Department of Fish and Game, Pierre.

TEXAS: All motorboats of more than 10 horsepower. Motor Vehicle Division, Texas Highway Department, 40th and Jackson Avenue, Austin.

UTAH: Every motorboat. State Park and Recreation Commission. Salt Lake City.

VERMONT: All mechanically propelled undocumented boats. Department of Public Safety, State of Vermont, Montpelier.

VIRGINIA: Every undocumented motorboat of 10 horsepower or more. Commission of Game and Inland Fisheries, 7 North Second St., Richmond 13.

WEST VIRGINIA: All motorboats of more than 5 horsepower. Boat Licensing Section, State Office Building No. 3, Charleston.

WISCONSIN: Every undocumented sailboat and motorboat. Wisconsin Conservation Department, 2158 Altwood Avenue, Madison 1.

CHAPTER XXI

State Boating Laws

The vast increase of pleasure boating in the United States during the past few decades has been accompanied by legislation in all of the "old" 48 states regulating pleasure boats and boating. At this time, in Alaska, Hawaii, and the District of Columbia there are no apparent provisions in the general statutes which cover pleasure boating.

In the other states, the laws are generally written with an emphasis on safety and the responsibility of the boat operator or owner for any damages caused by the operation of a pleasure boat.

In the following digest of State Boating Laws, the legislation is broken down into the categories listed below. This information has been compiled by the Outboard Boating Club of America and is reproduced with their permission.

Equipment for Boats

Lights, Fire Extinguishers, Whistles and Bells, Chlorinators, Flame Arrestors, Ventilators, Mufflers.

Rules of Operation

Careless Operation, Reckless Operation, Incapacity of Operator, Speed Regulated, Restricted Areas, Horsepower Limitations, Overpowering Prohibited, Overloading Prohibited, Accidents, Age of Operators, Traffic Rules, Water Skiing Regulations, Skin Diving, Interference With Navigation, Mooring to Buoys or Beacons, Riding on Decks or Gunwales, Races and Regattas, Owner's Civil Responsibility, Criminal Liability, Boat Pollution, Operator's Licensing.

Federal Regulations

At the outset, it should be noted that there are separate and distinct Federal laws controlling motorboat equipment for operation on navigable waters of the United States. In no case are these laws superseded by any of the state equipment requirements. A state law can be more stringent (or less) than the Federal rule, but it cannot *conflict* and still be valid on the navigable waters of the United States. The Federal laws and regulations are paramount.

Briefly the Federal law requires:

(a) Lighting for all motorboats;

(b) all motorboats, except outboards of open construction and less than 26 ft. in length, to have such number and type of fire extinguishers as the Coast Guard may prescribe;

(c) all motorboats to carry at least one approved life preserver or ring buoy for each person on board; craft under 40 ft. can use buoyant cushions or vests;

(d) every motorboat 16 ft. or more in length to be provided with an efficient whistle or other sound-producing mechanical appliance;

(e) motorboats other than outboards to be equipped with carburetor flame arrestors; and

(f) ventilators on inboard motorboats capable of removing gases from the bilges in the engine and fuel tank compartments, unless the greater portions of such bilges are open and exposed to the natural atmosphere at all times.

Lights

State laws vary. Match the letters follow-

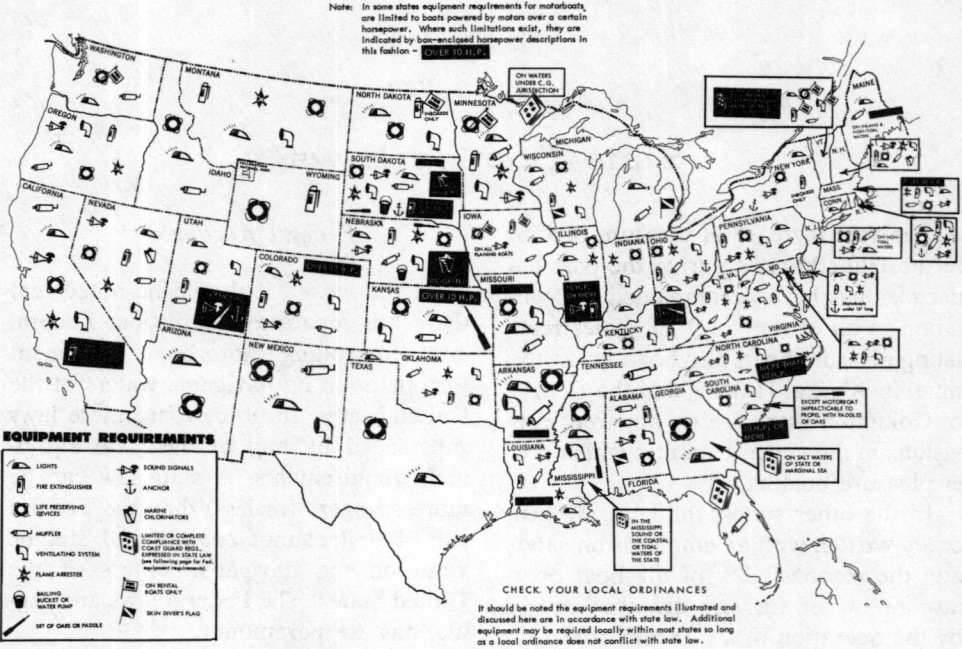

ing each state to the General Code for requirements of each state.

General Code

Motorboats shall carry and show lights when underway or when anchored in navigation channels after dark, as follows:

(a) Less than 26 ft. in length, a white light aft showing all around the horizon, visible for at least 2 miles; and a combination light in the forepart, lower than the white light aft, showing green to starboard and red to port, so fixed as to throw a light from dead ahead to 2 points abaft the beam on each side, and visible for at least 1 mile.

(b) Twenty-six feet in length or over, a white light aft showing all around the horizon, visible for at least 2 miles; two separate sidelights, showing green to starboard and red to port, so constructed as to show an unbroken light over an arc of the horizon of 10 points of the compass, so fixed as to throw the light from right ahead to 2 points abaft the beam on each side, and visible up to 1 mile; and a white light in the forepart, as near the stem as possible, lower than the white light aft, so constructed as to show an unbroken light over an arc of the horizon of 20 points of the compass, and visible for at least 2 miles. Sidelights shall be properly screened to prevent them from being seen across the bow.

(c) A light sufficient to make the motorboat's presence and location known to any and all other vessels within a reasonable distance.

(d) When propelled by sail and machinery any motorboat shall carry the same lights required for a motorboat propelled by machinery only.

(e) Motorboats under 26 ft. when propelled by sail alone, shall carry the combination light, but not the white light aft. Motorboats 26 ft. or over, when so propelled, shall carry the colored sidelights, suitably screened, but not the prescribed white lights. All motorboats, when so propelled, shall carry a lantern or flashlight showing a white light to be exhibited temporarily in sufficient time to avert a collision.

(f) Any motorboat may carry and exhibit the lights required by the Federal Regulations for Preventing Collisions at Sea, 1948, Federal Act of October 11, 1951 (33 USC 143-174D) as amended, in lieu of the lights required by state law.

(g) Flashing lights prohibited.

ALABAMA: (a), (b), (d), (e), (g).

ARIZONA: (a—Applies to all watercraft), (g—Visible throughout a full circle for not less than 1 mile.)

ARKANSAS: (c—Over 10 HP.)

CALIFORNIA: (a), (b), (d), (e—But 1 white stern light, so constructed as to show an unbroken light over an area of the horizon of 12 points of the compass, and so fixed as to show 6 points from right aft on each side, additionally required on each motorboat of every class), (f).

COLORADO: Over 10 HP. (a), (b), (d), (e), (f), (g).

CONNECTICUT: (a—Bow light shall be visible for not less than 300 ft. ahead; aft light, not less than 300 ft. from rear or side. One extra light required. Bow light may be combination or 2 separate lights. Minimum lens diameter of all lights: 3 inches.)

DELAWARE: (a), (b), (d), (e).

FLORIDA: (a), (b), (d), (e).

GEORGIA: (c — Fresh water regulations: Power boats operating at night shall be equipped with light sufficient to throw light not less than 150 ft. in direction of travel.)

IDAHO: (a—Applies to all motorboats.)

ILLINOIS: (a), (b), (d), (e), (h).

INDIANA: (a—Applies to all motorboats and sailboats equipped with a motor of 15 HP. or more.)

IOWA: (a—Applies to all inboard motorboats and outboard motorboats of plane or gliding type, capable of traveling 8 miles or more per hour. An additional white light is required in forepart, as near the bow as practicable. Its minimum lens diameter: 3-1/2 inches. When in use, this light shall be kept pointed in direction boat is traveling. On outboards of plane or gliding type (including combination plane displacement) not capable of exceeding 8 miles per hour: A constant white light in forepart, visible all around the horizon. On rowboats of displacement type, with outboard motor, when operated on any lake, and when over 300 ft. from shore: A constant white light so placed as to be visible from any direction.)

KANSAS: (c—Over 10 HP.)

KENTUCKY: (c).

LOUISIANA: Over 10 HP. (a), (b), (d—Also a bright white lantern or flashlight shall be carried aboard motorboat and vessels of all classes ready to be exhibited in sufficient time to avert collision), (e), (f).

MAINE: Over 10 HP. (c—Every kind of watercraft.)

MARYLAND: (a), (d), (e) (f).

MASSACHUSETTS: Over 10 HP. (a), (b), (d), (e—Motorboats of every class when propelled by sail alone if not otherwise required to carry one or more lights visible from aft, shall carry at their stern, a white light so constructed as to show an unbroken light over an arc of the horizon of 12 points of the compass, and so fixed as to show 6 points from right aft on each side. Such light shall be carried about the same level as the side lights), (f)

MICHIGAN: Motorboats shall be equipped with one bow light which can be plainly distinguished at a distance of 500 ft.

MINNESOTA: On waters under U. S. Coast Guard's jurisdiction: (a), (b). On State waters: (b). On every watercraft under 26 ft., when underway: A lantern or flashlight not necessarily fixed to any part of boat, showing a white light visible all around the horizon for at least 2 miles, which shall be temporarily exhibited in sufficient time to avert a collision.

MISSISSIPPI: (c—Every kind of watercraft.)

MISSOURI: (c—Over 10 HP.)

MONTANA: (c—Every kind of watercraft.)

NEBRASKA: (a—A lantern or flashlight additionally required), (b), (e), (f), (h).

NEVADA: (a), (b), (d), (e), (f). No motorboat of less than 16 ft. in length need exhibit the lights required during a period of one hour after sunset and during a period of one hour before sunrise.

NEW HAMPSHIRE: (a — Alternate white stern light authorized in place of white light aft so fixed as to show from straight astern to 2 points forward of the beam on both sides.), (b—Alternate white stern light authorized on boats 26 to 40 ft. in length,), (g—One white light high enough to show all around the horizon.)

NEW JERSEY: On non-tidal waters: (a—Combination light shall be placed so as to be visible over bow at any speed.), (b—Minimum diameter of side lights: 16 square inches; of white forelight: 19 square inches. All glasses or lenses prescribed shall be fresnel or fluted. Side lights shall be not less than 18 inches long.), (g—One clear white light 2 ft. above the deck visible over all points of the compass.)

NEW MEXICO: (a—Applies to every motorboat during the hours of darkness.)

NEW YORK: (a), (b—Up to 65 ft.), (d), (e), (g—Vessels under 150 ft. shall carry forward, where it can best be seen, but no higher than 20 ft. above the hull, a white light in a lantern, so constructed as to show clearly all around horizon for at least 1 mile. However, vessels 65 ft. or less at anchor in special anchorage areas need not exhibit such a light.)

NORTH CAROLINA: More than 10 HP. (a), (b), (d), (e), (f). During the hours between sunset and sunrise all motorboats of 10 HP. or less and all manually propelled vessels shall carry, ready at hand, a flashlight or lantern showing a white light which shall be displayed in time to avert collision.

NORTH DAKOTA: (c—Every kind of watercraft.)

OHIO: (a), (b), (d), (e), (f), (h—Except in emergency.)

OREGON: (a), (b).

PENNSYLVANIA: For public inland waters: (a), (b).

RHODE ISLAND: (a), (b), (d), (e), (f).

FIRE EXTINGUISHERS

Study the table below. The states listed below this table require fire extinguishers to be carried aboard motor boats as indicated in the table.

EQUIPMENT	CLASS A (Less than 16 ft.)	CLASS 1 (16 ft. to less than 26 ft.)	CLASS 2 (26 ft. to less than 40 ft.)	CLASS 3 (40 ft. to not more than 65 ft.)
Minimum number of B-1 Hand Portable Fire Extinguishers Required*				
When no fixed fire extinguishing system in machinery space.	1	1	2	3
When fixed fire extinguishing system in machinery space.	0	0	1	2

*One B-2 hand portable fire extinguisher may be substituted for two B-1 hand portable fire extinguishers.
   B-1 extinguishers contain: Foam, 1¼ (Minimum) gallons; or Carbon Dioxide, 4 (Minimum) pounds; or Dry Chemical, 2 (Minimum) pounds; or Vaporizing Liquid, 1 quart. "It should be noted that toxic vaporizing—liquid type fire extinguishers, such as carbon tetrachloride and chlorobromethane, will not be acceptable after January 1, 1962 as required approved extinguishers on private pleasure craft. Such extinguishers currently in use may be continued in service until that date if in good and serviceable condition".
   B-2 extinguishers contain: Foam, 2½ (Minimum) gallons; or Carbon Dioxide, 15 (Minimum) pounds; or Dry Chemical, 10 (Minimum) pounds.

SOUTH CAROLINA: (c—10 HP, or more.)

SOUTH DAKOTA: Over 6 HP. (a), (b), (d), (e—Vessels of all classes, when propelled by oars alone, shall carry a lantern or flashlight as a warning signal to avert collisions.) (h—Only authorized emergency rescue or law enforcement craft.)

TEXAS: (a), (b), (d), (e),(f).

UTAH: (a—Applies to all boats 16 ft. or over. Boats under 16 ft. required to carry a flashlight or lantern visible for at least 2 miles. Open deck boats over 16 ft. used exclusively for fishing may carry flashlight or lantern in lieu of required lights for boats 16 feet or over.), (g).

VERMONT: (a—Applies to all motorboats over 16 ft. in length), (c—Motorboats less than 16 ft. in length), (f).

VIRGINIA: (a), (b), (d), (e), (f), (g).

WEST VIRGINIA: (a), (b), (d), (e), (f).

WISCONSIN: (a), (b), (d), (f).

Fire Extinguishers—State Requirements

ALABAMA: (1) *All* inboard motor boats, and *all* outboard motor boats with enclosed bilges—one hand portable or semi-portable fire extinguisher using carbon dioxide (CO_2), foam, or other chemical ingredient commonly used to put out gasoline or petroleum product fires. Must be of a CG-approved type.

(2) All vessels equipped with any butane gas, propane gas, kerosene, gasoline or petroleum product consuming device (except outboard motors)—same as (1).

(3) All motor vessels having closed or semi-enclosed cabins and any vessel with sleeping accommodations—same as (1).

ILLINOIS: On motorboats with 10 or more horsepower at least one U.S. Coast Guard approved fire extinguisher is required.

IOWA: A fire extinguisher of type and size approved by Conservation Commission—on all motorboats when operated for hire. Shall be capable of extinguishing burning gasoline and be of the carbon dioxide, carbon tetrachloride, or foam type.

KENTUCKY: If boat has deck 30 inches or longer, a fire extinguisher of approved type (CO_2, dry chemical, or foam) is required.

MINNESOTA: Motorboats carrying or using fuel or other inflammable or toxic fluid in any enclosure of the boat shall be equipped with a fire extinguisher.

MONTANA: (1) All boats under 26 ft. of open construction* powered by an outboard motor and not carrying passengers for hire shall have one fire extinguisher. (2) All other motorboats shall carry at least the minimum number of fire extinguishers of adequate volume and approved by the National Board of Fire Underwriters as follows: Class 1—one; Class 2—two; Class 3—three.

*Open construction defined excludes (A) Vessels containing any enclosed compartment; (B) Vessels with bilges which are enclosed so as to permit accumulation of gasoline vapors; and (C) Vessels which have any compartment in which gasoline vapors may accumulate. After 4/1/60, all motorboats of closed construction in Class 1 and all motorboats in Class 2 and 3, shall carry U.S. Coast Guard approved fire extinguishers according to Federal regulations for boats of their class.

NEBRASKA: As defined by Nebraska law, Class 1 motorboats (less than 16 ft. in length and powered by outboard motors totalling 5 horsepower or less), Class 2 (less than 16 ft. in length and powered by outboard motors totalling more than 5 horsepower), and Class 3 (16 ft. to less than 26 ft. in length), shall carry one Coast Guard approved fire extinguisher. Class 4 motorboats (26 ft. to less than 40 ft. in length) shall carry two such extinguishers, and Class 5 motorboats (40 ft. or over) must carry three such extinguishers.

NEW HAMPSHIRE: Boats operated by gasoline or other inflammable fuel: (a) Less than 26 ft.: One quart of carbon tetrachloride or chlorobromethane, or 1-1/4 gallons of foam or 4 pounds of carbon dioxide, or 2 pounds of dry chemical. (b) 26 ft. to 40 ft.: Approved type extinguishers with double the total capacity of (a); (c) Over 40 ft.: Approved type extinguishers with three times the capacity of (a); (d) Power boats where passenger carrying space is divided by the engine: Double the capacity specified, and stationed each side of engine; (e) Boats propelled by outboard motor: one C/G approved or one of a type approved by State Public Utilities Comm.

On boats propelled by outboard motors, for use at the time on waters under Federal jurisdiction at least one U.S. Coast Guard approved fire extinguisher is required.

NEW JERSEY: On non-tidal waters, all inboard motorboats and outboard cruisers shall carry at least 1 fire extinguisher as approved by Dept. of Conservation & Economic Development. All vessels carrying passengers for hire shall be equipped with at least 2 fire extinguishers as approved by the Dept.

NEW YORK: All vessels propelled by petroleum fuels, except outboard motors, must at all times, carry at least 1 fire extinguisher of either the carbon dioxide, foam type, or other type approved by the Commissioner of Conservation.

NORTH DAKOTA: Every watercraft powered by an inboard motor shall be equipped with a chemical fire extinguisher.

OHIO: All powercraft shall carry fire extinguishers capable of extinguishing a burning gasoline fire and such fire extinguishers shall be so placed as to be readily accessible and in such condition as to be ready for immediate and effective use.

PENNSYLVANIA: On inland waters, on inboard motorboats under 26 ft. in length, 1 1-quart carbon tetrachloride or 1-1/4 gallon foam or 1 4-pound CO_2 extinguisher. None required on outboard motorboats. On motorboats 26 ft. and over, 2 1-quart tetrachloride or 2 1-1/4 gallon foam or 2 4-pound CO_2 extinguishers.

SOUTH DAKOTA: Class 1 motorboats shall carry at least one fire extinguisher. Class 2 motorboats shall carry at least two extinguishers. Class 3 motorboats shall carry at least one B-2 type and one B-1 type or three B-1 type extinguishers. All extinguishers must have the stamp of approval of the U.S. Coast Guard.

UTAH: All motorboats of closed construction, closed bilges, or having built-in gas tanks, must carry a Coast Guard approved fire extinguisher.

WYOMING: All inboard motorboats and all other watercraft 16 feet or over in length shall carry at least one U.S. Coast Guard approved fire extinguisher.

Boating acts of the states below make this Common Provision —

"Every motorboat shall be provided with such number, size and type of fire extinguishers, capable of promptly and effectively extinguishing burning gasoline, as may be prescribed by the regulations of the department, which fire extinguishers shall be at all times kept in condition for immediate and effective use and shall be so placed as to be readily accessible."

LOUISIANA: (Wild Life and Fisheries Commission)

NEVADA: (Dept. of Motor Veh.)

Fire Extinguishers—Exceptions

1. Outboard motorboats less than 26 ft. in length of open construction*, not carrying passengers for hire, are not required to carry fire extinguishers in the following states:
California
Delaware
Florida
Maryland
Massachusetts
North Carolina
Oklahoma
Utah
Virginia
West Virginia
Wisconsin—*All* outboards of open construction.

*A vessel of open construction may be defined as one which does not have enclosed areas in which inflammable vapors may collect and which, under all operating conditions, has adequate natural ventilation of all areas subject to penetration by inflammable vapors.

2. Motorboats engaged in any race which has been previously arranged or announced, or if such boats be designed and intended solely for racing while engaged in such navigation as is incidental to the tuning up of the motorboats and engines for the race.
California
Delaware - Florida - Maryland - Massachusetts—Motorboats propelled by outboard motors.
Nebraska
Nevada
Oklahoma
Rhode Island
South Dakota

3. Other Exceptions
California—Motorboats propelled by electric motors of 10 horsepower or less.
Illinois—Motorboats under 10 horsepower.
South Dakota—Motorboats less than 16 feet in length.

Lifesaving Devices

All states requiring such, generally provide every motorboat or vessel regulated shall have aboard one life preserver, buoyant vest, ring buoy or other device of the type approved by the U.S. Coast Guard or of the sort prescribed by regulations of the appropriate state agency, in good and serviceable condition for each person on board.

Note: A ski belt is legal equipment for skiing but does not fulfill the requirement of a Coast Guard approved life-saving device for each occupant of the boat.

In the following states children under a specified age are required to wear a life preserver at all times while aboard a motorboat, or other watercraft:

ARIZONA: Under 8 years old.

MONTANA: 12 years of age or younger. Law reads while occupying a vessel in motion.

NEBRASKA: Under 12 years old. Also, passengers aboard vessels for hire must wear life jackets while boats are in operation.

OHIO: Under 10 years old on any watercraft under 18 ft. in length.

Whistles and Bells

General Code: Match the letters following each state to this Code for the requirements of each state.

(a) Motorboats 16 ft. or over, but less than 26 ft. in length must carry a hand, mouth or power operated whistle or other sound-producing mechanical appliance capable of producing at least a 2-second blast and audible for at least 1/2 mile.

(b) Motorboats 26 ft. or over, but less than 40 ft. in length must carry a hand or power operated whistle or other sound-producing mechanical appliance audible for at least 1 mile;

(c) and also an efficient bell.

(d) Motorboats 40 ft. or over in length must have a power-operated whistle or other sound-producing mechanical device audible for at least 1 mile;

(e) and also an efficient bell.

(f) All boats subject to the State Boating Laws, irrespective of class or size, must carry a whistle or other sound-producing device.

(g) No siren shall be carried or used other than on a patrol boat or like official boat used in emergencies.

(h) Unnecessary sounding of whistles, horns, bells, etc. prohibited.

(i) Sound signal requirements do not apply to motorboats while competing in officially sanctioned race, or if such boats be designed and intended solely for racing, while engaged in tuning up for the race.

ALABAMA: (a)—hand or power operated only; (b); (d) — audible at least 1-1/2 miles; (g). These sound-signal devices are expressly required for nighttime operation and during inclement weather when visibility is greatly reduced. The state requirements shall not be construed as exempting a vessel from further sound signal devices which may be required by Federal law on the navigable waters of Alabama.

CALIFORNIA: (a); (b); (c); (d); (e); (h) — in harbor area; (i).

COLORADO: (f) — Every motorboat (defined as any boat propelled by machinery of more than 10 HP.)

DELAWARE: (a); (b); (c); (d); (e); (i). Every motorboat less than 16 ft. in length must carry a hand or mouth whistle.

FLORIDA: a; (b); (c); (c); (e).

GEORGIA: On salt waters or marginal sea adjacent to state: (a); (b); (c); (d); (e); (i).

ILLINOIS: (f) — All motorboats of 10 HP. or more; (g) — Use of sirens in violation of Boating Act shall be considered a public nuisance and sirens are subject to confiscation.

INDIANA: (g).

IOWA: (f)—All steamboats, commercially or privately operated inboard motorboats, and outboard motorboats of plane or grading type, including combination plane and displacement types; (g) — Sirens prohibited without exception.

LOUISIANA: (a); (b); (c); (d); (e).

MARYLAND: (a); (b); (c); (d); (e); (g)—on Deep Creek Lake; (i).

MASSACHUSETTS: (a); (b); (c); (d); (e); (i).

MINNESOTA: On waters under the jurisdiction of U.S. Coast Guard: (a); (b); (c); (d); (e); (g); (i). On state waters: Motorboats 26 ft. or more in length shall carry a power, hand, or mouth operated horn or whistle capable of a 2-second sound audible for at least 1/2 mile; (g).

MISSISSIPPI: In the Mississippi Sound or coastal or tidal waters of state: (a); (b); (c); (d); (e); (i).

NEBRASKA: (a); (b)—audible at least 1/2 mile; (c); (d)—audible at least 1/2 mile; (e); (g); (h); (i). Motorboats less than 16 ft. in length and powered by outboard motors shall also be equipped with an efficient whistle or other sound producing mechanical appliance.

NEVADA: (a); (b); (c); (d); (e); (i).

NEW HAMPSHIRE: (f)—all power boats including boats propelled by outboard motors.

NEW JERSEY: On non-tidal waters: (f)—every power vessel; (g); (i).

NEW YORK: (f)—every power vessel; (g); (i);. On vessels less than 26 ft. in length a mouth whistle capable of producing a 2-second or more blast and audible at least 1/2 mile, may be used.

NORTH CAROLINA: (a); (b); (c); (d); (e); i).

OHIO: (g).

OKLAHOMA: (a); (b); (c); (d); (e); (g).

OREGON: (f)—all power boats.

PENNSYLVANIA: For public inland waters: (a); (b); (c); (d); (e); (i).

RHODE ISLAND: (a); (b); (c); (d); (e); (i).

SOUTH DAKOTA: (a); (b); (c); (d); (e); (i).

UTAH: (f)—the State Park and Recreation Comm. suggests that all boat owners provide their boat with some type of horn or whistle; (g).

VERMONT: On interstate or international waters only: (a); (b); (c); (d); (e); (i).

VIRGINIA: (a); (b); (c); (d); (e); (i).

WEST VIRGINIA: (a); (b); (c); (d); (e).

WISCONSIN: (g); (h).

Chlorinators Required
(for Marine Toilets)

NEBRASKA: In order to protect the safety and health of the boating and water-using public and to promote uniformity of laws, every vessel equipped with kitchen or toilet facilities shall handle and treat solid and liquid wastes in a manner that will prevent water pollution.

NEVADA: No boat shall be so equipped as to permit discharge of inadequately treated sewage from its marine toilet, or in any other manner. Marine toilets shall have securely affixed to their interior discharge opening a suitable treatment device in operating condition, constructed and fastened according to State Dept. of Health regulations. All sewage passing through a marine toilet shall pass solely through such device.

NEW HAMPSHIRE: After December 31, 1958, every marine toilet on any boat operated on state waters must be equipped with a suitable treatment device designed to disinfect human wastes before discharge into the water. Applicants registering outboard motors and inboard boats shall indicate on their application form whether or not their boat has a marine toilet which meets the Water Pollution Commission's standards. If a boat is found inadequately equipped, the owner has 48 hours in which to remedy the defect. Registration will be suspended for failure to comply. Additionally, up to $500 in fines may be imposed and/or 1 year prison term may be ordered.

SOUTH DAKOTA: Every vessel equipped with kitchen or toilet facilities shall be so equipped and operated to handle or treat liquid and solid wastes in a manner that will prevent pollution of the receiving waters. Violation constitutes a misdemeanor punishable by up to $100 fine and/or up to 30 days in county jail.

Carburetor Flame Arrestors

It is generally required that every motorboat equipped with an inboard motor shall have the carburetor of every such motor fitted with an approved device for arresting backfire.

Ventilators

Every motorboat, except those of open construction, using as fuel any inflammable or toxic fluid in any enclosure, shall be provided with an efficient natural or mechanical ventilation system which is capable of removing inflammable or explosive gases.

Mufflers

Except for motorboats actually competing in authorized races or regattas, every motorboat propelled by an internal combustion engine shall be equipped with a stock factory muffler or other device capable of adequately muffling the sounds of the exhaust of the engine. The use of cut-outs is prohibited, except in regattas or races or trial runs therefor.

RULES OF OPERATION

*1. Careless Operation
(Operating in a Careless or Heedless Manner So As To Be Grossly Indifferent To The Safety Of Any Person or Property) Prohibited.*

ARIZONA: Any watercraft.
ILLINOIS: Any motorboat.
INDIANA: Any boat, including any motorboat, sailboat, rowboat, skiff, dingy or canoe of whatever length or size and whether or not used to carry passengers for hire.
LOUISIANA: Any watercraft.
MICHIGAN: Any watercraft.
MINNESOTA: Any watercraft other than duck boat during hunting season, sailboat, canoe, rice boat during harvest season, and seaplane.

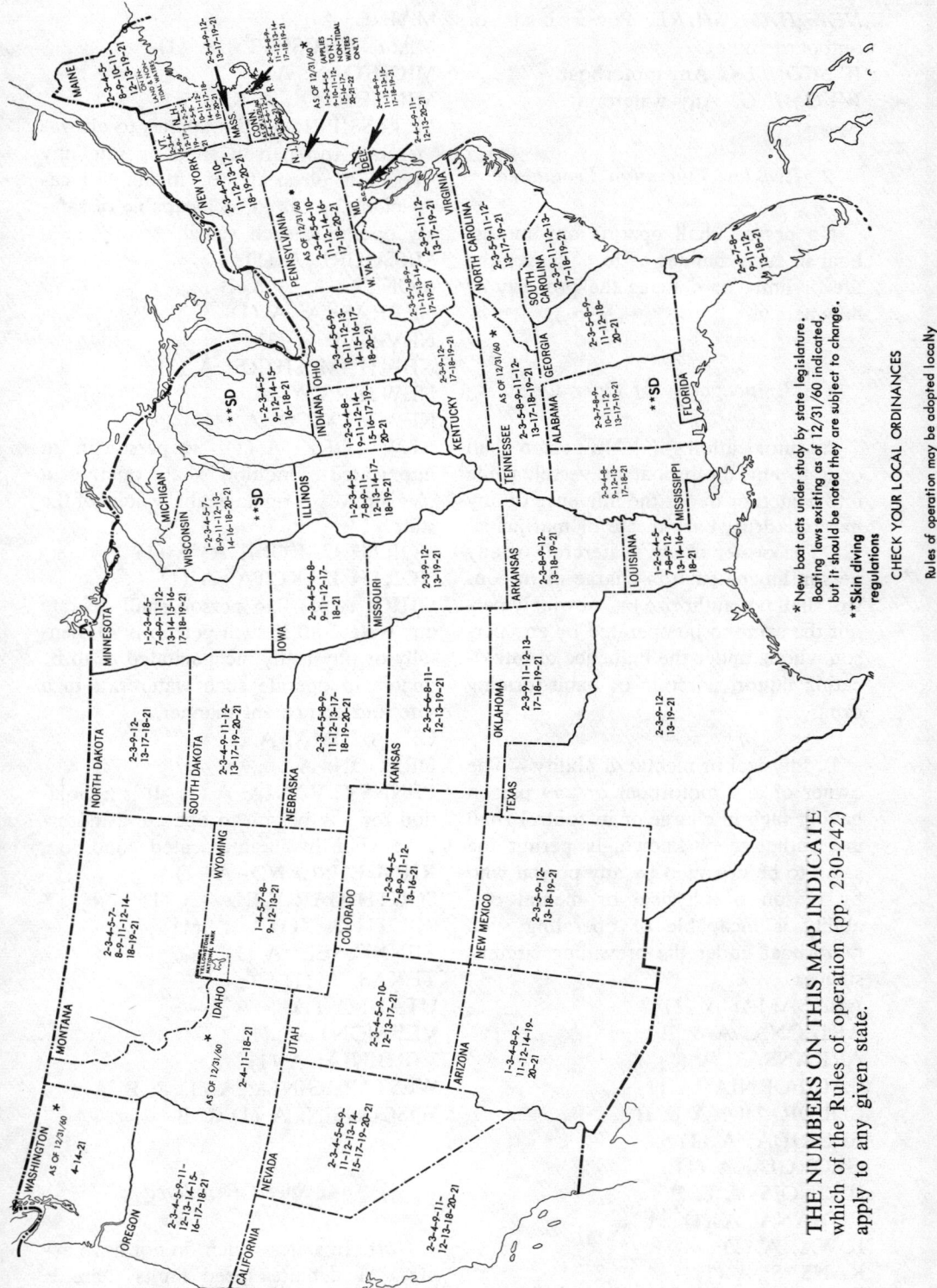

NEW HAMPSHIRE: Power boats or outboard motors.
WISCONSIN: Any motorboat.
WYOMING: Any watercraft.

2. Reckless Operation Prohibited

No person shall operate any motorboat in such manner as to endanger the life or limb, or damage the property of any person.

3. Incapacity of Operator

A. Intoxication — (1) No person shall operate any motorboat or vessel, while intoxicated or under the influence of any narcotic drug, barbiturate or marijuana. (2) The owner of any watercraft or any person having such in charge or in control shall not authorize or knowingly permit the same to be operated by any person who is under the influence of intoxicating liquor, narcotic or habit-forming drugs.

B. Physical or mental disability — The owner of any motorboat or any person having such in charge or in control shall not authorize or knowingly permit the same to be operated by any person who by reason of physical or mental disability is incapable of operating such motorboat under the prevailing circumstances.

ALABAMA: A (1)
ARIZONA: A & B
ARKANSAS: A (1)
CALIFORNIA: A (1)
COLORADO: A & B
FLORIDA: A (1)
GEORGIA: A (1)
ILLINOIS: A & B
INDIANA: A (1)
IOWA: A (1)
KANSAS: A (1)
KENTUCKY: A (1)
LOUISIANA: A & B
MAINE: A (1)
MASSACHUSETTS: A (1)
MICHIGAN: A
MINNESOTA: A & B
MISSISSIPPI: A (1)—Applies to all watercraft (no person shall operate any vessel if physically or mentally incapacitated so as to be incapable of safely operating such vessel.)
MISSOURI: A (1)
MONTANA: A & B
NEBRASKA: A (1)
NEVADA: A (1)
NEW HAMPSHIRE: A (1)
NEW JERSEY: A
NEW MEXICO: A (1)
NEW YORK: A (1)—No person in an intoxicated condition shall operate a pleasure vessel on navigable waters of the state.
NORTH CAROLINA: A (1)
NORTH DAKOTA: A (1)
OHIO: A (1)—No person shall operate any watercraft if such person is so mentally or physically incapacitated as to be unable to operate such watercraft in a safe and competent manner.
OKLAHOMA: A (1)
OREGON: A
PENNSYLVANIA: A (1)—It is a violation for any person to operate a motorboat while in an intoxicated condition.
RHODE ISLAND: A (1)
SOUTH CAROLINA: A (1)
SOUTH DAKOTA: A (1)
TENNESSEE: A (1)
TEXAS: A (1)
UTAH: A (1)
VERMONT: A (1)
VIRGINIA: A (1)
WEST VIRGINIA: A (1) & B
WISCONSIN: A (1) & B

4. Speed Regulated

Note: In states which do not have express or definite speed limits there is nevertheless a speed limitation implied in safe boat operation. Speed which is excessive under existing circumstances and which endangers persons or property, is a form of reckless operation which is prohibited by most state boating laws.

Exceptions to speed limits: Operators of watercraft competing in an officially sanctioned race or regatta on marked courses usually expressly exempt under state law.

COLORADO, ILLINOIS, LOUISIANA, MICHIGAN, MINNESOTA, MONTANA, NEVADA, OHIO (water areas under jurisdiction of Division of Parks),

OREGON, PENNSYLVANIA, WYOMING: No person shall operate at a rate of speed greater than will permit him, in the exercise of reasonable care, to bring the motorboat to a stop within the assured, clear, visible distance ahead. — In most states where this law exists violators are expressly guilty of the misdemeanor of careless operation.

ARIZONA, MISSISSIPPI, NEBRASKA, SOUTH DAKOTA, WISCONSIN: No person shall operate a boat at a speed greater than is reasonable and prudent under the conditions and having regard to the actual and potential hazards then existing.

In every event, speed shall be so controlled as may be necessary to avoid colliding with any person or other watercraft or otherwise endangering the lives of other persons from excessive wake or speed.

NEBRASKA AND SOUTH DAKOTA: Excessive speeds are illegal at all times in or near harbors, marinas, landings, piers, anchorages, bathing beaches, drifting or trolling fisherman, or anchored boats.

CALIFORNIA: On waters under jurisdiction of State Park Commission, to 5 m.p.h.—(a) within 200 ft. of the actual water edge except in open zones as declared and posted at the local post office; (b) within 200 ft. of any swimming float, diving platform, life line, dock, pier, or landing float; (c) within 100 ft. of any bather.

CONNECTICUT: To 6 m.p.h. when approaching or passing, and while within 200 ft. of (a) any wharf, pier or dock in the city of Hartford between the bridge over the Connecticut river and the southern limits of the city or in the city of New London, or in New London harbor, or in the city of Norwich, or on the Eight Mile River in Lyme between the northerly end of the channel at Hamburg village and the southerly end of the Connecticut river; (b) the wharf or pier in Bridgeport harbor known as Mather's dock; (c) any wharf, pier or marine railway in Norwalk harbor; (d) any wharf in the city of Middletown; (e) any wharf on either side of the Mystic river between Mystic bridge and a point 200 yards south of the Wharf of Joseph S. Avery; (f) while passing between Branford Point Dock and Sybil's creek in the Branford river.

Boats propelled by motors on specified state-owned lakes and ponds shall be operated in a safe, reasonable and considerate manner, not to exceed 8 m.p.h. Exception: This speed limit does not apply between 11:00 a.m. and 6 p.m., from June 15 to the first Sunday following Labor Day, both dates inclusive, on Amos Lake, Preston; Pataganset Lake, East Lyme; Pickerel Lake, Colchester and East Haddam; Silver Lake (Peat Works Pond), Berlin and Meriden; and Wyassup Lake, North Stonington; provided boats are operated at a safe, considerate and reasonable speed.

DELAWARE: To 5 m.p.h. on all state-owned ponds.

IDAHO: To 10 m.p.h. within 50 ft. of

another craft or when vision is obstructed up to 300 ft. ahead. No machinery propelled craft shall approach any dock, pier or shore of any lake except at safe, reduced rate of speed.

INDIANA: To 10 m.p.h. on all waters between sunset and sunrise; to 10 m.p.h. on lakes under 300 acres; to 10 m.p.h. within 200 ft. of the shoreline of any lake or channel; to a minimum speed within 200 ft. of the shoreline of any lake or channel at a point where such lake or channel is 500 ft. or more in width, and only for the purposes of trolling or approaching or leaving a dock, pier or wharf or the shore of such lake or channel.

IOWA: On state-owned lakes, to 5 m.p.h. within 250 ft. of another craft; to 10 m.p.h. on any lake within 300 ft. of shore; to 5 m.p.h. on any body of water when vision obstructed up to 300 ft. ahead.

MAINE: To a minimum speed within 200 ft. of the shoreline of any lake or channel at a point where such lake or channel is 500 ft. or more in width, and only for the purposes of trolling or approaching or leaving a dock, pier or wharf or the shore of such lake or channel.

MARYLAND: To 6 knots on Seneca Creek (Montgomery County).

NEW HAMPSHIRE: The speed restrictions below are part of the rules and regulations promulgated by New Hampshire Public Utilities Commission, effective April 1, 1960.

To 10 m.p.h. within 500 ft of shore: Baboosic and Contocock lakes; also in a designated area on Gregg Lake.

To 10 m.p.h. in designated portions of the following lakes: Cobbetts Pond, Bow Lake, Lake Sunapee (at Georges Mills Bay), Lake Winnipesaukee (Varney-Kenniston Island Channel).

To 10 m.p.h.: Spectacle Pond in the towns of Groton and Hebron.

To 10 m.p.h., except between certain hours when the restriction shall not apply: Back Lake (except 12:30 p.m. to 3:30 p.m. daily on a specified portion of the lake in the town of Pittsburg); Beaver Lake in Derry (except between 1:00 p.m. and 7:00 p.m. Mondays through Fridays, holidays excepted, when speeds up to 30 m.p.h. are permitted beyond 150 ft. from shore for water skiing and surfboard riding; Sunset Lake (or Gould Pond) in the town of Greenfield (except between 3:00 p.m. and 6:00 p.m., Mondays through Saturdays; a specified part of Lake Winnepocket in Webster (except between 12:30 p.m. and 3:30 p.m. daily).

To 12 m.p.h. in designated portions of the following lakes: Newfound Lake; Lake Winnipesaukee (on part of Alton Bay and in the channel between Loon Island and the Mainland in the town of Meredith).

To 6 m.p.h. in the following water areas: Squam Lake (in Squam River in the towns of Holderness and Ashland); Lake Sunapee (in Sunapee Harbor and in Burkehaven); Lake Winnipesaukee (in Lake Paugus southwest of the Laconia Water Works pumping station); The Weirs Channel; Sally's Gut; off the southeastern end of Locke's Island to a point 600 ft. north of the Island; at the entrance of Smith's Cove at Glendale and southwest of there; Pine Island-Meredith Neck Channel; Horse Island-Meredith Neck Channel; in the cove on the westerly shore of Welch Island between said Island and a line extended between marked buoys; Lake Winnisquam (from the flashing light beacon on the westerly end of Mohawk Island to a point 400 ft. northerly and in the Winnisquam River in the City of Laconia east of the light at Dixon Point).

Under bridges: Headway speed only, while passsing under all bridges.

Note: For further detail write to the

State of New Hampshire, Public Utilities Commission, Concord, N.H.

In addition, a law passed by the 1959 New Hampshire Legislature provides: "No person shall operate motorboats and outboard motors on Otter Lake in the town of Greenfield at greater than trolling speed, except in case of emergency or by special approval of the selectmen."

NEW YORK: To 5 m.p.h. within 100 ft. of shore, or a dock, pier, raft, float or an anchored or moored vessel; vessels approaching or passing any boat or bathing beach shall be slowed to a speed which will cause no damage; all vessels shall be operated at a rate of speed which will not endanger any person or property. In St. Lawrence River Motorboat Regulation Zone no motorboat shall be operated within the habor line at a speed exceeding 5 m.p.h., and no motorboat shall exceed 15 m.p.h. from one-half hour after sunset to one-half hour before sunrise. On State Canal System navigation speed is limited to 6 m.p.h. in land cuts and 10 m.p.h. in canalized river and lake sections.

OHIO: On state lakes under the jurisdiction of the Division of Parks — to 6 m.p.h. within any Shore Zone, i.e., up to 300 ft. from shore (indicated by yellow and black buoys); no greater than reasonable under prevailing traffic, surface and other hazardous conditions within a Class A Speed Zone (indicated by buoys painted green overall) from sunrise to sunset, and to 10 m.p.h. within said zone from sunset to sunrise; to 10 m.p.h. within any unzoned area at any time.

OREGON: To 10 m.p.h. during fishing season on the following lakes: East, Paulina, Elk, Magone, Crescent, Timothy, Davis, Diamond, and Squaw. To 10 m.p.h. at any time: On designated portion of Upper Klamath Lake and any stream, creek or canal that leads into it, including Crystal Creek, Recreation Creek and Four-Mule (Harrison) Creek; North Fork Reservoir, and Lake Simtustus behind Pelton Dam.

PENNSYLVANIA: To 8 m.p.h. within 100 ft. of shore or of a buoyed fishing ground, zoning area, or occupied boat, channel or bathing beach, except a water skier or surf boarder may be towed from a shoreline area, dock or float at such speed only as is necessary to plane.

UTAH: To 5 m.p.h. within 150 ft. of the following: (a) landing wharfs to which boats are made fast or other points of embarking or discharging of passengers; (b) any buoy; (c) designated "slow areas"; (d) designated bathing or swimming areas or any persons in the water wherever they may be; (e) other seafaring craft; (f) the shore-line; (g) water skiers, surfboard riders, etc.; (h) authorized boats in rescue operations or in pursuit of a violator; (i) any fish trolling boats. To 5 m.p.h. within buoyed-off launching area on Rockport Lake. To 10 m.p.h. on Navajo Lake outside buoyed eastern portion.

WASHINGTON: No greater than is reasonable and proper under conditions at time and place of operation.

WISCONSIN: To 8 m.p.h. on the Brule River or any of its tributaries in Douglas County.

5. Restricted Areas

COLORADO, ILLINOIS, NEVADA: It is unlawful to operate *a motorboat* within an area which has been marked off as a bathing, swimming or otherwise restricted area, except in case of emergency, or patrol or rescue craft.

CONNECTICUT: According to local ordinance.

KANSAS (on state lakes), LOUISIANA, MINNESOTA, MONTANA, OHIO, RHODE ISLAND, WISCONSIN, WYOMING: It is unlawful to operate *any watercraft* within an area which has been set aside as a bathing, swimming or otherwise restricted area, except in case of emergency or patrol or rescue craft.

GEORGIA: Launching, floating or operating any powerboat except life-saving or other emergency craft, prohibited in established fish sanctuary areas.

IOWA: Motorboating barred on certain parts of West Okoboji Lake.

KANSAS: Motorboats permitted on lakes located in state parks or state game refuges for fishing purposes only; houseboats and cabin boats prohibited. Lake McKinney in Kearny County and federal water impoundments are not included.

MAINE: Powerboats prohibited on Portage Lake in Floating Island Area (Aroostook County).

MARYLAND: No vessel, except those manually propelled, shall be operated inshore from yellow buoys which designate wharves, piers, docks and bathing beaches on Deep Creek Lake, except for departure and landing. No vessel over 30 ft. in length (measuring by the greatest overall length stem to stern) and no houseboat of any description shall be permitted on Deep Creek Lake.

NEBRASKA: Motorboats not permitted on state waters, except Victory Lake at Fremont and Cottonmill Lake at Kearney.

NEW HAMPSHIRE: Powerboats prohibited on Lucas Pond (Northwood) and Lake Whittemore (Bennington). Use or operation of houseboats barred on Squam Lake.

NEW JERSEY: Outboard motors not permitted on the Delaware and Raritan Canal and in congested spots on Navesink and Shrewsbury rivers. Power boats barred in all State Parks, except Hopatcong Park.

NEW MEXICO: Use of outboard motors not permitted on small lakes under jurisdiction of State Game Department.

NORTH CAROLINA: On state lakes operation of motorboats prohibited within designated safety zones except to leave or go to a landing place.

OHIO: Columbus — Griggs Reservoir: Boating permitted only between 6:00 a.m. and 11:00 p.m. (E.S.T.), from Griggs Reservoir northward to north north side of Fishinger Road Bridge. *O'Shaughnessey Reservoir:* Boating permitted only between 6:00 a.m. and 11:00 p.m. (E.S.T.) from O'Shaughnessey Reservoir northward to and including Eversole Run.

City of Mansfield — Cleafork Reservoir: Boating permitted only between 4:00 a.m. and 10:00 p.m. (E.S.T.). No boating permitted at any time within 500 ft. upstream from dam.

Hamilton County Park District — only watercraft used for fishing or patrol purposes allowed.

Youngstown Township Park District — Mill Creek Park; Boating permitted only between 6:30 a.m. and 10:30 p.m. (E.D.T.) during May 1 to Dec. 1 season.

Water Areas under jurisdiction of Division of Parks: Power craft prohibited on lakes of 500 acres or less.

Water under exclusive control of Division of Wildlife: Motor propelled boats prohibited on all lakes and ponds in District #1 through #5, except Hocking Lake in District #4.

Water under management of Department of Public Works: Motor propelled boats barred.

OREGON: Motorboats prohibited on Taylor, Irish, South Twin, North Twin, Three Creek, Devils, Lucky, Todd, Gold, Clear, Olallie, Horseshoe, Frog, Breitenbush, Lost, Timpanagos, and Opal lakes. No person shall try or test a racing motorboat near anchored boats, swimmers, populated beaches, water skiers, boats underway, or otherwise congested areas.

PENNSYLVANIA: Use of motorboats of 6 hp. or less on Pymatuning Lake restricted to that portion of lake extending from the main dam near Jamestown northwardly to the causeway across the Reservoir from Espyville, Pennsylvania to Andover, Ohio. Use of motor boats prohibited on Lake Le Boeuf and Twin Lakes and in state forest areas.

TENNESSEE: Outboards prohibited on a few small State Game and Fish Commission lakes.

UTAH: *Rockport Lake:* Allows no boating within 1,000 ft. of the dam, as marked by buoys. Before 12:00 p.m., no speed boating or water skiing allowed except for special events. After 12:00 p.m., until 1/2 hour past sundown, the buoyed area west of the harbor area is the only area in which water skiing and speed boating are allowed.

Navajo Lake: On eastern buoyed portion of lake, pleasure boating Thursdays through Sundays and holidays only from 12:00 p.m. to 1/2 hour after sunset.
Ruling of State Fish and Game Department zones lakes for boat racing and water skiing when in conflict with fishing.

VERMONT: Prohibits operating motorboat or vessel within 200 ft. of shores of a bathing beach or other recreational spot, or approaching within 100 ft. of a person swimming, or a canoe, rowboat, or other light craft conveying any person, except incident to mooring or landing, or leaving shore.

WEST VIRGINIA: Operation of pleasure vessels prohibited within 20 ft. of the exterior boundary of a clearly marked bathing or swimming area. Unlawful to operate a vessel or to knowingly permit another person to operate one's vessel within 20 ft. of a person engaged in fishing, without permission, or unless unavoidable.

6. Horsepower Limitations

CONNECTICUT: To 12 cubic inch total piston displacement on Wononscopomuc and Alexander lakes; to 6 hp. on Willimantic Reservoir.

DELAWARE: To 5 hp. on Noxentoon or Silver Lake.

IOWA: To 6 hp. on artificial lakes 100 acres or larger.

KANSAS: To 10 hp. on State Lakes.

OHIO: Water areas under supervision and control of Division of Parks — To 6 hp. on Pymatuning, Cowan, Burr Oak and Acton lakes; unlimited on 14 other lakes having a Class A Speed Zone; to 3 hp. on canoes; to less than 6 hp. (factory rated) on air-propelled boats. Waters under exclusive control of Division of Wildlife — No motors allowed except on Hocking Lake which has a limit of 3 hp. Muskingum Watershed Conservancy District — To 6 hp., except Atwood and Tappan lakes (18 hp.), Seneca Lake (65 hp.), and that part of Pleasant Hill Reservoir in Ashland County (no limit).
Note: State law allows use of motor of 65 horsepower or less on all lakes covering 3,500 acres or more. No conservancy district or political subdivision may impose horsepower limits on such lakes provided motors used in conjunction with properly matched boats in reasonable areas to be designated for use of motors and boats for water skiing.

PENNSYLVANIA: To 5 hp. on inland water 180 ft. or less in width; to 6 hp. on Pymatuning Lake; to 10 hp. on Canadohta Lake in Crawford County; to 7-1/2 hp. on Quaker Lake in Susquehanna County.

7. Overpowering Prohibited

No watercraft shall be equipped with any motor or other propulsion machinery beyond its safe power capacity taking into consideration the type and construction of such watercraft and other existing operating conditions.

FLORIDA: All vessels sold in Florida shall bear a manufacturer's plate or suitable inscription stating the maximum horsepower motor recommended for the safe operation of the vessel and the number of persons or maximum weight recommended for safety load. This shall not apply to resales.

8. Overloading Prohibited

No boat shall be loaded with passengers or cargo beyond its safe carrying capacity taking into consideration weather and existing operating conditions.

9. Accidents; Rendering Aid; Reporting

Boat operator involved in an accident required to stop, identify himself and the registration and ownership of his boat to the injured or damaged party, render aid, and report accident to designated law enforcement agency.

Note: All states which have adopted numbering acts aimed at conformity with the Federal Boating Act of 1958 require boat accidents involving personal injury or death or property damage generally in excess of $100 to be reported to the appropriate state agency, and that such agency compile and transmit statistics on such accidents to the Federal government.

10. Age of Operators Limited

ALABAMA: No person owning or having control of a mechanically propelled vessel shall permit any person under 12 years old to operate it unless accompanied by a competent person 12 years of age or older, except this regulation shall not apply to participants in officially recognized marine events.

MAINE: Prohibits any person under 12 years old from operating a motorboat with more than 10 hp. unless under the immediate supervision of a person in the boat who is at least 16 years old.

NEBRASKA: No person under 16 years old shall operate any vessel propelled by a motor of 10 hp. or more unless operating in a training course under direct supervision of an instructor at least 21 years old. Children under 14 shall not operate motorboats at any time whether accompanied by an adult or not.

NEW HAMPSHIRE: No private boat capable of attaining a speed of 25 m.p.h. or more shall be operated by any person under 12 years old. No certificate to act as operator of a commercial boat capable of attaining a speed of 25 m.p.h. or more shall be issued to a person under 18 years.

NEW JERSEY: On inland lakes and other waters not influenced by natural tides, no person under 13 years old shall be licensed to operate a power vessel equipped with an outboard motor; no person under 16 shall be licensed to operate a power vessel equipped with an inboard motor. Every applicant for an operator's license under 17 years old shall submit a birth, baptismal or school certificate showing applicant's age, and written consent to the granting of the license signed by applicant's parent or guardian.

NEW YORK: No person under 10 years old shall operate a mechanically propelled pleasure boat on navigable water, unless accompanied by a person over 14 years old. No one between 10 and 14 years old shall operate a mechanically propelled pleasure vessel on navigable waters, unless accompanied by a person over 14 years old, or the holder of a boating safety certificate issued by the Conservation Commissioner for the successful completion of a standard public training course for youthful boat operators.

OHIO: Bars any person under 12 years

old from operating any kind of boat unless under the direct visual and audible supervision of a parent, guardian, or other person over 16 years old.

PENNSYLVANIA: Persons under 16 years old prohibited from operating boats equipped with motors on Pymatuning Lake. (By regulation of Dept. of Forests and Waters.)

UTAH: No person under 16 years old shall operate a motorboat except when accompanied by a responsible adult experienced in motorboat operation, except as further provided in the rules and regulations of the State Park and Recreation Commission.

11. Traffic Rules

General Code: Compare letters following the states with this code for rules of the road in effect in each state.

(a) Passing head-on — keep to right.
(b) Overtaking — on either side but must grant right of way to overtaken boat.
(c) Passing from rear — keep to left.
(d) Passing at right angles — boat on right has right of way.
(e) Motorboats shall yield right of way to non-motor powered boats.
(f) Directed course for motorboats when passing sailboats.
(g) Any boat departing from a landing, dock or pier, has right of way over incoming boats.
(h) Any boat approaching shoreline area has right of way over departing boats.
(i) Do not abruptly change course without first determining that it can be safely done without risk of collision with another boat.
(j) On failing to understand course of an approaching boat — slow down immediately to a speed barely sufficient for steerage way until other boat has passed.
(k) Boat with right of way shall hold course and speed. Boat yielding right of way shall, if necessary, slacken speed, stop, reverse, or alter course.
(l) If danger of collision — slow down, stop, or reverse until danger averted.
(m) Special warning signals in fog, thick weather, or other conditions of poor visibility.
(n) No motorboat shall be operated in a circular course around any boat being used for fishing or any person swimming.
(o) In narrow channel — keep to right of mid-channel.
(p) When passing close to swimming areas, moored boats, boats engaged in fishing, or servicing buoys for markings, reduce speed so as to prevent wash or wake from causing damage or unnecessary inconvenience to occupants of area or other craft.
(q) All watercraft must be operated at reasonable speeds for given situations and must be under complete control of operator at all times.
(r) No watercraft shall intentionally obstruct or interfere with take-off, landing, or taxiing of aircraft.
(s) Appropriate stage agency may establish pilot rules in conformity with pilot rules under Federal navigation laws or Coast Guard Navigation rules.
(t) Miscellaneous.

ALABAMA: (a); (b); (c); (d); (e); (f); (g); (h); (i); (j); (k); (l); (m); (n); (o); (p); (q); (r).

ARIZONA: (a); (b) — Passing boat responsible for collision resulting from overtaking or for damaging wake; (d) — Area from point directly ahead to 112-1/2° of the compass to starboard side of watercraft is danger zone, and any other craft in this zone has right of way to avoid collision; (e); (h); (1) — Duty to use due caution; (t) — Normal traffic shall be counter-clockwise; approach shore from right and lead to left as observed from water looking toward shore.

CALIFORNIA: On "Inland Waters"; (a) — Motorboats approaching each other head-on shall exchange signal of intention to pass on port side of each other by 1 short distinct blast. If courses of such vessels are so far on starboard of each other as not to be considered meeting head-on, either vessel shall immediately give 2 short distinct blasts, which the other shall acknowledge promptly, and they shall pass on starboard side of each other. The foregoing applies only where head-on approach involves risk of collision. (b) — When motorboats are running in same direction, if vessel astern desires to pass on right or starboard side of vessel ahead, she shall give 1 short blast; to pass on left or port side, 2 short blasts. Vessel ahead shall acknowledge same if she thinks it safe to pass; but if she does not think it safe to pass at that point, she shall immediately signify this by not less than 4 short, rapid blasts, and vessel astern under no circumstances shall attempt to pass until vessel ahead blows proper clearance signals. Vessel ahead shall in no case attempt to cross the bow or crowd upon course of passing vessel; however, passing vessel shall keep out of way of overtaken vessel. (d); (e); (g) — When motorboats are moved from their docks or berths, and other boats are liable to pass from any direction toward them, they shall give 1 long blast, which signal shall be acknowledged by any approaching motorboat within hearing. If the signal is not answered, the outbound motorboat is to consider the way clear and govern herself accordingly, but immediately after clearing the berth so as to be fully in sight she shall be governed by steering and sailing rules. (j) — Vessel in doubt shall immediately signify by several short rapid blasts — the danger signal. (k); (l); (m); (o); (s) — Vessels operating on "High Seas" including San Francisco Harbor, San Pedro Bay and San Diego Harbor, shall adhere to International Regs. for Preventing Collisions at Sea, as amended. (t) — When a motorboat is nearing a point of land which cuts off view of any motorboat that may be approaching from opposite direction for 1/2 mile, she shall when within 1/2 mile of such curve or bend sound 1 long blast, which signal shall be acknowledged by an approaching motorboat that may be within hearing. If the signal is acknowledged, then the usual signals for meeting and passing shall, immediately upon sighting the other vessel, be exchanged; but if the first alarm signal is not answered, the first vessel shall consider the channel clear and govern herself accordingly.

COLORADO: (a); (b); (d); (e); (t) — Any person who fails to yield right-of-way shall be guilty of a misdemeanor.

DELAWARE: (s).

FLORIDA: (s) — Coast Guard rules and regulations applicable to motorboats of not less than 16 ft. nor more than 65 ft. in length adopted.

GEORGIA: On all fresh and salt waters and the marginal sea adjacent to this State: (d); (p). Fresh water regulations: (a); (c) — Keep out of way of overtaken boat, passing to left of it if that side is clear; (o); (p) — Power boats shall keep clear of row boats with occupants, approaching not nearer than 50 ft. Larger craft, approaching or passing smaller craft, shall reduce speed so that its wake does not endanger the smaller craft.

IDAHO: (a); (c); (d); (e) — Sailboats; (f); (g).

ILLINOIS: (a); (b); (d); (e).

INDIANA: (a); (b) — If it can be done with safety and within assured clear distance ahead: (d); (g); (n); (o); (p) — A motorboat approaching or passing another boat, shall be operated in such manner at such rate of speed as will not create a hazardous wash or wake.

IOWA: (a); (c); (d); (e) — Sailboats; (f); (g).
KANSAS: (a); (b); (d).
MAINE: (n).
MARYLAND: (s)—In navigating boats, the inland rules of the road, as set forth in Coast Guard pamphlet C-G-169 (May 1, 1959) and amendments thereto shall be observed.
MINNESOTA: (a); (b) — Craft being overtaken must hold course and speed, and overtaking craft must keep a sufficient distance to avoid collision or endangering other craft from its wake. (d); (i); (p); (q); (r).
MONTANA: (a); (b); (d); (e) — Sailboats; (t) — Operating motorboat within 20 ft. of person engaged in fishing prohibited unless consented to or unavoidable.
NEBRASKA: (a) — Each operator shall give one short whistle blast and indicate his course by swinging the bow of his boat substantially to starboard. (b) — A boat is considered to be overtaking another boat when approaching the course of the leading boat from more than 2 points abaft the beam (22 degrees to rear). (d); (e) — Also, swimmers have right of way at all times over all vessels, power operated or not. (m); (p)—Boats passing a tow must slow down when there is a chance their wash or wave will cause damage. (s)—Western River rules, as amended and supplemented by the Motorboat Act, the Pilot Rules of the Western Rivers and General Regs. of the Army Engineers followed. (t) — On failing to understand course of an approaching boat, or when in doubt as to safety of course or intention of approaching boat — so signify by 4 or more short, rapid whistle blasts, or 4 sharp bell rings.
NEVADA: (a); (b); (d); (p); (q); (r).
NEW HAMPSHIRE: (a) — When courses of 2 boats are so far on starboard of each other as not to be considered meeting head-on, they shall keep to left. (b) — Only when sufficient distance between boats to avoid collision, and passing boat reduces speed so as not to endanger boat being passed by its wake; (d); (e); (f) — Whenever it can be reasonably avoided, do not pass on sailboat's windward side. (i); (j); (k); (l); (m); (t) — All boats must keep at least 150 ft. distance from other boats, rafts, floats, or shore, except when prevented by a narrow channel or when approaching or leaving shore, etc. When approaching or leaving shore, etc. proceed at headway speed so as to provide full visibility and control, and prevent damaging wash.
NEW JERSEY: Power vessels on non-tidal waters; (a) — Either vessel shall signal intention to pass on port side of other by 1 short, distinct blast. If courses of 2 boats are so far on starboard of each other as not to be considered meeting head-on, either vessel shall sound 2 short, distinct blasts, which the other shall acknowledge, and they shall keep to left. (b) — Boat wishing to pass shall signal forward vessel intention to pass on port side, by 2 distinct blasts; on starboard side, by 1 distinct blast. Forward vessel shall acknowledge same. Passing boat shall keep out of way of vessel being passed, and forward vessel shall hold course. (d); (e) — Sailboats; (j) — Vessel in doubt signifies this by 4 rapid whistles. If vessels have approached within 300 yards of each other, both shall be immediately slowed to a speed barely sufficient for steerage way until the proper signals are given, answered and understood or until the boats have passed each other. (k); (l); (m); (p) — Speed of power vessels shall be regulated at all times to avoid danger of injury to other boats or waterfront constructions either directly or from wash or wave. (t) — When leaving a wharf or slip or running toward a point of land which cuts off view of waterway, sound 1 long whistle for not less than 4 seconds. — Continuous sounding of whistle or horn is distress signal. Operator of any

power vessel hearing this signal shall render all assistance in his power. — No boat shall move across or around course of race or regatta so as to unnecessarily endanger those competing in race or regatta.

NEW YORK: (a) — Vessels shall exchange signal of intention to alter course to right by 1 distinct blast. When courses of 2 boats are so far on starboard of each other as not to be considered meeting head-on, they shall immediately exchange 2 distinct blasts, and pass on starboard of each other. (b) — If overtaking vessel desires to pass on right side, she shall give 1 distinct blast, and forward vessel shall acknowledge; on left side, 2 distinct blasts to be acknowledged in same way. If forward vessel does not think it safe to pass, she shall sound 5 or more rapid blasts, and vessel astern shall not attempt to pass until forward vessel blows proper signal to indicate passing can be done safely. Neither vessel shall attempt to cross bow of or crowd the other. (d); (e); (j) — Vessel in doubt shall give 5 or more rapid blasts; (k); (l); (m); (o).

NORTH CAROLINA: (a) — If watercraft far enough to left of each other so that no change in direction is necessary for safe passage, both will maintain their course and speed to pass clear. (b); (d); (k); (p); (q); (r).

OHIO: (a); (b) — Every watercraft approaching another from any direction more than 22-1/2 degrees abaft the other's beam, so that at night she would be unable to see either of the other's side or combination bow lights is an overtaking craft. No subsequent alteration of bearing shall relieve overtaking craft of duty of keeping clear of overtaken craft until finally passed and clear. If overtaking craft is in doubt whether she is forward of or abaft this direction from other craft, she should assume that she is overtaking and yield right of way. (d); (e) — Except when a sailboat is overtaking a power craft; (h); (k); (t) — In rivers, streams and other water current areas, ascending watercraft shall yield right of way to descending watercraft — Operator shall keep proper lookout at all times. — Departure from these rules permitted to avoid dangers of navigation and collision and under special circumstances.

OKLAHOMA: (s).

OREGON: (a); (b); (d).

PENNSYLVANIA: (s) — Unless otherwise specified, Rules of the Road for U.S. Inland Waterways are assumed to obtain.

RHODE ISLAND: (s).

SOUTH CAROLINA: (a) — If watercraft far enough to left of each other so that no change in direction is necessary for safe passage, both will maintain their course and speed to pass clear. (b); (d); (k); (p); (q); (r).

SOUTH DAKOTA: (a) — If equipped with a horn, it is the duty of each vessel to give 1 short blast, and in addition each boat will indicate course by sharp swing of bow to starboard. (b); (g) — But the Rules of the Road do not apply nor do rights become applicable until such vessels are entirely clear of slips or piers. Passing craft may not block entrance to or exit from any slip or pier. (p); (q); (s).

TENNESSEE: (s).

UTAH: (p); (q).

VIRGINIA: (a) — If watercraft far enough to left of each other so that no change in direction is necessary for safe passage, both will maintain their course and speed to pass clear. (b); (d); (k); (p); (q); (r).

WEST VIRGINIA: (a); (b); (d); (e); (s) — All motorboats shall be operated in conformance with the Rules of the Road, Western Rivers.

WISCONSIN: (a); (b); (d); (e); (k); (n); (p) — Creating wash or wake hazardous to other boats prohibited; (s).

12. Water Skiing
(Aquaplaning, surfboarding, etc.)
Regulated

GENERAL CODE: Trace letters following each state to this Code for the law.

(a) Tow boat must be occupied by at least 2 competent persons.
(b) (a) shall not apply to any motorboat equipped with a rear view mirror.
(c) Prohibited after dark — unless otherwise specified this means the period from 1 hour after sunset to 1 hour before sunrise.
(d) (a) and/or (c) do not apply to a performer engaged in a professional exhibition, or a person or persons engaged in an authorized tournament, competition, marine parade, regatta, etc.
(e) Tow boat shall be operated in a careful and prudent manner and at a reasonable distance from persons and property so as not to endanger life or property.
(f) No person shall manipulate any vessel, tow rope, etc. by which the course of water skis or water skier may be influenced in such a way as to cause a collision or accident.
(g) (f) does not apply to collision with ski jumps, buoys and like objects normally used in competitive or recreational skiing.
(h) Water skiing in reckless or negligent manner prohibited.
(i) Water skiing while intoxicated or under the influence of drugs prohibited.
(j) Skier required to wear life preserver while underway.

ALABAMA: (a); (b); (c); (d); (f); (g); (h); (i); (j) — does not apply to performers in officially recognized marine events.
ARIZONA: (a); (c); (j) — applies only to persons unable to swim.
ARKANSAS: (f); (h); (i).
CALIFORNIA: (a) — second person must be at least 12 years old; (c) — between the hours of sunset to sunrise, unless otherwise fixed by local ordinances, laws or regulations enacted pursuant to state law; (d); (f) — does not apply to collisions of 2 or more persons being towed by same boat; (h); (i).
COLORADO: (a); (b); (c); (d) — exception to (c) only; (e).
DELAWARE: (a); (b); (c); (d) — exception to (c) only, where adequate lighting is provided; (e); (f); (g). Unlawful to water ski in the Rehoboth Canal, the Channel through Massey's Landing and any public swimming area.
CONNECTICUT: Water-skiing and surfboarding prohibited on specified state-owned lakes and ponds. Exceptions: Between 11:00 a.m. and 6:00 p.m. from June 15 to the first Sunday following Labor Day, both dates inclusive, on Amos Lake, Preston; Pataganset Lake, East Lyne; Pickerel Lake, Colchester and East Haddam; Silver Lake (Peat Works Pond), Berlin and Meriden; and Wyssup Lake, North Stonington, provided tow boat occupied by a person able to swim who shall act as observer and render assistance when necessary, and provided tow boat is operated at reasonable speed and remains at a safe, considerate and reasonable distance from other watercraft, swimmers, floats, docks and shoreline.
FLORIDA: (a); (b); (c) — from 1/2 hour after sunset to 1/2 hour before sunrise; (d); (f); (g); (h); (i).
GEORGIA: (c); (h); (j) — does not apply to performers in organized water ski tournaments, competitions, expositions, or trials therefor.
ILLINOIS: (a); (c); (d) — exception to (c) only, where adequate lighting is provided; (e); (f); (g); (h); (i).
INDIANA: (a); (h); (i).
IOWA: (a); (c); (d); (h); (i).
KANSAS: (c); (d); (f).
LOUISIANA: (a) — does not apply to motorboats used by ski school instruc-

tors in giving lessons, or used in authorized activities; (c); (d); (e).
MAINE: (h); (i).
MARYLAND: (a) — operator as well as second person in boat must be at least 12 years old; (c) — between the hours of sunset and sunrise; (d).
MASSACHUSETTS: (a); (d) — Tow boat must be equipped with a ladder, steps or similar means by which skier can be taken from water.
MICHIGAN: (c); (h).
MINNESOTA: (a); (b) — or a safety warning device approved by the Conservation Commissioner; (c) — from 1-1/2 hours after sunset to sunrise.
MISSISSIPPI: (a) — does not apply to the Mississippi Sound, or the coastal or tidal waters of the State; (d); (f); (g).
MISSOURI: (a); (b); (c); (d); (f); (h); (i).
MONTANA: (c); (d); (i); (j).
NEBRASKA: (a) — second person must be at least 12 years old, and not under the influence of alcohol, narcotics, or barbiturates; (b); (c); (h); (i). Operator of towboat responsible for conduct of skier. When not in use, towlines shall be stowed immediately aboard towboat.
NEVADA: (a) — on any congested waters. Motor Vehicle Dept. shall determine and arrange to give notice to the public what waters are congested; (b) — on waters determined as not congested; (c); (d); (h); (i).
NEW HAMPSHIRE: (a); (c) — between 1/2 hour after sunset and 1/2 hour before sunrise; (d).
NEW JERSEY: On non-tidal waters: (a); (c) — after sunset. Towboat must at all times keep at least 200 ft. from any shore, wharf or dock, or from any other craft that it may pass. Maximum length of tow rope, 75 ft.
NEW MEXICO: (a); (b); (c); (d); (f); (h); (i).
NEW YORK: (a) — second person must be 10 or more years of age; (c).
NORTH CAROLINA: (a); (b); (c); (d); (f); h); (i); (j).
NORTH DAKOTA: (c); (d); (f); (h); (i); (j) — except performer engaged in a professional exhibition or persons engaged in authorized activities.
OHIO: (a); (c) — between sunset and sunrise, except upon special permit issued by state department, conservancy district or political subdivision in control of water area; (j).
Except on Lake Erie, the Ohio River and immediately connected harbors and anchorages, water skiing shall be restricted to a designated ski zone wherever established. Towing more than 2 skiers simultaneously by same boat prohibited, except upon special permit.
Water skiing or surfboard riding prohibited on Lake Milton (City of Youngstown) between 8 P.M. (EDT) and sunrise of the following day and on Sundays and holidays after 1 p.m. (EDT).
OKLAHOMA: (a); (b); (c); (d); (h); (i).
OREGON: (c); (d); (f); (h); (i).
PENNSYLVANIA: (c); (d).
RHODE ISLAND: (a); (c); (d); (f); (h); (i).
SOUTH CAROLINA: (a); (b); (c); (d); (f); (h); (i).
SOUTH DAKOTA: (a); (b); (c); (d); (f); (h); (i).
TENNESSEE: (c); (d); (f); (h); (i).
TEXAS: (c); (d); (e); (h); (i).
UTAH: (a); (b); (c); (d); (f) — towboat must be operated in such as way as to keep water skier at least 100 ft. distant from any swimmer, canoe, rowboat, or other light craft conveying any person, but this is not meant to prohibit necessary mooring or landing, or leaving shore; (h); (i); (j).
VERMONT: (a); (d); (f) — towboat must be operated in such a way as to keep water skier at least 100 ft. distant from any swimmer, canoe, rowboat, or other light craft conveying any person, but this is not meant to prohibit necessary mooring or landing, or leaving shore; (h); (i); (j).

VIRGINIA: (a); (b); (c); (d); (f); (h); (i); (j).
WISCONSIN: (c) — between the hours of sunset to sunrise, unless otherwise fixed by local ordinances enacted pursuant to state law; (d) — exception to (c) only, where adequate lighting is provided; (h).
WYOMING: (c); (d); (e).

13. Skin Diving

ALABAMA: A diver's flag must be displayed on the surface of any water where skin divers are operating.
MICHIGAN: Any person diving or submerging in any waterway with the aid of a diving suit or other mechanical diving device may place a buoy in the water at or near the point of submergence. The buoy shall bear a red flag not less than 14 inches by 16 inches with a 3-1/2 inch white stripe running from one upper corner to a diagonal lower corner. The buoy shall be in place only while actual diving operations are in progress.
WISCONSIN: It is unlawful to engage in underwater skin diving, or to rise to the surface beyond a 50 foot radius of a flag having one diagonal white stripe on a red background of such size and height to be identifiable at 100 yards.

14. Interference with Navigation Prohibited

No person shall operate any motorboat in a manner which unreasonably or unnecessarily interferes with free navigation of the waterways. Example: Anchoring under bridges or in heavily traveled channels.

15. Mooring to Buoys or Beacons Prohibited

No person shall moor, attach or secure a boat in any manner to a buoy, other than a mooring buoy, or any other marking guide placed pursuant to legal authority.

16. Riding on Decks or Gunwales Prohibited

A person operating a motorboat shall not permit anyone to ride or sit on the gunwales or on the decking over the bow unless the boat is equipped with adequate guards or rails to prevent persons from falling overboard.

17. Races and Regattas

It is unlawful to hold or sponsor any race, regatta, tournament or other competition, exhibition, or trials for same, without first having obtained a written permit from the appropriate state agency, or where such events are to take place. In addition, most state boat acts exempt boats engaged in sanctioned races from certain regulations, such as speed limits and muffler and fire extinguisher requirements.

18. Owner's Responsibility (Civil Liability)

(A) Owner of vessel liable for damages due to negligent operation, whether a violation of statutory or common law, if vessel used with owner's express or implied consent. Owner's consent presumed if vessel operated by immediate member of family. This does not relieve any other person from liability he would otherwise have. Recovery limited to actual damages.
(B) Family purpose doctrine as applied to ownership and operation of motor vehicles followed: Owner of vessel liable for act of another who operates vessel for a family purpose.
(C) Nothing shall exonerate owner or operator from consequences of any neglect of any precaution which may be required by the ordinary practice of seamanship or by the special circumstances of the case.
ARKANSAS: (A) — Boat guest has

cause of action against owner or operator for damage due to operation of vessel if vessel was willfully and wantonly operated in disregard of the rights of others.

CALIFORNIA: (A) — Owner's liability, not based upon principal — agent or master — servant relationship, limited: to $10,000 for any death or injury in any one accident; up to $20,000 for death or injury involving more than one person in any one accident; to $10,000 for property damage. Operator shall be made party defendant in action against owner if personal service of process can be had upon him within Calif., and upon recovery of judgment, damages shall be sought to be collected first from operator. — Any owner against whom recovery is made has right of subrogation against operator, i.e., owner steps into shoes of injured person and may recover from operator total amount of any judgment plus costs recovered by injured person against owner. — If owner entrusts vessel to another who permits a third party to use it, with owner's express or implied consent, owner and bailee are both liable for damages. — Cause of action will survive death of any injured person or of any person liable under this Act.

DELAWARE: (A)

FLORIDA: All motorboats considered dangerous instrumentalities. Operator owes highest degree of care to prevent injuries to others. Liability for negligent operation of a motorboat confined to actual operator, and not the owner unless he is the operator or present in boat when any injury or damage is occasioned by negligent operation.

GEORGIA: (A)

IDAHO: (C)

ILLINOIS: Injury or damage resulting from negligent operation of a watercraft is primarily the operator's responsibility.

IOWA: (C) — or any neglect to carry lights, signals or equipment.

KENTUCKY: (B) — Liability for negligent operation of vessel or motorboat charged to actual operator, and not the owner unless the latter is in the boat at the time of injury or damage or unless the boat is being operated for the owner's business.

LOUISIANA: (A)

MICHIGAN: (A) — Owner personally responsible for any damages resulting from a wake or swell created by negligent operation of watercraft being operated with owner's consent.

MISSISSIPPI: Owner and operator of a vessel shall be jointly and severally liable in any civil action for damages arising out of negligent failure to comply with this Act. Cause of action shall be cumulative and supplemental to cause of action maintainable at common law, maritime law or in admiralty.

MONTANA: (A)

NEBRASKA: (A)

NEW HAMPSHIRE: (A)

NEW MEXICO: (A)

NORTH DAKOTA: (A)

OKLAHOMA: (A)

OREGON: (B) — Does not apply in actions in which courts of admiralty have jurisdiction.

PENNSYLVANIA: Every motorboat owner causing or knowingly permitting any person to operate his motorboat on any inland waters, and any person who leases or furnishes a motorboat to any other person, shall be jointly and severally liable with such other person for any damages caused by the negligence of such other person in operating such motorboat.

SOUTH CAROLINA: (A) — Provided a boat livery owner shall not be liable as an owner for any negligent injury or damage resulting from the operation of a vessel rented or hired. The operator of the vessel shall be liable as owner.

TENNESSEE: (B)

WISCONSIN: (C) — Comparative negligence doctrine followed: Motorboat owner may not recover damages arising from accident involving operation of owner's boat by spouse or minor child if the negligence of such spouse or minor child exceeds that of the operator of other boat.

(Criminal Liability)

KENTUCKY: Any person who, by negligent operation of a motorboat, causes the death of another, under circumstances not otherwise punishable as a homicide, shall be imprisoned in the county jail for not more than one year.

LOUISIANA: The operator of any watercraft who causes the death of another person through operating at an immoderate rate of speed, or in a careless, reckless, or negligent manner, is guilty of *negligent homicide*. Penalties: Imprisonment for not more than 1 year, or a fine of not more than $1,000, or both.

MICHIGAN: Any person who, by the operation of any watercraft at an immoderate rate of speed or in a careless, reckless or negligent manner, but not wilfully or wantonly, shall cause the death of another, shall be guilty of *negligent homicide*. Penalties: Imprisonment for not more than 2 years, or a fine of not more than $2,000, or both.

MINNESOTA: Any person who, by operating a watercraft in a reckless or grossly negligent manner, causes a human being to be killed, under circumstances not constituting murder or manslaughter, is guilty of *criminal negligence in the operation of a watercraft resulting in death*. Penalties: Imprisonment for not more than 5 years, or a fine of not more than $1,000, or both.

NEW YORK: A person who uses or operates a vessel upon any waters within the boundaries of the state, in a culpably negligent or reckless manner, whereby a human being is killed, is guilty of *criminal negligence in the use or operation of a vessel resulting in death*. Penalties: Imprisonment for not more than 5 years, or a fine of not more than $1,000, or both.

OHIO: Any person who unlawfully or unintentionally kills another while violating any law of this state applying to the use or operation of watercraft is guilty of *manslaughter in the second degree*.

19. Boat Livery Operator's Responsibility

All boat livery owners are required to keep records, including name and address of persons hiring boat, identification number of hired boat, departure date and time, and expected time of return. No rental boats shall be permitted to be used unless provided, either by livery owner or renter, with equipment required by state boat act.

20. Boat Pollution Prohibited

Most states have general laws which prohibit the pollution of the waters of the state. This section is concerned with additional laws which specifically prohibit the discharge of raw sewage or garbage from recreational watercraft.

ARIZONA: Dumping refuse, rubbish or debris on waterways unlawful. Violation is a misdemeanor punishable by fine and/or imprisonment.

CALIFORNIA: The mooring of a houseboat or boat used as a residence on any waters 2 miles above the intake or place where any city, town, or village takes its water from a river or stream for drinking or domestic purposes is unlawful except for temporary mooring.

CONNECTICUT: Unlawful to deposit any garbage, domestic refuse or other material of like nature from any watercraft into the waters of the State. Violation is punishable by a fine of not more than $1,000 or imprisonment for not more than 3 months, or both.

GEORGIA: Unlawful for boaters to dump trash within 2 miles of established fish sanctuaries.

INDIANA: Unlawful to keep, maintain or operate any boat equipped with a marine toilet unless the toilet is sealed or otherwise rendered inoperative so that no human wastes can be discharged into water. Boats operating solely on Lake Michigan excepted. First offense punishable by maximum fine of $50 and/or 30 days imprisonment; for subsequent offense, fine up to $100 and/or 60 days imprisonment.

NEBRASKA: Every vessel equipped with kitchen or toilet facilities shall handle and treat solid and liquid wastes in a manner that will prevent water pollution. No wastes or container of such wastes shall be placed, left or discharged in or near any waters of this state. See Marine Chlorinator under Equipment Requirements.

NEVADA: Every marine toilet on any boat operated on state waters must be equipped with a suitable treatment device designed to disinfect human body wastes before discharge into the water. See Marine Chlorinator under Equipment Requirements.

NEW HAMPSHIRE: Every marine toilet on any boat operated on state waters must be equipped with a suitable treatment device designed to disinfect human body wastes before discharge into the water. See Marine Chlorinator under Equipment Requirements.

NEW JERSEY: No vessel equipped with toilet shall be licensed to operate on non-tidal waters so long as any matter that might pollute the water, harm fish or wildlife, or litter the water or the shoreline can be discharged from its facility. Any person who discharges, or permits the discharge of any excrement, waste, debris, refuse, chemical, etc., from any vessel afloat is a disorderly person. First offense punishable by maximum fine of $100; for subsequent offense, a fine up to $200 and/or imprisonment up to 90 days.

NEW YORK: Unlawful to deposit offensive matter into navigable waters. Penalty: Up to $100 fine and/or imprisonment up to 1 year. No watercraft equipped with sanitary facilities may be launched, kept or used on Lake George unless said facilities are removed, sealed or made to drain into a portable tank which can be emptied ashore. Violation constitutes a misdemeanor punishable by a maximum fine of $100, and/or imprisonment up to 1 year.

OHIO: No person shall launch, moor, dock, use or operate any watercraft on state waters which contains a sanitary system capable of discharging human or household wastes into the water. Such sanitary system shall be removed, sealed or made to drain into a portable tank for disposal ashore according to local health regulations. Watercraft operating solely on Lake Erie, the Muskingum River, the Ohio River, and immediately connected habors and anchorages, excepted. Violation punishable by fine up to $100.

PENNSYLVANIA: On Pymatuning Lake no sewage or any nocuous or deleterious substances, liquid or solid, may be discharged into the water except after complete treatment and under permit first applied for to State Health Dept.

SOUTH DAKOTA: Every vessel equipped with kitchen or toilet facilities shall be so equipped and operated to handle or treat liquid and solid wastes in a manner that will prevent pollution of the receiving waters. See Marine Chlorinator under Equipment Requirements.

WISCONSIN: Unlawful to maintain or operate upon inland waters, except Lake Winnebago, the Mississippi River, and the Wisconsin River for 15 miles above and below the dam at Wisconsin Dells, any boat equipped with a toilet unless such toilet is sealed or otherwise rendered inoperative so that no human waste can be discharged into water.

21. Operator's Licensing

NEW JERSEY: Licensing of operators required on non-tidal waters. License fee ($1.50) shall be paid annually. Learner's permit issued for not more than 30 days.

CHAPTER XXII

Refunds on Gasoline Taxes

The primary expense of boat operation—except for sailboats—is the cost of the gasoline and oil used. Here, the operating cost can vary tremendously, depending on the weight, size and type of boat; the type and amount of engine power; the average speed at which the boat will run (most boats are run most of the time at full power) and the approximate number of running hours per season.

The first consideration here is a comparison between outboards and inboard engine boats. As a general observation, the inboard is accepted as superior for nearly any type of boat from 25 feet upward, where there is demand for better boat balance, seaworthiness and durability. On the other hand, the outboard engine is preferred for all boats up to about 22 feet in length because of its lower weight, higher speed per horsepower, greater maneuverability, and the fact that the outboard does not take up any of the available space in the boat. Also, the outboard is relatively easy to remove for repairs and storage and can be "traded in" on a specific basis, like an automobile. In the past few years, a new type of engine has appeared on the market, the outboard-inboard which uses an inboard engine, mounted close to the rear transom and an outboard propulsion unit.

The rate of gasoline consumption is important because it accounts for a considerable part of overall operating expense—a factor which is very often overlooked by prospective boat purchasers. There is no simple answer for estimating the rate of gasoline consumption because so many different factors enter into it: the design, horsepower, weight and condition of both the engine and the boat; the speed at which the boat is driven, and the variable factors such as wind resistance, strength and direction of wind and current.

Horsepower is the Important Factor

Basically, horsepower can be defined as energy for getting work done, and the more work to be done, the more horsepower required. Second, the more horsepower required, the more fuel is used in a given time. Keep in mind that in figuring fuel consumption in boats, you work on the basis of gallons per hour, rather than on distance travelled as is usually done in figuring automobile-gas usage.

The only reliable formula for fuel consumption must be on the basis of full-throttle operation, because engine manufacturers rate their engines at the maximum horsepower they develop. Also, most people are concerned with fuel consumption under cruising conditions; which usually means at or near wide-open throttle. On this basis, a reasonably accurate approximation for outboards can be made by using the following formula: *Advertised maximum horsepower divided by eight equals gallons of fuel consumed per hour.*

The gasoline companies estimate that the average outboarder uses his motor about 50 hours a year and consumes about $35 worth of gasoline-oil mix.

Because of the wide differences among inboard boats it is difficult to even estimate what the operating costs for fuel

Index

States	Refer to Part	Tax	Status	See Note
ALABAMA	4	7¢	NR	
ALASKA	3	6¢	PR	1
ARIZONA	2	5¢	FR	
ARKANSAS	4	6½¢	NR	
CALIFORNIA	2	6¢	FR	
COLORADO	1	6¢	FR	2
CONNECTICUT	2	6¢	FR	
DELAWARE	1	5¢	FR	3
DISTRICT OF COLUMBIA	2	6¢	FR	
FLORIDA	4	7¢	NR	4
GEORGIA	3	6½¢	PR	5
HAWAII	4	3½¢	NR	6
IDAHO	1	6¢	FR	7
ILLINOIS	2	5¢	FR	
INDIANA	1	6¢	FR	
IOWA	1	6¢	FR	
KANSAS	2	5¢	FR	8
KENTUCKY	4	7¢	NR	
LOUISIANA	4	7¢	NR	9
MAINE	3	7¢	PR	
MARYLAND	1	6¢	FR	
MASSACHUSETTS	2	5½¢	FR	
MICHIGAN	4	6¢	NR	
MINNESOTA	2	5¢	FR	

States	Refer to Part	Tax	Status	See Note
MISSISSIPPI	3	7¢	PR	10
MISSOURI	2	3¢	FR	
MONTANA	1	6¢	FR	
NEBRASKA	3	7¢	PR	11
NEVADA	2	6¢	FR	
NEW HAMPSHIRE	2	7¢	FR	
NEW JERSEY	4	5¢	NR	12
NEW MEXICO	2	6¢	FR	13
NEW YORK	2	6¢	FR	14
NORTH CAROLINA	3	7¢	PR	15
NORTH DAKOTA	4	6¢	NR	
OHIO	1	7¢	FR	16
OKLAHOMA	4	6.58¢	NR	
OREGON	1	6¢	FR	
PENNSYLVANIA	4	5¢	NR	
RHODE ISLAND	1	7¢	FR	17
SOUTH CAROLINA	3	7¢	PR	18
SOUTH DAKOTA	1	6¢	FR	19
TENNESSEE	4	7¢	NR	
TEXAS	1	5¢	FR	
UTAH	4	6¢	NR	
VERMONT	4	6½¢	NR	
VIRGINIA	1	7¢	FR	20
WASHINGTON	2	6½¢	FR	
WEST VIRGINIA	1	7¢	FR	21
WISCONSIN	2	6¢	FR	22
WYOMING	4	5¢	NR	

(FOR CANADIAN PROVINCES SEE PART 5)

Part 1 States granting full refund of tax on gasoline used in motorboats:

State (Note)	Tax	Form No.
Colorado (2) Motor Fuel Tax Division Dept. of Revenue 120 W. 6th Ave. Denver 4, Colorado	6¢	DR 189
Delaware (3) State Highway Dept. Dover, Delaware	5¢	Claim Form MF-14 and MF-15
Idaho (7) Tax Collector Motor Fuel Tax Division State House Boise, Idaho	6¢	Refund Claim Form
Indiana Dept. of State Revenue Motor Fuel Tax Division 111 South Meridian St. Indianapolis 25, Indiana	6¢	3-R
Iowa Treasurer of the State of Iowa Refund Department Des Moines 19, Iowa	6¢	R-1 and R-2
Maryland Comptroller of the Treasury Gasoline Tax Division State Office Building Annapolis, Md.	6¢	G.T. 100
Montana State Board of Equalization Gasoline Refund Dept. Helena, Montana	6¢	R 1550
Ohio (16) Dept. of Taxation Motor Fuel Tax Division 1104 State Office Building Columbus, Ohio	7¢	31, 4, 4A
Oregon Dept. of Motor Vehicles Fuels Tax Refund Salem, Oregon	6¢	1200
Rhode Island (17) Motor Fuel Tax Section Division of Taxation 49 Westminster St. Providence, R. I.	7¢	T-59
South Dakota (19) Department of Revenue Motor Fuel Tax Refund Section Pierre, South Dakota	6¢	Motor Fuel Tax Refund Forms
Texas Comptroller of Public Accounts Motor Fuel Tax Division Austin, Texas	5¢	7065-E
Virginia (20) Division of Motor Vehicles Bureau of Gasoline Tax P. O. Box 1298 Richmond, Va.	7¢	VGT-26
West Virginia (21) State Tax Commission Charleston, West. Va.	7¢	GT-509

will come to; the first season's experience should provide the new owner with that information.

There is an old rule-of-thumb formula for estimating the fuel consumption of an inboard motorboat. This is: *About 1 pint of fuel per horsepower per hour, at normal cruising speed*. This calls for a bit of further figuring. At normal cruising speed (2/3 to 3/4 of full throttle) you are using about half the rated horsepower of the engine and this formula should apply to the horsepower you are actually using, rather than the rated horsepower.

Federal Gasoline Tax

On July 1, 1956, the Federal Excise Tax on gasoline was increased from 2¢ to 3¢ a gallon. On October 1, 1959, this Tax was again increased; this time to 4¢ a gallon. Any amount of tax paid in excess of 2¢ per gallon is refundable if the fuel is used otherwise than in a highway vehicle.

Only one application for refund of the Federal Tax may be made each year. It must be made on Internal Revenue Service Form 843 and filed with the District Director of Internal Revenue between July 1 and September 30. It must cover purchases of gasoline during the previous fiscal year (July 1 to the following June 30).

United States State Gasoline Taxes

Listed in the index below are the various States and the part of this chapter

Part 2 States granting full refund of tax on gasoline used in motorboats under the non-highway use provisions of the motor fuel tax law:

State (Note)	Tax	Form No.
Arizona Gasoline Tax Refund Dept. Motor Vehicle Division State Highway Dept. Phoenix, Arizona	5¢	343A and 264
California State Controller Division of Tax Collection and Refund P. O. Box 1019 Sacramento, Calif.	6¢	SCGR-1
Connecticut Gasoline Tax Section Motor Vehicle Dept. State Office Building Hartford 15, Conn.	6¢	O-21
District of Columbia Finance Office Room 1134 Municipal Center Building Washington 1, D. C.	6¢	P-3900
Illinois Motor Fuel Tax Division Dept. of Revenue Springfield, Ill.	5¢	RMFT 11
Kansas (8) Director of Revenue Department of Revenue Topeka, Kansas	5¢	G-81
Massachusetts Bureau of Excises 40 Court Street Boston, Mass.	5½¢	GT-9
Minnesota Commissioner of Taxation Petroleum Division 555 Wabasha St. St. Paul 1, Minn.	5¢	PDR-1
Missouri Fuel Tax Supervisor Department of Revenue Jefferson City, Missouri	3¢	No. 8
Nevada Nevada Tax Commission Carson City, Nevada	6¢	E-9
New Hampshire Motor Vehicle Department State House Annex Concord, N. H.	7¢	Refund Application for boats
New Mexico (13) Gasoline Tax Division Bureau of Revenue Santa Fe, New Mexico	6¢	Invoice Refund Form 3
New York (14) Misc. Tax Bureau Dept. of Taxation & Finance Gov. Smith Building Albany 1, N. Y.	6¢	MT-390
Washington Director of Dept. of Licenses Olympia, Washington	6½¢	SF 4112
Wisconsin (22) Dept. of Taxation Motor Fuel Tax Division State Office Bldg. Madison 2, Wisconsin	6¢	No. 3

Part 3 States granting a partial refund of the tax on gasoline used in motorboats:

State (Note)	Tax	Form No.	State (Note)	Tax	Form No.
Alaska (1) Dept. of Taxation Alaska Office Bldg. Juneau, Alaska	6¢	Deptax MF 15, 17	Georgia (5) Gas Tax Refund Unit 682 State Labor Bldg. Atlanta 3, Georgia	5½¢ of 6½¢	RF-14, RF-15

REFUNDS ON GASOLINE TAXES

State (Note)	Tax	Form No.
Maine Division of Gasoline Tax State House Augusta, Maine	6¢ of 7¢	GT 27-56
Mississippi (10) Motor Vehicle Comptroller Jackson, Miss.	6¢ of 7¢	M V C 5(a)
Nebraska (11) Dept. of Agriculture & Inspection Division of Motor Fuels Lincoln, Nebraska	6¢ of 7¢	Application to purchase refund tax gasoline
North Carolina (15) Commission of Revenue Gasoline Tax Division Raleigh, North Carolina	6¢ of 7¢	Gas 1201
South Carolina (18) Tax Commission Columbia, S. C.	6¢ of 7¢	306 & 307

Part 4 States which do not grant any refund on gasoline used in motorboats (pleasure craft), and amount of gas tax per gallon:

State (Note)	Tax	State (Note)	Tax
Alabama	7¢	North Dakota	6¢
Arkansas	6½¢	Oklahoma	6.58¢
Florida (4)	7¢	Pennsylvania	5¢
Hawaii (6)	3½¢	Tennessee	7¢
Kentucky	7¢	Utah	6¢
Louisiana (9)	7¢	Vermont	6½¢
Michigan	6¢	Wyoming	5¢
New Jersey (12)	5¢		

Part 5 Canadian province gasoline taxes

There is no gasoline tax levied by the Dominion of Canada. The taxes levied by the individual Provinces, together with the refund status, follow:

Canadian Province	Tax	Status	See Note	Canadian Province	Tax	Status	See Note
ALBERTA	10¢	NT	23 & 33	NOVA SCOTIA	17¢	NT	27
BRITISH COLUMBIA	10¢	PR	24	ONTARIO	13¢	PR	28
MANITOBA	11¢	NR		PRINCE EDWARD IS.	16¢	NR	29
NEW BRUNSWICK	15¢	PT	25	QUEBEC	13¢	NR	
NEWFOUNDLAND	19¢	NR	26	SASKATCHEWAN	12¢	NR	

in which the information pertaining to them is found, together with their State gasoline tax and the status of the refund to pleasure craft if any, NT=no tax, PT =partial tax, FR=full refund, PR= partial refund, and NR=no refund.

Time Limits

In each state there is a time limit imposed within which the application for refund must be filed. The shortest is 60 days for the District of Columbia. Two states, Iowa and West Virginia, require filing within 90 days. All the rest are 4 months or more.

Province	Tax	Refund	Form	Note
Alberta Deputy Provincial Secretary Natural Resources Building Edmonton, Alberta	10¢	10¢		23+33
British Columbia Director Consumer Taxation Tax Branch Parliament Building Victoria, British Columbia	10¢	9¢		24
Nova Scotia Gasoline Tax Division Dept. of Highways & Public Works Halifax, N. S.	17¢	Not Taxable	M.V. 15P	27
Ontario Inspector of Gasoline Tax Refunds Treasury Department Parliament Buildings Toronto 2, Ontario	13¢	11¢	G.T. 1001	28

The other Provinces do not grant tax refunds for gasoline used in pleasure craft; however, "marked" gasoline (dyed purple) may be purchased in some cases, and this is not taxed at same rate. See notes.

Notes On Gasoline Tax

1. (Alaska) Pleasure boats pay the full tax of 6¢ and apply for a 3¢ refund. Commercial fishing boats pay only 2¢ a gallon. Request forms DEPTAX MF-15 for a refund permit and DEPTAX MF-17 for a refund. Include original invoices.

2. (Colorado) If purchased in lots of 20 or more gallons, refund permit required.

3. (Delaware) Request form MF-14 when buying gasoline. Apply for refund on form MF-15.

4. (Florida) Refunds 4¢ of 7¢ tax for commercial fishing purposes if 25 or more gallons are purchased at one time and refund amounts to $5.00 or more. But not refunded to pleasure craft.

5. (Georgia) 5-1/2¢ of 6-1/2¢ is refunded if purchased in lots of 25 or more gallons and used in watercraft on navigable waters.

6. (Hawaii) Each of major islands levy additional gasoline tax. Oahu (Honolulu) 5¢, Hawaii 8¢, Mau 5¢, Kauai 5¢

7. (Idaho) Refunded if purchased in lots of 50 or more gallons if purchaser holds refund permit and seller is licensed distributor.

8. (Kansas) Refunded if purchased in lots of 40 or more gallons.

9. (Louisiana) Refunded only to commercial fishing boats and boats transporting children to school. Application must be filed on January 1 and July 1 of each year, and not later than 10 days thereafter.

10. (Mississippi) 6¢ of 7¢ refundable when use is non-highway.

11. (Nebraska) 6¢ to 7¢ is refundable if purchased in lots of 40 or more gallons. Apply for permit.

12. (New Jersey) Refunded to motor boats used for commercial fishing, fishing parties or sea scouts.

13. (New Mexico) Refunded if purchased in lots of 50 or more gallons. However, no refund is granted on a to-

tal quantity if less than 100 gallons.
14. (New York) Record all purchases and manner of use. Save records for 3 years.
15. (North Carolina) 6¢ to 7¢ refundable, file annual claim before April 15.
16. (Ohio) Refund of the marine fuel tax is granted on fuel used in all vessels on inland lakes without a navigable inlet or outlet. Also granted on fuel used on navigable waters in the following vessels:
(1) Vessels up to 16 feet with detachable motors; (2) Vessels used in a person's chief business or as a means of livelihood; (3) Vessels used for commercial fishing; (4) Vessels used for training Sea Scouts; (5) Vessels used by a railroad or a railroad car ferry company; and (6) Vessels of the United States, the State and any political subdivision thereof.
17. (Rhode Island) Refunded only when operated on navigable waters of the State. These are defined as, in addition to Narragansett Bay and the Atlantic Ocean, those rivers and streams adjacent thereto which are navigable and subject to the ebb and flow of the tides.
18. (South Carolina) 6¢ of 7¢ refundable if dealer delivers gasoline directly to the tank of the boat. Request refund certificate L-307 issued by dealer at time of purchase.
19. (South Dakota) Full tax is refundable if refund claim is filed before 6 months. If refund claims are filed later than 6 months but not later than 13 months from date of purchase, only one-half of the tax is refundable. No refund is granted unless total gallonage is 25 gallons or more.
20. (Virginia) Refundable if purchased in lots of 5 or more gallons.
21. (West Virginia) Refundable to motorboats or other water craft operated on navigable streams if purchased in lots of 25 or more gallons.
22. (Wisconsin) Requires original invoice with words "Original Invoice" printed or rubber stamped on it, showing date, name and address of seller and purchaser, number of gallons sold, price per gallon, amount of Wisconsin tax paid shown separately, must be legible and receipted for payment. Submit this with Wisconsin form No. 3.
23. (Alberta) Pleasure boats and fishermen buy gasoline colored purple, on which no tax is levied.
24. (British Columbia) Marine outlets sell gasoline colored purple for marine use, taxed at 1¢ per gallon. This 1¢ is not refundable, nor is 10¢ tax levied on other gasoline.
25. (New Brunswick) No refund granted, but pleasure craft buy marked gasoline, on which tax is 3¢.
26. (Newfoundland) Gasoline for passenger carrying boats within the Province is not taxed.
27. (Nova Scotia) 17¢ tax is not refundable but pleasure craft and fishermen buy marked (purple) tax free gasoline. This requires a permit applied for on form M.V. 15P.
28. (Ontario) Pleasure craft receive 11¢ refund, commercial fishermen receive 13¢ refund.
29. (Prince Edward Is.) 11¢ refund to commercial fishermen.

Diesel Fuel Tax

There is no Federal Tax levied on diesel fuel when it is delivered into the tanks of a boat. In general the States do not levy a tax on diesel fuel delivered into the tanks of a boat. There are the following exceptions:

STATES		TAX STATUS	NOTE
District of Columbia	6¢	Refundable	(30)
Hawaii	1¢	Not Refundable	
Michigan	6¢	Not Refundable	(31)
North Dakota	6¢	Not Refundable	
West Virginia	7¢	Refundable	(32)

Notes On Diesel Fuel Tax

30. (Dist. of Columbia) Use same form for refund as gasoline tax, Form P3900.

31. (Michigan) Tax is not collected on diesel fuel sold to (a) Watercraft used for commercial fishing, (b) Watercraft used by sea scouts, (c) Watercraft owned by the State or political subdivision thereof, (d) Watercraft used in interstate or foreign commerce, or owned by any railroad. Otherwise all diesel fuel is taxed at 6¢ and the tax is not refundable.

32. (West Virginia) Diesel tax is refundable to watercraft operated on navigable waters when fuel is purchased in lots of 25 gallons or more. Apply on Form GT-509-B to same address as shown above for gasoline refunds.

33. (Alberta) 12¢ diesel fuel tax not levied on purple fuel—for licensed fishermen or pleasure boating.

Invoices

In most instances original invoices showing receipt for payment are required to support gasoline tax refund requests. It is therefore suggested that these be requested at time of sale and retained for possible refund.

CHAPTER XXIII

Yacht and Motorboat Insurance

Marine insurance is the oldest form of insurance of which there is any record, and yacht insurance has followed the principles applied to the insurance of ocean-going commercial vessels, with the necessary adaptations to meet the requirements and risks peculiar to the insurance of private pleasure craft.

Policy Forms

The following forms of insurance are available for insuring yachts and inboard motorboats, including sailboats (with or without auxiliary power) used for private-pleasure purposes. Other insurance forms, which will be described later, are available for outboard motorboats.

Rates for pleasure-boat insurance are based on a variety of factors peculiar to the individual case. The principal determining factors are the value of the vessel, her age, permanently installed fire equipment, gasoline or oil engines (if any), cruising limits and in-commission periods (whether more or less than six months of the policy-year). Rates on the higher valued yachts are lower than rates on yachts of low value. The companies explain that the reason for this is that the cost of repair on lower valued yachts is generally much higher in proportion to the value of the yacht than would be the case on those of higher value. In some instances, deductible insurance, in which the boat-owner assumes a part of the cost of covered repairs, may be purchased at a lower rate.

Generally, insurance for a pleasure boat will cost between 2 and 8 percent of the value of the boat per year.

The Yacht (Form "A") policy provides under Section "A" Hull (Marine) Insurance; under Section "B" Protection and Indemnity (Liability); under Section "C" Omnibus Clause; under Section "D" Medical Payment Insurance and under Section "E" Federal Longshoremen's and Harborworkers' Compensation Insurance covering the yacht owner's liability under this act. The protection and indemnity (liability) insurance is optional and when carried includes the Omnibus clause, Medical Payments insurance for not exceeding $1,000 per accident, and the Federal Longshoremen's and Harborworkers' Compensation insurance, without additional charge. This form of policy is used mainly to insure boats which are in commission some part of the year, but is also used to provide port risk insurance on boats laid up and out of commission during the term of the policy.

The Yacht—Fire and Lightning Policy insures against Fire and Lightning and usually covers vessels which are in commission some part of the year while afloat or ashore. Theft of the entire boat may be endorsed on the policy. This form of policy may also be used to insure boats which are laid up and out of commission during the entire term of the policy.

Yacht Liability Insurance (similar to Protection and Indemnity Insurance) is written to provide liability coverage on boats less than 36 feet at the waterline when the owner does not carry Hull (Marine) Insurance under the Yacht (Form "A") policy described above.

Builder's Risk Insurance is a form of policy that provides insurance against practically all risks of physical damage, except war and strikes, to yachts and motorboats while under construction at approved yards from the time of laying the keel until delivered to the owner at the yard. The risks of launching and trial trips are included. Insurance can also be provided on delivery trips for an additional premium.

Details of Marine Insurance

Yacht (Form "A") Policy Hull (Marine) Insurance: Property Covered; Insurance is provided on the hull, spars, sails, tackle, apparel, provisions, stores, machinery, boats and other furniture of and in the insured yacht or motorboat. According to this, there is a coverage on the entire vessel and its appurtenances, including the furnishings and fittings that are common to yachts. The word "boats" as used in the policy means the tender, dinghy, or row-boat that belongs to the yachts and includes yacht tenders propelled by outboard motors.

If any part of the furniture, tackle, boats or other property of the vessel is separated and laid up on shore, it is covered against the same perils as the vessel and the amount insured on the vessel and the property on board is decreased by the actual value of the property on shore. For example, if a yacht is insured for $3,000 and $500 worth of equipment is separately stored ashore, there would remain but $2,500 insurance on the yacht. The insurance company's liability on property separately stored on shore is limited to an amount not exceeding 50 per cent of the insured value of the vessel unless otherwise agreed upon in the insurance contract.

Privileges: The insured vessel is covered in port and at sea, under power or sail, in docks or graving docks and on ways, gridirons, and pontoons or on shore; with leave to sail with or without pilots, to tow and assist vessels or craft in all situations and to be towed and to go on trial trips. The assured is thus given the "privilege" of engaging in all of the operations necessary in connection with the ownership, maintenance and use of pleasure boats.

Perils Covered: Coverage is provided against fire, perils of the seas, assailing thieves, jettison and all other like perils. "All other like perils" does not mean all risks. Only perils *like* the perils insured against are covered. The term "perils of the seas" includes losses caused by stranding, sinking (caused by an insured peril), collision and stress of weather. Particular attention is called to the phrase "perils of the seas" so that the reader will not gain the erroneous impression that all damage to the vessel occurring on the seas is covered. The damage must be caused by a peril *of* the seas. "Assailing Thieves" as used in the Yacht policy means thieves making forcible entry of which there are visible marks; for example, theft due to thieves breaking into a locked cabin or locker of a boat.

Latent Defect, Negligence, Risk on Shore, etc., Clause: Since fire and assailing thieves are perils specifically mentioned in the policy, the yacht is insured against these perils at all times, either afloat or ashore. The additional coverage afforded by this clause can best be explained by quoting the clause in its entirety as follows:

This insurance also specially to cover, subject to any average warranty herein, loss of or damage to hull or machinery directly caused by the following:
1. Accidents in loading, discharging or handling stores and fitting or in taking fuel, or in hauling or launching or moving in shipyards;
2. While in shipyards or elsewhere on shore, windstorm, tornado, earthquake, hurricane, floods, collapse of shoring, blocking or staging; including collapse of buildings or other structures afloat or ashore;
3. Contact with aircraft (including articles falling therefrom) or motor vehicle;

4. Explosions on shipboard or elsewhere;
5. Bursting of boilers, breakage of shafts or any latent defect in the machinery or hull (excluding, however, the cost and expense of repairing or renewing the defective part);
6. Negligence of master, mariners, engineers or pilots; provided such loss or damage has not resulted from any want of due diligence by the owners of the yacht, or any of them, or by the manager, or by the assured.

This clause does not cover ordinary engine breakdown nor the repair of the hull and machinery necessitated by ordinary wear and tear.

Liability for Damage to Other Vessels: While the primary function of Hull (Marine) Insurance is to provide insurance against loss or damage to the vessel of the insured party, the "running down" clause gives some liability protection to the assured. In reality, this is separate liability insurance for an amount equal to the amount of the Hull (Marine) Insurance. If the insured yacht is involved in a collision with another vessel and the insured party is liable for damages to the other vessel, the insurance company will pay such damages up to the amount of insurance. The expenses of any litigation in connection with such claims against the assured are also covered. If the insured yacht negligently collides with another vessel owned by the insured, the amount of damages payable under the policy is determined by arbitration.

This coverage should not be confused with the insurance against collision damage to the assured's yacht. The latter applies to damage *sustained* by the insured yacht, while the "running down" clause applys to liability for damage *caused* to other vessels. Furthermore, it should be noted that this clause does not cover the assured's liability for personal injury under any circumstances.

Exclusions: There is no coverage under Hull (Marine) Insurance against:

(a) Loss or damage to spars and/or sails while racing. (A special endorsement may be attached to the policy for an additional premium to cover this risk with the exception, however, that loss or damage to spinnakers while racing is still excluded.)

(b) Wages or provisions. (This means that when a vessel sustains damage and is laid-up for repairs the insurance does not cover the wages of the crew during such layup, nor the cost of their provisions. However, physical loss or damages to provisions or stores of the yacht by perils insured is covered.)

In addition to the above exclusions there are various clauses that may be inserted in the policy depending on the particular type of boat being insured. For example, sometimes policies covering high powered speedboats or runabouts contain a clause known as the "propeller" or "machinery" clause stipulating that the insurance company is not liable for loss or damage to rudder, propeller, shaft, or machinery unless caused by stranding, sinking, burning, or collision with another vessel. Due to the very high speed of such boats, and because the propeller usually extends down below the line of the keel and is unprotected, the rudder, propeller, shaft or machinery are particularly susceptible to damage by striking floating logs or submerged obstructions, etc.; the clause relieves the company from liability for claims of this nature. Many companies do not insure boats having a speed of 45 miles per hour or more or those equipped with airplane motors.

Other Provisions of Hull Insurance: Salvage Charges: Claims under this insurance quite frequently involve salvage charges. Damage to the insured vessel may necessitate towing assistance and in some cases extensive salvage operations if the vessel has submerged. The cost of such salvage is covered by the policy. Charges for salvage, towing or other assistance rendered to the insured vessel by another vessel belonging to the assured are also covered, the amount payable being determined by arbitration.

Sue and Labor: In case of any loss or misfortune it is lawful for the assured, "their factors, servants and assigns, to sue labor and travel for, in and about the defense, safeguard and recovery of the insured yacht or any part thereof, without prejudice to the company." The expense of such actions is borne by the insurance company.

Protection and Indemnity Insurance

The Protection and Indemnity Insurance covers the insured boat-owner against claims for loss of life or personal injury by reason of his interest in the insured yacht or motorboat. The assured is protected whether the injured person is a guest on board, a member of the crew, or a member of the public.

Under Maritime Law a yacht owner's liability to his captain or a member of the crew for personal injuries sustained by them while in the performance of their yacht duties is for "maintenance and cure." The yacht owner is obliged to provide "maintenance and cure" whether the injuries were sustained accidentally or due to his negligence. The claimant may, however, disregard his right to receive merely "maintenance and cure" and bring a damage suit against the yacht owner for a certain amount if he feels that he may be able to prove that the injuries sustained were due to the owner's gross negligence. With respect to other persons such as guests or members of the general public, the yacht owner's liability is limited to only those injuries which are due to his negligence.

In addition to paying for injuries for which the assured is responsible, the insurance company will pay litigation expenses when the liability of the assured is contested, with the consent of the company, in lieu of settling the claim.

Limits of Liability: There are two limits to be observed under this clause. One is the limit for the injury or death of any one person, and subject to this limit is the limit for one accident. The limit for any one accident is not less than the amount of Hull (Marine) Insurance carried. The reason for this is that under the Protection and Indemnity plan of rating there is no rate or premium advantage to be gained by taking an accident limit lower than the amount of Marine Insurance on the hull. Higher protection and Indemnity limits may be purchased at additional rates.

Insurance companies point out that the need for adequate loss of life and personal injury limits can be realized when it is appreciated that under Maritime Law (which differs considerably from similar situations in civil law covering, for example, automobile accidents), there is no limit to the amount of a yacht owner's liability unless the loss was occasioned without his "privity" or knowledge. If the owner can demonstrate that the loss was caused without his privity or knowledge (and this often is difficult to do), the court will usually grant his petition to limit the amount of his liability to the value of his vessel in her condition after the accident.

Property Damage: Protection and Indemnity Insurance also supplements the "running down" clause, and covers the insured's *liability* or responsibility for damages to all other types of property of others by reason of his interest in his boat or yacht, as follows:

(a) Loss or damage to any other ship or boat or goods, merchandise, freight or other things or interests whatever on board such other ship or boat caused proximately or otherwise by the yacht insured so far as the damage would not be covered by the "running down" clause.

(b) Loss or damage to any goods, merchandise, freight or other things, or interests other than that included in (a) above, whether on said yacht or not, which may arise from any cause whatever.

(c) Loss or damage to any harbor, dock, slipway, way, gridiron, pontoon, pier, quay, jetty, stage, buoy, telegraph cable, or other

fixed or movable thing whatever or to any goods or property in or on the same, however caused.
(d) Any attempted or actual raising, removal or destruction of the wreck of the insured ship or the cargo thereof or any neglect or failure to raise, remove or destroy the same.

The insurance company's liability under Protection and Indemnity Insurance, for all property damage arising from any one accident or series of accidents arising out of the same event does not exceed the amount of Hull (Marine) Insurance carried or the *per person* limit for loss of life or personal injury, whichever is greater.

Omnibus clause: When Protection and Indemnity Insurance is carried, the Omnibus clause is included without additional premium. This clause extends the Running Down and Protection and Indemnity Clauses to protect other persons operating the insured vessel with the prior permission of the owner (excluding the crew and employees of boat yards, service or sales agencies or similar agencies.)

Federal Compensation Insurance

When Protection and Indemnity Insurance is carried, Federal Compensation Insurance covering the yacht owner's liability under the Federal Longshoremen's and Workers' Compensation Act is automatically included.

Coverage: This Federal Act provides that every employer shall secure the payment of compensation either by insurance or by qualifying as a self-insurer for the "disability or death of an employee resulting from an injury occurring upon the navigable waters of the United States (including any dry dock) if recovery for the disability or death through Workmen's Compensation proceedings may not validly be provided for by State Law. No compensation shall be payable with respect to the disability or death of—a master or a member of a crew of any vessel."

As the name implies, the Act was designed primarily to provide compensation for longshoremen and harbor workers when they were not subject to State workmen's compensation laws, but is broad enough to apply to the employees (other than the captain and crew) of a yacht owner if injured under the circumstances described.

Since this Federal Act does not apply to the captain and crew, if any (who are covered by the Protection and Indemnity Insurance), it is only *other* employees of a boat owner who might fall within the protection of the Act. In this category are chauffeurs, butlers, maids and other types of employees, who if injured aboard the yacht while it is upon the navigable waters of the United States or in any dry dock, might be construed as coming under the Act, if it were held that at the time of the accident they were engaged in maritime employment.

Medical Payments Insurance

When Protection and Indemnity Insurance is carried, it will include Medical Payments Insurance with payments not exceeding $1,000 per accident designed to cover reasonable medical, surgical, ambulance, hospital, etc., expenses incurred by guests as a result of sustaining bodily injury caused by accident while in, or upon, boarding or leaving the insured yacht, without additional premium. Higher Medical Payment limits (not exceeding $5,000 per accident) may be obtained at additional premiums.

Exclusions: This insurance does not apply to bodily injury to or death of any person
(a) to or for whom benefits are payable under any workmen's compensation act
(b) who, in being in or upon or in

boarding or leaving the yacht, is a trespasser

(c) who is an employee of the insured while engaged in the employment of the insured, except those in domestic service who are not covered by any workmen's compensation act.

It also does not apply to any liability assumed by the assured under any contract or agreement; while the insured yacht is being used for other than private-pleasure purposes; to bodily injury or to death of the assured or registered owner of the insured yacht.

General Provisions of the Yacht (Form "A") Policy

The following provisions are applicable to Hull (Marine) Insurance, Protection and Indemnity Insurance, Omnibus Clause, Medical Payments Insurance and Federal Compensation Insurance:

Private Pleasure Warranty: The policy warrants that the vessel will be used solely for private pleasure purposes and will not be chartered or hired unless approved by the insurance company and permission is endorsed on the policy.

Continuation Clause: If the insured vessel is at sea at the expiration date of the policy, the insurance may be continued until the arrival of the vessel at her port of destination provided notice is given to the insurance company and additional premium is paid as required.

Held Covered Clause: In the event of any unintentional deviation beyond the waters permitted by this policy, or unintentional violation of the lay-up warranty, if any, it is hereby agreed to hold this yacht covered, provided notice is given to the company as soon as it is known to the insured, and an additional premium paid for the extra coverage.

Exclusions: The "exclusions" are an important part of any policy and should be understood by the boat owner. Even the most comprehensive policy does not cover against everything, and this is one phase of the policy that should be discussed at length with the broker or agent.

"Strikes and Riots:" There is no coverage against loss or damage in consequence of strikes, lockouts, political or labor disputes, civil commotions, riots, martial law, military or usurped power or malicious acts. (Strike and Riot endorsement is usually available on payment of an additional premium.)

"War Risks": Unless removed from the policy by the underwriter, the following warranty is paramount and supersedes and nullifies and contrary provision of the policy:

F.C. and S. Clause: Notwithstanding anything to the contrary contained in this policy, this insurance is warranted free from any claim for loss, damage and expense caused by or resulting from capture, seizure, arrest, restraint or detainment, or the consequences thereof or of any attempt thereat, or any taking of the vessel, by requisition or otherwise, whether in time of peace or war and whether lawful or otherwise; also from all consequences of hostility or war-like operations (whether there be a declaration of war or not) but this warranty shall not exclude collision, contact with any floating object (other than a mine or torpedo), stranding, heavy weather or fire unless caused directly (and independently of the nature of the voyage or service which the vessel concerned, or, in the case of a collision any other vessel concerned therein, is performing) by hostile act or against a belligerent power; and for the purpose of this warranty "power" includes any authority maintaining naval, military or air forces in association with a power, also warranted free, whether in time of peace or war, from all loss or damage caused by any weapon of war employing atomic fission or radioactive force.

Further warranted free from the consequences of civil war, revolution, rebellion, insurrection, or civil strife arising therefrom, or piracy.

When war risks are added to the policy by endorsement, they apply only as they specifically outline conditions under which they supersede the above warranty.

Illicit Trade: No claims will be paid for claims arising from use of the vessel for illicit trade, or trade in articles under contraband, or from violation of any port regulation.

Other Conditions: Payment of Loss: Losses covered by the policy are payable within 30 days after proof of loss and interest in the vessel have been given. Any indebtedness to the company (premiums due) may be deducted. In case of dispute with the insurance company, suit must be brought within 12 months, unless some other time limit is provided by State laws.

Cancellation: Either the assured or the company may cancel the policy by 10 days written notice. The policy contains schedule for return of premium in proportion to time covered.

Navigation Privileges

The Yacht (Form "A") policy warrants that the yacht or motorboat will be confined to certain waters, such as "Coastwise and inland waters between Eastport, Maine and Cedar Keys, Florida" on the East Coast, or "Coastwise and inland waters between Point Reyes and Point Banda" on the West Coast or "Waters of the Great Lakes and tributaries including the St. Lawrence River not below Quebec", etc. The policy does not cover a vessel while outside the specified cruising limits except as provided in the "held covered" clause mentioned above. (On large ocean-going yachts unrestricted cruising may be granted.)

As used in the insurance contract "coastwise waters" means a limit of 15-20 miles from shore for larger motorboats. For smaller boats the term is interpreted to mean the usual and normal safe cruising range for such boats. For instance, a 14-foot outboard that is purposely taken 10 or 12 miles offshore would be considered as going beyond its normal "coastwise" range, and would not be covered by its policy.

Lay-Up Warranty

Policies covering boats with Great Lakes cruising limits, or Eastport-Cedar Keys limits (when the cruising is confined to northern waters), usually warrant that the vessels be laid up and out of commission during the winter, ordinarily from November 1st to May 1st, but the policy covers the boat during this period. The lay-up period may be amended to meet your individual requirements by a reduction for lesser use, an increase in premium for more use. If the vessel is unexpectedly placed in commission during the policy lay-up period the insurance company should be notified, otherwise there may be a loss of protection. In those territories where it is customary to navigate all year round, privilege of 12-month cruising without a lay-up warranty may be granted, as for example boats confined to southern waters, or northern yachts which proceed to southern waters in the winter.

Proportion of Loss Covered

In the policy, the valuation of the boat is specified as well as the amount of insurance. In order to receive full payment for any losses, the amount of insurance carried must equal the agreed valuation of the vessel. Otherwise, if a lesser amount of insurance is carried, the insurance company is liable only for "that proportion of any loss that the amount of insurance bears to the agreed valuation." In other words, you could cut down the cost of your insurance by insuring for only 50 percent of the value of your boat, but then any claim for losses would pay only one-half of the amount of the loss.

In case of loss or damage, prompt notice should be given to your insurance broker or directly to the insurance company. No damage should be repaired until inspected by the company surveyor and the amount of damage agreed upon, except where temporary repairs are necessary after an accident to place the boat "in good safety" to use the nautical term. But keep in mind that the agreement made with the surveyor is strictly without prejudice to the insurance, as the company will pass on its liability after the surveyor's report is received. A loss on a boat is usually adjusted by the company paying for the cost of repairs necessary to place the vessel in the same condition that she was in prior to the accident. Note that under the "new for old" clause in the policy, when it becomes necessary to repair damage to old or used material by replacing with new material, no deduction is made by the insurance company for depreciation.

How Rates Are Set

The rates for Hull (Marine) Insurance depend upon the amount insured, cruising limits, navigation period, age, construction, and physical condition of the vessel. There is a graduated scale of rates based on the type of vessel, i.e., gasoline, Diesel, runabout or sailboat.

On gasoline and Diesel yachts, a reduction is made in the rate for the installation of a built-in carbon dioxide system of fire extinguishing apparatus in the engine room.

The proper rate is applied to the amount of insurance, which, as stated above, should be the same as the agreed valuation. On new boats, the purchase price is usually fixed as the agreed valuation, and on second-hand boats, the purchase price plus amounts spent for reconditioning is usually used.

On Protection and Indemnity Insurance, the premiums depend upon the limits of coverage per accident and the period of navigation specified in the policy, and the premiums for Medical Payments Insurance are set similarly. The Federal Compensation Insurance is only granted when Protection and Indemnity insurance is carried and then it is included without additional premium.

Yacht "Increased Value on Hull" Policy

On yachts insured for more than $30,000 against marine risks, a saving in premium can usually be effected by dividing the insurance, covering part under a Hull policy and the balance under an "Increased Value on Hull" policy.

For example, on a yacht to be insured for $50,000, $40,000 could be carried under the Hull policy and $10,000 under the "Increased Value on Hull" policy. The coverage under the latter policy is limited primarily to total loss (excluding all partial loss) but including excess liability claims under the "running down" clause or excess General Average claims which are not recoverable under the Hull (Marine) insurance policy. In view of the restricted coverage, the rate for the "Increased Value on Hull" policy is approximately one-half of the rate applicable to the Hull policy. The combined premium, therefore, for the two policies is usually less than if the total amount to be insured was all carried under the Hull policy at full rate. The two policies together afford a total loss protection for the full amount and the amount insured on the hull is usually sufficient to cover partial losses. The "Increased Value on Hull" policy also provides that a total loss shall be paid under this policy if total loss is paid on the Hull policy.

The proportion of the total insurance to be carried which is permitted on "Increased Value on Hull" varies with the amount to be insured. However, it should be borne in mind that if the yacht is insured for $30,000 or less, no "Increased Value on Hull" insurance is permitted.

Fire and Lightning Only Insurance

If you are interested in protecting your boat only against fire and lightning, you can obtain the Yacht — Fire and Lightning Policy. This insurance is available to vessels that are in commission either year-round or only a part of the year. It can also be taken out on a boat that is laid-up and out of commisssion all year. The property coverage is about the same as that described under Hull (Marine) insurance and a certain percentage, usually not over 20 percent applies to movables belonging to the insured boat while stored separately on shore.

This form of insurance covers direct loss or damage caused by fire or lightning. The commonly accepted use of the term "lightning" applies and in no case does it include loss or damage by cyclone, tornado or windstorm.

Yacht Liability Policy (Protection and Indemnity)

The Yacht Liability Policy is available only on motor or sailboats that are less than 36 feet at the waterline and only when Hull (Marine) insurance is *not* carried. If Hull (Marine) insurance is carried, then liability protection, if desired, is provided under the Protection and Indemnity section of the Yacht (Form "A") Policy.

This policy is specially adapted to the needs of the owner of a smaller boat who is not interested in Hull (Marine) insurance and who carries only Fire and Lightning insurance, but who feels that he needs protection to cover any responsibility for loss of life or injury or property damage that may arise out of his ownership of a boat.

There are three separate coverages available under this policy and the boatowner may buy any one coverage or any combination among the three;

Section A covers the assured's liability for loss of life and personal injury. This insurance is subject to the limit per person and per accident specified in the policy.

Section B covers, subject to the limit specified, the assured's liability on account of loss or damage to any harbor, dock, slipway, gridiron, pontoon, pier, quay, jetty, stage, buoy, telegraph cable, or other fixed or movable thing whatsoever, or to property in or upon the same, except to any ship or boat or to any goods or property in or upon same, howsoever caused.

Section C covers up to the limit of liability specified, the assured's liability on account of loss or damage to any other ship or boat or to property in or upon same, caused proximately or otherwise by the boat insured.

Port Risk Insurance

Boats which are laid up and out of commission all year round may be insured against marine risks under the Yacht Form "A" policy including Protection and Indemnity, Medical Payments and Federal Compensation insurance, or they may be protected only against fire and lightning. The rates for this insurance vary considerably, depending on whether the storage is wet or dry, the amount to be insured and the specific Fire Contents rate at the shore location where the boat is laid-up.

Builders' Risk Insurance

A Builders' Risk Form is usually used to insure yachts or motorboats when a boat is being built under contract. Usually a boat under construction is at the risk of the builder until he makes delivery to the buyer, but in some cases the buyer agrees to carry the necessary insurance or desires it to protect his down payment and any additional payments made during construction and before delivery. This insurance may be written in the name of the builder or the owner or both.

This policy covers practically all risks, including the risk of launching and trial trips if required, and may be endorsed to cover delivery trips subject to specified insuring conditions. Insurance is required equal to the completed contact price and the premium rate is averaged in view of the fact that the total amount is not insured during the entire period of construction. At the time of loss, the insurance company is liable for the actual value of the vessel at time of loss based on labor and materials.

Engineering and Inspection Service

An important feature of the yacht and motorboat insurance is the safety engineering and inspection service that offered with no additional cost to the boat owner. Particularly in the case of older boats, the insurance is not granted until a physical inspection of the boat has been made.

Most insurance companies have a staff of marine surveyors trained to discover fire, explosion and other hazards so often found in pleasure boats. In some cases, modifications or changes in the boat will be required before the insurance will be issued. On a minimum basis the insurance company surveyors check and make recommendations on the following: adequate ventilation, number and type of fire extinguishers, proper vents and fills for fuel tanks, flame arrestors and drip pans for carburetors, exhaust pipe insulation and proper installation of galley stove and fuel tanks.

INSURANCE FOR THE OUTBOARD

Insurance for the outboard is usually sold in units of $100 based on the actual value of the boat and motor or motors. Generally the buyer of the outboard policy buys his insurance in units: (1) boat; (2) outboard motor(s); (3) boat trailer; (4) accessories; and most companies offer these policies on an installment payment plan.

The outboard policy covers loss or specified damage to the boating equipment against fire; theft (theft coverage on portable boat accessories applies only if such theft occurs at the same time as theft of boat or motor); motor overboard; sinking; wind damage; damage in transit; hitting a snag; vandalism; running aground.

Included generally is a minimum $500 property damage liability protection against collision with another boat and if the total of insurance taken is over $500, then this liability is increased to equal the amount of the insurance.

Liability insurance to cover responsibility for injury to guests aboard the outboard or injuries that may be inflicted through operation of the boat is available in the form of homeowners' liability, boat liability, or a comprehensive personal liability policy.

Rates for Outboard Insurance

The above table shows the rates generally in effect for outboard motorboat policies although they may vary slightly from company to company. In addition, several of the national boating associations have plans which offer similar protection to members at somewhat lower rates.

FOR BOATS NORMALLY USED ON INLAND LAKES AND RIVERS

Term	TERRITORY 1*			TERRITORY 2**		
	$100 Deductible	$50 Deductible	$25 Deductible	$100 Deductible	$50 Deductible	$25 Deductible
1 year	$2.50	$3.50	$4.50	$2.00	$2.50	$3.50
2 years	4.50	6.50	8.50	3.50	4.50	6.50
3 years	7.00	9.50	12.00	5.50	7.00	9.50

*TERRITORY 1 Inland waters of Alabama, Arizona, Arkansas, California, Florida, Georgia, Kansas, Kentucky, Louisiana, Mississippi, Missouri, New Mexico, North Carolina, Oklahoma, Oregon, South Carolina, Tennessee, Texas, Virginia, and Washington.

**TERRITORY 2 Inland waters of District of Columbia and all states not included in Territory 1.

FOR BOATS NORMALLY USED ON OCEAN, GULF AND TIDAL WATERS

Term	TERRITORY 3 PACIFIC COAST			TERRITORY 4 ATLANTIC and GULF COAST		
	$100 Deductible	$50 Deductible	$25 Deductible	$100 Deductible	$50 Deductible	$25 Deductible
1 year	$2.50	$3.50	$4.50	$3.00	$4.00	$5.00
2 years	4.50	6.50	8.50	5.50	7.50	9.00
3 years	7.00	9.50	12.00	8.00	11.00	13.50

Full protection, for all four territories, takes the same rate as $25 deductible plus a flat charge of $12.50 for one year, $23.00 for two years or $34.00 for three years.

Minimum premium:
1 year $10.00   2 years $18.50   3 years $27.00

Rates per $100 Protection.

CHAPTER XXIV

Something About Sailboats

Acquiring a sailboat is a highly personal matter. The amount which you wish to spend, the use for which you intend the boat, your sailing skill, and the waters which you plan to cruise, are all important factors.

Boatmakers today offer wind-driven craft in all sizes and types from the 8-foot pram dinghy to 70-foot ocean racing yachts with auxiliary motor power. They are available in wood, fiberglass (which is rapidly becoming more and more popular), and in larger yachts, in metal.

No one, even in the boating industry, knows exactly how many different types of sailing craft are available in the United States. One list compiled by the National Association of Engine and Boat manufacturers list 98 different types of standardized sailboats which are numerous enough to have active racing or cruising associations sponsoring them. These are the "one-design" classes which are built to uniform specifications under license from the sponsoring group, and are identifiable by the class insignia on the sail and the registered number of the individual boat. In addition to custom-built boats and numerous locally designed and built sailboats that do not have any "class" sponsorship, there are also mass-produced boats and an increasing number of imported boats that are unsponsored.

Selecting Your Sailboat

With this plenitude of craft, making a selection is no easy matter, and any advice will naturally not apply to all situations. One important matter that many fail to consider is that the original price of the boat — whether new or used — does not by any means represent the cost of enjoying sailing. There are always expected and unexpected expenses. In some areas mooring space must be rented, winter layup can be expensive, there is always some seasonal and yearly maintenance expense, sails and rigging must be replaced in time, and insurance should be considered. Also, many yacht club memberships are not inexpensive, although the bulk of present day yacht clubs are well beneath the millionaire's strata.

Perhaps one of the best ways to select the boat within your price range is to spend some time surveying the waters which you intend to cruise and noting which types of sailboat are most popular in the area. Generally you will find that a few types predominate and there is generally a logical reason for their choice because of their performance under local water and weather conditions. Speak to local sailors and accept their praise of their own type of boat with a grain of salt.

Keep the "resale" angle in mind when buying a sailboat. A boat that is not too expensive to begin with, and of a popular type should lose very little in resale value in a year or even in several years. Second-hand boats often sell at about the same price for year after year, if they are properly maintained. If you are a novice in the field it is well worth the additional expense of hiring a marine surveyor or a reliable ship's broker to check over the second-hand boat you may be planning to buy. Dry rot or other damage may not be visible to the untrained eye but can be readily spotted by the expert. Also keep in mind that the average sailboat buyer does not keep his first boat too long. The afternoon-with-family-on-the-water man may catch the bug and go in for racing. The day sailer may give way to a boat with accommodations for longer cruises, or a changing family situation may dictate a larger or a smaller boat.

For the average newcomer to sailboating, a sloop in the 14-20-foot range is a good starting size. Smaller than that, the boat becomes pretty cramped after a few hours on the water, and a much larger boat may be quite too much for the sailor. Also, note that larger sailboats are always faster than smaller sailboats.

Most of the present day sailboats are designed pretty much for specific purposes. The racing-type boat is very different in design from the family day sailor, and for family use, a broad-beamed heavy boat with a large, comfortable cockpit is far more desirable than the sleeker racing models whose tendency to "heel" over must be compensated by the shifting weight of the crew "hiking" over the rail.

Centerboard or Keel?

One of the basic differences among different designs of sailboats is the matter of keel *vs.* centerboard. A sailboat must have some projection beneath the hull to keep it from sliding sideways when under sail. The keel-type has a heavy weight of ballast under the keel or centerline of the boat projecting down into the water and increasing the draft of the boat. The centerboard type has a board which slides down from the centerboard trunk to serve this purpose.

Each type has its virtues.

The centerboard boat is unballasted and lighter, and since the center board can be raised it can run into shallow waters where the keel type cannot venture. Also, the smaller centerboard can be run right up on a sandy beach. Most centerboard boats are built a bit wider than keel boats of the same length in order to provide stability and more cockpit room. It is also easier to haul out a centerboard boat and much simpler to trailer it. Generally, the centerboard boats are faster off the wind than similar keel types.

One drawback of the centerboard types is the fact that most of them can capsize if not properly handled in strong winds. In some boats the centerboard trunk may be a source of trouble, being sometimes prone to leaks and to jamming of the centerboard itself.

A properly designed keel boat should not capsize under any wind condition, and although she can sink, she is normally faster to windward than a similar centerboard board. Elimination of the centerboard trunk from the middle of the boat provides more usable cockpit space, and in a cabin-boat the deeper body of the hull permits much better headroom.

Since much of the pleasure sailing in some parts of the country is in rather shallow bays, exploration of inlets being part of the fun of sailing, the deeper draft of the keeled boat that may restrict her to dredged or natural channels and keep her fairly far offshore in some areas is a drawback. Some manufacturers have provided a combination keel-centerboard type which has some of the features of each type, with a centerboard dropping through a slot in the ballast keel.

Generally the type of sailboat that you find in your cruising area is the type that has proven best, whether the keel or centerboard type.

Sloops and Other Rigs

The most popular type of sailboat in

the United States is the *Jib Headed Sloop* (Marconi Rig) and practically all the one-design classes are sloops. The sloop has one mast set forward, mainsail and one headsail, usually a "jib." This rig provides the most speed for the sail area and is fairly easy to handle.

The *Cat* is a single-masted boat, usually found in the smaller craft, dinghies and "training" boats, with a single sail that may be a gaff (suspended from a boom), or jib-headed.

The *Yawl* is similar to the sloop with the addition of a small *mizzen-mast* at the extreme stern. This rig is most often seen on larger ocean-going craft, seldom on those under 35 feet. In heavy weather the yawl often runs with only the mizzen and headsail set.

The *Ketch* is similar to the yawl except that the mizzen is larger and its mast is set further forward on the boat; the mainsail is relatively shorter on the foot. Slower than the yawl or the schooner, it has the advantage of being a somewhat easier rig to handle.

The *Schooner* is a two-masted boat, the largest sail being on the after mast. Forward sails may be gaff-headed and jibs. Usually found in older vessels over 40 feet in length, this is sea-going rig, adjustable to all kinds of weather.

Day Sailer or Cruiser?

An air mattress on the floorboards, "sterno" or a one-burner alcohol stove, the traditional bucket for toilet facilities are all possible in a 20 foot boat or even a smaller one, but it's a little uncomfortable once you are beyond the "college-kid" category.

As a rule, the sailboat that can make a comfortable cruiser is at least 25 feet, should be equipped with an icebox, a two-burner stove and a real "head." However, for four or five people, the minimum requirement is a 30-footer. In recent years, a number of 25-foot boats have appeared which advertise sleeping accommodations for five, but living aboard a boat that size with four other people can be rather confining.

Why Not Rent First?

In most popular cruising areas, it is possible to charter a sailboat of almost any type, either with or without a "captain." The novice might well consider trying out the boat he thinks he wants before putting down his cash; or, better still, it's possible to try out several types on charter before making a "buying" decision.

Portability?

Many of the one-design classes have frequent regattas and meets during the sailing months, the smaller boats traveling on car trailers to the various locations. If you plan such activities, make certain that the boat and its trailer can travel the highways of the states you plan to visit. Check the regulations on boat trailers in a later section of this book.

BASICS OF SAILING

When you step aboard your new sailboat for the first time you should find everything you need to sail her, as most boats are delivered fully equipped and ready to go. The majority of small pleasure sailing boats today are sloop-rigged, meaning that they have a single mast and a boom with a *mainsail* and a *jib*, similar to the "Explorer" shown in the drawing.

The mainsail is the larger of the two sails, and is attached to the mast by its forward edge or *luff*. The *foot* of the mainsail is attached to the boom. The *jib* is the smaller sail set ahead of the

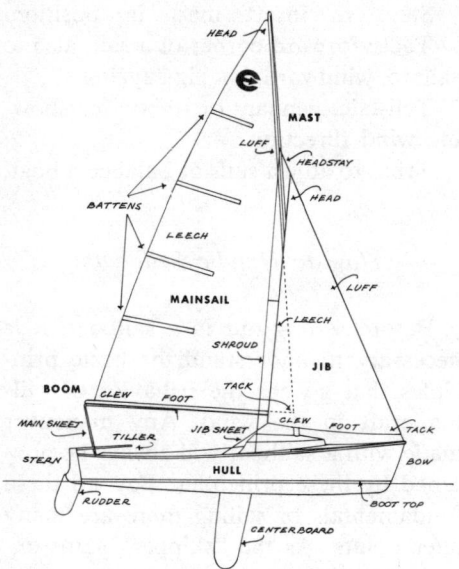

when hiking, or leaning to one side to counterbalance the tilt of the boat in stiff winds.

The *centerboard,* which is enclosed in the *centerboard trunk,* projects below the boat to keep it from sliding sideways in the wind. Other types of sailboats may have a fixed, heavy *keel* of lead which serves the same purpose as the centerboard and also counterbalances the weight of the masts and rigging.

The centerboard is dropped down when sailing at an angle against the wind and is lifted to reduce water drag when sailing in a downwind direction.

The Start

The first step in most small sailboats is to install the rudder by inserting the two pins (called "pintles") into the brackets attached to the transom. Then lower the centerboard (it should always be kept in a raised position when the boat is at a mooring or out of water).

Before hoisting the sails, make sure the bow is pointing into the wind — and check to see if the battens have been put into the mainsail. Hoist the mainsail first, after checking to be sure the main sheet is coiled neatly so it can run free. Coil the halyard, too, after the sail is up. Then raise the jib, and coil the jib halyard. Make sure both jib sheets can run free.

Now the boat can set off. The boat is still pointing directly into the wind and both sails are luffing. You have no forward motion yet and you cannot steer the boat until she has some headway.

If you are at a dock, held by stern and bow lines, cast off the stern line first to prevent the bow from swinging out and away from the wind before you are ready. At a mooring, secured by a bow line, simply cast off the line.

Now, swing the rudder to let the bow drift away from the wind. When it drifts off about 45 degrees, the wind will be-

mast. Its forward edge or luff is clipped to the *headstay.*

To raise or lower the sails, you take in or let out the *halyards* (also spelled "halliards"). Remember that in nautical language, the word "rope" is never used for the working rigging. These "ropes" are always called *lines.* The main halyard is used to raise or lower the mainsail; the jib halyards, the jib.

Sheets are the lines that control the position of the sails — set them at the correct angle in relation to the direction of the wind. The *main* sheet is used to trim, or adjust, the mainsail; the *jib sheet,* the jib. You will find two jib sheets, however, as one is needed on each side, according to which way the wind is filling the jib.

In brief, you raise the sail with halyards and control them with their sheets.

The *rudder,* which is pivoted on the stern of the boat, provides the primary means of steering. Some sloops have kick-up rudders, which simply means that the blade lifts up when it strikes an obstruction.

The rudder is controlled by means of the *tiller.* Sometimes it is necessary to use a *hiking stick,* which is a removable extension of the tiller to permit steering gin to fill the sails and the boat will start moving forward. At the same time, you will feel the rudder come to life so you can now steer the boat.

As you pick up speed, trim both sails so they are taut, without rippling or luffing. They are now properly trimmed ... and you are sailing!

Some "Sail" Language

You should know that *starboard* refers to anything and everything on the right-hand side as you face forward in a boat and *port* (old-timers called it "larboard") everything on the left hand side. Starboard and port never change sides, but directions equally important to the sailing boatman are *windward* and *leeward* (and get accustomed to calling it "loow'd") change sides with the wind. The windward side of anything is always the side *from which* the wind is blowing; leeward always the side *away* from the wind.

Here are some more nautical terms that are helpful to the sailboater (others are listed in the glossary at the back of this book):

Batten: thin strip of wood to keep sail in correct shape.
Block: a pulley.
Boom Crotch (or crutch): device for holding boom when boat is not sailing.
Cleat: device for securing lines.
Head: top corner of a sail.
Headstay: wire supporting mast from the bow, on which jib is snapped.
Helm: steering arm or tiller.
Leech: after edge of a sail.
Point: to sail as close as possible to the wind.
Reef: to lower sail part way to reduce its area when sailing.
Run: to sail with the wind nearly astern.
Shroud: wire supporting mast from the sides.
Spar: mast or boom.

Step: to insert mast in position.
Tack: forward corner of a sail; also to sail to windward by zig-zagging.
Tell-tale: pennant or ribbon for showing wind direction.
Trim: to adjust sails or balance a boat.

How to Handle Sailboats

Before setting out in a sailboat, it is necessary to understand the basic principles that govern the behavior of sailing craft in the wind. Any maneuver made with a sailboat will always be governed by these principles. Beyond these fundamentals of sailing there are many finer points. As the "skipper" gains experience and becomes more venturesome there are many excellent books on sailing and racing sailboats to help him, but again, experience is probably the best teacher.

Know Your Wind Direction

Since sailboats depend on the wind for their motion, you have to be aware of wind direction. It determines both the course you can sail and the way you must set or "trim" your sails.

There are any number of ways to tell which way the wind is blowing. Look for smoke drifting from a chimney, a flag snapping from its mast, the direction ripples travel over the water. Or just feel the wind on your face. Many sailors attach a "telltale" piece of cloth or string to the rigging, or fix a wind-direction-indicator atop the mast.

It's handy to think of wind direction as an imaginary line passing through the mast of your boat. This line shows the direction from which the wind is blowing.

If your boat is held by the bow and allowed to swing with the wind, she will line up with the wind and her sails will flap, or "luff." The boat cannot possibly move forward, at least not under sail.

It isn't until you point the bow about 45° off the wind direction that the wind can exert its force on one side of the sails and cause forward motion. When sails are no longer luffing, they are said to be filled.

As your boat heads away from the wind at an angle, the wind forces the sails to the "leeward" side of the boat. Thus, even though you trim the boom in towards the center, the wind will force it to the lee side. Therefore you must know the direction from which the wind is blowing so you can point the boat away from that direction and set sail so the wind can fill it.

Points of Sailing

If you were to sail your boat around in a complete circle, you would go through each of the "points of sailing" illustrated in the diagram.

Starting with your bow heading about 45 degrees off the wind, which is about as close as you can get to sailing directly into the wind, and with your jib and mainsail trimmed in, you are sailing "close hauled."

As soon as you point farther off the wind, you are "reaching." And the farther off the wind you point, the farther out you carry your sails. Letting out sails is called "easing your sheets."

When you are heading with the wind coming in at right angles to your course, or with the wind on the "beam," you are on a "beam reach." Any course between being close-hauled and beam reaching is known as "close reaching."

If this seems confusing, stop reading here and look at the "points of sailing" diagram. As you can see, it is really a lot simpler than it sounds.

A course off the wind from a beam reach is a "broad reach." As you continue heading off the wind, you are on a broad reach until you have the wind coming in over the stern. Now you are "running free" or sailing before the wind.

You have now covered all the points of sailing and yet have only gone around a half circle. This is because the points of sailing are divided into two "tacks," each having identical points.

The side over which the wind is coming determines which tack you are on. With the wind coming over the starboard side, the boat is on the starboard tack. She is on the port tack when the wind comes over the port or left hand side.

How to Change Tacks

Changing from the starboard tack to the port tack, or vice versa is known as "tacking." Tacking can be done by "coming about" if you are sailing into the wind, or "jibing" if you are running free.

The beginner should tack by "coming about" into the wind and never by jibing. Jibing can be a dangerous maneuver. It requires a sense of timing and close control of sails and rudder that can only be gained by experience.

In coming about, sail close-hauled and alert your crew by telling them, "Ready about," so they will be prepared

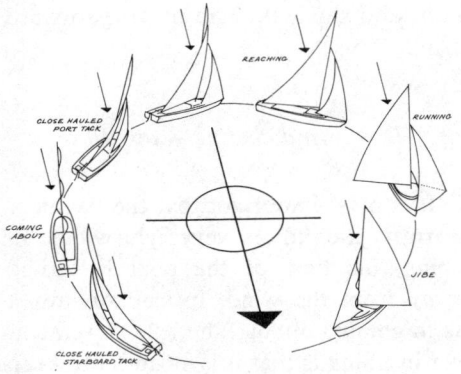

Points of sailing *(arrows show wind direction)*.

to tend the jib and main sheets and to change positions to correct "trim" as the wind side changes.

At the moment you decide to make your turn, call out "Hard-a-lee!" and pull your tiller towards the leeward of the boat. This turns the bow of the boat into the wind.

As the jib begins to luff, ease the leeward jib sheet. The main sheet takes care of itself because as the boat changes sides it forces the main boom across the boat. (And make sure there are no heads in the way!)

As the boat crosses the wind and the sails fill on the opposite side, the windward jib sheet of the previous tack now becomes the leeward jib sheet. So you trim the leeward jib sheet as the jib fills on the new tack.

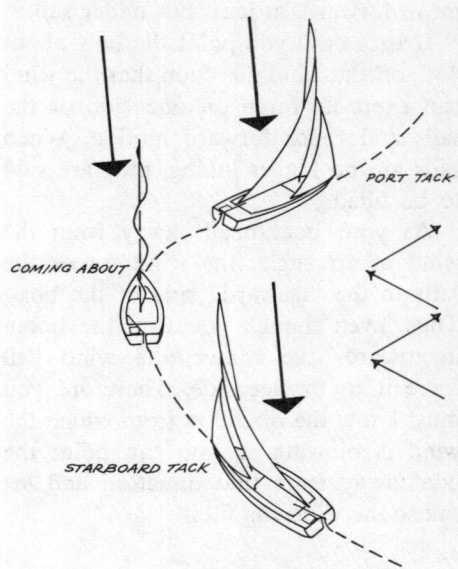

Tacking... coming about from starboard to port tack.

Beating to Windward

Since you cannot point your sailboat any closer to the wind direction than 45 degrees, how can you possibly sail against the wind and reach a place directly up-wind of you? Or in other words, how can you go against the wind-direction?

This can be accomplished by sailing close-hauled on one tack and coming about to the other tack, and repeating. This is called "beating to windward." You have a choice in the number of tacks you need. You can stay close-hauled on one tack and sail until you have the windward point abeam. Then, when you come about you can reach the point by sailing close-hauled on the other tack. Or you can also reach the same point by making a series of shorter tacks or legs. The diagram shows you how this is done.

Sometimes when you are sailing along close hauled and feeling pleased with yourself, you may decide to see how close you can point your boat into the wind. And perhaps you will point it so close that the wind spills out of your sails and leaves them luffing while the boat drifts to a stop. When this happens, you are "in irons," and you may find the situation a bit embarrassing if there are witnesses around.

The only consolation is that this has happened to many, many other skippers. To get out of it, just swing the tiller over to one side or the other — at this point it doesn't matter much which side. Doing this will encourage the boat to fall away from the wind enough to fill her sails, and she will begin moving forward again.

Downwind Sailing — the Jibe

It is most important that the beginner learn to jibe only in very light winds. In jibing, the bow of the boat is turned *away* from the wind, instead of into it as in coming about. The rule to remember in jibing is that it is essential to keep control of sails and tiller.

Just as in coming about, you must alert your crew. While keeping your same downwind course, you call out, "Ready for jibe!"

Next you must trim your mainsheet in until the boom lies "amidships." The leeward jib sheet should be held ready to release.

When you are ready to jibe, call out "Jibe ho!" and slowly turn the boat so that the bow crosses the wind direction heading downwind. As soon as the wind catches the other side of the mainsail, stop your turn and let your main sheet out rapidly until the boom is all the way out on the other side.

Now you can release the jib sheet and trim the sheet on the other side.

The "Flying" Jibe

When jibing, the mainsail does not luff as it does in coming about. Instead, the wind forces it across the boat and fills it immediately. While an intentional jibe is safe enough if properly executed, an accidental jibe can be dangerous.

If the wind is at all strong it can catch the mainsail from all the way out on one side and force it violently to the other side. The result can be a torn sail or broken rigging or worse. Such a jibe is called a "flying jibe" because the main boom is out of control. You can see the importance of trimming the main sheet before attempting a jibe.

Because of the danger of a flying jibe, it is best not to sail "dead before the wind" — that is, with the wind directly astern. A shift in the wind direction could easily cause you to sail "by the lee," or with the mainsail out on what is actually the windward side of the boat. In so doing, the boat's heading has crossed the direction of the wind. Such a heading is very likely to result in a flying jibe.

Sailing "Wing and Wing"

While the mainsail is the controlling factor in running free, you can also use

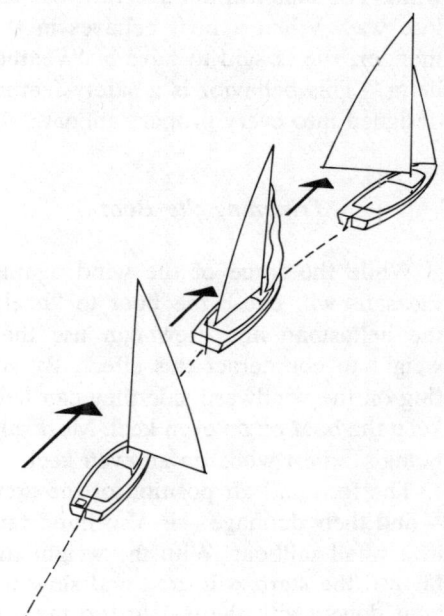

Jibing. Practice this only in light winds!

the jib for more pulling power. Because the mainsail is to the windward of the jib, it blankets the jib, which then lies idle in the lee of the main. By holding the clew of the jib to the windward side, you can cause the jib to fill. You can use a boathook or oar to hold the clew of the jib out.

With the mainsail to leeward and the jib filled, to windward, you are sailing "wing to wing" — that is, with the two sails on opposite sides of the boat.

Steering a Sailboat

The helmsman usually sits on the windward side of a small sailboat. He can watch the sails and wind direction best from this position and can balance the boat better. It is also advisable for the helmsman to sit far enough forward so that he is beyond the end of the tiller. He can thus turn the boat in either direction without getting in the way of the tiller.

When the tiller is left free, the boat will have a tendency to head up into the wind. The sails will luff and the boat will lose way. When a boat behaves in this manner, she is said to have a "Weather helm." This behavior is a safety feature designed into every proper sailboat.

Trimming the Boat

While the force of the wind against the sails will cause the boat to "heel," the helmsman and crew can use their weight to counteract this effect. By sitting on the windward side they can help keep the boat on an even keel. Most sailboats sail best when on an even keel.

The fore and aft position of the crew — and their dunnage — is also important in a small sailboat. With the weight too far aft, the stern will drag and slow the boat down; with the weight too far forward, the bow will be pushing too much water. Try to keep most of the "cargo" weight as near the middle of the boat as possible to get the best performance from the craft.

Anchoring and Mooring

Approaching an anchorage or mooring is a matter of stopping all forward motion on reaching the anchoring or mooring point. It is here that you make use of heading in the eye of the wind and letting the sails luff.

If, in coming about, you allow the boat to continue to head into the eye of the wind instead of swinging across the wind, the sails will luff and the boat comes to a standstill. The difference between doing this at your mooring and being "in irons" is that when mooring, you do it on purpose. Then just drop your anchor or reach out for the mooring buoy.

In maneuvering towards a mooring, head the boat into the wind from a point where the mooring lies directly ahead and within reach when the boat slows to

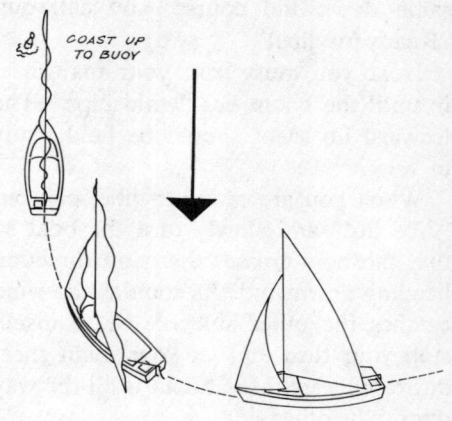

Approaching a mooring.

a stop. If you head into the wind from too great a distance, you will not reach the mooring before losing headway and starting to drift back. If you head up too close to the mooring, you will be going too fast when you reach it. This is called "overshooting" or "overrunning" the mooring. A little practice will develop the sense of timing to know just when and where to head into the wind.

Coming into a Dock

You can bring your boat alongisde a dock pretty much the same way you brought it up to a mooring. It is mainly a matter of controlling the vessel's headway. Whenever possible, it is advisable to approach a dock from its leeward, or downwind side. When the wind direction lies parallel to the side of the dock, try to make your landing parallel to the side. Head into the wind as you would in approaching a mooring and lose headway on reaching the landing point.

Where there is no leeward side to a dock — that is, when the wind is blowing directly against the only side available to you — there are two different ways of making your landing.

First you can head into the wind directly in front of the dock. On losing headway you lower your sails and let the wind drift you back to the dock. Or, you can make a landing on a reach. As you approach the dock let both sheets all the way out to spill the wind from the sails. With the sails luffing, the boat will lose most of her headway. Again, you must time your approach so as to lose your headway at the landing point.

Some Precautions

1. Learn to sail in light winds; if there's someone with good sailing experience available, invite him along to give you some pointers.

2. When the wind causes the boat to "heel" too far, ease or let out the main and jib sheets. This allows the sails to luff and reduces the force of the wind on the sails. You can also luff your sails by heading more nearly into the wind.

3. Never make fast or cleat the main sheet, unless or until you are an experienced sailor. Always have it coiled neatly so it can run freely.

4. Always keep your boat bailed and free of water. Too much water in the bilges will make your boat sluggish and hard to control.

5. A properly handled sailboat should not tip over or capsize. If it does, stay calm and *remain with the boat*. The boat will not sink and forms a support while you are waiting for help. Do not attempt to swim to shore.

6. Be sure to have at least one life preserver for each person aboard. Preservers should be kept clean, dry and always within easy reach.

7. Learn the rules of the road and respect the rights of others. Although power boats must always keep clear of sailboats, never force the issue. This is particularly true on meeting large vessels which cannot be quickly maneuvered or are operating in a restricted channel.

8. Wear soft, non-skid shoes, for safety as well as to protect the finish of your boat.

9. When making fast to a cleat, always take one full round turn before starting criss-cross turns.

10. Learn the basic knots and where to use them. (See Chapter on "Marlinspike Seamanship.")

CHAPTER XXV

The One-Design Sailboats

The one-design types of small sailboats described on the following pages include those which have found the most popularity with pleasure boatmen for racing or for club and family use. A study of the different types and their specifications may help the reader select a boat suitable to his needs. Price information has not been included as prices vary not only from year to year but also, in some cases, among the different boatyards which make the more popular types. Generally, writing to the source listed for information on the class will bring complete specification of the boat, prices, sources, and the addresses of local fleets and yacht clubs where the particular type boat is raced or widely used.

A number of the clubs have informative handbooks or yearbooks which are free or sent for a small charge, and it is suggested that it is always best to join a class through a local fleet when possible, as many fleets in addition to a program of races, have instruction classes and social activities geared to their common interest in sailing and in the particular type of boat.

EL TORO
Type and Dimensions: Centerboard catboard; plywood hull, may be finished with fiber-glass. Length overall 7′11″ to 8′.
Beam 46″
Over 2,200 boats active, mainly in California.
Association information: El Toro International Yacht Racing Ass'n., 43 Park Way, Piedmont, California.

SPRITE

Type and Dimensions: Training sloop; can be used as catboat; fiberglass hull; built-in buoyancy tanks; centerboard.
Length overall 10′
Waterline length 9′6″
Beam 4′7″
Weight 150 lbs. (approx.)
Sail area 53.2 sq. ft. main.
16.2 sq. ft. jib.

The Sprite was designed especially for training youngsters to sail. It has a convertible rig enabling the beginner to learn to handle the main sail first, then gain experience with jib and spinnaker.
Class information: The O'Day Corporation, 9 Newbury St., Boston 16, Massachusetts.

PENGUIN

Type and Dimensions: Centerboard catboat; plywood hull; fiberglass may be adopted.
Length overall 11′2″
Waterline length 11′5″

Over 5,500 boats throughout the world; national championship races held each year in the United States.
Association information: International Penguin Class Dinghy Association 1217 Fourth Road, Baltimore 20, Maryland.

DYER DHOW
Type and Dimensions: Centerboard catboat; fiberglass hulls since 1949; older models wooden hull.
Length overall 9'0"
Beam 4'5"
Sail area 45 sq. ft

Over 1,000 active, popular for frostbite dinghy racing on Long Island Sound, N.Y.; also used by Mystic Marine Museum, Mystic, Connecticut, for training and by Boy Scouts and military schools.
Association information: The Anchorage, Inc., Warren, Rhode Island.

PELICAN
Type and Dimensions: Sailing dinghy, crew of two; day sailer for six children or four adults; transom bow.
Length overall 11'2"
Beam 4'7"
Weight 140 lbs.
Draft 6"; 2'6" board down.
Sail area 62 sq. ft.

Suggested as a boat for beginners and women; 200 sailing in U.S.; Nassau; Venezuela and Colombia.
Association information; Pelican Sailing Dinghy Association; 5960 Southwest 78th St., South Miami, Florida.

INTER-CLUB
Type and Dimensions: Dinghy; old models woods, now fiberglass; built-in air tanks at bow and stern.
  Length overall 11'6"
  Beam 4'7"
  Weight 195 pounds
  Draft 3' (board down)
  Sailing area 72 sq. ft.
Used for training; also popular among "frost bite" dinghy racers.
Association Information: Robert R. Larsen, 1375 Post Road, Westport, Conn.

SAILFISH — SUNFISH
Type and Dimensions: Sport sailboats; Carry one or two persons.
  Plastic-surfaced plywood or fiberglass full. Daggerboard for stability.
  Length overall 11'7 1/2" to 13'10"
  Beam 31 1/2" to 48 1/2"
  Sail area 65-75 sq. ft.
  Weight 300-500 lbs.
Builders report more than 20,000 in active service, with regattas from Cape Cod to Bahamas and in many lake and shore areas.
Association information: Alcort, Inc., P.O. Box 1345, Waterbury Connecticut; in Canada, Sailfish Sportscraft Ltd., 59 Industrial Road, Richmond Hill, Ontario.

BLUE JAY
Type and Dimensions: V-bottom knockabout sloop; marine plywood hull; centerboard.
> Length overall 13'6"
> Waterline 11'5"
> Beam 5'2"
> Sail area 90 sq. ft.

Originally designed for junior sailing, this sloop has been adopted and raced by adults in many areas; 87 active fleets from Maine to Florida, Gulf Coast, California and Canada, include over 2,400 boats. Association information from International Blue Jay Class Ass'n., 11 East 44th St., New York 17, N.Y.

JET 14
Type and Dimensions: Centerboard Sloop, molded plywood or fiberglass hull
> Length Overall 14'
> Beam 4'8"
> Draft 6" and 4'6"
> Sail area 113 sq. ft.

Racing activity: Class numbers about 500 boats, mainly on East Coast. Fleets in Conn., Mass.; New York; N.J.; Ohio; Maryland; Wash. D.C.; North Carolina; Virginia; Florida Lousiana; Texas; Colorado, and Michigan.
Association information: Gwen Olsen, 66 Alexander Drive, Red Bank, N.J.

MERCURY
Type and Dimensions: Training Sloop, older models wood; newer fiberglass; keel and centerboard types; large flotation tanks.
Length Overall 15'
Waterline length 13'10"
Beam 5'5"

About 400 in service; popular eastern end of Long Island, N.Y., Fleets at North East Harbor, Maine; Bar Harbor, Maine; Sorrento, Maine; Cohasset, Gloucester and other Massachusetts ports.
Association information: Mr. Frederick M. Gilbreth, 590 Madison Ave., New York 22, N.Y.

WINDMILL
Type and Dimensions: Centerboard sloop; marine plywood hull; many made from plans.
Length overall 15'6"
Beam 58"
Sail area 119 sq. ft.
Weight 160 lbs.

Association reports that boat can be built for about $400 from plans; some 90 active fleets; hold several annual regattas. Suggested for 15-year olds and up.
Association Information: Windmill Class Association, 784 53rd Ave., So., Petersburg 5, Florida.

SNIPE
Type and Dimensions: Centerboard sloop; conventional wood; plywood or fiberglass hull.
- Length overall 13'
- Waterline 13'
- Beam 5'
- Sail area 103 sq. ft.
- Draft 6" hull; 33 1/2" board down.

About 13,000 numbers have been issued by this 30-year old class. About 4,000 boats in active racing in U.S.; fleets in 27 other countries.

Association information: Snipe Class International Racing Association 655 Weber Ave., Akron 3, Ohio.

OSPRAY
Type and Dimensions: Day sailer; fiberglass sloop; centerboat; fiberglass hull; small cabin.
- Length overall 15'6"
- Waterline length 14'
- Beam 6'
- Draft 9" centerboard up; 4' board down.
- Weight 450 lbs. (approx.)
- Sail area 125.7 sq. ft.

Association information: The O'Day Corporation. 9 Newbury St., Boston 16, Mass.

COMET
Type and Dimensions: Centerboard Sloop, wood or fiberglass
- Length Overall 16'
- Waterline 14'3" (approx.)
- Beam 5'
- Draft 6" (board up)
- Sail area 136 sq. ft.

One of the more popular classes. About 4,000 boats organized into 150 active fleets, throughout the U.S.

Association Information: Comet Class Yacht Racing Association, ℅ David H. Kingston, Gooseneck Point, Oceanport, N.J.

DAY SAILER
Type and Dimensions: Centerboard sloop; day sailer; fiberglass hull.
Length Overall 16'6"
Waterline length 16'
Beam 6'
Draft 6" centerboard up; 4' board down.
Sail area 145 sq. ft.

Designed in England for fishing, outboarding, camping and trailing, features roomy cockpit.

Association information: The O'Day Corporation, 9 Newbury St., Boston 6, Massachusetts.

EXPLORER
Type and Dimensions: Centerboard sloop; day cruiser; flotation tanks; fiberglass hull.
Length overall 17'
Beam 6'4"
Draft 9" centerboard up; 4'6" board down.
Weight 520 lbs. (approx.)

Association information: Sailstar Boats, 770 Main Street, West Warwick, Rhode Island.

THISTLE
Type and Dimensions: Centerboard sloop; wood or fiberglass hull.
    Length overall 17′
    Waterline length 17′ (approx.)
    Beam 6′
    Sail area 175 sq. ft.
About 1,400 boats organized into some 85 fleets; about 50 in foreign countries.
Association information: Douglass & McLeod, Inc., Box 311, Painesville, Ohio.

RHODES 18
Type and Dimensions: Sloop, cast iron keel or steel centerboard; fiberglass or wooden hull.
    Length overall 18′
    Waterline 16′
    Beam 6′3″
    Draft 32″ with keel; 4′ board down,
    Sail area 165 sq. ft.
A fleet of over 300 boats is active on Long Island Sound, N.Y.; about 500 others in service.
Association information: International Rhodes 18 Racing Association P.O. Box 1908, New Haven, Connecticut.

FLYING SCOT
Type and Dimensions: Centerboard sloop; fiberglass hull.
    Length overall 19′0″
    Waterline 18′4″
    Beam 6′9″
    Sail area 190 sq. ft.
This boat was designed for family and club use rather than emphasis on speed; considered a family day sailer; 15 fleets from Rockport, Mass. to San Francisco; about 220 boats since boat appeared in 1957.
Association information: Gordon K. Douglass, 3rd and Omar Streets Oakland, Maryland.

RHODES 19
Type and Dimensions: Keel or centerboard sloop; fiberglass hull.
Length overall 19′
Beam 6′8″
Draft 3′9″
Keel weight 450 lbs.
Sail area 176 sq. ft.

This is a keel version of the famous Hurricane Class designed by Philip Rhodes. Features cited by maker are stability and large, unobstructed cockpit.
Association information: The O'Day Corporation, 9 Newbury St., Boston 6, Massachusetts.

LIGHTNING
Type and Dimensions: Centerboard sloop; racer; wood, wood covered with resin and synthetic cloth, fiberglass hull; three-man crew.
Length Overall 19'0"
Waterline 15'3" (approx.)
Beam 6'6 1/4"
Sail area 177 sq. ft.

One of the largest classes with some 6,000 active boats in 313 fleets throughout the world. International regatta held yearly.

Class information: Lightning Class Association, 308 Center St., South Haven, Michigan.

CELEBRITY
Type and Dimensions: Centerboard or Keel Sloop
Length overall 19'9"
Beam 6'4"
Draft 8" centerboard up; 39" down; 29" keel model
Sail area: main & jib 172 sq. ft. Genoa 76 sq. ft.

Day sailer and racer.

Association information: Secretary, Thor Christensen, 600 S. 21st Ave., Maywood, Illinois.

THE ONE-DESIGN SAILBOATS

CUTLASS
Type and Dimensions: Racing cruiser; sloop; midget ocean racer; wood hull, glued strip construction; being built in Norway, Canada and California; centerboard and Keel types.
   Length overall 23'7"
   Waterline length 19'2"
   Beam 7'1"
   Draft 4'0"
   Sail area 242 sq. ft.
In the past six years, Cutlass has proved an excellent racer in ocean and overnight races.
Association information: Richard D. Carlson, N.A., Shelter Island, N.Y.

HIGHLANDER
Type and Dimensions: Centerboard sloop, planing hull, fiberglass or molded plywood.
   Length overall 20'
   Waterline length 19'3"
   Beam 6'8"
   Sail area 225 sq. ft.
Over 300 boats active in 15 fleets; largest groups in Ohio.
Association information: Douglass & McLeod, Inc., Box 311, Painesville, Ohio.

STAR
Type and Dimensions: Keel sloop; racer, planked wood hull only.
   Length overall 22'8-1/2"
   Waterline length 15'6" (approx.)
   Beam 5'8-1/4"
   Draft 3'4" (approx.)
   Sail area 281 sq. ft.
Star is the first of the one-design classes, designed in 1911 by Francis Sweisguth of New Rochelle, N.Y. Now being sailed in about 30 countries and more than 200 fleets. About 4,000 numbered boats.
Association information: International Star Class Yacht Racing Association, 51 East 42nd St., New York 17, N.Y.

INTERNATIONAL 110
Type and Dimensions: Keel sloop; racing boat; plywood hull; some covered with fiberglass
Length overall 24′
Beam 4′2″
Sail area 155 sq. ft (with large genoa)
Draft 2′10″
Keel weight 300 lbs.

Boat has limited sail area vs. weight of keel and should do well in heavy wind. Over 30 fleets in U.S., one in Philippines, about 650 boats. Association information from International 110 Yacht Racing Association 505 So. Birney St., Bay City, Michigan.

DOLPHIN
Type and Dimensions: Midget Ocean Racer, Centerboard-Keel; fiberglass.
Length overall 24′2″
Length at waterline 19′0″
Beam 7′8″
Draft, board up 2′10″
Sail area: main 158 sq. ft.; Fore triangle 138.5 sq. ft.; working jib 76 sq. ft.; small genoa 160 sq. ft; large genoa 215 sq. ft.

Five models: Day sailer; day sailer with engine; day sailer with head; cruising model; ocean racing model. Boats on Eastern Coast, Great Lakes and Florida.
Information: The O'Day Corporation, 9 Newbury St., Boston 6, Mass.

RAVEN
Type and Dimensions: Centerboard sloop
　　　　　　　　　　Length overall 24'3"
　　　　　　　　　　Waterline 21'7"
　　　　　　　　　　Beam 7'0"
　　　　　　　　　　Draft 5'4" (board down)
　　　　　　　　　　Sail area 300 sq. ft.

Raven can carry 8 to 10 people for day sailing; normal racing crew is four. About 300 boats range from Detroit, Cleveland, Long Island Sound and Marblehead to Canada, South America and Switzerland.
Association information: Raven Class Corporation, 6081 12th St., Detroit 8, Michigan. *(Photo: DeWitt Busch, Photo Illustrators, Inc.)*

PILOT
Type and Dimensions: Powered cruising sloop; sleeps four; wide beam.
    Length overall 32'11"
    Waterline length 24'
    Beam 9'6"
    Draft 4'9"
    Sail area 495 sq. ft.
    Power, Gray 422 engine
About 20 boats on the Great Lakes and East Coast; cruising races on the Great Lakes.
Association information; Sparkman and Stephens, Inc., 11 East 44th St., New York, N.Y.

OHLSON 35
Type and Dimensions: Yawl, planked hull, Swedish-built, racing-cruiser
    Length overall 35'6"
    Length at waterline 25'
    Beam 9'4"
    Draft 4'11"
    Sail area 545 sq. ft.
Boats racing on both coasts.
Information from The O'Day Corporation, 9 Newbury St., Boston, Mass., or 195 Hickory Grove, Larchmont, N.Y.

CHAPTER XXVI

Do It Yourself—Building from Kits or Plans

The do-it-yourselfer in the boating field has a wide choice of outlets for his creative skill. Almost any type of boat from a pram or dinghy to a 40-foot cruiser is available for the build-it-yourself addict, and this entree to boat ownership can be achieved at savings of up to 70 percent from the advertised price of the boat. Basically, the term "kit" as used in the boating field refers to sets of plans and instructions, plus a quantity of prepared building materials. The cost of the kit depends to a considerable extent on the amount of "prefabrication" which the manufacturer has done and the kind of work the buyer must complete to get his boat into the water. The man with proper power tools may work from a set of plans and instructions, buying his materials from a local shipyard or lumberyard. On the other hand, it is possible to buy a steel or aluminum hulled boat which requires merely finishing operations which can usually be done with a few simple hand tools.

Start Small

Frequent advertisements in the boating pages of newspapers offering for sale "partly constructed" kit boats highlight the wisdom of starting any kit building venture on a small scale. Even some of the manufacturers suggest that the novice try his hand at building one of the smallest boats before starting off on a larger craft. Generally, to complete a kit boat you need time and the proper tool equipment. Another factor is that many of the operations in boat-building require several pairs of strong and skillful hands and the "loner" who sets out on such a project may encounter insurmountable obstacles.

Almost any type of pleasure boat that is available on the market — inboard or outboard, sailboat, catamaran, etc. — is available in some form of kit.

Many of the dealers or manufacturers offer fairly long term financing (up to two years is offered by some of the larger mail-order houses) and some kits may be purchased on a "pay-as-you-build" basis. The usual arrangement is that payment is made first for the frame, then for the planking, finally for the cabin and/or the accessories as needed by the builder.

Types of Kits

The advertising of the kit manufacturers should be read carefully before making a final selection as there is a wide variance among the different types of kits.

The two basic materials used in most of the kits are wood and fiberglass. Simplest, and least expensive (although the finishing costs do mount up) is the frame kit, in which only the skeleton of the boat is provided in knock-down form. The builder must purchase the planking and other components. Other kits travel right up the range to almost-ready-to-launch boats requiring only finishing.

In some kits, the pieces are supplied rough, while in others the bevels are cut and the parts fitted. Still other kit boats are partially assembled at the factory, then knocked down, packaged and sent off to the purchaser. It is most important that the buyer read the specifications carefully to determine just what the kit offers and what must be done to finish the job.

Wood Kits

1. *Frame Kits:* These kits include the framework parts along with plans and instructions for building the boat. The framework parts usually provided are the stern, transom, frames and such small items as the breasthook and transom knee. These pieces have been cut to size at the factory. Some kits include the longitudinal members such as the keel, chines, and sheer clamps; others do not. Usually, the kit will include full sized patterns for cutting the wood parts the builder needs and specifications to aid him in purchasing the proper kind of wood. Of course, paint and hardware must be purchased separately. Estimates are that savings of 55 to 70 percent of the cost of a comparable factory-finished delivered boat may be achieved in building from a frame kit.

2. *Precut Kits:* These kits usually provide all the wood parts necessary to complete the boat, along with plans and instructions. In building from a precut kit, it is usually necessary for the builder to do the beveling and fairing-in of the framework to assure a good fit against the planking. The cut-to-measure sections are generally shipped slightly oversized to permit snug fitting, and this is usually true of seats, floorboards, cabin parts, etc. As a rule, paint and accessories must be bought separately. With this type of kit, savings generally amount to about 50 percent of the cost of the comparable factory craft.

3. *Preformed Kits:* These kits are in essence "pre-fabricated boats." All wooden parts are included along with instruction charts. The different parts of the kit are preformed or machined to fit the bevels on the framework. The entire boat may have been assembled at the factory, then broken down for shipping. Paint and hardware are not usually provided with the kit. Savings are said by the manufacturers to run about 40 percent of the cost of the boat factory-finished.

4. *Preassembled and Molded Kits:* The kits may run in cost to about 80 percent of the cost of a finished boat. The purchaser has a choice among one piece molded plywood hulls, pre-planked hulls, and some of the larger models, fully assembled hull frames, and fully assembled but unfinished boats, calling for paint and hardware installation.

Fiberglass Kits

Outboards, cruisers and sailing sloops are available in fiberglass boat kits. These kits include the various members, such as bottom, topsides, decks, seats, etc., which the purchaser assembles. These kits require little finishing and are a good choice for the man with limited mechanical skills.

In another form of fiberglass kit the home builder actually builds up the boat by laying the materials into a hollow form or by spreading layers of fiberglass and resin over the outside of a form. It should be noted that persons in the boating industry have expressed some concern about the physical strength of the home-molded-fiberglass boats and the danger of amateurs working with the highly flammable resins.

After the mold is constructed, different types of longitudinal and transverse supports may be placed in the hull, and wooden decks, seats, etc., are added.

Assembling a Frame Kit

The home craftsman with the proper tool equipment can find a wide variety of plans for pleasure boats of all types.

DO IT YOURSELF — BUILDING FROM KITS OR PLANS

Boat-Building Plans

1. The building form for building the "TUFFY" is one of the crates. It is mounted at a convenient level from the floor both lengthwise and athwartships.

2. The framework is aligned to position with a chalk line and plumb bob. The builder is using a plumb bob to accurately align the stem.

3. The longitudinal members are sprung around the framework. Minor beveling of the notches will be required to allow the longitudinal members to mate firmly to the framework.

4. The completed framework with battens, chine and sheer in position ready for fairing.

5. Minor fairing or beveling will be required on all members to enable the planking skin to mate firmly.

6. The short length of plywood is being used here to determine the amount of fairing to be done to assure that the planking will fit to all surfaces properly.

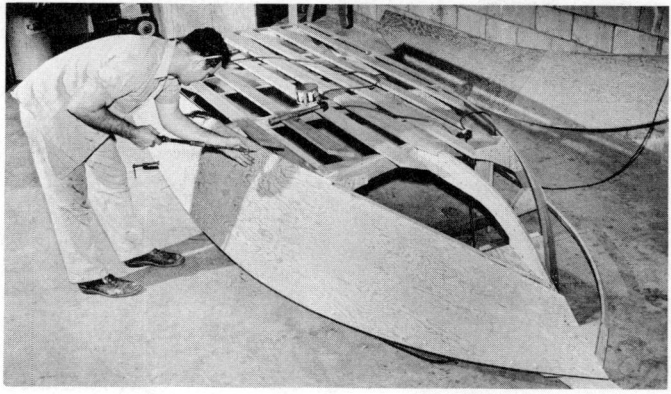

7. The precut planking or the panel cut from the full size template is fastened to the side of the hull. Close fitting of this panel is not necessary except in the forward position that will join with the bottom panel.

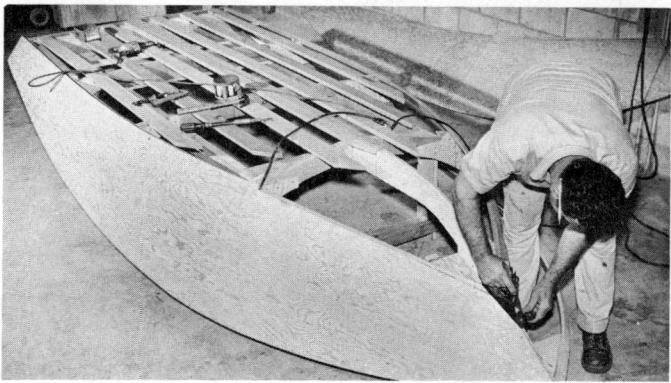

8. The overhang along the bow is planed flush. The second side panel to be applied is shown in the background and will lap the initially applied panel at the stem.

9. The bottom panel will again require fitting only along the portion that will meet with the side planking. The balance of the planking is left overhanging as shown on the left half bottom for subsequent trimming.

10. The carling member is precut to fit with minor trimming required on the end. It is fitted to the interior of the inside of the frame members. The deck is readily and simply applied from the precut members.

11. The completed hull with decking and cowling in position. All panelling for the deck is readily and simply applied from the precut members.

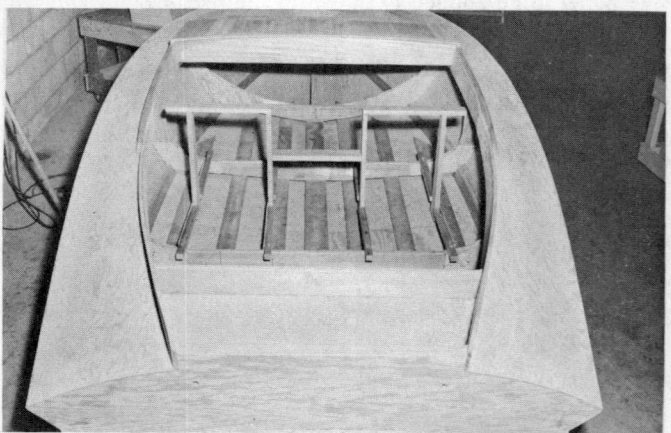

12. The templates provided even furnish such parts as the framework for the seats as shown in this figure. Note the self bailing motor well. This is a safety feature that could well be appreciated in the outboard craft.

13. The finished product. (*Glen Marine Designs*)

The following sets are available from the Douglas Fir Plywood Association, 1119 A Street, Tacoma 2, Washington:

20-Foot Sailboat

A day sailer along classic plywood construction linees. Hull is 3/8 inch DFPA plywood. Frame is oak or ash. Design is by C. P. and E. D. Burgess. Ask for boat plan #21 from Douglas Fir Plywood Association. Include 10 cents.

11-1/2-Foot Skiff

An easy boat for the do-it-yourselfer, this flatbottom boat uses 1/4, 3/8 and 3/4 inch DFPA Exterior-type Plywood. The boat is 14-1/2 inches deep amidships with a 48-inch beam. Ask for boat plan #22; include 10 cents.

9-Foot Skiff

Edwin Monk, naval architect, takes the beginner through the steps in building this simple boat. Only two panels of 4x8 foot DFPA Exterior-type plywood are required. Ask for boat plan #23; include 10 cents.

7-Foot, 9-Inch Pram Dinghy

An all-purpose plywood dinghy for the yachtsman who needs a strong, seaworthy craft or sportsman who needs a lightweight cartop boat. Planking consists of 2 pieces of 1/4 inch EXT-DFPA fir plywood A-A grade 4x8 feet. Plans include a bill of materials, construction procedures, finishing suggestions, information on selection of fir plywood panels. Ask for boat plan #30; include 25 cents.

11-Foot, 3-Inch Outboard

This boat design is simple to build with plywood and made-to-order for the amateur to construct at low cost. The boat, which can be used for fishing, family leisure or sports, is 58 inches in the beam and 24 inches deep. It weighs only 215 pounds. Easy to launch, the boat was designed for a 5 or 10 hp motor. Ask for boat plan #35; include 25 cents.

13-Foot, 4-Inch Outboard

A sportsman's boat that can be built by an amateur working on a modest budget. Can be modified for use as a runabout or as a utility boat. Speeds up to 35 miles an hour. Accepts 5 to 25 hp motors. It is 5 feet, 2 inches in the beam and 27 inches deep. Weight is 312 pounds. Plans include step-by-step instruction, construction photographs and materials list. Include 25 cents and ask for boat plan #40.

15-Foot Outboard

A true open-water boat, the craft takes a 25 hp motor with ease. Built with tough, lightweight plywood, the 15-footer weighs only 400 pounds. It is

5 feet, 3 inches in the beam and 22 inches deep. Designed by Frank E. Strickland, naval architect. Ask for boat plan #50; include 25 cents.

16-Foot Runabout

A trim plywood boat designed by David Beach, naval architect, to deliver speed and power. It will take 50 hp motors for speeds to 30 miles an hour. The craft was designed so that it could be built by the first-time boat builder who has average woodworking ability. Plans are available from Douglas Fir Plywood Association, 1119 "A" Street, Tacoma 2, Washington. Plans include alternate deck arrangements, step-by-step instructions and photographs as well as drawings and materials list. Runabout is 6 feet in the beam, 28 inches deep and weighs about 620 pounds. Ask for plan #55 and include 25 cents.

18-Foot Day Cruiser

This plywood boat can be built by amateurs — but it requires time, skill and patience. The craft has a 7 foot beam and is 36 inches deep. It weighs about 1125 pounds. It was designed as a family boat — it is safe, roomy and offers all-weather protection as well as good cabin visibility. The hull was designed for motors up to 40 hp. Plans are by Edwin Monk, naval architect. Ask for plan #60 and include 25 cents.

20-Foot Cabin Cruiser

A wide-roaming cabin cruiser with big boat comfort and convenience. The generous-sized cabin has full sitting head room with plenty of space for two berths, galley and head. The craft will take two outboards or a single unit up to 50 hp. Or, it will take an inboard up to 70 hp. The beam is 7 feet, 10 inches with a depth of 44 inches. Cabin headroom is 4 feet 8 inches. The boat weighs about 1475 pounds. Design is by David Beach, naval architect. Ask for plan #65 and enclose 25 cents.

5-Foot Sailer

This little boat can be built in a weekend with two panels of DFPA Exterior type plywood. The pudgy 5-footer is ideal for teaching children how to sail in swimming pool or lake. The craft was designed by John Burroughs. Ask for boat plan #70 and include 25 cents to cover handling costs.

7-Foot, 9-Inch Pram Dinghy and Sailboat Conversion

An amateur who has never before tackled a boat will find this small plywood craft easy to put together. It can be a rowboat, sailboat or outboard. Ask for plan #70 and include 25 cents.

15-Foot Knockabout

This simple, well-designed plywood knockabout is a safe, stable sailboat for family fun on inland waters — but it also has performance characteristics that make it fun for the expert to sail. Anyone can build it — the carpentry is straightforward. Detailed instructions, drawings and pictures are included with plans. Ask for boat plan #80 and include 25 cents.

26-Foot Racing-Cruising Sloop (Thunderbird)

This boat is designed so that it performs both as a racing boat and as a cruising boat. It has a roomy cabin, can sleep four; it also has a galley and head. Hatch cover raises up and forward to make cabin light and airy. A national class has been formed for the Thunderbird and its popularity is growing rapidly, particularly on the West Coast. The Thunderbird was designed by Ben Seaborn, naval architect. He developed a racing form that takes advantage of the hard chine in plywood craft and designed a hydrofoil fin that gives the Thunderbird extraordinary stability. Plans include four sheets with detailed instructions. The plans are sufficiently detailed that an amateur could follow

This is the 7'9" Pram Dinghy, and Sailboat Conversion. It is plan #75.

This is plan #40, a 13'4" Outboard Utility-Runabout.

This is plan #50, a 15-Foot Outboard Utility.

This is the 16-Foot Outboard Runabout. Plan #55.

This is plan #60, an 18-Foot Day Cruiser.

DO IT YOURSELF — BUILDING FROM KITS OR PLANS

These are the 20-Foot Outboard — Inboard Cruiser and the 16-Foot Outboard Runabout DFPA boat plans #65 and #55.

Here are two youngsters thoroughly enjoying themselves with a good breeze and two five-foot sailers. These photographs were taken on a small lake — ideal for using the "Pipsqueak". This is plan #70.

This is the 15-Foot Knockabout Sailboat. Plan #80.

This is the 26-Foot Thunderbird Racing Sloop. Plan #85

This is plan #35, a 13'3" Outboard Utility.

them. Verbal instructions are detailed; step-by-step photographs of the construction processes are included. Ask for boat plan #85 and include two dollars.

DO IT YOURSELF — IN FIBERGLASS

In the past few years, a number of fiberglass kits have appeared on the market. While these kits do not require the amount of frame-work necessary in assembling a wooden boat kit, they do require the construction of a mold on which to lay the resins. Several of the kit manufacturers provide a factory mold on a loan basis; others provide prefabricated cardboard frames on which waxed composition board may be taped to form a mold.

One unique approach to the "mold" problem has been met by the Sock Boat Corporation which provides a large "sock" of cotton jersey fabric which is stretched over a die-cut corrugated paper framework and the cloth is then used as the base to which the resin is added.

The fiberglass kits are usually available in smaller size boats up to about 15 feet. On some models of the fiberglass kits, wood veneer may be applied to form the deck of the boat; interior fixtures of wood are usually added after the hull has been "cured" and removed from the mold.

While the advertising of the fiberglass kit manufacturers state that the whole job can be finished in 20 hours over a four day period, others in the boating field have expressed some concern over the strength and dependability of the finished product without the rigid temperature and other controls which are used in factory construction of fiberglass boats. Also, there is some fire hazard connected with working with highly flammable resins and a minor problem, removing waste resins that spill during the application to the hull.

Steps in Construction of a Fiberglass Kit

The following illustrations show the various stages of construction of a "sock" fiberglass craft:

1. You make the jig (frame) by assembling die-cut pieces of corrugated board by inserting numbered tabs into slots.

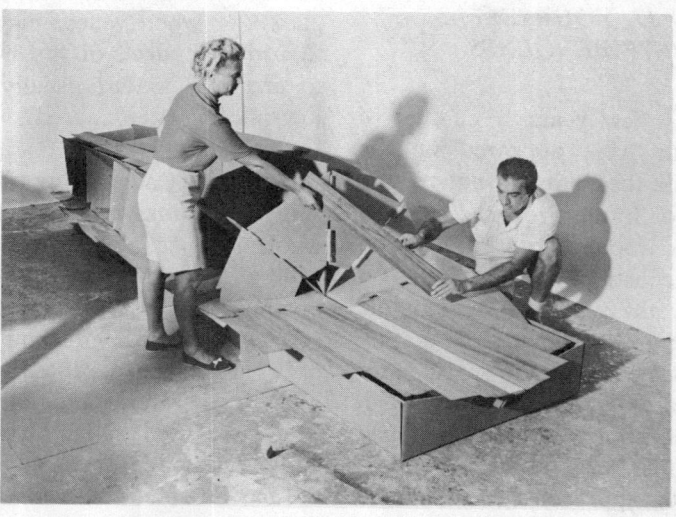

2. You make the mahogany topsides by temporarily gluing mahogany veneer planks onto the corrugated deck and gunwale area.

DO IT YOURSELF — BUILDING FROM KITS OR PLANS

3. You attach precut solid mahogany coamings and dashboard and sheer rail and then cover it with a layer of fiberglass and saturate with resin.

4. You lay on a one-inch-thick honeycomb and cover it with a second layer of heavy woven roving fiberglass and saturate with resin.

5. You install bow section, attach first half of of the double transom, notch in seat rails, slide seats into slots, and attach steering pulleys and guides. You glue a precut stringer to each chine and lay on a tempered masonite floor panel, then resin on a one-inch thick honeycomb.

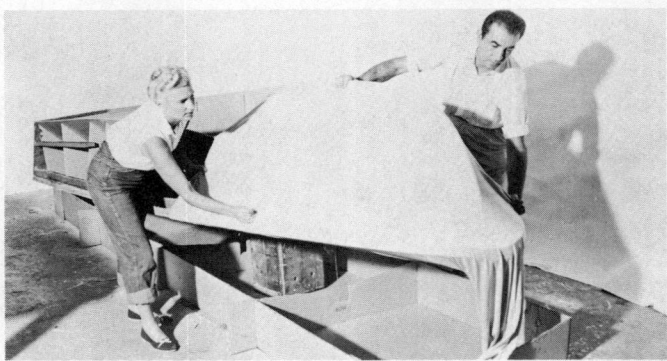

6. The next day you draw a preformed sock over the jig and paint the sock with resin, which hardens it overnight into a firm mold.

7. You cover the mold with two layers of woven roving fiberglass cloth and saturate each with resin spread on with a squeegee.

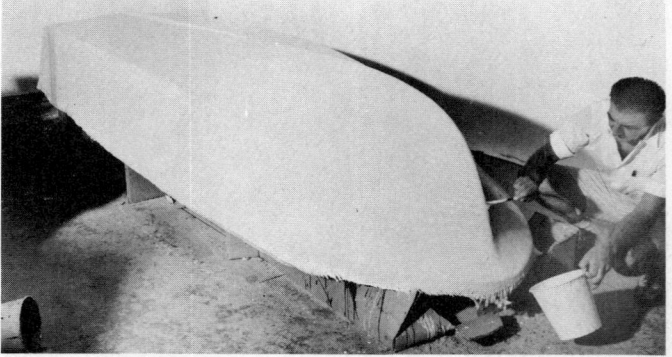

8. You stretch on a third layer of fine fiberglass and this time saturate it with the selected colored resin, which imparts the color to the boat. The next day, turn the boat over, tear out the corrugated frame and she is complete, except for hardware, wheel and splash rails.

9. After a few hours on the "finishing" projects, the fiberglass kit boat is off on the waters of Long Island Sound. *(Photos courtesy Sock Boat Corp.)*

CHAPTER XXVII

Galley Cookery

A Word to the Galley Detail

On board your boat, the food you provide can make or break your cruise. Fine weather afloat can't make up for poor meals, but when the weather closes in to keep you at anchor, tasty food on the cabin table can make you forget a lot of rain on the deck.

It takes a great deal of forethought and no little physical effort to produce tempting fare for four or five on a two-burner stove and with a minimum of of working area. If you don't understand the job, or don't like it, turn it over to someone who does. It can be a lot of fun, and on the water the results of your labors will be fully appreciated by appetites whetted on fresh air.

Planning Supplies

Many factors enter into your initial grocery list: (1) How many persons are to be served how many meals? (2) How long between ports where you can get fresh supplies? (3) What storage areas do you have and how much perishable food can be put in your icebox along with the minimum ice you want to carry — allowing plenty for cold drinks? (4) What size and type of stove do you have, and can you plan on oven-cooking? (5) What utensils do you have — if you plan a mess of crabs or fresh corn do you have the pot to cook them in? (6) Finally, what are the food preferences of your crew?

With these ideas in mind (and after a couple of times around they become second nature), you can devise a series of menus which will include simple, appetizing food, and plenty of it.

As a guide in figuring quantities, a table of the approximate needs per man per day which was used successfully on several long passages is as follows:

	Oz. per man per day
Meats, poultry, fish	14.5
Beverages (not milk)	4.0
Dairy Products (incl. milk)	22.0
Cereals & Bread	13.0
Fruits	8.0
Vegetables	11.0
Sweets (sugar, syrup, chocolate, jam)	12.5
	88.0 oz.

or 5½ pounds per man per day

First, to the Butcher

Meat, of which the foregoing table says you should plan almost a pound per day per man, will be the mainstay of at least one meal and probably more, so order generously. A roast of beef or lamb or veal can be brought aboard cooked and ready to slice for sandwiches, or to have as cold cuts with gravy, or a special sauce poured over. It will keep well while you have a quick-cook meat the next night — chops or fried chicken — and will probably end up as sandwich filling or in stew ladled over stale bread. A baked ham, especially the boned and rolled variety which gives more meat per pound, keeps several days, can be served in numerous ways for lunch and dinner, and is a welcome replacement for bacon for breakfast. Nothing smells quite as delicious as ba-

A typical two-burner Marine stove. *(Photo-Homestrand Co.)*

con in the morning, but its grease is treacherous in the galley. When you do cook it, have a large empty can standing in the sink to receive the grease, which should never go down the drain. If you toss it overboard, see that it won't float along the bottom of your own or a neighboring boat.

Before buying a thick, juicy porterhouse steak with which to dazzle your crew, be sure that your marine stove will do it justice. Many a luscious piece of meat has stewed to tastelessness over a too-faint flame.

For the unexpected — when guests come aboard for a drink and stay for dinner, or when the weather prevents your making the next supply port on schedule — keep the larder stocked with tasty canned meats. Whole chickens, chicken fricassee, canned hamburgers, and your favorite meat-heavy brand of stew or corned beef hash provide hearty, quickly-prepared dishes.

Such popular fare as Swedish meat balls in their own gravy, a meaty spaghetti sauce, and other seasoned dishes whose flavor improves if left standing a day while the seasonings go to work, can be prepared at home and are even better when you get around to serving them on board. Of course, with a pressure cooker you can always do a fresh roast with which to start the hot-cold-sandwiches-hash sequence all over again.

Take along plenty of eggs, whether you're off for a weekend, a week or a month. They keep well in a locker, not necessarily on ice, and will serve in a variety of ways for any meal.

Don't overdo any one meat at a stretch just because you have it aboard. Wrap it in foil after a couple of meals and stow it while you serve alternates. You might even end up taking it home after the weekend, to get your money's worth, but your menus won't have become tiresome.

Add Complementary Vegetables

According to the quantity table, each person requires about 3/4-lb of vegetables a day, and there is such a wide selection available, your chief concern need only be what best complements the meats you plan to serve.

For weekend cruising, you can count on the time-saving frozen variety. But for longer cruises when supply ports are scarce, frozen vegetables take up valuable icebox space and soon thaw so that they must be used anyhow. Fresh vegetables — potatoes, asparagus, beets, spinach, especially the gritty ones— should be washed before being taken aboard, or before stowing, particularly items which will be put on ice. If the lettuce is leafed, carrots are scraped, asparagus cropped, and cauliflower denuded when you go to use them, you miss just that much less fun in the cockpit during the cocktail hour.

Canned vegetables should be stowed in a semblance of order so that you can find what you want when you want it. A list of what and how many cans you bring aboard, checked off as they are used, will help you to know what you have left, without having to take inventory. If there's even a remote chance that labels may come off, mark the contents on the up-end of the can with a grease pencil. Any cans stowed in the bilge should certainly be marked this way.

Whatever your vegetable purchases are, be sure there is enough variety to add color and interest to your meals.

You can use your ingenuity in dovetailing cooking processes in a number of ways. If you must use the pressure cooker for asparagus, save time and use a quick-cooking rice, instead of potatoes for a starch. The rice must then stand for 10 minutes before being served. Incidentally, using consommé as the liquid in cooking rice, instead of water, gives an unusual taste lift.

If you plan to cook two vegetables together in a sectioned pot, use two which won't impart their respective tastes or colors to each other. On the other hand, you can mix some new partners together in the same undivided pot to good effect. Peeled onions and peas or string beans, sliced onions in stewed tomatoes, and peas with mushrooms are all tempting companions.

You can do yourself a service by cooking more than enough at one meal for use the next time the crew sits down. Do extra potatoes to serve hash-browned in the morning. Extra bacon goes on sandwiches, left-over string beans go in salad, or can be creamed, for example.

Salad ingredients don't last too long on board; first because they're eagerly devoured and secondly, because they lose their crispness fast. However, after you've been cruising for a few days and eating out of cans, the sudden appearance of a cool, fresh vegetable salad, born of a recent trip to town, hits the spot with everyone, even the big meat and potato specialists. Incidentally, a tablespoon of sugar added to any tossed salad adds a nice flavor, and be sure to take a good basic dressing which can be doctored with blue cheese, oregano, etc., to individual tastes.

Cater to a Sweet Tooth

Dessert is a problem. It is often passed up after you've gone to work and prepared one, but if you don't provide it, there is sure to be a howl from some quarter. You can usually get away with the usual run of bakery products, but you'll really make a hit if you bake a cake for the occasion. A moist fruit or spice cake won't dry out — if it lasts that long — and can sit securely in its own pan until served. Layer cakes don't stow as happily — in fact, they're adept at upsetting and ending up as pudding. Canned fruit and cookies top off a cruising meal nicely and, of course, if you have an oven and enjoy baking in it, anything you produce will be sensational, especially after the crew has been primed by the homey aroma from the oven.

Whether you have dessert or not,

some allowance for sweets should be made in the form of candy, syrup, jellies, etc. Our quantity chart says a little more than 3/4 lb. per man per day. Other enjoyable nibblers include raisins, dried prunes and apricots, nuts, cracker and cheese or peanut butter, apples and oranges.

Hearty Sandwiches Hit the Spot

For sandwiches, if you get around to preparing fillings at home and bringing them aboard in mason jars, you'll be able to produce greater variety and and save yourself more time for fun. Otherwise the first half day of your cruise finds you in the galley. You surface for a breath of air only to find the skipper and crew yelling for lunch, and down you go again. Salad mixes such as egg, tuna, chicken and ham keep for a long while on ice. And sandwiches should be hearty. Few men will smack their lips over a cream cheese and jelly sandwich and after a morning of rigorous crew work in the fresh air.

Hollow Leg Fillers—Bread and Cereal

If you carry a bun-warmer you can heat old bread to a delicious warmth and freshness (wrap it in foil first), putting this on a burner as the plates are served, and it will be ready just as everyone gets settled. Breakfast buns, doughnuts, coffee cake and loaf bread all respond favorably to this treatment.

There are some especially nice canned breads on the market, besides date-nut and brown breads, and you'll never be without if you stow some of these in the dry locker.

As for cereals, you'll find people eating them afloat who never do ashore, and a hot cereal makes the heartiest one-dish breakfast you can have, particularly in rough weather when your crew needs a hot and filling meal and you feel least like producing one.

Beverages—a Variety is Welcome

Don't dismiss your liquid supplies with "a pot of coffee will do." Fruit juices are more popular than ever as eye-openers, and, while the frozen juices are fine for short hauls, be sure to stow plenty of cans of orange, grapefruit, pineapple and apple juice too. The flavor of canned juices improves a great deal if you aerate them just before serving.

Coffee, tea and soup alternate each other for cool weather sailing. Orangeade or lemonade go well for hot weather, and you'll always have some on tap if you make a thermos full in the morning for anyone to help himself as he pleases. As in other foods, variety in liquids will be appreciated, and even the inveterate coffee drinker may sidle up to tea or cocoa for a welcome change.

Stowing—Not a Hit-or-Miss Affair

Stowing your food aboard should not be a hit-or-miss operation. All like items should be placed together as you unpack the carry-all, and then the group stowed in icebox, locker or cabinet all at once.

If you can pre-cool your icebox, after a thorough scrubbing and airing, by filling with ice and leaving it a day or two before you bring food aboard, your ice will last longer and foods stay colder. You're also more fortunate in this respect if your box is of the top-opening type rather than side-opening, as the latter dumps a certain amount of the settled cold air every time you open the door. Wash the ice before putting it in and wipe off all containers and milk bottles. Stow things with a semblance of order so you know just where to find what you want without losing valuable cold air.

Fresh meats should be taken out of their store paper, rinsed and wrapped in wax paper. It's the juice around the meat that deteriorates first, and might give the idea that the meat itself is bad when it really is not. Vegetables should be washed and made ready for use before stowing, and special attention should be given to placing the milk so that it won't be upset with the motion of the boat. Incidentally, waxed milk cartons sometimes give way after being soaked and squeezed in the icebox, so check yours to be sure all is well, or transfer the milk to your own plastic or glass containers. Have plenty of the latter on hand for stowing left-overs and dry staples.

To prevent butter from absorbing other food odors, and to keep the icebox generally sweet, a container of charcoal or charcoal derivative placed in the box will help a lot.

In stowing dry goods, place the most-used containers where they're handiest, and keep a roll of scotch tape handy to tape opened boxes when there's a possibility of spoiling.

Crackers, cookies, nuts and other foods which get stale when soggy can be kept in a dehumidifying can, which has a dehydrating unit in the lid to absorb moisture from the can's contents. Sugar, salt and flour are best kept in jars with screw tops, particularly if left aboard from weekend to weekend.

Clean-up detail, when the weekend cruise is over, is also preparation for the following trip, and requires a thorough job if you want to enjoy yourself the next time you come aboard. The icebox should be cleared of food and washed out, the remaining ice thrown overboard, and the lid left off when you depart. Unused perishables should all go in the homebound duffle and, as a finale, take the last bag of garbage ashore for disposal in a trash can.

Good Galley Gear Lightens the Chores

When assembling galley equipment, don't make the mistake of saying, "It's only for the boat, I'll get a cheap pot." The cheap pot may not last through the season; it will be the devil to clean, will dent and not sit squarely on the

Chow time and the cockpit of this outboard cruiser becomes a dining salon afloat. *(Photo-Homestrand Co.)*

burners, will not have an insulated handle, will tip unless half full, and won't give an even heat to its contents. In a good grade of cooking ware, an adequate complement of utensils could include (10"frying pan; one or two 4-qt. pots; a 6-qt. pot (or a several-utensils-in-one unit); pressure cooker, bunwarmer; coffee pot, tea kettle and some flat pans. If you have an oven, include a casserole dish, baking square and muffin tin. A large roasting pan with a 2-inch lip serves many purposes, from serving as a dish drainboard to holding condiments, silver, napkins, bread and butter and other accessories for passing to the cockpit or around the cabin in one easy motion.

Icepick and its holder, bottle opener, beer can openers, and a special screw-top jar for matches are essentials, as are a strainer and sufficient sharp knives and mixing spoons, measuring cups and tongs or asbestos mittens for grasping hot foods or containers. A chopping board which doubles as a sink cover, thermos with pouring spigot, and a scrap-trap garbage bag unit are also helpful gear. But the greatest help of all will be your favorite cooking text supplemented with one or two cookbooks giving special attention to the intricacies of the galley detail.

Remember that a well-fed crew is a happy crew.

SUGGESTED MENUS

Following is a sample list of menus for a week's cruise for four persons, and a list of the groceries necessary to provide them. One midweek stop is allowed for.

SATURDAY

NOON
Tomato Soup
Egg Salad Sandwiches
(Eggs prepared at home beforehand)
Cupcakes Milk

DINNER
Sliced Ham (baked at home)
Boiled Sweet Potatoes
Succotash Salad
Tea Bananas & Cream

SUNDAY

BREAKFAST
Pineapple Juice Dry Cereal
Bacon & Eggs
(cook extra bacon to use at noon)
Corn Muffins (packaged, heated)
Coffee Jam

NOON
Tomato Juice
Peanut Butter & Bacon Sandwiches
Egg Salad Sandwiches
(if some remain from previous day)
Cake Milk

DINNER
Spaghetti with vegetable-meat sauce made at home (or canned sauce with some spices and hamburg added)
Salad Italian Bread
Elberta Peaches Cookies Beverage

MONDAY

BREAKFAST
Prunes Dry Cereal
French Toast Syrup
Bacon Coffee

NOON
Vegetable Soup
Ham & Cheese Sandwiches
Tea Cookies

DINNER
Fried Chicken
Candied Sweet Potatoes
(made from leftovers from Saturday dinner)
Canned Asparagus Warm Bread
Tea Coffee Milk

TUESDAY

BREAKFAST
Fruit Salad
Dry Cereal (Canned Milk)
Ham and Eggs
Warmed Doughnuts, Coffee Cake
(warmed to restore freshness)
Coffee

NOON
Tomato Juice
Spaghetti   Beer
Cheese & Crackers

DINNER
Ham & Corned Beef Hash
(or ham and canned stew mixed)
Lima Beans   Boiled Potatoes
Pilot Crackers & Canned Butter
(if fresh supply is gone)
Tea   Coffee   Milk
Vanilla Pudding,
Canned Raspberry Sauce

WEDNESDAY (Shopping Trip in the Morning)

BREAKFAST
Apple Juice
Cereal & Bananas (Canned Milk)
Coffee
Datenut bread (Canned Butter)

NOON
Hamburgers on Rolls
Potato Chips
Cake   Tea   Coffee   Milk

DINNER
Roast Beef (cooked in pressure cooker)
Potatoes   Peas
Sliced Tomatoes
Blueberries & Cream
Cake   Tea   Coffee   Milk

THURSDAY

BREAKFAST
Apple Sauce   Dry Cereal
Sausage & Eggs
Buns   Coffee

NOON
Vegetable Juice
Roast Beef Sandwiches
Cake
Tea   Coffee   Milk   Beer

DINNER
Pork Chops & Beans Grill
(Brown chops, add beans, sprinkle with brown sugar, put cover on and finish cooking—until chops are done and beans very hot—over very low flame)
Brown Bread
Broccoli   Salad
Canned Berries on Pound Cake
Tea   Coffee   Milk

FRIDAY

BREAKFAST
Prune Juice
Fried Potatoes & Eggs
(potatoes left over from Tuesday dinner)
Warmed Buns   Coffee

NOON
Tuna Salad or Cold Cuts Sandwiches
Tea   Coffee   Milk
Bananas   Cake

DINNER
Creamed Crabmeat
on
Rice with Pimento
String Beans   Beets
Tea   Coffee   Milk
Fruit Cookies

THE FOOD SUPPLY LISTS

Planned for four persons—midweek shopping day provided for.

First Supply List
Meat and Fish

10-12 lb. ham (boned and rolled)
3 lbs. bacon
1 frying chicken
2 cans tuna fish
4 cans hash
4 cans fricassee

Vegetables and Soup

2 lbs. sweet potatoes
5 lbs. white potatoes
2 #2 cans succotash
4 #2 cans asparagus
2 #2 cans lima beans
2 #2 cans string beans
1 large can beets
1 can pimento
2 cans baked beans
2 cans Spanish rice
5 fresh tomatoes
2 heads lettuce
  carrots
6 onions
2 green peppers
  celery
pkg. minute rice, spaghetti, macaroni
4 cans tomato soup
4 cans vegetable soup

Bread and Cereal

pkg. of assorted cereals
corn muffins (pkgd.)
4 loaves bread
loaf cake
1/2 doz. cupcakes
cookies-assortment
  orange ⎫
  toll house ⎬ one box each kind
1 doz. doughnuts
2 cans datenut bread
2 cans brown bread
1 can of bread
1 loaf of Italian bread
saltines
crackers

Other items which could be included:

peanuts
dried apricots, prunes
candy
cheese spreads

Beverages

tea bags or liquid tea
pineapple juice (2 #2 cans)
coffee (1 large, 1 small instant brand)
tomato juice (2 #2 cans)
beer — 1-1/2 doz. cans or more
soft drinks—1-1/2 doz. or more
apple juice (4 #2 cans)
vegetable juice (4 #2 cans)
prune juice (2 #2 cans)

Dairy

2 lbs. butter
2 pints cream
3 doz. eggs
5 qts. milk
1-1/2 lbs. cheese
canned milk, canned butter

Dry Staples

sugar, brown and white
1 pkg. flour
1 pkg. oatmeal (or other hot cereal)
salt & pepper
mustard
jam
peanut butter
salad dressing
oil
syrup
ketchup
onion salt, garlic salt, celery salt
meat tenderizer
pint of mayonnaise
nutmeg
cloves

Fruit

bananas—6
Elberta peaches—large can
prunes—large can
fruit salad—4 #2 cans
raspberries—2 cans
applesauce—2 cans
figs—2 cans
oranges—1 doz.

Second Supply List
(On Midweek shopping trip)

Meat

8 pork chops
6-lb. roast of beef
1 lb. sausage
1 lb. bacon
2 lbs. ground steak

Vegetables

Frozen peas (2 pkgs.)
Tomatoes—3 fresh
Lettuce—large head
Broccoli—bunch fresh
celery

Bread

Hamburger Rolls—8
buns
3 loaves bread
cakes
coffee cake

Dairy

butter
2 pts. cream
5 qts. milk
eggs

Fruit

blueberries — 1 qt.
melon—green when purchased
grapefruit

CHAPTER XXVIII

Water Skiing and Water Skis

The sport of water skiing is about 40 years old, and has become so popular that in some localities separate water areas have been set aside for this sport, while in others it is governed by local water regulations.

In the booklet, "Recreational Boating Guide," the U.S. Coast Guard suggests the following safety hints:

1. Install a wide-angle, rear-view mirror or take along a second person to act as lookout. This will permit watching the skier and the waters ahead. Some state laws require this mirror or a second person in the boat to assist the operator.

2. Don't tow the skier in heavily traveled or restricted waters such as swimming areas; narrow, winding channels; and areas containing docks, floats and buoys.

3. Make sure the skier is wearing a proper lifesaving device. If he tumbles, the boat should approach him from the lee side.

4. Stop your motor before taking the skier on board.

5. In taking the skier on board, take precautions not to swamp your boat. In smaller craft, it is normally safer to take a person aboard at the stern.

For communication between the water skier and the operator of the boat, a standard set of signals is recommended

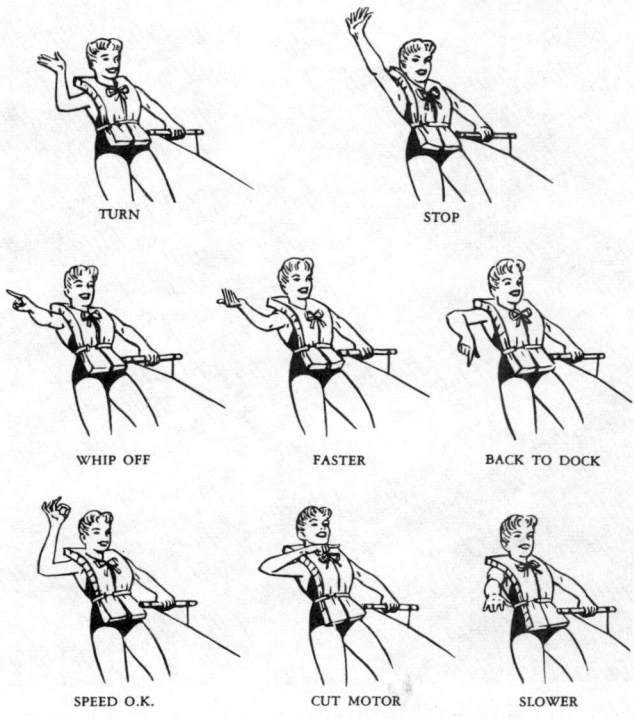

Recommended Water Skiing Signals

About Water Skiing

The first water skiers back in the twenties used regular snow skis—which differ from modern water skis mainly in being longer and narrower and grooved on the undersurface. Today's typical water ski is about 5-12 feet long, 6-1/2 inches wide, and 5/8 of an inch thick. It does not taper. The upcurve starts about a foot from the rounded tip. At the rear end of the painted or varnished undersurface there is a fin (sometimes two fins) about 1-1/2 feet long and 1 inch deep. The slipper-like adjustable rubber "binding" into which the foot fits, is placed with its opening about 2-1/2 feet from the trailing end of the ski.

While these dimensions are descriptive of a conventional water ski, there are many variations. The specifications of the American Water Skiing Association state only that the ski should be no less than four feet long, and not less than four inches nor more than eight inches wide.

Many resorts that boast water sports offer water skiing along with somebody to teach those who don't know how. The instructor will supply not only the boat, but the skis as well. (For specific information on where to find schools and individual instructors, write to the American Water Ski Association, 307 North Michigan Avenue, Chicago.) Also, many children's summer camps offer water skiing as part of their waterfront activities programs.

But isn't this a sport strictly for aquatic athletes? Not at all. As far as the physical strain goes, water skiing may safely be indulged in by any sound person in good health who can swim fairly well. It is much more a matter of coordination than of strength. As for the

Water skiing continues to grow as a participation sport: these girls ski as well as their boy friends and everyone takes a turn in the spray. *(Mercury Outboard Motors photo)*

danger, it exists, but it is small if common sense is exercised.

A beginner may learn to ride the skis, at least after a fashion, the first day he tries. But Jack Andresen in his textbook, "Skiing on Water" (A.S.Barnes & Co.), calculates that it will take the average beginner about five hours of actual skiing, or some 60 five-minute rides, really to master the basic maneuvers—starts, landings, turns and jumping the wake.

In the most basic of maneuvers, the start, the pupil and the instructor squat in shallow water with their ski's ends on the bottom. As the tow-boat starts, it pulls the skiers into proper take-off position, with knees bent at right angles and arms out straight. As the boat speeds up, the skis plane along the surface as the skiers rise. Bending arms or straightening legs at this point may mean a spill. Once under way, the proper form is arms straight, shoulders squared, chin up, chest out, knees slightly bent.

Another way to start is from a sitting position on the edge of a dock or float. When properly done, this method allows you to get going without getting wet. However, some people, finding the timing tricky, become very wet indeed before getting the knack of it.

A much harder way is to start from water deep enough so that the skis do not touch bottom. Beginners may find this difficult. Even though you're wearing a life jacket, as you should, you may find it hard to put on the skis while floating. But learning to start off in deep water pays, for it means you won't have to go all the way back to shore to get going again every time you fall off the skis.

Successful water skiing depends not only on the skill of the skier; the person who drives the boat also has to know a thing or two. Nearly all the danger of

Waterskiing is a safe, fun-filled family sport if certain basic precautions are observed. Here, skier wears safety belt and observer watches her continuously, allowing boat operator to keep his eyes focused ahead.

being seriously injured in water skiing lies in striking other objects such as boats, docks or the shore. While one can sustain minor cuts and bruises on his legs from hitting his own skis, this very seldom happens. And at ordinary speeds it's rare indeed that anybody gets badly hurt by falling in the water.

Safety in water skiing depends largely on the boat driver. A good boat driver who knows the limitations of his skier can keep beginners out of most troubles.

The Proper Boat

If the boat is an inboard, the ideal one for skiing is a utility runabout 14 to 18 feet long, with a 60 to 160 horsepower motor, a short foredeck, no centerdeck, and only enough deck behind the rear seat to house the gasoline tank.

For inboard motorboats, a very desirable feature is a towing post or pylon, placed about half way back from the stern, to which the tow-rope may be tied three feet or so above the waterline. It provides three advantages: the driver can see the rope better and judge how much slack there is, reducing the danger of fouling the rope on the propeller; the rope being higher is less likely to sag when the boat is going slowly, especially when towing a light skier; and it allows the boat to turn more easily.

However, a pylon won't work well on an outboard. It can make a light boat rock badly; and the pull of the rope on the pylon pulls the stern down during take-off.

An outboard for skiing should be between 12 and 16 feet in length. The load should be placed well forward. Because an outboard and an average skier on an ordinary pair of skis plane at about the same speed (10 to 15 miles per hour), both the boat and the skier are trying to "get over the hump" at the same time, and some medium powered outboard boats may be unable to shoulder this double burden. All outboard boats for water skiing should be equipped not only with remote steering, but also with remote shift and throttle, all operated from the front seat.

With an exceptionally light boat, small women and children can be skied with an outboard motor of as little as 15 horsepower, and sometimes even 10 horsepower will do. But as the skier becomes more proficient, he usually wants more speed to enable him to perform more complicated maneuvers and a 25 horsepower—or higher—engine is desirable. Tests made by Consumers Union of Mount Vernon, New York, indicate that two average adults are about the maximum possible load for an ordinary outboard equipped with a 25 horsepower engine to pull out of the water and ski satisfactorily.

Unless you have one of the few outboard motors made with left hand propeller rotation (as viewed from the rear), the steering wheel should be placed on the right hand side, where the driver's weight counteracts the propeller's twisting action.

When you're driving, always bear in mind that you have a very sharp, powerful meat-chopper under your boat. Treat it with the caution and respect it deserves. Always switch the motor off when taking skiers or swimmers aboard. Always have someone in the boat whose sole job is to watch the skier.

Don't operate near swimmers, or allow waiting skiers to swim anywhere near the boat-operating area. They may be hit by the boat or they may be run into by an inexperienced skier coming in for a landing.

Never allow anyone to stand up in the boat while it is moving or to sit on the bow deck or the side. A fall from here can land one in the propeller.

Whenever possible avoid driving close to stationary objects such as other boats, docks and piers. Even if your skier is experienced he may not be looking, or he may take it into his head at that moment to show off—and make a bad error of judgment.

Never reverse if there are swimmers in the water anywhere near you, or if you are near your skier. One of the most dangerous mistakes made by amateur drivers is to pull in a dropped tow rope and then back up to the skier to pass him the tow bar. *Never back up to a skier!* Always circle around again, constantly keeping the skier in view so that you do not inadvertently drift too close to him. Always keep the dangerous propeller away from him. If you do find yourself coming too close, *don't use reverse*. Stop the engine and put it in neutral.

After your skier has fallen off or dropped off, throttle down your engine, turn at low speed, and then open up to get back. Sharp turns at high speed are cowboy tactics. You stress the boat severely, wear the engine, burn gasoline unnecessarily, and make the water rough.

Never take your skier into shallow water—except, naturally, when he's starting out. At least four feet is necessary with a sandy or muddy bottom, and six feet if the bottom is at all hard or rocky. (Remember that a nautical chart of unfamiliar waters will give you "bottom" information.) Otherwise, the skier may injure himself by hitting the bottom if he goes off the skis while traveling at a good clip. Contrary to popular belief, skiing is not easier if the boat goes fast. The easiest speed for beginners is the lowest speed at which they are fully planing, about 10 to 16 miles per hour.

Be sure you have a good view. Use extra cushions to raise you up really high. A windshield is a disadvantage in a skiing boat, unless you can look over it, as it is often partially obscured by spray.

As the nation's eight million water skiers become more accomplished, many of them are learning that even spectacular stunts such as riding on this single slalom ski are not as hard as they once thought. *(Mercury Outboard Motors photo)*

Never follow a skier being towed by another boat. He may fall and you may not be able to avoid him. Similarly, if another boat starts to follow your skier, alter course (gently so that you do not disturb your skier) and wave the following boat away.

If space permits, run the boat straight down its own wake with large turning circles at either end. If the boat is run constantly in a circle, it is awkward for the skier and the water gets very rough.

Towing Gear

The bar should be about one inch in diameter and about 15 inches long. It should be made of ash or other very strong wood and unpainted, as the bare wood provides a better grip.

A wooden float is usually used on the rope just ahead of the handle to help keep the rope on the surface when it's free in the water. Even better are the inexpensive two-inch cork floats used to support fishing nets. Floats should be brightly painted for easy visibility.

The most popular rope used for towing today is made of polyethylene. This type of rope is available in colors, and its wet strength is claimed to be as high as its dry strength. While it is slightly more elastic than Manila rope, the excessive stretching which was its disadvantage some years ago has been corrected. Another point in its favor is that it floats!

Also used to some extent is 1/4-inch twisted Manila rope. Cotton, nylon and linen line have disadvantages as skiers' tow lines. The tow line is usually about 75 feet long.

How to Choose a Ski That Fits

Any general-purpose water ski (about 5-1/2 feet long and 6-1/2 inches wide) has the right dimensions for almost any adult. Very heavy people may find a somewhat wider ski advantageous. In addition to the general-purpose skis, there are several types of "special" skis. The jumping skis are especially strong, made to stand the impact of landing after a jump. Slalom skis are single skis fitted with two foot bindings, one behind the other.

A variation of the water ski is the "water saucer" or disc. These have no bindings. Skiers stand on them and hold on to the tow rope as in skiing, and they can be used with relatively low-powered outboard motors since they plane at low speed.

The weight of the ski is of relatively little importance except that heavier skis are awkward to handle out of the water. Far more important is that the buoyancy of the ski be low because before the start, the wearer has to resist the tendency of the skis to float his feet to the surface.

The ski bindings are generally adjustable through a wide range of sizes. However, if your foot is longer or shorter than the limits of adjustment provided, the bindings can usually be shifted to suit you. Try the bindings in your bare feet before you buy. If you find that the molded-rubber binding is uncomfortable choose a binding without a thick molded edge. But if you've decided to buy a ski despite an uncomfortable binding, you can make another binding (sometimes the shops are willing to do this) out of a piece of rubber from a discarded inner tube—the material that most experts use on their water skis. (Make screw holes in the rubber with a leather punch. Unless you own a punch, let a shoemaker make the holes.)

Water skis are also available from a number of manufacturers in children's sizes.

CHAPTER XXIX

Automobile-Marine Engine Conversion

For about 30 years converting auto to marine engines has been a way of powering pleasure boats used most often when pleasure boats have been re-powered. However, the "new" boat buyer might well consider the possibility of acquiring an older hull in good condition and installing a converted automobile engine.

A survey of the "marine" engines shows that many of them are conversions of automobile, truck or industrial engines. For example the following listing of marine engines shows the engine blocks from which they are made:

Gray: in-line blocks are Continental; V-8's are American Motors Rambler.

Universal-Norseman: in-line blocks are Hercules; V-8's are Lincoln.

Brennan: Minneapolis-Moline Tractor engines.

Palmer: International truck motors.

Crusader: Cadillac and Chevrolet.

Chris-Craft: Hercules Industrial engines (in-line) and Chevrolet V-8's.

Owens: Chevrolet and Ford V-8's, industrial blocks for 4-cylinder motors.

The actual converting process is fairly simple with the available kits and components; the really big job is the proper installation of the engine in the boat, and this requires expert knowledge regardless of the type of engine being installed.

Full conversion equipment is available from a number of sources for all of the Ford Motor Company line (Ford, Edsel, Mercury, Thunderbird, Lincoln); Chrysler (Plymouth, Dodge, DeSoto, Chrysler and Imperial); and General Motors (Chevrolet, Pontiac, Buick, Oldsmobile and Cadillac). Equipment is still available for some models dating back to the late '30 models. Currently and for the past few years, the Chevrolet V-8 has been popular as a conversion "job." The Oldsmobile "Rocket" engine has also been popular and the Cadillac has been a favorite on the West Coast for many years. Since Pontiac came out with the "hot" engine in 1959, it has been praised by ski-boat and drag enthusiasts.

Selecting the Automobile Engine for Marine Duty

First, there are several points which are advanced as arguments for considering an automobile power plant for marine duty.

Price: This is the thought most commonly associated with conversions. Many satisfactory marine installations have been made from "junkyard" engines, and even a new auto engine with a conversion kit is considerably less expensive than a comparable marine engine.

Parts and Service: Parts and service are readily available from auto dealers, auto supply stores, gas stations, auto junkyards, etc. All engines need parts and service at some time; and auto supply outlets are generally more available than dealers in specific marine lines. If you are not a do-it-yourselfer, the smaller inboard can be trailered right into a garage. Also, parts prices are generally lower than for comparable marine parts.

Adaptability: A great variety of optional equipment is readily available for most auto engines for stepping up power for drag-boating; ski-towing, etc., such as special cams, carburetors, "hot" ignition equipment, etc.

Closed cooling system: The auto engine in its natural habitat operates on a closed heat exchanger system. While there is no difference in internal cooling passages between auto and marine engines, there is a big difference at the coolant inlet and outlet points. Because the marine engine is usually used with a raw water cooling system (and raw water is colder than recirculating water) the ports are smaller. Conversely, because the auto engine is cooled with "warmer" water, the inlet ports are larger for higher water flow as is the water pump capacity. The closed system is considered to preserve engine life (no salting, etc.), but gives better performance. The internal combustion engine operates most efficiently in the 160-180 degree range. However, with a raw water system the operating temperature should be kept below 140° as salting increases rapidly above that temperature. Also, with a raw water system the temperature variations among cylinders may be too great for truly efficient performance. Incoming water may be 60-65 degrees, cooling the front cylinders greatly, but by the time it reaches the back cylinders it is warmed considerably. In a closed system, the maximum variation is only 15° to 20° from inlet to outlet, and the use of a thermostat also helps to maintain optimum engine temperature.

Down-draft carburetion: All auto engines have downdraft carburetors (as do the newer marine V-8's), but all in line and many older V-8 marine engines have updraft carburetion. In case of engine flooding this makes a big difference. With the downdraft, excess gas merely flows into the combustion chamber where it is burned off. But with an updraft carburetor, flooding may spill gas outside the carburetor where it constitutes a great fire and explosion hazard. Although the flame arrestor helps, gas in the engine compartment presents a great danger from many possible spark sources. (Incidentally, all complete conversion kits include Coast Guard approved flame arrestors.)

Choice of Reverse and Reduction Gears: Marine engines are usually sold with a choice of only one or two gear boxes. With a conversion engine, you can choose from a variety of manual and hydraulic gears. The conversion equipment manufacturer or dealer can recommend the gear ratio to best suit your particular hull and use requirements. Frequently to keep the "package price" as low as possible, the marine engine will be outfitted with an adequate (but not heavy-duty) gear box. With the conversion engine, you decide for yourself how much "extra" to allow.

Operating Economy: A switch from a large (or twin) outboard power plant to a converted auto engine should reduce fuel consumption considerably. (Conversion kit manufacturers say from 20 to 50 percent depending on all factors involved; although at a sacrifice of interior space and maneuverability.)

Guide to Buying a Motor for Conversion

First, of course, is to make sure that conversion equipment is available for the engine you want. While this seems elementary, every manufacturer of conversion kits receives calls for conversions which are not available in the field. And always give the dealer or manufacturer the year and *model* of the engine, not just the make. If you are in doubt about the model, give the engine serial number.

Also, keep away from "off" brands. Certain makes of automobiles are notorious for substandard engines and while such engines may be obtainable "at a price," the owner will pay much more in excessive maintenance.

Don't go power-mad unless you know your hull will take high speed running. Select your engine on the basis of your hull and the purpose you hope to achieve. If you use your boat primarily for fishing or family cruising, select an engine in the medium horsepower range and mate it with a reduction gear so you can swing a good sized propeller. Even on boats in the 25'-36' bracket, a reduction gear is advisable for smoother ride plus greater maneuverability and gas economy. The extra grip you get from a larger screw is particularly advantageous in inlets or in rough water and in "playing" fish. Also, you will be less affected by wind, waves and changes in load with a reduction gear.

If you are primarily interested in "thrill" boating or fast take-off for ski-towing, such engines as the "Thunderbird," the large Chevrolet with the power-pack, the Plymouth Fury, the Dodge 345 cu. in., the Oldsmobile and the Cadillac are all ideally suited. For example a "Thunderbird" conversion in 20-foot runabout which had an 85" beam and 12" draft with a 13"x18" prop developed better than 60 m.p.h.

If you are replacing an existing inboard engine with a conversion, there are several things to look for:

1. Make sure your engine bed is ample if you are going into a larger engine. If in doubt, ask the dealer or conversion manufacturer.

2. In going from a smaller to a larger engine, make sure your water intake is ample in size for the engine — enlarge it if it is not.

3. Be sure your propeller shaft is adequate to handle an increase in power.

4. Check to see if your clearance will allow you to swing a large enough prop to make sufficient use of a power increase.

5. Be sure that the design of your boat will enable you to benefit from stepped-up power. A "squatting" hull will require wedges or shingles to get up and plane.

6. Give first consideration to a V-8 over an in-line because you get more power in less space and less weight. Some of the larger in-lines are so cumbersome and heavy that the excessive weight defeats the very purpose of the change.

Many experts in the field strongly advocate that the conversion-minded boatman should consider purchasing a late model, low-mileage used engine whenever feasible. Thanks to the nation's careless drivers, auto graveyards are full of excellent engines with many years of good life left in them. Never buy an engine from a head-on wreck; but you can often get an excellent buy from a car which was smashed amidships (aft of the engine area) or in the rear. There are two reasons for this advice:

1. Price: You can get a late model V-8 with less than 10,000 miles on it for less than $300 (sometimes as low as

Working on the water. Here, two Edsel engines have been converted to provide a nautical power plant.
(Barr Marine Products photo)

$200 depending on make, model and your bargaining ability). This means you can repower — including all conversion equipment and marine reverse gear — for less than $700 in many cases.

By checking the general appearance of the wrapped-up car (interior condition, lube stickers, etc.) you can tell if the car had been well cared for and thereby get a good idea of the motor's shape.

When you bargain for the engine, make sure you get all the necessary accessories — voltage regulator, coil, distributor, starter, solonoid switch, etc. — with your purchase. You get them at no extra charge at purchase time, but if you forget and come back later, you will be charged extra for the needed parts.

2. Any "bugs" which were in the engine initially will have been discovered and rectified in the first few thousand miles. A new engine, be it marine or auto, is fully guaranteed, but this will do little to soothe your temper if you get stranded at sea, or have to remove the engine for make-good.

For those who prefer to start with a factory-fresh block, some engines are available only in "short block" form — block, crankcase and pistons — which will have to be built up.

If you lean towards a new engine, auto dealers will "wheel and deal" on engines just as they do on complete cars. Many will start talking "discount" even before you ask for it. For example, a recent-year's Chevrolet V-8 engine complete sold to dealers at $541 net and listed at $701.25 retail. In most cases a deal could be struck for a price halfway between the two figures. If you lean towards the Ford V-8, it may pay you to know that for only $30 more you can get the "Thunderbird" engine; in the Chrysler family, you can get the Windsor V-8 for about $100 more than the Plymouth V-8.

A dealer can get for you any engine made by the parent corporation of his new car line. For example, if you want an Oldsmobile or a Cadillac engine, you may be able to make a better deal through a Chevrolet dealer than through an Oldsmobile or Cadillac dealer, especially if the smaller car dealer is a volume operator.

Disadvantages of Conversion Engines

There are certain disadvantages of the automobile engine even after conversion that should be considered:

1. Steel oil pan — this is thinner and more subject to corrosion than the cast iron or cast aluminum pans of marine engines.

2. Smaller oil capacity — this does not mean less lubrication, but as the engine gets older and starts to burn oil you have less reserve.

3. Low position of starter. This applies only to V-8's not to 6's where there is no difference in position. The slight actual difference in inches does not give a safety factor, but if the hull is leaky, a low-placed starter can get flooded or submerged.

4. The height of an auto engine above the crankshaft is generally greater than a marine engine which sometimes necessitates adding height to the engine hatch.

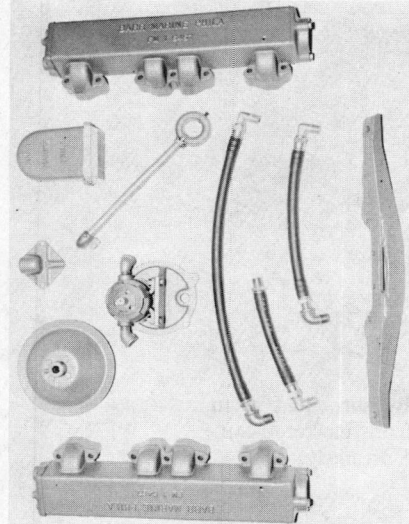

Pictured here is a full "conversion kit" for marine-izing a Ford or Mercury V-8. The water-cooled exhaust manifolds are at the sides (a 6-cyl or straight 8 would require only one manifold). Top left is vee-belt pulley for marine water pump. Top center is cast-iron water outlet plate. Top right is the required, Coast Guard-approved flame arrestor which must be placed atop the carburetor (this serves as a backfire trap). Below the pulley is the water pump which replaces the automotive type pump originally on the engine — marine use requires rubber impeller type ball bearing pump such as this. Beside it is the crankcase breather which vents any oil fumes into the carburetor flame arrestor. The three hoses are for the circulation of the cooling water. Bottom is the front motor support.

Step-by-step process of converting auto engine for marine duty.

1. After removing automotive exhaust manifold, remove the automotive water pump assembly on this 292 cu. in. Ford V-8.

2. Next take off the flywheel housing.

3. Remove rust and scale; clean engine. Be sure, just as in auto engine work, to remove all particles from gasketed surfaces so that new gaskets will fit cleanly and properly.

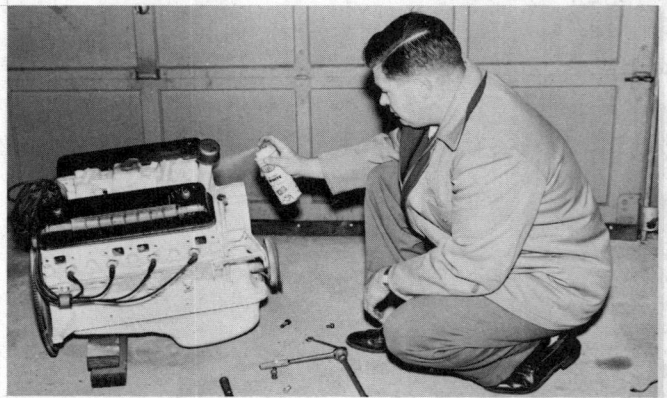

4. Not necessary, but makes for cleaner looking job. Before bolting on the conversion parts paint the engine block. In using spraypaint, as here, tape over oil fill pipe, manifolding and other openings to keep paint *outside* of engine.

5. Bolt the marine reverse gear drive flange to the flywheel. In buying your engine, if possible get one with "straight stick" transmission; otherwise you will have to purchase a heavy-duty flywheel as the flywheel from an automatic transmission is too light for marine use.

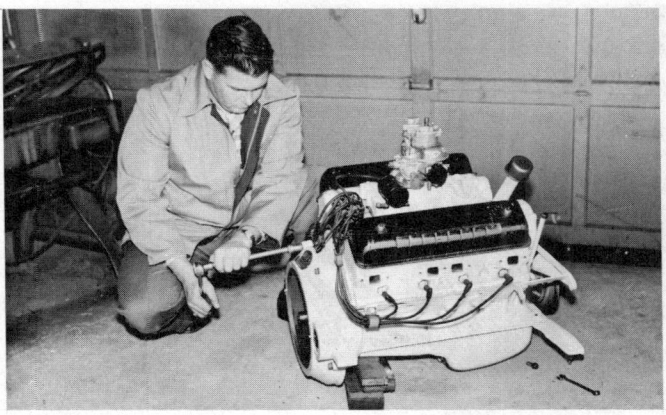

6. Bolt the flywheel housing into position. This comes with the marine reverse gear and as you will notice also serves as the rear motor support.

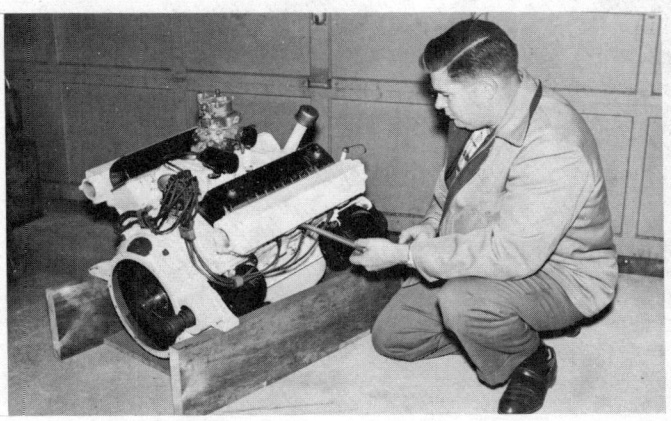

7. The engine has been mounted on skids for easier, safer handling. The water-cooled marine exhaust manifolds are now being bolted on.

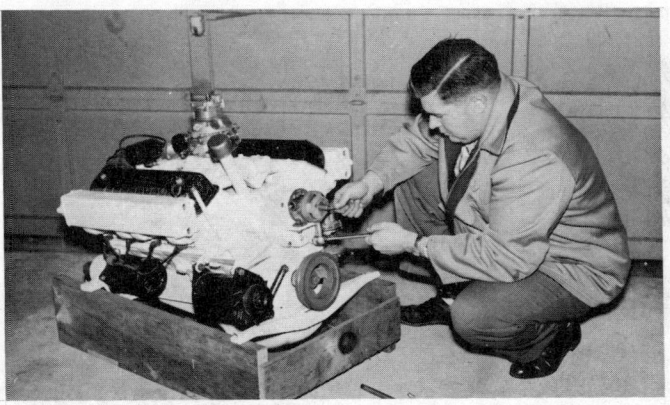

8. The marine type water pump is then bolted into position on the front of the engine replacing the automotive type.

9. The water circulating lines are connected to the pump, the exhaust manifolds and the block.

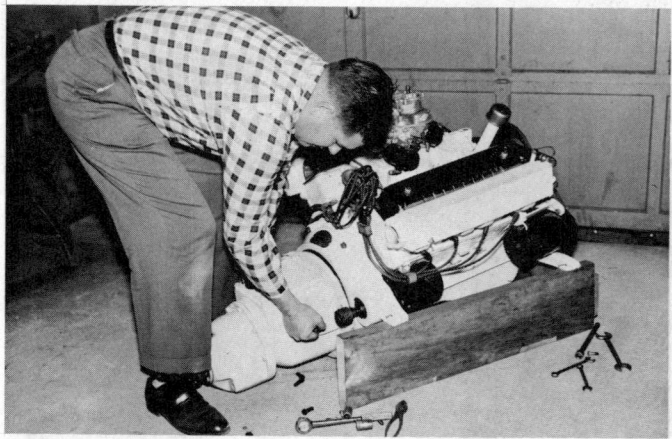

10. Reverse gear is then bolted to the flywheel housing. Note that a reduction gear which is attached directly behind the marine reverse gear is also used. This is advisable in boats of 25 feet or more in length enabling a larger, more efficient propeller to be used.

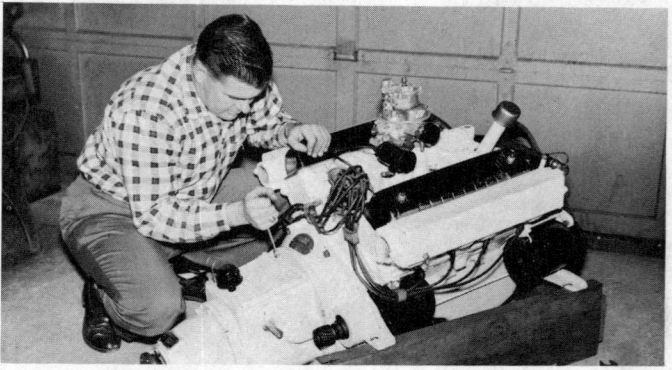

11. The original automotive ignition equipment is put back on (distributor, coil, voltage regulator, starter and solenoid switch).

12. The finishing touch is the bolting on of the Coast-Guard-approved flame arrestor.

13. The completed "marine" engine. Note that no special tools or mechanical skills are required for the conversion job since all conversion components bolt on. *(Photos courtesy Barr Marine Co.)*

CHAPTER XXX

Looking Ahead

Rubber-Coated Pleasure Boats

Rubber-coated pleasure boats may be the next step in the development of craft to move through the water faster. This may result from an idea by a former German scientist who wondered why porpoises can swim so swiftly with so little apparent effort. His studies led to the development of a specially designed rubber coating that will permit vessels to travel faster without any increase in power, or at the same speed with less power than is now required. When the rubber coating is applied to an object, it reduces the turbulence normally created as the object moves through the water.

Dr. Max O. Kramer of Los Angeles is the developer of the coating and an authority on the theory of anti-turbulence which is technically "boundary layer stabilization by distributed damping." The U.S. Rubber Company which is producing the coating believes that this development will be as important to boating as the pneumatic tire is to land transportation. The company's technologists have already developed coatings which have reduced drag by about 50 percent on underwater measuring devices, and they feel that the most efficient application will be for boats that plane on the water. Larger displacement vessels are less likely to benefit from the coating because they generate larger

TURBULENT FLOW
UNDERWATER OBJECT IS SLOWED BY TURBULENCE

LAMINAR FLOW
PORPOISE ELIMINATES TURBULENT CURRENTS

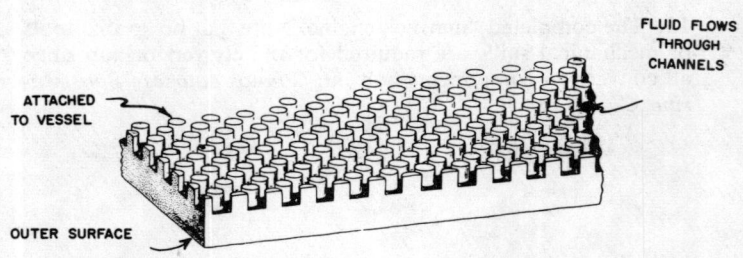

SCHEMATIC VIEW OF LAMIFLO COATING

New rubber coating shown in schematic view, reduces turbulence created by objects moving through water, permitting vessels to travel faster without any increase in power, or at the same speed with less power than now required. Dr. Max Kramer developed this theory of boundary layer stabilization after wondering why porpoises could swim so swiftly with so little apparent effort. Turbulence does not form along body of porpoise, which has a 1-16 inch hydraulic skin that is elastic and ducted. *(Courtesy U.S. Rubber Co.)*

Streamlined test device is put in place by Frank Marty as Dr. Max Kramer, developer of anti-turbulence theory, prepares to start boat in Long Beach, Calif., harbor. This coating developed by U.S. Rubber Co. has brought approximately 50 percent reduction in drag of underwater object. Scientists anticipate benefits for pleasure craft as well as submarines. *(Courtesy U.S. Rubber Co.)*

bow waves, unless their design is modified considerably.

The scientists report that an object being propelled though the water actually uses from 70 to 90 percent of the propulsive energy to overcome the drag due to turbulence, which is created by the object itself. Reduction of this turbulence reduces the power required for propulsion. The two main factors in achieving maximum speed through water have been the smoothness and shape of the object. These are now joined by a third factor, the elimination of turbulence by "damping."

Dr. Kramer began his anti-turbulence research before World War II while he was heading the Aerodynamic Institute of the German Research Center for Aeronautics near Berlin. He obtained the first German patent on high-speed drag reduction by damping. Following the war, he accepted an invitation to work for the United States Navy. He came to this country in 1946.

On his voyage from Europe, Dr. Kramer happened to notice a school of porpoises passing his ship. Based on his observations and calculations, he came to the conclusion that the porpoise (technically the dolphin) must have only about 1/10 the drag that would be normally be expected from an animal of its size and shape. Working with porpoise-skin samples, he found that the animal is completely covered with a 1/16-inch hydraulic skin that is elastic and ducted. In his experiments, he utilized streamlined test bodies towed at the side of a small motorboat containing measuring instruments.

The most practical development thus far is a thin layer of rubber supported by a multitude of tiny rubber pillars. Inter-connecting channels between the pillars contain a freely-flowing viscous liquid. The channels face the surface of the boat; the outside or water side of the coating is smooth. The channels give the coating flexibility, and the liquid provides the necessary damping to suppress potential turbulence.

Hydrofoils

Another approach to the problem of reducing water-drag, this time by trying to eliminate it, is found in the Hydrofoil, or water wings for the boat. A hydrofoil is a plane surface, either flat or curved, designed to obtain a lifting action from the water through which it moves. In principle, it is much the same in theory as the airplane wing, except that the plane uses air for support; the hydrofoil uses water. Also, in principle, water being about 800 times more dense than air, should give about 800 times the "lift." However, this is neutralized to some degree by the drag or resistance of the water.

The idea and use of the hydrofoil principle is not new. The first development work was done as far back as 1898 by Alexander Graham Bell, who experimented with a hydrofoil boat in Nova Scotia in 1918. In Italy at least one large passenger ferry Hydrofoil has been operating for several years, reaching reported speeds of 80 miles an hour.

Basically, the Hydrofoil consists of two main foils and a tail foil which are attached to the hull. Water flows both beneath and over the surfaces of the foils. Just as the wings of an airplane give the plane lift, hydrofoils lift the hull *out* of the water. When the boat accelerates, the main foils begin lifting the bow. They lift the bow faster than the stern thus producing the necessary "angle of attack." As speed is increased, the tail foil produces sufficient lift to overcome hull suction. The Hydrofoil equipped boat normally becomes "foil borne" at about 18-20 miles an hour. Normal cruising speed is 34-36 m.p.h.; maximum speed is about 40 miles per hour. These figures are for a 14-16 foot outboard boat equipped with a 35 horsepower motor. On a boat of this type, the transom would have to be cut down to 15 inches and a 20-inch-shaft outboard motor used.

Hydrofoil kits are available for the do-it-yourselfer from several companies.

HELI-BOUT, 16-foot outboard runabout which incorporates the principle of the helicopter, was displayed at the 1961 National Motor Boat Show in New York. A prototype design, Heli-Bout is for use in the air and on the water. Designed by Brooks Stevens, boat is powered with 75 horsepower Evinrude motor. In the air, the Heli-Bout makes use of a rotor with a 16-foot blade. Rotor is linked to the boat's outboard engine by flexible shafting and reduction gears. *(Courtesy Evinrude)*

They retract for docking and may be removed for ordinary cruising. The draft with foils submerged is about 20 inches. Steering devices vary with the different types of Hydrofoils; some installations use a control stick, somewhat like a pilot's control; others use conventional steering methods.

Users of Hydrofoils claim they enjoy a dry ride, out of reach of all but the largest waves and greater maneuverability than in conventional boating, and freedom from any motion due to water action.

The Heli-Bout

You can't buy it yet, but a combination helicopter-pleasure boat has been made and according to the Evinrude Corporation, it should work when it is tried out on the water and in the air.

The Jet-Powered Pleasure Boat

One of the new developments in the pleasure boating industry is the introduction of jet propulsion as a means of powering pleasure craft. As an engineering problem this required the designing of a suitable turbine for small boat use; this turbine was then attached to the drive shaft of a standard four-cycle inboard engine in place of the transmission and propeller.

In operation, when the engine is started, water is sucked into the turbine through an intake port in the bottom of the hull. As the throttle is advanced, the water is forced out through a nozzle, mounted either on the boat's transom or under the hull, under pressure from the turbine's spinning blades. This flow provides the forward thrust. No external rudder is used on the jet craft. Steering is accomplished by directing the powerful water flow to the right or left. In some units this is done by turning the nozzle itself, in other units by turning vanes similar to Venetian blinds, or by a small "rudder" inside the nozzle. To put the boat into reverse, the nozzle is closed and the jet stream is forced down and forward through a port. In some units, the port moves to the right and left to provide reverse steering. In neutral, the flow is divided fore and aft and there is no motion of the boat.

The makers of these craft point out that elimination of the outside rudder and propeller reduces projections below the hull enabling the turbo-craft to be operated in extremely shallow water or among weeds and debris.

Among some of the advantages claimed by jet-propulsion are these:

A jet-powered boat can be launched in extremely shallow water and its operation is not hampered by debris or sand.

In maneuverability, it is claimed that the jet-power is even more versatile than the outboard. It can make a complete 180-degree turn at full speed in its own length. Some models have the jet nozzle on a gimbal mount so that the power stream can be deflected downward to

TURBOCRAFT FISHERMAN is driven by a two-stage jet unit that is coupled to a Gray 109-horsepower engine.

TURBOCRAFT FIREBOAT, a converted 19-foot pleasure boat, pumps 3,400 gallons per minute through four pressure hoses plus two fog nozzles. Capable of 30 m.p.h., the fireboat is made by Indiana Gear Works, Inc., Indianapolis, Inc.

trim the boat by adjusting the bow angle for proper planing under varying load conditions. Some models also have bow jet outlets which permit the boat to be moved sideways. For instance, in docking, the boat can be brought alongside the dock, then moved sideways into its berth. Then, by keeping the power on, the boat can be held firmly against the dock to allow people to get on or off without the need for tie lines.

Forward, reverse, and bow steering are controlled in some models by means of a single "joy stick" located in the cockpit, somewhat like a plane's control stick. When you want the boat to go forward or backwards, you push the control stick forward or back. To go right or left, the stick is moved in the desired direction. A foot throttle, like the gas pedal of an automobile is used for speed control, and it can be locked in position for any desired speed.

On a small pleasure boat installation, the jet stream leaves the nozzle under pressure of 5,500 gallons per minute, with an estimated thrust of 1,100 pounds.

The first models appeared on the markets in 1960 and were offered by the Buehler Corporation in 16 different sizes and types of boats. A number of other manufacturers expect to enter the market in the near future.

The Inboard-Outboard Motor

Another recent development in powering the boat is the inboard-outboard motor. Basically, this is a small inboard gasoline engine, mounted on the transom of the boat, with an outboard propulsion unit.

One of the arguing points for this type of unit is that it allows use of a full height transom as extra protection against swamping. The outboard-type

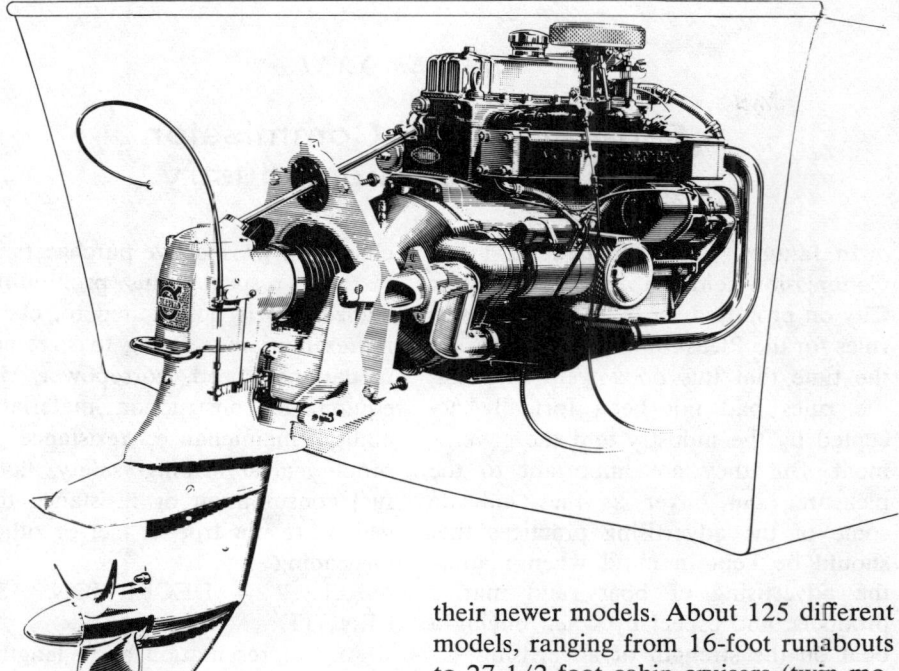

An Inboard-Outboard Motor. *(Courtesy Turbocraft)*

propulsion unit provides the full maneuverability of the outboard. The unit tilts when in low water or when striking an obstacle, and can be tilted up for trailering or beaching the boat.

The 4-cycle engine burns regular gasoline, rather than the gas-oil mixture used in outboards, and the makers claim that the average gas consumption is about half that of comparable horsepower outboards.

For installation in an outboard hull, the makers say that any transom able to carry outboard motors from 50 horsepower up is adequate for the inboard-outboard. However, it might be wise to follow the OBC suggested maximum horsepower for the hull to avoid overpowering a smaller boat. Generally, this power installation is probably best for boats in the 16-35 foot length range. Twin installations are suggested for larger craft, but for racing, twin installations have been made in 21-foot boats.

A number of boat builders are offering the inboard-outboard installations in their newer models. About 125 different models, ranging from 16-foot runabouts to 27-1/2-foot cabin cruisers (twin motors), are currently available in fiberglass, different types of wooden construction, and aluminum.

The motor and drive unit weigh about 440 pounds, compared to the approximate 200-pound weight of the outboard of the same horsepower, 30. In cost, the inboard-outboard runs about $300 to $400 more than the comparable outboard motor with controls. There are also 100-horsepower units available.

A minor saving is effected in that boats with the inboard-outboard motor installations pay the lower inboard insurance rates.

The "Cons"

On the negative side, it has been pointed out that the horsepower-weight ratio is in favor of the outboard; that some cockpit space is sacrificed, although this is made up in part by elimination of the outboard well. Also, the portability of the outboard motor is lost and repairs must be made in the boat; and off-season storage is more of a problem.

CHAPTER XXXI

Federal Trade Commission and the Boating Industry

In January 1961, the Federal Trade Commission held hearings in New York City on proposed set of "Trade Practice rules for the Pleasure Boat Industry." At the time that this book went to press, the rules had not been formally accepted by the industry and the government. But they are important to the pleasure boat buyer as they indicate some of the advertising practices that should be kept in mind when reading the advertising of boats and marine products, and especially when buying a boat on the strength of advertising.

The portions of the proposed rules that are of most importance to the public are these:

The Industry and Its Products Defined

Members of this industry are persons, firms, corporations, and organizations engaged in the manufacture, sale or distribution of pleasure boats. Products of the industry consist of pleasure boats of all types (row boats, motor boats, sail boats, etc.), the length of which does not exceed 65 feet, and equipment therefore, such as engines, propellers, rigging and tanks, which are installed on such boats when the boats are offered for sale.

Rule 1 – GENERAL DECEPTION:

No representation shall be made concerning a boat which directly, by implication, or by failure to adequately disclose significant facts, has the capacity and tendency or effect of deceiving purchasers or prospective purchasers in any material respect. This prohibition includes, but is not limited to, claims or representations relating to size, accommodations, speed, horsepower, rigging, equipment, construction, material, durability, maintenance, resistance to or proof against leaking, safety, flotation, fuel consumption or resistance to fire, which are not true in fact or otherwise misleading.

Rule 2 – DECEPTION AS TO LENGTH:

Any representation as to length of a boat, either direct or indicated as by use of model numbers suggesting length, or otherwise, must state the exact distance measured end to end over the deck of such boat excluding sheer. If in addition a representation of the length of a boat measured by any other method (as for example at the water line or on the gunwale) is made, the nature of such measurement must be conspicuously disclosed.

Rule 3 – DECEPTIVE SPEED CLAIMS:

Claims that a boat is capable of a specified speed by the use of such terms as "up to X miles per hour," or by similar representation, shall not be used unless such boat will attain the specified speed under usual conditions as represented. If a boat is capable of attaining the claimed specified speed only under conditions such as when not having usual tools, or a reasonable quantity of water or fuel on board or under ideal water or weather conditions such as with a favorable wind or current, such speed claims shall be accompanied by a conspicuous disclosure of the conditions which must be present to achieve the claimed speed.

In case of speed claims made for boats which are not equipped with engines, such claims shall be accompanied by a conspicuous disclosure of the horsepower of the engine which must be used in such boat to customarily achieve the claimed speed.

Rule 4 – DECEPTION AS TO MAINTENANCE:

No representation to the effect that a boat is "maintenance free" shall be used unless the boat so described, including installed components such as its propulsion machinery, sails, etc. will not rot, rust, or otherwise deteriorate during the expected life of such boat, and will require no sanding, scraping, painting, patching or other repair, except for accidental damage sustained, and will require no replacement of a part or parts as a result of wear during the life expectancy of such boat.

When equipped with a motor or engine, which will need replacement of a part or parts such as spark plugs, etc., the boat shall not be represented as "maintenance-free" unless such motor is clearly excepted from the representation.

(Note: It is the consensus of the industry that no boat of present manufacture is completely maintenance free under all normal conditions of use.)

Rule 5 – DECEPTIVE USE OF WOOD NAMES:

No representation to the effect that a boat is "(name of wood)" shall be used unless the boat so described is throughout, except for minor braces, etc., solidly of the named wood. When a representation regarding the wood composition of a boat is properly applicable to only certain portions of the boat, such fact shall be clearly stated, e.g., "solid cyprus planking," "teak decks."

The word "Mahogany" shall not be used unqualifiedly to describe any wood other than genuine mahogany (Swietenia). However, the non-mahogany Philippine woods Tanguile, Red Lauan, White Lauan, Tiaong, Almon, Mayapis and Bagtikan may be called "Philippine Mahogany," and the wood of the genus Khaya may be called "African Mahogany."

Rule 6 – DECEPTIVE PRICING:

Members of the industry shall not make any direct or indirect representation concerning the price at which a boat is offered for sale which has the capacity and tendency or effect of misleading or deceiving purchasers or prospective purchasers in any material respect. Accordingly, such members shall not represent or imply that a boat may be purchased at a specified price when such is not the fact. Specified prices in conjunction with pictorial representations shall be the prices for which purchasers may purchase the advertised boat as pictured unless otherwise stated. For example, pictorial representations of a boat equipped with top, engine, anchor, sails or other equipment or accessories shall not be used in conjunction with the specified price of a stripped model unless it is conspicuously disclosed that the price does not include such items as the case may be.

Additionally, no representation shall be made to the effect that the price of a boat has been reduced from a price which, in fact, is a fictitious price; or that the price is a special or sale price when in fact it is the regular selling price of the boat.

Any unqualified reference to a "list price" shall be with respect to the advertiser's bona fide regular established current selling price of the advertised boat. A retailer referring to a list price not his own shall conspicuously disclose whose "list price" is referred to (e.g. "manufacturer's list price"). Manufacturers and other distributors of boats shall not publish or distribute as "manufacturer's list prices" or "list prices" etc. any price list showing prices higher that those at which the boats are regularly and customarily sold in the trading areas in which such price lists are published or distributed.

Members of the industry shall not make or publish any false, misleading or deceptive representation, through advertising or otherwise, concerning installment sales contracts to be used in the sale of boats, the terms or conditions of such contracts, the down payment to be required, the rate of interest or the financing to be charged, or respecting any other matters relative to such contracts.

Rule 7—GUARANTEES, WARRANTIES, ETC.:

Advertising of products shall not contain representations that a product is guaranteed without clear and conspicuous disclosure of:

(1) the nature and extent of the guarantee, *and*

(2) any material conditions or limitations in the guarantee which are imposed by the guarantor, *and*

(3) the manner in which the guarantor will perform thereunder, *and*

(4) the identity of the guarantor.

Representations that a product is guaranteed "for life" or has a "lifetime guarantee" in addition to meeting the above requirements, shall contain a conjunctive and conspicuous disclosure of the meaning of "life" or "lifetime" as used (whether that of the purchaser, the product, or otherwise).

Guarantees shall not be used which under normal conditions are impractical of fulfillment or which are for such a period of time or are otherwise of such nature as to have the capacity and tendency of misleading purchasers or prospective purchasers into the belief that the product so guaranteed has a greater degree of serviceability, durability or performance capability in actual use than is true in fact.

Rule 8 — DISCLOSURE OF CAPACITY LIMITATIONS OF BOATS AS TO WEIGHT AND ENGINE:

In the offering for sale of boats, members of the industry shall clearly and conspicuously disclose material facts as to the safe maximum weight and engine capacity of such boats when the failure to so disclose has the capacity and tendency or effect of misleading or deceiving prospective boat purchasers. For example, sellers of boats with seats for X number of passengers, but which are not capable of carrying that number without subjecting such passengers to hazards from overloading, shall disclose the safe maximum capacity of such boats, under normal use, e.g. "maximum recommended capacity 800 lbs." Likewise sellers of boats which cannot be used safely under normal conditions with an engine having in excess of X horsepower shall disclose such limitations, e.g. "takes motors up to 15 H.P."

The remainder of the proposed trade rules cover trade practices such as exclusive deals, price fixing, defamation of competitors, trade discrimination and other matters which only indirectly affect the boat buyer. The rules were drawn up after lengthy investigation by the Federal Trade Commission and the practices listed and prohibited above were widely enough exercised, in the opinion of the FTC, to call for remedial action.

CHAPTER XXXII

A Boatmanship Quizzer—
How Are Your Skipper Skills?

1. What basic piloting equipment should be carried on every boat no matter how small?
    a. Don't need any as I never go out of sight of land! . . . . _____
    b. Those listed in the Federal Boating Act of 1958 . . . . _____
    c. Compass and deviation card, chart of water cruised, dividers, course protractor, watch or clock, tide and current tables, lead line . . . . _____
    d. The equipment on the boat when I bought it . . . . _____
2. Your watch shows that you required 7-1/2 minutes to cover a measured mile on your chart; what was the speed of your boat?
    a. Eight miles per hour ——— b. Seven & one half miles per hour_____
    c. No idea, but I know the dealer said my boat would do 30 knots. . _____
    d. Eight nautical miles per hour . . . . _____
3. Careful skippers carry a sounding line (lead line) on board their boat at all times; how are depths of water corresponding to 1, 2, 3, 4, 5, 6, and 7 fathoms indicated?
    a. With pieces of colored string tied in every six feet. . . . . _____
    b. Depth of 1 fathom by one strip of leather; of 2, by two strips of leather; of 3, by three strips of leather; of 4, by one rag; of 5, by two rags; of 6, by three rags; then repeat the sequence . . . . . _____
    c. Don't mark mine, just tie knots in it! . . . . _____
    d. Depths of 1 fathom with nothing; of 2, with two strips of leather; of 3, with three strips of leather; of 4, with nothing; of 5, with a white rag; of 6, with nothing; of 7, with a red rag . . . . _____
4. When sailing in localities of westerly variations, on a boat heading with deviation west, do you steer to right or left of the true course?
    a. To right . . . . ——— b. To left . . . . _____
    c. The compass points "North," so I steer by what it says . . . . . . _____
    d. Don't need a compass . . . . _____
5. What is your compass reading when converting (uncorrecting) a true course of 037 to a compass course, with a variation of 6W and a one point westerly deviation?
    a. 032 . . . . . _____ b. 037 . . . . _____ f. 020 . . . . _____
    d. 030 . . . . . _____ e. 044 . . . . _____ c. 054 . . . . _____
6. What is a way of determining the deviation of your compass?
    a. By asking another skipper cruising with you what his deviation is . . . . _____
    b. By a simultaneous comparision of compass bearings on a known object with its magnetic bearing . . . . _____

c. By asking the compass manufacturer to provide me with a "Deviation Card" ....
　　d. By taking the deviation from the chart and/or local coast pilot..
7. In turning a single engine, right-hand wheel, power boat in a narrow or restricted area, is it better to turn to port or to starboard?
　　a. It makes no difference ....
　　b. Turn to port when going ahead and to starboard when going astern ....
　　c. Put the helm hard over and full power will get you around in the shortest possible space ....
　　d. To port, if turn may be safely made in one movement; if alternate ahead and astern must be used, go ahead to starbord with short "shots" of power and astern to port with short "shots" of power until you get around to new heading ....
8. In coming alongside a float or pier with a single engine, right-hand wheel, power boat; the preferable method is to:
　　a. Head into wind or current, whichever is stronger, if both are negligible make a port side landing ....
　　b. Boats with 177 or more horsepower should come alongside on either port or starboard ....
　　c. Always make a port side landing with a single engine boat since it's right-hand screw backs best to port ....
　　d. Come as near as possible under power and ask attendants to pull the boat in with lines that are there for that purpose .....
9. What is an anchor sentinel? What is its use?
　　a. Some one on board that is detailed to watch that the anchor isn't dragging. This sentinel work is a job no one likes ....
　　b. A light anchor, or a weight sometimes called a "Kellet," which is sent down the anchor line about halfway to the anchor. Such a device lowers the pull on the anchor line and greatly increases its holding power in bad weather or in anchorages with restricted space ....
　　c. This is a new patent anchor that has incorporated into its design an automatic warning device to indicate if it is dragging. Is very useful for boat protection ....
　　d. An anchor sentinel is a small buoy secured by light line to the anchor crown just prior to lowering. Its purpose is to show the skipper the exact location of his anchor. It is also an aid in preventing another skipper from crossing his anchor line with yours since he can readily see the relative position of both your boat *and* anchor ....
10. You are bringing your power boat down river with an appreciable current; what is the preferred method of picking up a mooring?
　　a. Approach the mooring with the boat's keel in line with the current; with hard astern, stop the boat and hold position with throttle and rudder so the mooring can be picked up over the bow ....
　　b. Go past the mooring and circle back to it upstream, slow down with the boat headed directly into mooring and current (do

not let the bow swing out of the line of the current), the mooring may now be picked up over the bow or alongside as headway and position is controlled with the throttle .... _____

    c. With a powerful enough boat you approach a mooring from any direction, hold the boat in position with rudder and throttle, and have any person on board pick up the mooring without trouble or danger .... _____

    d. Approach mooring directly, but carefully; station crew or guests along the side you will pass on so some one may grab the mooring as it is momentarily alongside, reverse hard if you chance to overshoot and pick the mooring up over the stern or quarter .... _____

11. What are some advantages of patent anchors (such as the "CQR", Sea-Claw, Danforth & Northill) over the Navy and other heavy stockless types?
    a. Lighter weight so they and the anchor line can be thrown out farther when anchoring .... _____
    b. There are no advantages, the anchor that comes with the boat is the proper one .... _____
    c. Lighter weight, but with much greater holding power per pound; stows and handles easier, depends on design rather than weight to dig in and hold .... _____
    d. No real advantage other than advertising value; if there is an advantage, why do the Navy and big vessels use stockless "Navy" anchors? .... _____

12. What is the proper speed of a motorboat?
    a. The speed the boat was designed to go, depending on the condition of the water .... _____
    b. The speed the boats around me are going .... _____
    c. At a speed suitable to the time and place at which I can readily change course from headway to sternway .... _____
    d. As fast as I want. I'm insured and it's my boat, isn't it? ...... _____

13. What are the objects of the "Rules of the Road"?
    a. To make boating more difficult by having to remember details .. _____
    b. "Rules of the Road"? Never heard of them .... _____
    c. They apply only to commercial boats and are of no interest to me .... _____
    d. They are to prevent collisions at sea or on the water, and apply to all types of boats when not aground, at anchor, or made fast to the shore, a dock or a mooring .... _____

14. The boat whistle ("horn" to landlubbers) is always used for passing signals. What do you do if you have signaled one whistle blast for a port side passing and are answered by two blasts?
    a. Speed up and get the - - - - out of the way .... _____
    b. Reverse to stop headway, give the danger signal, and do not proceed until signals are straight and understood .... _____
    c. Report the other boat to authorized officials as a menace to navigation or as a slaphappy "tooter" .... _____
    d. Do nothing and continue on your way .... _____

15. What organization publishes the charts of coastwise waters?
    a. Hydrographic Office of the Navy Department .... _____
    b. Coast and Geodetic Survey Office of the Commerce Department .... _____
    c. The Government Printing Office, Washington, D.C. .... _____
    d. The U.S. Coast Guard .... _____
16. What organization publishes the tide and current tables predicting height and flow of water at reference stations, and difference data at subordinate stations?
    a. Hydrographic Office of the Navy Department .... _____
    b. Coast and Geodetic Survey Office of the Commerce Department .... _____
    c. Government Printing Office, Washington .... _____
    d. United States Coast Guard .... _____
17. What organization publishes the lights lists describing the characteristics of aids to navigation?
    a. Hydrographic Office of the U.S. Navy Department .... _____
    b. Coast and Geodetic Survey Office of the Commerce Department .... _____
    c. Government Printing Office, Washington, D.C. .... _____
    d. U.S. Coast Guard .... _____

The following are Correct (C) or Wrong (W). Indicate your choice.
18. The "Rules of the Road" is a list of the various aids to navigation found in inland waterways. .... _____
19. A privileged vessel is one which has the right of way. .... _____
20. A burdened vessel is one which is never required to answer signals. _____
21. A vessel indicates it is backing by three blasts on the whistle. .. _____
22. The only purpose of buoys is to mark out the channels leading to various points. .... _____
23. Combination buoys are lighted buoys with some form of sound signal. .... _____
24. Red buoys mark the left hand sides of channels, entering from seaward. .... _____
25. White buoys mark anchorages. .... _____
26. Numbers on buoys increase from seaward. .... _____
27. Even numbered buoys mark the left hand sides of channels entering from seaward. .... _____
28. Can buoys are cylindrical with flat tops. .... _____
29. Green lights are used only on buoys marking the left hand sides of channels entering from seaward. .... _____
30. Fixed lights are found on black buoys only. .... _____
31. Flashing lights are placed on either black or red buoys. .... _____
32. The order "rudder amidships" means put the rudder indicated on zero degrees. .... _____
33. The reverse course of SW x S1/4S is NE x N 3/4N. .... _____
34. The reverse course of 315 degrees is 135 degrees. .... _____
35. A red woolen rag on the hand lead line marks both seven fathoms and seventeen fathoms. .... _____

A BOATMANSHP QUIZZER

36. A binnacle is a marine growth which fouls the boat's bottom. ..... _____
37. Brass is a metal which retains magnetism. .... _____
38. A point is equal to 11-1/4 degrees. .... _____
39. A marlinspike is used to manipulate a capstan. .... _____
40. The way to check a line which is running out rapidly is to throw a turn around a bollard. .... _____
41. A fathom is a unit of length measuring six feet. .... _____
42. A knot is a unit of speed on water equal to 1 mile on land. ...... _____
43. A fire cannot burn in a cloud of carbon dioxide due to the lack of free oxygen. .... _____
44. A soda and acid extinguisher is serviceable for use on an electrical fire. .... _____
45. A simple overhand knot may be used to keep the end of a rope from unlaying. .... _____
46. A figure eight knot should never be used to keep the end of a rope from fraying. .... _____
47. A sheepshank may be used to take the strain off the weak part of a rope. .... _____
48. The sheet or becket bend is an imperfect square knot. .... _____
49. A square or reef knot will slip if used to tie together lines of different sizes. .... _____
50. A running bowline is obtained by tying a bowline with a small loop and passing the line through the loop. .... _____
51. When using two half hitches to make fast to a pile, the knot consists of a turn around the pile and a clove hitch around the standing part of the line. .... _____
52. A good knot is just as strong as a good splice. .... _____
53. Wire rope has a tendency to stretch when heated. .... _____
54. Wire rope is made of steel and copper alloy. .... _____
55. Fiber rope has a tendency to stretch when wet. .... _____
56. Fiber rope should be washed down with a high pressure steam to remove dirt and grit. .... _____
57. New fiber rope should be treated with oil at regular intervals to make it water resistant. .... _____
58. Manila rope has a higher working strain than sisal rope, the diameters being equal. .... _____
59. A rope of sufficient tensile strength to handle a load of 600 lbs. should not be selected to lift a load of 500 lbs. .... _____
60. The sea anchor is a cone-shaped canvas bag. .... _____

Column I lists various tidal terms, preceded by a question number. Column II lists, in irregular order, the explanation of these terms, preceded by a representative letter. In the space, write the letter which correctly fits the term.

Column I

61. Ebb tide _____

Column II

A. The water has no motion due to tides.

62. Flood tide _____
63. High water _____
64. Low water _____
65. Range _____
66. Slack water _____
67. Stand _____
68. Tidal currents _____

B. The greatest height to which water rises.
C. Moment when no vertical movement occurs.
D. Flowing of water in and out.
E. The tide is setting in.
F. Difference in height between low and high water.
G. The tide is running out.
H. Lowest level to which the tide falls.

The following are Correct (C) or Wrong (W). Indicate your choice.

69. A vessel, although aground, is legally under way. ...._____
70. The term "steam vessel" includes any vessel propelled by machinery, so far as the Rules of the Road are concerned. ...._____
71. When a vessel receives no answer within one minute to a signal requesting permission to overtake another vessel in a narrow channel, it may pass without assent by the other vessel. ...._____
72. Once an overtaking vessel's stern is ahead of the bow of the overtaken vessel, it may change course and speed at will. ...._____
73. When two vessels are meeting head on each should pass to the port side of the other. ...._____
74. One short blast of the whistle in an overtaking or head on meeting situation means that the vessel giving the signal wishes to keep the other vessel on its port side while passing. ...._____
75. When a vessel agrees with the action proposed by another vessel through a 1 or 2 blast signal it need not reply. ...._____
76. In a crossing or meeting situation a 1 blast signal may be answered by a 2 blast signal if the answering vessel does not agree with the signal. ...._____
77. Cross signals, that is answering 1 blast by 2 blasts, or vice versa, are not permissible under any circumstances. ...._____
78. Passing signals are given whenever vessels are in sight of each other. ...._____
79. Passing signals are never given at night. ...._____
80. Passing signals are not given during fog or when visibility is poor for other reasons. ...._____
81. The danger zone extends from dead ahead to 2 points abaft the starboard beam. ...._____
82. A burdened vessel has the burden of maintaining course and speed. ...._____
83. A government-owned vessel is called a privileged vessel. ...._____
84. The danger signal is 3 or more short blasts of the whistle. ...._____
85. All fog signals in inland waters must be given at 1 minute intervals. ...._____
86. Fog signals are not given at night. ...._____
87. Running lights must be lighted from 8:00 p.m. to sunrise while under way. ...._____
88. The inland rules apply only in waters that are completely surrounded by land. ...._____

89. "Lateral system" refers to marking the edges of channels by means of aids to navigation. .... _____
90. The shape of a buoy has no particular significance. .... _____
91. Conical buoys with pointer tops are known as nun buoys. .... _____
92. Can buoys are always painted black. .... _____
93. When can buoys are painted black, they always mark the left hand side of channels entered from seaward. .... _____
94. When nun buoys are painted red, they always mark the right hand side of channels entered from seaward. .... _____
95. Odd numbered buoys may be either black or red. .... _____
96. Even numbered buoys mark the right hand sides of channels entered from seaward. .... _____
97. Heading seaward from a harbor, the buoys on your starboard side are always red. .... _____
98. Coming from seaward the buoys are odd numbered nuns on your port side. .... _____
99. Striped buoys are sometimes numbered. .... _____
100. Mid-channel buoys may be either nuns or can. .... _____
101. Red lights are never placed on black buoys. .... _____
102. Green lights are never placed on red buoys. .... _____
103. A flashing light always shows white and red. .... _____
104. A light located on shore is called a fixed light. .... _____
105. Quick flashing lights indicate that special caution is required. .... _____
106. White buoys mark anchorages. .... _____
107. Quarantine anchorages are marked with yellow buoys. .... _____
108. You can always rely on a buoy being where it should be in accordance with an up-to-date chart. .... _____
109. A vessel aground at night with no anchors out is required to display running lights. .... _____
110. When a vessel is adrift with the engine shut down it should not display its running lights. .... _____
111. When the wind blows against the side of a boat the bow has a tendency to turn down wind. .... _____
112. When the wind blows against the port side of a boat the bow tends to turn to starboard. .... _____
113. It is easier to learn to handle a twin screw boat than one with a single propeller. .... _____
114. A twin screw boat will turn to starboard when the port engine is going forward while the starboard engine is in reverse. .... _____
115. A twin screw boat may be turned in the same manner as a single screw boat by using the rudder only. .... _____

Listed below in Column I are various knots. In Column II are listed the uses for these knots. For each item in Column I select the proper use in Column II and place the letter preceding that term in the space.

Column I   *Column II*

116. Two half hitches _____   A. Used to shorten a bight of rope.
117. Clove hitch _____   B. Used to make fast to a stanchion.

118. Round turn and half hitch _____   C. Used for bending a line to an anchor.
119. Sheepshank _____   D. An imperfect reef knot.
120. Blackwall hitch _____   E. Used to make fast, temporarily to a pile.
121. Granny knot _____   F. Used to secure hook to bight of rope quickly.
122. Figure of eight _____   G. Used to sling a man over the side.
123. Bowline _____   H. Used to prevent rope from unreeving through block.
124. Bowline on a bight _____   I. Used on mooring lines to pass over cleats.

The following are Correct (C) or Wrong (W). Indicate your choice.

125. Boats of all classes are required to carry a whistle. .... _____
126. The taffrail log is the boat's journal. .... _____
127. Athwart means a boat is off balance laterally. .... _____
128. Abaft means to stop. .... _____
129. A kedge is a small anchor used for warships. .... _____
130. Neap tides are the same as ebb tides. .... _____
131. A windlass is an instrument which determines the direction of the wind. .... _____
132. In a fog, the distance of a vessel from a pier can be determined by taking a sounding. .... _____
133. Latitude is the distance north or south of the equator. .... _____
134. A lubber's line represents the boat's center line. .... _____
135. The lubber's line follows the direction of the boat's bow. ..... _____
136. It is bad practice to use lye to clean a painted surface. .... _____
137. When painting a surface, the paint brush should be held at right angles to the wood. .... _____
138. The proper way to paint on wood is to stroke the brush against the grain of the wood. .... _____
139. Oily waste will not burn if oxygen is present. .... _____
140. Carbon dioxide extinguishers should be used on electrical equipment fires. .... _____
141. Carbon tetrachloride extinguishers should not be used in confined spaces. .... _____
142. Carbon monoxide is used in some types of fire extinguishers. ... _____
143. Lights on harbor and ocean-going boats do not differ. .... _____
144. A single flash at regular intervals is an occulting light. .... _____
145. Wet lines should be stowed in an air-tight locker. .... _____
146. Belayed lines should be slacked when wet. .... _____
147. Faking down means to coil a rope in a spiral fashion. .... _____
148. Flemish down means to lubricate a wire rope. .... _____
149. A boat not under control is subject to rules of the road. .... _____
150. Sailing vessels are not subject to rules of the road. .... _____
151. When meeting head on, vessels should bear port to port. ...... _____
152. An overtaking vessel is always the burdened vessel. .... _____
153. Boats coming out of a slip should give one short and one long blast. .... _____
154. A black spar buoy denotes an anchorage area. .... _____

155. Nun buoys are never all black. .... _____
156. Black can buoys are even numbered. .... _____
157. Red buoys are on the port side going seaward. .... _____
158. Boats may not pass close to a buoy colored black and white vertically. .... _____
159. Vessels at anchor are required to give whistle signals in a fog. ...... _____
160. Whistle signals should be sounded every four to six seconds. .... _____
161. The intervals on high seas are longer than those on inland waters. .. _____
162. The type of blast is the same whether on inland waters or high seas. .... _____
163. On high seas in a fog, vessels give two prolonged blasts every minute. .... _____
164. Red lights show through or around 10 points. .... _____
165. One blast answered by one blast is a cross signal. .... _____
166. Water should not be used on gasoline fires. .... _____
167. A red pennant signifiies small craft warning. .... _____
168. Hemp ropes should never be lubricated. .... _____
169. Two half hitches is the same as a clove hitch. .... _____
170. Some wire rope has hemp core. .... _____
171. Red buoys are even numbered. .... _____
172. Buoys painted red and black are odd numbered. .... _____
173. Red and black horizontal stripes indicate an obstruction buoy. .... _____
174. Spar buoys are not found on both sides of the channel. .... _____
175. Nun buoys are painted all black. .... _____
176. Can buoys are placed on starboard sides of channels entering from the sea. .... _____
177. Green buoy lights are placed on port side of channel entering from the sea. .... _____
178. White lights may be found on both sides of the channel. .... _____
179. If a boat requires 15 minutes to cover one mile, then the speed of the boat is four miles per hour. .... _____
180. 6-1/2 fathoms measures 39 feet. .... _____
181. 5 knots represents 5 nautical miles. .... _____
182. "Dead ahead" means a partially submerged spar is sighted. .... _____
183. "Purchase" is a tackle consisting of blocks and falls. .... _____
184. A "right hand line" is a line which is twisted from right to left, counterclockwise. .... _____
185. A "dinghy" is a small boat pennant. .... _____
186. "Diesel" refers to an oil burning internal combustion engine. .... _____
187. A "thwart" is a cross piece used in a bosun's chair. .... _____
188. A "float" refers to any kind of a raft. .... _____
189. A "gangway" is a portable bridge. .... _____
190. "Grapnel" is a light anchor. .... _____
191. "Snub" means to check a line temporarily. .... _____
192. 5 land miles equals 4.44 nautical miles. .... _____
193. 3 nautical miles equals 3.45 land miles. .... _____
194. Lights must be shown from 6 p.m. to 6 a.m. .... _____
195. Windward is the direction in which the wind is going. .... _____
196. Marrying a set of falls is to bind them together. .... _____
197. In a fog, the rapid ringing of a bell indicates a boat at anchor. .... _____

198. Spring lines are used at dock to prevent boats from moving ahead or astern. ....
199. A "painter" is the line at the bow of a small boat used for the purpose of towing. ....
200. The lee side of a boat is always on the starboard side. ....

ANSWER KEY

1-C	26-C	51-C	76-W	101-C	126-W	151-W	176-W
2-D	27-W	52-W	77-C	102-C	127-W	152-C	177-C
3-D	28-C	53-C	78-W	103-W	128-W	153-W	178-C
4-A	29-C	54-W	79-W	104-W	129-C	154-W	179-C
5-C	30-W	55-C	80-C	105-C	130-W	155-C	180-C
6-B	31-C	56-W	81-C	106-C	131-W	156-W	181-W
7-D	32-C	57-W	82-W	107-C	132-W	157-C	182-W
8-A	33-W	58-C	83-W	108-W	133-C	158-W	183-C
9-B	34-C	59-C	84-W	109-W	134-C	159-W	184-W
10-B	35-C	60-C	85-C	110-W	135-C	160-W	185-W
11-C	36-W	61-G	86-W	111-C	136-C	161-C	186-C
12-C	37-W	62-E	87-W	112-C	137-C	162-C	187-W
13-D	38-C	63-B	88-W	113-W	138-W	163-W	188-C
14-B	39-W	64-H	89-C	114-C	139-W	164-C	189-W
15-B	40-C	65-F	90-W	115-C	140-C	165-W	190-C
16-C	41-C	66-A	91-C	116-B	141-C	166-C	191-C
17-C	42-W	67-C	92-W	117-E	142-W	167-C	192-C
18-W	43-C	68-D	93-C	118-C	143-W	168-C	193-C
19-C	44-W	69-W	94-C	119-A	144-W	169-W	194-W
20-W	45-C	70-C	95-C	120-F	145-W	170-C	195-W
21-C	46-W	71-W	96-C	121-D	146-C	171-C	196-C
22-W	47-C	72-W	97-W	122-H	147-W	172-C	197-C
23-C	48-W	73-C	98-W	123-I	148-W	173-C	198-C
24-W	49-C	74-C	99-W	124-G	149-C	174-W	199-C
25-C	50-C	75-C	100-C	125-W	150-W	175-W	200-W

CHAPTER XXXIII

Free for the Boatman— Sources of Information

The oil companies are not overlooking the buying potential of the some 8,000,000 pleasure boat operators in the United States, and they are extending themselves in efforts to provide the boat-owners with material on all phases of boating. Among the free material available on request, are the following:

Mobile Oil Company. America's Waterways — a pamphlet listing the sources for charts and state recreational information, widely used as a general reference book and carries the Library of Congress Number 60-1843.

Radio-Weather Pamphlets — available for the East Coast, Central Area, and West Coast, showing the radio-telephone channels, procedures, commercial broadcasting stations and radio beacons.

Mobile Care for Your Boat and Engine — a listing of inboard and outboard engines and the lubricants and fuel recommendations.

Mobile Cruising Guides as follows:
  No. 1 Eastport, Maine to Barnegat Inlet, N.J.
  No. 2 Sandy Hook, N.J. to Jack-Jacksonville, Florida.
  No. 3 New York Waterways, Great Lakes and Mississippi River.
  No. 4 Puget Sound to San Diego, California.
  Southern Guide, Florida and Gulf Coast (published by the Standard Oil Company of Kentucky).

—*Available from the Mobil Oil Company, Small Craft Division, 150 E. 42nd Street, New York 17, N.Y.*

Texaco, Inc. Texaco Cruising Charts — ten charts in all covering every principal waterway throughout the breadth of the United States.

Texaco Lubrication Chart — covering all the lubricating points of inboard and outboard engines; plus the covering of all Diesel engines.

Texaco Navigators Cruise Plan — a unique cruising plan, aiding the boat operator in coordinating all the vital statistics necessary in laying out a cruise.

Texaco Conversion Card — convenient card for converting RPM's to knots to miles per hour.

Texaco Mixing Ratio Chart — Graphical relation for the proper blending of outboard oil with gasoline, relative to all manufacturers recommendations.

Buoyage Charts — depicting in color all major aids to navigation covering chief buoys and markers of the Intracoastal Waterway.

Texaco Waterway Bulletins — interesting and timely waterway bulletins covering the main channels and waterways in specified areas; also information on State and Federal taxation.

Available from the Small-Craft Department, Texaco, Inc., 135 East 42nd Street, New York 17, N.Y.

Gulf Oil Corporation: Current Tide Charts

Down the Hatch — a pamphlet on boating.

Gulf "Cruiseguides" as follows:

Harbors of Long Island Sound and Nearby Waters
Harbors of the South
Harbors on Inland Lakes and Rivers
Harbors of the Middle Atlantic States
Harbors of New England

Available from Public Relations Department, Gulf Oil Corporation, 17 Battery Place, New York 4, N.Y.

Esso Standard Oil Co. Safe Cruising is Happy Cruising —booklet.
Cruising Guides
Esso Log
Slide Rule for Calculating Distances
Weather Warning Card

Available only at Esso marinas in the 18 states and the District of Columbia in which Esso Standard conducts its business.

From the U.S. Government. A number of government publications are available free of charge. Some of these have been referred to earlier in this book.

From the U.S. Coast Guard, Washington 25, D.C. Rules of the Road, International-Inland, CG-169. Required whistle signals, and rules of the road for Inland Waters and oceans.

Rules of the Road, Great Lakes, CG-172. Required lights, whistle signals, and rules of the road.

Rules of the Road, Western Rivers, CG-184. Required lights, whistle signals, and rules of the road.

Equipment Lists (Lists of approved equipment) CG-190. Contains lists of approved and acceptable equipment as required by inspection laws.

From the Hydrographic Office, Navy Department, Washington 25, D.C. Notice to Mariners (weekly). To keep charts and Coast Pilots up to date. Contains discontinuances, establishments, and changes to aids, reports obstructions, danger areas, etc.

From Commander, Local Coast Guard District. Local Notice to Mariners. Items of interest within the District Boundaries.

From Commander, 9th Coast Guard District, Main Post Office Building, Cleveland, Ohio. Notice to Mariners, Great Lakes (weekly). To keep charts and Great Lakes Pilot up to date. Concerns discontinuances, establishments, and changes to aids. Reports obstructions, danger areas, etc.

FREE COURSES IN BOAT HANDLING AND SEAMANSHIP

The United States Power Squadrons

The United States Power Squadrons is a nationwide association of boatmen, established in 1914 "to establish a high standard of skill of the handling and navigation of yachts; to encourage the study of the science of navigation; to cooperate with the agencies of the United States Government charged with the enforcement of laws and regulations relating to navigation; and to stimulate interest in activities which will tend to the upbuilding of our Navy, Coast Guard and Merchant Marine."

In recent years, with the huge expansion of boating, the free courses offered by the USPS have become their most prominent activity. Over 275 squadrons in the continental United States, Alaska, Hawaii, the Canal Zone, Okinawa and Japan offer the basic course in elementary piloting without charge to all those interested in boating. While membership in the association is restricted to men who have passed the basic courses and are invited to join, most classes are open to both men and women, and most squadrons encourage youngsters to attend. On completion of the course, certificates are awarded. Members are privileged to fly the USPS flag, to wear its uniform and to participate in its social and educational activities.

The Courses

Classes are generally held one evening a week for about ten weeks. There is no charge for the course or for materials, although most students buy a text book and a set of dividers and parallel rules or a course protractor for use in the later sessions. While the course of study is designed to prepare for the examination at the end of the course, there is no obligation to take the test.

The Piloting and Small Boat Handling Course covers the following subjects:

Safety Afloat: Avoiding accidents. Safeguarding against fire. Proper installation of fuel system. Handling gasoline safely. Ventilation of engine and fuel compartments. Fire fighting and life saving equipment. First aid. Signalling for assistance. Radio telephone. Weather reports and weather maps. Operation in fog. Danger of carbon monoxide poisoning. Grounding. Overloading.

Seamanship: Common nautical terms and their meanings. Types of motor and sailing vessels. Ground tackle and its use. Various types of anchors, their advantages and disadvantages. Rules for anchoring. Maneuvering in close quarters. Getting under way. Docking and mooring under various conditions of wind and current. Marlinspike seamanship. Rope and its care. Knots, bends, hitches and splices. Whipping, coiling, faking and flemishing. Making fast to a cleat and bollard. Man overboard.

Small Boat Handling: The basic limitations of small boats. Safe power for outboards. The capacity and stability of small boats. The steering capability of outboard-powered boats. Maintenance of outboard motors while underway. Special precautions for small boats in rough water and when passing large ships. Swamping and rescue. Towing and anchoring.

Equipment and Government Regulation: The Motor Boat Act. Equipment required by law. Other equipment that should be aboard. The numbering act. Documenting, licensing and inspection Tools and spare parts. Accident reports. Electronic equipment. The flying of flags on various types of boats. The flag of our country. The yacht ensign.

Rules of the Road: Rules governing right of way. Various situations. Passing whistle signals. Essential differences among International, Inland and Great Lakes rules. Fog signals given by various types of craft. Arc of visibility. Distance of visibility required. Location on vessel. Meanings of light combinations. Inland and International rules.

Aids to Navigation: Lighthouses, lightships, buoys and other aids to navigation installed and manned by the Coast Guard. Lighthouses — structural features, characteristics of lights, and of fog signals. Visibility. Range. Lights. Lightships. Radio beacons and distance finding station. Buoys — types, coloring and numbering. Characteristics of buoy lights. Unlighted aids. Intracoastal Waterway aids. Government publications. Light lists, Notice to Mariners, Coast Pilots.

The Mariner's Compass: Kinds of compasses. Their construction, installation and care. Various kinds of cards. Variation and deviation. True, magnetic and compass courses. Rules for applying variation and deviation to convert from one type of course to another.

Charts and Piloting: Types of charts used by mariners. Sources from which charts may be obtained. Symbols and abbreviations. Piloting instruments. The lead and lead line. Logs. The course protractor. The pelorus or bearing finder. Laying a course. Bearings.

Advanced Grade USPS Courses

The Seamanship Course: This course is open to all members in good standing

— and usually to women who have completed the first course. It has been organized primarily as a source of information for the benefit of the newcomer to the water, and should also prove of value to the experienced boatman as a refresher. The subject matter includes material applying to sail as well as power boats.

The subjects include: types of boats used by yachtsmen, equipment required by law and for safety and comfort, conditions affecting the handling of boats under power, principles of sailing, anchoring and mooring, docking and undocking, handling under adverse conditions, and personnel relations afloat. These topics are dealt with from the viewpoint of the practical boatman. The purpose is to afford the student background he would otherwise acquire only by long experience on the water, to give him an understanding of the forces with which he has to deal in operating a yacht, and to bring to his attention practical solutions for the problems he will sooner or later encounter afloat. A portion of each class period is devoted to marlinspike seamanship in order to develop a working knowledge of the more useful knots, bends, hitches and splices.

The Advanced Pilot Course: This course is concerned with the basic principles and more important practices of piloting. It includes a thorough review of the mariner's compass with particular emphasis on course conversion, allowance for the so-called "compass errors," and the use of the Napier diagram. Charts and chart work are treated and instruction given in the laying of courses and in the determination of position by bearings, angles and soundings. The student is acquainted with the various government publications of value to the pilot. Problems involving the computation of height of tide and strength of current at a given time are worked out by reference to the Tide Tables and Current Tables. As a means of emphasizing the practical applications of the principles taught and developing skill in plotting, homework problems in the form of imaginary cruises are assigned, for which the student is expected to do the necessary chart work and provide the important plotting information that would be required by the skipper. With the information in this course, a member is well qualified to enter any of the predicted log races or navigators' contests.

The Junior Navigator Course: This course is intended to afford a working knowledge of the principles of dead-reckoning and to serve as an introduction to the techniques employed in determining position at sea by means of celestial observations. It is open to squadron members who have attained the Seaman and Advanced Pilot grades.

Consideration is given to the earth as a sphere and to the methods employed for delineating its surface on a plane for use as a chart. The Mercator chart and the small area plotting sheet are studied. Emphasis is placed on plotting methods for solving dead-reckoning problems, but the course also includes a brief treatment of the "sailings" including Mercator sailing, mid-latitude sailing and great circle sailing. To add interest and to aid in developing practical skill in plotting, an imaginary voyage is carried on for the period of the course and the homework assignments require the student to do the associated dead-reckoning work.

The introductory work on celestial navigation includes lessons on the subject of time, the nautical almanac and its use for obtaining the coordination of celestial bodies, star identifications, solution of the astronomical triangle or azimuth and intercept by one method, the Sumner line of position, and the practical use of the sextant. One of the requirements for the course is that the student shall take, work up and plot a number of practical sights.

The Navigator Course: After the JN course, this course is intended not only to develop greater skill in the taking of sights and higher precision in position finding, but also to afford the student insight into, and schooling in, the fundamental principles which underlie the practical work. The course supplements the work done in the JN course, and deals with alternative methods, special cases and more advanced techniques.

Starting with the basic concepts and definitions of nautical astronomy, consideration is given to the system of coordinates employed in describing the positions of celestial bodies. The civil, solar and sidereal systems are studied together with the commonly used instruments for determining time — the chronometer and watch. The theory, use and care of the sextant are treated and the student is required to take and compute a considerable number of practical sights in order to become familiar with the instrument and to develop skill in its use. Thorough instruction is given in the solution of an astronomical triangle, lines of position, meridian altitudes, determination of azimuth, star identification, and the computation of time of sunrise, sunset, moonrise and moonset. Considerable emphasis is placed on the development of orderly methods for carrying on the day's work of the navigator at sea, and the final examination includes a short imaginary voyage for which the student is required to work out the various steps in the navigator's day's work.

Weather Course: This is a course in assembling and interpreting weather information and signs to enable the skipper to prepare his own local forecasts. The work is intended to foster an awareness of weather phenomena, to enable him to understand and anticipate weather developments.

The subjects treated include: the characteristics and structure of the atmosphere, what weather is and its basic causes, the normal development and movement of weather over the world, and the fundamental factors that enter into weather forecasting. The instrumental and visual observations which the skipper can make afloat are considered. Cloud sequences and the weather they predict are studied. Air masses, fronts, storms and fog are the subjects of lectures. The use of the daily weather map is stressed and other sources of useful weather information, including radio weather broadcasts, are brought to the student's attention. Throughout the course the student is encouraged to make observations and predictions in order to gain experience in applying the principles taught and develop greater insight into weather phenomena.

Engine Maintenance Course: This course is offered on an elective basis to members. It is designed to familiarize the student with the general construction, operating principles, maintenance and repair of marine engines, both gasoline and diesel, with their cooling, electrical, fuel and lubricating systems, and with the associated propulsion components — clutches, shafting and propellers. Since one of the major objectives is to make the boat owner more self-reliant afloat, "trouble-shooting" is given considerable emphasis. Safety measures are also stressed. The course is not intended to produce trained mechanics, but rather more resourceful boat engine operators. Approximately ten class sessions are involved.

Sail Course: This elective course is also open to members. It covers such things as terminology, types of rigs and hulls, auxiliaries under power and sail, signals and rules of the road, theory of sailing, balance of hull and sails, stability, true and apparent wind, points of sailing, sailing in heavy weather, rigging and sails, handling, piloting, anchoring, mooring and docking, getting underway, fog and night sailing, trouble, cruising and laying up and fitting out.

For Information on USPS Classes

The opening of classes by a local USPS is generally announced in the community newspapers; through posters in schools, boatyards, marine dealers, etc. Also, for locations and dates you may write to USPS Headquarters, Box 510, Englewood, New Jersey.

The Coast Guard Auxiliary

In 1939 the Coast Guard Auxiliary was authorized by an act of Congress to assist the Regular Coast Guard to promote safety on the water. It is the only boating organization having such official recognition. In addition to its work of patrolling boating areas, its inspection service and the award of approval decals, the Auxiliary also conducts numerous courses in safe boating.

The primary course is "Basic Seamanship and Safe Boathandling," which is an eight-lesson course followed by an examination. Completion of the course and passing the examination will win a certificate for the amateur boatman. Members of the Coast Guard Auxiliary enjoy a program of instruction, activity and social life afloat and ashore.

For membership in the Coast Guard Auxiliary, completion of the basic course is *not* required. Applicants for membership must be at least 17 years of age, United States citizens, and have at least one-fourth interest in a boat, radio station or aircraft. However, the "ownership" requirement may be waived for applicants with special qualifications, such as long boating experience, prior Coast Guard or Navy service, etc. Women are also eligible for membership. There is an all-girl flotilla in New Jersey and there are a number of "mixed" flotillas.

The Coast Guard Course

The basic Coast Guard Auxiliary course is somewhat less comprehensive than the Power Squadron course. It includes the following lessons:

Lesson One — "Preview and Prospectus"
Lesson Two — "Seamanship (Part I)"
Lesson Three — "Seamanship (Part II)"
Lesson Four — "Aids to Navigation"
Lesson Five — "Charts and Compass"
Lesson Six — "Rules of the Road"
Lesson Seven — "Safe Motorboat Operation (Part I)"
Lesson Eight — "Safe Motorboat Operation (Part II)"
Final Examination (9)

The copyrighted booklet used in the instruction course explains the scope of the course as:

How the rudder and propeller effect a boat's motion.
How to anchor and secure to a dock or mooring.
What to do when the going gets rough.
How to handle an outboard.
How to tie knots and make splices in line.
How buoys, lighthouses and other aids to navigation can assist you.
How to use your compass and chart.
Your rights and responsibilities in operating your boat.
How to get your boat numbered or documented.
How to equip your boat properly.
What to do in case of engine failure.
What to do in case of distress.

A nominal charge is made for the text used in the course, which was prepared by the Auxiliary National Headquarters. There is no charge for the course, but in some areas an additional charge for building services may be assessed; for example, to pay for the school custodian or a "use" charge for the use of a public building.

*For Information on
Coast Guard Auxiliary Courses*

These courses, too, are generally announced in the press and often by posters and notices on local bulletin boards. Information on coming classes, enrollment dates, etc. is available from the Coast Guard District offices.

For information on the instruction courses, and also on boat safety checks, and auxiliary membership, write to the Director of Auxiliary nearest you, at the following offices:

1st Coast Guard District
703 Customhouse
Boston 9, Mass.

2nd Coast Guard District
805 Olive Street
St. Louis 1, Mo.

3rd Coast Guard District
Customhouse
New York 4, N.Y.

U.S. Coast Guard
Room 804, Customhouse
Philadelphia 6, Pa.

5th Coast Guard District
P.O. Box 540
Norfolk 1, Va.

7th Coast Guard District
150 S.E. Third Avenue
Miami 32, Fla.

8th Coast Guard District
Room 328, Customhouse
New Orleans 16, La.

9th Coast Guard District
Main Post Office Building
Cleveland 13, Ohio

11th Coast Guard District
706 Times Bldg.
Long Beach 2, Calif.

12th Coast Guard District
630 Sansome Street
San Francisco 25, Calif.

13th Coast Guard District
618 Second Avenue
Seattle 4, Wash.

14th Coast Guard District
P.O. Box 4010
Honolulu, Hawaii

17th Coast Guard District
P.O. Box 2631
Juneau, Alaska

A STATE TRAINING PROGRAM

New York, in 1960, was the first state to institute a statewide training program for young boat operators. This project was instituted as a result of changes in the State Boating Law which provided that motorboats on State waters may be operated by:
1. all persons over 14 years of age.
2. all persons between 10 and 14 years of age who have earned safety certificates.
3. all persons 14 years or younger who are accompanied by a person over 14 or a person who has earned a safety certificate.

The "safety certificates" referred to are issued by the Commissioner of Conservation to children 10 to 14, who have satisfactorily completed the New York State Boating Safety Course. It was anticipated that about 20,000 certificates would be issued during the first nine months of the program.

The courses are given by volunteers from boating organizations, camp counsellors, teachers and others who have attended training institutes for this purpose and who have been certified by the Division of Motor Boats as instructors.

The course consists of eight units that can be taught in a minimum of four hours. Students in the course will be provided with a manual, workbook and examination. The course and the training materials are furnished free by the State, the instructors are unpaid, and local organizations furnish the classrooms or other teaching areas. There are no restrictions on those taking the course except the age requirement (10-14). Classes consist of not less than 6 nor more than 30 students.

According to the State Conservation Department, all funds received from boat registration fees are earmarked for boating activities in New York State, and these funds will support the program.

The Department reports that it has received inquiries from a number of other states who are planning similar programs. Information is available from the Division of Motor Boats, Conservation Department, State Campus Site, Albany, N.Y.

Glossary of Nautical Terms

Abaft — Astern of, toward the stern; at the rear of, with reference to a boat or any part of it. Opposite to forward of.

Abeam — In a direction 90° from the centerline of a vessel; opposite the waist of the vessel. Used to refer to an object outside the vessel.

Aid to navigation — A charted mark to assist navigators, such as buoys, beacons, lights, radio beacons, etc. Generally, any information published for the assistance of mariners.

Amidships — Generally speaking, the word amidships means in the middle section of a vessel. The point of intersection of two lines, one drawn from the stem to the stern, the other across the beam (or widest part) is the actual amidships. By extension, amidships is also employed to locate any object or part of the ship lying in the line of the keel.

Apron — 1. The portion of a wharf lying between the waterfront edge and the warehouse or wharf shed. 2. An inner stem fitted behind the stem to reinforce it.

Athwartships — At right angles to the fore-and-aft line of a vessel; across the vessel in a direction at right angles to the keel.

Atmospheric pressure — The pressure exerted by the weight of the earth's atmosphere. Its standard value at sea level is about 14.7 pounds per square inch, corresponding to a barometric height of 30 inches.

Autoalarm — Radio-electrical apparatus connected to a ship's wireless set for the reception of emergency radio signals. The use of this device relieves the radio operator of continuous radio watch.

Auxiliaries — A term applied on ships to all machinery and apparatus forming the nonpropulsive equipment of the vessel; in sailing boats to the supplementary engine or motor used for propulsion.

Bar — A ridge or succession of ridges of sand or other substances, especially such a formation extending across the mouth of a river or harbor, and which may obstruct navigation.

Batten — 1. Long strip of metal or wood used aboard ship for various purposes. 2. To "batten down" the hatches means cover up and fasten down. Usually said of hatches when they are covered with tarpaulins that are fastened down with hatch battens. (See sail batten in text.)

Belay — 1. To take one or more S turns with a rope around a cleat, set of butts, or any other fixed point. 2. To cancel an order.

Bending shackle — Device used to secure an anchor chain to the anchor.

Bight — 1. The bend or loop in a rope; the double part when it is folded. In knotting, that part of the rope between the bitter end and the standing part. 2. A bend in a coast line, in a river, or a mountain range.

Bitt (s) — A strong post of wood or metal for belaying, fastening and working ropes, cables and mooring lines. They are usually found in pairs.

Blinker signaling — The transmission of optical signals by the Morse code, using fixed electric lamps or portable signaling lamps.

Bollard — Single or double cast metal posts or wooden posts secured to a wharf and used for mooring vessels by means of lines extending from the vessel and fastened to the posts.

Bower, bower anchor — One of the anchors carried on each bow and designated as port bower and starboard bower. They are the main anchors by which a ship rides.

Bow Line — A line leading from the bow of a vessel.

Breast — 1. To "breast the sea" is to meet a wave or swell head on. 2. To "breast in" is to heave a vessel sideways toward a wharf or another vessel. 3. To "breast off" is to shove out from a wharf or another vessel. 4. Breast line is a mooring line leading at an angle of about 90° from the fore-and-aft line of the vessel to a wharf or another vessel.

Bridge deck — A partial deck extending from side to side of a vessel over a comparatively short length amidships, forming the top of a bridge house or partial superstructure.

Bull nose — A closed chock at the bow of a vessel.

Bulwark — Light plating or wooden extension of the hull above an exposed deck, furnishing protection against weather.

Buoyed trip line — A line with one end fastened to the fluke of an anchor and the other to a buoy. Used on rocky bottom where the flukes may be caught and cannot be dislodged by the pull on the cable.

Catenary — The curve assumed by a chain or rope hanging freely between two points of support.

Chafing gear — A guard of canvas, rope or similar material placed around spars, lines or rigging to prevent wear.

Cleat — 1. A short piece of wood nailed transversely to a sloping gangway to provide sure footing. 2. A fitting of wood or metal with two horns used for securing lines.

Compass rose — A circle graduated in degrees, clockwise from 0° to at the reference direction to 360° and sometimes also marked to show compass points. Compass roses are placed at convenient locations on charts to facilitate measurement of direction.

Counter — The underside of the stern overhang abaft the rudder. Also known as the fantail.

Cross bearings — The bearings of two or more objects, crossing each other at the position of the observer. Used for plotting a boat's position on a chart when near a coast.

Deadlight — Strong shutters that screw down upon airport holes and keep water out in heavy weather.

Deadwood — The structure between the keel line and the sternpost.

Dividers — An instrument consisting in its simplest form of two pointed legs jointed by a pivot, and used principally for measuring distances or coordinates on a chart or map.

Drift lead — A heavy lead used when a

vessel is riding at anchor to a heavy sea, wind, or current to indicate whether the anchor is holding or dragging.

Dunnage — A term applied to loose wood or other material used in a ship's hold for protection of cargo.

Easing-out line — The line used to hold back a strain on something being eased out to prevent it from going out too quickly.

Eddy — A current of water or air running contrary to the main current, especially one moving circularly. Eddies occur principally on the downstream side of obstructions.

Fag end — The frayed end of a rope, also called cow's tail.

Fair-lead — Any fitting used for "running rigging" to pass around or through to guide it in the required or desired direction.

Fairway — The parts of the river or harbor where the navigable channel lies; also called ship channel.

Fathometer — The trade name for a widely used echo sounder. Used to determine depth of water.

Fender — Term applied to various devices, fixed or portable, serving to cushion the shocks and protect the hull when a vessel comes in contact with another object or vessel; also called bumper.

Fid — A tapering pin of wood or metal used to open the strands of a rope for splicing, to stretch eyes, etc. 2. A square bar of wood or iron used to support the topmast.

Forefoot — A term applied to the intersection of the curved portion of the stem with the keel.

Founder — To fill with water and sink at sea.

Freshen the nip — An expression used to describe the shifting of position of a rope or chain to reduce friction caused by chafing.

Gaff — The spar that stands or hoists on the after side of the mast and supports the head of a sail. A vessel so fitted is termed gaff-rigged.

Guy — A rope used to steady an object when hoisted or lowered or a steadying rope used to support a spar in a horizontal or inclined position.

Headland — A precipitous promontory or cape.

Headsail — Any sail set forward of the foremast.

Headway — A vessel's motion forward or ahead.

Heaver — A smooth, round wooden staff used for twisting or heaving tight a rope or strap.

Intercardinal point — Any of the four directions midway between the cardinal points; northeast, southeast, southwest, northwest.

Jew's harp — A lyre-shaped shackle for joining the chain cable to the anchor so that another cable may be fastened in addition to the ordinary chain.

Jib-headed sails — A general term for all sails of triangular shape, such as jibs, staysails, etc.

Jury rig — Any makeshift device or apparatus contrived as a substitute for regular gear.

Leadsman — One who takes soundings or determines the depth of water by using a leadline or hand lead.

Light stuff — Small line aboard a boat, such as 12-thread stuff, marline, seizing stuff or spun yarn. Also called small stuff.

Limber hole — In general holes in a structure near a deck or flat worked in to facilitate drainage where desired. Also called watercourse, drainage hole.

Load waterline — The waterline to which a vessel is immersed when loaded and on an even keel.

Loran — Derived from the words "long range navigation." An electronic navigation system by which lines of position are determined by measuring the difference in the time of reception of synchronized pulse signals from two fixed transmitters.

Manrope — A general name used for ropes used as safety lines; the ropes which hang down a vessel's sides to aid in ascending or descending.

Maximum ebb — The greatest speed of an ebb current. The ebb is the tidal current moving away from land or down a tidal stream.

Maximum flood — The greatest speed gf a flood current. The flood current is the tidal current moving toward land or up a tidal stream.

Messenger — A light line made fast to a heavier line or hawse and used to take the heavier line across an intervening space. The messenger line is thrown, and then the heavier line is hauled in.

Mooring line — The cables or ropes used to tie a vessel to another vessel or to a wharf.

Mooring pendant — A small chain which has one end fastened to a mooring buoy and the other to the ground chain of the anchor.

Nautical mile — The standard unit of measure for marine navigation and for work with the Mercator chart. The nautical mile is 6,080 feet, being for practical purposes the length of one minute of arc of a meridian or of the equator. Also called Admiralty mile (Great Britain).

Oakum — A calking material of tarred hemp fiber. Used to calk seams in wooden decks or between strakes of planking.

Outhaul — A rope for hauling out the corners of a sail to the end of the boom or gaff.

Outrigger — A projecting support for a rowlock, or a projecting contrivance at the side of a boat to prevent capsizing.

Pelican hook — A quick release hook used wherever rapid release is desired. Consists of a hinged hook held together by a ring or bridgepiece. When the ring is knocked off, the hook swings open.

Pendant — A length of wire or rope with a block or thimble spliced in one end to connect rigging.

Pitch — The motion of a boat as the bow and stern move up and down in opposite directions — bow up, stern down (motion along the boat's transverse axis). Pitching as caused by the boat's bow and stern being raised and lowered as the vessel passes through successive crests and troughs of waves.

Pitch pole — The motion of a boat which, through the force of a breaking sea, is turned stern over bow, or vice versa, in a sort of half-somersault action.

Plotting — Laying down on a chart the

position of a vessel, or of a place, or of the boat's course.

Quay — A wharf approximately parallel to the shore line and accommodating boats or ships on one side only, the opposite side being attached to the shore.

Range finder — An optical instrument for meaasuring the distance to an object.

Reeve — The act of threading a line or wire through an opening; especially referring to the process of threading the fall on a purchase; setting a pulley.

Relative bearings: See diagram at end of chapter.

Relative humidity — The percentage of water saturation of the air; the ratio of actual vapor pressure to the vapor pressure corresponding to saturation at the prevailing temperature.

Residual magnetism — Magnetism that remains after removal of the magnetizing force.

Rigging — The lines and/or wires of a vessel; collective term for all the stays, shrouds, halyards and lines that support a vessel's masts and booms and operate its movable parts. Rigging is known as *standing* or *running* rigging. Standing rigging is rigging that is fixed in place to support masts, king posts, etc. Running rigging is rigging that is movable within its fairleads and blocks.

Roadstead — An area of water where ships and boats can ride safely at anchor. An open anchorage generally protected by shoals.

Roller — A stout bar rotating on its longitudinal axis, often tapered to a minimum diameter at its midpoint, used to protect a rope from friction wear, as at a mooring chock.

Rollers — A succession of long, heavy swelling waves caused by a recent gale or distant storm.

Rolling — The motion of a ship swinging from side to side (motion along the longitudinal axis) caused by the pressure of the waves on the side of the vessel.

Rose box — The bilge pump suction point in the bilges or in the double bottom of larger craft.

Running block — A block fixed or attached to the object to be raised or moved.

Sea buoy — The first buoy encountered, coming from seaward, marking a channel or entrance to a harbor.

Sea painter — A long line leading from a dinghy or lifeboat to a boat or ship, used to steer the towed craft clear of the tower when afloat and under way.

Seaway — 1. The progress a vessel is making through water. 2. The navigable portion of the sea or the position of vessel when a moderately heavy sea is running.

Secure — To make fast or safe; a signal to stop engines.

Selvage strap — A strap made by warping a piece of small stuff around two or more nails or spikes placed some distance apart. The ends of the small stuff are spliced or tied together with a reef knot and the whole is parceled. It is stronger than a spliced strap.

Semaphore — A method of signaling, employing moving arms or plates affixed to a high post or pole; a method of hand signaling with two flags.

Sextant — An instrument for measuring the angle between two objects.

Shackle bolt — A bolt which passes through the eye of a shackle and is secured by a shackle pin.

Sheave — A grooved wheel in a block over which a rope passes.

Sheer — 1. The longitudinal upward curve of a deck. 2. Sudden change in course. 3. To decline or deviate from a course, or cause a vessel to do so.

Sheer off — To move away from. The opposite of to bear toward.

Shoran — Derived from the words "short range navigation." A precision electronic position fixing system using a pulse transmitter and receiver and two transponder beacons at fixed points.

Short stay — A term used to describe the location of the anchor when it is directly underfoot.

Shroud — One of a set of strong wires or hemp ropes extending on each side of a masthead to the sides of a boat to support the masts laterally.

Signal halyard — Light lines running through sheaves at the gaff end for hoisting flags.

Skeg — 1. A knee timber connecting the stern post and keel. 2. A wood or metal arm extending abaft the keel with a bearing at its after end. It acts as a support for the rudder and protects the propeller. 3. The extension of the after part of the keel in a single screw vessel that supports the rudder post and stern post.

Slewing — 1. The action of yawing from side to side while at anchor or while being towed. 2. When a boom, spar, etc. sways on a fixed point.

Snatch block — A block which can be opened on one side to receive a bight of a rope.

Snub — 1. To let go of the anchor and bring the boat up quickly with a short range of cable. 2. To check a line or rope from running out by taking a turn around a cleat or bitt.

Sounding — The act of ascertaining the depth of water by sending a lead to the bottom.

Spar — A pole, such as a mast or boom.

Sponson — A projecting structure on the hull of a boat.

Stay — A strong rope, generally of wire, forming part of the standing rigging, used as a support for spars or masts. Stays lead from the head of a mast down to another mast or down to the deck. The stays leading forward or aft are called fore-and-aft stays; those leading across the boat are back-stays.

Steerageway — Sufficient headway for the vessel to respond to the rudder.

Stem — The most forward part of a vessel, the vertical or nearly vertical forward extension of the keel, to which the forward ends of the strakes are attached.

Sternway — The backward motion of a boat; the movement of a vessel being carried or impelled backward.

Still water level — Mean level, or that to which water surface would subside if wave action ceased.

Stream — 1. To place overboard and secure, as to stream a log or stream a sea anchor. 2. A current in the sea formed by the action of the wind. 3. A course of water flowing along a bed in the earth.

Superstructure — Any structure extending above the upper or main deck. Also called deck erection.

Swivel — A hoop or link in which provision is made, by means of a shank and collar, for circular movement.

Tackline — A line spliced into the eye at the bottom of the sail border for securing a flag to the halyards and separating the different flags of a signal. Can be used to separate each group of flags when more groups than one are shown on the same halyard.

Thimble — A round or heart-shaped fitting of metal, with a deep score in its outer surface, around which the eye may be spliced in hemp or wire rope. Protects the eye from the destructive effect of a link or shackle pin passing through it.

Three-arm protractor, station pointer — An instrument consisting of a circle whose outer circumference is graduated in degrees and minutes to which is attached one fixed arm and two arms pivoted at the center and provided with clamps so that they can be set to make any required angle with the fixed arm.

Thrust — The impulse or push exerted by a propeller in driving, or by a jet stream.

Thwart — Plank set athwartships just below the gunwales in an open boat; acts as a seat and also supports the sides.

Toggle — Any wood or metal pin fixed transversely through a line or wire, or through an eye or bight drawn through an eye.

Topmark — A characteristic shape secured at the top of a buoy or beacon to aid in its identification.

Transponder beacon — A beacon used in the Shoran system, which is activated by the transmitter on the ship and emits a signal when "triggered" to provide a fix.

Triatic stay — A wire, extending from the fore topmast to the main topmast or from the fore topmast to the top of the stack, used for signaling, Also called the signal stay.

Tricing line — A small rope used to haul up or lift any object either to stow or remove it.

Trick — A period of two hours of the helmsman at the wheel; a turn or spell of duty.

Trim — The longitudinal deviation of vessel from her designed waterline at a given draft. The condition of the boat with reference to her longitudinal position in the water. The difference between the draft forward and aft.

Trough — A wide depression in the ocean bottom, with gently sloping sides.

Tumbler lanyard — A small line made fast to the device for tripping or casting loose a stocked anchor (one which has a cross member atop the shank which turns the flukes into biting position).

Underfoot — A condition existing when the anchor is under the vessel's bow; said of an anchor dropped while the boat had headway.

Union jack — Flag consisting of the blue, star-studded field in the corner of

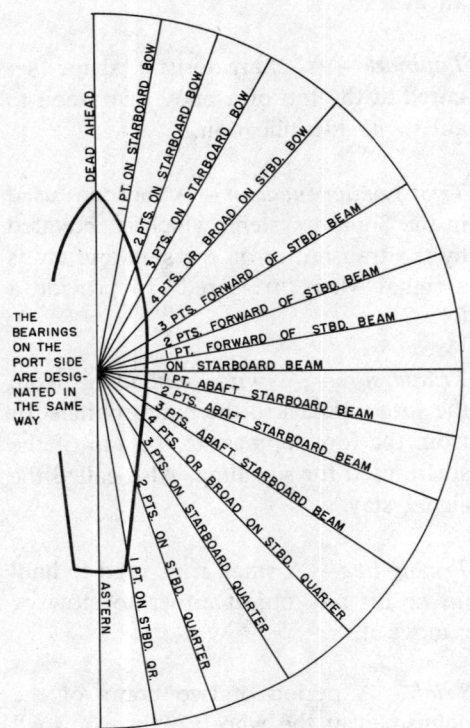

the national ensign, flown at the jackstaff by ships at anchor.

Vector diagram — A diagram of more than one vector (a straight line representing both direction and magnitude) drawn to the same scale and reference direction and in correct position relative to each other.

Veer — 1. To pay out cable or line. 2. To change direction of a vessel in reference to wind.

Waist — The amidships section of the main deck.

Warp — The act of moving a vessel broadside, or one end of a vessel broadside, by heaving on a line to a laid-out anchor or to the dock.

Weather deck — Any uncovered deck exposed to the weather.

Whipping — The binding of twine tied around a rope to keep it from fraying or unraveling.

Windsail — A sort of tube or tunnel made of canvas spread by wooden hoops or wire rings, serving to convey a current of fresh air below deck. On each side of the top are canvas wings designed and set to catch the wind. It is suspended from a stay by halyards and the wings are held by guys.

Yardarm — The outer quarter of a horizontal spar attached to the mast athwartships, equipped with blocks for reeving halyards.

Yardsail — Two or more sets of halyards for hoisting flags, shapes or lights for a signal secured to a cross spar.

Yaw — The motion of a boat as the bow and stern move from side in opposite directions (motion along the boat's vertical axis).

Acknowledgments

Material on "Guide to Outboard Cruising" is largely from the "Evinrude Guide to Outboard Cruising" by Fessenden S. Blanchard, courtesy the Evinrude Foundation.

"Care of the Boat, Motor and Equipment" is based on material provided by the Evinrude Foundation.

Material on "Fiberglass Boat Construction" from "The Future of Pleasure Boating," permission of Boating Associates, Cambridge, Massachusetts.

Material on propellers courtesy of Columbian Bronze Corporation, Freeport, New York.

Material on "Boating Safety" is adapted with the permission of the Marine Office of America from their "Safety Savvy," prepared by William H. Taylor.

Material on "Lightning Protection" from "Fire Protection Standards for Motor Craft," National Fire Protection Association.

"More About Ground Tackle" adapted from "Boat Security" by Edmund S. Terwilliger, manager, the Yacht Safety Bureau, by permission of Marine Office of America.

Information on the buoyage system and other navigational aids is largely from the U.S. Coast Guard publication "Aids to Navigation." The chapter, "Cautions Concerning Aids to Navigation" is largely from the monthly publication "Proceedings of the Merchant Marine Council." Readers should note that material in this book is not intended to be used for purposes of marine navigation. For actual marine navigation, reference should be made to current charts, light lists and other Coast Guard and Hydrographic Office publications.

Information and illustrations on the radio direction finder courtesy The Bendix Corporation, Pacific Division.

Information on "Marlinspike Seamanship" courtesy Plymouth Cordage Corp.

Information on "Refunds on Gasoline Taxes" is from the "Tax Refund Bulletin" of the Mobil Oil Company, and is reproduced with their permission.

The material on Marine Insurance is largely from the Marine Division, The Aetna Casualty and Surety Company and the Standard Fire Insurance Company of Hartford, Connecticut. Information was also provided by the Atlantic Mutual Insurance Company of New York City. The data on Outboard Insurance courtesy of Hardware Mutual Insurance of Wisconsin.

Suggestions and sketches in "Something About Sailboats" courtesy Talman Bigelow, President, Sailstar Boats.

Material on "Galley Cookery" is from "Making the Most of Meals Afloat," by Marcia Wiley, assistant editor of *Yachting,* used with the permission of Marine Office of America.

The material on Water Skiing and Water Skiing equipment, where not otherwise credited, is reprinted from "Consumer Reports," published by Consumers Union of Mount Vernon, N.Y., with the permission of that organization. The information on tow ropes was provided by the Plymouth Cordage Corporation and Abercrombie & Fitch, New York City.

Water Skiers' signals and other information on small-boat safety from the U.S.C.G. "Recreational Boating Guide," an informative booklet which is available from the Government Printing Office, Washington 25, D.C., for forty cents.

Material on engine conversion courtesy Barr Marine Products Co. and William J. Barber, Jenkintown, Pa.

Questions 1-17 in "A Boatmanship Quizzer" are by Lt. Col. Edward V. Chandler, USA, from the "Crow's Nest" of the American Yachtsmen's Association; other questions and answers are from maritime examinations given by the New York City department of personnel.

Numerous diagrams throughout this book are from the Department of the Army manual "Harbor Craft Crewman's Handbook."

STATE	TAIL LIGHT MOUNTED ON BOAT TRANSOM	HITCH REQUIRED?	SAFETY CHAIN REQUIRED?	MINIMUM GROSS WEIGHT BOAT TRAILERS REQUIRING BRAKES	WIDTH	LENGTH	HEIGHT	MAXIMUM LEGAL SPEED Towing Trailer On Open Highway DAY	NIGHT
MONTANA	LEGAL in addition to other lights	NO	NONE	1500 lbs.	8'	60' Single 60' L.O.A.	13½'	50 m.p.h.	50 m.p.h.
NEBRASKA	LEGAL	YES	SINGLE	—	8'	40' Single 60' L.O.A.	13½'	50 m.p.h.	50 m.p.h.
NEVADA	ILLEGAL	YES	SINGLE	1500 lbs.	8'	NONE	NONE	Reasonable and proper	Reasonable and proper
NEW HAMPSHIRE *NEW HAMPSHIRE TOLL ROADS	ILLEGAL	YES	NONE	3000 lbs.	8'	50' L.O.A.	13½'	50 m.p.h. (T) As posted	50 m.p.h. (T) As posted
NEW JERSEY *NEW JERSEY TOLL ROADS	LEGAL	YES	SINGLE	3000 lbs. (6d)	8'	35' Single 50' L.O.A. (T) 45' L.O.A.	13½'	50 m.p.h. (T) 60 m.p.h.	50 m.p.h. (T) 60 m.p.h.
NEW MEXICO	LEGAL	YES	NONE	3000 lbs.	8'	65' L.O.A.	13½'	70 m.p.h.	60 m.p.h.
NEW YORK *NEW YORK THRUWAY	LEGAL	YES	NONE	over 1000 lbs. uniladen	8' (T) to 12' under special hauling permit	50' L.O.A. (T) No maximum under special hauling permit	13' (T) to 13½' under special hauling permit	50 m.p.h. (T) 60 m.p.h.	50 m.p.h. (T) 60 m.p.h.
OHIO *OHIO TURNPIKE	ILLEGAL / LEGAL	YES	SINGLE	more than 2000 lbs.	8'	35' Single 60' L.O.A. (T) 50' L.O.A. with permit	13½' (T) 13½' to 14' with permit	65 m.p.h. (T) 50 m.p.h. (T) 55 m.p.h.	55 m.p.h. (T) 50 m.p.h. (T) 55 m.p.h.
NORTH CAROLINA	ILLEGAL	YES	NONE	4000 lbs.	8'	35' Single 50' L.O.A.	12½'	45 m.p.h.	45 m.p.h.
NORTH DAKOTA	LEGAL	YES	NONE	—	8'	60' L.O.A.	13½'	50 m.p.h. (T) 70 m.p.h. Max.; (T) 40 m.p.h. Min.	50 m.p.h. (T) 70 m.p.h. Max.; (T) 40 m.p.h. Min.
OKLAHOMA *OKLAHOMA TURNPIKES	LEGAL	YES	DOUBLE	3000 lbs.	8' (T) to 11½' by special permit	50' L.O.A. (T) No maximum under special hauling permit	13½' Turner (T) to 14½' by special permit; Will Rogers (T) to 15½' by special permit	50 m.p.h. (T) 70 m.p.h. Max.; (T) 40 m.p.h. Min.	50 m.p.h. (T) 70 m.p.h. Max.; (T) 40 m.p.h. Min.
OREGON	LEGAL	YES	DOUBLE	—	8' (T) 10'	35' Single 50' L.O.A. (T) 70' L.O.A.	12½' (T) 13½'	Reasonable and proper	Reasonable and proper
PENNSYLVANIA *PENNSYLVANIA TURNPIKE	LEGAL	YES	NONE (T) House trailers, or trailers similarly constructed or hitched, when being towed under adverse weather and/or road conditions may be excluded.	Over 1000 lbs. chassis & body wt.	8' (T) 10' Vehicles over 8' and not more than 10' in width are permitted on the Turnpike daylight hours only, Monday through Saturday noon from Labor Day to Memorial Day and daylight hours only, Monday through Friday noon from Memorial Day to Labor Day. Travel is prohibited for all vehicles in excess of 8' in width from one full day before to one full day after the following holidays: Good Friday, Easter, Memorial Day, Independence Day, Labor Day, Thanksgiving and Christmas.	35' Single 70' L.O.A.	12½' (T) 13½'	On four lane highways—50 m.p.h. On three lanes or less, restricted by local signs—40 m.p.h. (T) 50 m.p.h. Max.; (T) 35 m.p.h. Min.	On four lane highways—50 m.p.h. On three lanes or less, restricted by local signs—40 m.p.h. (T) 50 m.p.h. Max.; (T) 35 m.p.h. Min.
RHODE ISLAND	LEGAL	YES	DOUBLE	4000 lbs.	8½'	50' L.O.A.	12½'	35 m.p.h.	35 m.p.h.
SOUTH CAROLINA	LEGAL	YES	NONE	1500 lbs.	8'	40' Single 55' L.O.A.	12½'	55 m.p.h.	55 m.p.h.
SOUTH DAKOTA	LEGAL	YES	SINGLE	—	8'	35' Single 60' L.O.A.	13'	Reasonable and proper, subject to limitation by State Highway Commission	Reasonable and proper, subject to limitation by State Highway Commission
TENNESSEE	LEGAL	NO	NONE	1500 lbs.	8'	50' L.O.A.	13½'	65 m.p.h.	55 m.p.h.
TEXAS *DALLAS-FT. WORTH TURNPIKE	LEGAL	NO	NONE	3000 lbs.	8'	35' Single 50' L.O.A.	13½'	45 m.p.h.	45 m.p.h.
UTAH	ILLEGAL	NO	NONE	—	8'	60' L.O.A.	14'	60 m.p.h.	50 m.p.h.
VERMONT	LEGAL	YES	NONE	more than 1500 lbs.	8'	50' L.O.A.	12½'	45 m.p.h.	45 m.p.h.
VIRGINIA *RICHMOND-PETERSBURG TURNPIKE	ILLEGAL	YES	SINGLE	3000 lbs.	8' (T) to 10' by special permit	12½' (T) 13½' to 14' by special permit		45 m.p.h. (T) 60 m.p.h. Max.; (T) 40 m.p.h. Min.	45 m.p.h. (T) 60 m.p.h. Max.; (T) 40 m.p.h. Min.
WASHINGTON	LEGAL	YES	SINGLE	more than 2000 lbs.	8'	40' Single	13½'	Obey posted truck speed signs; usually 10 m.p.h. less than cars	Obey posted truck speed signs; usually 10 m.p.h. less than cars
WEST VIRGINIA *WEST VIRGINIA TURNPIKE	LEGAL	YES	SINGLE	more than 1500 lbs.	8'	35' Single (T) 60' L.O.A.	12½' (T) 13¾'	55 m.p.h. (T) 60 m.p.h.	55 m.p.h. (T) 60 m.p.h.
WISCONSIN	LEGAL	YES	DOUBLE	more than 3000 lbs.	8'	35' Single 50' L.O.A.	13½'	65 m.p.h.	55 m.p.h.
WYOMING	LEGAL	NO	NONE	1500 lbs.	8'	60' L.O.A.	13½'	60 m.p.h.	60 m.p.h.

	TAIL LIGHT MOUNTED ON BOAT TRANSOM	HITCH REQUIRED?	SAFETY CHAIN REQUIRED?	GROSS WEIGHT OF BOAT TRAILER REQUIRING BRAKES	WIDTH	LENGTH	HEIGHT	MAXIMUM LEGAL SPEED Towing Trailer On Open Highway DAY	NIGHT
ALABAMA	LEGAL	YES	NONE	———	7′	50′ L.O.A.*	13′	60 m.p.h.	50 m.p.h.
ALASKA	LEGAL	NO	NONE	more than 1500 lbs. (6a)	8′	35′ Single 60′ L.O.A.	12½′	50 m.p.h.	50 m.p.h.
ARIZONA	ILLEGAL	YES	NONE	1500 lbs.	8′	40′ Single 65′ L.O.A.	13½′	Reasonable and prudent	50 m.p.h.
ARKANSAS	LEGAL	YES	SINGLE	1500 lbs.	8′	35′ Single 50′ L.O.A.	13½′	50 m.p.h.	50 m.p.h.
CALIFORNIA	LEGAL	NO	EITHER SINGLE OR DOUBLE	——— (6b)	8′	35′ Single 60′ L.O.A.	13½′	45 m.p.h.	45 m.p.h.
COLORADO *DENVER-BOULDER TURNPIKE	ILLEGAL	YES	SINGLE	more than 1500 lbs. (6c)	8′	35′ Single 60′ L.O.A.	12½′ 13½′ on certain designated highways	Trailers of gross weight 1500 to 3000 lbs.— 45 m.p.h. Other trailers—reasonable and proper	45 m.p.h.
CONNECTICUT *CONNECTICUT TURNPIKE	LEGAL	YES	NONE	3000 lbs.	8½′	50′ L.O.A.	12½′	Reasonable and proper (T) 60 m.p.h.	(T) 60 m.p.h.
DELAWARE	LEGAL	NO	NONE	more than 4000 lbs.	8′	40′ Single 60′ L.O.A.	12½′	55 m.p.h.	55 m.p.h.
DIST. OF COLUMBIA	LEGAL	YES	SINGLE—for 2 wheel trailer; DOUBLE, if gross wt. in excess of 1500 lbs., or 4-wheel trailer	1500 lbs.	8′	35′ Single 50′ L.O.A.	12½′	25 m.p.h.	25 m.p.h.
FLORIDA *SUNSHINE STATE PARKWAY	LEGAL	YES	NONE	3000 lbs.	8′	40′ Single 50′ L.O.A.	12½′	50 m.p.h. (T) 65 m.p.h.	45 m.p.h. (T) 65 m.p.h.
GEORGIA	LEGAL	YES	NONE	1500 lbs.	8′	50′ L.O.A.	13½′	60 m.p.h.	50 m.p.h.
HAWAII	ILLEGAL	NO	NONE	1500 lbs.	9′	40′ Single 55′ L.O.A.	13′	45 m.p.h.	45 m.p.h.
IDAHO	LEGAL	NO	SINGLE	1500 lbs. unladen	8′	60′ L.O.A.	14′	60 m.p.h.	55 m.p.h.
ILLINOIS *ILLINOIS TOLLWAY SYSTEM	LEGAL	YES	NONE	1500 lbs.	8′ (T) over 8′ and not more than 10′ by special $10 permit only	50′ L.O.A. (T) Over 50′ L.O.A. by special $10 permit only	13½′ (T) to 14¾′ by special $10 permit only.	55 m.p.h. (T) 55 m.p.h. Max.; 40 m.p.h. Min.	55 m.p.h. (T) 55 m.p.h. Max.; 40 m.p.h. Min.
INDIANA *NORTHERN INDIANA TOLL ROAD	LEGAL	YES	DOUBLE	1500 lbs.	8′	36′ Single 50′ L.O.A.	13½′	65 m.p.h. (T) 65 m.p.h.	65 m.p.h. (T) 65 m.p.h.
IOWA	LEGAL	YES	SINGLE	3000 lbs.	8′	50′ L.O.A.	13½′	55 m.p.h.	55 m.p.h.
KANSAS *KANSAS TURNPIKE	ILLEGAL	YES	DOUBLE	3000 lbs.	8′ (T) to 10′ by special permit	50′ L.O.A. (T) 60′ L.O.A.	13½′ (T) to 14′ by special permit	70 m.p.h. If towed by truck with gross weight of 5000 lbs. or more, 50 m.p.h. day or night (T) 80 m.p.h. Max.; 40 m.p.h. Min.	60 m.p.h.
KENTUCKY *KENTUCKY TURNPIKE	LEGAL	YES	DOUBLE	———	8′	48′ 50′ Class AA Hys.	12½′ 13½′ Class AA Hys.	60 m.p.h.	50 m.p.h.
LOUISIANA	LEGAL	YES	NONE	1500 lbs. net load	8′	50′ L.O.A.	13½′	Reasonable and proper	
MAINE *MAINE TURNPIKE	LEGAL	YES	SINGLE—for trailers having more than 2 wheels	———	8′ (T) 8½′; to 10′ by permit	50′ L.O.A. (T) 55′ L.O.A. By permit in excess of 55′	12½′ (T) 13½′	45 m.p.h. (T) 70 m.p.h.	45 m.p.h. (T) 65 m.p.h.
MARYLAND	LEGAL	YES	NONE	1500 lbs.	8′	55′ L.O.A.	12½′	50 m.p.h. Dual Lane Highways— 50 or 60 m.p.h.	50 m.p.h.
MASSACHUSETTS *MASSACHUSETTS TURNPIKE	ILLEGAL	NO (T) RIGID BAR Connection between hauling unit and trailer required	NONE	———	8′ (T) 8½′—if wider, a special hauling permit is required	33′ Single (T) 50′ L.O.A. If longer, a special hauling permit is required	NONE (T) 13′—if higher, a special hauling permit is required	Reasonable and proper (T) 50 m.p.h. Max.; 40 m.p.h. Min.	(T) 50 m.p.h. Max.; 40 m.p.h. Min.
MICHIGAN	ILLEGAL	YES	DOUBLE	1500 lbs.	8′	40′ Single 55′ L.O.A.	13½′	65 m.p.h. If trailer has more than 2 wheels and/or weighs in excess of 750 lbs. gross, maximum speed is 50 m.p.h.	55 m.p.h.
MINNESOTA	LEGAL if within 20 inches of extreme left edge of trailer	YES	DOUBLE	1000 lbs.	8′	40′ Single 50′ L.O.A.	13½′	60 m.p.h.	50 m.p.h.
MISSISSIPPI	LEGAL	YES	NONE	2000 lbs.	8′	35′ Single 50′ L.O.A.	12½′	45 m.p.h.	45 m.p.h.
MISSOURI	LEGAL	YES	NONE	———	8′	50′ L.O.A.	12½′	On divided Federal Highways: 70 m.p.h. On undivided Federal Highways: 70 m.p.h. On all other highways: 65 m.p.h.	 70 m.p.h. 65 m.p.h. 60 m.p.h.

	LICENSE REQUIRED?	COST OF VEHICLE LICENSE:	VEHICLE LICENSE VALID FROM:	WHERE TO APPLY FOR LICENSE:	TAIL LIGHT(S) REQUIRED?	STOP LIGHT(S) REQUIRED?	DIRECTIONAL LIGHT(S) REQUIRED?	REFLECTOR LIGHT(S) REQUIRED?	LICENSE LIGHT REQUIRED?
MONTANA	YES	$2.00 up to 2,500 lbs. plus personal property tax	JAN. 1 THRU DEC. 31	County Treasurer's Office—County of Owner's Residence	YES (2i)	YES	YES	YES	YES
NEBRASKA	YES	$1.00 per 1,000 lbs. net	JAN. 1 THRU DEC. 31	Division of Roads & Irrigation, Motor Vehicle Division—Lincoln	YES	NO	NO	YES	YES
NEVADA	YES	$2.50 plus personal property tax	JULY 1 THRU JUNE 30	Division of Motor Vehicle Registration—Carson City	YES	YES	YES	YES	NO
NEW HAMPSHIRE *NEW HAMPSHIRE TOLL ROADS	YES	$.35 per 100 lbs. up to 4,001 lbs.	APRIL 1 THRU MARCH 31	Motor Vehicle Department—Concord	YES	NO	NO	YES	YES
NEW JERSEY *NEW JERSEY TOLL ROADS	YES	$5.00 for a gross load not in excess of 2,000 lbs; all other trailers, $10.00	APRIL 1 THRU MARCH 31	Department of Law and Public Safety, Division of Motor Vehicles—Trenton	YES (2j)	YES (3a)	YES (4f)	YES	YES
NEW MEXICO	YES	$5.00 plus $1.00 for each 100 lbs. or fraction thereof in excess of 5,001 lbs.	JAN. 1 THRU DEC. 31	Department of Motor Vehicles—Santa Fe	YES (2k)	YES	YES	YES (5m)	YES
NEW YORK *NEW YORK THRUWAY	YES	$2.50 per 500 lbs. gross vehicle wt. or any part thereof.	JAN. 1 THRU JAN. 15 following year	Department of Motor Vehicles—Albany	YES	YES	YES (4g)	YES	YES
OHIO *OHIO TURNPIKE	YES	$3.00 up to 2,500 lbs. gross wt.	JAN. 1 THRU FEB. 15 following year	Department of Motor Vehicles—Raleigh	YES (2l)	YES	YES	YES	YES
NORTH CAROLINA	YES								
NORTH DAKOTA	NO (1c)	$.85 per 100 lbs. up to 2,000 lbs.; $1.40 per 100 lbs. from over 2,000 lbs. to 3,000 lbs.; $1.90 per 100 lbs. from over 3,000 lbs. to 4,000 lbs.; etc.	APRIL 1 THRU MARCH 31	Motor Vehicle Department—Bismarck	YES (2m)	NO	YES	YES (5n)	NO
OHIO *OHIO TURNPIKE	YES			Bureau of Motor Vehicles—Columbus, or local Deputy Registrar	YES	YES	YES	YES	YES
OKLAHOMA *OKLAHOMA TURNPIKES	NO				YES (2n)	YES	YES	YES	NO
OREGON	YES (1d)	$10.00	JUNE 1 THRU MAY 31	Department of Motor Vehicles—Salem	YES (2o)	YES	YES (4h)	YES	YES—if trailer licensed
PENNSYLVANIA *PENNSYLVANIA TURNPIKE	YES	$10.00 up to 1,000 lbs. (chassis wt.), $30.00—more than 1,000 but less than 2,000 lbs; $45.00—more than 2,000		Department of Revenue, Bureau of Motor Vehicles—Harrisburg	YES	YES (3f)	YES	YES	YES—if trailer licensed
RHODE ISLAND	YES	$.15 per 100 lbs. gross wt.	APRIL 1 THRU MARCH 31	Registry of Motor Vehicles—Providence	YES	YES	YES	YES	YES
SOUTH CAROLINA	YES (1e)	$5.00—classified as utility trailer	NOV. 1 THRU OCT. 31	Highway Department, Motor Vehicle Division—Columbia	YES	YES	NO	YES (5o)	YES
SOUTH DAKOTA	YES	To County Treasurer—$2.00 up to 1,200 lbs; $10.00—1,201, 1,500 lbs; and $5.00 additional for each 500 lbs. $5.00—1,200 lbs. to 2,000; $10.00—2,001 to 3,250 lbs; $15.00—3,251 to 5,000 lbs. for State Hy. Fund	APRIL 1 THRU FEB. 28 of succeeding year	Department of Motor Vehicles—Pierre	YES	NO	NO	YES	YES
TENNESSEE	NO								
TEXAS *DALLAS-FT. WORTH TURNPIKE	YES	$.33 per 100 lbs. up through 6,000 lbs.	JAN. 1 THRU DEC. 31	County Tax Collector—County where owner resides	YES	YES	YES	NO	NO
UTAH	YES (1f)	$2.50—750 lbs. or less uniden wt.; $5.00—over 750 lbs.	JAN. 1 THRU FEB. 28 of succeeding year	Tax Commission, Motor Vehicle Division—Salt Lake City	YES	YES	YES	YES	YES
VERMONT	YES	$7.50	APRIL 1 THRU MARCH 31	Department of Motor Vehicles—Montpelier	YES	YES	YES	YES	YES
VIRGINIA *RICHMOND-PETERSBURG TURNPIKE	YES	$3.50 if gross wt. is 1,000 lbs. or less; others, $12.00	JAN. 1 THRU MARCH 31	Division of Motor Vehicles—Richmond	YES	YES	YES (4i)	YES (5p)	YES
WASHINGTON	YES	$3.00 up to 2,000 lbs.; $6.50 up to 4,000 lbs.	JAN. 1 THRU DEC. 31	Department of Licenses—Olympia	YES (2p)	YES (3g)	YES	NO	YES
WEST VIRGINIA *WEST VIRGINIA TURNPIKE	YES	$6.00—less than 2,000 gross lbs.; $17.50—more than 2,000 gross lbs.	JULY 1 THRU JUNE 30	Department of Motor Vehicles—Charleston	YES	YES	YES	YES	YES
WISCONSIN	YES (1g)	$12.50—3,000 to 4,500 lbs.	JAN. 1 THRU JUNE 30	Motor Vehicle Department—Madison	NO	YES	NO	YES	NO
WYOMING	YES	den weight of trailer	JAN. 1 THRU JAN. 31 € succeeding yr.	D ment of Revenue, Motor Division—Cheyenne	YES	NO	YES	YES	YES

Appendix — OBC Digest of State Boat Trailer Laws

State		Fee	Valid From	For License	Required?	Required?	Required?	Required?	Required?
ALABAMA	NO				YES	YES	YES	YES	YES
ALASKA	YES	$4.00	MARCH 1 THRU FEB. 28	Department of Taxation—Juneau	YES	YES	NO	NO	NO
ARIZONA	YES	$.400—Unladen wt. 1,000 lbs. or less; $6.00 plus tax up to 3,000 lbs.		Highway Department, Motor Vehicle Division—Phoenix	YES	NO	YES	YES	YES
ARKANSAS	YES	$3.00	JULY 1 THRU JUNE 30	Revenue Department, Motor Vehicle Division—Little Rock	YES	NO	NO	NO	NO
CALIFORNIA	YES	$8.00 plus 2% market value	JAN. 1 THRU DEC. 31	Department of Motor Vehicles—Sacramento	YES (2a)	YES	YES (4a)	YES (5a)	YES
COLORADO *DENVER-BOULDER TURNPIKE	YES	$2.00 reduced quarterly, plus specific ownership tax	JAN. 1 THRU DEC. 31	Department of Revenue—Denver	YES (2b)	YES	YES (3b)	YES (5b)	YES
CONNECTICUT *CONNECTICUT TURNPIKE	YES	$2.00	APRIL 1 THRU MARCH 31	Motor Vehicles Department—Hartford	YES (2c)	YES	YES (3c)	YES (5c)	YES
DELAWARE	YES	$1.75 per 500 lbs. up to 5,000 lbs.; $2.30 for every 500 lbs. over 5,000 lbs.	Registration by year—4 year expirations MARCH 31, JUNE 30, SEPT. 30, DEC. 31	Motor Vehicle Division—Dover	YES (2d)	YES	YES (4b)	YES	YES
DIST. OF COLUMBIA	YES	$8.00 up to 500 lbs.; $12.00—1,000 to 1,500 lbs.; $20.00—1,500 to 2,500 lbs.; $32.00—2,500 to 5,000 lbs.	APRIL 1 THRU MARCH 31	Department of Motor Vehicles—Washington, D.C.	YES	YES	YES	YES	YES
FLORIDA *SUNSHINE STATE PARKWAY	YES	$2.50 for the first 500 lbs. and $.75 for each additional 100 lbs.	JAN. 1 THRU DEC. 31	Motor Vehicle Department—Tallahassee	YES	YES	YES	YES	YES
GEORGIA	YES	$5.00 up to 1,000 lbs.; $10.00 over 1,000 lbs.	JAN. 1 THRU DEC. 31	Department of Revenue, Motor Vehicle License Unit—Atlanta	YES	YES	YES	YES	YES
HAWAII	YES	1¢ per lb. of weight of trailer	JAN. 1 THRU DEC. 31	Treasurer's Office—County of Owner's Residence	YES	NO	YES	YES	YES
IDAHO	YES	$2.50 to $8.00 depending on weight	JAN. 1 THRU DEC. 31	Department of Law Enforcement—Boise	YES (2e)	YES	YES (3d)	YES (5f)	YES
ILLINOIS *ILLINOIS TOLLWAY SYSTEM	YES	$6.00 up to 2,000 gross lbs.; $20.00 for a gross wt. exceeding 2,000 lbs. but not more than 5,000 lbs.	JAN. 1 THRU DEC. 31	Office of Secretary of State, Auto Department—Springfield	YES (2f)	YES	YES (4c)	YES (5g)	YES
INDIANA *NORTHERN INDIANA TOLL ROAD	YES	$3.00 up to 3,000 gross lbs.; $8.00 up to 5,000 gross lbs.	MARCH 1 THRU FEB. 28	Bureau of Motor Vehicles—Indianapolis	YES (2g)	YES	YES (4d)	YES	YES
IOWA	YES	Trailers with a gross weight of 1,000 pounds or less, $3.00. Trailers with a gross weight exceeding 1,000 pounds, and not exceeding 2,000 pounds, $10.00, and a $10.00 increase in license fee for every two ton increase thereafter. Trailers whose empty weight is 2,000 pounds or less are exempt from Certificate of Title and Lien provisions of the Iowa Motor Vehicle Laws.	JAN. 1 THRU DEC. 31	County Treasurer's Office—County of Owner's Residence	YES	YES	YES	YES	YES
KANSAS *KANSAS TURNPIKE	YES (1a)	$5.00, reduced quarterly, (Owner's Option); $10.00, reduced quarterly, if gross wt. exceeds 2,000 lbs. and trailer not for hire.	JAN. 1 THRU DEC. 31	County Treasurer's Office—County where owner lives or is in business	YES	YES	NO	YES (5h)	NO
KENTUCKY *KENTUCKY TURNPIKE	NO (1b)			Department of Motor Transportation—Frankfort	YES	YES	NO	NO	NO
LOUISIANA	YES	$3.00 for a gross wt. not to exceed 500 lbs.; $10.00 for a gross wt. not to exceed 3,500 lbs.; $20.00 up to 6,000 lbs.	JAN. 1 THRU DEC. 31	Department of Revenue—Baton Rouge	YES	YES	YES	YES (5i)	YES
MAINE *MAINE TURNPIKE	YES	$5.00 for a gross wt. in excess of 2,000 lbs. but not more than 4,000 lbs.	MARCH 1 THRU FEB. 28	Office of Secretary of State, Motor Vehicle Division—Augusta	YES	YES	NO	YES (5j)	YES
MARYLAND	YES	$7.00 to $23.00 depending on gross wt.	MAY 1 THRU APRIL 30	Department of Motor Vehicles—Baltimore	YES	YES	NO	NO	NO
MASSACHUSETTS *MASSACHUSETTS TURNPIKE	YES	$3.00 per 1,000 lbs.	JAN. 1 THRU DEC. 31	Division of Registry of Motor Vehicles—Boston	YES	YES	NO (f) YES	NO (f) YES	YES
MICHIGAN	YES	$.55 per 100 lbs. up to 1,000 lbs.; $1.40 per 100 lbs. from 1,000 lbs. to 6,000 lbs.	MARCH 1 THRU FEB. 28	Office of Secretary of State, Division of Driver and Vehicle Services—Lansing	YES	YES	YES (4e)	YES	YES
MINNESOTA	YES	$2.35 for two-wheel trailers under 3,000 lbs.; $4.20 a ton or fraction thereof for other trailers (Class "Z")	JAN. 1 THRU DEC. 31—each biennium beginning with even numbered year	Office of Motor Vehicle Division—St. Paul	YES (2h)	YES	YES	YES (5k)	YES
MISSISSIPPI	YES	$3.00	NOV. 1 THRU OCT. 31	Department of Motor Vehicles—Jackson	YES	YES	YES	YES (5l)	YES
MISSOURI	YES	$7.00	JAN. 1 THRU DEC. 31	Department of Revenue, Motor Vehicle Registration—Jefferson City	YES	YES	YES	YES	YES

LEGEND FOR BOAT TRAILER LAWS

(1) LICENSE REQUIRED

a) KANSAS: Owner's option if gross weight is 2,000 lbs. or less.
b) KENTUCKY: Special permit necessary for any four-wheel boat trailer. Fee: $15; good for 10 days, one trip only.
c) NORTH DAKOTA: Identification plates issued for private trailers at cost of $2.00 per calendar year.
d) OREGON: Utility and small boat trailers weighing not more than 750 lbs. and carrying a load weighing not more than 1,000 lbs. are exempt from registration. All other such trailers having a gross weight of 4,500 lbs. or less must be registered annually.
e) SOUTH CAROLINA: Trailers weighing less than 500 lbs. and carrying a load weighing less than 1,000 lbs. are exempt from registration.
f) UTAH: Under 1959 law, all one-wheel or two-wheel trailers of 1,000 lbs. or less actual weight are no longer exempt from registration. Also, whenever a trailer is registered on or after July 1, the fee for such registration shall be 60% of the regular fee, provided the minimum fee shall be $2.00.
g) WISCONSIN: Boat trailers weighing under 3,000 lbs. are not required to carry vehicle license.

In most states, trailers exceeding maximum length, width or weight limits may be operated for continuous or single trips over designated highways and/or at stated times by special permit.

Non-resident's license honored:

All states permit non-residents to tow their trailers on the highways of the state for a limited time without requiring them to register the vehicle and obtain a driver's license. This privilege is generally based upon reciprocity, which means the state will extend to a non-resident the identical privileges granted by his home state to non-resident motorists. Most states require persons who intend to reside there permanently to buy new plates and secure a new driver's license immediately, or within a certain time. Generally, obtaining employment or placing one's children in a public school is considered intention to reside permanently. In some states licenses are honored other than on a reciprocal basis, as follows:

a) ALASKA: 90 days
b) ARIZONA: Until expiration of home state plates or establishment of residence. Visitors must obtain permit after 10 days.
c) ARKANSAS: 90 days
d) CALIFORNIA: Until expiration of home state plates or establishment of residence.
e) GEORGIA: 30 days
f) INDIANA: 60 days
g) MISSISSIPPI: 30 days
h) MONTANA: 30 days for recreational travel. Extension for same period upon request.
i) NEVADA: Until expiration of home state plates or establishment of residence.
j) NEW JERSEY: 60 days
k) NEW MEXICO: 30 days
l) NORTH DAKOTA: 90 days
m) OKLAHOMA: 60 days
n) SOUTH CAROLINA: 90 days
o) SOUTH DAKOTA: 60 days
p) TENNESSEE: 30 days
q) VIRGINIA: 60 days
r) WEST VIRGINIA: 90 days
s) WYOMING: 90 days

(2) TAIL LIGHT(S) REQUIRED

Most states require at least one tail lamp on the rear of every trailer. Some state laws have the proviso that the trailer shall be equipped with a tail light, provided the trailer is so loaded or of such construction as to obscure the view of the tail light on the towing vehicle. Generally, the statutes do not specify what size the lamp must be, but there are specifications on color (red), range of visibility (most frequently 500 feet to the rear, and location.

Some unique requirements are noted for—

a) CALIFORNIA: One tail light is legal on trailers registered prior to 1/1/58. On all new trailers first registered after 1/1/58, two red tail lamps, one at each side on the rear, are required.
b) COLORADO: One tail light is legal on trailers manufactured before 1/1/58 and registered in Colorado. On trailers manufactured after 1/1/58 and registered in Colorado, two red tail lamps, one at each side on the rear, are required.
c) CONNECTICUT: Minimum lens diameter—3 inches.
d) DELAWARE: After 7/1/56, two red tail lamps are required on all vehicles.
e) IDAHO: Minimum lens diameter—3½ inches.
f) ILLINOIS: Boat trailers are classified as a semi-trailer or a trailer depending on how they are constructed. The two-wheel (single-axle) and the four-wheel (tandem-axle) trailer are *semi-trailers*. The four-wheel (two-axle) trailer is a *trailer* when it is so constructed that no part of its weight rests upon the towing vehicle. On every semi-trailer and trailer having a gross weight in excess of 3,000 pounds, at least one red tail light is required. On every trailer having a gross weight of 3,000 pounds or less (including the weight of the trailer and maximum load), two red tail lights, one on each side on the rear, are required.
g) INDIANA: One tail light is legal on trailers manufactured in Indiana before 1/1/56 and registered in Indiana. On trailers manufactured or assembled after 1/1/56 and registered in Indiana, two red tail lamps, one at each side on the rear, are required.
h) MINNESOTA: One red tail lamp is legal on trailer manufactured and assembled before 1/1/60. Two red tail lamps are required on every trailer manufactured or assembled after 1/1/60 and registered in Minnesota. These lamps shall be mounted on the rear, on the same level and as widely spaced laterally as practicable.
i) MONTANA: One tail light is legal on trailers manufactured and assembled before 1/1/56 and registered in Montana. On trailers manufactured and assembled after 1/1/56 and registered in Montana, two red lamps, one on each side on the rear, are required.
j) NEW JERSEY: One tail light is legal on trailers manufactured before 7/1/54 and registered in New Jersey. On trailers manufactured after 7/1/54 and registered in New Jersey, two red tail lamps, one on each side on the rear, are required.
k) NEW MEXICO: One tail light is legal on trailers manufactured or assembled before 7/1/53 and registered in New Mexico. On trailers manufactured after 7/1/53 and registered in New Mexico, two red tail lamps, one on each side on the rear, are required.
l) NORTH CAROLINA: One red tail lamp, of an approved type, is required on every trailer licensed for not more than 2,500 pounds. It shall not be necessary for a trailer licensed for not more than 2,500 pounds gross to carry a rear lamp, provided such vehicle is equipped with 2 red reflectors at the rear, each not less than 4 inches in diameter, of an approved type, and so designed and situated as to be visible for at least 500 feet to the rear.
m) NORTH DAKOTA: Minimum lens diameter—3 inches.
n) OKLAHOMA: Two red tail lamps required.
o) PENNSYLVANIA: Two red tail lamps are required on trailers initially registered in Pennsylvania on or after 7/1/56; otherwise, only one.
p) WASHINGTON: Two red tail lamps required.

(3) STOP LIGHT(S) REQUIRED

Most states require one red stop lamp on every trailer weighing more than 3,000 pounds gross; and one on every trailer 3,000 pounds gross or less, provided the trailer is so loaded or of such dimensions as to obscure the stop light on the towing vehicle or hand signals by the driver of the towing vehicle.

Some unique provisions are noted for—

a) CALIFORNIA: Two red or amber, one on each side, are required on new trailers first registered after 1/1/58. One stop light is legal on trailers registered before 1/1/58. Minimum lens diameter, 2⅛ inches (3½ square inches).

b) COLORADO: Two stop lights are required on trailers manufactured after 1/1/58 and registered in Colorado. One stop light is legal on trailers manufactured before 1/1/58 and registered in Colorado.

c) CONNECTICUT: Minimum lens diameter—3 inches.

d) ILLINOIS: One stop light is required on any combination of vehicles when the distance from the center of the top of the steering post of the towing vehicle to the left outside limits of the trailer body or load exceeds 24 inches, or when the distance from the center of the top of the steering post to the rear limit of the trailer body or load exceeds 14 feet.

e) NEW JERSEY: Two stop lights are required on trailers manufactured and registered in New Jersey after 7/1/54. One stop light is legal on trailers manufactured and first registered before 7/1/54. The law states that stop lights shall provide a substantial increase in illumination.

f) PENNSYLVANIA: Two stop lights are required on all trailers initially registered in Pennsylvania on or after 7/1/56. One stop light is legal on trailers first registered before 7/1/56.

g) WASHINGTON: Two stop lights are required.

(4) DIRECTIONAL LIGHTS REQUIRED

Most states require two red or amber signal lights on the rear of every trailer <u>under one or more of the following conditions:</u> a) If trailer so loaded or constructed as to prevent hand and arm signal by operator of towing vehicle, or mechanical turn signals on towing vehicle, from being visible both to front and rear; b) if distance from center of steering wheel of towing vehicle to rear limit of trailer body or load exceeds 14 feet; c) if distance from center of steering wheel to left outside limit of trailer body or load exceeds 24 inches.
Directional signals on trailers are required in the states listed below under the following conditions (notwithstanding the above)—

a) CALIFORNIA: If only lamp type signals are used on towing vehicle, or if trailer is first registered on or after 1/1/58, and has a gross weight of 6,000 pounds or more. If vehicle or load is 80 inches or less in width, the minimum lens diameter of a signal light shall be 2⅛ inches (3½ square inch minimum Class B lamp); if vehicle or load exceeds 80 inches in width, 4 inches (12 square inch minimum Class A lamp).

b) DELAWARE: On all new vehicles licensed in this state after 7/1/53.

c) ILLINOIS: In the event the turn signals on the rear of the towing vehicle are visible 100 feet to the rear in normal sunlight while towing a boat trailer, it is not necessary to have turn signals on the trailer.

d) INDIANA: On all trailers manufactured after 1/1/56; on all trailers manufactured prior to 1/1/56 when distance from center of steering column to left side of trailer load exceeds 24 inches, or if distance from center of steering column at top to extreme rear of trailer or load exceeds 14 feet.

e) MICHIGAN: On all trailers manufactured or assembled after 1/1/55, except boat trailers weighing less than 2,500 pounds, which are exempt from certificate of title requirements under state law.

f) NEW JERSEY: On all trailers exceeding 3,000 pounds gross vehicle weight manufactured after 7/1/54 and registered in New Jersey. Also, on trailers of 3,000 pounds gross vehicle weight or less, manufactured after 7/1/54 and registered in this state if trailer obscures sight of turn signals on towing vehicle for at least 500 feet to the rear.

g) NEW MEXICO: On all trailers manufactured after 1/1/54 and registered in this state.

h) OREGON: May use Class B lamp (no specific size required so long as plainly visible, day or night, 100 feet to rear), but State Motor Vehicle Department strongly recommends Class A lamp (minimum lens diameter, 4 inches; minimum illuminated area, 12 square inches) instead.

i) VIRGINIA: Directional signals are required if hand signal cannot be seen; however, installation of turn signals on all trailers is recommended.

(5) REFLECTOR LIGHT(S) REQUIRED

Many states differentiate between trailers having a gross vehicle weight exceeding 3,000 pounds and trailers weighing 3,000 pounds or less as to the number of reflector lights required. <u>*Typically, as many as 6 reflectors are required on every trailer over 3,000 pounds gross:*</u> 2 on each side, 1 amber at or near the front and 1 red at or near the rear; and 2 on the rear, 1 on each side. <u>*On every trailer 3,000 pounds gross or less, usually 2 red reflectors, 1 on each side of the rear, are required.*</u> In most states, reflectors are not required to be of any specific size, but they must be of such size and characteristics and so maintained as to meet prescribed visibility requirements, e.g., "readily visible at night from all distances within 500 to 50 feet from a following vehicle when directly in front of the lawful upper beams of its headlamps". The statutes generally tell you where reflector lights shall be mounted on your trailer, e.g., "not less than 24 inches nor more than 60 inches above the ground on which the trailer stands; except that if the highest part of the permanent structure of the vehicle is less than 24 inches, the reflector at such point shall be mounted as high as that part of the permanent structure will permit". In many cases, at least one reflector may be combined with the tail lamp. It should be borne in mind, however, that the foregoing is only to show you the general requirements. There are variations in some states as to the total number of required reflectors, size, location, etc.

Some unique requirements (different from the above) are noted for—

a) ALASKA: Minimum lens diameter—3 inches.

b) ARKANSAS: Only 1, on the rear.

c) CALIFORNIA: Only 1, (Class B, i.e., ⅞ inch minimum diameter) if towed by passenger car. May be mounted on boat when no practical place for installation on trailer, but must be transferred to trailer when not loaded.

d) COLORADO: If trailer manufactured after 1/1/58 and registered and operated in this state, 2 reflectors, visible at night from all distances within 350 feet; otherwise, only 1, except that every motor drawn vehicle or vehicle combination exceeding 35 feet in length shall be equipped with 4 side marker reflectors, 1 amber on each side near the front and 1 red on each side near the rear.

e) CONNECTICUT: If width of trailer or boat is 6 feet or more, two are required. Minimum lens diameter—3 inches. Otherwise, only one required, at cross member of trailer.

f) IDAHO: Minimum lens diameter—3½ inches.

g) ILLINOIS: On every trailer (defined as four-wheel or two-axle vehicle so constructed that no part of its weight rests upon the towing vehicle) having a gross weight of 3,000 pounds or less including maximum load: 2 red reflectors required on the rear of the trailer body, not more than 12 inches from the lower left hand and right hand corners. Must be visible when hit by headlight beams 300 feet away at night.

h) KANSAS: Only 1, on the rear. Minimum lens diameter—3 inches.

i) MAINE: Only 1, on the rear. Must be visible at least 200 feet away at night on an unlighted highway when directly in front of headlight beams of vehicle approaching from rear. On every trailer of 7 feet or more in width, an additional reflector, green or amber, is required, attached to extreme left front so as to indicate extreme left lateral extension of trailer or load. Must be visible not less than 200 feet in direction towards which vehicle is facing or proceeding.

j) MARYLAND: Only 1, on the rear. Must be visible at night from 300 to 50 feet away when directly in front of headlamp beams of approaching vehicle.

k) MINNESOTA: At least two reflectors of a type approved by the commissioner are required on the rear. They shall be mounted as close as practicable to the extreme right and left rear edges of the trailer. Must be visible at night from 300 to 50 feet away when directly in front of headlamp beams of vehicle approaching from rear.

l) MISSISSIPPI: Minimum lens diameter—3 inches.

m) NEW MEXICO: On every trailer less than 80 inches in over-all width, 2 required, 1 at each side of rear.

n) NORTH DAKOTA: Minimum lens diameter, not less than 3 inches.

o) SOUTH DAKOTA: Only 1, on the rear. Shall be maintained not less than 24 nor more than 42 inches above ground. Must be visible at night from 300 to 50 feet away when directly in front of headlamp beams of approaching vehicle.

p) VIRGINIA: On any combination of vehicles whose over-all length exceeds 35 feet and does not exceed 7 feet in height or in width. Shall be mounted on widest part of trailer or load so as to be visible from front and sides. Also, on all combination of vehicles requiring clearance lamps. Amber on the side at or near front and red on rear.

q) WISCONSIN: <u>*Every trailer*</u> or semi-trailer shall carry on the rear 2 reflectors, one on each side. Reflectorized material extending across the full width of the vehicle and otherwise meeting the mounting and visibility specifications for reflectors may be used in lieu of the reflectors required.

(6) BRAKES REQUIRED

a) ALASKA: Brakes are required for trailer of more than 1,500 pounds gross weight, if manufactured *after* 1/1/58. Brakes are required for trailer of 3,000 pounds or more gross weight, if manufactured prior to the above date.

b) CALIFORNIA: Brakes are not required, provided a combination of vehicles can stop within 40 feet from a speed of 20 m.p.h.

c) COLORADO: Whenever the weight of a boat trailer does not exceed 1,500 pounds gross weight, such trailer shall not be required to have brakes, provided the towing vehicle shall have brakes adequate to stop the combination of vehicles at 20 m.p.h. within 40 feet on dry asphalt concrete free from loose material where the grade is less than 1%, and under the same conditions, a hand brake shall be capable of stopping the combination of vehicles within a 55 ft. distance and hold such combination on any grade.

d) NEW JERSEY: Brakes are not required on trailers with a gross weight under 3,000 pounds; provided, however, that the gross weight of any such trailer without brakes shall not exceed 40% of the gross weight of the towing vehicle and that the gross weight of any such semi-trailer without brakes shall not exceed 40% of the gross weight of the towing vehicle when the vehicles are connected.

(7) MISCELLANEOUS

a) *License light required*—Virtually all of the state laws requiring illumination of the trailer registration plate provide that either the tail lamp or a separate lamp shall be so constructed and placed as to illuminate the plate with a white light rendering it legible 50 or 60 feet to the rear. The license light is supposed to be so wired as to be lighted whenever the headlamps are lighted.

b) *Clearance and side marker lights required*—Many states (e.g. Arizona, Delaware, Florida, Indiana, Iowa, Michigan, Mississippi, Montana, North Carolina, Ohio and Oregon) require that every trailer having a gross weight in excess of 3,000 pounds shall be equipped with 4 clearance lamps and 4 side marker lamps, typically as follows: (a) on the front, 2 amber clearance lamps, 1 at each side; (b) on each side, 2 side marker lamps, 1 amber at or near the front and 1 red at or near the rear; (c) on the rear, 2 red clearance lamps, 1 at each side. It is usually specified these clearance lamps shall be mounted on the permanent structure of the trailer in such a manner as will indicate its extreme width, and as near the top as practicable. Clearance lamps and side marker lamps may be mounted in combination.

In several other states (e.g. Colorado, Maryland, Minnesota, New Hampshire, South Dakota and Wisconsin) every trailer having a width at any part in excess of 80 inches must be equipped with 4 clearance lamps, 2 amber-colored, 1 at each side on the front; and 2 red-colored, 1 at each side on the rear.

In some states every motor-drawn vehicle or combination of vehicles which exceeds a certain over-all length (e.g. 30 feet in Colorado, Minnesota and South Dakota) must be specially equipped with side marker or identification lights.

c) *Flag or light on protruding load*—Most states require that when a boat extends 4 feet or more beyond the rear of the trailer on which it is being carried, a red flag or cloth shall be displayed at or near the end of the load during daylight, and a red light shall be displayed in place of the flag between ½ hour after sunset and ½ hour before sunrise. The prescribed size of the red flag varies between states—either 12 or 16 inches square, but the red light at night, for the most part, must be visible 500 feet to the rear.

d) *Identification*—A general provision under the Illinois Highway Traffic Act requires all second division vehicles (which includes vehicles used for the conveyance of property) to have painted or otherwise firmly affixed to both sides of the vehicle in a color or colors vividly contrasting to the color of the vehicle, the owner's name and address and the maximum empty weight of the vehicle. It has been seriously questioned whether this law applies to boat trailers. *Until an official legal opinion is received, there will be no enforcement by the Illinois State Highway Police in regards to identification on boat trailers.*

TURNPIKE AND EXPRESSWAY FARES

CALIFORNIA: NONE, except for bridge tolls in San Francisco Bay Area.

COLORADO: DENVER-BOULDER TURNPIKE: For information concerning fares, write to: Denver-Boulder Turnpike, Department of Highways, 4201 East Arkansas Avenue, Denver 22, Colorado.

CONNECTICUT: CONNECTICUT TURNPIKE (129 miles): Passenger car with 1-axle trailer: Full length trip, $2.70. Cost per mile, 2.09¢.

Passenger car with 2-axle trailer: Full length trip, $4.05. Cost per mile, 3.14¢.

DELAWARE: NONE—Only one Toll Bridge.

FLORIDA: SUNSHINE STATE PARKWAY (109 miles): Single-axle semi-trailer (CLASS 6): Full length trip, (day), $2.40; (nights) $1.75 for passenger car plus $1.20 for Trailer.. Cost per mile, 3.03¢ (day); 2.70¢ (night).

Two-axle semi-trailer with pulling vehicle (CLASS 4): Full length trip, (day) $5.00; (night) $3.00. Cost per mile, 4.59¢ (day); 2.75¢ (night).

ILLINOIS: ILLINOIS TOLLWAY SYSTEM: NORTHWEST TOLLWAY (Chicago, Elgin, Rockford, Beloit); EAST-WEST TOLLWAY (Chicago, Aurora & U. S. 30); TRI-STATE TOLLWAY ("Belt" route around Chicago from Ind. to Wisc.) (187 miles). On all of the TOLLWAY system except that part located west of Elgin on the Northwest Tollway you pay as you pass through each toll plaza. The tolls for vehicles with 3 or more axles are 25¢ for each ramp plaza and 50¢ for each main plaza.

TRI-STATE: Full length trip (77 miles) through 6 main plazas—$3.00; less for shorter trips. Cost per mile, 3.89¢.

EAST-WEST: Full length trip (28 miles) through 2 plazas—$.75. Cost per mile, 2.67¢.

NORTHWEST: Between West Elgin and South Beloit (Wisconsin line)—Passenger car with one-axle trailer $1.45. Cost per mile 2.75¢. Passenger car with two-axle trailer $1.85. Cost per mile 3.50¢. Also one main plaza—50¢.

INDIANA: NORTHERN INDIANA TOLL ROAD (157 miles): Single-axle boat trailers under 21 ft. in length (Ticket Class No. 4): Full length trip, $2.80. Cost per mile, 1.78¢. Two-axle boat trailer under 21 ft. in length (Ticket Class No. 5): Full length trip, $5.60. Cost per mile, 3.51¢.

KANSAS: KANSAS TURNPIKE (233 miles): Passenger car with 1 or 2-axle trailer (Class 8): Full length trip, $5.40. Cost per mile, 2.32¢.

KENTUCKY: KENTUCKY TURNPIKE: For information concerning fares, write to: Kentucky Turnpike, Box 374, Elizabethtown, Kentucky.

LOUISIANA: PONTCHARTRAIN CAUSEWAY: Connecting U.S. 61 and U.S. 190.

MAINE: MAINE TURNPIKE (106 miles): Full length fare passenger car with trailer, combined length not exceeding 40'—$3.25.

MARYLAND: NONE—Except on Bay, Potomac River and Susquehanna River bridges.

MASSACHUSETTS: MASSACHUSETTS TURNPIKE (123 miles): Passenger car with single-axle trailer: Full length trip, $3.10. Cost per mile, 2.5¢. Passenger car with two-axle trailer: Full length trip, $3.70. Cost per mile, 3.0¢.

MISSISSIPPI: NONE—Except bridges at Greenville, Bay St. Louis & Pascagoula.

NEW HAMPSHIRE: EVERETT TURNPIKE (Nashua-Concord, 40 miles): Full length trip, 50¢ (25¢ at Merrimack and 25¢ at Hooksett Station).

SPAULDING TURNPIKE (Portsmouth-Rochester, 23 miles): Full length trip, 30¢ (15¢ at Dover Station and 15¢ at Rochester Station).

NEW HAMPSHIRE TURNPIKE (Seabrook-Portsmouth, 15 miles): Full length trip, 20¢ for hauling vehicle plus 20¢ per axle (up to 2 axles) for trailer 1,000 lbs. gr. wt. or over.

Approximate cost per mile for entire turnpike system, 25¢.

THE HAMPTON RIVER TOLL BRIDGE (Hampton-Seabrook): All vehicles, 10¢.

Discount tokens may be purchased at any toll station for any vehicle classification, and may be used interchangeably between all toll facilities of the State regardless of point of purchase.

NEW JERSEY: NEW JERSEY TURNPIKE (118 miles): Full length trip for combination, $3.00. Cost per mile, 2.54¢.

GARDEN STATE PARKWAY (173 miles): Passenger car with one-axle boat trailer: Full length trip, $3.85. Cost per mile, 2.33¢. Passenger car with two-axle boat trailer: Full length trip, $5.50. Cost per mile, 3.18¢.

NEW YORK: NEW YORK THRUWAY (Spring Valley to Buffalo, 495 miles): Class 2 (Passenger cars or light trucks with 4 tires, and hauling 1, 2 or 3-axle trailers): Full length trip, $8.10; less for shorter trips. Cost per mile, 1.64¢.

*Class P passenger cars hauling one-axle trailers: Full length trip, $2.00; less for shorter trips. Cost per mile, 40¢.

*Class P = passenger cars and suburbans registered with the Bureau of Motor Vehicles of the State of New York.

Barrier Station Tolls for passenger cars or light trucks hauling 1, 2, or 3-axle trailers: Tappan Zee Bridge (Hudson Section) 75¢; Tuckahoe Road (Yonkers) 30¢; New Rochelle (New England Section) 30¢; Buffalo City Line (N1) Niagara Section 20¢; Black Rock (N8) Grand Island Bridges 30¢.

OHIO: OHIO TURNPIKE (241 miles): Passenger car with trailer having combined gross wt. of not more than 16,000 lbs.: Full length trip, $5.00. Cost per mile, 2.07¢.

OKLAHOMA: OKLAHOMA TURNPIKES: TURNER (86 miles)—Combination: Full length trip, $4.00. Cost per mile, 4.65¢.

WILL ROGERS (88 miles)—Combination: Full length trip, $4.00. Cost per mile, 4.55¢.

PENNSYLVANIA: PENNSYLVANIA TURNPIKE (470 miles): Pasenger car and any two-axle vehicle not exceeding 7,000 lbs. gross wt.: Full length trip, $4.80. Cost per mile, 1.08¢.

RHODE ISLAND: NONE—Except Mt. Hope Bridge and Jamestown Bridge.

TEXAS: DALLAS - FT. WORTH TURNPIKE (30 miles): Three-axle combinations (Class 3): Full length trip, $1.00. Cost per mile, 3.33¢. Four-axle combinations (Class 4): Full length trip, $1.25. Cost per mile, 4.17¢.

VIRGINIA: RICHMOND-PETERSBURG TURNPIKE (34.7 miles): Pasenger car with one-axle boat trailer (Class 4): Full length trip, $1.20. Cost per mile, 3.46¢. Passenger car with two-axle boat trailer (Class 5): Full length trip, $1.40. Cost per mile, 4.03¢.

WEST VIRGINIA: WEST VIRGINIA TURNPIKE (88 miles): Passenger car with one-axle boat trailer (Class 3): Full length trip, $3.00. Cost per mile, 3.49¢. Passenger car with double-axle boat trailer: Double the fare for the towing vehicle. Full length trip, $3.90. Cost per mile, 4.43¢.

Index

Abbreviations, on charts, 160-163
Accessory drives, 64-65
Accidents, boating, 213
    cause of, 102
    reports of, 213, 238
Actuator, 59
Advertising of boats, 336-338
Aids to navigation (*see* Navigational aids)
Air cleaner elements, 64
Air compressor, maintenance procedure, 67-68
Air control, 59-60
Air pressure, maintenance check, 58
Alcohol or "canned heat," use of, 105
Alternators, 37
American Institute of Electrical Engineers, 106
American Marc, 21
American Water Ski Association, 316
Ammeter and voltmeter, 58
Amphibious cruising, 32, 36, 40-42
Anchorages, 32, 121-122
    buoys to mark, 135, 136
    chart of, 120
    supply ports, 35
Anchors and anchoring, 37, 71, 120-126
    anchorage areas, 32, 121-122
    anchoring technique, 120-122
    bower anchor, 120
    cable, 125-126
        catenary (curve), 125
        Manila rope, 120, 125
        nylon rope, 125
        wire, 125
    cement blocks, 120
    Danforth Shearpin, 120, 122-123
    definition, 120
    effects of wind, current and surge, 122, 124
    freeing fouled anchors, 122-123
    holding characteristics of bottoms, 120-121
    holding power of anchors, 123-124
    kedge anchor, 120
    Manila line, 120, 125
    mooring, 126-129 (*see also* Moorings)
    mushroom type, 126
    near other boats, 122
    parts of an anchor, 121
    precautions, 123
    rode, 125
    sailboats, 272
    scope or length of anchor line, 120

Anchors and anchoring—
    sea, 98-101
    selecting the right anchor, 124-125
    size of anchor needed, 123
    stern anchors, 120, 122
    storm anchors, 123-125
    stream anchor, 120
    tackle inspection, 126
    types of, 120-121
    used as a turning aid, 96-97
    weighing anchors, 122
    weights and holding requirements, 123
Andresen, Jack, 317
Anemometer, 183-184
Antifreeze, 65
Apron, definition, 73
Architects, marine, 26
Automatically rotated loops (ADF), 149-150
Back stay, 78
Balsa wood, used in construction of fiberglass boats, 82
Bank cushion, 96
Bank suction, 96
Barges, 24
    staying clear of, 99-100
Barnacles, removing, 52
Barometers, 181-182
    use of, 181
    weather table, 182
Batteries
    checking, 56, 67
    safety precautions, 107
Beacon Band, for radio direction finding, 151
Beams, deck, 75
Bearings, 173-174
    pelorus used for taking, 165-166
    reliable bearing distance, 153
    special, 176
Beaufort wind scale, 183-184
Bell, Alexander Graham, 332
Bells and whistles, 132
Bight knot, 201
Bilges
    cleaning, 51, 109
    keeping free of grease and oil, 109
    pumps, 69
    ventilating, 107
Binnacle for compass, 165
Binoculars, 38
Bitts, cleats and chocks, 126
Blanchard, Fessenden S., 40, 47

Blocks, snatch, 71
Blue Jay, V-bottom sloop, 278
Boats
　buying pointers, 32-33
　care of, 49-56
　characteristics of, 89-90
　family boating, 11-12
　growth of interest in pleasure boating, 9-17
　　outboard boating, 12-17
　inboard (*see* Inboard boats)
　outboard motorboats (*see* Outboard motorboats)
　sailboats (*see* Sailboats)
　yachts (*see* Yachts)
Bollards, 127
Boom, boating, 9-17
　growth of interest in boating, 9
Bottoms, sea
　depth sounder gives contour of, 153-156
　hard, 156
　holding characteristics of, 120-121
　mud, 156
　obstructions in, 134
　rocky, 156
Bow-and-beam method, to determine position, 174-175
Breadth of boat, 79
　extreme breadth, 79
　molded breadth, 79
Breast hooks, definition, 73
Briggs, Stephen F., 15
Briggs-Stratton Corporation, 13
Broadcast Band, for radio direction finding, 151
Brokers, marine, 26, 264
Buehler Corporation, 334
Builder's risk insurance, 255
Bulkheads, 70
Bundy line of outboard motors, 21
Buoys and buoyage system, 134-138
　bell, 135
　black, 136
　black and white vertically striped, 136
　can and nun buoys, 135, 137
　caution in relying upon, 143-144
　channels marked by, 130, 135
　coloring, 136
　combination, 135-136
　corner radar reflectors, 136
　fog signals, 132
　gong, 135
　guide for the novice, 130
　Intracoastal Waterway, 138-139
　lateral system, 135
　light phase characteristics, 135, 137-138
　　flashing lights, 137
　　interrupted quick flashing lights, 138
　　quick flashing lights, 137-138
　　short-long flashing lights, 138

Buoys —
　lighted, 135-137
　　color of, 137
　　green, 136
　　red, 137
　　white, 137
　marking wrecks, 144
　numbering of, 136-137
　optical reflectors, 137
　primary function of, 134
　red, 136
　red and black horizontally banded, 136
　ring, 216-217
　shapes of, 137
　shifted, capsized or sunk, 143
　spar, 135
　special purpose, 135-136
　types of, 135-136
　whistle, 135
　white, 136
　white and black alternate horizontally banded buoys, 136
　white with green tops, 136
　with sound signals, 135
　yellow, 136
Butt blocks, definition, 74
Buying a boat, points to consider, 32-34

Cabin heaters, 105
Cable-laid rope, 196-197
Camber, decks, 78
Camp sites, public, 35
Camshifting interlock valve, 59
Canadian gasoline taxes, 252
Carburetors, 322
　air cleaners, 64
　care of, 66
　flame arrestors, 108, 215, 217
　　state laws, 230
　maintenance check, 53
Care of boat, motor and equipment, 49-56
　dock and anchor lines, 62
　end-of-the-season program, 56
　in salt water, 51
　maintenance procedures for large inboard boats, 56-72
　removing marine growths, 51-52
　spring-cleaning program, 56
Carlines, 75
Carvel construction, 75
Catboats, 266, 275
Ceiling, marine construction, 74
Celebrity, sloop, 284
Cement blocks used as anchor, 120
Centerboard, sailboats, 267
Centrifugal advance, 67
Chairs, folding, 37
Chamois cloth, use of, 51
Channels
　boats nearing bend or curve in, moving from docks, 193

INDEX

Channels —
  buoys to mark, 130, 135
  daybeacons, 138
  lateral system of buoyage, 135
  navigating in narrow, 96-97
Charts
  abbreviations, 160-163
  Coast and Geodetic Survey charts, 157-158
  corrections on, 159, 160-163
    published in *Notice to Mariners,* 159
  datum plane, 160
  frame of reference, 157
  Gnomonic, 157-158
  government agencies issuing, 157
  government nautical publications to use with, 162-164
  Great Lakes, 160
  labeling, 173
  lines of position, 173
  Marine, 151
  measuring distance on, 159
  Mercator, 134, 157
  notes and dates on, 159
  outboard cruising, 38
  planes of reference, 157, 160
  plotting a safe course, 134
  Polyconic, 157
  scales used, 158-159
  Small Boat Charts, 158-159
  small boat piloting, 157-162
  symbols and abbreviations, 160-163
  temporary changes on, 160-163
  types of, 157-158
Chicago World's Fair, 1893, 12
Children
  entertaining aboard cruiser, 44-48
  making frequent stops for, 44-46
  planning duties for, 46
Chine of hull, 24
Chocks, cleats and bitts, 126, 195
Choke, 66
Citizen's Band Radio Service, 112, 116-117
  Western Long Island System, 117-118
Clay, anchoring in, 121
Cleaning the boat, 39, 49-56
  end-of-the season program, 56
  maintenance procedures for large inboard boats, 56-72
  spring-cleaning program, 56
Cleats, bitts and chocks, 126, 195
Clinker construction, wooden boats, 75
Clouds, 186-187
  as weather indicators, 186-187
  cumulus and cirrus, 186
  formations, 187
Clubs, yacht and boat, 12
  cruising information obtained from, 48
Clutch drive, 59

Coast Guard Auxiliary
  addresses of offices, 355
  courses in "Basic Seamanship and Safe Boat handling," 89, 354-355
  membership in, 354
  safety inspection, 108-109
Coast Pilots, 163
Cockpit cover, runabouts, 37
Codes
  "International Code of Signals," 119
  Morse, 152
Coil and wiring, marine engines, 66
Collisions, avoiding, 190-191
Comet, centerboard sloop, 280
Commands, steering, 90-91
Communications, 111-119
  Citizens' Band Radio Service, 116-119
    Western Long Island System, 117-119
  distress signals, 111
  flags and pennants, 119
  intership, 114-115
  ship radiotelephone, 111-119
    interim licenses, 114
    regulations, 112-116
    station and operator licensing, 113-114
  "wave" for help, 111
Commutator, care of, 65, 69-70
Compartments, checking, 70
Compass course, 170
Compasses, 71
  adjusting, 170
  binnacle for, 165
  compass error, 170
  compass rose, 165
  correcting variation errors, 169
  deviation, 169-170
  deviation card, 170
  deviation table, 171-173
    dating, 173
  gyrocompass, 169
  liquid, 38
  magnetic, 148, 164-165
    deviation and variation, 165
  mariner's, 169
  Napier diagram, 170-172
  plotting a deviation curve on a Napier diagram, 171-173
  radio direction finder used with, 148
  using, 169-173
Compression test
  diesel, 61-62
  gasoline, 61
Construction, small boat, 73-88
  Builders' Risk Insurance, 262-263
  carvel construction, 75
  clinker, 75
  diagonal construction, 78
  do-it-yourself kits and plans, 289-305
    boat-building plans, 295-301
    frame kits, 290-295

Construction, small boat —
  fiberglass boats, 80-83, 290, 301-304
  measurements of pleasure boats, 79-80
  metal boats, 78
  plywood construction, 78
  propellers, 83-88 (see also Propellers)
  wooden boats, 75-78
Consumer Reports, outboard motors rated by, 19, 318
Controlair, 59
Convertible top, runabouts, 37
Cooking aboard boats, 306-313 (see also Galley cooking)
Cooling system, 322
  cleaning, 65
  maintenance check, 56
Converting automobile engine to marine, 321-329
  Cord, string and twine, 196
Cordage, 196 (see also Ropes)
Corrosion, galvanic, 87
Course of ship, 170, 179
  compass course, 170
  laying out line, 179
  magnetic course, 170
  plotting a safe, 134
  true course, 170
Courses in boat handling and seamanship, 350-355
  Coast Guard Auxiliary, 354-355
    "Basic Seamanship and Safe Boathandling" course, 354
  New York State training program, 355-356
  safety certificates awarded, 355
  United States Power Squadrons, 89, 130, 170, 350-355
    Advanced Grade Courses, 351-354
    Advanced Pilot Course, 352
    Engine Maintenance, 353
    Junior Navigator Course, 352
    Navigator Course, 353
    Piloting and Small Boat Handling, 351
    Sail Course, 353-354
    Weather Course, 353
Crankcase oil change, 63-64
Chris-Craft Company, 10, 11, 21
  operator's manual, 130
Cruisers, 11-12 (see also Outboard motorboats)
  inboard, 23
Cruising, outboard, 27-49
  amphibious cruises, 32, 36, 40-42
  care of outboard motor, 48, 56-72
  children, entertaining, 28, 44-48
    duties for, 46
    frequent stops, 44-46
  Coast Guard courtesy inspection, 39-40
  cost of, 30, 42
  equipment needed, 37-40
  exploratory side-trips, 29-30

Cruising, outboard —
  filing a float plan, 34
  Florida, 28
  houseboat, 42-44
  in groups, 42
  meals, 44
  mileage that can be covered, 35
  New York, 28
  overland cruising, 40-42
  planning a cruise, 32-34, 37
    overnight accommodations, 28-29, 32, 35-37
    selecting the water way, 34-35
  popularity of, 29-30
  rough water, 32
  runabout for, 32-34
  selecting type of boat for, 32-34
  sources of cruising information, 47-48
  speed limits, 35
  supply ports, 35
  swimming, 44-46
  weather conditions, 32
  winter cruising, 42
Crutches, definition, 73
Current Tables, 163
Currents
  discharge, 89
  effects on boat handling, 95-96
  screw, 89
  suction screw, 89
  Tidal Current Charts and Diagrams, 163
Cushions, buoyant, 216
Cutlass, racing cruiser, 285
Cyclones, 189

Dacron rope, 197
Daily Memorandum for pilots, 164
Daimler, Gottlieb, 12
Danforth Shearpin Anchor, 120, 122-123
Day Sailer, centerboard sloop, 281
Daybeacons, 138
Dead reckoning, 178-179
  course line, 179
  data for, 178
  plotting sheets, 178
  track line, 179
Deadweight tons, 79
Deadwood, definition, 73
Dealers, information obtained from, 48
Decks, 70
  beams, 75
  construction of, 78
  fill plates, 104
  riding on decks prohibited, 245
Depth finder
  hand lead line, 166-167
  sonic, 166
Depth sounder, 152-156
  "fathometer," 155-156
  indicator depth sounders, 153-154
  interpreting bottom conditions, 154-156

Depth sounder —
  operation of, 153
  parts, 153
  portable, 155
  recorder models, 154
  types of, 153
  used for navigation, 154
  used to locate fish, 153, 156
Design of a boat, affects control, 89
Deviation table, 171
Dewpoint and dewpoint spread, 184
Diagonal construction, wooden boats, 78
Diesel engines
  compression test, 61-62
  timing, 68
Diesel fuel
  nozzles and lines, 61
  safety precautions, 105
  tax refund, 252-253
Dimensions, 79-80
  sailboats, 274-288
Dipping the eye, 127
Discharge current, 89
Distress signals, 111
  "Distress Information Sheet," 111
  flare gun, 111
  recognized, 113
  "wave" for help, 111
Distributor, 66-67
Do-it-yourself kits and plans, 10, 289-305
  boat-building plans, 295-301
  fiberglass kits, 290, 301-304
  frame kits, 290-295
    assembling, 290-295
  hydrofoil kits, 332-333
  preassembled and molded kits, 290
  precut kits, 290
  preformed kits, 290
  starting small, 289
  types of kits, 289-305
Docks and docking, 128-129
  bringing sailboat into, 272-273
  information about, 48
  lines, 37
Documents, ship's papers, 214
Doldrums, 184
Dolphin, midget ocean racer, 286
Double-ender, definition, 73
Doubling the angle on the bow, piloting, 175
Douglas Fir Plywood Association, 295
Draft, measuring, 79
Dredging areas, buoys to mark, 135, 136
Drives, accessory, 64-65
Driving units
  checking, 59
  direct drive reverse gear, 59
Drogue, 98-101
Dry rot, preventing, 107
Dyer Dhow, centerboard catboat, 276

Echo-sounding devices, 166
El Toro, centerboard catboat, 275
Electrical installations on shipboard, 106-107
  fuses or circuit breakers, 107
  placed as high as possible, 107
  safety suggestions, 106-107
"Electronic Aids to Navigation," Coast Guard publication, 134
Electronic aids to navigation, 134, 148-156
  depth sounder, 152-156
  "fathometer," 156
  radio direction finder, 148-152
Elgin line of outboard motors, 19
Elk Marine of England, 21
Elto Outboard Motor Company, 13, 15
Engine space, ventilating, 107
Engines
  acceleration, power and noise, 60
  carburetors 54, 64, 322
  coil and wiring, 66
  compression, 53
  compression test, 61-62
  converting automobile to marine, 321-329
    adaptability, 321-322
    choice of reverse and reduction gears, 322
    closed cooling system, 322
    disadvantages, 324
    down-draft carburetion, 322
    guide to buying a motor for conversion, 322-324
    list of engines and the engine blocks from which they are made, 321
    operating economy, 322
    parts and services, 321
    price, 321
    selecting the automobile engine, 321-322
    step-by-step process, 324-329
  cylinder head and gaskets, 60-61
  development of, 9-10
  factory checks, 57
  fuel fires, 102-104
  generators, 37, 65, 69
  governed speed, 60
  Hickman Sea-Sled, 11
  idle, 60
  ignition system, 53-54
  inboard-outboard, 249, 334-335
  instruments and gauges, 58-59
  leaks, 60
  maintenance procedures, 56-72
  manifolds and heat control, 62
  mounting and braces, 62
  naphtha-gas, 10
  outboard motors (*see* Outboard motors)
  regulator units, 65
  temperature gauge, 59

Engines —
  timing, 68
  valve mechanism, 61
Entertaining children on cruises, 44-48
  activities, 44-46
  duties for teen-agers, 46
Equipment
  care of, 49-56
  "Coast Guard Approved Equipment," 40, 107-108, 216-218
  houseboats, 44
  legal requirements, 214-218
  for outboard cruising, 37-40
  outboard motorboats, 34, 39-40, 214-215
  safety (see Safety devices)
  state laws, 221
  unapproved, 217
Evinrude, Ole, 13-17
Evinrude Foundation, 17
  cruising information, 48
Evinrude Motors Company, 13, 19
Examination of piloting skills, 339-348
Exhaust pipes and mufflers, 62
Expenses
  inboard boats, 26
  operating and maintenance, 26, 249
  outboard cruising, 30, 42
Explorer, centerboard sloop, 281
Explosions and fire, 102-104

Fair-leaders, 195
"Fathometer," 155-156
Federal Boating Act of 1958, 211-220
  boating accidents, 213
  documentation and "yachts," 214
  equipment required, 214-218
  law enforcement, 213-214
  numbering, 212-213
Federal Boating Stamp, 218
Federal Communications Commission
  inspection and monitoring by, 116
  marine radiotelephones controlled by, 112
  radio stations and operators licensed by, 113-114
  violation notices, 115
Federal Compensation Insurance, 258
Federal Trade Commission, proposed set of "Trade Practice Rules for the Pleasure Boat Industry," 336-338
Fenders and fender board, 37
Fiberglass boats, 80-83
  advantages, 80
  do-it-yourself kits, 290, 301-304
    assembling, 302-304
  ease of maintenance, 80-81
  hull-making, 81-85
    cloth-laminated method, 81
    core construction, 81-82
    gel coat, 82

Fiberglass boats, hull making —
  matched metal die molding, 83
  open mold fabrication, 82-83
  pressure-molded hulls, 82
  sandwich type of construction, 81, 82
  spray-up process, 83
  temperature and humidity control, 81
  use of balsa wood, 82
  vacuum bag molding, 83
  virtually unsinkable, 81
  reinforced plastic, 80
Films, boating, 89
Filters
  fuel screens and, 62
  oil, 64
Fire extinguishers, 70-71
  Coast Guard requirements, 107-108, 217-218
  hand, 108
  required on outboards, 215
  state requirements, 225-227
  types of, 107-108
  yearly check of, 108
Fire prevention, 102-110 (see also Safety, boating)
"Fire Protection Standards in Motor Craft," 102
Fireboats, 334
First aid kits, 72
Fish and fishing, 46
  depth sounder used to locate fish, 153, 156
Fish net area, buoys to mark, 135, 136
Fittings, for wire rope, 209-211
"Fix," method of making, 173
  cross-bearing, 173
  from two visible objects, 173-174
  obtaining from one visible object, 174
  relative bearings, 174
Flags, communicating with, 119
Flagstaff, 78
Flame arrestors, 108
  approved, 217
  required on outboards, 215
  state laws, 230
Flare gun, 111
Flashlights, 38
Flight Information Manual, 152
Float plan, filing, 34
Floors, marine construction, 73
Florida, outboard cruises, 28, 42
Flying Scot, centerboard sloop, 282
Fog, 187-188
  dropping anchor, 178
  forecasting, 188-189
  formation of, 187-188
  piloting in, 176-178
  radiation, 187
  reducing speed, 177
  sounding the way, 177-178
  weather reports, 177

Fog signals
  apparatus for, 133
    bells, 133
    diaphones, 133
    diaphragm horns, 133
    reed horns, 133
    whistles, 133
  bells and whistles on buoys, 132, 135
  cautions in using, 140-142
  characteristics of, 132
  distance finding in the fog, 134
  identifying, 132-133
  lighthouses, 132-133
  on light ships, 132
  radiobeacons synchronized with, 133-134
  rules governing, 194
  sound often unpredictable, 142
  time given in "Light Lists," 133
Foremast, 78
Forestay, 78
Frames, definition, 73
Freeboard, 79
Fuel tanks
  carburetor air intakes, 104
  cleaning, 63-64
  drip pans, 104
  fill pipes, 104
  filling precautions, 52, 104-105
  filters and screens, 62-63
  fittings, 63
  fuel lines, 104
  inboard boats, 25
  inspection of, 62
  maintenance check, 56
  measuring oil, 63
  outboard cruising, 39
  portable, 53, 56
  safety precautions, 104-105
    installation essentials, 104
  strainers, 104
  vent lines, 104
Fuels and fueling
  cutoff valve, 60
  diesel fuel
    nozzles and lines, 61
    safety precautions, 105
  engine fuel fires, 102-104
  gas-and-oil mixture, 49, 52
  gauges, 58
  handbooks published by oil companies, 52
  kerosene, 105-106
  liquified petroleum, 106
  maintenance check of fuel system, 53
  outboard motors, 48-49, 52
  pump, 63
  rate of consumption, 249
  refunds on gasoline taxes, 249-253
  safety precautions

Fuels, safety precautions —
  diesel fuel, 105
  liquid fuels, 105-106
  liquified petroleum fuel, 106
  solid fuel, 105
  white gasoline, 49
Fuses or circuit breakers, 107

Gaff, definition, 78-79
Gale line of outboard motors, 19-20
Gales, warning signals, 180
Galley cookery, 44, 306-313
  beverages, 309
  desserts and sweets, 308-309
  eggs, 307
  food supply lists, 312-314
  gear, 310-311
  icebox, 310
  meat, 306-307, 310
  planning supplies, 306, 312-314
    quantities per man per day, 306
  safety precautions, 105
  salads, 308
  sandwiches, 309
  stowing food, 309-310
  suggested menus, 311-312
  types of stoves for, 105, 307
  vegetables, 307-308, 310
Garboard, 74
Gaskets, 60-61
Gasoline
  compression test, 61
  danger of fire, 102-104
  for outboard motors, 48-49
  rate of consumption, 249
  refunds on taxes, 249-253
  safety precautions, 105-106
  white, 49
Gauges, maintaining, 58
Gear case, maintenance check, 56
Gear drive, 59
Gear oil levels, 68
Generating plants, installation of, 107
Generators, 37
  care of, 65
  maintenance check, 69
Geographic range of light, 132
Glossary
  of nautical terms, 356-364
  of sailing terms, 266-268
Gnomonic charts, 157-158
Goniometer or direction finder loop, 144
Governor, 66
Grab rails, 70
Great Lakes
  charts, 160
  lighthouses, 130
  Rules of the Road, 190
Gross tonnage, 79
Ground strap, 62

Ground tackle, 123-124
 definition, 120
 inspection of, 126
Groups, outboard cruising, 42
Gulf coast, buoys, 135
Guns, flare, 111
Gunwales, 74
 riding on decks or, 245
Gyrocompass, 169

Halyards, 267
Handcrank ratchet and lever, 68
Handling, safe boat, 89-101
 action of the tides, 96
 commands, 91
 condition and direction of the sea, 95
 crossing bow waves, 99
 design affects control, 89
 effects of current, 95-96
 effects of wind and sea on turning, 94-95
 free courses in, 89, 350-355 (see also Courses in boat handling and seamanship)
 heaving to, 101
 in heavy seas, 95
 kicking the stern, 90
 natural factors affecting, 90
 navigating in narrow channels, 96-97
 oil used to calm the seas, 101
 outboard boats, 93
  in heavy seas, 95
  reverse power, 93
 passing another boat in a narrow channel, 97
 power affects control, 89
 propeller action, 89-90
 rudder action, 90
 sea anchor as a safety device, 98-101
 single-screw vessels, 92-93
  turning in a limited space, 96
  vessel and propeller going forward, 92
  vessel with headway, propeller backing, 92-93
  vessel with sternway, propeller backing, 92
  vessel with sternway, propeller going ahead, 93
 staying clear of barges and tows, 99-100
 steering orders, 90-91
 turning in a bend, 97-98
 turning in a limited space, 96
 twin-screw vessels, 93-94
  turning in a limited space, 96
 using an anchor as a turning aid, 96-97
 vessels' characteristics affecting control, 89-90
Harbors, *Tidal Current Charts and Diagrams,* 163
Harmsworth International Trophy, 11
Hatches, coamings, 78
Hawser ropes, 196

Headstay, 267
Heat exchangers, 65
Heaters, cabin, 105
Heaving lines, 127
Heaving to, 101
Heavy seas, navigating in, 95, 126
Heel, of mast, 78
Heli-Bout, 332-333
Helicopter-pleasure boats, 333
Helm of the boat, steering commands, 90-91
Hemp rope, 197
Hickman Sea-Sled, 11
Highlander, centerboard sloop, 285
Historical background of boating, 9-17
Hitches, 203-206 (see also Knots, bends and hitches)
Hood ends, of planks, 75
Hook, boat, 71
Horn timbers, definition, 73
Horns, fog, 58, 135
Horse latitudes, 184
Horsepower
 design of hull and, 23-24
 inboard boats, 23-24
 "OBC Horsepower Curve" chart, 18
 outboard motors, 18, 335
Hour meter, 58
Houseboats, 42-44
 advantages of, 44
 cruising, 42-44
 equipment, 44
 outboard motors for, 44
 popularity of, 42-44
 price ranges, 44
 sleeping accommodations, 45
 types of, 44
 wiring systems, 44
Hulls, 10
 care of, 51
 characteristics of, 24-25
 chine, 24
 displacement type, 24
 do-it-yourself kits and plans, 290-295
 fiberglass, 81-85
 flat-bottom, 10, 24
 freeboard, 25
 horsepower and design of, 23-24
 inboard boats, 24-25
 insurance, 255-257
 maintenance procedure, 70
 outboard boats, 18
 rounded bottom, 24
 speed, 24-25
 stability of, 24
 types of wooden boat construction, 75-78
 V-bottom, 10, 24
 wind resistance, 25
Hurricanes, 189
 warning signals, 180

Hydrofoils, 332-333
  "angle of attack," 332
  kits for, 332-333
Hydrographic Bulletin, 164
Hydrographic Office (*see* United States, Hydrographic Office)
Hydroplane, 10
Hygrometer, 183-184

Icebox, marine, 310
Identification of boats, 71, 212 (*see also* Numbering)
Ignition system, 52-53
  maintenance check, 53
Inboard boats
  advantages, 23
  fuel and water tanks, 25
  fuel consumption, 250
  functional layout, 25
  horsepower needed, 23-24
  hull characteristics, 24-25
  maintenance procedure, 56-72
  number of, 12
  operating and maintenance costs, 26, 249
  runabouts, 25
  selecting, 23-26
  size of boat to buy, 26
  sleeping accommodations, 25
  storage, 25
  water skiing, 318
  wiring and piping, 25
Inboard-outboard engines, 249, 334-335
  gas consumption, 335
  installation of, 335
Information, boating
  cruising and cruises, 47-48
  on rules of the road, 190
  sources of, 349-356
Innocenti firm in Italy, 21
Inspections
  by Coast Guard Auxiliary, 39-40, 108-109
  by insurance companies, 263
  of lines, 195
Instrument and gauges, maintaining, 58
Insurance, yacht and motorboat, 254-263
  Builders' Risk Insurance, 262-263
  details of, 255-257
  engineering and inspection service, 263
  Federal Compensation Insurance, 258
  fire and lightning only, 262
  for outboard boats, 263
    rates, 263
  hull insurance, 255-257
  lay-up warranty, 260
  Medical Payments Insurance, 258-259
  policy forms, 254-255
    builder's risk insurance, 255
    fire and lightning, 254
    Yacht (Form "A"), 254-256, 259-260

Insurance, policy forms —
    yacht liability insurance, 254
  port risk insurance, 262
  proportion of loss covered, 260-261
  protection and indemnity, 257-258, 262
    omnibus clause, 258
  rates, 261-262
    outboard motors, 263
  salvage charges, 256-257
  Yacht (Form "A") Policy, 254-256
    general provisions, 259-260
    Hull (Marine) Insurance, 255-256
    navigation privileges, 260
  Yacht Liability Policy, 262
Inter-Club, sailing boat class, 277
International and Inland Rules, 177
"International Code of Signals," 119
International Morse Code, 152
International 110, keel sloop, 286
Intracoastal Waterways, 138-139
  charts, 138
  distinctive markings, 138-139
  dual markings, 139
  lateral system of buoyage, 135
  navigational aids, 138-139
  New Jersey to the Mexican Border, 138
  range lights, 176

Jackstaff, 78
Jet-14, centerboard sloop, 278
Jet-powered pleasure boats, 333, 334
Jib, 266-267
Jib Headed Sloop (Marconi Rig), 266
Jibe, 270-271
  "flying," 271
Johnson Motor Company, 15, 17, 18, 20

Kedge anchor, 120
Keel, definition, 73
Keelson, definition, 73
Kerosene, safety precautions, 105-106
Ketches, 266
Kicking the stern, 90
Kiekhaefer Company, 20
Kits and plans for boats, 289-305
Knees, used in hull structure, 73
Knots, bends and hitches, 200-206
  bight, 201
  bitter end, 201
  Blackwall Hitch, 201
  bowline, 201
  bowline on a bight, 201
  cat's paw, 201
  Double Carrick bend, 203
  figure of eight, 201
  hitches, 203-206
    clove hitch, 206
    fisherman's bend, 203
    rolling hitch, 203-204
    round turn and two half hitches, 204-206

Knots —
    Spier knot, 206
    studding sail halyard bend, 203
    studding sail tack bend, 203
    timber hitch, 203
    timber hitch and half hitch, 203
    two half hitches, 206
  in a single line, 201-202
  overhand knot, 201
  reeving line bend, 203
  running bowline, 201
  sheepshank, 201
  sheet bend, double, 203
  sheet or Becket Bend, 203
  Single Carrick bend, 203
  square or reef knot, 203
  standing part, 201
  two bowlines, 203
  used for bending two lines together, 201-204
  used in securing a line to a ring or spar, 203-206
Kramer, Dr. Max O., 330-332

Lateral system of buoyage, 135
Launching the boat, 30
  number of sites, 12
Laws
  boating accidents, 213
  documentation and "yachts," 214
  enforcement of, 213-214
  equipment required, 214-218
  Federal Boating Act of 1958, 211-220
  numbering boats, 212-213, 218
  state boating laws, 218-248 (*see also* State boating laws)
Lay-up of vessels
  insurance coverage, 260
  port risk insurance, 262
Lead line, 132, 166-167
  arming the lead, 167
  disadvantages, 154
  marking the line, 166-167
  taking a sounding, 167
Length of boat, measuring, 79
Licenses
  operators, 248
  radiotelephone station and operators, 113-114
Life jackets, 33
Life preservers, 72
  construction and markings, 216
Lifesaving devices
  buoyant cushions, 216
  buoyant vests, 217
  Coast Guard approved equipment, 216-218
  fire extinguishers, 217-218
  life preservers, 72, 216
  required on outboards, 215

Lifesaving devices —
  ring buoys, 216-217
  state laws, 227-228
Light Lists, 134, 164
  fog signals given, 133
  radiobeacons, 134, 151
Lighthouses, 130-133
  appearance, 131
  atmospheric conditions affect visibility, 140
  automatic apparatus, 131
  brilliant shore lights can confuse, 140
  caution in relying on, 140-143
  characteristics of lights, 140-141
  danger in passing too close to, 143
  Execution Rocks, 146
  fog signals, 132-133
  geographic range, 132
  Harbor Refuge, 146
  how flashes are produced, 131
  identification of lights, 140-141
  location, 130-131
  luminous range, 132
  minor lights, 131
  nighttime means of distinguishing, 131
  purpose, 130
  resident keepers, 131
  secondary lights, 131
  sectors, 132
    problems with, 141-142
  timing devices, 131
  visibility of lights, 131-132
Lighting interior, 25
Lightning, centerboard sloop, 284
Lightning protection, 110
  cone of protection, 109
Lights
  cautions in using, 140-142
  Coast Guard requirements, 38
  color of, on buoys, 137
  geographic range of, 132
  inland waterways, 132
  range, 176
  required on outboard motorboats, 215
  rip-rap mounds, 142
  state laws, 221-225
Lightships, 96
  Ambrose, 146
  fog signals, 132
  off station, 143
Limber holes, definition, 73
Lines (*see also* Rope)
  heaving, 127
  hints for care of, 195-196
  Marlinspike seamanship, 195-211
  mooring, 127-129, 185
  reversing, 195
Lines
  sailboats, 267
  towing, 71

INDEX

"List of Lights and Other Marine Aids," 134, 151, 164
Liverpool splice, wire rope, 207-208
Livery, boat, 247
Lockwood Motor Company, 13-15
Logs
  radio, 116
  taffrail, 167
Lubber's line, 164, 166
Lubrication of motor, 48-49, 67
Luminous range of light, 132

McCulloch Corporation, 20
Magazines, boating, cruising information, 47
Magnetic compass, 164-165
  compass rose, 165
  use of, 165
  variation and deviation, 165
Magnetic course, 170
Magnetos (points), 66
Mainmast, 78
Mainsail, 266
Maintenance procedures, inboard pleasure boats, 56-72
  air cleaners, 64
  air-compressor, 67-68
  air control, 59
  air pressure, 58
  batteries, 67
  bilge pumps, 69
  carburetor, 66
  clutch drive, 59
  coil and wiring, 66
  compression test, 61-62
  diesel fuel nozzles and lines, 61
  distributor, 66-67
  engine, 60
  engine oil, 63-64
  fire extinguisher system, 70-71
  fuel tanks, filters and screens, 62-63
  gear drive, 59
  generator, 65, 69
  heat exchangers, 65
  hull, 70
  instruments and gauges, 58
  magnetos (points), 66
  manifolds and heat control, 62
  propeller, 69
  rudder, 69
  safety devices, 60
  spark plugs, 61
  starting motor, 68
  steering wheel, 59
  supercharger, 60
  superstructure, 70
  throttle, 63
  tools and equipment, 71-72
  water pumps, 64
  windshield, horns, 58
Manifolds and heat control, 62

Manila rope, 125, 197
  for mooring lines, 127
Manuals
  familiarity with, 38-39, 49, 52
  fire safety, 102-104
Manufacturers, marine equipment, 89
  list of, 21-23
Maps, weather, 185-186
Marconi Rig, 266
Marinas and boat yards, 35
  information about, 48
  number of, 12
Marine Band, for radio direction finding, 151
Marine growths, 51
  removing, 52
Marine Motors, 21
"Marine Radio Telephony," 112
Mariner's compass, 169
Maritime Service, radiotelephone, 112
Markings and identification, 71
Marlinspike seamanship, 195-211
  hints for care of lines, 195-196
  how rope is made, 196
  knots, bends and hitches, 200-206
  rope fibers, 197
  seizing rope, 200
  selecting rope, 198
  size and type of rope, 196
  splicing rope, 198-200
  types of fiber rope, 196-197
  wire rope, 206-211
    care of, 207
    fittings for, 211
    working with, 207-211
  worming, parceling and serving, 200-201
Masts, 78
Measurements of pleasure boats, 79-80
  breadth, 79
  length, 79
  weight, 79-80
Measuring, taffrail log, 167
Medical Payments Insurance, 258-259
Menus, suggested, 311-312
Mercator chart, 134, 157
Mercury, training sloop, 279
Mercury line of outboard motors, 20
Metal boats, 78
  air tanks for buoyancy, 78
  lightning protection, 110
Meyer, C. J., 13
Mildew, 107
Minor lights, 131
"Miss Minneapolis," hydroplane, 11
Mississippi River, numbering of buoys, 136-137
Mizzenmast, 78
Moorings, 126-129
  affect of tides on, 128-129
  anchors and anchoring, 120-126 (*see also* Anchors and anchoring)

Moorings —
  costs, 26
  handling a vessel around a wharf, 128-129, 272-273
  heaving lines, 127
  heavy weather conditions, 126
  lines, 127-129
    care of, 127
    names and location of, 127-128
    use of Manila rope, 127
    making landings, 129
  pendants, 127
  permanent, 126-127
  rented, 126
  sailboats, 272
  state laws, 245
  technique of, 126-129
    using the lines, 127-129
  winding ship or warping, 129
Morse Code, 152
"Motogobile" and "Motogobille," 12
Motor Boat Shows, 10, 11, 13, 79, 332
Motor boats
  insurance, 254-263
  number of, 12
Motors (*see also* Engines)
  automobile-marine engine conversion, 321-329
    disadvantages, 324
    guide to buying, 322-324
    selecting the engine, 321-322
    step-by-step process, 324-329
  inboard-outboard motor, 334-335
  outboard (*see* Outboard motors)
Mounting and braces, engines, 62
Mud, anchoring in, 121
Mufflers, state laws, 230
Muncie Gear Works, 21

Napier diagram, 170-172
  plotting a deviation curve on, 171-173
National Fire Protection Association, 102
National Motor Boat Show, 10, 11, 12, 13, 79, 332
National Safe Boating Association, 89
Nautical terms, 267-268
Navigational aids, 130-139
  cautions concerning, 140-147
    buoys, 143-144
    fog signals, 142
    hazard in rip-rap, 142
    lights and fog signals, 140-141
    lightships, 143
    problems with "sectors," 141-142
    radiobeacons, 144-147
  daybeacons, 138
  depth sounder, 152-156
  electronic, 148-156
    depth sounder, 152-156
    radio direction finder, 148-152

Navigational aids —
  fog signals, 132-133
  Intracoastal Waterway, 138-139
  lighthouses, 130-133
  maritime radiobeacons, 133-134
  radio direction finder, 148-152
  sectors, 132, 141-142
Net tonnage, 79
New York
  outboard cruising, 28, 35, 40-42
  statewide training program for young boat operators, 355-356
Newspapers, boating information, 48
Notice to Mariners, 159, 163
Numbering boats
  application for renewal, 212-213
  certificates, 212
  Coast Guard regulations, 212-213, 218
  Federal laws, 212-213
  fee, 212
  numbers of boat dealers and manufacturers, 213
  position of number on boat, 213
  state regulations and address of state agency, 218-220
  system, 213
Nylon rope
  splicing, 199
  to hold anchors, 125

Ohlson 35, yawl, 288
Oil
  changing crankcase, 63-64
  gasoline-and-oil mixture, 49, 52
  used to calm the seas, 101
Oil companies
  cruising information published by, 47, 349-350
  handbooks on lubricating and fueling procedures, 52
  material on boating available from, 349-350
  waterway guides, 47
Oil pressure, 58
Oil temperature, 58
Oliver Corporation, 21
Operating and maintenance costs, 249
  inboard boats, 26
Operation, rules of (*see* Rules of operation)
Operators
  age of 238-239
  incapacity of, 232
  licensing, 248
  radio, 113-114
Optical reflectors
  on buoys, 137
  on daybeacons, 138
Osprey, day sailer, 280
"Outboard Boating" (periodical), 48

Outboard Boating Club of America
  cruising information, 48
  Horsepower Curve chart, 18
  horsepower rating formula, 18
  state boating laws, 221-248
Outboard Marine and Manufacturing Company, 17-18
Outboard motor industry, 12-17
  in the depression, 17
  World War II, 17
Outboard motorboats
  buying, 32-34
  care of, 49-56
  equipment required, 34, 37-40, 214-215
    fire extinguishers, 215
    flame arrestor, 215
    lifesaving devices, 215
    lights, 215
    signalling equipment, 215-216
    ventilation, 215
  for water skiing, 318
  guide to outboard cruising, 27-49 (see also Cruising)
  insurance, 263
  length of, 28
  number of, 12
  sleeping accommodations, 39
Outboard motors (see also Engines)
  angle of the propeller, 48
  carburetor sediment bowl, 53-54
  care of, 48-56
    at beginning of the season, 53
  choosing, 18-21
    horsepower rating, 18
    list of manufacturers, 21-23
    list of models, 19-21
    objective report, 19, 318
  coil and condenser, 56
  common causes of trouble, 52-53
    at end of the season, 56
    ignition, 52-53
  compression, trouble with, 53
  development of, 12-17
  80 horsepower, 16
  electric starters, 56
  Elgin line, 19
  Elto Quad, 13, 15
  Evinrude line, 19
  four cylinder, two-cycle, 15
  fuel, 48-49, 52-53 (see also Fuels and fueling)
  Gale line, 19-20
  horsepower ratings, 18, 335
  houseboats, 44
  ignition system, 53-54
  Johnson line, 20
  list of manufacturers, 22-23
  lower unit, checking, 53, 55
  lubricating, 48-49
  maintenance check, 52-56
  Mercury line, 20
  mounting, 48

Outboard motors —
  new, 52
  operating costs, 249
  operating manual for, 49
  origin of, 12
  owner's manual, 38-39, 49, 52
  package units, 18
  prices, 18
  protecting internal parts, 48-49, 56
  rate of gasoline consumption, 249
  rated by "Consumer Reports," 19, 318
  removing salt deposits, 56
  SAE 30 outboard motor oil, 49
  sales and trade-ins, 18
  Scott line, 20-21
  spark plugs, 53-54
  specification and details of models, 19-21
  throttle linkage, 53
  tilt of the motor, 48
  tools and spare parts kit, 52
  West Bend line, 21
Outboard Motors Corporation, 13, 17
Overland cruising, 40-42
Overpowering prohibited, 237-238
Owner's responsibility, 245-247
  civil liability, 245-247
  criminal liability, 247

Paint and markings, 51, 71
  filling dents, nicks and gouges, 52
  preparation of surface, 51
  sealing seams, 51
  touch-up jobs, 52
Parceling rope, 200-201
Passengers, overloading prohibited, 238
Patents, boating, 9
Pelican, sailboat class, 276
Pelorus, 165-166
  radio direction finder augments, 148
Pendants, mooring, 127
Pennants, signalling with, 119
Penguin, sailboat class, 275
Piers, making landings, 129
Pilot, powered cruising sloop, 288
Pilot Charts, 164
Pilot Rules, 164
Piloting
  basic small boat, 157-168
  bow-and-beam method of determining position, 174-175
  charts, 157-162
  compass course, 170
  courses in, 351-352
  cross bearing, 173
  dead reckoning, 178-179
    course line, 179
    data for, 178
    plotting sheets, 178
    track line, 179
  definition, 169
  deviation card, 173
  dividers, protractor or parallel rule, 167

Piloting —
  doubling the angle on the bow, 175
  examination of piloting skills, 339-348
  fundamentals, 169-179
  hand lead line and depth finder, 166-167
  in fog, 176-178
  instruments, 164-167
  labeling a chart, 173
  magnetic compass, 164-165
  magnetic course, 170
  making a deviation table, 171
  Napier diagram, 170-172
  navigator's "tools," 167
  obtaining a fix from one visible object, 174
  obtaining a fix from two visible objects, 173-174
  pelorus, 165-166
  plotting a course, instruments for, 167
  plotting a deviation curve on a Napier diagram, 171-173
  ranges and their uses, 176
  relative bearings, 174
  seven-eights rule, 175
  seven-tenths rule, 175
  small boat, 157-168
    charts, 157-162
    government nautical publications, 162
  special bearings, 176
  taffrail log, 167
  test of, 339-348
  true course, 170
  using the compass, 169-173
    variation and deviation, 169-170
Planning a cruise, 32-34
  selecting the water way, 34-35
Plans, boat-building, 295-301
Plastic wood, use of, 52
Plates, checking, 70
Pleasure boating
  birth of the boating boom, 9-17
  development of, 9-17
  growth of interest in, 9
  popularity of, 27-28
  statistics on, 12
Plotting sheets, use of, 178-179
Plumb, definition, 73
Plywood boat construction, 78
Pneudyne, 59
Polar fronts, 184
Pollution of waters, state laws, 247-248
Polyconic charts, 157
Port, definition, 268
Port risk insurance, 262
Power, handling affected by, 89
Pre-fabricated boats, 290
Prohibition, effect on boating, 12
Propeller, 83-88
  action of, 85-86, 89-90
  blades, 85
  carrying an extra, 52

Propeller —
  cavitation, 89-90
  checking, 53-55
  dimensions, 85
  direction of rotation, 85
  factors affecting, 89-90
  galvanic corrosion, 87
  handling affected by, 89
  maintenance check, 53, 69
  metallurgy, 88
  multi-pitch, 88
  ogival section, 85
  pitch, 85, 89
  pitch ratio, 87
  post, 73
  selection of efficient shaft speed, 87
  slip, 86, 89
  thrust, 85-86
Publications, government nautical, 162-164
Pumps
  bilge, 51, 69, 71
  fuel, 63
  water, 64

Quarantine areas, buoys to mark, 135, 136
Quarter knees, definition, 73

Rabbeted frame members, 74-75
Races and regattas, state laws, 245
Racing boats, 10
  hydroplane, 10-11
Racing records, 11
Radar
  corner radar reflectors on buoys, 136
  reflectors for wood and plastic boats, 111
Radio Bearing Conversion tables, 134
Radiobeacons, maritime, 133-134
  airways, 151
  cautions in using, 144-147
    accuracy problems, 144
    erroneous radio direction finder bearings, 145-147
    land effect, 145-146
    local disturbing effects, 145
    night effect, 145
    skywave signals, 144-145
  checking radio direction finder installations, 145
  frequencies, 133
  limitations on use of, 144-147
  lists of, 151-152
  location of, 151
  the 180° error problem, 146-147
  publications on, 152
  radio bearing conversion tables, 134
  signals emitted by, 134
  stations maintained and operated by Coast Guard, 133-134
  taking bearings on commercial or aeronautical stations, 146

Radio Corporation of America, Western Long Island System, 117-119
Radio direction finder, 148-152
  automatically operated fixed loop, 150
  automatically rotated loops (ADF), 150
  basic principle of operation, 150-151
  Beacon Band, 151
  construction of, 149
  landbased and mobile finders, 148
  list of radio transmitting stations, 148
  manually operated fixed loop, 150
  manually rotated loops, 150
  Marine Band, 151
  necessary equipment, 148
  portable, 149
  price range, 148
  radiobeacons (*see* Radiobeacons)
  sense antenna, 149
  types of, 149-150
  using radio stations, 151-152
"Radio Navigational Aids," 134, 164
Radio stations, used for radio direction finding, 151
Radio Technical Commission for Marine Service, 112-113
Radio Weather Aids, 164
Radios
  grounding antennas, 110
  portable, 46
Radiotelephone, 111-119
  calling and distress frequency, 114
  certification of transmitter, 115
  Citizen's Band Radio Service, 112, 116-117
  FCC controls, 112
  frequency measurement, 114-115
  grounds required, 115
  harmonics, 115
  inspection and monitoring, 116
  intership communication, 114-115
  Maritime Service, 112
  modulation, 115-116
  operating procedures, 115
  operator, 114
  prevention of interference, 115
  radio log, 114, 116
  regulations, 112-113, 114-116
  sign-off announcements, 114
  station and operator licensing, 113-114
    interim licenses, 114
    Restricted Radiotelephone Operator Permit, 114
  type available for small boats, 112
  violation notices, 116-117
  Western Long Island System, 117-119
Raked, definition, 73
Range lights, piloting by means of, 176
Raven, sailboat class, 287
Raytheon Manufacturing Company, 155, 156

Reclaimers, 64
"Recommended Practices for Electrical Installations on Shipboard," 106
Reducing valves, 60
Refunds on gasoline taxes, 249-253
  Canadian gasoline taxes, 252
  diesel fuel tax, 252-253
  Federal gasoline tax, 250
  horsepower is the important factor, 249-250
  invoices required, 253
  state gasoline taxes, 250-253
Regulator units, marine engines, 65
Relative bearings, 174
Relay air valve, 60
Rental boats, 29, 266
Reports, boating accidents, 213, 238
Restricted areas, state laws, 235-237
Revolution counter, 58
Rhodes 18, sailboat class, 282
Rhodes 19, sailboat class, 283
Rigging, 78
Rigging screw, 207
Ring buoys, 216-217
Ringbolts, 73
Rip-rap, hazards in, 142
River cruising, 26
Rock, anchoring on, 122
Rode, anchor, 125
Ropes (*see also* Lines)
  cable-laid, 196
  care of, 195-196
  characteristics of, 198
  cotton and flax, 197
  dacron, 197
  deterioration of, 195
  different parts of line, 201
  "dry-rot," 196
  fibers, 196-198
  hawser, 196
  hemp, 197
  inspection of, 195
  knots, bends and hitches, 200-206 (*see also* Knots, bends and hitches)
  Manila, 125, 127, 197
  marlinspike seamanship, 195-211
  nylon, 125, 197-198
    splicing, 199
  parceling, 200-201
  polyethylene, 197
  polypropylene, 197
  protecting, 195
  ropemaking 196
    right-laid or plain-laid, 196
  seizing, 200
    throat seizing, 200
  serving, 200-201
  shroud, 196
  sisal rope, 197
  sizes and types of, 196

Ropes —
  small stuff, 196
  some hints on selecting, 198
  splicing, 198-200
    eye splice, 199
    long splice, 199-200
    short splice, 198-199
  wire, 206-211 (*see also* Wire rope)
    construction of, 207
  worming, 200-201
Rowboats, canoes, dinghies, number of, 12
Rubber-coated pleasure boats, 330-332
Rudders, 69
  action of, 90
  sailboats, 267
Rules of operation, 221, 230-248
  accidents, 238
  age of operators limited, 238-239
  careless operation, 230-232
  incapacity of operator, 232
  interference with navigation prohibited, 245
  mooring to buoys or beacons prohibited, 245
  overloading prohibited, 238
  overpowering prohibited, 237-238
  reckless operation prohibited, 232
  restricted areas, 235-237
  state laws, 221, 230-248
  traffic rules, 239-242
Rules of the road, 190-194
  boats approaching each other at right angles or obliquely, 193
  boats approaching each other head and head, end on, 191-193
  boats nearing bend or curve in channel, moving from docks, 193
  boats passing each other, 191
  boats running in same direction, overtaking vessel, 193
  cross signals are forbidden, 191
  five "situations," 191-193
  fog signals, 194
  for sailing vessels, 194
  four or more short, 191
  general provisions, 190-191
  official source of information on, 190
  purpose of, 190
  sound (whistle) signals, inland rules, 191
    one short blast, 191
    two short blasts, 191
    three short blasts, 191
"Rules of the Road, Great Lakes," 190
"Rules of the Road, International-Inland," 190
"Rules of the Road, Western Rivers," 190
Runabouts, 25
  amphibious cruising, 40-42
  buying, 32-34
  cockpit cover, 37
  convertible tops, 33, 37

Runabouts —
  inboard boats, 25
  outfitting, 37
  planning a cruise, 32-34
  sleeping accommodations, 35
Rust prevention, 71
Ryan, John J., 10

Safety, boating, 102-110
  alcohol, 105-106
  Coast Guard safety inspection, 39-40, 108-109
    sticker given, 108
  diesel fuel, 105
  electric wiring, 106-107
  engine fuel fires, 102-104
  extra gas for outboards, 109-110
  filing a float plan, 34
  fire extinguishers, 107-108
  "Fire Protection Standards in Motor Craft," 102
  flame arrestors, 108, 215, 217, 230
  fuel tanks
    filling precautions, 104-105
    installation essentials, 104
  "Fundamentals of Fire on Pleasure Boats," 104
  galley stoves, 105-106
  gasoline, 104-105
  heaving the anchor, 122, 123
  inboard craft, 108
  installation essentials, 104
  keeping the air moving, 107
  keeping bilges free of grease and oil, 109
  kerosene, 105-106
  life vests or pillows, 108
  lightning protection, 110
  liquid fuels, 105-106
  liquified petroleum gas, 106
  outboard boats, 108, 109-110
  standards, 102-104
  water skiing, 315-316, 318-320
Safety devices
  Coast Guard approved equipment, 216-218
  inspection of, 72, 263
  legal requirements, 214-218
  lifesaving devices, 216-218
  low oil safety shutdown, 60
  maintenance check, 60, 71-72
  overspeed safety trip, 60
  straps and grab rails, 70
Sailboats, 264-273
  association information, 274-288
  auxiliary propulsion units, 22
  Cat type, 266
  centerboard or keel, 265-266
  day sailer or cruiser, 266
  dimensions of various types, 274-288
  insurance, 254
  Jib Headed Sloop, 266

Sailboats —
    ketches, 266
    list of types and their dimensions, 274-288
    one-design classes, 273-288
        association information, 274-288
        listed by name, 274-288
        number of active boats, 274-288
        types and dimensions, 274-288
    renting, 266
    selection of 264-265
        resale angle, 264
        second-hand boats, 264
    sizes and types, 264
    sloops and other rigs, 265-266
    yawls, 266
Sailfish & Sunfish, sailboat class, 277
Sailing, 266-273
    anchoring and mooring, 272
    basics of sailing, 266-273
    beating to windward, 270
    coming into a dock, 272-273
    downwind sailing — the jibe, 270-271
    "flying" jibe, 271
    how to change tacks, 269-270
    how to start, 267
    points of sailing, 269
    rules of the road, 194
    schooners, 266
    some precautions, 273
    steering a sailboat, 271-272
    terminology, 266-268
    trimming the boat, 272
    wind direction, 268-269
    "wing and wing," 271
Sailing Directions, 164
Salt water, removing salt deposits, 51, 56
Salvage, insurance and, 256-257
Sand, anchoring in, 121
Schooners, 266
Scope or length of anchor line, 120
Scott line of outboard motors, 20-21
Screw current, definition, 89
Scrubbing boat, 51
Sea anchors, 98-101
Sea-Sled, 11
Seagull line of outboard motors, 22
Seamanship
    courses, 89 *(see also* Courses in boat handling and seamanship)
    dipping the eye, 127
    Marlinspike, 195-211
    safe small boat handling, 89-101 *(see also* Handling)
Seams
    calking, 74
    compounds for, 51
    paved, 74
    sealing, 51
Seasonal overhaul, checklist for, 58-72
Sectors, lighthouses, 132

Sectors —
    boundaries indicated in Lights List, 141
    problems with, 141-142
    visibility problems, 141
Serving rope, 200-201
Seven-eights rule, piloting, 175
Seven-tenths rule, piloting, 175
Shafts, 67
    logs, definition, 73
    selection of efficient shaft speed, 87
Sheer, decks, 78
Sheer strake, 74
Sheets, main and jib, 267
"Shipshape and Bristol fashion," 49
Shipyards, service, 26
Shoals
    sectors used to mark, 141
    shifting, 143
Shoe, attached to keel, 73
Shroud ropes, 78, 196
Side pans, 62
Signalling equipment
    Coast Guard approved, 215-216
    required on outboards, 215-216
    state laws, 228-229
Signals
    boats passing each other, 191
    distress, 111, 113
    flags and pennants, 119
    "International Code of Signals," 119
    sound (whistle) signals, inland rules, 191
Single-screw vessels, handling, 92-93
Sintz, Charles, 10
Sisal rope, 197
Skiing, water, 315-320 *(see also* Water skiing and skis)
Skiing on Water (Andresen), 317
Skin diving, state laws, 245
Skywave signals, radiobeacons affected by, 144-145
Sleeping accommodations
    ashore, while cruising, 35-37
    houseboats, 45
    inboard boats, 25
    outboard boats, 28-29, 39-40
    runabouts, 35
Slip, propeller, 86
Slips, mooring vessel, 129
Sloops, 265-266
    Jib Headed Sloop, 266
Small Boat Charts, 158-159
Small craft warning, 180
Small stuff, 196
Smith, Christopher Columbus, 10
Smith-Ryan Company, 10
Snatch blocks, 71
Snipe, sailboat class, 280
Sockets, for wire rope, 211
Sonic depth finder, 166
Sound (whistle) signals
    inland rules, 191

Sound signals —
  state laws, 228-229
Sounding the way, in fog, 177-178
Sources of information
  boating, 349-356
  cruising, 47-48
  rules of the road, 190
Spare parts, outboard motors, 52
Spark plugs, maintenance check, 53, 56, 61
Spars, vertical, 78
Specifications, of boats, 79
Speed
  outboard boats, 18
  state laws, 232-235
Splicing rope, 198-200
  eye splice, 199
  Liverpool splice, 207-208
  long splice, 199-200
  nylon rope, 199
  short splice, 198-199
  wire rope, 207-208
Spring stay, 78
Sprite, sailboat class, 275
Stamp, Federal Boating, 218
Star class, 285
Starters, outboard motors, 56, 68
State agencies
  addresses of, administering state laws, 218-220
  cruising information published by, 47-48
State boating laws, 218-248
  addresses of state agencies administering, 218-220
  boat livery, 247
  boat pollution prohibited, 247-248
  carburetor flame arrestors, 230
  chlorinators required for marine toilets, 229-230
  equipment for boats, 221
  fire extinguishers, 225-227
  lifesaving devices, 227-228
  lights, 221-225
  mufflers, 230
  operator's licensing, 248
  owner's responsibility, 245-247
    civil liability, 245-247
    criminal liability, 247
  races and regattas, 245
  rules of operation, 230-248
    accidents, reporting, 238
    age of operators limited, 238-239
    careless operation, 230-232
    incapacity of operator, 232
    interference with navigation prohibited, 245
    moorings to buoys or beacons prohibited, 245
    overloading prohibited, 238
    overpowering prohibited, 237-238
    reckless operation prohibited, 232

State boating laws, rules of operation —
    restricted areas, 235-237
    riding on decks on gunwales prohibited, 245
    speed regulated, 232-235
    traffic rules, 239-242
  skin diving, 245
  traffic rules, 239-242
  trailers, 366-374
  ventilators, 230
  water skiing, 243-245
  whistles and bells, 228-229
State gasoline taxes, refunds, 250-253
"Stations on Shipboard in the Maritime Services," 112
Statistics, pleasure boating, 12
Steam launches, 9
Steel, wire rope, 206-211
Steering, by teen-agers, 46
Steering mechanism, checking, 56, 59
Stem, definition, 73
Stem bands, definition, 73
Stemson, definition, 73
Step, mast rests in, 78
Stern, kicking the, 90
Stern hook, 73
Sternpost, 73
Stevens, Brooks, 332
Storage
  supplies for galley cooking, 309-310
  inboard boats, 25
  stowage compartments, 70
  winter, 26, 79
Storms
  causes and types of, 189
  warnings, 180
Stoves, galley, 105, 307
  kerosene and alcohol, 106
  safety precautions, 105-106
Strake, marine construction, 74
Suction screw current, 89
Supercharger, 60
Superstructure, maintaining, 70
Surveyors, marine, 264
Symbols, on charts, 160-163

Tachometer, 58
Tackle, ground, 120, 123-124
  inspection of, 126
Taffrail, 74
Taffrail log, 167
Tanks
  fuel (*see* Fuel tanks)
  water, 25
Tarpaulins, 70
Taxes, refunds on gasoline taxes, 249-253
  Canadian gasoline, 252
  Diesel fuel tax, 252-253
  Federal gasoline, 250
  state gasoline taxes, 250-253

Television, on outboard cruisers, 46
Temperature gauges, 59
Terminology, nautical
  glossary of, 356-364
  sailing, 266-268
  small boat construction, 73-75
Test of piloting skills, 339-348
Thistle, sailboat class, 282
Throttle, 63, 66
  maintenance check, 53, 59
Thrust, propellers, 85-86
Thwarts, folding chairs attached to, 37
Tidal Current Charts and Diagrams, 163
Tide Tables, 163
Tides, effect on mooring boat, 128-129
Tiller, sailboats, 267
Timing, engines, 68
Toilets, marine, 229-230
Tonnage, definition, 79
Tools and equipment
  care of, 52, 71
  outboard cruising, 38, 52
Topsides, 74
Towing lines, 71
Tows, staying clear of, 99-101
Track line, laying out, 179
"Trade Practice Rules for the Pleasure Boat Industry," 336-338
Trade winds, 184
Traffic rules for ships, 190-194 (*see also* Rules of the Road)
  state laws, 239-242
Trailers, boat, 29
  advantages of, 41-42
  amphibious cruising, 40-42
  care of, 56
  dropping bolster, 41
  light and flag for, 39
  number of, 12
  OBC Digest of State Boat Trailer Laws, 366-374
  tilting frame, 41
Transom, outboard boats, 34, 74, 79
Transom knee, definition, 73
Transportation, water transportation to boat, 26
Tropical disturbances, 189
Truck, of mast, 78
True course, 170
Twin-screw vessels, handling, 93-94

U-bolt clamps, for wire rope, 211
United States
  Coast and Geodetic Survey
    charts issued by, 157
    Coast Pilots, 164
    Current Tables, 163
    Tidal Current Charts and Diagrams, 163
    Tide Tables, 163

United States Coast Guard
  addresses of District Offices, 355
  approved equipment, 216
  courtesy inspection, 39-40
  "Distress Information Sheet," 111
  "Equipment Lists," 216
  fire extinguishers required by, 107-108
  law enforcement by, 213-214
  "List of Lights and Other Marine Aids," 134, 164
  numbering, 212-213
  Pilot Rules, 164
  "Recreational Boating Guide," 315
  "Rules of the Road," 190
  Department of Commerce, 180
  free government publications, 350
  Hydrographic Office, 119
    charts issued by, 157
    Flight Information Manual, 152
    Notice to Mariners, 163
    Radio Bearing Conversion tables, 134
    "Radio Navigational Aids," 134
    special publications for pilots, 164
  Weather Bureau, 180
United States Power Squadrons, 350-355
  Advanced Grade Courses, 351-354
  Advanced Pilot Course, 352
  Engine Maintenance, 353
  free courses in boat handling, 89, 130, 170, 350-355
  Junior Navigator Course, 352-353
  membership in, 350
  Navigator Course, 353
  Piloting and Small Boat Handling Courses, 351
  Sail Course, 353-354
  Weather Course, 353
U. S. Rubber Company, 330-332

Vacuum bag molding, fiberglass boats, 83
Varnish, use of, 51
Ventilation, problem of, 107
  electric fans, 107
  elimination of fire risks, 107
  required on outboards, 215
Ventilators, 70
  state laws, 230
Vests, buoyant, 108, 217
Voltmeter, 58

Walkie-talkie communications, 116
Warping or winding ship, 129
Water pumps, 64
Water skiing and water skis, 315-320
  boat driver, 317-318
  proper boat, 318-320
  safety hints, 315-316, 318-320
  ski bindings, 320
  skis, 316, 320
  starting to ski, 317

Water skiing and water skis —
  state laws, 243-245
  towing gear, 320
  "water saucer" or disc, 320
Water tanks, inboard boats, 25
Waterfront facilities, information about, 48
Waterman Porto Motor, 12-13
"Wave" for help, 111
Weather, 180-189
  anemometer, 183-185
  aneroid barometer, 181-182
  atmospheric pressure, 180-182
  barometers, 180-183
    use of, 181-183
    weather table, 182
  basic elements of, 184
  Beaufort wind scale, 183-184
  clouds as indicators, 186-187
  cyclones, 189
  dewpoint, 184
  fogs, 187-189
  fronts, 184, 188-189
  hurricanes, 189
  hygrometer, 183-184
  instruments, 180-181
  maps and forecasts, 180
    isobars, 185
    pressure gradient, 185-186
  obtaining information, 32
  polar fronts, 184
  pressure gradient, 185-186
  storm signals
    gale warnings, 180
    hurricane warning, 180
    small craft warning, 180
  storm warnings, 180
  storms, 189
  winds, 184
    land and sea breezes, 184-185
    velocity and direction, 186
Weight of boat, methods of measuring, 79-80
  deadweight tons, 79
  gross tons, 79
  net tons, 79
West Bend line of outboard motors, 21
Western Long Island radiotelephone system, 117-119
Wharves
  handling a vessel around, 128-129
  making landings, 129
  slips, 129

Whistle signals
  boats passing each other, 191
  rules of the road, 191
  sounding the way, in fog, 177-178
  state laws, 228-229
Wind resistance, of hulls, 25
Winding ship or warping, 129
Windlass, 120
Windmill, sailboat class, 279
Winds
  Beaufort wind scale, 183-184
  doldrums, 184
  effect on boat handling, 94-95
  horse latitudes, 184
  land and sea breezes, 184-185
  measuring velocity, 184
  polar fronts, 184
  prevailing westerlies, 184
  trade winds, 184
Windshields and wipers, care of, 58
Windward and leeward, 268
Winter cruising, 42
Winter storage, 26
Wire rope, 206-211
  care of, 207
  construction, 207
  fittings, 209-211
    sockets, 211
    U-bolt clamps, 211
  Liverpool splice, 207-208
  size of, 207
  splicing, 207-208
  stays, 78
  working with, 207-211
    rigging screw, 207
Wiring, checking, 70
Wood, Gar, 11
Wooden boats
  care of, 51
  hulls, 51
  types of construction, 75-78
Worming rope, 200-201
Wrecks, buoys marking, 144

Yacht Safety Bureau, 104, 123
Yachts
  clubs, 12, 26
  insurance, 254-263 (*see also* Insurance)
  ships documented as, 214
Yawls, 266

Wrecks, buoys marking, 144

Yacht Safety Bureau, 104, 123
Yachts
    clubs, 12, 26
    insurance, 254-263 (*see also* Insurance)
    ships documented as, 214
Yawls, 266